Strategic Marketing Management

University of Strathclyde Business School
MBA Programme

McGraw-Hill Custom Publishing

http://create.mheducation.com/uk/

Published by McGraw-Hill Education, 2 Penn Plaza, New York,
NY 10121.

ISBN: 9780077188948

About the Authors

John Fahy is Professor of Marketing at the University of Limerick in Ireland and Adjunct Professor of Marketing at the University of Adelaide, Australia. He has a distinguished track record of teaching and research in the fields of marketing and business strategy. In particular, he is known for his work in the area of marketing resources and capabilities and how these factors impact on organizational performance. He is a founder member of the MC21 group which has conducted research on marketing resources and performance across 15 countries. An eclectic thinker, his work draws on insights from marketing strategy, behavioural economics, evolutionary psychology and neuroscience. Other current research interests include customer value, evolutionary perspectives on marketing and strategic decision making. He is the author of dozens of referred journal articles on marketing and strategy that have been published in leading titles, including *Journal of Marketing, Journal of International Business Studies, Journal of Business Research, Journal of Marketing Management, European Journal of Marketing, International Business Review* and *Sloan Management Review*. He is also the winner of several major international research awards such as the AMA Services Marketing Paper of the Year Award and the Chartered Institute of Marketing Best Paper Award at the Academy of Marketing Annual Conference.

Professor Fahy is also a renowned teacher with a particular expertise in working with MBA and executive groups and he was awarded the prestigious *Shannon Consortium Regional Teaching Excellence Award* in 2012. His skills have been in demand around the world and he has worked with students in Australia, Japan, Hungary, Ireland, New Zealand, Russia, Singapore, the UK and the USA. The focus of his executive work is on bridging the gap between academic insight and the commercial realities facing organizations and he has been extensively involved in both open and in-company programmes in Ireland and the UK. As part of this activity he is the author of several award-winning business case studies and has also been involved in the development of new pedagogical materials such as a series of business videos where he interviews some leading marketing managers about recent strategic initiatives in their organizations. Further details can be found at *www.johnfahy.net*.

Professor Fahy currently holds the Chair in Marketing at the University of Limerick. Prior to this he worked at Trinity College, Dublin, and he holds a Master's degree from Texas A&M University and a Doctorate from Trinity College. Outside of work his passions include family, music, sport, food and travel.

David Jobber is an internationally recognized marketing academic. He is Professor of Marketing at the University of Bradford School of Management. He holds an Honours Degree in Economics from the University of Manchester, a Master's Degree from the University of Warwick and a Doctorate from the University of Bradford.

Before joining the faculty at the Bradford Management Centre, David worked for the TI Group in marketing and sales, and was Senior Lecturer in Marketing at the University of Huddersfield. He has wide experience of teaching core marketing courses at undergraduate, postgraduate and post-experience levels. His specialisms are industrial marketing, sales management and marketing research. He has a proven, ratings-based record of teaching achievements at all levels. His competence in teaching is reflected in visiting appointments at the universities of Aston, Lancaster, Loughborough and Warwick in the UK, and the University of Wellington, New Zealand. He has taught marketing to executives of such international companies as BP, Croda International, Allied Domecq, the BBC, Bass, Royal & Sun Alliance, Rolls-Royce and Rio Tinto.

Supporting his teaching is a record of achievement in academic research. David has over 150 publications in the marketing area in such journals as the *International Journal of Research in Marketing, MIS Quarterly, Strategic Management Journal, Journal of International Business Studies, Journal of Management, Journal of Business Research, Journal of Product Innovation Management* and the *Journal of Personal Selling and Sales Management*. David has served on the editorial boards of the *International Journal of Research in Marketing, Journal of Personal Selling and Sales Management, European Journal of Marketing* and the *Journal of Marketing Management*. David has acted as Special Adviser to the Research Assessment Exercise panel that rates research output from business and management schools throughout the UK. In 2008, he received the Academy of Marketing's Life Achievement award for distinguished and extraordinary services to marketing.

Brief Table of Contents

Detailed Table of Contents

Case list

Vignette list

Preface to the Fifth Edition

Since the last edition of this book, it has been another remarkable three years in the marketing landscape. In terms of practice, the pace of change continues to be relentless. Technology continues to revolutionize both the ways in which consumers behave and the ways in which organizations both respond to and, in some cases, lead this change. Social media continues to grow to become one of the most pervasive influences on consumer behaviour. The 'old stalwarts' like Facebook and Twitter (which in truth are just a decade old) have been joined by a variety of other social media platforms like Pinterest and Tumblr. Typical of the social networking platforms of today is WhatsApp, a messaging service that was bought by Facebook in 2014 for almost $20 billion. The company was founded in 2009 but, by the time it was sold, it had over 500 million users worldwide and just 32 employees. The scale of the business and its small employee base is indicative of many of today's technology start-ups and highlights as well the ubiquitous nature of social networking.

Social media has significantly enhanced customer power. Recommendations on products and services can be found instantly by simply asking friends and contacts. Online reviews have become a key source of influence for consumers considering a purchase decision. With the rapid penetration of smartphones, these reviews can be accessed instantly right at the point of purchase with significant marketing implications. Bad customer experiences (as well as good) can be blogged or tweeted about, often invoking immediate responses from service providers. Customers can also choose the extent to which they want to become involved with a brand, with many becoming powerful advocates for brands through their posts and comments on social media.

But technology has also provided organizations with enhanced power. The phrase 'big data' has entered the general lexicon in the past three years. With so much of consumers' lives being lived through technology, data gathering, analysis, aggregation and distribution has become big business. In particular, aggregation of data about customers which has been collected across multiple platforms has enabled marketers to build up very accurate profiles of buyers to assist with their marketing efforts.

Changes in marketing theory move in tandem with these changes in practice. While many of the fundamentals of marketing stay the same over time, new questions also arise and subtle changes continue to take place. Some of the questions that currently occupy the mind of marketing thinkers include the following: (i) how much control do organizations have over their brands in our current information-rich environment, (ii) have consumers become jaded by the efforts of organizations to market themselves and what factors influence a consumer's sense of engagement with a brand, and (iii) what are the most appropriate metrics and analytics to be used by organizations as part of their marketing efforts. As we highlighted in the previous edition, organizations of whatever type need to be clear about what value they are offering and communicate this value to their audiences. But the process is no longer one-way. In a networked world, value is often co-created between organizational partners and often jointly by organizations and consumers. A value-centred approach to marketing is more important than ever.

The fifth edition

Some of the exciting features of the fifth edition include the following.

Digital Marketing

The rapid developments in theory and practice in the field of digital marketing means that we have included a full chapter dedicated to this subject.

A Focus on Value

Value remains the central theme of this book. As well as outlining the nature of customer value in Chapter 1, we have expanded this chapter to show how value plays a central role in an organization's strategic activities.

Market Research

The chapter on market research has been extensively revised to include a discussion on the uses of 'big data' and market intelligence in market research.

Social Media Marketing

The nature of social media marketing remains a core focus throughout the book. We examine the nature of effective social media marketing and also include 12 social media marketing vignettes. These contain insights on developing themes and effective practice and include questions for discussion and critical reflection.

Marketing and Society Debates

The book emphasizes a critical approach to both the theory and practice of marketing. For example, throughout the book, ten marketing and society debates are highlighted. These inserts provide conceptual arguments both for and against certain aspects of marketing with questions added to encourage critical reflection and debate.

Learning about marketing

Marketing is an interesting and exciting subject that is at the core of our lives both as consumers and as employees or managers in organizations. Therefore the focus of this book has always been on blending conceptual insights with the contemporary world of marketing practice. As such it retains the popular features of previous editions and adds several new ones.

Insights from the world of practice feature in myriad ways. Each chapter begins with a marketing spotlight focusing on the marketing activities and challenges facing some well-known global enterprises that sets the scene for the content that follows. In addition to the social media marketing inserts discussed above, there are 26 marketing in action vignettes that focus on the activities of a variety of organizations, large and small, public and private. Roughly one-third of these organizations are based in the UK/Ireland, one-third in Western Europe and one-third are from around the world giving a wide geographic breadth. Each of these inserts contains discussion questions designed to improve critical thinking and learning. New and updated end of chapter cases are included to provide more detailed problems for analysis and discussion.

Although the text is foundational, it also provides students with an introduction to many of the emerging themes in the marketing literature. Included, to name but a few, are consumer culture theory, semiotics, multisensory marketing, experiential marketing, search engine optimization, ambient marketing, value co-creation, marketing metrics, and so on. These concepts are presented in an accessible way to enable students to learn both the classic and contemporary elements of effective marketing.

Acknowledgements

Our thanks go to the following reviewers for their comments at various stages in the text's development:

Maged Ali, Brunel University
David Brown, Northumbria University
Craig Cathcart, Queen Margaret University
Jo Cartwright, Manchester University
Dr. Marius Claudy, University College Dublin
Dr. Sean Ennis, University of Strathclyde
Pfavai Nyajeka, University of Hertfordshire
Gary Harden, Nottingham Trent University
Sofia Isberg, Umea University
Reulene Kusel, Tshwane University of Technology

Nanne Migchels, Radbound University
Dr. Elizabeth Nixon, University of Nottingham
Danita Potgieter, University of Pretoria
Neil Richardson, Leeds Metropolitan University
Vicky Roberts, Staffordshire University
Beejal Shah, University of Hertfordshire
Dr. Alex Thompson, University of Exeter
Paul Trow, Avans University
Nick Yip, University of East Anglia

We would also like to thank the following contributors for the material which they have provided for this textbook and its accompanying online resources:

Dr. Seamus Allison, Nottingham Trent University
Fiona Armstrong-Gibbs, Liverpool John Moores University
Glyn Atwal, Burgundy School of Business
Dr. Abraham Brown, Nottingham Trent University
David Brown, Northumbria University
Douglas Bryson, ESC Rennes School of Business, France
Jane Burns, University College London
David Cosgrave, Limerick University
Irena Descubes, ESC Rennes School of Business, France
Mark Durkin, University of Ulster
Dr. Michael Gannon, Dublin City University
Thomas Gulløv Lohghi, University of Southern Denmark.
Alex Hiller, Nottingham Trent University
Lynsey Hollywood, University of Ulster
Tom McNamara, ESC Rennes School of Business, France
Christina O'Connor, National University of Ireland Maynooth
Marie O'Dwyer, Waterford Institute of Technology
Roisin Vize, University College Dublin
Anna Wos, University of Coventry

Authors' acknowledgements

We would like to thank colleagues, contributors and the reviewers who have offered advice and helped develop this text. We would also like to thank our editors Jennifer Yendell, Peter Hooper and Caroline Prodger for their invaluable support and assistance, and extend our gratitude to Alice Aldous, Alison Davis and Gill Colver.

Every effort has been made to trace and acknowledge ownership of copyright and to clear permission for material reproduced in this book. The publishers will be pleased to make suitable arrangements to clear permission with any copyright holders whom it has not been possible to contact.

Picture acknowledgements

The authors and publishers would like to extend thanks to the following for the reproduction of images, advertising and logos:

Exhibits

1.1: © studiomode / Alamy; 1.2: © Mediablitzimages / Alamy; 1.3: Reproduced with permission from United Biscuits; 1.4: © Jeffrey Blackler / Alamy; 2.1: © Holger Burmeister / Alamy; 2.2: Reproduced with permission from Amnesty International and Walker Werbeagentur AG; 2.3: © Justin Kase zfivez / Alamy; 2.4: Reproduced with permission from Honda; 3.1: reproduced with permission from The AA Ireland and Brando; 3.2: © Cultura Creative (RF) / Alamy; 3.3: © Mark Richardson / Alamy; 3.4: Reproduced with permission from Peugeot and Loducca; 3.5: © Islandstock / Alamy; 3.6: © david pearson / Alamy; 4.1: © Newscast / Alamy; 4.2: © Jeffrey Blackler / Alamy; 4.3: © Google; 4.4: iStock; 4.5 © mediaphotos / iStock; 5.1: Reproduced with permission from BMW; 5.2: ©Peggy Sirota, reproduced with permission; 5.3: reproduced with permission from The Gro Company; 5.4: © Mark Bourdillon / Alamy; 5.5 © Art Directors & TRIP / Alamy; 6.1: © Justin Kase z12z / Alamy; 6.2: © Justin Kase zsixz / Alamy; 6.3: reproduced with permission from Continental Tyres; 6.4: reproduced with permission from Audi; 6.5: © Roberto Herrett / Alamy; 7.1 © Jeff Morgan 09 / Alamy; 7.2 Photo/image by Ross Silcocks (www.livephotography.co.uk), reproduced with permission; 7.3: © WENN Ltd / Alamy; 7.4: reproduced with permission from Breakthrough Breast Cancer; 7.5: reproduced with permission from The Rainforest Alliance; 8.1 © Ian Dagnall / Alamy; 8.2: © epa european pressphoto agency b.v. / Alamy; 8.3: © M.Flynn / Alamy; 8.4: © Amazon; 8.5: reproduced with permission from Dollar Shave Club; C8.1 © razorpix / Alamy; 9.1: reproduced with permission from PRS research; 9.2: © Danny Callcut / Alamy; 9.3: © wonderlandstock / Alamy; 9.4: reproduced with permission from McDonald's; 9.5: reproduced with permission from IKEA Australia; C9.1: © Judy Unger / Alamy; 10.1: © Rakoskerti / iStock; 10.2: © AW Photography / Alamy; 10.3: © Matthew Chattle / Alamy; 10.4: © Nike; 10.5: reproduced with permission from Megx; C10.1: © Newscast / Alamy; 11.1: © david pearson / Alamy; 11.2: © ersler / iStock; 11.3: © zeljkosantrac / iStock; C11.1 © Brendan Donnelly / Alamy; C11.2: reproduced with permission from Donal Fallon; 12.1: © Gov.uk; 12.2: © Chris Ridley - Internet Stock / Alamy; 12.3: reproduced with permission from Nielsen Norman Group; 12.4: © Google; 12.5: © LDProd / iStock.

Part Opening Images

1: © AleksandarNakic / iStock; 2: © bluecinema / iStock; 3: © zuzlik / iStock.

Chapter Opening Images

1: © Dima_Oris / iStock; 2: © penfold / iStock; 3: © Bernhard Classen / Alamy; 4: © Courtney Keating / iStock; 5: © ALAN OLIVER / Alamy; 6: © diego_cervo / iStock; 7: © Hemis / Alamy; 8: © Frank and Helena / Alamy; 9: © BRIAN HARRIS / Alamy; 10: © Bon Appetit / Alamy; 11: © Dieter Wanke / Alamy; 12: © David J. Green - lifestyle themes / Alamy.

Case Images

1: © JJMaree / iStock; 2: © lofilolo / iStock; 3: © Michał Krakowiak / iStock; 4: © Nemanja Radovanovic / Alamy; 5 © Mlenny / iStock; 6: © Dangubic / iStock; 7: © Islandstock / Alamy; 8: © laartist 2004 iStock; 9: © thomasmax / iStock; 10: © BlakeDavidTaylor / iStock; 12: © Web Pix / Alamy.

Guided Tour

Chapter Outline and Learning Outcomes

The topics covered and a set of outcomes are included at the start of each chapter, summarizing what to expect from each chapter.

Chapter outline	Learnin[...]
What is marketing?	By the end of this chap[...]
The development of marketing	1 Understand what [...]
	2 Understand the na[...]
Marketing planning and strategy	3 Describe how mar[...] the years
	4 Explain the scope [...]
Marketing and business performance	5 Analyse the impac[...] organisational per[...]
	6 Critique the role o[...]
The scope of marketing	7 Explain the differe[...] and marketing tac[...]
	8 List the main com[...]

Marketing Spotlight

A lively vignette begins each chapter to introduce the main topic and show how marketing works in real life.

MARKETING SPOTLIGHT

Spotify

Music is something that stirs the passions of people right a[...] changes in the industry during the past 20 years demonstrate[...] marketing. The traditional business model for music is one th[...] years of popular music. Aspiring artists sought to win a covete[...] music label that then created a permanent record of the art[...] technology of the day, which evolved from vinyl to tape to [...] distributed through music stores and artists were promoted t[...] radio play and live concerts. Some of the best known names i[...] the Beatles to Bruce Springsteen were developed in this way. But by the turn of this century, developments in digital te[...]

Marketing in Action

In each chapter you'll find these fun informative examples of marketing in action, which show how the issues covered in the chapter affect real life companies and products. Each Marketing in Action vignette has a Critical Thinking box to provoke discussion and encourage critical reflection on that topic.

Marketing in Action 1.1 LEGO b[...] and physical divide

Critical Thinking: Below is an example of how a toy manuf[...] the real-life relevance of its physical products. Can compa[...] ries use a similar method to bridge the digital and physical[...]

With more and more children possessing the com-petences necessary to engage in online interac-tions, toy manufacturers are increasingly using their online presence to provide greater levels of value by enriching the play experience that

To su[...] content i[...] LEGO Fr[...] specific [...] beach or[...]

Social Media Marketing

There are several brand new social media marketing vignettes throughout the book. These contain insights on developing themes and effective practice and include questions for discussion and critical thinking.

Social Media Marketing 1.1 The[...]

Critical Thinking: Below is a review of the phenomenal g[...] cally reflect on the reasons for its success. One of the key[...] to spot and exploit new and rapidly growing markets. S[...] spoken about for several years, most people still only ha[...] actually is or have considered the kinds of opportunities[...] think of it, is that you store and access data and programs [...] hard drive. The cloud, in other words, becomes a metapho[...] to think of computing like this, a world of opportunity ope[...] this opportunity has been Dropbox Inc.

Marketing and Society

Marketing and Society boxes are located throughout the book, designed to highlight ethical issues, provoke discussion and critical reflection.

Marketing and Society 1.1 good or evil?

It is possible to look at marketing from different standpo[...] provides significant benefits to society. For example, the [...] as consumers, with a world of choice and diversity. A sea[...] on anything that we want; with an Apple app on their iPh[...] to examine patients, and websites like Amazon and eBay[...] desks. The innovations of tomorrow will bring us new and[...] Second, as the practice of marketing improves, our part[...] we eat only gluten-free products, love skydiving and hav[...] organizations that will fulfil these needs. As firms collec[...]

Exhibits, figures and tables

We've included a hand-selected array of contemporary adverts and images to show marketing in action. Key concepts and models are illustrated using figures, tables and charts.

End of chapter case studies

Every chapter has its own case study, directly relating to the issues discussed and designed to bring the theories to life. See page x for a full list of companies and issues covered. Questions are included for class work, assignments, revision and to promote critical reflection.

Summary

This chapter has introduced the concept of marketing and discussed ho
In particular, the following issues were addressed.

1. What is meant by the marketing concept? The key idea here is tho
at the centre of things. Implementing the marketing concept requ
effort throughout the company and a belief that corporate goals c

2. The idea of customer value, which is the difference between the pe
service and the perceived sacrifice involved in doing so. Customers
instances, therefore companies need to clearly spell out what value
value proposition.

3. That marketing as both a field of study and a field of practice is co
marketing has moved from an internal focus on production and sal
customers and markets. These market-driven organizations are bet

End of chapter material

The chapter summary reinforces the main topics to make sure you have acquired a solid understanding. Study questions allow you to apply your understanding and think critically about the topics. Suggested reading and References direct you towards the best sources for further research.

Tour our video and digital resources

In addition to the great study tools available for student and lecturers through Connect there are a host of support resources available to you via our website:

Online Learning Centre

Visit **www.mheducation.co.uk/textbooks/fahy5** today

Resources for students:

- New case studies
- Self test questions
- Internet exercises
- Glossary
- Ad Insight video

Also available for lecturers:

- Case study teaching notes
- Animated PowerPoint slides
- Additional case studies
- Image bank of artwork from the textbook
- Marketing Showcase videos

Ad Insight

Throughout the book you will find QR codes that link to carefully selected TV advertising campaigns via company YouTube videos. To access the videos, download a QR code reader app to your smartphone and scan the code with your camera.

Multiple choice questions that encourage you to analyse and relate the adverts to what you have learned in the book are offered within the Self-Quiz and Study area of **Connect™**.

Marketing Showcase SHOWCASE

We are excited to offer an exclusive set of new video cases to lecturers adopting this text. Each video illustrates a number of core marketing concepts linked to the book to help students to see how marketing works in the real world. This fantastic video resource will add real value to lectures, providing attention-grabbing content that helps students to make the connection between theory and practice.

What do the videos cover?

The videos offer students insights into how different organisations have successfully harnessed the elements of the marketing mix, including discussions about new product development, pricing, promotion, packaging, market research, relationship and digital marketing. The videos feature interviews with business leaders and marketing professionals, researched and conducted by Professor John Fahy to ensure seamless integration with the content of the new edition of this text.

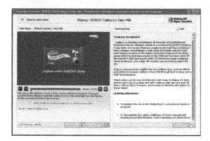

How can I use them?

To ensure maximum flexibility for teaching purposes, the videos have been edited to focus on key topics so that short extracts can be easily integrated into a lecture presentation or be delivered in a tutorial setting to spark class discussion. To ensure painless preparation for teaching, each video is accompanied by PowerPoint slides, teaching notes and discussion questions.

Some highlights of the video package include:

- An interview with **Paddy Power**, Communications Director of the eponymous bookmaker, who reveals the story behind their ground-breaking and often controversial marketing campaigns
- A first-hand account of how a young student entrepreneur set up the thriving **SuperJam** brand, taking his homemade preserves from the kitchen table to the supermarket
- The marketing director of **Burnt Sugar**, luxury toffee confectioners, explaining how his company has used innovative online forums, events and other customer feedback to develop and promote their products.

How do I get the videos?

The full suite of videos is available exclusively to lecturers adopting this textbook. For ultimate flexibility, they are available to lecturers:

- through **Connect**
- online at **www.mheducation.co.uk/textbooks/fahy5**

If you are interested in this resource, please contact your McGraw-Hill representative or visit **www.mheducation.co.uk/textbooks/fahy5** to request a demonstration.

McGraw-Hill Connect Marketing is a learning and teaching environment that improves student performance and outcomes while promoting engagement and comprehension of content.

You can utilize publisher-provided materials, or add your own content to design a complete course to help your students achieve higher outcomes.

PROVEN EFFECTIVE

INSTRUCTORS

With McGraw-Hill Connect Plus Marketing, instructors get:

- Simple **assignment management,** allowing you to spend more time teaching

- **Auto-graded** assignments, quizzes and tests

- **Detailed visual reporting** where students and section results can be viewed and analysed

- Sophisticated **online testing** capability

- A **filtering and reporting** function that allows you to easily assign and report on materials that are correlated to learning outcomes, topics, level of difficulty, and more. Reports can be accessed for individual students or the whole class, as well as offering the ability to drill into individual assignments, questions or categories

- **Instructor materials** to help supplement your course.

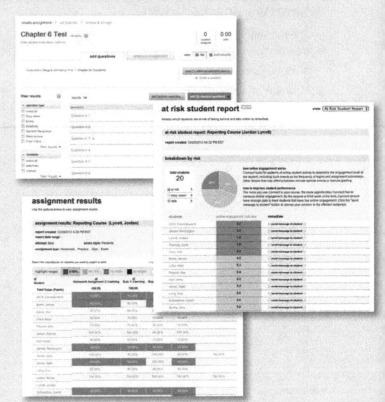

Get Connected. Get Results.

STUDENTS

With McGraw-Hill Connect Plus Marketing, students get:

Assigned content

- Easy **online access** to homework, tests and quizzes

- **Immediate feedback** and 24-hour tech support.

Self-Quiz and Study

- **Practice tests** help you to easily identify your strengths and weakness and create a clear revision plan.

- A fully searchable **e-book** allows you to brush up on your reading.

- **Study tools** – give you extra learning materials on individual topics.

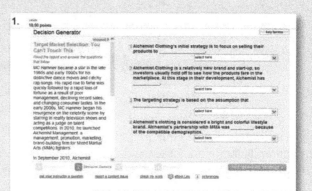

If your instructor is **not** prescribing Connect as part of your course, you can still access a full range of student support resources on our Self Study platform at http://connect.mheducation.com/selfstudy.

ACCESS OPTIONS

Is an online assignment and assessment solution that offers a number of powerful tools and features that make managing assignments easier, so faculty can spend more time teaching. With Connect Marketing, students can engage with their coursework anytime and anywhere, making the learning process more accessible and efficient.

Interactives

Encourage students to formulate a marketing strategy or illustrate a concept in an engaging and stimulating activity format with step by step guidance, to ensure conceptual understanding is tested and applied.

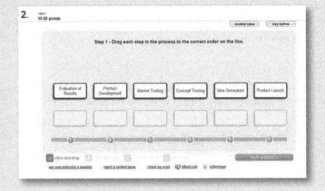

Videos

Promote engagement and student understanding, offering content in a fresh format and reinforcing key concepts. Videos feature interviews from business leaders and marketing professionals, allowing students to learn from real world strategies and campaigns.

Cases

Allow the student to learn how to analyse cases and check they have understood what they have read, while learning from market leading brand names.

Multiple Choice Questions

Check students' knowledge and conceptual understanding. Quick to answer and give students immediate feedback.

Pre-built assignments

Assign all of the autogradable end of chapter material as a ready-made assignment with the simple click of a button.

Seamlessly integrates all of the Connect Marketing features with:

- An integrated e-book, allowing for anytime, anywhere access to the textbook
- Dynamic links between assigned and self-study problems and the location in the e-book where that problem is covered
- A powerful search function to pinpoint and connect key concepts.

LearnSmart™

LearnSmart is the most widely used and intelligent adaptive learning resource that is proven to strengthen memory recall, improve course retention and boost grades. Distinguishing what students know from what they don't, and honing in on concepts they are most likely to forget, LearnSmart continuously adapts to each student's needs by building an individual learning path so students study smarter and retain more knowledge. Real-time reports provide valuable insight to instructors, so precious class time can be spent on higher-level concepts and discussion.

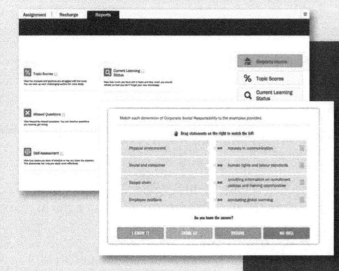

Let us help make our content **your** solution

At McGraw-Hill Education our aim is to help lecturers to find the most suitable content for their needs delivered to their students in the most appropriate way. Our **custom publishing solutions** offer the ideal combination of content delivered in the way which best suits lecturer and students.

Our custom publishing programme offers lecturers the opportunity to select just the chapters or sections of material they wish to deliver to their students from a database called CREATE™ at

http://create.mheducation.com/uk/

CREATE™ contains over two million pages of content from:
- textbooks
- professional books
- case books – Harvard Articles, Insead, Ivey, Darden, Thunderbird and BusinessWeek
- Taking Sides – debate materials

Across the following imprints:
- McGraw-Hill Education
- Open University Press
- Harvard Business Publishing
- US and European material

There is also the option to include additional material authored by lecturers in the custom product – this does not necessarily have to be in English.

We will take care of everything from start to finish in the process of developing and delivering a custom product to ensure that lecturers and students receive exactly the material needed in the most suitable way.

With a Custom Publishing Solution, students enjoy the best selection of material deemed to be the most suitable for learning everything they need for their courses – something of real value to support their learning. Teachers are able to use exactly the material they want, in the way they want, to support their teaching on the course.

Please contact **your local McGraw-Hill representative** with any questions or alternatively contact Warren Eels e: **warren.eels@mheducation.com**.

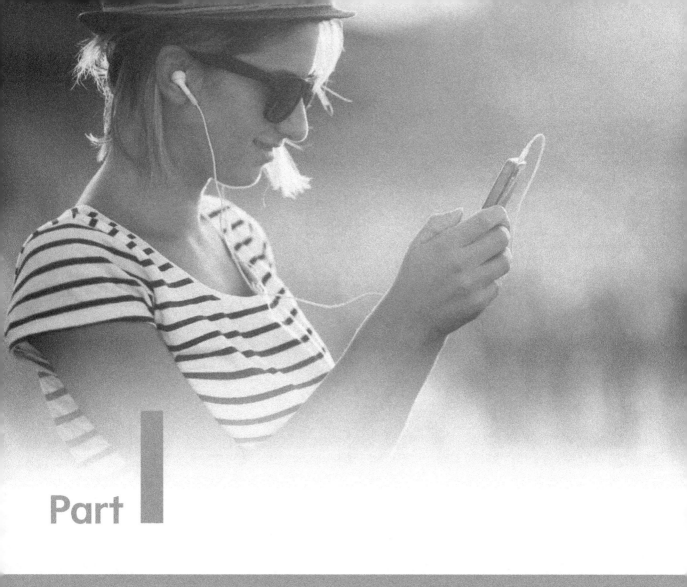

Part 1

The Market-Led Organization

Chapter 1

The Nature of Marketing

Chapter outline

What is marketing?

The development of marketing

Marketing planning and strategy

Marketing and business performance

The scope of marketing

Learning outcomes

By the end of this chapter you will:

1 Understand what marketing is

2 Understand the nature of customer value

3 Describe how marketing thought has developed over the years

4 Explain the scope of marketing

5 Analyse the impact of marketing activity on organisational performance

6 Critique the role of marketing in society

7 Explain the difference between marketing strategy and marketing tactics

8 List the main components of a marketing plan.

Spotify

Music is something that stirs the passions of people right around the world. But the dramatic changes in the **industry** during the past 20 years demonstrate the dynamic nature of business and marketing. The traditional business model for music is one that was established during the early years of popular music. Aspiring artists sought to win a coveted recording deal with an established music label that then created a permanent record of the artist's work through the appropriate technology of the day, which evolved from vinyl to tape to compact disc. These products were distributed through music stores and artists were promoted through marketing communications, radio play and live concerts. Some of the best known names in the industry from Elvis Presley to the Beatles to Bruce Springsteen were developed in this way.

But by the turn of this century, developments in digital technology began to change all that. Music could be stored on digital (MP3) files that were shared freely by computer users. One of the pioneering firms in this space was Napster, a company that operated between 1999 and 2001, whose technology enabled people to freely transfer music files that were stored on their computers. However, this activity violated the copyright owned by either record companies or artists and the service was forced to shut down. Nevertheless the rapid growth in the use of MP3 players (devices that could play MP3 music files) gave rise to the development of the iPod by Apple and the iTunes music store (where digital music could be legally purchased) which helped propel the firm to global dominance.

But once music lovers had developed a taste for consuming music for free, the industry was changed forever. Entrepreneurs rushed in with new models and concepts. One of the most successful of these has been the Swedish firm, Spotify, which has sought to bring to consumers the music that they want but also provide a revenue stream to the owners of that music. Like previous music streaming services, Spotify provides users with access to millions of tracks as well as the facilities to browse through genres and playlists and to share playlists with friends. But it also provided a revenue stream to the music owners – initially through an advertisement-supported free service and then through encouraging users to upgrade to a premium service that costs a set monthly fee but has the added benefit of enabling customers to download music and listen offline.

In seeking to build its brand in a competitive industry, Spotify employed some clever marketing tactics. The first was to exploit the principle of scarcity – in other words, making your product difficult to get paradoxically increases demand for it. Initially, users could only sign up to Spotify if invited to do so by a friend, a tactic which generated lots of word-of-mouth promotion for the brand. This social effect was then greatly enhanced by partnerships with leading social media sites such as Facebook and Twitter which allowed users to send songs to Facebook friends and have played songs appear on news feeds. By 2013, it was estimated that Spotify had 24 million users worldwide of which 6 million were paying customers generating revenues estimated to be in the region of €500 million.

The activities of companies both reflect and shape the world that we live in. For example, some have argued that the invention of the motor car has defined the way we live today because it allowed personal mobility on a scale that had never been seen before. It contributed to the growth of city suburbs, to increased recreation and to an upsurge in consumer credit. It gave us shopping malls, theme parks, motels, a fast-food industry and a generation of road movies. In a similar vein today, the development of wearable technology such as Google Glass could have a profound impact on everything from how people navigate their worlds, to how they interact with each other to how they even store and retrieve the memories of their lives.

Therefore, the world of business is an exciting one where there are new successes and failures every day. The newspaper industry was once all powerful and the main means by which consumers learned about what was happening in the world. It continued to thrive with the arrival of radio and television and complemented these media. But the Internet has changed the way that news is both captured and communicated, with the result that many newspapers are either struggling or failing. Not too long ago, Sony dominated the gaming business with its PlayStation consoles and exciting range of games. While trying to strengthen the functionality of its PlayStation 3, it wasn't alive to the threat posed by the Nintendo Wii, whose ease of use, lower price points and broader appeal enabled it to capture a leading share in the market. And now both organizations must respond to an increasing customer preference for online play in virtual worlds.

At the heart of all of this change is marketing. Companies succeed and fail for many reasons but very often marketing is central to the outcome. The reason for this is that the focus of marketing is on customers and their changing needs. If you don't have customers, you don't have a business. Successful companies are those that succeed not only in getting customers but also in keeping them through being constantly aware of their changing needs. The goal of marketing is long-term customer satisfaction, not short-term deception or gimmicks. This theme is reinforced by the writings of top management consultant Peter Drucker, who stated:[1]

> *Because the purpose of business is to create and keep customers, it has only two central functions – marketing and innovation. The basic function of marketing is to attract and retain customers at a profit.*

What does this statement tell us? First, it places marketing in a central role for business success since it is concerned with the creation and retention of customers. The failure of many products, particularly those in sectors like information technology, is often attributed to a lack of attention to customer needs. For example, Microsoft developed a new version of its Windows operating system, Windows 8, in order to appeal to a growing segment of consumers using hand-held tablet devices rather than traditional personal computers. However, its launch was generally considered a failure as poor design and usability issues meant a low level of uptake of the system by existing Microsoft users while it also failed in its important task of kick-starting sales of Microsoft's own tablet devices. Second, it is a reality of commercial life that it is much more expensive to attract new customers than to retain existing ones. Indeed, the costs of attracting new customers have been found to be up to six times higher than the costs of retaining existing ones.[2] Consequently, marketing-orientated companies recognize the importance of building relationships with customers by providing satisfaction and attracting new customers by creating added value. Grönroos stressed the importance of relationship building in his definition of marketing, in which he describes the objective of marketing as to establish, develop and commercialize long-term customer relationships so that the objectives of the parties involved are met.[3] Third, since most markets are characterized by strong competition, the statement also suggests the need to monitor and understand competitors, since it is to rivals that customers will turn if their needs are not being met. The rest of this chapter will examine some of these ideas in more detail.

What is marketing?

The modern **marketing concept** can be expressed as 'the achievement of corporate goals through meeting and exceeding customer needs better than the competition'. For example, Netflix has added to its successful movie rental and streaming services by providing original TV show content. In addition, all of its content is available on mobile devices, allowing customers to watch their favourite movies and shows while on the move – a significant advantage over cable operators. Three conditions must be met before the marketing concept can be applied. First, company activities should be focused on providing **customer satisfaction** rather than, for example, simply producing products (see Exhibit 1.1). This is not always as easy as it may first appear. Organizations almost by definition are inward-looking with a focus on their people, their operations and their products.

Exhibit I.I The Duracell brand owned by P&G has built a strong reputation in the marketplace as a longer-lasting battery

 Duracell Ad Insight: Brand advertising focuses on key benefits such as battery life.

The customer may often appear to be at some remove from the organization and when their needs are changing rapidly, companies can lose touch with them. For example, until recently, Finland's Nokia was the world's dominant mobile-phone manufacturer by some distance. However, its failure to recognize the shift in consumer tastes towards more technologically advanced smartphones meant that its sales collapsed and it was rapidly overtaken by Apple and Samsung.

Its Mobile Devices and Services division was subsequently sold off to Microsoft in 2013.

Second, the achievement of customer satisfaction relies on integrated effort. The responsibility for the implementation of the concept lies not just within the marketing department but should run right through production, finance, research and development, engineering and other departments. The fact that marketing is the responsibility of everyone in the organization provides significant challenges for the management of companies. Finally, for integrated effort to come about, management must believe that corporate goals can be achieved through satisfied customers (see Figure 1.1). Some companies are quicker and better at recognizing the importance of the marketing concept than others. For example, Nike was a late entrant into the running shoe business dominated by brands such as Reebok and Puma, but it has established itself as the world's leading sportswear company, through the delivery of powerful brand values.

In summary, companies can be viewed as being either inward looking or outward looking. In the former, the focus is on making things or providing services but with significant attention being paid to the efficiency with which internal operations and processes are conducted. Companies that build strategy from the outside in start with the customer and work backwards from an understanding of what customers truly value. The difference in emphasis is subtle but very important. By maintaining an outside-in focus, companies can understand what customers value and how to consistently innovate new sources of value that keep bringing them back.[4] Doing so efficiently, ensures that value is created and delivered at a profit to the company – the ultimate goal of marketing.

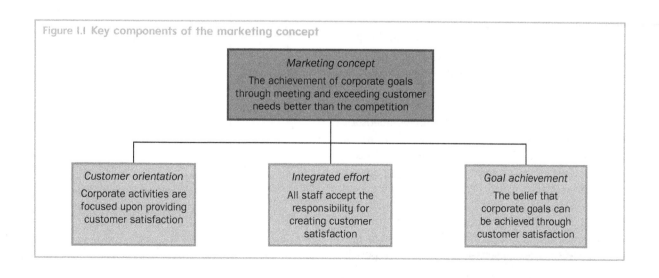

Figure I.I Key components of the marketing concept

Marketing concept
The achievement of corporate goals through meeting and exceeding customer needs better than the competition

Customer orientation
Corporate activities are focused upon providing customer satisfaction

Integrated effort
All staff accept the responsibility for creating customer satisfaction

Goal achievement
The belief that corporate goals can be achieved through customer satisfaction

The nature of customer value

If delivering **customer value** is the key to building a successful business, how can a firm know if it is creating such value? This has proven to be a troublesome problem for many companies. For example, some firms add new features to products and hope that this will attract customers. Others engage in new marketing activities such as advertising campaigns, Facebook competitions or the creation of retail experiences. And still others may seek to exploit consumer preferences for economy by offering products or services at lower prices. But the key question is: do consumers see any of these changes as being beneficial to them and worth any of the costs that they may have to incur in order to obtain these benefits? Consequently customer value is often expressed in terms of the definition below and it is important to note that it is customers and not organizations who define what represents value:

customer value = perceived benefits – perceived sacrifice

Perceived benefits can be derived from the product (for example, the hotel room and restaurant), the associated service (for example, how responsive the hotel is to the specific needs of customers) and the image of the company (for example, is the image of the company/product favourable?). Conveying benefits is a critical marketing task and is central to positioning and branding, as we shall see in Chapters 5 and 6.

Perceived sacrifice is the total cost associated with buying the product. This consists not just of monetary costs, but also the time and energy involved in the purchase. For example, with hotels, good location can reduce the time and energy required to find a suitable place to stay. But marketers need to be aware of another critical sacrifice in some buying situations: this is the potential psychological cost of not making the right decision. Uncertainty means that people perceive risk when purchasing. Therefore, hotels like the Marriott or restaurants like McDonald's aim for consistency so that customers can be confident of what they will receive when they visit these service providers.

A further key to marketing success is to ensure that the value offered exceeds that of competitors. Consumers decide on purchases on the basis of judgements about the value offered by different suppliers. Once a product has been purchased, customer satisfaction depends on its perceived performance compared to the buyer's expectations and will be achieved if these expectations are met or exceeded. Expectations are formed through pre-buying experiences, discussions with other people and suppliers' marketing activities. Companies need to avoid the mistake of setting customer expectations too high through exaggerated promotional claims, since this can lead to dissatisfaction if performance falls short of expectations.

In the current competitive climate, it is usually not enough simply to match performance and expectations. Expectations need to be exceeded for commercial success so that customers are delighted with the outcome. In order to understand the concept of customer satisfaction, the Kano model (see Figure 1.2) helps to separate characteristics that cause dissatisfaction, satisfaction and delight. Three characteristics underlie the model: 'must be', 'more is better' and 'delighters'.

Those characteristics recognized as 'must bes' are expected and thus taken for granted. For example, commuters expect planes or trains to depart on time and for schedules to be maintained. Lack of these characteristics causes annoyance but their presence only brings dissatisfaction up to a neutral level. 'More is better' characteristics can take satisfaction past neutral and into the positive satisfaction range (see Marketing in Action 1.1). For example, no response to a telephone call can cause dissatisfaction, but a fast response may cause positive satisfaction. The usability of search results is an example of 'more is better' and has become a key differentiating factor in the search engine industry, which has allowed Google to become the dominant player. 'Delighters' are the unexpected characteristics that surprise the customer. Their absence does not cause dissatisfaction, but their presence delights the customer. For example, tourists who have found that a holiday destination

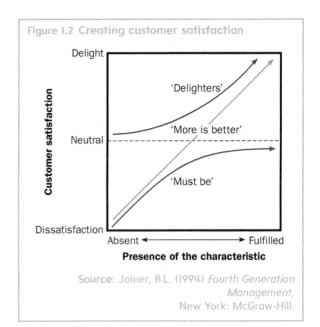

Figure I.2 Creating customer satisfaction

Source: Joiner, B.L. (1994) *Fourth Generation Management*, New York: McGraw-Hill.

Marketing in Action 1.1 LEGO bridging the digital and physical divide

Critical Thinking: Below is an example of how a toy manufacturer uses online content to increase the real-life relevance of its physical products. Can companies marketing other product categories use a similar method to bridge the digital and physical divide?

With more and more children possessing the competences necessary to engage in online interactions, toy manufacturers are increasingly using their online presence to provide greater levels of value by enriching the play experience that children get out of the products that they buy in toy stores. LEGO, the Danish toy manufacturer with one of the strongest brands in the world, is no exception to this development. Not only does LEGO manufacture a product that is renowned for its quality and flexibility, but by integrating online content with the physical product line, LEGO can enrich the experience that children have when interacting with LEGO's products in both the online and offline environments

The LEGO 'Friends' product line is targeted towards girls between the ages of five and 12. The LEGO Friends sets are characterised by pink, purple and pastel coloured elements and are designed around themes such as horse riding, camping in the forest and being at the beach. While LEGO has been criticized by some for entrenching gender stereotypes with the Friends product line, the sets have been well received by the target segment. Children derive value from all of LEGO's physical products through, for example, the activity of building, the sense of accomplishment with the finished model and the opportunities for storytelling afterwards. The play experience in conjunction with the LEGO Friends line has been enriched by creating online content that supports the storytelling element; not only this, but LEGO has leveraged what the target segment is doing in real life – helping out in the kitchen – to make the LEGO sets relevant to children in their everyday lives.

To support the physical product, the online content is placed on microsites under the main LEGO Friends web pages. On the microsite, a specific LEGO set, for example a juice bar on the beach or a bakery shop, is singled out for special attention. In the case of the juice bar LEGO set, the child is able to download recipes for different smoothies and juices; in the case of the bakery shop LEGO set, the child is able to download cupcake recipes. The choice of which LEGO set to support is also based on the time of year; in this way, LEGO is able to leverage what the child is doing in 'real life' in order to increase the value provided by the online supporting content. The juice bar downloads are available in the summer when the hot weather makes a refreshing juice a welcome drink, while the bakery shop downloads are available in the winter when the cold weather makes a warm cupcake a treat.

In order to leverage the real-life activities that the child is engaging in, LEGO makes the online content available to all microsite users, irrespective of whether the child owns the LEGO set or not. This means that by linking a LEGO set to a particular real-life activity, the child is made aware of the existence of the juice bar and bakery shop LEGO sets. In this case, LEGO is leveraging what the child is doing in the kitchen in order to increase the value provided by the LEGO sets: the child can recreate the kitchen experience through storytelling with the juice bar or bakery LEGO set. So LEGO is not just providing supporting online content to increase the value of its sets, it is also using the target segment's real-life activities as a marketing tool for LEGO's sets, bridging the digital and physical divide.

has exceeded their expectations through the quality of customer service that they have received will often be delighted and are likely to recommend the destination to friends and colleagues.

Four forms of customer value

Though modern organizations offer an innumerable variety of products and services, four core forms of customer value have been identified as follows:[5]

Price value: one of the most powerful customer motivations to purchase is because a product is perceived as being cheaper than those offered by competitors. This has been exploited in many industries such as air travel (Ryanair), food retailing (Aldi), car rental (EasyCar), and so on. These types of organizations recognize that, in their markets, some consumers will forego extra product features in order to avail themselves of low prices (see market segmentation in Chapter 5). They respond by providing basic products at low prices. For example, low fares airlines have stripped away many of the features that used to characterize air travel such as in-flight meals, airport check-ins and no baggage restrictions. Consumers who want these features are now charged extra for them and the profitability of low price companies is further enhanced by a high degree of attention that they pay to the efficiency of their operations. The food retailer Aldi has an estimated annual turnover of €40 billion and is one of Germany's most successful companies. Its business proposition is to offer customers a limited range of own-label products at permanently low prices in a no-frills environment.

Performance value: in the same way that some customers have a preference for low price, others are more concerned about product performance. What they are looking for is the latest features and they are attracted to products by their functionality and perceived quality levels. The priority for companies operating in this space is to be consistently innovative, exploiting changes and discontinuities in technology in order to deliver products with attractive features and functionality. For example, the UK electronic products manufacturer, Dyson, has a team of 420 engineers and scientists working on product ideas and the firm has been responsible for innovations like the cyclonic vacuum cleaner, the Airblade electric hand dryer and the Contrarotator, which was the world's first washing machine with two counter-rotating drums for a better clean. Firms like Dyson aim to provide value to customers based on the functionality and performance features of their products and services.

Emotional value: one of the big challenges facing the modern firm is to find effective ways to differentiate products based on performance elements. If one looks at the car industry for example, the technical differences between cars in particular categories such as economy cars and family saloons are marginal. Most have very similar designs, functionality and features, and different manufacturers frequently share time on the same production lines. Similarly for a whole array of consumer products such as basic electrical appliances, the brands of competing firms are regularly manufactured by a small number of companies and technical differences between them are minimal. Consequently, the only real difference that exists between these brands is in the mind of the consumer and this is what is known as emotional value. Some consumers may prefer Volvo cars because they believe them to be safer than competing brands (technically this is not the case) and as a result remain loyal Volvo buyers. This kind of emotional value is created through marketing activity as we shall discuss throughout the book. It also helps to explain why some consumers will pay huge premiums for luxury brands (Chanel, Hermès) and why others will queue for hours to be the first among their peers to own certain products (iPad, Kate Moss clothing).

Relational value: another important motive to purchase is the quality of service received by the customer. This presents a particular opportunity in the case of service businesses (see Chapter 7) such as a restaurant meal or business taxation services which are not easy to evaluate in advance of purchase. When the customer finds a good quality service provider, they may be willing to stay with this provider and as the relationship builds a high level of trust becomes established between the parties. Central to this is the notion of the **lifetime value of a customer** which is recognition by the company of the potential sales, profits and endorsements that come from a repeat customer who stays with the company for several years. But relational value is not restricted just to service businesses. All kinds of organizations are now becoming proficient users of **customer relationship management** (CRM) systems to get to know their customers better and to interact with them on a regular basis (see Chapter 7). Even fast-moving consumer goods brands such as innocent and Walkers have sought to build stronger relationships with core customers through running events that customers can enjoy (innocent village fetes, Walkers 'Do Us a Flavour') while in turn the company benefits from not only customer loyalty but also creation of new product ideas that come from the market place. In other words, value is increasingly being seen as not something that is created by organizations for customers but rather something that is co-created between organizations and customers.[6]

The challenge for organizations then is to try to become a value leader on one of these four dimensions (see Social Media Marketing 1.1). Those that do achieve these leadership positions such as Ryanair (price value leader in aviation) or Louis Vuitton (emotional value leader in luxury fashion goods) tend to be significantly more successful than their peers. This is because they have a clearly defined **customer value proposition** or unique selling point (USP) which is a reason why customers return to them again and again. It is not normally possible for companies

Social Media Marketing 1.1 The rise of Dropbox

Critical Thinking: Below is a review of the phenomenal growth of Dropbox. Read it and critically reflect on the reasons for its success. One of the keys to success in business is the ability to spot and exploit new and rapidly growing markets. So though cloud computing has been spoken about for several years, most people still only have a vague understanding of what it actually is or have considered the kinds of opportunities that it can create. A simple way to think of it, is that you store and access data and programs online rather than on your computer's hard drive. The cloud, in other words, becomes a metaphor for the Internet and once you begin to think of computing like this, a world of opportunity opens up. One of the new firms to exploit this opportunity has been Dropbox Inc.

Dropbox is a file hosting service that was founded in San Francisco, California in 2008. Because computer users today typically have or use more than one computer, store files on hand-held devices and travel a lot, file management can be a major problem. For example, you are at a meeting in another country but the file you need is on your home or office computer. Emailing files between computers and carrying them on USB sticks is time consuming and inefficient. This problem is solved by Dropbox's technology which allows users to set up a storage 'box' on their computers that is automatically synchronized and updated when any one device is used. The files are also stored on the Dropbox website so if a computer is lost or crashes, the files are saved. Dropboxes can be shared with friends or business colleagues resulting in applications in consumer and business markets.

Dropbox's rise has been spectacular. By 2012, it was estimated to have over 200 million users worldwide who were saving a billion files to Dropbox every 24 hours. The service is free initially with a monthly subscription fee applying once larger quantities of storage are required. This enabled annual revenues to rise to an estimated $116 million in 2012. A huge part of its growth and popularity stemmed from effective word-of-mouth marketing and use of social media. When one friend invites another to join on Dropbox, they get an extra 500MB of storage space, with the result that 60 per cent of new customers were referrals. Each new Facebook and Twitter connection also received an additional 125MB of storage.

Based on: Rogowsky (2013).[7]

to compete on more than one dimension as to do so would mean presenting a confusing message in the marketplace. However, the proposition may evolve over time. For example, innocent drinks initially captured a share of the market through the quality of its smoothies (performance value) but this was quickly supplanted by the personality of the brand – its humorous, quirky approach to business and its cause-related activity (emotional value). And as discussed above, some of its recent initiatives suggest a drive towards relational value.

The key role of customer value enables us to offer the following definition of **marketing**:

Marketing is the delivery of value to customers at a profit.

Therefore we see that the two core elements of marketing are value and profit. Organizations must create and deliver some form of value for some customer group. But they also must be able to do this in a manner that enables them to generate a profit, otherwise their business will be unsustainable. Being consistently able to provide value and generate profit is a characteristic of the most successful companies such as Apple and Tesco.

The development of marketing

The origins of modern marketing can be traced to the Industrial Revolutions that took place in Britain around 1750 and in the USA and Germany around 1830.[8] Advances in production and distribution, and the migration of rural masses to urban areas, created the potential for large-scale markets. As business people sought to exploit these markets, the institutions of marketing such as advertising media and distribution channels began to grow and develop. Marketing as a field of study began in the early part of the twentieth century, growing out of courses that examined issues relating to distribution.[9] The focus of marketing courses in the 1950s and 1960s was on 'how to do it', with an emphasis on the techniques of marketing.[10] In more recent times, attention has been paid to the philosophy of marketing as a way of doing business, and to the nature and impact of marketing on stakeholders and society in general.

Despite this long tradition, there is no guarantee that all companies will adopt a **marketing orientation**. Many firms today are characterized by an inward-looking stance, where their focus is on existing products or the internal operations of the company, that can be traced all the way back to the emergence of mass production in the USA in the 1920s and 1930s. Figure 1.3a illustrates **production orientation** in its crudest form. The focus is on current production capabilities. The purpose of the organization is to develop products or services and it is the quality and innovativeness of these offerings that are considered to be the key to success. For example, a report on the funds management industry in the UK found that, in general, the sector was characterized by a lack of customer focus and a lack of effective market segmentation, with the result that many products being offered were unsuitable and potential sales were being lost.[11]

Many other organizations are characterized by what can be described as an excessive sales focus. They may possess good products and services but believe that the focus of marketing should be on ensuring that customers buy these offerings (see Figure 1.3b). This is an approach that is often traced back to the post-Second World War period in the United States when the engines of mass production generated a surplus of products in the market and aggressive sales efforts were required in order to persuade customers to buy. Many industries such as pharmaceuticals rely heavily on sales forces to push products in the marketplace.

The failure of many businesses that were excessively product or sales focused then led to increasing attention to the needs of customers. This orientation is shown in Figure 1.3c. Because customer-orientated companies get close to their customers, they understand their needs and problems. Market research is a critically important activity that will be discussed in more detail in Chapter 4. Customer needs and preferences change rapidly and close contact with them is necessary to understand these changes. Throughout the book we will describe examples of organizations that have changed their marketing strategies in response to customer changes.

One of the great benefits of having satisfied customers is that they tell others of their experiences, further enhancing sales (see Social Media Marketing 1.1). For example, recent research has shown that the experience of other customers with a product or service has a significant impact on purchase decisions in sectors like automobiles and financial services. Online businesses are significant users of word-of-mouth marketing. For example, TripAdvisor is a website where satisfied and dissatisfied customers post their reviews of hotels and destinations that they have stayed at, and these kinds of reviews influence the purchase decision of other customers.

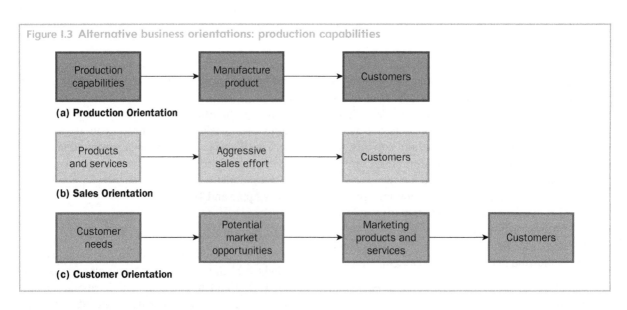

Figure 1.3 Alternative business orientations: production capabilities

(a) Production Orientation

(b) Sales Orientation

(c) Customer Orientation

Sometimes these three orientations are presented as being chronological, with the production orientation (c.1930s), followed by the **sales orientation** (c.1950s) and then the customer orientation emerging in the 1960s and 1970s. But it is quite clear that in the world of practice all three orientations are still commonplace. Significant attention has also been paid to newer business orientations that have been emerging in recent years, particularly the **societal marketing concept** which is frequently referred to as sustainable marketing. One of the major concerns for both business and society is that the resources of the planet are finite and business activity places significant demands on these limited resources. The societal marketing concept holds that marketing strategy should deliver value to customers in a way that maintains or improves both the consumer's and society's well-being. This means that as well as meeting customer needs, businesses should also engage in activities such as reducing pollution as well as developing corporate social responsibility programmes. The societal marketing concept will be dealt with in greater detail in Chapter 2.

Finally, there is also an increasing recognition that a focus on customer needs does not always deliver the kinds of insights that businesses expect. Consumers may not always be able to articulate their needs and wants and that it is also up to organizations to lead markets from time to time. These **market-driven or outside-in firms** seek to anticipate as well as identify consumer needs and build the resource profiles necessary to meet current and anticipated future demand. In the same vein, Vargo and Lusch have called for a move away from the economic model of marketing based on notions of manufactured goods and transactional exchanges to one that is based more clearly on relational exchanges between entities where value is co-created rather than determined by one entity and exchanged with another.[12] Recent developments such as the rapid growth of social media further illustrate the important role of the customer in co-creating value

In short, the differences between market-orientated businesses and internally orientated businesses are summarized in Table 1.1. These can be considered to be two ends of a spectrum. Market-driven businesses display customer concern throughout the business; they understand the criteria customers use to choose between competing suppliers; they invest in market research, and track market changes; they regard marketing spend as an investment, and are fast and flexible in terms of their pursuit of new opportunities.

Marketing planning and strategy

In some organizations, marketing can be a haphazard activity done in response to particular opportunities or in times of difficulty or crisis. But attention to marketing must be consistent as markets change and nothing lasts forever. For example, even the book that you are reading is right at the centre of a rapidly changing market environment. In 2010, the world's largest bookstore, Barnes and Noble, was put up for sale following the pattern of many other bookstores around the world that struggle to cope with the combined developments of Internet book selling, e-books and the recent emergence of e-book readers or e-readers such as Amazon's Kindle, the Apple iPad and Sony's e-reader.

Table I.I Market-orientated businesses versus internally-orientated businesses

Market-orientated businesses	Internally orientated businesses
Customer concern throughout business	Convenience comes first
Know customer choice criteria and match with marketing mix	Assume price and product performance key to most sales
Segment by customer differences	Segment by product
Invest in market research (MR) and track market changes	Rely on anecdotes and received wisdom
Welcome change	Cherish status quo
Try to understand competition	Ignore competition
Marketing spend regarded as an investment	Marketing spend regarded as a luxury
Innovation rewarded	Innovation punished
Search for latent markets	Stick with the same
Be fast	Why rush?
Strive for competitive advantage	Happy to be me-too

Table 1.2 The marketing planning process

Main stages in the marketing planning process	Relevant chapters in the book
Business mission and strategy	Chapter 1
The marketing audit	Chapters 1–4
Marketing objectives	Chapter 1
Marketing strategy	Chapter 5
Marketing actions	Chapters 6–12
Evaluation of performance	Chapter 1

For marketing efforts to be effective, it is essential that a planned approach is taken. The process by which businesses analyse the environment and their capabilities, decide upon courses of marketing action and implement those decisions is called **marketing planning**. The following key questions need to be asked when thinking about marketing planning decisions:

- Where are we now?
- Where would we like to be?
- How do we get there?

The process of answering these questions involves some analyses and choices which are detailed in Table 1.2. The themes and issues emerging during each of these stages will be developed in greater detail at certain times throughout specific chapters of this book.

Business mission and strategy

Marketing does not operate in splendid isolation but is intrinsically linked to all the other activities that take place in organizations such as human resource management, design and production, research, financial management and so on. The glue that links all of these diverse activities together is the **business mission**. Ackoff defined the business mission as:[13]

a broadly defined, enduring statement of purpose that distinguishes a business from others of its type

This definition captures two essential ingredients in mission statements: they are enduring and specific to the individual organization.[14] For example, Coca Cola's mission statement is 'to refresh the world in mind, body and spirit: to inspire moments of optimism through our brands and actions; to create value and make a difference everywhere we engage'. Effective mission statements infuse organizations with a sense of purpose as well as defining the domains in which they operate. Both of these elements are crucially important. For example, Samsung claims that it wants to devote its talent and technology to creating superior products and services that contribute to a better global society. Mission statements like these can be inspiring and appealing to a variety of key stakeholders such as employees, investors and customers. Second, they clarify the domain that the organization operates in. This is something that marketing can both contribute to and be influenced by. For example, Levitt argued that a business should be viewed as a customer-satisfying process and not a goods-producing process.[15] By adopting a customer perspective, new opportunities are more likely to be seen. He famously argued that the US railroads would not have declined had they defined themselves as being in the transportation business and acknowledged that airlines were significant competitors. Businesses today face the same kinds of questions. For example, how retail banks choose to define their domain of operations is very important in a fast-changing environment where they face competition from several new sources such as grocery stores, online payment firms like Paypal and even peer-to-peer lending platforms like Lending Club.

The personalities and beliefs of the people who run businesses shape the business mission. This emphasizes the judgemental nature of business definition. There is no right or wrong business mission in abstract. The mission should be based on the vision that top management and their subordinates have of the future of the business. This vision is a coherent and powerful statement of what the business should aim to become. The business mission will serve as an overriding influence on the nature of the marketing plan and should also serve to motivate all staff to attain the targets set out in the plan.

In tandem with the business mission is the organization's strategy which seeks to answer the question of how it intends to gain a competitive advantage in the marketplace. The key to superior performance in competitive markets is to gain and hold a competitive advantage. Firms can gain a competitive advantage through differentiation of their product offering, which provides superior customer value, or by managing for lowest delivered cost. Evidence for this proposition was provided by Hall, who examined the competitive strategies pursued by the two leading firms (in terms of return on investment) in eight mature industries characterized by slow growth and intense competition.[16] In each industry, the two leading firms offered either high product differentiation or the lowest delivered cost. In most cases, an industry's return-on-investment leader opted for one of the strategies, while the second-place firm pursued the other. When combined with the competitive scope of activities (broad vs narrow) these two means of competitive advantage result in four generic strategies: differentiation, cost leadership, differentiation focus and cost focus. The **differentiation strategy** and cost leadership strategy seek competitive advantage in a broad range of market or industry segments, whereas differentiation focus and cost focus strategies are confined to a narrow segment. Seeking one of these positions of advantage is critical to survival. For example, the only players remaining in the fashion business are either megabrands with a billion dollars in sales, such as Gucci, Louis Vuitton, Burberry, Prada and others, or niche brands with sales of between $1 million and $100 million, such as Rochas and Balenciaga.

These two positions of advantage embrace the four forms of value explained earlier. For example, organizations can pursue a strategy of differentiation on the basis of offering superior emotional performance or relational value; alternatively they may use a cost leadership position to offer a price value proposition. The model also takes account of competitive scope or the arena in which the business operates. Some organizations such as start-ups, small-to-medium sized firms or firms that are pursuing a niche strategy choose to have a narrow focus. For example, some small speciality chemical companies thrive on taking orders that are too small or specialized to be of interest to their larger competitors. Microbreweries have been on the rise around the world to meet the niche tastes not catered for by the big brewers. In contrast, larger firms like Tesco and Philips attempt to have a broad appeal, offering a wide range of products to a broad spectrum of customers. Whether an organization chooses to differentiate or to be a cost leader will have important implications for the amount and type of marketing activity that takes place.

Other aspects of organizational strategy will also drive marketing planning decisions. As we shall see in Chapter 6, some companies carry a very large portfolio of brands or products. Some of these may be seen as flagship products and receive a significant level of marketing investment while others may be viewed as being of less importance in the overall portfolio and are forced to operate within a tighter marketing budget which limits what they can do. Also, as we shall examine in the next chapter, many businesses compete on a global scale with operations spread right around the world. How they are structured to operate across borders has a significant impact on how marketing happens at a local level. For example, some firms find that it is more efficient to make all the key marketing decisions in one location with the result that the marketing conducted by a national subsidiary may amount to no more than simply implementing locally, concepts and campaigns that have been created at head office.[17]

The marketing audit

Information is required to develop an effective marketing plan. Therefore, one of the starting points of planning is an analysis of the organization's current situation or what is known as a **marketing audit**. This is a systematic examination of a firm's marketing environment, objectives, strategies and activities, which aims to identify key strategic issues, problem areas and opportunities. An internal audit concentrates on those areas that are under the control of marketing management, whereas an external audit focuses on those forces over which management has no control. The results of the marketing audit are a key determinant of the future direction of the business and may give rise to a redefined business mission statement. A checklist of those areas that are likely to be examined in a marketing audit is given in Tables 1.3 and 1.4. Aspects of the external marketing audit will be addressed in more detail in Chapters 2–4 while the remainder of the book will inform aspects of the internal marketing audit.

A comprehensive marketing audit is a time-consuming activity and may only be conducted periodically. In rapidly changing industries, organizations may prefer to focus on some key elements such as market and competitive changes in order to produce timely and responsive plans.

One concise way of presenting the outcomes of a marketing audit is through a summary of the strengths, weaknesses, opportunities and threats facing the organization, or a **SWOT analysis** (see Figure 1.4).

For a SWOT analysis to be useful a number of guidelines must be followed. First, it should focus on relative rather than absolute strengths and weaknesses. In other words, it should take account of what the competition are doing. Thus, if everyone produces quality products this is not identified as a relative strength. Unique resources and capabilities that a firm has may provide it with a relative strength.[18] Second, strengths need to be looked at objectively as they can sometimes turn into weaknesses. A case in point is Sony, one of whose strengths has been its product innovation capabilities. Such was the success of its products that it took its eye off the market and technological trends. For example, its dominance of cathode ray tube television technology caused it to

Table 1.3 External marketing audit checklist
(Chapters 2–4)

Macroenvironment
Economic: inflation, interest rates, unemployment
Social/cultural: age distribution, lifestyle changes, values, attitudes
Technological: new product and process technologies, materials
Political/legal: monopoly control, new laws, regulations
Ecological: conservation, pollution, energy
The market
Market: size, growth rates, trends and developments
Customers: who are they, their choice criteria, how, when, where do they buy, how do they rate us vis-à-vis competition on product, promotion, price, distribution
Market: segmentation: how do customers group, what benefits does each group seek
Distribution: power changes, channel attractiveness, growth potential, physical distribution methods, decision-makers and influencers
Suppliers: who and where they are, their competences and shortcomings, trends affecting them, future outlook
Competition
Who are the major competitors: actual and potential
What are their objectives and strategies
What are their strengths (distinctive competences) and weaknesses (vulnerability analysis)
Market shares and size of competitors
Profitability analysis
Entry barriers

Table 1.4 Internal marketing audit checklist
(Chapters 5–12)

Operating results (by product, customer, geographic region)
Sales
Market share
Profit margins
Costs
Strategic issues analysis
Marketing objectives
Market segmentation
Competitive advantage
Core competences
Positioning
Portfolio analysis
Marketing operations effectiveness
Product
Price
Promotion
Distribution
Marketing structures
Marketing organization
Marketing training
Intra- and interdepartmental communication
Marketing systems
Marketing information systems
Marketing planning system
Marketing control system

miss the trend towards flat-screen televisions.[19] Third, only those strengths that are valued by the customer should be included.[20] Thus, strengths such as 'We are a large supplier' or 'We are technologically advanced' should be questioned for their impact on customer satisfaction. Finally, opportunities and threats should be listed as anticipated events or trends *outside* the business that have implications for performance. They should not be couched in terms of strategies. For example, 'To enter market segment X' is not an opportunity but a strategic objective that may result from a perceived opportunity arising from the emergence of market segment X as attractive because of its growth potential and lack of competition.

Figure 1.4 Strengths, weaknesses, opportunities and threats (SWOT) analysis

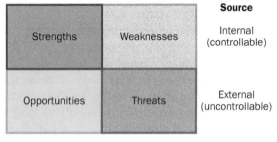

		Source
Strengths	Weaknesses	Internal (controllable)
Opportunities	Threats	External (uncontrollable)

Marketing objectives

The definition of **marketing objectives** may be derived from the results of the marketing audit and the SWOT analysis. Two types of objective need to be considered: strategic thrust and strategic objectives.

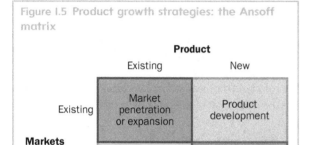

Figure 1.5 Product growth strategies: the Ansoff matrix

Decisions regarding how the company chooses to grow are incorporated within its **strategic thrust**. The four generic options available are summarized in the Ansoff growth matrix, as shown in Figure 1.5. These are:

- Existing products in existing markets (market penetration or expansion). Tactics used to increase penetration include getting existing customers to use the brand more often (e.g. eat breakfast cereals as daytime snacks) and to use a greater quantity when they use it (e.g. two teaspoons of coffee instead of one), and changes to packaging
- New products for existing markets (product development). For example, many companies provide additional products and services to their customers. Global accounting firms like KPMG and Deloitte provide management consulting services to clients.
- Existing products in new markets (market development). For example, Nestlé, the world's biggest food group, has been able to grow sales of its brands such as Kit Kat confectionery and Nescafé instant coffee by over 10 per cent in emerging markets such as Africa, Asia and Oceania compared with relatively stagnant sales growth in Western Europe.[21]
- New products for new markets (diversification). This is the most risky strategy but may be necessary when a company's current products and markets offer few prospects of future growth.

Aside from decisions regarding how the business should grow, **strategic objectives** for each product also need to be agreed. Choices have to be made whether to build, hold, harvest or divest products in the range. The important point to remember at this stage is that *building* sales and market share is not the only sensible strategic objective for a product. As we shall see, *holding* sales and market share may make commercial sense

under certain conditions; *harvesting*, where sales and market share are allowed to fall but profit margins are maximized, may also be preferable to building; finally, *divestment*, where the product is dropped or sold, can be the logical outcome of the situation analysis.

Finally, marketing objectives need to be SMART; that is, they should be specific, measurable, achievable, realistic and timed. There is little point in having vague objectives such as to grow the business or to increase sales in a new market. What needs to be established is, for example – what is the specific target for sales growth: a 10 per cent increase or 50 new customers? What is the time frame to achieve this growth – six months, one year? It is only when very precise objectives are set that their attainment can be assessed.

Exhibit 1.2 Variations in the sizes of packaging such as mini Peperami can be used as a means of generating greater sales

Marketing strategy

The **core** elements of marketing strategy involve decisions related to market segmentation, targeting and positioning and these will be explored in greater detail in Chapter 5. As we shall see in that chapter, there may be many reasons why firms may not choose to try to serve all customers in the market but rather to make careful choices regarding which customers to serve and how to go about serving them. Inevitably all the main planning stages outlined above such as the business mission, the marketing audit and marketing objectives will feed into the marketing strategy that is developed.

Marketing actions

Any strategy will be ineffective unless it is converted into actions. Each of the actions that may need to be undertaken is discussed in detail in Chapters 6–12. This set of decisions has traditionally been described as the company's **marketing mix** which normally comprises the 4Ps of product, price, promotion and place. **Product** decisions refer to choices that are made regarding the products/services and benefits that are going to be offered to a particular customer group. **Price** refers to all the decisions that are made regarding the different price points used for products in the company's range as well as all those decisions regarding the raising or reducing of prices in response to competitor activity and consumer demand. The breadth of promotional activity that can be carried out by an organization is such that it has been labelled the promotions mix, a large and significant subset of the marketing mix. Decisions that are made regarding Facebook and Twitter campaigns, sponsorship, radio advertising and so on all constitute elements of a **promotional mix**. **Place** refers to distribution activity, that is, the processes by which products and services are delivered to customers. It entails decisions regarding which channels to use, for example selling online versus through retail stores, as well as the processes by which goods are physically moved from factories to shops.

Finally, several other Ps have also been identified that can be considered as part of the marketing mix. These include people, process and physical evidence which are particularly relevant in the case of services industries (see Chapter 7). A total of 12 variables were initially identified by Borden which demonstrates the breadth of activities that need to be considered when putting marketing programmes into action.[22] These are the day-to-day responsibilities of the organization's marketing staff and are what make up the rich variety of marketing careers outlined in Appendix 1.1.

Evaluation of performance

Finally, all marketing plans need to be evaluated to determine whether the objectives set out at the beginning of the plan have been achieved or not. One of the criticisms frequently levelled at the marketing profession is that it does not do a good job of demonstrating how its efforts benefit the organization. We shall explore the issue of marketing and organizational performance in greater detail in the next section of this chapter.

Research into the marketing planning approaches of commercial firms has discovered that most companies did not practise the kinds of systematic planning procedure described in this chapter and, of those that did, many did not enjoy the rewards described above.[23] However, others have shown that there is a relationship between planning and commercial success (e.g. Armstrong and McDonald).[24, 25] The benefits of taking a planned approach to marketing are said to include strategic consistency, the encouragement of organizational adaptation, the stimulation of achievement and a logical process for resource allocation. But in practice, planning involves many difficulties. Not least among these is that it involves choices which may have consequences

for people in the organization such as in a case where a decision is made to delete a product line for example. As a result, planning can become a highly political activity as individuals or organizational sub-units seek to defend their territory and/or gain access to more resources. Therefore strong leadership and clear communications are the hallmarks of effective planning.

Marketing and business performance

Does marketing work? Surprisingly this is a controversial question, with many people arguing that, yes, of course it does, while others are less sure. The difficulty surrounds both the definition and the intangibility of marketing. Many organizations think they are engaging in marketing but may simply be engaging in selling or promotion and, if these activities do not achieve their intended objectives, they may feel that their marketing efforts have been ineffective. But what we will learn throughout this book is that selling or promotion is only part of the marketing process. It can also be difficult to predict in advance whether a marketing or promotional campaign is going to work. Sometimes campaigns can be stunningly successful (see Marketing in Action 1.2). New campaigns can drive the sales of stagnant brands as happened in the case of Magnum ice cream which had been suffering flat sales throughout Europe. Aimed at women and using a combination of television advertising, outdoor advertising and Internet advertising, the Magnum 7 Deadly Sins campaign lifted sales of the brand by 20 per cent in one year.[26]

In other companies, marketing is seen as the central engine of business growth. For example, Nestlé is a huge global company with 8,000 products (a figure that grows to 20,000 when local variations are included) and an annual marketing budget of $2.5 billion. Reckitt Benckiser, the world's largest manufacturer of household cleaning products, spends an average of 12 per cent of sales on marketing and is a market leader in its business. These kinds of firms see marketing expenditure as an investment, not a cost, and continue to spend money on marketing even during recessions when sales and demand drops (see Exhibit 1.3). A case in point is the Berocca vitamin tablet brand, owned by the German corporation, Bayer. It was launched on the Irish market in 2001 but thanks mainly to an investment level of 25 per cent of turnover on marketing, it has seen sales rise from an initial level of just €500,000 to over €4 million by 2010. This has given it a 40 per cent share of the Irish market, making it one of the best markets in the world for Berocca on a per capita basis.[27] But, for some, the issue is not whether marketing works but rather that it works too well. Marketing has been the subject of a great deal of criticism.[28] It has been equated

Marketing in Action 1.2 Volkswagen Passat

Critical Thinking: Below is a review of the successful 'The Force' campaign run by Volkswagen for its Passat brand in the US. Read it and reflect on the effectiveness of this campaign. What are its implications for marketing generally?

The turnaround of the Volkswagen Passat brand in the US is a classic example of the potential effectiveness of a marketing campaign. The challenges faced by the brand in this market were significant. A mid-sized car, it was selling about 10,000 units per year and posing little threat to the market leaders, the Toyota Camry and the Honda Accord, models that were selling about 200,000 units in the same category. Worse still, the brand was perceived negatively by consumers who viewed it as under-sized and over-priced.

Shifting these attitudes and improving sales required an innovative marketing approach for the 2012 version of the car. While its main competitors dominated on attributes like reliability, safety and value, the Passat adopted a different appeal. Its analysis of the market revealed some interesting customer insights. In an economy hurting from the global recession, Americans were shifting their attitude from material success and focusing more on the importance of family and friends. In targeting the parents of young families, the Passat

delivered an emotional appeal that focused on the important things in life. The central character in the advert, Max, is dressed as Darth Vader from Star Wars and his dad uses the remote keyless engine start facility of the Passat to give him 'the Force'.

The advert was a huge success. It was voted the number one Super Bowl advert for 2011 and became the most viewed commercial on YouTube for that year. Its powerful emotional appeal was also evident in it becoming the most shared branded video of all time. It scored well above the car industry average on attributes like entertainment and involvement. And these positive attitudes quickly translated into increased sales. In the four months after the car was launched, sales exceeded over 20,000 units generating incremental revenue for the company of over $210 million. When compared with the cost of the marketing campaign of $8.2 million, this represents a return-on-investment for the company of 25:1, making it money very well spent.

Based On: Feldman and Dorsett (2012)[29]

with trickery and deception, and with persuading people (often those on low incomes) to buy products they do not really need. Some of the main controversies surrounding marketing are summarized in Marketing and Society 1.1.

In short, marketing works. Succeeding in making it work in any particular situation is the challenge. In this regard some issues relating to the nature and impact of marketing need to be borne in mind.

Marketing and performance

The adoption of the marketing concept will improve business performance – that is the basic premise. Marketing is not an abstract concept; its acid test is the effect that its use has on key corporate indices such as profitability and market share. Extensive research has been conducted that has sought to examine the relationship between marketing and performance. The results suggest that the relationship is positive.

Narver and Slater, for instance, looked closely at the relationship between marketing orientation and

business performance.[30] They collected data from 113 **strategic business units (SBUs)** of a major US corporation. In the main, their study found that the relationship between market orientation and profitability was strongly linear, with the businesses displaying the highest level of market orientation achieving the highest levels of profitability, and those with the lowest scores on market orientation having the lowest profitability figures. As the authors state: 'The findings give marketing scholars and practitioners a basis beyond mere intuition for recommending the superiority of a market orientation.'

It is surprising, then, that marketing has not had the influence in corporate boardrooms that its importance would seem to justify. A study in the UK found that only 21 per cent of chief executive officers (CEOs) in the FTSE 100 had worked in marketing before going into general management, and only five of the FTSE 100 companies had dedicated marketing directors on their boards.[31] Research in the USA

Exhibit 1.3 United Biscuits spent £12 million on this hugely popular advert for its McVitie's brand. The ads aimed to connect with consumers on an emotional level and were designed to encourage sharing on social media to amplify their effect

shows that the majority of chief executives in recent decades have had a finance background.[32] Doyle argues that the reason for marketing's relatively low status is that the links between marketing investments and the long-term profitability of the organization have not been made clear.[33] Too often, marketers justify their investments in terms of increasing customer awareness, sales volume or market share. Doyle proposes the concept of **value-based marketing**, where the objective of marketing is seen as contributing to the maximization of **shareholder value**, which has become the overarching goal of chief executives in more and more companies. This approach helps clarify the importance of investment in marketing assets such as brands and marketing knowledge, and helps to dissuade management from making arbitrary cuts in marketing expenditure, such as advertising, in times of economic difficulty.

To further explore the link between marketing activities and firm performance, Rust et al. have identified a **chain of marketing productivity** which demonstrates how marketing investments eventually are reflected in firm outcomes. The chain begins with a firm's strategy such as its product strategy or promotion strategy which is then translated into specific tactics such as an advertising campaign or a loyalty programme, for example. These campaigns have an impact on customers (attitudes or satisfaction) which in turn feed through to market impacts (e.g., market share) and financial impacts (e.g., profitability) and ultimately to the value of the firm. In other words, a variety of factors

influenced by marketing activity such as marketing capabilities, marketing assets and marketing actions can impact upon firm value.[34,35] Further research has found that where this marketing activity is measured, significant performance benefits accrue.[36] As a result, the title Chief Marketing Officer (CMO) has emerged to reflect the importance of marketing to the overall performance of the organization. Chief marketing officers usually have a seat in the corporate boardroom.

Marketing metrics

A key emerging area of **control** is that of marketing metrics. The marketing discipline has traditionally been criticized for the quality of its metrics. For example, sales revenues are an important metric but many of the factors influencing sales levels are outside the control of marketers, such as economic conditions or competitor activity. And because marketers have not been good at measuring what they do, they are often poorly represented in corporate boardrooms compared with disciplines such as production and finance. In addition, marketing budgets are often the first to be cut when companies need to make cost savings.

As a result, more attention than ever is being paid to the metrics used to measure marketing activity. A vast array of potential metrics can be identified.[37] In short there are two key elements of marketing measurement, namely, the effectiveness of operational marketing activity and the impact of marketing on the bottom line. Measuring the former

Marketing and Society 1.1 Marketing – good or evil?

It is possible to look at marketing from different standpoints. A positive view holds that marketing provides significant benefits to society. For example, the innovative efforts of companies provide us, as consumers, with a world of choice and diversity. A search on Google allows us to find information on anything that we want; with an Apple app on their iPhones, doctors no longer need a stethoscope to examine patients, and websites like Amazon and eBay allow us to shop from the comfort of our desks. The innovations of tomorrow will bring us new and appealing products, services and solutions. Second, as the practice of marketing improves, our particular needs are increasingly being met. If we eat only gluten-free products, love skydiving and have a passion for Japanese origami, there are organizations that will fulfil these needs. As firms collect more information about their customers, they will tailor solutions to meet specific user requirements. Finally, the competition between firms continually forces them to improve their services and products, and deliver extra value to customers. For example, low-fares airlines have revolutionized air travel and enabled people who traditionally flew infrequently to travel to new destinations much more often.

At the same time, marketing is also the subject of some trenchant criticism. For example, it is seen as not only fulfilling needs but creating unnecessary wants. Critics argue that companies use sophisticated marketing techniques to create aspirations and to get consumers to buy products that they don't really need, with the result that many consumers find themselves building up significant debts. Consumer credit levels are at an all-time high in many developed countries. Related to this is the rise of materialism in society. Proponents of this view suggest that the modern consumer has become obsessed with consumption, as illustrated, for example, by the growth in Sunday shopping. Psychologists argue that this rise in consumption has done little to make people feel happier and better about themselves. At the same time as materialism is rising, there are growing concerns that the world's resources are being rapidly depleted and that current levels of consumption are not sustainable into the future. Third, there are concerns with the way that marketers target vulnerable groups like children, where the skills of child psychologists are used to find more and novel ways to instil brand preferences in the very young. Finally, there are concerns with the ways that marketing activity appears to have invaded all aspects of society. Public leisure events such as sports, shows and concerts now usually have a corporate partner, with the result that events aimed at teenagers may be sponsored by an alcoholic drinks organization, for example. Pressures on the public funding of schools, hospitals, and so on also create opportunities for corporations to tie in with these entities, which is often ethically questionable.

Resolving such a debate is very difficult, but the core of the issue lies in the key components of the definition of marketing – namely, value and profit. When organizations provide genuine value to customers, marketing is doing what it should, and both firms and society benefit. When firms create an illusion of value or seek to exploit customers for profit, then consumers and society do not benefit. Like all professions, marketing has its unscrupulous practitioners and there will always be individuals and organizations who will seek to exploit vulnerable customers. But, in an information-rich world, such practitioners can and should be named and shamed.

Suggested reading: James (2007);[38] Klein (2000);[39] Linn (2004).[40]

Reflection: Critically evaluate the arguments above and develop your own opinion on whether marketing is good or evil.

is contingent on the type of marketing activity undertaken. For example, distribution activity can be measured by inventory levels, markdowns, facings and out-of-stock levels. But, ultimately, marketing decisions must contribute to increasing profits by increasing sales volumes, increasing prices or reducing unit costs.[41] The most common metrics in use in UK firms are shown in Table 1.5.

The scope of marketing

Up to now our focus has been on the application of marketing in commercial contexts – that is, its use by companies with products or services to sell. But it is clear from simple observation that the marketing concept, and marketing tools and techniques, is in evidence in many other contexts too. For example, political parties are often criticized for their overuse of marketing. They are heavy users of marketing research to find out what the views of the voting public are; the candidates they put forward for election are often carefully selected and 'packaged' to appeal to voters. They are also extensive users of advertising and public relations to get their message across. This is because value exchange is a key element of marketing. Organizations create some form of value and exchange it for something that they need. In the case of politics it is the creation of policy platforms in exchange for votes in an election.

Evidence of the application of marketing can be found in many other contexts (see Marketing in Action 1.3 and Exhibit 1.4). Educational institutions have become more market-led as demographic changes have given rise to greater competition for students, whose choices

Table 1.5 The use of marketing metrics in UK firms

Rank	Metric	% using measure	% rating it as important
1	Profit/ profitability	92	80
2	Sales, value and/ or volume	91	71
3	Gross margin	81	66
4	Awareness	78	28
5	Market share (value/volume)	78	37
6	Number of new products	73	18
7	Relative price	70	36
8	Customer dissatisfaction	69	45
9	Customer satisfaction	68	48
10	Distribution/ availability	66	18

Source: Ambler, Kokkinaki and Puntoni (2004)[42]

Exhibit 1.4 Social marketing where marketing is used to promote important societal causes has grown dramatically.

Blue Light Ad Insight: Advertising can be used to present powerful social messages.

are increasingly being influenced by the publication of performance-based league tables. Universities are responding by developing new logos and rebranding themselves, conducting promotional campaigns, and targeting new markets such as mature students and those from other countries around the world. They are also using the kinds of segmentation techniques employed by companies to identify potential 'customers', as well as customer service training to convert enquiries into 'sales'.[43] The use of marketing takes many forms in the arts and media. It has been argued that many media vehicles, such as newspapers and television channels, are being 'dumbed down' in order to appeal to certain market segments and to maximize revenues, in the same way many artistic organizations would be criticized for putting revenues ahead of quality and originality by producing art that appeals to a mass audience.

The range of potential applications for marketing has given rise to much debate among marketing scholars regarding the scope of marketing.[44] In particular, the challenge has been to find a core concept that effectively integrates both business and non-business or social marketing. For example, initially the idea of a transaction was put forward, but not all marketing requires a transaction or sale. Kotler then put forward the notion of exchange, implying that any exchange between two parties can be considered marketing.[45] However, this is also clearly problematic as many exchanges, such as favours given by family members, are not marketing activities. Throughout this book we place customers at the core of marketing and detail the processes through which organizations understand and respond to their ever changing needs and wants.

Marketing in Action 1.3 VisitScotland

Critical Thinking: Below is a review of some of the marketing activity conducted by the VisitScotland tourism organization. Read it and critically reflect on the role of marketing in building a tourism destination. What are the key challenges and opportunities in doing so?

For many countries around the world tourism is an extremely important industry generating high levels of employment, increased national income and improved quality of life brought about by a diversity of people. The responsibility for promoting tourism in a country is usually vested in a national tourism authority. While countries may have natural advantages such as great history, superb cuisine or beautiful scenery, marketing destinations is also extremely challenging. Consumers have a wide variety of choices so tourism organizations need to adopt high-quality marketing practices in order to be successful.

One of the first challenges to think about is the range of different visitors that may be interested in coming to your country. In the case of Scotland, visitors will come from the rest of the UK and Ireland, as well as Europe, America and further afield such as China and Japan. Age, lifestyle and interests are other factors to consider. Some visitors will be interested in history, others in outdoor activities such as hiking and water sports. The choices regarding what to promote,

who to promote it to and how to promote it will all have a critical bearing on success.

A case in point is VisitScotland's campaign to target affluent, 35- to 55-year-old couples from Spain, Germany, France and the Netherlands whom they termed cultural explorers. These are visitors who travel not for relaxation but rather to engage with countries and cultures. The also fitted with VisitScotland's goal of promoting sustainable tourism by attracting not necessarily larger numbers of visitors but rather high-value customers. The integrating theme of the campaign was entitled 'welcome to our life' which aimed to promote Scotland in an authentic rather than staged way. So while the iconic images such as castles, kilts and bagpipes continued to play a big part, visitors were invited to 'meet the real people behind the kilts'. This invitation was communicated through print advertising, direct mail and online advertising. It proved a popular appeal with visitors both staying longer and spending more than the campaign had targeted.

Based on: von Matt (2011)[46]

Summary

This chapter has introduced the concept of marketing and discussed how and why organizations become market-oriented. In particular, the following issues were addressed.

1. What is meant by the marketing concept? The key idea here is that it is a business philosophy that puts the customer at the centre of things. Implementing the marketing concept requires a focus on customer satisfaction, an integrated effort throughout the company and a belief that corporate goals can be achieved through customer satisfaction.

2. The idea of customer value, which is the difference between the perceived benefits from consuming a product or service and the perceived sacrifice involved in doing so. Customers are faced with a wide variety of choices in most instances, therefore companies need to clearly spell out what value they are offering and this forms their customer value proposition.

3. That marketing as both a field of study and a field of practice is constantly evolving. The way that we think about marketing has moved from an internal focus on production and sales towards a more outward-looking focus on customers and markets. These market-driven organizations are better placed to succeed in rapidly changing competitive environments.

4. That marketing planning is an important activity to ensure marketing effectiveness. There are a number of critical steps in the marketing planning process, namely the business mission and strategy, the marketing audit, marketing objectives, marketing strategy, marketing actions and evaluation of performance.

5. That marketing works and there is a strong relationship between a marketing philosophy and business performance. Academic research in the field of market orientation and ample evidence from practice attest to the power of marketing in assisting organizations to achieve their goals.

6. That the scope of marketing is broad, involving non-business as well as business contexts. Political parties, educational institutions, sporting organizations, religious organizations and others are regular users of marketing.

7. That marketing is also controversial and that it has many negative connotations relating to the creation of unnecessary desires among consumers, that it exploits vulnerable groups and that it results in depletion of the world's resources. An informed perspective on both the merits and risks associated with marketing and commerce generally is important.

Study questions

1. Discuss the development of marketing. What are the critical ways in which marketing has changed over the years?

2. Identify two examples of organizations that you consider provide customer value, and describe how they do it.

3. Marketing is sometimes considered to be an expensive luxury. Respond to this claim by demonstrating how a marketing orientation can have a positive impact on business performance.

4. Marketing is central to how we live our lives. Discuss.

5. Rather than assisting in the creation of value, marketing is responsible for many of society's ills. Discuss.

6. Visit www.marketingpower.com and www.cim.co.uk and discuss the different definitions of marketing presented by two of the world's leading marketing organizations.

Suggested reading

Court, D. (2007) The Evolving Role of the CMO, *McKinsey Quarterly*, **3**, 28–39.

Dawar, N. (2013) When Marketing is Strategy, *Harvard Business Review*, **91** (12), 100–108.

Karababa, E. and D. Kjellgaard (2014) Value in Marketing: Toward Socio-Cultural Perspectives, *Marketing Theory*, **14** (1), 119–27.

Levitt, T. (1960) Marketing Myopia, *Harvard Business Review*, **38**, 45–56.

Rust, R., C. Moorman and G. Bhalla (2010) Rethinking Marketing, *Harvard Business Review*, **88** (1/2) January– February, 94–101.

Vargo, S. and R. Lusch (2004) Evolving to a New Dominant Logic for Marketing, *Journal of Marketing*, **86** (1), 1–17.

Verhof, P. and K. Lemon (2013) Successful Customer Value Management: Key Lessons and Emerging Trends, *European Management Journal*, **31**, 1–15.

When you have read this chapter

log on to the Online Learning Centre for
Foundations of Marketing at
www.mheducation.co.uk/textbooks/fahy5
where you'll find links and extra online study tools for marketing.

References

1. **Drucker, P.F.** (1999) *The Practice of Management,* London: Heinemann.
2. **Rosenberg, L.J.** and **J.A. Czepeil** (1983) A Marketing Approach to Customer Retention, *Journal of Consumer Marketing,* **2,** 45–51.
3. **Gronroos, C.** (1989) Defining Marketing: A Market-oriented Approach, *European Journal of Marketing,* **23** (1), 52–60.
4. **Day, G. S.** and **C. Moorman** (2010) *Strategy From the Outside-in: Profiting From Customer Value,* New York: McGraw-Hill.
5. **Fahy, J.** (2012) Creating a Winning Customer Value Proposition, in *Best Practices in Successful Businesses: A Collection of Tutorials,* S. Harwood (ed.), USA: Walker Publications, 78–87.
6. **Vargo, S.** and **R. Lusch** (2004) Evolving to a New Dominant Logic for Marketing, *Journal of Marketing,* **86** (1), 1–17.
7. **Rogowsky, M.** (2013) Dropbox is Doing Great But Maybe Not as Great As We Believed, *Forbes.com,* 19 November.
8. **Fullerton, R.** (1988) How Modern is Modern Marketing? Marketing's Evolution and the Myth of the 'Production Era', *Journal of Marketing,* **52,** 108–25.
9. **Jones, D.** and **D. Monieson** (1990) Early Development of the Philosophy of Marketing Thought, *Journal of Marketing,* **54,** 102–13.
10. **Benton, R.** (1987) The Practical Domain of Marketing, *American Journal of Economics and Sociology,* **46** (4), 415–30.
11. **Davis, P.** (2005) Attack on 'Outdated' Marketing, *Financial Times,* Fund Management Supplement, 30 May, 1.
12. **Vargo, S.** and **R. Lusch** (2004) Evolving to a New Dominant Logic for Marketing, *Journal of Marketing,* **86** (1), 1–17.
13. **Ackoff, R.I.** (1987) Mission Statements, *Planning Review,* **15** (4), 30–2.
14. **Hooley, G.J., A.J. Cox** and **A. Adams** (1992) Our Five Year Mission: To Boldly Go Where No Man Has Been Before . . . , *Journal of Marketing Management,* **8** (1), 35–48.
15. **Levitt, T.** (1984) Marketing Myopia, *Harvard Business Review,* **4** (4), 59–80.
16. **Hall, W.K.** (1980) Survival Strategies in a Hostile Environment, *Harvard Business Review,* **58** (September/October), 75–85.
17. **Hewett, K** and **W.O. Bearden** (2001) Dependence, Trust and Relational Behaviour on the Part of Foreign Subsidiary Marketing Operations: Implications for Managing Global Marketing Operations, *Journal of Marketing,* **65** (4), 51–66.
18. See **Barney, J.** (1991) Firm Resources and Sustained Competitive Advantage, *Journal of Management,* **17** (1), 99–120 for a discussion on the resource-based view of the firm, and **Teece, D.J., G. Pisano** and **A. Sheun** (1997), Dynamic Capabilities and Strategic Management, *Strategic Management Journal,* **18** (7), 509–33 for a discussion on dynamic capabilities.
19. **Nakamoto, M.** (2005) Caught in its Own Trap: Sony Battles to Make Headway in a Networked World, *Financial Times,* 27 January, 17.
20. **Piercy, N.** (2008) *Market-Led Strategic Change: Transforming the Process of Going to Market,* Oxford: Butterworth-Heinemann, 259.
21. **Simonian, H.** (2010) Emerging Markets Drive Sales for Nestlé, *Financial Times,* 12 August, 20.
22. **Borden, N.** (1964) The Concept of the Marketing Mix, *Journal of Advertising Research,* June, 2–7.
23. **Greenley, G.** (1987) An Exposition of Empirical Research into Marketing Planning, *Journal of Marketing Management,* **3** (1), 83–102.
24. **Armstrong, J.S.** (1982) The Value of Formal Planning for Strategic Decisions: Review of Empirical Research, *Strategic Management Journal,* **3** (3), 197–213.
25. **McDonald, M.H.B.** (1984) The Theory and Practice of Marketing Planning for Industrial Goods in International Markets, Cranfield Institute of Technology, PhD thesis.
26. **Coulter, D.** (2004) Magnum 7 Sins: Driving Women to Sin across Europe, *Warc.com.*
27. **O'Connell, S.** (2009) Vitamin Ad Provides Flat Market with Some Fizz, *Irish Times,* 15 October, 22.
28. **Klein, N.** (2000) *No Logo,* London: HarperCollins.
29. **Feldman, J.** and **J. Dorsett** (2012), VW Passat: How a Single Spot Can Create a Social Phenomenon, *Warc.com.*
30. **Narver, J.C.** and **S.F. Slater** (1990) The Effect of a Market Orientation on Business Profitability, *Journal of Marketing,* **54** (October), 20–35.
31. **Terazono, E.** (2003) Always on the Outside Looking In, *Financial Times,* Creative Business, 5 August, 4–5.
32. **Fligstein, N.** (1987) Intraorganisational Power Struggles: The Rise of Finance Personnel to Top Leadership in Large Corporations, 1919–1979, *American Sociology Review,* **52,** 44–58.
33. **Doyle, P.** (2000) *Value-based Marketing,* Chichester: John Wiley & Sons.
34. **Rust, R., T. Ambler, G. Carpenter, V. Kumar** and **R. Srivastava** (2004) Measuring Marketing Productivity: Current Knowledge and Future Directions, *Journal of Marketing,* **68** (4), 76–89.
35. **Hanssens, D., R. Rust** and **R. Srivastava** (2009) Marketing Strategy and Wall Street: Nailing Down Marketing's Impact, *Journal of Marketing,* **73** (6), 115–18.

36. **O'Sullivan, D.** and **A. Abela** (2007) Marketing Performance Measurement Ability and Firm Performance, *Journal of Marketing*, **71** (2), 79–93.

37. **Farris, P.W., N.T. Bendle, P.E. Pfeifer** and **D.J. Reibstein** (2006) *Marketing Metrics*, Upper Saddle River, NJ: Wharton.

38. **James, O.** (2007) *Affluenza*, London: Vermilion.

39. **Klein, N.** (2000) *No Logo*, London: Flamingo Press.

40. **Linn, S.** (2004) *Consuming Kids: The Hostile Takeover of Childhood*, New York: The New Press.

41. **Shaw, R.** and **D. Merrick** (2005) *Marketing Payback: Is Your Marketing Profitable?* London: Pearson Education.

42. **Ambler, T., F. Kokkinaki** and **S. Puntoni** (2004) Assessing Marketing Performance: Reasons for Metrics Selection, *Journal of Marketing Management*, **20**, 475–98.

43. **Boone, J.** (2007) Private School's Marketing Pays Off, *Financial Times*, 4 May, 3.

44. See, for example, **Foxall, G.** (1984) Marketing's Domain, *European Journal of Marketing*, **18** (1), 25–40; **Kotler, P.** and **S. Levy** (1969) Broadening the Concept of Marketing, *Journal of Marketing*, **33**, 10–15.

45. **Kotler, P.** (1972) A Generic Concept of Marketing, *Journal of Marketing*, **36**, 46–54.

46. **von Matt, J.** (2011) Visit Scotland: Welcome to Our Life, *Warc.com*.

Appendix I.I Careers in marketing

Choosing a career in marketing can offer a wide range of opportunities. Table A1.1 outlines some of the potential positions available in marketing.

Table AI.I Careers in marketing

Marketing positions	
Marketing executive/co-ordinator	Management of all marketing-related activities for an organization.
Brand/product manager	A product manager is responsible for the management of a single product or a family of products. In this capacity, he or she may participate in product design and development according to the results of research into the evolving needs of their customer base. In addition, marketing managers develop business plans and marketing strategies for their product line, manage product distribution, disseminate information about the product, and co-ordinate customer service and sales.
Brand/marketing assistant	At the entry level of brand assistant, responsibilities consist of market analysis, competitive tracking, sales and market share analysis, monitoring of promotion programmes, etc.
Marketing researcher/analyst	Market researchers collect and analyse information to assist in marketing, and determine whether a demand exists for a particular product or service. Some of the tasks involved include designing questionnaires, collecting all available and pertinent information, arranging and analysing collected information, presenting research results to clients, making recommendations.
Marketing communications manager	Manages the marketing communications activity of an organization manager such as advertising, public relations, sponsorships and direct marketing.
Customer service manager/executive	Manages the service delivery and any interactions a customer may have with an organization. Role can be quite varied, depending on industry.
Sales positions	
Sales executive/business development	Aims to develop successful business relationships with existing and potential customers. Manages the company's sales prospects.
Sales manager	Plans and co-ordinates the activities of a sales team, controls product distribution, monitors budget achievement, trains and motivates personnel, prepares forecasts.
Key account executive	Manages the selling and marketing function to key customers (accounts). Conducts negotiations on products, quantities, prices, promotions, special offers etc. Networks with other key account personnel influential in the buying decision process. Liaises internally with all departments and colleagues in supplying and servicing the key account. Monitors performance of the key account.
Sales support manager	Provides sales support by fielding enquiries, taking orders and providing phone advice to customers. Also assists with exhibitions, prepares documentation for brochures and sales kits, and commissions market research suppliers for primary data.
Merchandiser	Aims to maximize the display of a company's point-of-sale displays, and ensures that they are stocked and maintained correctly.
Sales promotion executive	Aims to communicate product features and benefits directly to customers at customer locations through sampling, demonstrations and the management of any sales promotion activities.
Telesales representative	Takes in-bound or makes out-bound calls, which are sales related.
Advertising sales executive	Sells a media organization's airplay, television spot or space to companies for the purpose of advertising.

Table AI.I *Continued*

Retailing positions	
Retail management	Plans and co-ordinates the operations of retail outlets. Supervises the recruitment, training, conduct and work of staff. Maintains high levels of customer service. Manages stock levels.
Retail buyer	Purchases goods to be sold in retail stores. Manages and analyses stock levels. Obtains information about the range of products available. Manages vendor relations.
Advertising positions	
Account executive	Helps devise and co-ordinate advertising campaigns. Liaises with clients, obtaining relevant information from them such as product and company details, budget and marketing goals, and marketing research information. Briefs other specialists in the agency (such as creative team, media planners and researchers) on client requirements, to develop the details of a campaign. May present draft campaign suggestions to clients along with a summary of the expenditure involved, and negotiate and arrange for modifications if required. May supervise and co-ordinate the work of the relevant production departments so that the campaign is developed as planned to meet deadlines and budget requirements.
Media planner/buyer	Organizes and purchases advertising space on television, radio, in magazines, newspapers or on outdoor advertising. Liaises between clients and sellers of advertising space to ensure that the advertising campaign reaches the target market.
Public relations positions	
Public relations executive	Helps to develop and maintain a hospitable, friendly public environment for the organization. This involves liaising with clients, co-ordination of special events, lobbying, crisis management, media relations, writing and editing of printed material.
Press relations/ corporate affairs	Develops and maintains a good working relationship with the media. Creates press releases or responds to media queries.

Case 1

Primary care trust: helping to save lives

PREGNANT? BREAST-FEEDING? YOUR SMOKING CAN HARM YOUR BABY

Introduction

Despite its well documented dangers, smoking during pregnancy is still common in the UK and remains a significant problem, primarily because of the health dangers to the child and mother, and the concern that many pregnant smokers find it difficult to quit or reduce smoking despite being aware of the health consequences. In the UK smoking rates, having initially dropped, settled at a steady rate before dropping again following the ban on smoking in public. In response to the need to address social issues such as smoking, public sector bodies, such as those responsible for public health initiatives, have started to embrace the techniques of marketing in order to encourage more healthy behaviours among the population. A key target of this activity is smoking during pregnancy. A range of interventions offered to promote smoking cessation in pregnancy includes community and individual level programmes and this remains a focus for health practitioners because it is seen as a significant opportunity for effective intervention.

Focus of the intervention

In England, the bodies responsible for commissioning health services at the time were the local primary care trusts (PCTs). A PCT in the English Midlands had a target to reduce smoking rates at delivery by 6 per cent from current levels. It commissioned the production of a DVD as part of a small-scale, locally focused, practitioner-led intervention to address the issue of smoking in pregnancy. The film was designed to carry a promotional/ educational message based on the experiences of a successful ex-smoker, 'Amy'. It was the principal piece of material used in the local cessation campaign. The film was distributed on DVD for use in face-to-face settings by midwives, for use in hospital settings and as material for the PCT's website. Given the public sector budget cuts in the UK, the low budget, local focus of this case is particularly relevant.

The objectives of campaign were to:

- encourage pregnant women to inform their midwife if they smoke
- make women aware of the benefits of nicotine replacement therapies (NRTs).

Background: the environment

The effect of smoking during pregnancy is well documented and includes increased risk of miscarriage, preterm birth, low birth weight, stillbirth and antenatal depression, and research shows an association between preterm birth and mortality rates in the first four weeks after birth, low birth weight and coronary heart disease in adulthood, and miscarriage and sudden infant death syndrome. This evidence suggests that smoking during pregnancy is the single most modifiable risk factor for adverse outcomes in pregnancy and contributes to 40 per cent of all infant deaths. Despite this, a significant proportion of pregnant women continue to smoke despite their knowledge of the health risks. Tobacco use has been identified as the principal reason for the inequalities in death rates between rich and poor. This is relevant because the case study was drawn from a county with high levels of deprivation where smoking-attributable mortality rates for women are higher than the national average. Efforts to promote smoking cessation in pregnancy, such as social marketing campaigns, are therefore important to reduce the health impacts and promote better health among the wider population.

Understanding behaviour: unreliable data

The number of women in the UK smoking during pregnancy is unclear. Current official figures suggest that less than 10 per cent of pregnant women smoke (ONS). However, academic research reveals that 13 per cent of women smoke during pregnancy and anecdotal evidence from midwives suggests that this is likely to be understated, with actual rates at least at the level of the population norm of 19 per cent (ONS). This observation is supported by several studies suggesting self-reporting by women is unreliable and that actual smoking rates may show little difference between pregnant women and others. Additionally, general smoking rates in the county are higher than the national average with a self-reported rate of 23 per cent. Even this higher figure has been questioned with a recent study revealing that 34 per cent of women smoked during pregnancy, showing the extent of the under-reporting. This tendency among consumers to under-report their behaviour results in there being unreliable market data on which to base appropriate social marketing efforts.

Pregnant smokers as significant target segments

It has been claimed that tobacco manufacturers target customers through careful segmentation and have developed brands aimed at women, low-income consumers and underage consumers, recent starters and those concerned about health risks. Using social marketing techniques the PCT recognized the need to carefully segment its audiences to ensure the effectiveness of its messages. It identified a number of key groups based on the extent to which they are personally at risk and also influence other groups. In addition to being a key target audience in UK health policy, pregnant women are a useful segment to target with anti-smoking campaigns for a number of reasons: they are at a pivotal stage of their life and are open to health interventions; health interventions among pregnant women will impact the health outcomes for their baby; these women may influence upwards to their own and their partners' parents who, the data suggests, are likely to be smokers and whose smoking behaviour may be controlled by the women; similar influences may take place horizontally as partners, friends and other relatives' behaviours are controlled by the woman, possibly leading to reduction or quitting; and, if the pregnant woman quits, the generational cycle of smoking may be broken.

Resourcing the campaign: county-wide stop-smoking services

The DVD was designed to support the 'stop smoking' service in the county. The delivery of these services is based on partnership work between NHS Stop Smoking Service 'New Leaf' and the maternity service providers. Midwifery services are well established throughout the county and provide a universal service to all pregnant women and families. Recent changes to delivery offer women greater choice, more local services and earlier identification of social and economic need. The Stop Smoking Service is provided as soon as possible during pregnancy until delivery, assuming tobacco smoking has been identified. It has four components:

- assessing the service user's nicotine dependence at the start of the intervention
- providing behavioural support
- providing NRT
- establishing the service user's smoking status at the end of the intervention.

The service user's progress in stopping smoking is assessed after four weeks and following delivery. Service user interventions are delivered by a 'stop smoking advisor', who has received appropriate Stop Smoking in Pregnancy Services training. Midwives are in a unique position to respond to the needs of pregnant smokers, as they will have contact from the earliest stages of pregnancy and are often a trusted support in a woman's life. Midwives assess the smoking status of all pregnant women at the booking visit, throughout pregnancy, at delivery and during the postnatal period. It is in this environment, among others, that the DVD was intended to be used in a face-to-face setting.

Producing the DVD

In response to the PCT's cessation targets, the health impacts of smoking in pregnancy and the relatively low proportion of pregnant smokers who use cessation services during pregnancy, this campaign was developed to inform and encourage pregnant smokers of the importance of using these services. The campaign centred around the production of a film to be distributed online via the county PCT's website and on DVD for use in antenatal (while pregnant) face-to-face settings by community midwives and for use in hospital pregnancy day care and postnatal ward settings (following birth). As the local maternity unit had been a centre for a trial that investigated the efficacy of NRT patches during pregnancy, the film was produced to highlight the effectiveness of the use of NRT in addition to the efficacy of face-to-face counselling.

Members of the Tobacco Control Team (TCT) in the PCT had been on training courses to introduce them to social marketing techniques and make them aware of a number of best practice case studies. They were introduced to the National Social Marketing Centre's benchmark criteria for effective social marketing campaigns (see Table CI.I). This framework informed elements of the design of the campaign, in particular the decision to concentrate on the comments of a successful quitter, the selection of material designed to provide genuine insight into what moved and motivated Amy and that was included in the final edit, and the inclusion of comments that had clear links to behavioural theory.

The TCT in the PCT felt that smoking cessation messages would be better received if they came from a successful ex-smoker, rather than from a health care professional, and focusing on the things that the customer believes to be most important to her. Amy was recruited to the campaign following contact with the maternity unit's research midwife. She was the only one of seven people contacted willing to take part in the filming. It was anecdotally believed that the reason so few women wanted to get involved with the campaign was that women were generally unwilling to admit that they smoked while pregnant, an insight that supported one of the campaign's objectives.

Amy's responses to the questions she was posed during the filming were spontaneous; she was not given the questions prior to the filming and she chose to be filmed in her own home with her baby and partner. The total filming time was three hours and the footage edited to five minutes for the finished DVD. In effect therefore, the message, media and research are virtually congruent. Selection of content was on the basis of revealing new insights, highlighting the pre-quitting relationship with cigarettes, avoiding the well-rehearsed statements regarding smoking and ill health and focusing on the subject's experiences, feelings and motivations.

Using the DVD

The £500 budget allowed for 300 copies to be produced and for it to be made available on the PCT's website. The DVD was distributed to all community midwives and maternity units in the county. Midwives were able to use the DVD in a clinic or home setting where it could support the intervention they provided at the booking interview or at a point in pregnancy where the key message was to quit smoking. The DVD was also disseminated to Sure Start Children's Centres and health visitors in the county for use with families with babies and young children

Behavioural change among service users

The PCT sought to influence its target audience in order to encourage a number of specific behaviours. So, in the DVD, behaviour is addressed in a subtle way. There are no messages about the health implications of smoking; it is generally believed that the majority of people are well aware of these. There is also no encouragement to give up smoking. Practitioners are aware that given that people understand the dangers of smoking

they would have already given up if this was easy. There is an acknowledgement that moving from smoker to ex-smoker is a large step that many find difficult and that such a direct approach carries the dangers that other important messages may be disregarded by the audience because they cannot envisage taking the big step. Also, many midwives are reluctant to address smoking for fear of alienating women due to the social stigma attached to smoking in pregnancy. In the DVD the first targeted behaviour change is to encourage the trial of NRT. The second is to encourage the woman to make the midwife aware of their smoking behaviour, despite the tendency among pregnant smokers to under-report. These small steps are much easier than trying to give up and they help to promote the individual sense of self-efficacy. Amy describes contacting her midwife about her desire to give up smoking as the best thing she ever did ('Don't be ashamed or embarrassed to say that you smoke because I was, but if I hadn't told the midwife then I wouldn't have got the support which helped us (sic) quit'). She also confirms that she had not been aware that NRT was an appropriate therapy in pregnancy. Thus the two targeted behavioural changes are directly addressed in the DVD.

Delivering value to service users

Amy's comments in the DVD address the social and emotional benefits of quitting smoking while acknowledging some of the sacrifices that the smoking quitter has to make. The Tobacco Control Team selected these comments in order to frame the messages as honest and credible; this was an attempt to show the value that the customer could derive, notwithstanding some of the enjoyable aspects of smoking that they would have to either give up or replace. These benefits emerged from the insights gained by allowing Amy to discuss her experiences in an unscripted way.

One of the key motivations for her was the ability to smell her baby, in contrast to the situation if she were still a smoker:

> 'I used to just cuddle him in and smell the top of his head and you'd just smell it, new baby, and it was the most amazing smell because before I couldn't smell anything.'
> 'He would have smelt like me and he would have smelt like cigarettes.'

She also describes enjoying the extra time in bed ('I hadn't appreciated that I was building smoke time into my daily routine') and how the support of her partner had a positive effect on their relationship. A key benefit was the self-efficacy of taking control of aspects of her life, in particular the ability to cope with stress without having to resort to cigarettes ('We'd find things to do together like go for a walk') and enjoying the sense of achievement of recording a zero in the carbon monoxide readings ('I got really excited about seeing the zero, because it felt like I had achieved something, it was a physical confirmation that you're a non-smoker now'). Amy also describes the sacrifices, including the difficulty of and loneliness in quitting, the removal of the 'social' benefits of smoking and work breaks ('*I had to not see some of my smoking friends for a couple of weeks*'), and the shame involved in telling the midwife about her smoking behaviour ('*The thought of the midwife knowing that I was putting harm, potentially, in my baby's way made us (sic) feel really, really ashamed*').

Conclusions

Interventions to promote smoking cessation in pregnancy are important to improve pregnancy and infant outcomes, and reduce complications during pregnancy. However, smoking prevalence in pregnancy remains high, and interventions to address the problem have had mixed results to date. The Tobacco Control Team (TCT) at the PCT showed how formal approaches to social marketing can be used to develop novel and low-cost interventions. It demonstrated how success stories to inform and influence smoking cessation in pregnant smokers is potentially a cost-effective way of communicating directly to specific social groups. The TCT applied its training in the techniques of social marketing to address a significant local health issue within the constraints of a limited budget. The result demonstrates how the tools and methods of marketing can be effectively applied in a non-business setting and how customer value can be understood in terms other than the price and performance of products and services.

Questions

1. Explain the main differences between social marketing and a 'traditional' approach to marketing. Consider the roles of the customer and marketer, segmentation and targeting and the 'product' being sold along with the other elements of the marketing mix.
2. What do you consider to be the main marketing challenges to the PCT reaching its stated target of a 6 per cent reduction in smoking in pregnant women?
3. Consider each of the elements of the NSMC's criteria in the context of the DVD identifying how each element applies.
4. Is this genuinely a case of how marketing can be used for the good of society? Can you think of any ethical problems with the social marketing approach?

Table CI.I The NSMC's Benchmark Criteria for Effective Social Marketing

Benchmark element	Description
Behaviour	Aims to change people's actual behaviour
Customer orientation	Focuses on the audience. Fully understands their lives, behaviour and the issues using a mix of sources and research methods
Theory	Uses behavioural theories to understand behaviour and inform the intervention
Insight	Customer research identifies 'actionable insights' – pieces of understanding that will lead intervention development
Exchange	Considers benefits and costs of adopting and maintaining a new behaviour; maximizes the benefits and minimizes the costs to create an attractive offer
Competition	Seeks to understand what competes for the audience's time, attention and inclination to behave in a particular way
Segmentation	Avoids a 'one size fits all' approach: identifies audience segments which have common characteristics, then tailors interventions appropriately
Methods mix (the marketing mix)	Uses a mix of methods to bring about behaviour change. Does not rely solely on raising awareness

Source: The National Social Marketing Centre

Case contributed by Dr Seamus Allison, Senior Lecturer, Nottingham Business School, Nottingham Trent University, Alex Hiller, Head of MSc Programmes, Nottingham Business School, Nottingham Trent University and Dr Abraham Brown, Senior Lecturer, Nottingham Business School, Nottingham Trent University.

Chapter 2

The Global Marketing Environment

Chapter outline

The macroenvironment

Economic forces

Social forces

Political and legal forces

Ecological forces

Technological forces

The microenvironment

Environmental scanning

Learning outcomes

By the end of this chapter you will:

1 Understand what is meant by the term 'marketing environment'

2 Explain the distinction between the microenvironment and the macroenvironment

3 Analyse the impact of economic, social, political and legal, physical and technological forces on marketing decisions

4 Critique the nature of corporate social responsibility and ethical marketing practices

5 Analyse the impact of customers, distributors, suppliers and competitors on marketing decisions

6 Explain how companies respond to environmental change.

The Pepsi Global Refresh Project

One of the main themes of this book is the interaction between marketing and society. Businesses do not operate in a vacuum but have a huge impact on society at large. The extent to which existing practices are sustainable into the future is a question that occupies the minds of many. The world's stock of resources such as water, rainforest and clean air is finite. Yet competition between enterprises and consumers' desire to have a better standard of living for themselves continues to negatively impact upon the planet and drain its limited resources.

It was this recognition that underpinned an ambitious initiative launched by the Pepsi brand in 2010 labelled the Global Refresh Project. In it, individuals, businesses and not-for-profit organizations from around the world were invited to submit ideas that they felt would positively impact on their local communities. Suggestions were sent to the refresheverything.com website with a monthly limit of 1,000 ideas. These were then assessed and vetted before the public was invited to vote for selected entries. A fund of $20 million was set aside to support the various causes, and awards from $5,000 to $250,000 could be made. In its first year, the project provided funds to 108 schools, 68 parks and playgrounds and 20 children's homes, shelters and affordable houses.

While businesses engage in these kinds of social initiatives on a regular basis, there are usually commercial advantages to doing so as well. For example, the Global Refresh Project helped to position Pepsi as a positive, optimistic force for change in communities that people cared about. This was very important at a time when soft drinks have been widely criticized for contributing to rising levels of obesity particularly among young people. The initiative also exploited the growing popularity of social media as a marketing tool. As both suggestions for funding and votes for selected entries were done through social media channels, this offered Pepsi the opportunity to engage in dialogue and build relationships with customers around the world. Initial results were very promising. In the first year, the project got 4 million 'likes' on Facebook, 60,000 Twitter followers and over 87 million votes were cast. Pepsi continued the conversation with its customers through a crowdsourcing initiative in 2011, asking fans and followers how they would like to see the project evolve.

However, despite the worthiness of the causes and the popularity of the project, one major problem began to surface in 2011. Pepsi sales throughout 2010 had fallen. The brand lost market share and for the first time in decades also the coveted number two slot, behind Coke, to Diet Coke. Furthermore, the weaknesses of the project began to become clearer. First, the range of funded projects was so diffuse that their overall impact was lower than had the initiative focused on one big idea. Second, there were problems with vetting projects that were so widely scattered around the world. And finally, there was no direct product linkage, which contributed to the fall in sales. The Pepsi Global Refresh Project was quietly shelved in 2012.[1]

Pepsi Refresh Project Ad Insight: can a soft drink make the world a better place?

Figure 2.1 The marketing environment

A market-orientated firm needs to look outward to the environment in which it operates, adapting to take advantage of emerging opportunities and to minimize potential threats. In this chapter we will examine the **marketing environment** and how to monitor it. In particular, we will look at some of the major forces that impact upon organizations, such as economic, social, legal, physical and technological issues. Firms need to monitor the rapid changes taking place in these variables in order to exploit potential opportunities and to minimize potential threats.

The marketing environment is composed of the forces and actors that affect a company's ability to operate effectively in providing products and services to its customers. Distinctions have been drawn between the **microenvironment** and the **macroenvironment** (see Figure 2.1). The microenvironment consists of the actors in the firm's immediate environment or business system that affect its capabilities to operate effectively in its chosen markets. The key actors are suppliers, distributors, customers and competitors. The macroenvironment consists of a number of broader forces that affect not only the company, but also the other actors in the microenvironment. These can be grouped into economic, social, political/legal, physical and technological forces. These shape the character of the opportunities and threats facing a company, and yet are largely uncontrollable.

The macroenvironment

This chapter will focus on the major macroenvironmental forces that affect marketing

decisions. Typically there are six forces that need to be examined – namely, economic, social, political and legal, ecological and technological, with the result that the acronym PESTEL is often used to describe macroenvironmental analysis. Later in the chapter we will introduce the four dimensions of the microenvironment, some of which will then be dealt with in greater detail throughout the book. The changing nature of the supply chain and customer behaviour will be dealt with in detail in the next chapter while the issue of distributors is explored in depth in Chapter 9.

Economic forces

Through its effect on supply and demand, the economic environment can have a crucial influence on the success of companies. It is important to identify those economic influences that are relevant and to monitor them. We shall now examine three major economic influences on the marketing environment of companies: economic growth and unemployment; interest rates and exchange rates; and taxation and inflation.

Economic growth and unemployment

The general state of both national and international economies can have a profound effect on an individual company's prosperity. Economies tend to fluctuate according to the 'business cycle'. Most of the world's economies went through a period of significant growth from the early to mid-2000s, driven mainly by rising demand in developing economies like China and the availability of cheap credit in the developed markets of the West. The fortunes of many sectors, such as retailing, services, consumer durables and commodities, closely mirror this economic pattern. For example, the rising demand for oil meant a rapid growth in wealth for oil-rich states like the United Arab Emirates (UAE) resulting in a retail, hotel and property boom in states such as Dubai. The global financial crisis (GFC) of 2007 followed by a sudden scarcity of credit gave rise to a significant downturn in the economies of Europe particularly. Several countries such as Greece, Portugal, Italy, Ireland and Spain suffered severe financial crises caused by excess levels of personal, corporate and sovereign debt built up during the boom years. Greece's economy collapsed with growth levels at zero and unemployment doubling since 2011 to almost one third of the population (see Table 2.1). Spain's youth unemployment rate is estimated to be close to 50 per cent, all of which has a very negative effect on levels of consumer demand for products and services. A major marketing problem is predicting the next boom or slump. Germany, which for years lagged average growth in Europe, has become the quickest country to recover from the GFC with many of its major firms reporting record profits. Investments made during periods of low growth can yield rich returns when economies recover.

Low growth rates and high unemployment levels have a direct impact on the way consumers behave. Because they feel less well off, they are likely to purchase less, buy smaller quantities and/ or switch to cheaper alternatives such as discount or retailer brands. But opportunities can also arise. Because consumers pay fewer visits to beauty salons and spas, for example, manufacturers may sell more beauty products to be applied at home. This is also the time when companies tend to cut back on advertising budgets, which has particular implications for marketing. It was estimated that the advertising budget of the UK government was cut by 75 per cent in 2010.[2] The variety of growth rates and unemployment levels throughout some of the world's major economies is illustrated in Table 2.1.

A key challenge for marketers will be to try to anticipate the implications of the changing patterns of global economic growth. While growth in the traditional powerhouses of the world economy such as Europe and the USA remains slow (see Table 2.1), other economies are racing ahead. China has grown so rapidly in the past decade that it is now the world's second largest economy. The remaining BRIC nations (Brazil, Russia and India, as well as China) have also experienced strong growth, while the term CIVETS (Colombia, Indonesia, Vietnam, Egypt, Turkey, South Africa) has been coined to describe the newest group of countries likely to grow rapidly. As these countries build factories, roads and shopping centres, they need resources such as oil, copper, coal and so on, and the continent of Africa – traditionally the world's poorest region – is rich in these resources, with the result that huge levels of Chinese investment have poured into Africa (see Marketing in Action 2.1). In specific industries, new opportunities are emerging all the time. For example, Nokia has been very successful in its efforts to gain a large share of the Indian market through its provision of low-cost telecommunications products. But many others have found these new markets very challenging. IBM reported a sales fall of 23 per cent in China in the last quarter of 2013, while consumer goods firms like L'Oréal and Revlon have either reduced their investments or exited the country completely due

Table 2.1 Growth rates and unemployment rates (percentage) in selected countries, 2014

Country	Growth Rate[1]	Unemployment Rate[2]
Canada	+2.3	7.0
United States	+2.8	6.6
Australia	+2.6	6.0
Japan	+1.4	3.7
Austria	+1.3	4.9
Belgium	+1.2	8.5
Czech Republic	+1.6	8.6
Denmark	+1.3	5.4
France	+0.8	10.9
Germany	+1.8	6.8
Greece	0.0	28.0
Italy	+0.4	12.9
Netherlands	+0.8	8.6
Norway	+2.2	3.6
Poland	+2.9	14.0
Spain	+0.7	25.8
Sweden	+2.3	8.6
United Kingdom	+2.8	7.2
Euro Area	+1.1	12.0
China	+7.2	4.1
India	+6.0	9.9
Russia	+2.9	5.6
Brazil	+1.8	4.8

[1] Projected growth rate for 2014
[2] Unemployment rate, January 2014
Source: *The Economist*.

to competition of discount online operators.[3] These dramatic trends mean that European marketers need to be aware of the emerging opportunities and challenges.

Interest rates and exchange rates

One of the levers that the government uses to manage the economy is interest rates; the interest rate is the rate at which money is borrowed by businesses and individuals. Throughout the world, interest rates are at historically low levels. One of the results of this has been a boom in consumer borrowing for capital investments such as housing. This has meant significant sales and profit rises for construction companies and global furniture retailers like IKEA. While taking on debt to buy homes and cars has traditionally been considered acceptable, what is

Marketing in Action 2.1 Tecno Telecom Ltd

Critical Thinking: Below is a review of the successful growth of Tecno Telecom Ltd in Africa. Read it and critically reflect on the implications of the growth of companies like Tecno for global business.

The current global business landscape gives rise to companies like Tecno Telecom Ltd. It was founded in Hong Kong in 2006 but the major focus of its operations is in Africa. It is a manufacturer of mobile phones but competes effectively against the titans of the industry like Samsung and Apple. In 2013, it achieved sales of 37 million units making it one of the dominant mobile phone brands in Africa.

Though the company initially began competing in Asian markets, it quickly spotted the opportunities presented by the growth of some major African economies and opened its first offices in Nigeria in 2008. Africa quickly became the focus of its operations and it moved both R&D and manufacturing facilities to the continent in order to develop products that were suited to local markets both in terms of design and affordability. For example, power supplies in many African regions can be erratic so the company developed a phone that came with its own power pack so that it could be recharged whenever the battery was depleted. Another

innovation was the development of a dual-SIM phone which allowed the user to separate business and personal use, for example, without the need to possess two devices. It operated a two-brand strategy. Its main brand Tecno was seen as a leader in terms of design and functionality while its itel brand offered a more affordable option in countries where disposable income is a fraction of that in other parts of the world.

By 2012, smartphone penetration was rising to about 30 per cent of the population in some African countries so Tecno launched its first smartphone using the Android platform. Again, its strategy was to produce devices that were high on functionality while being more affordable than leading brands. Tecno's mission has been not just to sell phones in Africa but to bring modern communications to the continent embodied by its slogan 'we can'. It operated the largest network of after-sales service outlets throughout the continent which helped it to serve customers, understand their needs and build its brand.

worrying policymakers is the high levels of consumer debt arising particularly from the overuse of credit cards. Total household borrowing as a percentage of gross domestic product (GDP) has risen considerably over the past two decades, but the rate of growth has been variable. Debt levels are below 40 per cent of GDP in Italy but over 100 per cent in the UK, the Netherlands and Denmark. Overall, changes in interest rates are usually followed quickly by changes in consumer behaviour.

Exchange rates are the rates at which one currency buys another. With the formation of the European Union (EU), exchange rates between most European countries are now fixed. However, the rates at which major currencies like the US dollar, the euro, sterling and the yen are traded are still variable. These floating rates can have a significant impact on the

profitability of a company's international operations. For example, the booming Australian economy and rising interest rates there in 2009 and 2010 led to a significant strengthening of the Australian dollar against currencies like the euro and the US dollar. This in turn has meant that Australian goods became more expensive in Europe and the USA, creating challenges for Australian companies operating in these markets. However, the rising dollar also brings positive results, such as making the cost of travel abroad cheaper for Australian citizens.

Taxation and inflation

There are two types of personal taxes: direct and indirect. Direct taxes are taxes on income and wealth, such as income tax, capital gains tax, inheritance tax, and so on. Income tax is important for marketers because it determines the levels of disposable income that consumers have. When taxes fall, consumers keep a greater portion of their earnings and have more money to spend. It also increases the levels of discretionary income that they have – that is, the amount of money available after essentials, such as food and rent, have been paid for. At this point consumers move from needs to wants, and a great deal of marketing activity is aimed at trying to convince us where we should spend our discretionary income.

Indirect taxes include value added tax (VAT), excise duties and tariffs, and are taxes that are included in the prices of goods and services that we buy. They have major implications for marketing mix variables such as price. Changes in VAT rates need to be passed on to customers and this can cause problems for firms trying to compete on the basis of low price. Differences in indirect tax levels across national boundaries give rise to the problem of *parallel importing*, whereby goods are bought in a low-cost country for importation back into a high-cost country. This presents a challenge for distributors in the high-cost country, who are not permitted to get access to this source of supply. Variations in tax levels impact on consumer demand. For example, lower tax levels on wine have resulted in consumers switching from beer. As a result, some interesting disputes have arisen with regard to how products should be classified. For example, Marks & Spencer (M&S) had consistently argued that its teacakes should be classified as cakes (which carry a zero VAT rating) as opposed to chocolate biscuits, which carry a VAT rate of 20 per cent. The long-running legal battle between the company and the UK Treasury was finally ended in the European Court in 2008 when the court ruled in M&S's favour, resulting in a £3.5 million rebate to the company for VAT paid on the product.

Finally, inflation is a measure of the cost of living in an economy. The inflation rate is calculated by monitoring price changes on a basket of products such as rent/mortgage repayments, oil, clothing, food items and consumer durables. The rising price of commodities like oil and wheat feed through to consumers in the form of higher fuel bills and higher bread and pasta prices. Rapid rises in inflation also reduce the future value of savings, investments and pensions. Governments are acutely sensitive to inflation figures and increase interest rates to keep inflation under control.

Overall economic movements feed through to marketing in the form of influencing demand for products and services, and the level of profitability that accrues to the firm from the sales of goods.

Social forces

When considering the social environment, two major aspects need to be examined, namely demographic changes and the cultural differences that exist within and between nations. Further aspects of the social environment will be explored in the next chapter when we examine consumer behaviour in greater detail.

Demographic forces

The term demographics refers to changes in population. The most significant factor from society's point of view is the dramatic growth in the world's population in the past 200 years (see Figure 2.2). On the one hand, this presents opportunities for marketers in the form of growing markets but on the other hand it raises questions about the sustainability of this global growth. The planet's resources are finite, meaning that pressure is increasing on the limited supplies of water, food and fuel. For example, the fishing industry supports 520 million people or 8 per cent of the global population but if current overfishing levels continue, commercial fishing will collapse before 2050. Some species such as tuna, marlin and swordfish have fallen by as much as 90 per cent since the 1950s. Innovative solutions to this challenge are likely to generate significant returns for organizations. Variations in population growth are also important.

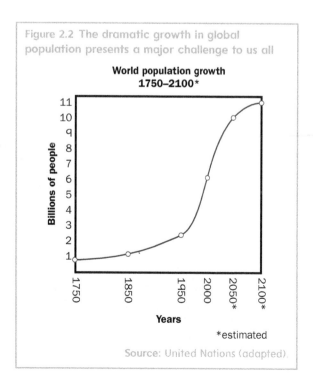

Figure 2.2 The dramatic growth in global population presents a major challenge to us all

World population growth 1750–2100*

*estimated

Source: United Nations (adapted).

China has a one-child policy, growth is slowing in the developed world and most increases are forecast in Africa, Asia and Latin America. In response, Unilever is trying to sell more soap in African countries, which improves hygiene and cuts down on diseases, while mobile phone companies like Vodafone in Africa and Digicell in the Caribbean have generated significant profits from providing telephony in these regions.

Globalization has given rise to two other interesting demographic effects, namely, population migration between countries and the rise of middle and wealthy classes in countries with a low average GDP per capita. The continued integration of Europe has resulted in significant movements of labour from the poorer areas of Central and Eastern Europe to the wealthier Western European countries. These patterns are being played out around the world, and the United Nations estimates that, in 2013, 232 million people settled outside the country in which they were born and that this number could reach 405 million by 2050. Changes in immigration controls such as the number of student visas issued impacts upon the level of demand for university places. Global economic prosperity has also given rise to significant segments of wealthy consumers in countries with low average wages, such as Russia and Indonesia. For example, advertising expenditure in Nigeria has grown sixfold

since 2000 as global companies seek to reach its growing middle class.[4]

A major demographic change that will continue to affect demand for products and services is the rising proportion of people over the age of 60 and the decline in the younger age group. Figure 2.3 shows projections for the growth of this segment up to 2050. The rise in the over-55-year-old group creates substantial marketing opportunities because of the high level of per capita income enjoyed by this group in developed countries. They have much lower commitments in terms of mortgage repayments than younger people, tend to benefit from inheritance wealth and are healthier than ever before. Pharmaceuticals, health and beauty, technology, travel, financial services, luxury cars, lavish food and entertainment are key growth sectors for this market segment. The overall implication of these trends is that many consumer companies may need to reposition their product and service offerings to take account of the rise in so-called 'grey' purchasing power. For example, almost one fifth of skiers at US resorts are aged over 55 and have been locally dubbed as the 'greys on trays!'

Finally, one of the emerging demographic trends is the growth in the number of household units and falling household sizes. People are choosing to get married later or stay single, divorce rates are rising

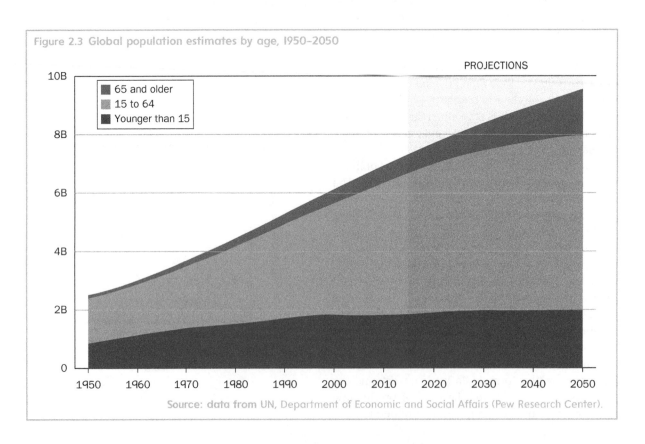

Figure 2.3 Global population estimates by age, 1950–2050

PROJECTIONS

Legend:
- 65 and older
- 15 to 64
- Younger than 15

Source: data from UN, Department of Economic and Social Affairs (Pew Research Center).

and family sizes are smaller than they traditionally have been. Combined with high incomes and busy lives, these trends have led to a boom in connoisseur convenience foods and convenience shopping. Companies like Northern Foods and Marks & Spencer, in particular, have catered for this market very successfully. Demand for childcare and homecare facilities has also risen.

Cultural forces

Culture is the combination of values, beliefs and attitudes that is possessed by a national group or subgroup. Cultural differences have implications for the way in which business is conducted. For example, because of the growth of markets like China, India and Singapore, more and more westerners are doing business in these countries and are finding significant differences in the way things are done. Westerners tend to view contracts as set in stone, while those from the East take a more flexible view. In the East, a penchant for harmony means that decision-making tends primarily to be a rubber-stamping of a consensus already hammered out by senior management. The Western obsession with using logic to unravel complex situations is likely to be viewed as naive by those in the East. These kinds of differences are deeply culturally bound in the complex social networks of the East versus the greater levels of independence experienced by those living in the West.[5]

International marketers need to pay particular attention to the possible impact of culture. For example, MTV – which was the traditional, all-American music channel – developed 141 channels broadcasting in 32 languages to 160 countries. While these could be viewed as vehicles for the export of American culture to new countries, the company is careful to reflect local cultures; for example, 45 per cent of what is shown on MTV Arabia in the Middle East is locally produced and the remainder is translated.[6]

Even within particular countries, however, it is important to bear in mind that many subcultures also exist (see Exhibit 2.1). The rapid movement of global populations, described above, has meant that ethnically based subcultures have sprung up in most developed countries, creating potentially lucrative niche markets for products and services. For example, there is an estimated 3.5 million people of Turkish origin living in Germany, over 5.5 million Moroccans living in Spain, and over 800,000 people living in Italy are of Albanian origin. In addition, social trends and fashions give rise to their own particular subcultures, whose members dress and behave in certain ways.

Guinness Ad Insight: The story of the Sapeurs.

Political and legal forces

Marketing decisions can also be influenced by political and legal forces, which determine the rules by which business is conducted. Political forces describe the close connections that politicians and senior business people often have, sometimes called crony capitalism. These relationships are often cultivated by organizations, both to monitor the political mood and also to influence it. Companies sometimes make sizeable contributions to the funds of political parties in an attempt to maintain favourable relationships. The types of sectors where crony capitalism is most pervasive include resources, defence, ports and airports, real estate and utilities and telecoms while the problem is greatest in countries like Hong Kong, Russia, Malaysia, Ukraine and Singapore.[7] The importance of political connections has been demonstrated by a study which showed that 'politically connected firms' are three times more likely to be bailed out during a financial crisis than those that are not.[8] During the global financial crisis, Lehman Brothers was allowed to fail but Goldman Sachs was rescued, leading it to earn the nickname – 'Government Sachs'. The extent to which businesses try to influence the political process is illustrated by the level of lobbying that takes place. Earlier in this chapter, we saw how world fishing stocks are being depleted yet successful lobbying by national fishing groups has given the industry globally an estimated $35 billion a year in cheap fuel, insurance and so on.[9] It is estimated that there are 15,000 lobbyists in Brussels trying to influence EU policy-making by its 732 Members of the European Parliament (MEPs).[10] Some of the proposals that businesses have lobbied against include restrictions on online and mobile phone advertising to reduce spam, tougher packaging rules to reduce waste, and stricter testing and labelling for chemicals.

Political decisions can have major consequences for businesses. For example, it can lead to the creation or removal of industries and businesses. Producing and selling marijuana is illegal in most countries but, in 2014, Colorado became the first state in the USA to allow the legal sale of the substance creating a new industry with producers, distributors and customers as well as a new source of tax revenue for the state. In 2013, the Spanish oil firm Repsol had its assets in Argentina taken over by the state. Decisions can severely impact existing business such as the US decision to invade Iraq, which resulted in some leading American companies becoming the targets for attack and some American products being boycotted. German businesses lobbied against proposed sanctions for Russia following its intervention in Ukraine in 2014 as it is Germany's 11th biggest export market worth an estimated €36 billion and supporting 300,000 jobs. Political turmoil in Egypt shattered its very important tourism industry, with estimates putting hotel occupancy rates in Cairo at 15 per cent in 2012. Usually, political forces have a more gradual and subtle effect, as illustrated by European politicians' pursuit of a common European union.

The European Union

In the past, the basic economic unit has been the country, which was largely autonomous with regard to the decisions it made about its economy and levels of supply and demand. But for the past three decades, all this has been changing rapidly, driven mainly by the globalization of business. The world's largest companies, like Google, General Electric, Walmart and others, are now larger than most countries in economic terms. At the same time, countries have been merging together into economic areas to more effectively manage their affairs. Most European countries are now part of the European Union (EU), the North American countries have grouped together into an economic area known as NAFTA (North American Free Trade Agreement), and the Pacific Rim countries are part of a group known as the ASEAN (Association of South East Asian Nations).

The advent in 1986 of the Single European Act was the launch pad for an internal market in the EU. The intention was to create a massive deregulated market of 320 million consumers by abolishing barriers to the free flow of products, services, capital and people among the then 12 member states. The current EU members are Austria, Belgium, Bulgaria, Croatia, the Czech Republic, Cyprus, Denmark, Estonia, Finland, France, Germany, Greece, Hungary, Ireland, Italy, Latvia, Lithuania, Luxembourg, Malta, the Netherlands, Poland, Portugal, Romania, Slovakia, Slovenia, Spain, Sweden and the UK. The common currency, the euro, is in use in 23 countries, making travel, price comparisons and cross-border trade easier.

One of the main outcomes of economic union is that the prospects for adopting what is known as a pan-European or standardized strategy across Europe are improved. Standardization appears to depend on product type. In the case of many industrial goods, consumer durables (such as cameras, toasters, watches, radios) and clothing (Gucci shoes, Benetton sweaters, Levi's jeans) standardization is well advanced. However, for many fast-moving consumer goods (fmcg), standardization of products is more difficult to achieve because of differences in local tastes. Nevertheless, it is an approach that is being increasingly adopted by companies. For example, Lastminute.com, which is aiming to position itself as a leisure, entertainment and travel retailer, has created a Europe-wide promotional campaign based on the idea of customers telling unforgettable stories under the tagline 'Stories start here…'.

Pro-competitive legislation

Political action may also translate directly into legislation and less formal directives, which can have a profound influence on business conduct. One of the key areas in which regulators act is ensuring that competition is fair and legal and operates in a way so that consumers and society benefit. Formerly, the control of monopolies in Europe was enacted via Article 86 of the Treaty of Rome, which aimed to prevent the 'abuse' of a dominant market position. However, control was increased in 1990 when the EU introduced its first direct mechanism for dealing with mergers and takeovers: the Merger Regulation. This gave the Competition Directorate of the European Commission jurisdiction over 'concentrations with a European dimension'. Over the years, the Commission has challenged the activities of major global companies, most notably Microsoft. After a legal battle lasting nine years, Microsoft finally admitted defeat in 2007 after the European Commission charged that it had abused its dominance in the software market. It had to pay fines totalling €777 million and was forced to provide information to other companies in order that their software would 'interoperate' with Microsoft's software. In 2011, the Commission ordered an investigation into Google after three online companies alleged that its search functions were penalizing their businesses.[11] Competition bodies also operate at a national level, such as the Office of Fair Trading in the UK and the Competition Authority in Ireland, where they monitor local-level competition issues.

Consumer legislation

Regulators also enact legislation designed to protect consumers. Many countries throughout Europe have some form of Consumer Protection Act that regulates how businesses interact with consumers and how they advertise their products. These acts typically outlaw practices that are deemed to be unfair, misleading or aggressive. For example, promotions and product information must be clear and claims – such as that a product is friendly to the environment – must be backed up with evidence. This legislation is then enforced through a body such as the National Consumer Agency in Ireland. For example, because of a global obesity epidemic, restaurants around the world are being required to state the number of calories in everything on their menus. The need for this kind of consumer protection is illustrated by the marketing of products like breakfast cereals and soft drinks which frequently portrays these products as being much healthier than they actually are.

In short, political and legal decisions can change the rules of the business game very quickly. For example, in 2006, the mayor of San Paulo in Brazil introduced the Clean City Law requiring that all of the city's extensive outdoor advertising be removed, with the result that Brazilian advertisers quickly adapted to using social media to reach their customers.[12] Similarly, the European Court's ruling in 2007 that the Baileys Minis series could remain on sale represented an important victory for Diageo, which had invested heavily in the development of the brand extension. In many instances, firms and industries create voluntary codes of practice in order to stave off possible political and legal action.

Codes of practice

On top of the various laws that are in place, certain industries have drawn up codes of practice – sometimes as a result of political pressure – to protect consumer interests. The UK advertising industry, for example, has drawn up a self-regulatory Code of Advertising Standards and Practice designed to keep advertising 'legal, decent, honest and truthful' and in 2010 this code was extended to cover Facebook pages, Twitter feeds and online banner advertising. However, these codes are frequently violated as advertisers push the boundaries of what is socially acceptable in order to increase the level of likes, shares and comments on social media. Similarly, the marketing research industry has drawn up a code of practice to protect people from unethical activities such as using marketing research as a pretext for selling. However, many commentators are critical of the potential effectiveness of voluntary codes of conduct in industries like oil exploration and clothing manufacture.[13] Firms like Coca-Cola and PepsiCo in the USA have begun to restrict sales of soft drinks in schools, in an effort to appease critics and stave off regulation such as that imposed in France, which banned school-based vending machines.

Marketing management must be aware of the constraints on its activities brought about by the political and legal environment. It must assess the extent to which there is a need to influence political decisions that may affect operations, and the degree to which industry practice needs to be self-regulated in order to maintain high standards of customer satisfaction and service.

Ecological forces

As we noted above, the explosion in the world's population and the resulting economic growth has brought the issue of environmental sustainability to centre stage. Everything that we need for our survival and well-being depends directly or indirectly on the natural environment. Some of the key sustainability challenges that have emerged in recent decades are outlined below.

Climate change

Climate change has been one of the most hotly debated topics in recent years. Most commentators argue that human activity is hastening the depletion of the ozone layer, resulting in a gradual rise in world temperatures, which is melting the polar ice caps and causing more unpredictable weather extremes like droughts, floods and hurricanes. Movies like Al Gore's *An Inconvenient Truth* have helped to bring the debate into the mainstream. Contrarian views suggest that global warming is largely the result of a natural cycle and find supporting evidence in the fact that global temperatures grew at a far slower rate between 1998–2013 than they had in the 1990s. In effect, for businesses, this means seeking ways to reduce CO_2 emissions and a ban on the use of chlorofluorocarbons (CFCs). For example, Land Rover, whose sports utility vehicles (SUVs) are a prime target for green-minded law-makers, aimed to cut its fleet's average CO_2 by 20 per cent before 2012. Such initiatives will be necessary as higher taxes on SUVs have caused their sales levels in Western Europe to fall quickly. Opportunities are also being created by the use of route-planning software for transport companies to reduce emissions, and Internet matching systems to fill empty vehicles.

Climate change has the potential to have a major impact on business and society (see Exhibit 2.2). For example, air travel is very much taken for granted and has boomed in recent years due to economic prosperity and the marketing activities of low-cost airlines. But airplanes are significant users of limited fossil fuels like oil, and CO_2 emissions from international aviation have doubled since 1990. Ultimately, this may mean consumers choosing to

Exhibit 2.2 Droughts and famines brought on by climate change have been the focus of attention of numerous non-governmental organizations (NGOs) such as Amnesty International

Exhibit 2.3 The 'greening' of the iconic London red bus is a pilot project between Arriva London and Volvo to manufacture hybrid buses that are 25% more fuel efficient than conventional diesel buses

fly less or even being encouraged to fly less, which will have significant implications for the aviation industry. These kinds of changes have already happened in the business of patio heaters, which grew in popularity due to smoking bans and a preference by consumers for eating and drinking outdoors. But the gas-powered heaters can emit as much CO_2 per year as one and a half cars, and companies like B&Q have stopped selling them.

Pollution

The quality of the physical environment can be harmed by the manufacture, use and disposal of products. The production of chemicals that pollute the atmosphere, the use of nitrates in fertilizer that pollutes rivers, and the disposal of by-products into the sea have caused considerable public concern. Rapidly growing economies like China and India have particular problems in this regard, with China having overtaken the USA as the world's biggest emitter of CO_2. Coal provides 80 per cent of China's energy and it is anticipated that it will continue to do so for the next half-century. Factory and car emissions have meant that air pollution has become a major problem in Beijing. Water pollution has also reached serious levels, with an estimated 90 per cent of the water running through cities being polluted.[14]

Pressure from regulators and consumer groups helps to reduce pollution (see Exhibit 2.3). Denmark has introduced a series of anti-pollution measures including a charge on pesticides and a CFC tax. In the Netherlands, higher taxes on pesticides, fertilizers and carbon monoxide emissions are proposed. Not all of the activity is simply cost raising, however. In Germany, one of the marketing benefits of its involvement in green technology has been a thriving export business in pollution-control equipment.

Conservation of scarce resources

Recognition of the finite nature of the world's resources has stimulated a drive towards conservation. This is reflected in the demand for energy-efficient housing and fuel-efficient motor cars, for example. In Europe, Sweden has taken the lead in developing an energy policy based on domestic and renewable resources. The tax system penalizes the use of polluting energy sources like coal and oil, while less polluting and domestic sources such as peat and woodchip receive favourable tax treatment. The UK is experiencing a boom in the installation of solar panels in response to the creation of incentives for households that generate surplus electricity which is exported back into the grid.[15] Companies manufacturing solar panels and related products stand to benefit from this trend. Toyota's development of its Prius model – a hybrid petrol-electric car – has been an unprecedented success; so much so, that the company has struggled to meet demand for it.

There is increasing recognition that water may become the next scarce resource that needs to be conserved as it is estimated that only 1 per cent of the world's water is fit for human consumption. This has major implications for the lucrative global bottled water industry. A US study has found that global consumption of bottled water had grown by over 57 per cent in the five-year period to 2006 and the amount being spent on it was seven times the sum invested in providing safe drinking water in developing countries.[16] The lifestyle brand, Fiji water is sourced in Fiji but travels 10,000 miles to Europe and beyond while one in three Fijians do not have access to safe drinking water. Furthermore, millions of barrels of crude oil are used in the making of 300 billion plastic bottles per year, 90 per cent of which are disposed of after one use and take 1000 years to biodegrade. Water scarcity also has implications for soft drinks manufacturers like PepsiCo and Coca-Cola, which are accused of causing water shortages near production plants in developing countries.

Organizational responses to the issue of scarce resources can have interesting effects. For example, European law commits countries to generate 30 per cent of their electricity from renewable sources by 2020. This has given rise to a rapidly growing wind turbine industry which has had two consequences. First, wind turbines are very unpopular with local residents due to their size and impact on the skyline. As a result, many wind farms have been moved offshore but the cost of producing electricity this way is estimated to be three times the current wholesale price.[17]

Recyclable and non-wasteful packaging

The past 20 years or so have seen significant growth in recycling throughout Europe. Cutting out waste in packaging is not only environmentally friendly but also makes commercial sense. Thus companies have introduced concentrated detergents and refill packs, and removed the cardboard packaging around some brands of toothpaste, for example. The savings can be substantial: in Germany, Lever GmbH saved 30 per cent by introducing concentrated detergents, 20 per cent by using lightweight plastic bottles, and the introduction of refills for concentrated liquids reduced the weight of packaging materials by a half. Many governments have introduced bans on the ubiquitous plastic bags available at supermarkets and convenience stores as they give rise to pollution and are slow to biodegrade, which has major implications for packaging manufacturers.

The growth in the use of the personal computer has raised major recycling issues as PCs contain many harmful substances and pollutants. EU legislation is forcing manufacturers to face up to the issue of how these products are recycled, with some of the costs being absorbed by the companies and the rest by the consumer. Hewlett Packard set up a team to re-examine how PCs are made and to design them with their disposal in mind. The team conducted projects such as using corn starch instead of plastic in its printers, redesigning packaging and cutting down on emissions from factories.[18] The Waste Electrical and Electronic Equipment (WEEE) Directive became European law in 2003 and imposed the responsibility for the disposal of electrical products on manufacturers. Consumers are entitled to return old electrical goods to sellers, which are charged with recycling them, though the cost of this activity has largely been passed on to consumers through an additional recycling levy. One of the consequences of the Directive has been an increased focus by manufacturers on the ease of recycling of their products.

Use of environmentally friendly ingredients

The use of biodegradable and natural ingredients when practicable is favoured by environmentalists. The toy industry is one that has come in for criticism for its extensive use of plastics and other environmentally unfriendly products. Consequently, startup companies like Green Toys and Anamalz have used a different approach. The former makes toys from recycled plastic milk containers, which are sold in recycled cardboard, while Anamalz uses wood instead of plastic. The humble light bulb is a classic example of a product made from environmentally unfriendly ingredients. It wastes huge amounts of electricity, radiating 95 per cent of the energy it consumes as heat rather than light, and its life span is relatively short. This is because existing light bulbs use electrodes to connect with the power supply and also include dangerous materials like mercury. Researchers at a company called Ceravision in the UK have developed an alternative that does not require electrodes or mercury, uses very little energy and should never need changing. These types of innovations illustrate the business opportunities that are created through the monitoring of the marketing environment.

Animal testing of new products

To reduce the risk of them being harmful to humans, potential new products such as shampoos and cosmetics are tested on animals before launch. This has aroused much opposition. One of the major concepts key to the initial success of UK retailer the Body Shop was that its products were not subject to animal testing. This is an example of the Body Shop's ethical approach to business, which also extends to its suppliers. Other larger stores, responding to Body Shop's success, have introduced their own range of animal-friendly products.

In summary, the demands that global economic growth are placing on the natural environment are very significant. Consequently, attention is now being given to the extent to which businesses behave responsibly and ethically.

Corporate social responsibility

Corporate social responsibility (CSR) is a widely used term that describes a form of self-regulation by businesses based on the ethical principle that a person or an organization should be accountable for how its actions might affect the physical environment and the general public. Concerns about the environment, business and public welfare are represented by pressure groups such as Greenpeace, Corporate Watch and Oxfam.

Marketing managers need to be aware that organizations are part of a larger society and are accountable to that society for their actions. Such concerns led Perrier to recall 160 million bottles of its mineral water in 120 countries after traces of a toxic chemical were found in 13 bottles. The recall cost the company a total of £50 million, even though there was no evidence that the level of the chemical found in the

water was harmful to humans. Perrier acted because it believed the least doubt in the consumers' minds should be removed in order to maintain its brand's image of quality and purity. In contrast, Coca-Cola took a week to accept responsibility for a wave of sickness caused by the contamination of its products in Belgium, and faces continued criticism over anti-union violence, worsening water shortages and childhood obesity. Companies are increasingly conscious of the need to communicate their socially responsible activities. The term 'Green marketing' is used to describe marketing efforts to produce, promote and reclaim environmentally sensitive products.[19]

The societal marketing concept is a label often used to describe how the activities of companies should not only consider the needs of customers but also society at large. This notion has given rise to movements like the Fairtrade Foundation and also to the formation of companies like Edun, the Dublin-based fashion company owned by the luxury goods group LVMH. Founded by U2's Bono and his wife Ali Hewson, the company manufactured a line of organic cotton shirts, jeans and hemp blazers. Its fashion line was made from non-subsidized cotton sourced in Peru and manufactured in Africa, while its second brand, Edun Live, comprised mass-market clothes made from Tanzanian cotton and manufactured in Lesotho. The company's ethical goal was to support manufacturers in Africa and world farmers by championing organic, environmentally sustainable cotton products.[20]

Corporate social responsibility is no longer an optional extra but a key part of business strategy that comes under close scrutiny from pressure groups, private shareholders and institutional investors, some of whom manage ethical investment funds (see Marketing in Action 2.2). Businesses are increasingly expected to adapt to climate change, biodiversity, social equity and human rights in a world characterized by greater transparency and more explicit values.[21] Two outcomes of these developments have been the growth in social reporting and cause-related marketing.

Social reporting is where firms conduct independent audits of their social performance and report the results. The practice is a form of self-regulation and some firms like Baxter International Inc. and Shell have been producing such reports since the mid-1990s. Currently, most of the world's largest companies produce sustainability reports.

Cause-related marketing is a commercial activity by which businesses and charities or causes form a partnership with each other in order to market an image, product or service for mutual benefit. Cause-related marketing works well when the business and charity have a similar target audience.

Marketing in Action 2.2 Novo Nordisk

Critical Thinking: Below is a brief overview of some of the sustainability activities conducted by Novo Nordisk. Read it, visit novonordisk.com/sustainability and critically evaluate the extent to which CSR is a core part of the organization's marketing strategy.

Novo Nordisk is a global healthcare company that was founded in 1989 with the merger of two Danish businesses, Novo Industri A/S and Nordisk Gentofte A/S. It has over 40,000 employees in 75 countries and markets its products in over 180 countries around the world. It is a global leader in the treatment of diabetes care as well as having leading positions in sectors like haemophilia care, growth hormone therapy and hormone replacement therapy. It is one of the largest publically traded companies in the Nordic region and had annual sales revenues in excess of DDK83 billion in 2013. Some of its leading brands include Levemir, Novolog and NovoSeven.

Sustainability is a big part of its business strategy. For example on climate change it has partnered with the World Wildlife Fund (WWF) Climate Savers programme and committed to reduce CO2 emissions from global production sites by 10 per cent between 2004 and 2014. It partnered with another Danish firm, Dong Energy, in 2007 and pledged to purchase all energy for its Danish production plants from an offshore wind farm. It produced a policy on animal ethics which sought to limit the testing of new drugs on animals to instances where there

was no other alternative. It also developed policies and actions on many of the other contentious issues within medicine such as counterfeit medicine, stem cell research and gene technology. Another of its hallmarks has been its commitment to social reporting which it has been engaged in since 1994. Its business is managed in accordance with the triple bottom line (TBL) principle which means that it is financially, socially and environmentally responsible and reports on these three dimensions in its communications with stakeholders. Its *TBL Quarterly* contains details of actions on these criteria.

Novo Nordisk has been a frequent award winner for both its sustainable activities and its social reporting. For example in 2012 at the World Economic Forum in Davos, Switzerland, it was awarded the top position in the Global 100 Most Sustainable Corporations in the World Index and received a best in category award in the same ranking in 2013. Among the aspects that it has been commended on are its energy use and greenhouse gas emissions as well as its CEO compensation as a percentage of employee pay – an issue that has become very significant in global business in the past two decades.

For example in 2010, the Indian telecommunications company Aircel partnered with the World Wildlife Fund (India) to launch a 'Save the Tigers' initiative, in response to the dwindling number of tigers, India's national animal. The centrepiece of the campaign was a powerful television advertising campaign, featuring Stripey, eagerly waiting for its mother to return while gunshots interrupt the scene. One of the strongest commitments to cause-related marketing has been given by Canadian company MAC cosmetics, which is now part of the Estée Lauder group. It gave away all of the sales revenues for its Viva Glam lipstick range to the MAC AIDS Fund, which in turn distributed it to HIV groups. To date, it has given away over $100 million.[22]

Marketing ethics

Ethics are the moral principles and values that govern the actions and decisions of an individual or group.[23] They involve values about right and wrong conduct. There can be a distinction between the legality and ethicality of marketing decisions. Ethics concern personal moral principles and values, while laws reflect society's principles, and standards that are enforceable in the courts.

Not all unethical practices are illegal. For example, it is not illegal to include genetically modified (GM) ingredients in products sold in supermarkets; however, some organizations (such as Greenpeace) believe it is unethical to sell GM products when their effect on health has not been scientifically proven. However, regulators so far appear to favour the stance taken by businesses. For example in 2013, the Obama administration in the USA signed legislation preventing biotech companies from litigation in regard to the making, selling and distribution of genetically modified seeds and plants despite environmental concerns. Similarly, mobile phone manufacturers are ensuring that handsets conform to international guidelines on the specific absorption rate of radiation emissions and the industry has contributed millions of dollars to research on the issue.[24]

Many ethical dilemmas derive from a conflict between profits and business actions. For example, by using child labour the cost of producing items is kept low and profit margins are raised. In 2006, secret footage aired on a news bulletin on the UK's Channel 4 showed clearly underage workers making Tesco own-label clothing in a factory in Bangladesh. Tesco, it emerged, was unaware that the factory produced clothes for it – it is a member of the Ethical Trading Initiative, which is a UK-based group that requires independent monitoring of the global supply chain. In 2013, an eight-storey building housing another clothing firm in Dhaka, Bangladesh, collapsed resulting in over 1,000 deaths. Significant concerns were raised about the safety and working conditions in these factories that produce cheap products for sale by firms such as Walmart, Benetton and JC Penney. Because of the importance of marketing ethics, each of the chapters in this book includes a key ethical debate discussing the positions taken by supporters and critics of marketing on a variety of core themes. The debate on corporate social responsibility (CSR) is summarized in Marketing and Society 2.1.

The consumer movement

The 'consumer movement' is the name given to the set of individuals, groups and organizations whose aim is to safeguard consumer rights. For example, various Consumers' Associations in Europe campaign on behalf of consumers and provide information about products, often on a comparative basis, allowing consumers to make more informed choices between products and services.

As well as offering details of unbiased product testing and campaigning against unfair business practices, consumer movements have been active in areas such as product quality and safety, and information accuracy. Notable successes have been improvements in car safety, the stipulation that advertisements for credit facilities must display the true interest charges (annual percentage rates), and the inclusion of health warnings on cigarette packets and advertisements.

Such consumer organizations can have a significant influence on marketing practices. For example, the Belgian consumer group Test-Achats brought a case to the European Court of Justice on the equal treatment of males and females in the provision of goods and services. The court ruled in its favour meaning that insurance companies who have traditionally offered cheaper car insurance to female drivers will no longer be able to do so from December 2012 with the result that the price of premiums for young female drivers is likely to rise.[25] In the UK, the Office of Fair Trading is seeking to enable consumers to more easily take legal action against companies that have harmed them through anti-competitive practices.

The consumer movement should not be considered a threat to business, but marketers should view its concerns as offering an opportunity to create new products and services to satisfy the needs of these emerging market segments. For example, growing concern over rising obesity levels in the developed world has led McDonald's to make significant changes to its menu items and marketing approach. It introduced a number of healthy options to its menus, including salads and fruit bags, which helped the company to return to profitability after some years of poor performance. Its *Global Best of Green* social report highlights advances made in energy efficiency, sustainable packaging and anti-littering that it hopes will boost its image. European firms that have made it to the list of the world's most ethical companies are included in Table 2.2.

Technological forces

People's lives and companies' fortunes can both be affected significantly by technology. Technological advances have given us body scanners, robotics, camcorders, computers and many other products that have contributed to our quality of life. Many technological breakthroughs have changed the rules of the competitive game. For example, the launch of the computer has decimated the market for typewriters and has made calculators virtually obsolete. Companies, like Skype, that have pioneered telephone calls over the Internet have revolutionized the telecoms business and reduced revenues for international calling to virtually zero. Mobile phone services are being used by pharmaceutical companies to tackle the damaging trade in counterfeit drugs in developing countries like Ghana and Nigeria.

Marketing and Society 2.1 CSR or PR?

For many years now, debate has raged regarding how socially responsible companies should be. Businesses do not operate in isolation, but are intrinsically linked to the economic, social, physical and political environments in which they operate. To many, their record in being sensitive to the needs of these environments is not one to be proud of. The abuse of human resources in the form of poorly paid workers, working in dangerous conditions, and child labour has been highlighted. Environmental damage through pollution, deforestation and the illegal dumping of waste has rightly been criticized. There is also the exploitation of consumers through the maintenance of artificially high prices and the corruption of the political process throughout the world. The list goes on. Riots between protesters and police at major government and economic conferences highlight the extent of the divide between business and some sections of society.

As a result of societal pressure for change, corporate social responsibility (CSR) has become part of the language of the corporate boardroom. All major corporations have CSR initiatives and many publicize these in their annual reports and/or social reports. As far back as 1953, Shell Oil Company set up the Shell Oil Foundation, which, since its formation, has contributed in the region of $500 million to the development of the communities where Shell employees live and work. In 2014, the food giant Kellogg's caved in to public pressure and announced that it would only buy palm oil from suppliers who can prove that they actively protect rainforests and peat lands, and respect human rights. Some 30,000 square miles of rainforest has been destroyed in the past 20 years to supply the global food industry with a cheap source of palm oil to make packaged foods, ice cream and snacks, endangering indigenous peoples and local habitats. Triple bottom-line accounting has grown, whereby firms demonstrate not only their economic performance but also their social and environmental performance.

At the same time, however, there are commentators who trenchantly argue that these kinds of investments are completely wrong. This stance has been most famously taken by the US economist Milton Friedman. In his view, the mission of a business is to maximize the return to its owners and shareholders; he advocated that anything that detracts from that mission should be avoided, and that society's concerns are the responsibility of government. Similarly, Robert Reich, who served as US Labor Secretary under Bill Clinton, has argued that companies cannot be socially responsible and that activists are neglecting the important task of getting governments to solve problems. Added to this is the growing line of research which shows that CSR does not work – in other words, that CSR has a negative effect on corporate performance.

So it remains very much a matter of debate as to whether the current trend in CSR activity reflects a greater concern from businesses about their impact on the environment or whether this is simply a rather large public relations exercise. Many critics would suggest the latter as companies respond to increasing scrutiny from non-governmental organizations and the public at large. The term 'greenwashing' has been coined to describe organizations that have an environmental programme while at the same time their core business is inherently polluting or unsustainable. A CSR initiative may create a feel-good factor within a business and may satisfy commentators and shareholders, but the ultimate test is whether businesses will consistently put principle before profit. This dilemma has been illustrated by the trials of brands like The Body Shop, Ben & Jerry's and innocent Ltd that have faced the challenge of staying true to their ethical values as they have grown in scale. Enlightened long-term self-interest would appear to be the best approach for corporations to take.

Suggested reading: Bakan (2004)[26]; James (2007)[27]; Sekerka and Stimel (2011)[28]

Reflection: Is it appropriate that business should put society's interests ahead of its own?

Table 2.2 The world's most ethical companies, 2013 (European firms only)

Name	Business	Country
ABB Asea Brown Boveri Ltd	Electrical equipment	Switzerland
Accenture	Business services	Ireland
Atlas Copco AB	Industrial manufacturing	Sweden
Capgemini	Business services	France
Coloplast A/S	Medical devices	Denmark
CRH plc	Construction	Ireland
EDP Energais de Portugal	Energy and utilities: Electrical	Portugal
Ethical Fruit Company	Agriculture	UK
H&M Hennes & Mauritz AB	Apparel	Sweden
Henkel AG	Consumer products	Germany
illycafe	Consumer products	Italy
L'Oréal	Health & beauty	France
Marks & Spencer	Retail	UK
Northumbrian Water Group	Energy and utilities: Water	UK
Portugal Telecom	Telecommunications services	Portugal
Premier Farnell plc	Electronics	UK
SCA Svenka Cellulosa AB	Forestry, paper & packaging	Sweden
Schneider Electrical	Electrical equipment	France
SONAE	Retail: Food stores	Portugal
Stora Enso	Forestry, paper & packaging	Finland
Swiss Re	Insurance: Reinsurance	Switzerland
The Cooperative Group	Retail: Food stores	UK
The Rezidor Hotel Group	Leisure & hospitality	Germany
Unibail-Rodamco	Real estate	France

Source: Forbes

Consumers in these countries that buy medicines scratch off a panel on the packaging that reveals a code. They text this code to a computer system that comes back with a message that the drug is genuine and safe.[29] Monitoring the technological environment may result in the spotting of opportunities and major investments in new technological areas. For example, Google has invested heavily in the development and testing of Google Glass, a miniature computer that is worn like a pair of spectacles. It has a wide variety of potential applications including taking photographs, sending messages and searching for things online. New technologies like this are also a source of concern for many people. Google Glass raises privacy issues such as people being photographed without their permission or whether Glass will have the facility to enable users to do a quick Internet search on people they have just met.[30]

New potential applications for technology are emerging all the time. For example, money – which has been the foundation for the market economy for generations – is becoming increasingly redundant. In Japan there has been a huge growth in the use of e-cash facilities where consumers buy smart cards which are topped up on a monthly basis and can be used for everything from transport systems to shops and cafés. Other consumers pay using their mobile phones with the result that leading firms like 7 Eleven and McDonald's have installed e-money readers.[31] Marketers are constantly on the lookout for new ways in which to utilize technology. For example, in 2013 Tesco installed high-tech screens in their petrol stations that scanned customer's faces as they waited at checkouts to determine their age and sex. This information is then used to tailor the types of adverts that are broadcast while customers are in the store.[32]

The speed with which technology can become part of our lives is illustrated by the rapid penetration of application software or apps. An app is a computer

Table 2.3 Software applications and their uses

Context	Applications
Travel	Hailo (taxi services), Airbnb (accommodation), Google Maps (maps)
Social media	Facebook (social networks), Snapchat (picture messaging), Tumblr (blogging), Pinterest (photographs)
Games	*Planets Versus Zombies, Temple Run, World of Warcraft Armory, Scrabble*
Communication	WhatsApp (messaging), Viber (calls and messages), Skype (calls)
Entertainment	Netflix (TV/movies), YouTube, BBC iPlayer (TV), TED (talks, speeches)
Sport	LiveScore (scores), Sky Sports (information, video), BetFair (betting)
Music	Spotify (music streaming), Shazam (finding music), Soundcloud (store recordings), Ticketmaster (buying tickets)
Holidays	TripAdvisor (reviews), XE Currency (currency exchange rates), Google Translate (translation), Trivago (price comparison)
Education	Khan Academy (maths and science), iTunes U (university courses), My Class Schedule (timetabling)
Work	Evernote (note taking), Box (file storage), Google Search (search)

Source: *Irish Independent,* October 2013.

program that allows a user to perform a single or several related tasks (see Table 2.3). The frustrating task of finding a cab has been revolutionized by apps such as Hailo, Uber and SnappCab. The application allows users to hail and pay for the cab using an app. Drivers accept the journey on their phones and passengers can see the driver's name and photo so they know who to accept. The key to successful technological investment is, however, market potential, not technological sophistication for its own sake (see Exhibit 2.4 and Social Media Marketing 2.1). The classic example of a high-technology initiative driven by technologists rather than pulled by the market is Concorde. Although technologically sophisticated, management knew before its launch that it never had any chance of being commercially

Exhibit 2.4 The popular Honda viral advert 'Hands' shows the possibilities that arise when technology and an inventive spirit are combined and featured a wide range of past, present and future Honda models including scooters and bikes

Social Media Marketing 2.1 Airbnb

> **Critical Thinking:** Below is a review of the rise of the sharing economy as illustrated by firms like Airbnb. Read it and critically reflect the ways in which changes in technology impact upon society.

Airbnb is a classic example of a sharing economy pioneer. Like many great start-ups, its founders stumbled on the idea when, tight for cash, they decided to rent out a room in their apartment to delegates attending a design conference in San Francisco. Incorporated in 2008 and still privately held, Airbnb offers members an opportunity to rent all forms of accommodation to those travellers looking for a place to stay. Very popular in major cities where accommodation can be scarce, the site has grown rapidly with offices around the world. By 2014, it had found accommodation for 11 million guests in 34,000 cities. As it takes fees of about 3 per cent from hosts and 6–12 per cent from guests, it has a significant revenue stream. In the spirit of the social media age, the community regulates itself as profiles of potential users can be checked in advance and all users can post reviews of their experiences. One of the unique aspects of this venture is that it shows how we as humans have tended to trust brands more than people in that we will be comfortable staying in a strange hotel but not (up to now, at any rate) comfortable letting a stranger into our home!

Another key insight relates to the issue of ownership. To date our consumer society is predicated on the idea of ownership of goods but this could be about to change. Not only can we share our houses for an income but what about our high-end household items such as cameras and musical instruments (SnapGoods), our cars (RelayRides, Lyft), our time (Task-Rabbit) and even our cash (LendingClub)? As the idea gains traction, the possibilities are endless. The threat for many established businesses such as hotels/motels and taxi services are very real. One study in Texas found that while Airbnb was not having much impact on the business or luxury hotel sector, its presence had cut revenues in the budget sector by 5 per cent in the two years to 2013. Incumbent sectors like these have been complaining loudly and have found a receptive ear among the regulators who are looking at issues like insurance and taxes. For example, Airbnb's host city of San Francisco charges a hotel tax of 14 per cent. Anyone who is privately renting accommodation via a site like Airbnb should also do the same.

The combination of technology (users can find services and pay via an app), social media (ease of sharing reviews) and changing consumer attitudes may all just be coalescing to give the sharing economy a new lease of life. Once again opportunities and threats abound!

Based on: Anonymous (2014)[33]; Geron (2013)[34]

viable. Large numbers of Internet businesses have failed for the same reason.

In summary, there are a wide variety of forces in the macoenvironment that impact upon business. Their common characteristics are that they are outside the control of the organization and can represent either an opportunity or a threat to its future. Analysing all of these potential variables and being able to anticipate the kind of impact that they can have is a particularly demanding task which we shall examine in more detail in the section on environmental scanning below.

The microenvironment

In addition to the broad macroeconomic forces discussed above, a number of microeconomic variables also impact on the opportunities and threats facing the organization. While these are also generally outside the control of the organization, managerial decisions and activities can exert some influence on them. We shall introduce each of these in turn, and deal with them in greater detail throughout the book.

Customers

As we saw in Chapter 1, customers are at the centre of the marketing effort and we shall examine customer behaviour in great detail in the next chapter. Ultimately customers determine the success or failure of the business. The challenge for the company is to identify unserved market needs and to get and retain a customer base. This requires sensitivity to changing needs in the marketplace and also having the adaptability to take advantage of the opportunities that present themselves.

Distributors

Some companies, such as mail-order houses, online music companies and service providers, distribute directly to their customers. Most others use the services of independent wholesalers and retailers. As we shall see in Chapter 9, these middlemen provide many valuable services, such as making products available to customers where and when they want them, breaking bulk and providing specialist services such as merchandising and installation. Developments in distribution can have a significant impact on the performance of manufacturers. For example, the growing power of grocery retailers such as Walmart and Tesco has affected the profitability of consumer foods manufacturers.

Suppliers

Not only are the fortunes of companies influenced by their distributors, they can also be influenced by their suppliers. Supply chains can be very simple or very complex. For example, the average car contains about 15,000 components. As a result the car industry is served by three tiers of suppliers. Tier-one companies make complete systems such as electrical systems or braking systems. They are served by tier-two suppliers, who might produce cables, for example, and are in turn supplied by tier-three suppliers who produce basic commodities such as plastic shields or metals. Just like distributors, powerful suppliers can extract profitability from an industry by restricting the supply of essential components and forcing the price up.

Competitors

Levels of competition vary from industry to industry. In some instances, there may be just one or two major players as is often the case in formerly state-run industries like energy or telecommunications. In others, where entry is easy or high profit potential exists, competition can be intense. For example, when messaging apps were developed to replace traditional SMS messaging, a wide range of brands quickly entered the space and tried to achieve market dominance including WhatsApp, GroupMe, Line, WeChat, MessageMe, Kik, Tango and many others. To be successful in the marketplace, companies must not only be able to meet customer needs but must also be able to gain a differential advantage over competitors. As we saw in the previous chapter, this can be done by gaining a leadership position in the delivery of some form of customer value.

A very popular tool for analysing the microenvironment is Porter's 'five forces' model. Porter was interested in why some industries appeared to be inherently more profitable than others, and concluded that industry attractiveness was a function of five forces: the threat of entry of new competitors; the threat of substitutes; the bargaining power of suppliers; the bargaining power of buyers; and the rivalry between existing competitors. Each of these five forces, in turn, comprises a number of elements that combine to determine the strength of each force, as shown in Figure 2.4. So, for example, industries that have high barriers to entry but relatively low levels of buyer/supplier power, low threat of substitutes and relatively benign competition will be more attractive than industries with the opposite set of forces. For example, high barriers to entry and high levels of competitive rivalry between major players such as Amazon, Sony and Apple may already have made the e-reader business unattractive for some potential entrants. We shall now look briefly at each of the forces in turn.

The threat of new entrants

Because new entrants can raise the level of competition in an industry, they have the potential to reduce its attractiveness. The threat of new entrants depends on the barriers to entry. High entry barriers exist in some industries (e.g. pharmaceuticals), whereas other industries are much easier to enter (e.g. restaurants).

Key entry barriers include:

- economies of scale
- capital requirements
- switching costs
- access to distribution
- expected retaliation.

The bargaining power of suppliers

The cost of raw materials and components can have a major bearing on a firm's profitability. The higher the bargaining power of suppliers, the higher these

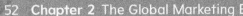

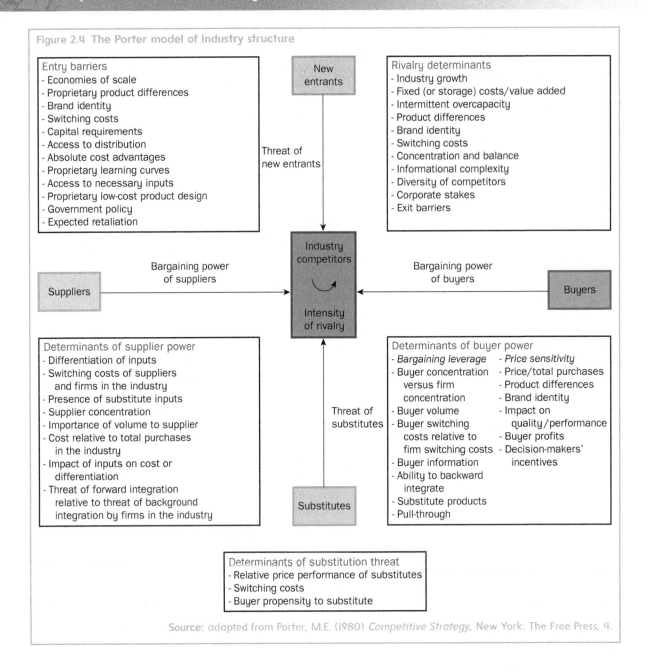

Figure 2.4 The Porter model of industry structure

Source: adapted from Porter, M.E. (1980) *Competitive Strategy*, New York: The Free Press, 4.

costs. The bargaining power of suppliers will be high when:

- there are many buyers and few dominant suppliers
- they offer differentiated, highly valued products
- suppliers threaten to integrate forward into the industry
- buyers do not threaten to integrate backward into supply
- the industry is not a key customer group to the suppliers.

A firm can reduce the bargaining power of suppliers by seeking new sources of supply,

threatening to integrate backward into supply and designing standardized components so that many suppliers are able to produce them.

The bargaining power of buyers

As we shall see in Chapter 9, the concentration of European retailing has raised buyers' bargaining power relative to that of manufacturers. The bargaining power of buyers is greater when:

- there are few dominant buyers and many sellers
- products are standardized

- buyers threaten to integrate backward into the industry
- suppliers do not threaten to integrate forward into the buyer's industry
- the industry is not a key supplying group for buyers.

The threat of substitutes

The presence of substitute products can lower industry attractiveness and profitability because they put a constraint on price levels. For example, tea and coffee are fairly close substitutes in most European countries. Raising the price of coffee, therefore, would make tea more attractive. The threat of substitute products depends on:

- buyers' willingness to substitute
- the relative price and performance of substitutes
- the costs of switching to substitutes.

The threat of substitute products can be lowered by building up switching costs, which may be psychological – for example, by creating strong distinctive brand personalities and maintaining a price differential commensurate with perceived customer values.

Industry competitors

The intensity of rivalry between competitors in an industry depends on the following factors.

1 *Structure of competition*: there is more intense rivalry when there are a large number of small competitors or a few equally balanced competitors; there is less rivalry when a clear leader (at least 50 per cent larger than the second) exists with a large cost advantage.
2 *Structure of costs*: high fixed costs encourage price cutting to fill capacity.
3 *Degree of differentiation*: commodity products encourage rivalry, while highly differentiated products that are hard to copy are associated with less intense rivalry.
4 *Switching costs*: when switching costs are high because a product is specialized, the customer has invested a lot of resources in learning how to use a product or has made tailor-made investments that are worthless with other products and suppliers, rivalry is reduced.
5 *Strategic objectives*: when competitors are pursuing build strategies, competition is likely to be more intense than when playing hold or harvest strategies.

6 *Exit barriers*: when barriers to leaving an industry are high due to such factors as lack of opportunities elsewhere, high vertical integration, emotional barriers or the high cost of closing down a plant, rivalry will be more intense than when exit barriers are low.

Environmental scanning

The practice of monitoring and analysing a company's marketing environment is known as **environmental scanning**. Two key decisions that management need to make are what to scan and how to organize the activity. Clearly, in theory, every event in the world has the potential to affect a company's operations, but a scanning system that could cover every conceivable force would be unmanageable. The first task, then, is to define a feasible range of forces that require monitoring. These are the 'potentially relevant environmental forces' that have the most likelihood of affecting future business prospects – such as, for example, changes in the value of the yen for companies doing business in Japan. One popular technique for managing this complex task is the development of scenarios, that is, the creation of fictitious future situations that combine a number of possible variables. The advantage of scenario planning is that it enables managers to consider and discuss how they would handle likely future changes in the business environment.[35] The second prerequisite for an effective scanning system is to design a system that provides a fast response to events that are only partially predictable, emerge as surprises and grow very rapidly. This has become essential due to the increasing turbulence of the marketing environment.

In general, environmental scanning is conducted by members of the senior management team, though some large corporations will have a separate unit dedicated to the task. The most appropriate organizational arrangement for scanning will depend on the unique circumstances facing a firm. A judgement needs to be made regarding the costs and benefits of each alternative. The size and profitability of the company and the perceived degree of environmental turbulence will be factors that impinge on this decision. Environmental scanning provides the essential informational input to create strategic fit between strategy, organization and the environment (see Figure 2.5). Marketing strategy should reflect the environment even if this requires a fundamental reorganization of operations.

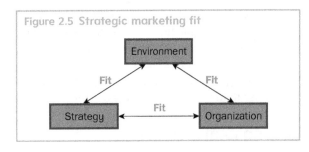

Figure 2.5 Strategic marketing fit

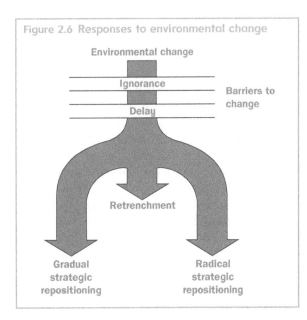

Figure 2.6 Responses to environmental change

Companies respond in various ways to environmental change (see Figure 2.6).

Ignorance

If environmental scanning is poor, companies may not realize that salient forces are affecting their future prospects. They therefore continue as normal, ignorant of the environmental issues that are threatening their existence, or the opportunities that could be seized. No change is made.

Delay

The next response, once the force is understood, is to delay action. This can be the result of bureaucratic decision processes that stifle swift action. The slow response by Kodak to the threat posed by the popularity of digital cameras and smartphones, for example, was thought, in part, to be caused by the bureaucratic nature of their decision making. 'Marketing myopia' can slow response through management being product focused rather than customer focused. A third source of delay is 'technological myopia'; this occurs where a company fails to respond to technological change. The fourth reason for delay is 'psychological recoil' by managers who see change as a threat and thus defend the status quo. These are four powerful contributors to inertia.

Retrenchment

This sort of response deals with efficiency problems but disregards effectiveness issues. As sales and profits decline, the management cuts costs; this leads to a period of higher profits but does nothing to stem declining sales. Costs (and capacity) are reduced once more, but the fundamental strategic problems remain. Retrenchment policies only delay the inevitable.

Gradual strategic repositioning

This approach involves a gradual, planned and continuous adaptation to the changing marketing environment. Faced with a customer base that was increasingly critical of its poor customer service, resulting in falling profits, the low-cost airline Ryanair hired a chief marketing officer (CMO), redesigned its website to make it more user-friendly and introduced a host of other changes to try to improve its reputation in the marketplace.

Radical strategic repositioning

If its procrastination results in a crisis, a company could have to consider a radical shift in its strategic positioning – the direction of the entire business is fundamentally changed. For example, Dell Computer Corporation, a former leader in personal computer manufacturing, had suffered several years of decline as customers switched to the attractive products offered by rivals like Apple and Samsung. In 2013, it was taken private by a consortium of investors as part of a strategy to try to rebuild the business by moving away from PC manufacturing and focusing instead on the provision of business services to the corporate sector. Radical strategic repositioning is much riskier than gradual repositioning because, if unsuccessful, the company is likely to fold.

Summary

This chapter has introduced the concept of the marketing environment. In particular, the following issues were addressed.

1. That the marketing environment comprises a microenvironment and a macroenvironment. What happens in these environments is largely uncontrollable by firms but can have a significant impact on organizational performance.

2. There are six key components of the macroenvironment: economic forces, social forces, legal and political forces, technological forces and ecological forces. Changes on each of these dimensions can present either opportunities or threats to the firm.

3. Economic forces comprise economic growth and unemployment, interest rates and exchange rates, as well as taxation and inflation. They largely impact upon how well-off consumers feel, and their resulting propensity to buy goods and services.

4. Social forces are made up of demographic changes and cultural differences. Sensitivity to cultural differences between countries is a particularly crucial issue in international marketing.

5. 'Political and legal forces' describes the regulatory environment in which organizations operate. Regulation may be enacted at a national or European level, and is mainly designed to protect the interests of consumers and to ensure a fair competitive playing field for organizations.

6. Changes in the ecological environment have been the focus of a great deal of attention in recent years. This encompasses concerns regarding climate change, pollution, scarce resource conservation, recycling and non-wasteful packaging, environmentally friendly ingredients and animal testing. Sustainability is a central challenge facing businesses and the relationship between marketing and society is a central theme of this book.

7. The term technology is used widely to describe information technology but also developments in nanotechnology, automation and so on. Technology is the engine as well as one of the outputs of modern business and needs to be carefully monitored as changes in this area can make businesses obsolete very quickly.

8. There are four key components of the microenvironment: suppliers, distributors, customers and competitors. They combine and interact to influence both the profitability of industries and the performance of individual organizations.

9. That environmental scanning is the process of examining the company's marketing environment. Firms exhibit a number of different responses to environmental change, including no change through ignorance, delay and retrenchment, through to gradual or radical repositioning.

Study questions

1. Visit www.trendwatching.com. Read its latest trend briefing and consider the impact of this trend for a brand of your choice.

2. Corporate social responsibility (CSR) activities are largely an exercise in public relations by major corporations. Discuss.

3. Discuss the alternative ways in which companies might respond to changes in the macroenvironment.

4. In 2013, Shell's scenario planning department presented two visions of the future labelled 'mountains' and 'oceans'. See http://www.shell.com/global/future-energy/scenarios/new-lens-scenarios.html. Select one scenario and outline its implications for energy companies.

5. Visit www.business-ethics.com/. Select any two of its 'popular stories' and discuss their implications for both business and society.

Suggested reading

Bakan, J. (2004) *The Corporation*, London: Constable & Robinson.

Jackson, R. W. and **C. M. Wood** (2014) The Marketing Environment: A New Paradigm, *Academy of Marketing Studies Journal*, **17** (1), 35–50.

James, O. (2007) *Affluenza*, London: Vermilion.

Roxburgh, C. (2009) The Use and Abuse of Scenarios, *McKinsey Quarterly*, November, 1–10.

Royte, E. (2008) *Bottlemania: How Water Went on Sale and Why We Buy It*, London: Bloomsbury Publishing Inc.

Sekerta, L. and **D. Stimel** (2011) How Durable is Sustainable Enterprise? Ecological Sustainability Meets the Reality of Tough Economic Times, *Business Horizons*, **54**, 115–24.

Webster, F. E. and **R. F. Lusch** (2012) Elevating Marketing. Marketing is Dead! Long Live Marketing!, *Journal of the Academy of Marketing Science*, **41**, 389–99.

When you have read this chapter

log on to the Online Learning Centre for *Foundations of Marketing* at
www.mheducation.co.uk/textbooks/fahy5
where you'll find links and extra online study tools for marketing.

References

1. **Brady, S.** (2012) Pepsi Refresh Project Expands in Canada with $1 million in Grants, *Brandchannel.com*, 2 January; **Ritson, M.** (2011) When it Comes to Social Media Coke is it! *Marketingweek.co.uk*, 7 April.

2. **Bradshaw, T.** (2010) Government Advertising Cuts Concern Agencies, *Financial Times*, 18 October, 5.

3. **Anonymous** (2014) China Loses Its Allure, *Economist*, 25 January, 7.

4. **Green, M.** (2008) Nigerians Heed the Call of Marketing, *Financial Times*, 8 April, 10.

5. **Matthews, R.** (2005) US Grapples with 'Language of Love', *Financial Times*, 13 January, 9.

6. **Edgecliffe-Johnson, A.** (2007) MTV Tunes into a Local Audience, *Financial Times*, 16 October, 16.

7. **Anonymous** (2014) Planet Plutocrat, *Economist*, 15 March, 53–54.

8. **Faccio, M., R. Masulis** and **J. McConnell** (2006) Political Connections and Corporate Bailouts, *Journal of Finance*, 61 (6).

9. **Anonymous** (2014) In Deep Water, *Economist*, 22 February, 47–49.

10. **Minder, R.** (2006) The Lobbyists Have Taken Brussels By Storm, *Financial Times*, 19 January, 11.

11. **Ahmed, K.** (2011) Google under Investigation for Alleged Breach of EU Competition Rules, *Telegraph.co.uk*, 11 June.

12. **Bevins, V.** (2010) Advertising Goes Underground, *Financial Times*, 7 September, 14.

13. **Klein, N.** (2000) *No Logo*, London: HarperCollins.

14. **Coonan, C.** (2008) Great Pall of China, *Innovation*, January, 36–7

15. **Harvey, F.** and **L. Simpson** (2010) Outlook Sunny for Solar Panels as Homeowners Go Green, *Financial Times*, 25 August, 8.

16. **Ward, A.** (2006) Global Thirst for Bottled Water Attacked, *Financial Times*, 13 February, 9.

17. **Anonymous** (2014) Rueing the Waves, *Economist*, 4 January, 23–24.

18. **Harvey, F.** (2004) PC Makers Set to Face Costs of Recycling, *Financial Times*, 4 February, 13

19. For a discussion of some green marketing issues, see **Pujari, D.** and **G. Wright** (1999) Integrating Environmental Issues into Product Development: Understanding the Dimensions of Perceived Driving Forces and Stakeholders, *Journal of Euromarketing*, 7 (4), 43–63; **Peattie, K.** and **A. Ringter** (1994) Management and the Environment in the UK and Germany: A Comparison, *European Management Journal*, 12 (2), 216–25.

20. **Carter, M.** (2005) Ethical Business Practices Come into Fashion, *Financial Times*, 19 April, 14.

21. **Elkington, J.** (2001) The *Chrysalis Economy*, Capstone.

22. **Hunt, B.** (2005) Companies with Their Reputations on the Line, *Financial Times*, 24 January, 10.

23. **Berkowitz, E.N., R.A. Kerin, S.W. Hartley** and **W. Rudelius** (2000) *Marketing*, Boston, MA: McGraw-Hill.

24. **Jack, A.** (2008) An Unusual Model for Good Causes, *Financial Times*, 5 June, 16.

25. **Anonymous** (2011) A Boy-Racer's Dream, *The Economist*, 5 March, 74.

26. **Bakan, J.** (2004) *The Corporation*, London: Constable.

27. **James, O.** (2007) *Affluenza*, London: Vermilion.

28. **Sekerta, L.** and **D. Stimel** (2011) How Durable is Sustainable Enterprise? Ecological sustainability meets the reality of tough economic times, *Business Horizons*, **54**, 115–24.

29. **Anonymous** (2011) Not Just Talk, *The Economist*, 29 January, 61–2.

30. **Anonymous** (2013) Every Step You Take, *The Economist*, 16 November, 13.

31. **Birchall, J.** (2005) US Supermarket Encourages Shoppers to Keep in Touch, *Financial Times*, 13 July, 22.

32. **Hawkes, S.** (2013) Shoppers' Faces to Be Scanned in Advertising Push at Tesco Petrol Stations Across the UK, *Telegraph.co.uk*, 3 November.

33. **Anonymous** (2014) Boom and Backlash, *Economist*, 55–6.

34. **Geron, T.** (2013) Airbnb and the Unstoppable Rise of the Share Economy, *Forbes.com*, 23 January.

35. **Roxburgh, C.** (2009) The Use and Abuse of Scenarios, *McKinsey Quarterly*, November, 1–10.

Hidesign: the emergence of a global fashion brand

Popular entertainment, whether Hollywood's *Sex and the City*, Bollywood's *Aisha*, or China's blockbuster *Tiny Times*, has helped to bring the catwalks of international designer brands into the homes of millions of consumers. The democratization of luxury is a global phenomenon with a plethora of implications for the bottom line of luxury companies. The global personal luxury goods industry is valued in excess of €200 billion and is forecast to grow at a compound annual growth rate of 7.9 per cent over the period 2012-16.[1] Buoyant growth in emerging markets has helped to sustain industry growth with luxurious profit margins. The luxury goods industry is dominated by the French holding group LVMH, which manages a portfolio of over 50 luxury brands, including Louis Vuitton and Fendi. Its main competitor is the French multinational Kering (formerly PPR), which owns brands such as Gucci and Bottega Veneta, and is followed by the Swiss company Richemont (Dunhill, Chloé), and the Italian Prada Group (Prada, Miu Miu). There are still a small number of independent luxury companies such as Chanel, Hermès and Burberry that have recently been speculated to be potential acquisition targets.

Fashion's fickle future

The luxury fashion competitive landscape is continually evolving and is at times unpredictable. Brands that were once 'must haves' can quickly become outmoded. Mulberry, for example, experienced a dramatic decline in sales and profits in 2013, which was reflected in the rapid fall of its stock market value. Remarkably, an increasing number of so-called affordable luxury brands, such as US designer brands Ralph Lauren and Michael Koors, have started to steal the limelight as their lifestyle designs connect with the contemporary aspirations of a global 'fashionista' audience. Likewise, fashion brands originating from emerging markets such as Brazil (e.g. Osklen) and China (e.g. Shanghai Tang) are extending their reach beyond their domestic markets to appeal to new consumers in new geographical markets. This is also the case for the Indian leather goods brand Hidesign. The manufacturer of handbags, clutches, briefcases and leather accessories for both men and women has not only over 70 exclusive retail stores in India, but a distribution network in 23 countries including John Lewis, Selfridges and House of Fraser in the UK. Does an Indian luxury brand have the mettle and sparkle to compete against the stature and glamour of the world's Guccis and Pradas?

From humble beginnings...

The story of Hidesign started less as a corporate business venture and more as a hobby. Dilip Kapur grew up in an ashram in Auroville, Pondicherry (a former French colony on India's south-eastern coast) and moved to the USA to pursue his education. After his studies that included a PhD in international relations, Dilip moved back to Pondicherry and helped out at the Aurobindo Ashram. It was during his free time that he started to make leather bags inspired by his nine-month experience working for a Denver-based leather house. The natural, rugged-looking bags that used a vegetable tanning process were soon being sought after by western visitors who were staying in Pondicherry. It was just a matter of time before Dilip could no longer cope with the number of orders he was receiving, which included several large orders from overseas. In 1978, a two-person artisan workshop was created, and Hidesign (derived from two words 'hide' and 'design') was born.

...and with Indian irony

Hidesign is one of the few fashion brands whose market success originated outside of its domestic market. Hidesign started to export its bags for sale in independent stores in Australia and the USA. It soon found new distribution outlets in the UK and Continental Europe, but its major breakthrough was in 1985 when John Lewis was the first UK department store to carry Hidesign's complete line of products. Word-of-mouth had soon elevated Hidesign as a leather goods brand for consumers who appreciate classic and natural looking designs made with traditional craftsmanship techniques. In 1992, Hidesign's Boxy Bag won the 'Accessory of the Year' award from the UK magazine, *Accessory Magazine*. However, many customers were not always aware of Hidesign's country of origin, as acknowledged by Dilip Kapur in an interview with the *Financial Times*: 'People thought of us more as a UK company than an Indian company.'[2] It was only in 1999 that Hidesign started selling in India, and in 2000 domestic sales accounted for only 6 per cent of total revenues.[3]

A home run

The market liberalization reforms in India that had started in 1991 soon created a dynamic consumer market driven by the aspirations of the growing middle classes. These were consumers who were overwhelmingly young, ambitious and optimistic, with a desire to live the Indian dream. International fashion and luxury brands started to enter the Indian market and were expanding their footprint in the increasing number of swanky shopping malls that were opening in Mumbai, Delhi and Bengaluru (Bangalore). The launch of glossy magazines such as *Vogue, Elle* and *GQ*, and India's obsession with Bollywood trends and styles were further influences of how fashion was starting to enter the mainstream. The rise of India as a fashion market destination was a catalyst for Hidesign's success in India. Its success did not go unnoticed, and LVMH acquired a minority stake in the company in 2007. India now contributes approximately 70 per cent of Hidesign's global sales and there seems to be no slowing down in Hidesign's plans to expand.[4] It has extended its retail network to include outlets at Mumbai, Delhi, Bengaluru and Hyderabad airports, and is set to open 200–300 stores in India within five years.[5] It has also set up its own e-commerce portal, with free shipping and cash payment on delivery, which is able to reach out to customers in smaller cities and towns where retail infrastructure is still very much underdeveloped.

Luxurious, but not snobbish

There is little doubt that there has always been a close association between image and fashion. Fashion brands invest millions in building a brand image that often uses celebrities to create positive associations. Lady Gaga was for example the face of Versace's Spring 2014 campaign. What sets Hidesign apart, however, is less about image and more about the product. Although Hidesign invests in print advertising campaigns in its home market, it is not perceived as a glamour brand for Bollywood stars. What Hidesign is able to offer is a higher level of quality than other brands in the category, while remaining not so expensive as to be out of reach, whether in India or abroad. For example, a Hidesign Charles Leather Briefcase can be bought online via John Lewis for £209. In other words, this is luxury for the masses, or affordable luxury. However, Hidesign has increasingly recognized that image cannot be completely ignored. For example, Hidesign was part of *Vogue India's* Fashion's Night Out 2013, and its 2012–13 Lady Godiva advertising campaign featured top models such as Kanishtha Dhankhar (ex-Miss India 2011 and Miss World 2011 contestant).

A quality green brand, by design

Hidesign's emphasis on traditional handcraftsmanship skills and techniques has helped to shape a distinctive brand identity as underlined by a long-standing slogan: 'Real Leather Crafted the Forgotten Way'. Hidesign products are all individually handcrafted and follow a natural and eco-friendly process. While the overwhelming majority of fashion and luxury brands use chemically treated chrome leathers, Hidesign's use of eco-friendly leathers that are considerably more expensive and take longer to produce means that Hidesign products represent a distinctive look and feel that is typical of natural grained leather. Even the solid brass buckles are individually sand cast and hand polished, reflecting traditional saddlery manufacture. The emphasis on quality is also demonstrated in attention to detail. Workers at the Hidesign factory in Pondicherry take an average of 13 hours to make a bag, which a Chinese worker could produce in three.[6] Incentives to increase quality also include rewards for efficiency in using leather which is in stark contrast to many other manufacturing operations.

However, within a wider context, Hidesign's ethical corporate philosophy could potentially give the brand a sustainable competitive advantage. Following a series of serious health and safety violations such as the collapse of a Bangladesh factory in 2013 that led to over a thousand casualties, the international fashion industry has come under increasing scrutiny to improve working conditions. Hidesign, on the other hand, has led by example when it established its customer-designed factory in Pondicherry back in 1990. Its design by an eco-architect ensured that the factory located in a plush green area did not only provide a safe and healthy working environment (e.g.

zero asbestos tolerance, red brick workshops), but importantly respected the natural environment. For example, all waste water is filtered and reused, while waste material is either reused or sold for reuse.

Out of the bag and into new markets

The rapid development of the fashion market in India has in turn created new market growth opportunities. As a result, Hidesign has attempted to broaden its appeal and target more narrowly defined lifestyle segments. For instance, the sub-brand Alberto Ciaschini, Handcrafted by Hidesign was launched in 2012. The luxury collection that includes handbags, evening bags and clutches, has a stronger design element and is priced at a premium compared to other Hidesign products. The Milanese designer attempts to integrate a more modern and cutting-edge design that uses, for example, pastel colours and effects such as Swarovski crystals with the distinctive quality of Hidesign's leather material. The collection is available in selected Hidesign outlets. At the other end of the spectrum, in 2009 Hidesign entered a joint venture with Future Group, one of India's biggest retailers, to launch the lifestyle brand Holii. The brand offers a selection of more glamorous and colourful designs of women's bags and accessories priced approximately 30–40 per cent below Hidesign. It is a brand that celebrates its heritage as reflected in its slogan, 'Real leather. Born in India' and sets out to appeal to a younger and style conscious target group. There is no reference that the brand is part of Hidesign's portfolio and is available across India through 12 exclusive stores and over 50 multi-brand outlets. Moreover, Hidesign has also diversified to introduce new products for new markets. For example, in 2013 Hidesign launched a line of sunglasses that includes leather on the arms, which according to the website is handcrafted from natural acetate and leather. Other new product categories under consideration include footwear, scarves and even watches.[7]

Growth: steps to an international footprint and future paths

Hidesign continues to flourish in India and is expanding its market presence in international markets. Besides India, Hidesign products are available across the globe including for example Jamaica, the USA, Germany, South Africa, Russia, Malaysia, Oman and Australia. The next stage of international development will challenge Dilip Kapur and his management team. Can Hidesign, 'Handcrafted. Since 1978,' capture an enduring place in the future of global luxury consumption?

Useful resources

www.hidesign.com
www.holii.in

References

1. *Research and Markets: Global Personal Luxury Goods Market 2012–2016: With Louis Vuitton SA, Luxottica Group S.p.A., and Ralph Lauren Corp. Dominating,* 8 January: http://www.reuters.com/article/2014/01/08/research-and-markets-idUSnBw086107a+100+BSW20140108
2. Yee, A. (2010) From hippies to handbags, *Financial Times,* 28 December.
3. Yee, A. (2010) From hippies to handbags, *Financial Times,* 28 December.
4. *The Economist* (2012) On a hiding to something, 29 September.
5. *The Economist* (2012) On a hiding to something, 29 September.
6. *The Economist* (2012) On a hiding to something, 29 September.
7. Pawar, N.J. (2013) Hidesign plans to enter footwear category, 25 September: http://retail.economictimes.indiatimes.com/news/apparel-fashion/footwear/hidesign-plans-to-enter-footwear-category/23062451

Questions

1. Evaluate the macroenvironment of the global luxury fashion market. Is India any different? Discuss implications for Hidesign.
2. Using Porter's 'five forces' framework, discuss competitiveness within the global luxury fashion market.
3. Evaluate Hidesign's marketing mix. What are its strengths and weaknesses?
4. Discuss issues of compatibility of a corporate social responsibility (CSR) strategy with competition for a global luxury fashion brand such as Hidesign.

Case contributed by Glyn Atwal, Burgundy School of Business, France and Douglas Bryson, ESC Rennes School of Business, France.

Chapter 3

Understanding Customer Behaviour

Chapter outline

The dimensions of customer behaviour

Who buys?

How they buy

What are the choice criteria?

Influences on consumer behaviour

Influences on organizational buying behaviour

Learning outcomes

By the end of this chapter you will:

1 Understand the key dimensions of customer behaviour

2 Explain the different roles played in a buying decision

3 Compare and contrast different theories of the buying decision process

4 Understand the differences between consumer and organizational buyer behaviour

5 Analyse the main influences on consumer behaviour – personal and social influences

6 Analyse the main influences on organizational buying behaviour – the buy class, product type and purchase importance

7 Critique the role of marketing activities in consumption decisions

8 Develop a better understanding of one's own consumption choices.

Supercell

One of the most fascinating dimensions of the rise of the Internet has been the growth in popularity of virtual worlds which are essentially interactive, usually three-dimensional (3D) environments where users create objects, communicate with each other and play games. At their simplest, virtual worlds take the form of chat rooms or forums where interactions between visitors are simply text based, but with improved functionality many now allow users to represent themselves graphically using 3D multisensory avatars visible to others. As such, these virtual worlds can depict a real world with all of its rules, actions and communications or fantasy worlds limited only by the imagination. Second Life, founded in 1999, was one of the earliest entrants into this space and other leaders include *World of Warcraft* – the multiplayer online game developed by Blizzard Inc, *League of Legends* developed by Riot Games and Mojang AB's *Minecraft*. The growing penetration of smartphones has substantially increased the amount of time that people around the world play online games with a consequential increase in revenues for the leading brands.

One of the fastest-growing companies in the gaming space is the Finnish company, Supercell which follows that country's tradition of producing gaming leaders such as Rovio and Habbo. The company was founded in 2010 and operates out of an office in Helsinki that used to house some of Nokia's R&D division. It started out developing games for Facebook but shifted focus to concentrate on the rapidly growing smartphone and tablet markets. In a short space of time, its growth has been staggering. Its two main products, *Clash of Clans* and *Hay Day* are among the most popular smartphone games in the world. *Clash of Clans*, released in 2012, is a multiplayer game where players can build their community, train troops and attack other players to earn gold and elixir while building their defences to protect against attackers. Players can also use the chat feature to connect with each other and to join forces to help each other. *Hay Day* is a social farming game where players tend a farm and earn coins which can be used to buy production, building and decoration items, as well as experience points (XPs) which help players to move onto new levels. The social nature of the games and the fact that they are distributed through Apple's App Store has helped to spread their popularity.

Both games have been popular because they are simple to play and contain highly impressive graphics and features. Supercell also aims to create services rather than products. It tries to avoid creating games that players play for a short while and then forget about by supporting the games and adding features that keep players coming back. As a result, its games spend much longer periods of time at or near the top of the charts than competitors.

Supercell also employs what is known as a 'freemium' pricing model for its games – in other words, the games are free to play but spending money can enhance the playing experience. For example, players can spend money to speed up farm production on *Hay Day* or buy more troops to win battles on *Clash of Clans*. These in-app purchases have generated significant returns for the company. It reported total revenues of $892 million in 2013 while employing just 132 people. One of the other interesting features of the company is that it celebrates failure as well as success. For example, while its two most popular games were released in 2012, five others were 'retired'. To mark this process, employees come together to discuss what can be learned from the game's failure before champagne is handed out to 'celebrate' the end of the game.

The speed with which users are keen to create virtual worlds to sit alongside the real world that we live in raises all sorts of interesting questions about consumer behaviour which is the focus of this chapter.[1]

Our lives are full of choices. We choose which universities we would like to attend, what courses we would like to study, what careers we would like to pursue. On a daily basis we make choices about the food we eat, the clothes we buy, the music we listen to, and so on. The processes by which we make all these choices and how they are influenced are of great interest to marketers as well as to consumer researchers. Companies with products or services to sell want to know us, what we like and dislike, and how we go about making these consumption decisions. As we saw in Chapter 1, this kind of in-depth knowledge of customers is a prerequisite of successful marketing; indeed, understanding customers is the cornerstone upon which the marketing concept is built. How customers behave can never be taken for granted and new trends emerge all the time, such as the current popularity of social networking. There are a variety of influences on the purchasing habits of customers and our understanding of these influences is constantly improving. Successful marketing requires a great sensitivity to these subtle drivers of behaviour and an ability to anticipate how they influence demand.

In this chapter we will explore the nature of customer behaviour; we will examine the frameworks and concepts used to understand customers; and we will review the dimensions we need to consider in order to grasp the nuances of customer behaviour and the influences upon it.

The dimensions of customer behaviour

At the outset, a distinction needs to be drawn between the purchases of private consumers and those of organizations. Most consumer purchasing is individual, such as the decision to purchase a chocolate bar on seeing an array of confectionery at a newsagent's counter, though it may also be by a group such as a household. In contrast, in organizational or business-to-business (B2B) purchasing there are three major types of buyer. First, the industrial market concerns those companies that buy products and services to help them produce other goods and services such as the purchase of memory chips for mobile telephones. These industrial goods can range from raw materials to components to capital goods such as machinery. Second, the reseller market comprises organizations that buy products and services to resell. Online retailers and supermarkets are examples of resellers and we will look at these in some detail in Chapter 9. Third, the government market consists of government agencies that buy

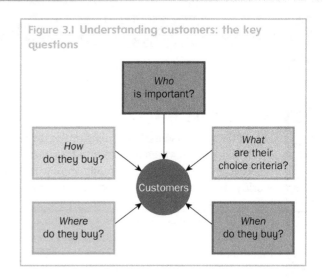

Figure 3.1 Understanding customers: the key questions

products and services to help them carry out their activities. Purchases for local authorities and defence are examples of this.

Understanding the behaviour of this array of customers requires answers to the following core questions (see Figure 3.1).

- *Who* is important in the buying decision?
- *How* do they buy?
- *What* are their choice criteria?
- *Where* do they buy?
- *When* do they buy?

The answers to these questions can be derived from personal contact with customers and, increasingly, by employing marketing research, which we will examine in Chapter 4. In this chapter we examine consumer and organizational buyer behaviour. The structure of this analysis will be based on the first three questions: who, how and what. These are often the most intractable aspects of customer behaviour; it is usually much more straightforward to answer the last two questions, about where and when customers buy.

Who buys?

Blackwell, Miniard and Engel[2] describe five roles in the buying decision-making process.

1 *Initiator*: the person who begins the process of considering a purchase. Information may be gathered by this person to help the decision.
2 *Influencer*: the person who attempts to persuade others in the group concerning the outcome of the decision. Influencers typically gather information and attempt to impose their choice criteria on the decision.

3   *Decider*: the individual with the power and/or financial authority to make the ultimate choice regarding which product to buy.

4   *Buyer*: the person who conducts the transaction. The buyer calls the supplier, visits the store, makes the payment and effects delivery.

5   *User*: the actual consumer/user of the product.

Multiple roles in the buying group may, however, be assumed by one person. In a toy purchase, for example, a girl may be the initiator and attempt to influence her parents, who are the deciders. The girl may be influenced by her sister to buy a different brand. The buyer may be one of the parents, who visits the store to purchase the toy and brings it back to the home. Finally, both children may be users of the toy. Although the purchase was for one person, in this example marketers have four opportunities – two children and two parents – to affect the outcome of the purchase decision. For example, Samsung sponsored the European Computer Gaming Championships in a bid to build its brand image among young people and the company's research has found that positive attitudes towards its brand increased by 25 per cent in the 18–29 age group since it changed its marketing focus.[3]

The roles played by the different household members vary with the type of product under consideration and the stage of the buying process (see Exhibit 3.1). For example, men now do a very significant portion of household grocery shopping, while women are increasingly visitors to DIY and hardware shops. Other interesting differences have also been observed. Women, who tend to take their time and browse in a retail environment, are more time conscious and goal directed online, while males tend to surf and browse many websites when shopping on the Internet. Also, the respective roles may change as the purchasing process progresses. In general, one or other partner will tend to dominate the early stages, then joint decision making tends to occur as the process moves towards final purchase. Joint decision making is more common when the household consists of two income earners.

Most organizational buying tends to involve more than one individual and is often in the hands of a decision-making unit (DMU), or **buying centre**, as it is sometimes called. This is not necessarily a fixed entity and may change as the **decision-making process** continues. Thus a managing director may be involved in the decision that new equipment should be purchased,

Exhibit 3.1 Brands like the AA are significant users of emotional advertising in their brand-building efforts

but not in the decision as to which manufacturer to buy it from. The marketing task is to identify and reach the key members in order to convince them of the product's worth. But this is a difficult task as the size of the decision-making groups in organizations is on the increase. It can also be difficult as the 'gatekeeper' is an additional role in organizational buying. Gatekeepers are people like secretaries who may allow or prevent access to a key DMU member. The salesperson's task is to identify a person from within the decision-making unit who is a positive advocate and champion of the supplier's product. This person (or 'coach') should be given all the information needed to win the arguments that may take place within the DMU.

The marketing implications of understanding who buys lie within the areas of marketing communications and segmentation. An identification of the roles played within the buying centre is a prerequisite for targeting persuasive communications. As we saw earlier, the person who actually uses or consumes the product may not be the most influential member of the buying centre, nor the decision-maker. Even when they do play the predominant role, communication to other members of the buying centre can make sense when their knowledge and opinions act as persuasive forces during the decision-making process. For example, recommendations from plumbers influence the majority of shower purchase decisions by consumers planning to install or replace shower units in their homes. Therefore, brands like Mira (see Exhibit 3.2) have sought to build awareness in the consumer market to reduce the influence of these 'deciders' in the purchasing decision.

How they buy

Attempting to understand how consumers buy and what influences their buying decisions have been the core questions examined in the field of consumer behaviour. It is a rich arena of study drawing on perspectives from disciplines as wide ranging as economics, psychology, sociology, cultural anthropology and others. The dominant paradigm in consumer behaviour is known as the **information processing approach** and has its roots in cognitive psychology. It sees consumption as largely a rational process – the

Exhibit 3.2 Advertising by shower manufacturers such as Mira has enabled them to build a high level of consumer recognition and hence reduce the influence of 'deciders' making choices in-store

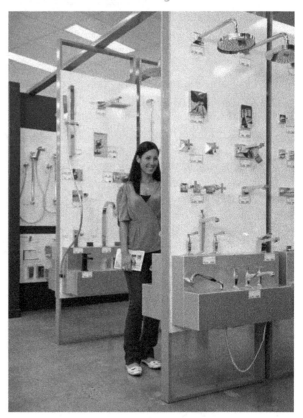

outcome of a consumer recognizing a need and then engaging in a series of activities to attempt to fulfil that need. But an alternative paradigm, known as **consumer culture theory (CCT)** (Arnould and Thompson, 2005),[4] has emerged in recent years which views consumption as a much less rational or conscious activity. In it, consumption is seen as a more sociocultural or experiential activity that is laden with emotion and helps to explain, for example, why consumers derive pleasure from shopping or search for certain meanings in the brands that they choose. The main differences between the two modes of thinking about consumer behaviour are summarized in Table 3.1. While this chapter is largely structured

Table 3.1 The information processing approach vs. consumer culture theory

Attribute	Information processing approach	Consumer culture theory
Level of analysis	Individual	Society
Focus	Cognitive processes	Context of consumption
Purpose of consumption	Utilitarian	Experiential
Process of consumption	Logical	Random
Key consumption influence	Rationality	Social

Figure 3.2 Types of consumer decisions	
Extended problem solving	Habitual problem solving
Limited problem solving	Variety seeking behaviour

around the information processing approach, the broader perspectives brought by consumer culture theory are incorporated into the discussion.

Both traditions enrich our understanding of why consumers behave as they do and we also need to take account of the different kinds of decisions that consumers engage in (see Figure 3.2). *Extended problem solving* occurs when consumers are highly involved in a purchase, perceive significant differences between brands and there is an adequate time available for deliberation.[5] It involves a high degree of information search, as well as close examination of the alternative solutions using many choice criteria.[6] It is commonly seen in the purchase of cars, consumer electronics, houses and holidays, where it is important to make the right choice. Information search and evaluation may focus not only on which brand/model to buy, but also on where to make the purchase. The potential for post-purchase dissatisfaction or **cognitive dissonance** is greatest in this buying situation.

A great deal of consumer purchases come under the mantle of *limited problem solving*. The consumer has some experience with the product in question so that information search may be mainly internal through memory. However, a certain amount of external search and evaluation may take place (e.g. checking prices) before the purchase is made. This situation provides marketers with some opportunity to affect the purchase by stimulating the need to conduct a search (e.g. advertising) and reducing the risk of brand switching (e.g. warranties).

Habitual problem solving occurs in situations of low consumer involvement and a perception of limited differences between brands. It will take place, for example, when a consumer repeat buys a product while carrying out little or no evaluation of the alternatives, such as groceries purchased on a weekly shopping trip. He or she may recall the satisfaction gained by purchasing a brand, and automatically buy it again. Advertising may be effective in keeping the brand name in the consumer's mind and reinforcing already favourable attitudes towards it.

Finally, consumers also engage in *variety seeking behaviour* in situations characterized by low product involvement but where there are significant perceived differences between brands. For example, consumers may switch from one brand of biscuit to another, simply to try something new. The use of sales promotions by firms such as extra free products and product sampling are designed to encourage variety seeking behaviour.

From the perspective of the information processing approach, the typical decision-making process for consumers and organizations is shown in Figure 3.3. This diagram shows that buyers typically move through a series of stages, from recognition that a problem exists to an examination of potential alternatives to a purchase and the subsequent evaluation of the purchase. Organizational buying is typically more complex and may involve more stages. However, as we saw above, the exact nature of the process will depend on the type of decision being made. In certain situations some stages will be omitted; for example, in a routine re-buy situation such as reordering photocopying paper, the purchasing officer is unlikely to pass through the third, fourth and fifth stages of organizational decision making (search for suppliers and analysis, and evaluation of their proposals). These stages will be bypassed as the buyer, recognizing a need, routinely reorders from an existing supplier. In general, the more complex the decision and the more expensive the item, the more likely it is that each stage will be passed through and that the process will take more time.

Need recognition/problem awareness

Need recognition may be functional and occur as a result of routine depletion (e.g. petrol, food) or unpredictably (e.g. the breakdown of a car or washing machine). In other situations, consumer purchasing may be initiated by more emotional needs or by simply imagining or day-dreaming about what an experience may be like. Marketing campaigns frequently try to tap directly into emotional needs as a way of initiating consumption and driving brand preference.

The need recognition stage has a number of implications for marketing. First, marketing managers must be aware of the needs of consumers and the problems they face. Sometimes this awareness may be due to the intuition of the marketer who, for example, spots a new trend (such as the early marketing pioneers who spotted the trend towards fast food, which has underpinned the global success of companies like McDonald's and KFC). Alternatively, marketing research could be used to assess customer problems or needs (see Chapter 4). Second, marketers should be aware of need inhibitors, that is, those factors that prevent consumers from moving from need recognition to the next stage of the buying decision process. For example, eBay recognized that

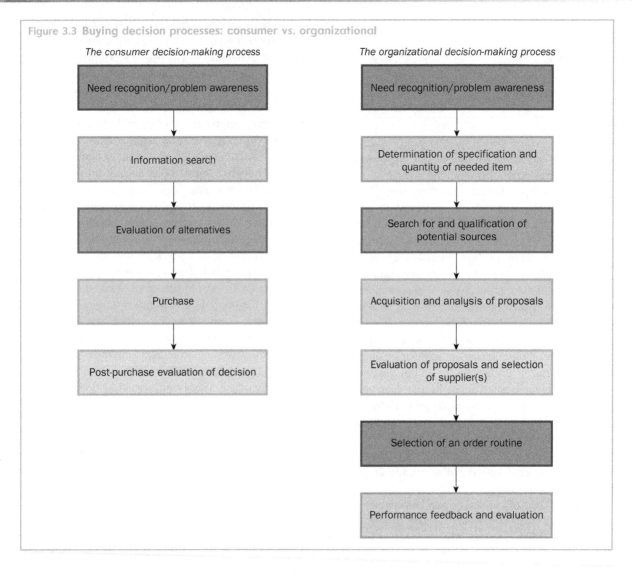

Figure 3.3 Buying decision processes: consumer vs. organizational

The consumer decision-making process

- Need recognition/problem awareness
- Information search
- Evaluation of alternatives
- Purchase
- Post-purchase evaluation of decision

The organizational decision-making process

- Need recognition/problem awareness
- Determination of specification and quantity of needed item
- Search for and qualification of potential sources
- Acquisition and analysis of proposals
- Evaluation of proposals and selection of supplier(s)
- Selection of an order routine
- Performance feedback and evaluation

overcoming the need inhibitor – lack of trust in being sent the product – is important. To overcome this inhibitor, it introduced its PayPal system, which acts as financial insurance against non-receipt of goods and has developed a feedback system that allows buyers to post information on their transactions and their experiences with particular buyers. Third, marketing managers should be aware that needs may arise because of stimulation. Their activities, such as developing advertising campaigns and training salespeople to sell product benefits, may act as cues to need arousal.

Information search

The second stage in the buyer decision-making process will begin when problem recognition is sufficiently strong. In the case of an organizational buying decision, the decision-making unit (DMU) will draw up a description of what is required and then begin a search for potential alternatives. When

marketers can influence the specification that is drawn up, it may give their company an advantage at later stages in the buying process.

In a consumer situation, the search may be internal or external. Internal search involves a review of relevant information from memory. This review would include potential solutions, methods of comparing solutions, reference to personal experiences and marketing communications. If a satisfactory solution is not found then an external search begins. This involves personal sources such as friends, family, work colleagues and neighbours, and commercial sources such as advertisements and salespeople. Third-party reports, such as *Which?* reports and product testing reports in print and online media, may provide unbiased information, and personal experiences may be sought such as asking for demonstrations, and viewing, touching or tasting the product. Information search largely takes place online and one of the significant growth businesses has been intelligent agents – that is, websites such as buy.com and trivago.com, which allow buyers to find out information about a wide range of products and compare online vendors. The increased use of social media has further assisted information search as outlined in Social Media Marketing 3.1. The objective of **information search** is to build up the **awareness set** – that is, the array of brands that may provide a solution to the problem.

Social Media Marketing 3.1 TripAdvisor Media Group

Critical Thinking: Below is a review of the role of TripAdvisor in the information search phase of the buying decision process. Read it and critically evaluate the extent to which consumer behaviour is rational (information processing approach) or social (CCT approach).

Almost invariably at some point in a purchase decision, the consumer will wish for more information about the choice that he or she faces. That frequently means an online search and a visit to a trusted website. Peer-to-peer review websites have grown dramatically in the past two decades and consumer decisions are heavily influenced by what other consumers have to say. This is often called word-of-mouth marketing, something that has long been seen as the most important influencer of consumer decisions. But in a digitally connected society, both good and bad word-of-mouth can spread very dramatically. This is why websites like TripAdvisor.com have become so popular.

As we will see in Chapter 7, the more intangible the product the more difficult it is to evaluate in advance and the higher the risk and consequences of making a poor decision. Selecting a travel destination or hotel to stay in is one of these risky decisions. Therefore TripAdvisor has become an enormously popular vehicle for assisting travellers with their decisions. The company was founded in 2000 and began life as a portal where users could post reviews of destinations and lodgings that they had stayed in. It quickly grew in popularity. It has been a heavy user of social media to grow its user base. It used Facebook to enable users to find and connect with friends who then identified hotels and restaurants in other cities that they liked. Reviews from friends generally rank higher than those from strangers and TripAdvisor also shows the number of reviews that individuals post as some consumers may rate a review posted by someone who has posted 20 others higher than one from a reviewer who has posted just one review. Prolific reviewers are given 'badges' in recognition of their work. This enabled TripAdvisor to develop an online community of people sharing insights and recommendations.

By 2014, the company operated local sites in 33 countries and had compiled over 125 million reviews of around 775,000 hotels and other accommodation, 590,000 holiday rentals, 139,000 destinations and 2 million restaurants worldwide. It has expanded into an integrated media group operating sub-brands like BookingBuddy, Cruise Critic, Jet Setter and Virtual Tourist. It generated almost $1 billion in revenues in 2013 largely on the back of pay-per-click advertising on its websites and was a publicly quoted company with a market valuation of almost $13 billion.

A key to success for companies like TripAdvisor is to ensure the accuracy and validity of the reviews posted on its website. The great benefit of user-generated content is that it is always up to date. The potential for deception though is high and the company is said to have blacklisted up to 30 hotels for suspicious reviews including one in the UK that allegedly bribed guests to leave positive reviews. However, many other enterprises have embraced TripAdvisor, using its website to engage in conversations with customers – thanking them for positive reviews or trying to resolve problems encountered by other guests.

Based on: Seave (2013)[7]

Trivago Ad Insight: Digital marketing has changed the nature of information search.

Evaluation of alternatives and the purchase

Reducing the awareness set to a smaller group of options for serious consideration is the first step in evaluation. The awareness set passes through a screening filter to produce an **evoked set**: those products or services that the buyer seriously considers before making a purchase. In a sense, the evoked set is a shortlist of options for careful evaluation. The screening process may use different choice criteria from those used when making the final choice, and the number of choice criteria used is often fewer.[8] In an organizational buying situation, each DMU member may use different choice criteria. One choice criterion used for screening may be price. For example, transportation companies whose services are below a certain price level may form the evoked set. Final choice may then depend on criteria such as reliability, reputation and flexibility. The range of choice criteria used by customers will be examined in more detail later in this chapter.

Consumers' level of involvement is a key determinant of the extent to which they evaluate a brand. Involvement is the degree of perceived relevance and personal importance accompanying the brand choice.[9] When engaging in extended problem solving, the consumer is more likely to carry out extensive evaluation. High-involvement purchases are likely to include those incurring high expenditure or personal risk, such as car or home buying. In contrast, low-involvement situations are characterized by simple evaluations about purchases. Consumers use simple choice tactics to reduce time and effort rather than maximize the consequences of the purchase.[10] For example, when purchasing baked beans or breakfast cereals, consumers are likely to make quick choices rather than agonize over the decision. Research by Laurent and Kapferer has identified four factors that affect involvement.[11]

1 *Self-image*: involvement is likely to be high when the decision potentially affects one's self-image. Thus purchase of jewellery, clothing and cosmetic surgery invokes more involvement than choosing a brand of soap or margarine.

2 *Perceived risk*: involvement is likely to be high when the perceived risk of making a mistake is high. The risk of buying the wrong house is much higher than that of buying the wrong chewing gum, because the potential negative consequences of the wrong decision are higher. Risk usually increases with the price of the purchase.

3 *Social factors*: when social acceptance is dependent upon making a correct choice, involvement is likely to be high. Executives may be concerned about how their choice of car affects their standing among their peers in the same way that peer pressure is a significant influence on the clothing and music tastes of teenagers.

4 *Hedonistic influences*: when the purchase is capable of providing a high degree of pleasure, involvement is usually high. The choice of restaurant when on holiday can be highly involving since the difference between making the right or wrong choice can severely affect the amount of pleasure associated with the experience.

The distinction between high-involvement and low-involvement situations is important because the variations in how consumers evaluate products and brands lead to contrasting marketing implications. The complex evaluation in the high-involvement situation suggests that marketing managers need to provide a good deal of information to assist the purchase decision such as through employing a well-trained, well-informed sales force. In low involvement situations, providing positive reinforcement through advertising as well as seeking to gain trial (e.g. through sales promotion) is more important than providing detailed information.

Post-purchase evaluation of the decision

The creation of customer satisfaction is the real art of effective marketing. Marketing managers want to create positive experiences from the purchase of their products or services. Nevertheless, it is common for customers to experience some post-purchase concerns; this is known as cognitive dissonance. Such concerns arise because of an uncertainty surrounding the making of the right decision. This is because the choice of one product often means the rejection of the attractive features of the alternatives.

There are four ways in which dissonance is likely to be increased: owing to the expense of the purchase; when the decision is difficult (e.g. there are many alternatives, many choice criteria, and each alternative offers benefits not available with the others); when the decision is irrevocable; and when the purchaser is inclined to experience anxiety.[12] Thus it is often associated with high-involvement purchases. Shortly after purchase, car buyers may attempt to reduce dissonance by looking at advertisements and brochures for their model, and seeking reassurance from owners of the same model. Some car dealers, such as Toyota, seek to reduce this 'buyer remorse' by contacting recent purchasers by letter to reinforce the wisdom of their decision and to confirm the quality of their after-sales service.

Many leading US retailers are aiming to reduce dissonance by posting customer reviews of products and services online. Companies like Target, Home Depot and Macy's have all launched online product reviews. The risks of a negative review are outweighed by the value of obtaining customer feedback and also by providing future customers with a better idea of what to expect.[13] Managing expectations is a key part of reducing dissonance.

What are the choice criteria?

The various attributes (and benefits) a customer uses when evaluating products and services are known as **choice criteria**. They provide the grounds for deciding to purchase one brand or another. Different members of the buying centre may use different choice criteria. For example, purchasing managers who are judged by the extent to which they reduce purchase expenditure are likely to be more cost conscious than production engineers who are evaluated in terms of the technical efficiency of the production process they design. Four types of choice criteria are listed in Table 3.2, which also gives examples of each.

Table 3.2 Choice criteria used when evaluating alternatives

Type of criteria	Examples
Technical	Reliability Durability Performance Style/looks Comfort Delivery Convenience Taste
Economic	Price Value for money Running costs Residual value Life cycle costs
Social	Status Social belonging Convention Fashion
Personal	Self-image Risk reduction Morals Emotions

Technical criteria are related to the performance of the product or service, and include reliability, durability, comfort and convenience. Many consumers justify purchase decisions in rational technical terms but as we shall see, the true motives for purchasing are often much more emotional. Some technical criteria such as reliability are particularly important in industrial purchasing. Many buying organizations are unwilling to trade quality for price. For example, Qantas Airlines had significant problems with the Rolls-Royce engines in its Airbus A380 planes in 2010 resulting in the grounding of flights while inspections were carried out. Rolls-Royce's quick and effective diagnosis of the problem not only limited any potential damage but also resulted in the company winning further orders from British Airways and Air China.

Economic criteria concern the cost aspects of purchase and include price, running costs and residual values (e.g. the trade-in value of a car). However, it should not be forgotten that price is only one component of cost for many buying organizations. Increasingly, buyers take into account life-cycle costs – which may include productivity savings, maintenance costs and residual values as well as initial purchase price – when evaluating products. Marketers can use life-cycle cost analysis to break into an account. By calculating life-cycle costs with a buyer, new perceptions of value may be achieved.

Social and personal criteria are particularly influential in consumer purchasing decisions. Social criteria concern the impact that the purchase makes on the person's perceived relationships with other people, and the influence of social norms on the person. For example, in the early days the manufacturers of personal computers and mobile phones, such as Apple, IBM and Motorola, sought to sell them on the basis of their technical and economic criteria. But as the technology underpinning these products becomes similar for all vendors, new forms of differentiation, such as colour, shape, appearance and emotional attributes all became important. Recent research has demonstrated the powerful social effects of consumption. Simply wearing clothes sporting well-known labels such as Lacoste and Tommy Hilfiger has been shown to generate perceptions of higher status, increase participation in shopping mall surveys and improve the wearer's job prospects and ability to solicit funds for a charity.[14]

Personal criteria concern how the product or service relates to the individual psychologically. Emotions are an important element of customer decision making (see Exhibit 3.3).

Personal criteria are also important in organizational purchasing. Risk reduction can affect choice decisions

Exhibit 3.3 Even brands like Budweiser have been known to use emotional advertising

since some people are risk averse and prefer to choose 'safe' brands. The IBM advertising campaign that used the slogan 'No one ever got fired for buying IBM' reflected its importance. Suppliers may be favoured on the basis that certain sales people are liked or disliked, or due to office politics where certain factions within the company favour one supplier over another.

Marketing managers need to understand the choice criteria being used by customers to evaluate their products and services. Such knowledge has implications for priorities in product design, and the appeals to use in advertising and personal selling.

Influences on consumer behaviour

The main influences on consumer behaviour are summarized in Figure 3.4. Personal influences describe those drivers that relate to the individual while social influences take account of the drivers that arise from the contexts in which we live.

Personal influences

The six personal influences on consumer behaviour are: information processing, motivation, **beliefs** and **attitudes**, personality, lifestyle and life cycle.

Information processing

The term **information processing** refers to the process by which a stimulus is received, interpreted, stored in memory and later retrieved.[15] It is therefore the link between external influences including marketing activities and the consumer's decision-making process. Two key aspects of information processing are perception and learning.

Perception is the complicated means by which we select, organize and interpret sensory stimulation into a meaningful picture of the world.[16] We receive these external stimuli through our different senses such as hearing a familiar jingle, seeing a YouTube video or encountering the familiar smell of a favourite coffee shop. The sensation of touch has been important in the success of Apple's products. Companies now place a significant emphasis on trying to present a multi-sensory experience for their customers as a way of attracting our attention (often subconsciously) and of differentiating their offerings from competitors. For example, Peugeot ran a print campaign to demonstrate the safety of its cars which invited readers to hit a spot on a page that caused a mini airbag to inflate (see Exhibit 3.4).

Three processes may be used to sort, into a manageable amount, the masses of stimuli that could be perceived. These are **selective attention**, **selective distortion** and **selective retention**. Selective attention is the process by which we screen out those stimuli that are neither meaningful to us nor consistent with our experiences and beliefs. In our information-rich world, selective attention represents a major challenge for marketers. Various studies have shown that consumers are exposed to a huge volume of marketing messages but attend to a very small percentage of them. For example, one study has found that consumers could recall only an average of 2.21 advertisements that they had ever seen.[17] Creative approaches such as humour, shock, sex and mystery are used by advertisers to try to capture consumer attention. Position is also critical; objects placed near the centre of the visual range are

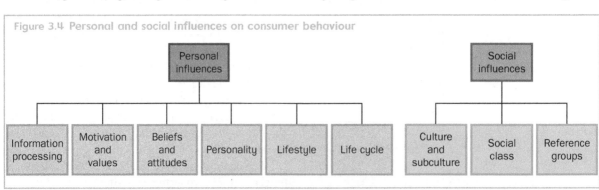

Figure 3.4 Personal and social influences on consumer behaviour

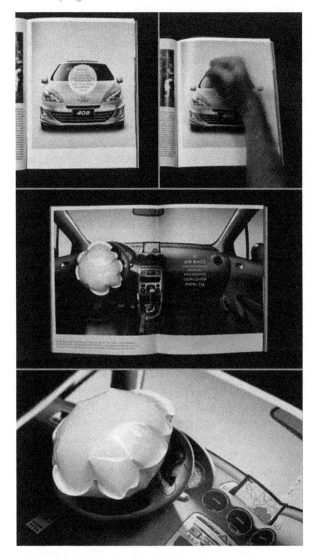

more likely to be noticed than those on the periphery. This is why there is intense competition to obtain eye-level positions on supermarket shelves. We are also more likely to notice those messages that relate to our needs (benefits sought)[18] and those that provide surprises (e.g. substantial price reductions).

When consumers distort the information they receive according to their existing beliefs and attitudes this is known as selective distortion. We may distort information that is not in accord with our existing views. Methods of doing this include thinking that we misheard the message, and discounting the message source. Consequently it is very important to present messages clearly without the possibility of ambiguity and to use a highly credible source. **Information framing** or priming can affect

interpretation. 'Framing' refers to ways in which information is presented to people. Levin and Gaeth[19] asked people to taste minced beef after telling half the sample that it was 70 per cent lean and the other half that it was 30 per cent fat. Despite the fact that the two statements are equivalent, the sample that had the information framed positively (70 per cent lean) recorded higher levels of taste satisfaction.

Priming involves using stimuli to encourage people to behave in certain ways. For example, when consumers arrive at a supermarket it takes a while for the mind to get into shopping mode. Therefore retailers term the area just inside the entrance as the decompression zone – where people are encouraged to slow down and look at special offers which is then followed by the chill zone containing books, magazines and DVDs.[20] Colour is another important influence on interpretation. Blue and green are viewed as cool, and evoke feelings of security. Red and yellow are regarded as warm and cheerful but have also been found to have an aphrodisiac effect on men without an awareness on their part that this so.[21] By using the appropriate colour in pack design it is possible to affect the consumer's feelings about a product. However, it is important to remember that colour is also subject to different interpretations across different cultures.

Selective retention refers to the fact that only a selection of messages may be retained in memory. We tend to remember messages that are in line with existing beliefs and attitudes. Marketers are also interested in how we make sense of marketing stimuli such as the processes by which a leading sportsperson can cause us to select particular brands.

Learning takes place in a number of different ways. These include conditioning and cognitive learning. **Classical conditioning** is the process of using an established relationship between a stimulus and a response to cause the learning. Thus, advertising of soft drinks will typically show groups of people having fun and when this type of advertising is constantly repeated a certain level of conditioning takes place creating an association between drinks consumption and happiness. This helps to explain why big, well-known brands repeatedly advertise. For example, the energy drink Red Bull repeatedly uses quirky, humorous advertising to appeal to its target market of young adults.

Operant conditioning differs from classical conditioning in terms of the role and timing of the reinforcement. In this case, reinforcement results from rewards: the more rewarding the response, the stronger the likelihood of the purchase being repeated. Operant conditioning occurs as a result of product trial. The use of free samples is based on the principles of operant conditioning. For example, free samples of a new shampoo are distributed to a large number of households. Because the use of the shampoo is costless it is used (desired response), and because it has desirable properties it is liked (reinforcement) and the likelihood of its being bought is increased. Thus the sequence of events is different for classical and operant conditioning. In the former, by association, liking precedes trial; in the latter, trial precedes liking. A series of rewards (reinforcements) may be used over time to encourage the repeat buying of the product.

The learning of knowledge, and the development of beliefs and attitudes without direct reinforcement is referred to as **cognitive learning** which stresses the importance of internal mental processes. The learning of two or more concepts without conditioning is known as **rote learning**. Having seen the headline 'Lemsip is for flu attacks', the consumer may remember that Lemsip is a remedy for flu attacks without the kinds of conditioning and reinforcement previously discussed. **Vicarious learning** involves learning from others without direct experience or reward. It is the promise of the reward that motivates. Thus we may learn the type of clothes that attract potential admirers by observing other people. In advertising, the 'admiring glance' can be used to signal approval of the type of clothing being worn or the alcoholic beverage being consumed. We imagine that the same may happen to us if we dress in a similar manner or drink a similar drink.

Reasoning is a more complex form of cognitive learning and is usually associated with high-involvement situations. For example, a detailed online product review or a sales presentation enables the consumer to draw their own conclusions through reasoning, having been presented with some facts or assertions. Whatever form of learning is used, marketers are particularly interested in both the recognition and recall of messages as we shall see in Chapter 10.

Our understanding of how people perceive stimuli and learn is improving all the time. **Semiotics** is the study of the correspondence between signs and symbols and their roles in how we assign meanings. Symbols in logo design and advertising are given meanings by the consumers that interpret them as such. For example, the striding man on a bottle of Johnnie Walker whisky symbolizes the journey we take through life and this journey was the centrepiece of the Johnnie Walker 'Keep Walking' campaign. In psychology and brain research, significant attention is being devoted to trying to understand the subconscious as it would appear that much of our decision making is done there without us realizing it. For example, it has been argued that we often make snap judgements that are superior to those that we think a great deal about.[22]

Motivation

Given the endless array of choices that are available to us, what are the motives that cause us to select one experience over another or choose to spend our time or money in certain ways? A key part of this issue (and of the debates about marketing generally) is the distinction between needs and wants. Critics of marketing argue that it creates excessive wants and desires among consumers leading to all types of maladaptive behaviours such as addictive consumption, compulsive shopping disorder (CSD), consumer debt and the waste of the planet's scarce resources.

One of the best known theories of motivation is Maslow's Hierarchy of Needs. The psychologist Abraham Maslow sought to explain how people grow and develop and proposed that we move through a hierarchy of motives. First we must satisfy our basic *physiological needs* for food, clothing and shelter, then we move to *safety needs* such as protection from danger and accidents, then to the need for *belongingness* such as love and family relationships, then to the needs for *esteem and status* and then to the final highest level of need, namely, *self-actualization* which is essentially our understanding of whatever the meaning of life is for us. From a marketing point of view, different products can be seen as fulfilling different needs, such as security systems for safety, club memberships for status, and travel and education for self-actualization. However, consumers do not progress rigidly up the hierarchy but may place emphasis on different levels at different times and the same product may satisfy different needs for different people.

Consequently, new explanations of fundamental human needs are becoming more popular. For example, evolutionary psychologists argue that we have four basic human needs that have derived from our evolution as a species and can be observed in different cultures during different time periods. These are the need to survive, to reproduce, to select kin and to reciprocate. These fundamental motives can be observed in the consumption of everything from cookery books (survival) to cosmetic surgery (reproduction) to Christmas gift giving (reciprocation).[23]

Beliefs and attitudes

A thought that a person holds about something is known as a 'belief'. Beliefs about oneself, which is known as the **self-concept**, are very important because this drives a signification element of consumption. For example, the viral video from Dove called *Evolution*, which was part of the Real Beauty campaign, was a significant hit because it shows how perceptions of beauty are distorted in the media.

Consumers increasingly use brands to convey their identity by wearing branded clothes or even having brands tattooed on their bodies. Marketing people are also very interested in consumer beliefs because these are related to attitudes. In particular, misconceptions about products can be harmful to brand sales. Duracell batteries were believed by consumers to last three times as long as Ever Ready batteries, but in continuous use they lasted over six times as long. This prompted Duracell to launch an advertising campaign to correct this misconception.

An 'attitude' is an overall favourable or unfavourable evaluation of a product or service. The consequence of a set of beliefs may be a positive or negative attitude towards the product or service. Changing attitudes is an important step in convincing consumers to try a brand. For example, the marketers of Skoda cars first had to overcome significantly negative attitudes towards the brand before they succeeded in growing its sales levels in the UK market. By changing the brand name and packaging of its value range to M Savers, the UK supermarket chain Morrisons was successful in changing attitudes and growing sales of this sub-brand.

Understanding beliefs and attitudes is an important task for marketers. For example, the attitudes of the 'grey market', those over the age of 50 years, are not well understood. Some companies, such as Gap, have explicitly targeted this segment, but Gap was forced to close its Forth & Towne outlets after heavy losses. Brands like Amazon's Kindle and Apple's iPhone and iPad have proved to be particularly popular with the grey market because they are larger than other portable devices and are very easy to use. This large and relatively well-off group is likely to be the subject of significant marketing effort in the years to come.

Personality

Just from our everyday dealings with people we can tell that they differ enormously in their personalities. **Personality** is the sum of the inner psychological characteristics of individuals, which lead to consistent responses to their environment.[24] There are several theories of personality but the most accepted today is the big five, and the extent to which one varies on these dimensions ranges from high to low.[25] The big five are openness to new experience, novelty seeking etc.; conscientiousness, which is self-control, reliability etc.; agreeableness, which is warmth, friendliness etc.; stability such as emotional stability; and extraversion, that is, the extent to which people are outgoing and talkative or not. The extent to which we possess each of these traits will be reflected in our behaviour and in our consumption choices. For example, conscientiousness is generally low in juveniles and it increases with age. The consumption of high-maintenance products, pets, personal grooming and home fitness equipment are all indicators of high conscientiousness.

This concept – personality – is also relevant to brands (see Marketing in Action 3.1). 'Brand personality' is the characterization of brands as perceived by consumers. Brands may be characterized as 'for young people' (Tommy Hilfiger), 'for winners' (Nike), or 'self-important' (L'Oréal). This is a dimension over and above the physical (e.g. colour) or functional (e.g. taste) attributes of a brand. By creating a brand personality, a marketer may generate appeal to people who value that characterization. For example, one of the longest-running fictional brands is James Bond; a variety of car makers and technology companies have attempted to bring his cool, suave and sexy personality into their brands by placing them in Bond movies.

Lifestyle

Lifestyle patterns have been the subject of much interest as far as marketing research practitioners are concerned. The term 'lifestyle' refers to the pattern of living as expressed in a person's activities, interests and opinions (the AIO dimensions). Lifestyle analysis (psychographics) groups consumers according to their beliefs, activities, values and demographic characteristics (such as education and income). For example, the advertising agency Young & Rubicam identified seven major lifestyle groups that can be found throughout Europe and the USA.

- *The mainstreamers*: the largest group. Attitudes include conventional, trusting, cautious and family centred. Leisure activities include spectator sports and gardening; purchase behaviour is habitual, brand loyal and in approved stores.

Canon Ad Insight: An award winning campaign celebrates amateur photographers.

Marketing in Action 3.1 Deutsche Telekom's brand personality!

Critical Thinking: Below is a review of the creation of some successful brand personalities. Read it and critically evaluate the role of brand personalities in building brand loyalty in consumer markets.

Consumer brands frequently invest heavily in imbuing themselves with personality. A classic example is in the mundane world of batteries. Perhaps the most famous is the Energizer bunny – an iconic pink rabbit that was the centrepiece of Energizer advertising for many years. The pink toy rabbit, wearing sunglasses and blue and white striped sandals would feature in commercials beating his drum and outlasting rival products. Adverts generally featured the tagline 'still going' and both the bunny and the tagline were embraced in general culture by everybody from presidential candidates to sports stars. The bunny was invented to match advertising by rival brand Duracell who had created their own 'long-lasting rabbit' several years earlier in 1973.

Aside from creating fictitious, cartoon-style personalities, brands also aim to incorporate consumer personality. A recent case in point is Deutsche Telekom's pan-European advertising campaign 'Move On'. The German telecom company's brand promise is that 'Life is for Sharing' and it sought to develop a campaign that would convey this idea. Its creative strategy was to produce a road movie filmed across 11 European countries. However, as part of the life is for sharing theme, people throughout these countries were invited to participate in the creation of the movie. A variety of tasks were set such as choosing the car, suggesting pets, the soundtrack, the front page of a newspaper, etc. Over 6,000 entries for each task were received. The winners were then selected and joined the Move On crew as extras on a journey across Europe. Entries were submitted via Facebook and behind the scenes footage of the creation of the movie was broadcast to a growing community on YouTube. The final production premiered in Berlin in 2012.

The campaign generated a big social media following and significant press coverage. However it was also effective in building the association between Deutsche Telekom and the 'Life is for Sharing' brand personality. For example, post-campaign research in Austria demonstrated a 17 per cent growth in this brand attribute.

Based on: Anonymous (2013)[26]

2 *The aspirers*: members of this group are unhappy, suspicious and ambitious. Leisure activities include trendy sports and fashion magazines; they buy fads, are impulse shoppers and engage in conspicuous consumption.

3 *The succeeders*: those that belong to this group are happy, confident, industrious and leaders. Leisure activities include travel, sports, sailing and dining out. Purchase decisions are based on criteria like quality, status and luxury.

4 *The transitionals*: members of this group are liberal, rebellious, self-expressive and intuitive. They have unconventional tastes in music, travel and movies; and enjoy cooking and arts and crafts. Shopping behaviour tends to be impulsive and to involve unique products.

5 *The reformers*: those that belong to this group are self-confident and involved, have broad interests and are issues orientated. They like reading, cultural events, intelligent games and educational television. They have eclectic tastes, enjoy natural foods, and are concerned about authenticity and ecology.

6 *The struggling poor*: members of this group are unhappy, suspicious and feel left out. Their interests are in sports, music and television; their purchase behaviour tends to be price based, but they are also looking for instant gratification.

7 *The resigned poor*: those in this group are unhappy, isolated and insecure. Television is their main leisure activity and shopping behaviour is price based, although they also look for the reassurance of branded goods.

Lifestyle analysis has implications for marketing since lifestyles have been found to correlate with purchasing behaviour.[27] A company may choose to target a particular lifestyle group (e.g. the mainstreamers) with a product offering, and use advertising that is in line with the values and beliefs of this group (see Exhibit 3.6). For example, Benecol's range of cholesterol-lowering foods are marketed at consumers who seek to have a healthy lifestyle. As information on the readership/viewership habits of lifestyle groups becomes more widely known so media selection may be influenced by lifestyle research.

A typical example of a niche lifestyle that has grown significantly in recent years is surfing. Originating in the south Pacific, surfing was formerly popular in just some select areas such as Hawaii, California and Australia. In the past decade, its popularity has soared and participation rates around the world have grown dramatically. It is characterized by its own surf culture such as dressing in boardshorts or driving 'woodies', that is, station wagons used to carry boards. Many brands have capitalized on this opportunity, most notably the Australian clothing brand Billabong, and marketers aiming to target surfers can do so through particular magazines, events, television programmes and social networks.

Life cycle

In addition to the factors we have already examined, consumer behaviour may depend on the 'life stage' people have reached. A person's life-cycle stage is of particular relevance since disposable income and purchase requirements may vary according to life-cycle stage. For example, young couples with no children may have high disposable income if both work, and may be heavy purchasers of home furnishings and appliances since they may be setting up home. When they have children, their disposable income may fall, particularly if they become a single-income family and the purchase of baby and child-related products increases. At the empty-nester stage, disposable income may rise due to the absence of dependent children, low mortgage repayments and high personal income. Research has shown that when children leave a home, a mother is likely to change 80 per cent of the branded goods she buys regularly and that they are more likely than any other group to decide which brands they want to buy once in a store than beforehand.[28] Both these issues have important marketing implications.

Social influences

The three social influences on consumer behaviour are: culture, social class and reference groups.

Culture

As we noted in Chapter 2, **culture** refers to the traditions, taboos, values and basic attitudes of the whole society within which an individual lives. It provides the framework within which individuals and their lifestyles develop, and consequently affects consumption. For example, in Japan it is generally women that control the family finances and make all the major household spending decisions. As a result, many financial services firms are developing investment products targeted specifically at Japanese women. Within cultures there are also a variety of sub-cultures that influence consumer behaviour and marketing as we saw in Chapter 2.

The most notable trend in the past three decades has been the increased internationalization of cultures. Products and services that, previously, may only have been available in certain countries are now commonplace. For example, speciality cuisines like Japanese sushi, Korean barbeque and Cajun food can now be found in major cities throughout the world. Allied to this, though, is the growing domination of some cultures. For example, the success of American fast-food chains and movie production companies represents a major challenge to smaller, local enterprises in many parts of the world.

Social class

Long regarded as an important determinant of consumer behaviour, the idea of social class is based largely on occupation (often that of the chief income earner). This is one way in which respondents in marketing research surveys are categorized, and it is usual for advertising media (e.g. newspapers) to give readership figures broken down by social class groupings. Some countries are significantly more class conscious than others, such as the UK and India, and movement between the classes is difficult. In others, such as Brazil and China, rising incomes are creating large new middle- and upper-class segments which is significantly driving demand for international and luxury brands respectively. For example, such is the demand for golf courses in China that many are being built without planning permission and others are not being called golf courses to get around planning legislation.

However, the use of traditional social class frameworks to explain differences in consumer behaviour has been criticized because certain social class categories may not relate to differences in disposable income (e.g. many self-employed manual workers can have very high incomes). The National Statistics Socioeconomic Classification system (NSSEC) in the UK aims to take account of this situation by identifying eight categories of occupation, as shown in Table 3.3. Consumption patterns are likely to vary significantly across these categories. For example, research on the social class of British grocery shoppers has found that the highest proportion of AB (managerial/professional) shoppers frequent Sainsbury's; Asda attracts a significantly higher

Table 3.3 Social class categories

Analytic class	Operational categories	Occupations
1	Higher managerial and professional occupations	Employers in large organizations; higher managerial and professional
2	Lower managerial and professional occupations	Lower managerial occupations; higher technical and supervisory occupations
3	Intermediate occupations	Intermediate clerical/administrative, sales/service, technical/auxiliary and engineering occupations
4	Small employers and own-account workers	Employers in small, non-professional and agricultural organizations, and own-account workers
5	Lower supervisory and technical occupations	Lower supervisory and lower technical craft and process operative occupations
6	Semi-routine occupations	Semi-routine sales, service, technical, operative, agricultural, clerical and childcare occupations
7	Routine occupations	Routine sales/service, production, technical, operative and agricultural occupations
8	Never worked and long-term unemployed	Never worked, long-term unemployed and students

share of people in lower supervisory and technical occupations; while Tesco's profile mirrors that of society in general.[29] An interesting trend in the growing middle-class segment is that consumers are becoming more cost-conscious but are also willing to splash out on luxury items. Brands that have targeted the middle market such as Maxwell House coffee owned by Kraft will be challenged by this development.[30]

Reference groups

A group of people that influences an individual's attitude or behaviour is called a **reference group**. Where a product is conspicuous (for example, clothing or cars) the brand or model chosen may have been strongly influenced by what buyers perceive as acceptable to their reference group; this may consist of the family, a group of friends or work colleagues. Some reference groups may be formal (e.g. members of a club or society), while others may be informal (friends with similar interests). Reference groups influence their members in a number of ways such as providing peers with information about products, by influencing peers to buy products and by individual members choosing certain products because they feel that this will enhance their image within the group. The role of reference groups is now more important than ever given that certain groups choose to live a very 'public' life through social networks. Different types of reference groups exist. *Membership* groups are those to which a person already belongs and can be with friends, club members or class mates. An interesting marketing development has been the growth of brand communities which are social relationships based around interest in a product (see Chapter 6). *Aspirational* groups are those which a person would like to belong to, for example, people often aspire to the lifestyle of sports stars or celebrities.

Finally, *avoidance* groups are those that people choose to distance themselves from because they do not share the values of such a group.

A key role in all reference groups is played by the opinion leader. Opinion leaders are typically socially active and highly interconnected within their groups. They also have access to product information and influence the behaviour and purchase choices of group members. Given advances in social networking technology, their influence can be highly significant. Therefore, they are the focus of attention from marketers who aim to identify them and to encourage them to influence their peers through buzz marketing techniques (see Chapter 11). They are also critical to the adoption of new products as demonstrated in Figure 3.5.

A related issue is the 'herd mentality' of consumption behaviour. People are social animals and tend to follow the crowd, therefore companies are looking at ways of exploiting this to increase sales. For example, researchers in the USA created an artificial music market in which people downloaded previously unknown songs. What they found was that when consumers could see how many times the tracks had been downloaded, they tended to select the most popular tracks. As a result, many websites now include features like 'other customers have bought' tabs. Similarly, 'smart cart' technology is being pioneered in supermarkets to exploit this herd instinct. Each cart has a scanner that reads products that have been chosen and relays it to a central computer. When a shopper walks past a shelf of goods, a screen on the shelf can tell her/him how many people in the shop have already selected that particular product. Studies have shown that if the number is high, he or she is more likely to choose it, so this method can be used to increase sales without offering discounts, for example.

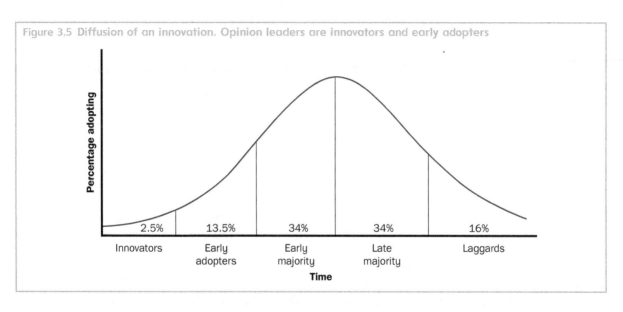

Figure 3.5 Diffusion of an innovation. Opinion leaders are innovators and early adopters

In summary, the behaviour of consumers is affected by a variety of factors. There is a range of personal influences and some social influences that all combine to make up the nature of the relationships that individuals have with products and services. We will now turn to the factors that influence the buying behaviour of organizations.

Influences on organizational buying behaviour

Organizational buying is characterized by a number of unique features. Typically, the number of customers is small and order sizes large. For example, in Australia just two companies, Coles and Woolworths, account for over 70 per cent of all products sold in supermarkets, so getting or losing an account with these resellers can be crucial. Organizational purchases are often complex and risky, with several parties having input into the purchasing decision as would be the case with a major information technology (IT) investment. The demand for many organizational goods is derived from the demand for consumer goods, which means that small changes in consumer demand can have an important impact on the demand for industrial goods. For example, the decline in the sale of DVDs has had a knock-on effect on the demand for DVD component parts. When large organizational customers struggle, this impacts on their suppliers. Most major car manufacturers such as Ford, General Motors, Daimler Chrysler and Volkswagen have all demanded significant price cuts from their suppliers in recent years. However, at the same time suppliers have faced rising steel and raw material costs, which has affected profitability and forced some out of business.[31] On the other hand, some suppliers like Intel have done an exceptional job of building their brands and creating an awareness of the presence of their products in the offerings of other companies. Organizational buying is also characterized by the prevalence of negotiations between buyers and sellers; and in some cases reciprocal buying may take place where, for example, in negotiating to buy computers a company like Volvo might persuade a supplier to buy a fleet of company cars.

Figure 3.6 shows the three factors that influence organizational buying behaviour and the choice criteria that are used: the buy class, the product type and the importance of purchase.[32]

The buy class

Organizational purchases may be distinguished as either a **new task**, a **straight re-buy** or a **modified re-buy**.[33] A new task occurs when the need for the product has not arisen previously so that there is little or no relevant experience in the company, and a great deal of information is required. A straight

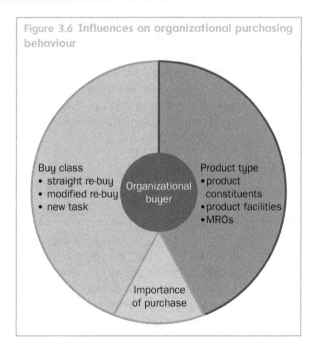

Figure 3.6 Influences on organizational purchasing behaviour

re-buy occurs where an organization buys previously purchased items from suppliers already judged acceptable. Routine purchasing procedures are set up to facilitate straight re-buys. The modified re-buy lies between the two extremes. A regular requirement for the type of product exists, and the buying alternatives are known, but sufficient change (e.g. a delivery problem) has occurred to require some alteration to the normal supply procedure.

The buy classes affect organizational buying in the following ways. First, the membership of the DMU changes. For a straight re-buy possibly only the purchasing officer is involved, whereas for a new buy senior management, engineers, production managers and purchasing officers may be involved. Modified re-buys often involve engineers, production managers and purchasing officers, but not senior management, except when the purchase is critical to the company. Second, the decision-making process may be much longer as the buy class changes from a straight re-buy to a modified re-buy and to a new task. Third, in terms of influencing DMU members, they are likely to be much more receptive to new task and modified re-buy situations than straight re-buys. In the latter case, the purchasing manager has already solved the purchasing problem and has other problems to deal with.

The first implication of this buy class analysis is that there are big gains to be made if a company can enter the new task at the start of the decision-making process. By providing information and helping with any technical problems that can arise, the company may be able to create goodwill and 'creeping commitment', which secures the order when the final decision is made. The second implication is that since the decision process is likely to be long, and many people are involved in the new task, supplier companies need to invest heavily in sales personnel for a considerable period of time. Some firms employ 'missionary' sales teams, comprising their best salespeople, to help secure big new task orders.

The product type

Products can be classified according to four types: materials, components, plant and equipment, and maintenance, repair and operation (MRO):

1 materials – to be used in the production process, e.g. aluminium
2 components – to be incorporated in the finished product, e.g. headlights
3 plant and equipment – for example, earth-moving equipment
4 products and services for MRO – for example, spanners, welding equipment and lubricants.

This classification is based on a customer perspective– how the product is used – and may be employed to identify differences in organizational buyer behaviour. First, the people who take part in the decision-making process tend to change according to product type. For example, senior management tend to get involved in the purchase of plant and equipment or, occasionally, when new materials are purchased if the change is of fundamental importance to company operations, e.g. if a move from aluminium to plastic is being considered. Rarely do they involve themselves in component or MRO supply. Similarly, design engineers tend to be involved in buying components and materials, but not normally MRO and plant equipment. Second, the decision-making process tends to be slower and more complex as product type moves along the following continuum:

$$MRO \rightarrow components \rightarrow materials \rightarrow plant\ and\ equipment$$

The importance of purchase

A purchase is likely to be perceived as being important to the buying organization when it involves large sums of money, when the cost of making the wrong decision, for example in terms of production downtime, is high and when there is considerable uncertainty about the outcome of alternative offerings. In such situations, many people at different organizational levels are likely to be involved in the decision and the process will be long, with extensive search for and analysis of information. Thus extensive marketing effort is likely to be required, but great opportunities present themselves to sales teams who work with buying organizations to convince them that their offering has the best pay-off; this may involve acceptance

trials (e.g. private diesel manufacturers supply railway companies with prototypes for testing), engineering support and testimonials from other users. Additionally, guarantees of delivery dates and after-sales service may be necessary when buyer uncertainty regarding these factors is pronounced.

Features of organizational purchasing practice

Within the purchasing function, a number of trends have occurred that have marketing implications for supplier firms. The relentless drive for efficiency by businesses has been one of the key factors behind the growth of just-in-time purchasing, online purchasing and centralized purchasing. At the same time, these developments have often strengthened relationships between buyers and their suppliers, and we have seen a significant growth in relationship marketing and reverse marketing.

The **just-in-time (JIT)** concept aims to minimize stocks by organizing a supply system that provides materials and components as they are required. The total effects of JIT can be enormous. Purchasing inventory and inspection costs can be reduced, product design can be improved, delivery streamlined, production downtime reduced and the quality of the finished item enhanced. Very close co-operation is required between a manufacturer and its suppliers. An example of a company that employs a JIT system is the Nissan car assembly plant in Sunderland in the UK. Nissan adopts what it terms 'synchronous supply': parts are delivered only minutes before they are needed. For example, carpets are delivered by Sommer Allibert, a French supplier, from its facility close to the Nissan assembly line in sequence for fitting to the correct model. Only 42 minutes elapse between the carpet being ordered and its being fitted to the car. This system also carries risks, however: the 2011 earthquake in Japan caused delays to the introduction of two new Toyota Prius models and impacted on production in other global companies such as Caterpillar and General Motors.

The growth in the use of the Internet has given rise to the development of online purchasing. Two main categories of marketplaces, or exchanges, have been created: **vertical electronic marketplaces** are industry specific, such as sites for the paper industry (e.g. www.paperexchange.com) or the automotive and healthcare industries (e.g. www.covisint.com); **horizontal electronic marketplaces** cross industry boundaries and cater for supplies such as MROs (e.g.www.dgmarket.com) and services (www.elance. com). Companies seeking supplies post their offers on these websites. Potential vendors then bid for the contracts electronically. Some companies report significant improvements in efficiency from managing their purchasing this way, through reducing the number of procurement staff involved in processing orders and increasing the potential global spread of vendors. This heightened competition presents challenges for suppliers. Social media platforms such as Facebook and LinkedIn have become a popular mechanism for firms to source employees and suppliers.

Where several operating units within a company have common requirements and where there is an opportunity to strengthen a negotiating position by bulk buying, centralized purchasing is an attractive option. Centralization encourages purchasing specialists to concentrate their energies on a small group of products, thus enabling them to develop an extensive knowledge of cost factors and the operation of suppliers.[34] For example, increasing concerns over the costs of healthcare has meant that many hospitals have centralized purchasing in procurement departments rather than devolving the activity to doctors and nurses as had been the case in the past. As

a result, many contracts are put out to tender, often on a pan-European basis, with vendors selected on the basis of quality, cost and ability to deliver over a number of years. The net effect of this is that orders are much more difficult to secure but, once secured, are likely to be more long lasting. At the same time, organizational buying has become increasingly characterized by very close relationships between buyers and sellers. **Relationship marketing** is the process of creating, developing and enhancing relationships with customers and other stakeholders (see Social Media Marketing 3.2). For example, Marks & Spencer has trading relationships with suppliers that stretch back almost a century. Such long-term relationships can have significant advantages for both buyer and seller. Risk is reduced for buyers as they get to know people in the supplier organization and know who to contact when problems arise. Communication is thus improved, and joint problem solving and design management can take place with suppliers becoming, in effect, strategic partners. Sellers gain

Social Media Marketing 3.2 Kern & Sohn

Critical Thinking: Below is a review of some innovative marketing conducted by the German firm Kern & Sohn. Read it and consider how social media marketing could be used by other business-to-business firms.

While examples of innovative marketing activity abound in the business-to-consumer (B2C) arena, less well-known but equally powerful examples are to be found in business-to-business (B2B) contexts. A typical example is an innovative marketing campaign conducted by the German precision scales firm, Kern & Sohn, a firm that was founded in 1844 and has grown to be a sixth generation family business. It is a leading player in the precision scales industry, manufacturing products such as laboratory balances and industrial scales for sectors like healthcare, production, education and jewellery. Its budget for marketing was limited but yet it came up with a novel campaign designed to demonstrate its global leadership in the industry.

What it did was to exploit a little known fact that, because of gravity, items weigh slightly differently depending on where they are in the world. These differences do not show up

on ordinary scales but are captured by Kern's precision equipment. The company carefully selected customers and scientists around the world and sent them a kit containing a set of scales and a special test weight – a chip-proof garden gnome. Scientists weighed the gnome, recorded the results on the website, took photographic evidence and passed him on. As the gnome travelled to different landmarks around the world, he generated highly shareable imagery and positive associations for Kern.

The results were exceptional. The story captured the attention of the world's media reaching an audience of over 350 million people in 150 countries and even becoming the subject of a Ted talk. After two weeks, over 16,000 websites had linked to gnomeexperiment.com, driving Kern & Sohn from page 12 to page 1 of the Google rankings and resulting in a 200 per cent increase in traffic. Within a month, Kern sales had risen by 21 per cent.

through closer knowledge of buyer requirements, and many companies have reorganized their sales forces to reflect the importance of managing customer relationships effectively – a process known as key account management. New product development can benefit from such close relationships. The development of machine-washable lamb's wool fabrics and easy-to-iron cotton shirts came about because of Marks & Spencer's close relationship with UK manufacturers.[35] The issue of relationship marketing will be dealt with in more detail in Chapter 7.

The traditional view of marketing is that supplier firms will actively seek out the requirements of customers and attempt to meet those needs better than the competition. However, purchasing is now taking on a more proactive, aggressive stance in acquiring the products and services needed to compete. This process, whereby the buyer attempts to persuade the supplier to provide exactly what the organization wants, is called **reverse marketing**.[36] Syngenta, an international supplier of chemicals, uses reverse marketing very effectively to target suppliers with a customized list of requirements concerning delivery times, delivery success rates and how often sales visits should occur. The growth of reverse marketing presents two key benefits to suppliers who are willing to listen to the buyer's proposition and carefully consider its merits: first, it provides the opportunity to develop a stronger and longer-lasting relationship with the customer; second, it could be a source of new product opportunities that may be developed to a broader customer base later on.

Finally in B2B contexts, a firm may not actually make a purchase but rather it simply leases a product. A lease is a contract by which the owner of an asset (e.g. a car) grants the right to use the asset for a period of time to another party in exchange for the payment of rent.[37] The benefits to the customer are that a leasing arrangement avoids the need to pay the cash purchase price of the product or service, is a hedge against fast product obsolescence, may have tax advantages, avoids the problem of equipment disposal and, with certain types of leasing contract, avoids some maintenance costs. These benefits need to be weighed against the costs of leasing, which may be higher than outright buying.

Summary

This chapter has examined the nature of customer behaviour and the key influences on customer behaviour. The following key issues were addressed.

1. The differences between consumer and organizational buying behaviour. In the latter, the buying decision process involves more stages, the input of more parties and greater levels of negotiation. Technical and economic choice criteria tend to play a greater role in organizational buying.

2. Who buys – the five roles in the buying decision-making process: initiator, influencer, decider, buyer and user. Different people may play different roles, particularly in a family purchase and, for marketers, identifying the decider is critical.

3. There are two main theories of consumer behaviour: the information processing approach which sees consumption as a rational, utilitarian process, and consumer culture theory which sees consumption as a social activity rooted in contexts.

4. The buying decision process, involving the stages of need recognition, search for alternatives, evaluation of alternatives, purchase and post-purchase evaluation. In the case of high-involvement purchases, consumers will typically go through all these stages, whereas in a low-involvement situation, they may move directly from need recognition to purchase.

5. The main choice criteria used in making purchase decisions – namely, technical, economic, social and personal criteria. In consumer buyer behaviour, social and personal criteria are very important as consumers build their identities through product and service selection.

6. The main influences on consumer buying behaviour: personal influences and social influences. At any given time, there are myriad factors that may influence a consumer's purchase decision. Deeply embedded emotional elements such as conditioning, learning, attitudes and personality are key drivers of consumption decisions.

7. The main influences on organizational buying behaviour: the buy class, the product type and the importance of purchase. For example, a major investment in plant and equipment that is critical to the organization and is a new task purchase will necessitate the involvement of many parties in the organization and will take time before a decision is made.

8. The key features of organizational purchasing practice: just-in-time purchasing, online purchasing, centralized purchasing, relationship marketing, reverse marketing and leasing. Organizational purchasing at one level presents opportunities for reverse marketing and relationship building with suppliers, but at a different level is driven by efficiency concerns that are managed through centralized and online purchasing.

Study questions

1. What are the differences between organizational buying behaviour and consumer buying behaviour?
2. Choose a recent purchase that included not only yourself but also other people in making the decision. What role(s) did you play in the buying centre? What roles did these other people play and how did they influence your choice?
3. Compare and contrast the information processing approach and the consumer culture approach to our understanding of how consumers behave in the ways that they do.
4. Review the choice criteria influencing some recent purchases such as a hairstyle, a meal, etc.
5. Describe the recent trends in just-in-time purchasing, online purchasing and centralized purchasing. Discuss the implications of these trends for marketers in vendor firms.

Suggested reading

Anderson, J.C., J.A. Narus and **W. van Rossum** (2006) Customer Value Propositions in Business Markets, *Harvard Business Review,* **84** (3), 90-9.

Arnould, E. and **C. Thompson** (2005) Consumer Culture Theory (CCT): Twenty Years of Research, *Journal of Consumer Research,* **31** (4), 868-82.

Gladwell, M. (2005) *Blink: The Power of Thinking Without Thinking,* London: Allen Lane.

Miller, G. (2009) *Spent: Sex, Evolution and the Secrets of Consumerism,* London: William Heinemann.

Spenner, P. and **K. Freeman** (2012) To Keep Your Customers, Keep it Simple, *Harvard Business Review,* **90** (5), 108-14.

Wisenblit, J., R. Priluck and **S. Pirog** (2013), The Influence of Parental Styles on Children's Consumption, *Journal of Consumer Marketing,* **30** (4), 320-7.

When you have read this chapter

log on to the Online Learning Centre for
Foundations of Marketing at
www.mheducation.co.uk/textbooks/fahy5
where you'll find links and extra online study tools for marketing.

References

1. **Gilbert, D.** (2014) Supercell Earns $30M a Month from Clash of Clans and Hay Day, *InternationalBusinessTimes.co.uk,* 12 February; **Rossi, J., S. Grundberg** and **J. Stoll** (2013) Supercell: Zero to $3 Billion in 3 Years, *WallStreetJournal.com,* 16 October; **Strauss, K.** (2013) Is This the Fastest Growing Game-Company Ever?, *Forbes.com,* 17 April.
2. **Blackwell, R.D., P.W. Miniard** and **J.F. Engel** (2000) *Consumer Behavior,* Orlando, FL: Dryden, 174.
3. **Pesola, M.** (2005) Samsung Plays to the Young Generation, *Financial Times,* 29 March, 11.
4. **Arnould, E.** and **C. Thompson** (2005) Consumer Culture Theory (CCT): Twenty Years of Research, *Journal of Consumer Research,* **31** (4), 868-82.
5. **Engel, J. F., R. D. Blackwell** and **P.W. Miniard** (1990) *Consumer Behavior,* Orlando FL: Dryden, 29.
6. **Hawkins, D. I, R. J. Best** and **K. A. Coney** (1989), *Consumer Behavior: Implications for Marketing Strategy,* Boston, MA: Irwin, 30.
7. **Seave, A.** (2013) How TripAdvisor Grows in Scale and Network Effects: Expertise in Gathering UGC, *Forbes.com,* 20 June.
8. **Kuusela, H., M. T. Spence** and **A. J. Kanto** (1998) Expertise Effects on Prechoice Decision Processes and Final Outcomes: A Protocol Analysis, *European Journal of Marketing,* **32** (5/6), 559-76.
9. **Blackwell, R.D., P. W. Miniard** and **J. F. Engel** (2000) *Consumer Behavior,* Orlando, FL: Dryden, 34.
10. **Elliot, R.** and **E. Hamilton** (1991) Consumer Choice Tactics and Leisure Activities, *International Journal of Advertising,* **10,** 325-32.
11. **Laurent, G.** and **J. N. Kapferer** (1985) Measuring Consumer Involvement Profiles, *Journal of Marketing Research,* **12** (February), 41-53.
12. **Hawkins, D.I., R.J. Best** and **K.A. Coney** (1989) *Consumer Behavior: Implications for Marketing Strategy,* Boston, MA: Irwin.
13. **Birchall, J.** (2006) Retailers Give Customers the Final Word, *Financial Times,* 6 October, 13.

14. **Anonymous** (2011) I've Got You Labelled, *The Economist*, 2 April, 74.

15. **Engel, J.F., R.D. Blackwell** and **P.W. Miniard** (1990) *Consumer Behavior*, Orlando, FL: Dryden, 363.

16. **Williams, K.C.** (1981) *Behavioural Aspects of Marketing*, London: Heinemann.

17. **Lindstrom, M.** (2009) *Buyology: How Everything We Believe About Why We Buy is Wrong*, London: Random House Books, 38.

18. **Ratneshwar, S., L. Warlop, D.G. Mick** and **G. Seegar** (1997) Benefit Salience and Consumers' Selective Attention to Product Features, *International Journal of Research in Marketing*, 14, 245-9.

19. **Levin, L.P.** and **G.J. Gaeth** (1988) Framing of Attribute Information Before and After Consuming the Product, *Journal of Consumer Research*, 15 (December), 374-8.

20. **Anonymous** (2008) The Way the Brain Buys, *The Economist*, December 20, 99-101.

21. **O'Morain, P.** (2008) The Fascinating Facts About Ladies in Red, *Irish Times HealthPlus*, November 11, 14.

22. **Gladwell, M.** (2005) *Blink: The Power of Thinking Without Thinking*, London: Allen Lane.

23. **Saad, G.** (2007) *The Evolutionary Bases of Consumption*, Hillsdale, NJ: Lawrence Erlbaum.

24. **Kassarjan, H.H.** (1971) Personality and Consumer Behavior: A Review, *Journal of Marketing Research*, November, 409-18.

25. **Miller, G.** (2009) *Spent: Sex, Evolution and the Secrets of Consumerism*, London: William Heinemann.

26. **Anonymous** (2013) Deutsche Telekom: Move On, *European Association of Communication Agencies*, Warc.com.

27. **O'Brien, S.** and **R. Ford** (1988) Can We At Last Say Goodbye to Social Class?, *Journal of the Market Research Society*, **30** (3), 289-332.

28. **Carter, M.** (2005) A Brand New Opportunity in the Empty Nest, *Financial Times*, 5 December, 14.

29. **Anonymous** (2005) This Sceptred Aisle, *The Economist*, 6 August, 29.

30. **Anonymous** (2006) The Disappearing Mid-Market, *The Economist*, 20 May, 70-2.

31. **Simon, B.** (2005) Car Parts Groups Face a Depressed Future, *Financial Times*, 18 May, 31.

32. **Cardozo, R.N.** (1980) Situational Segmentation of Industrial Markets, *European Journal of Marketing*, 14 (5/6), 264-76.

33. **Robinson, P.J., C.W. Faris** and **Y. Wind** (1967) *Industrial Buying and Creative Marketing*, Boston, MA: Allyn & Bacon.

34. **Briefly, E.G., R.W. Eccles** and **R.R. Reeder** (1998) *Business Marketing*, Englewood Cliffs, NJ: Prentice-Hall, 105.

35. **Thornhill, J.** and **A. Rawsthorn** (1992) Why Sparks Are Flying, *Financial Times*, 8 January, 12.

36. **Blenkhorn, D.L.** and **P.M. Banting** (1991) How Reverse Marketing Changes Buyer-Seller Roles, *Industrial Marketing Management*, 20, 185-91.

37. **Anderson, F.** and **W. Lazer** (1978) Industrial Lease Marketing, *Journal of Marketing*, 42 (January), 71-9.

Fiat and consumer behaviour in the UK market

Today most consumers would agree that Fiat, the Italian car manufacturer, is an industrial powerhouse - one of the most successful and recognizable commercial organizations in the world, with a fresh, youthful product line-up and a brand image which combines the heritage of classic European motoring with the modernity and chic of cutting-edge fashion. This strength has provided Fiat with the financial muscle to compete with the very biggest players, acquiring control of several major rivals along the way. However, in relatively recent times, the position of Fiat was so precarious that it almost ceased to exist. At the turn of the millennium, Fiat was struggling, but the company reinvigorated itself through the following actions:

- concentrating on making small, stylish cars such as the 500, Panda and Grande Punto, rather than the larger saloon/sedan cars where Fiat's brand is weaker
- bringing in energetic, proactive executives
- seeking alliances with other carmakers in underexploited markets (e.g. Chrysler in the USA).

The UK car market

The UK is Europe's third largest car market and car ownership levels are high. A small hatchback (e.g. Toyota Yaris) can cost around £10,000 and a family saloon (e.g. Hyundai i40) around £17,500. Until mid-2008, the UK economy was healthy, consumer credit was readily available, and consumer confidence high. As a result, the new car and light commercial vehicle (LCV) market was strong. The UK new car market peaked in 2007 at around 2.2 million units.

However, as a result of the economic crisis, new car sales volumes almost halved during 2008, recovering very gradually over the intervening years. Manufacturers and dealers struggled to sell vehicles and reduce their stock inventories, which increased the financial burden upon them. Some dealers were forced to cease trading as their cash flows dried up. The UK government helped with a scheme which incentivized owners of aged vehicles to have them scrapped in an environmentally sound manner at government-appointed sites, in return for a voucher to be redeemed against part of the value of a new car (with a further contribution from the motor manufacturer). This scheme – which generated more tax revenues for the UK in incremental sales tax than it cost – helped reduce emissions from aged vehicles and stimulated the market, but had a restricted time frame. The average age of UK cars is now 7.5 years (with approximately 32 million still in use), as UK consumers postpone replacing them due to financial considerations. However, the Society of Motor Manufacturers and Traders (SMMT) explain that this may be false economy, as the average new car is 20 per cent more efficient than the equivalent seven-year-old car, equating to a typical fuel and tax saving of £400 per year.

UK consumers use cars for a number of purposes: the average UK commute to work is 30 minutes each way per working day, with 75 per cent of such journeys outside London being made in private transport; many UK citizens use their cars to holiday within the UK, and a substantial proportion of these will take self-catering holidays, which often necessitate carrying more luggage; it is not uncommon for UK families to take day trips by car for leisure; most shopping trips, particularly for buying groceries, are undertaken by car.

Half of all UK new car sales are to fleet operators – organizations which run vehicles to carry out their business. Fleet drivers are usually sales representatives, engineers and other field-based staff. The largest companies and councils operate fleets in excess of 1,000 cars. While both consumers and fleet operators purchase new vehicles outright, the vast majority source them through contract hire and leasing companies, paying a predetermined monthly rate for three or four years, which covers servicing, maintenance and repair costs, depreciation, the 'Road Fund Licence' tax and often insurance. Leasees (the people to whom the vehicles are leased) pay a surcharge for exceeding the predetermined contract period or mileage, and for refurbishment of vehicles at the end of contract if they are damaged or unclean.

Market share is of particular concern to companies in the motor industry because:

- customer perceptions of a manufacturer's success are greatly influenced by how many of their vehicles they witness on the roads – in making 'big ticket' (expensive) purchases, consumers look for reassurance that many other people have made the same decision
- although a manufacturer's market share is usually similar to their percentage 'share of market spend' (i.e. the amount they spend on marketing communications compared to their competitors), recovering lost market share is expensive and difficult
- if factory production slows or stops, economies of scale are lost, meaning that manufacturers often sell a significant proportion of their vehicles at a net loss.

Half of UK car sales are in March and September, when the government introduces new age-identifying numbers on the registration plates placed on each vehicle. Many buyers postpone purchases until new registration dates, because cars depreciate in steps with each new plate change. Sales volumes are also influenced by rental companies, the most famous being Hertz and Avis. For carmakers, rental companies are unprofitable but necessary: they buy in bulk and help demonstrate vehicles to potential customers, but demand large discounts and sell old stock at prices which can cheapen a car's brand image and damage resale values. Fiat is reducing its dependency on rental sales.

Fiat's new vehicle range has the lowest average CO_2 (carbon dioxide) emissions of any major European manufacturer. Each UK car owner pays a government tax based upon their vehicle's CO_2 emission levels (unless their car is very low-polluting). Company car drivers are taxed based on the undiscounted price of their vehicle and its CO_2 emission level. These stepped taxes have led to many UK drivers abandoning larger family saloons in favour of more tax-efficient, smaller cars.

Consumer buyer behaviour in the UK car market

For UK consumers, a new car purchase is likely to be an infrequent event – drivers of company-owned 'fleet' vehicles and those supplied by contract hire and leasing companies usually change cars every three or four years, whereas other private buyers using their savings or loans would tend to keep a car even longer. The infrequency of the purchase and its high price (which is usually a consumer's third highest-value purchase after a house and wedding) mean that choice of new car is a 'high risk' decision. If a consumer makes a poor purchase decision (e.g. by failing to realize the tax implications or fuel costs of an uneconomical car), then he or she will probably have to suffer the consequences for several years. This is exacerbated by the tendency of UK drivers to use their vehicles as status symbols and to express their desired personal images, consciously or otherwise. For example, although a consumer may believe that his or her reason for choosing a high performance car was the advanced engineering or reliability stated in the manufacturer's advertisement, a deeper motivation may well have been a desire to be seen by others in an expensive, stylish car – to be associated with the trappings of success; to convey sportiness; to instil envy in neighbours and friends; to demonstrate that he or she is 'doing well in life'; to attempt to recapture his or her youth; or to stay ahead of peers.

Organizational buyer behaviour in the UK car market

Organization-based decision-makers – fleet managers – must consider how a vehicle will reflect their corporate brand image, but are likely to focus much more heavily on financial considerations. If purchasing vehicles outright for cash, they must consider their predicted residual value at a predetermined age and mileage, to avoid disposal of vehicles becoming a financial burden. This is not a consideration if the vehicle is to be leased to the organization, as the leasing company would take the burden of disposal and the risk of overestimating residual values, although leasing rates would reflect this. Reliability is key, as vehicle down-time (when a vehicle is undergoing servicing, maintenance or repair) can prevent an organization from undertaking its core activities, impacting on business performance. An operator of a large fleet is also likely to spread risk by using vehicles from several manufacturers. Therefore, if one of the manufacturers ceases to operate, as did Rover in 2005, the resulting drop in residual values and dealer back-up would only affect a proportion of its fleet.

In addition to fuel consumption and tax considerations, a fleet operator may wish to choose low-polluting vehicles as part of a wider corporate social responsibility policy. If choosing alternatively fuelled vehicles, fleet decision-makers must also consider the range of the vehicle (the distance it can travel before refuelling), and the local refuelling infrastructure, to avoid major inconvenience. Risk-aversion may be a factor in fleet operators' vehicle choices – a fleet manager is very unlikely to have to justify to his or her managing director the decision to purchase market-leading vehicles, whereas if a more unusual choice of vehicle proves unreliable or unpopular with company drivers, his or her decision may fall under scrutiny. Also, the company car policy is highly emotive to the company drivers themselves – who may be considered 'end consumers'. Very restricted choices of low prestige cars may damage staff morale and retention. Some organizations offer an open 'user/chooser' policy whereby drivers are allowed to select whichever car they wish within certain price brackets or leasing rates (and may even be able to make contributions from their payroll to 'trade up' to better vehicles). Other organizations operate a restricted choice policy, perhaps limited to a small number of manufacturers and models. Some organizations have a 'solus' (i.e. single manufacturer) policy which allows them to negotiate a strong volume-related discount from the manufacturer, but prevents them from using company car policy as a tool for raising staff retention and morale.

Fiat in the UK

Around 250 people work for Fiat UK, based near London. The company's role is to import Fiat vehicles from the factories and sell them within the UK. Although many aspects of Fiat's marketing are globalized, Fiat UK (and other nation-level counterparts) enjoy significant autonomy in addressing the needs of their local market. For example, Fiat UK is able to import vehicles which have product specifications specifically aimed to satisfy the needs and wants of British customers; it is responsible for appointing a dealer network which can represent the company and its products in towns and cities throughout the country; it develops a national customer relationship management (CRM) strategy to help increase customer satisfaction and retention.

In addition to the people employed by Fiat UK, there is a much greater number of outsourced service providers and channel partners who help to connect Fiat UK with the British market: staff employed by field marketing agencies play a significant role in promoting Fiat at shows, conferences and other events, and in prospecting and other sales activities; transport, logistics and events management companies help Fiat to deliver products to their clients (cars to customers, parts to dealerships) and in their below-the-line marketing; and above-the-line agencies work with Fiat UK in designing promotional campaigns for traditional and new media.

Fiat UK has around 160 independently owned but franchised dealerships, many being 'multi-franchise' sites, where Fiat cars are sold alongside rival manufacturers' products. Their dealer network is diverse, with multi-million-pound city sites owned by multinational companies and banks, and family businesses in small towns. Most manufacturers occasionally sell large numbers of discounted cars to dealers to meet sales objectives. This has let wealthy dealers sell cars cheaper than smaller dealers, producing pricing fluctuations, customer uncertainty and dealer unrest. Fiat endeavours to circumvent this model by adding customer value and avoiding commoditization.

During Fiat and Alfa Romeo's renaissance, they found that their average UK customers had an older age profile than was desirable for sustained brand growth. They subsequently launched a marketing campaign which distributed an online car racing game to middle-income professionals under the age of 40. This infectious game was intended to be circulated via email and social media, encouraging word of mouth within a target audience. The game was then beamed onto building walls in prominent 'cool' places, like London's Brick Lane, where young, affluent people spend their leisure time. This further built word of mouth and encouraged more conspicuous brand engagement.

The Fiat 500 in the UK

In early 2008, Fiat UK launched the '500' supermini car in Britain. The launch event was attended by celebrities such as pop star Mika. The subsequent marketing strategy for the 500, and the Fiat brand as a whole, was moved away from a previous over-dependence on magazine and television advertising, towards a more holistic approach. Despite the 500 being a 'retro-mini', Fiat did not overstate the heritage aspect, instead emphasizing brand values like youthfulness, fun and individuality.

While 'Fiat' has often been a difficult brand to push, '500' and 'Fiat 500' have enjoyed significantly more brand appeal, particularly among younger drivers and female audiences. It has been so successful that Fiat has extended this sub-brand with products such as the 500l, a larger, higher mini-estate version with panoramic windscreen, spacious cabin and characteristic Fiat 500 styling – a similar move to BMW's launch of the Mini Clubman. Fiat also owns the 'Abarth' brand. Abarth-badged versions of Fiat cars such as the 500, Punto and Panda are available at a much higher price than the Fiat models on which they are based, but offer substantially improved sportiness through faster engines, racing seats, lowered suspension and tyre profiles, and other changes which help target a more profitable and loyal, if relatively niche, market segment.

Each 500 is customizable with thousands of options like bespoke colour schemes and livery. Fiat's marketing strategy changed from explaining the brand in a 'one-size-fits-all' manner, to engaging each customer as personally as possible, allowing them to build their individual ideas of how the Fiat brand could enrich their everyday lives and help them express their identities. In this shift towards more consensual customer relationship management, Fiat sought to add value in new ways.

Fiat UK's recent promotional messages for the 500 car include the following:

- 'More style, lower monthly payments': The Fiat 500 can be personalised in over half a million ways. Competitive finance offers with attractive monthly payments can make the Fiat 500 yours;

- The 2014 UK television advertising campaign, 'Life's too short to wear a boring car: The Fiat 500 Spring / Summer Collection';

- 'Sport up' with the Fiat 500S. Features include satin chrome body trim, body coloured side skirts and spoiler, matt silver dashboard, red-stitched gear knob and seats, embroidered seat logos, and racing steering wheel;

- 'Colour Therapy' – a choice of many paint colours, including 'vintage' colours, on the Fiat 500;

- The chance to win £2,000 worth of free fuel when buying and registering a new Fiat 500 in the key month of September;

- Fiat 500 has Euro NCAP 5 star rating – which means it is in the safest category for occupants and pedestrians in the event of a collision. Also, 'it has 7 airbags';

- Fiat 500 is made of 95 per cent recoverable material;

- Fiat 500 has up to 14 body colours;

- Fiat introduced the 500byGucci, a special edition of the iconic hatch – a convertible customized by Gucci Creative Director Frida Giannini in collaboration with Fiat Centro Stile, Fiat's design team;

- The 500 has one diesel and three petrol engines – including 'Twinair' engines – with very low CO_2 emissions.

Questions

1. What might be the main decision-making criteria for (i) retail customers, and (ii) fleet managers? How might the decision-making process differ between the two?

2. When a family decides that they need to replace their current car, what actions in the decision-making process are they likely to undertake before purchasing a new Fiat 500?

3. If Fiat is currently targeting 'early adopters' with the Fiat 500 car, what should its marketing messages say in order to be effective?

This case was prepared by David Brown, Northumbria University, from various published sources as a basis for class discussion rather than to show effective or ineffective management.

Chapter 4

Marketing Research and Customer Insights

Chapter outline

The role of customer insights

Marketing information systems

Internal market information

Market intelligence

Approaches to conducting marketing research

Stages in the marketing research process

Learning outcomes

By the end of this chapter you will:

1 Understand the importance of marketing information and customer insights
2 Explain what is meant by a marketing information system
3 Analyse the main types of internal market information
4 Explain what is meant by market intelligence
5 Understand the different dimensions of marketing research
6 Explain the main stages in the marketing research process
7 Describe the differences between qualitative and quantitative research
8 Critique the role of marketing information in society.

Mondelez chocolate lovers

Good marketing is rooted in a deep knowledge of customer needs and preferences. As we saw in the previous chapter customers make decisions on the basis of a combination of rational and emotional attributes. Rational motives are somewhat easier to assess than emotional ones. So, for example, a hotel chain might change some aspects of its service based upon customer feedback information supplied through comment cards or posted on online review sites. Because hotel guests have just had an experience, their ability to articulate what they liked and disliked about it is relatively easy. But the motives behind why a consumer might be loyal to a particular shampoo brand may be much more difficult to uncover. Marketing research specialists use a variety of sophisticated methods to try to reveal these deep-seated drivers which then form the basis for the design and implementation of appropriate marketing campaigns.

A case in point is a project that was conducted by Mondelez International (formerly Kraft Foods) which is a major global manufacturer of chocolate, biscuits and gum. Some of its best known brands include Cadbury, Jacobs, Toblerone and Trident. Its challenge was to find new ways to present and package a mature product like chocolate. At the same time, many of the tried and trusted ways of conducting market research were showing some declines. For example, it is estimated that response rates to telephone surveys has fallen from 36 per cent in 1997 to just under 10 per cent in 2012 in Europe. Therefore, the company sought to interact with its customers in a less formal way. It created a competition called the Mondelez Chocolate Lovers Contest which invited customers to come up with new designs for a chocolate bar and its packaging. The contest was online in November/December 2012 and awarded prizes totalling $11,000 for the best submissions. Over 1,000 contestants from 69 countries generated a pool of 551 ideas.

However, as well as providing product ideas, the competition generated a huge amount of descriptions, comments and messages. To stimulate this activity, Mondelez also had a prize for the Most Valuable Participant, that is, the person who made the most submissions and comments. All of this qualitative data was content analysed to gain insights into chocolate lovers. Some novel insights were uncovered. For example, while 'ingredient' suggestions represented the largest cluster of ideas submitted, these were not necessarily the most preferred ones. So while most chocolate manufacturers try to innovate with new ingredients, consumers were much more moved by ideas that involved more emotional elements like relationships and love. A more detailed netnographic analysis of the comments revealed seven scenarios or 'chocolate moments' where the emotional appeal of chocolate comes through. This insight enabled the company to identify which of their own (and competitor products) 'owned' these particular moments or not! Market research like this helps to identify both new market opportunities and new ways of marketing existing products.[1]

The role of customer insights

Would the likes of New Coke, WAP technology or Google Wave not have been such disastrous failures had more or better consumer research been conducted in advance? We will never know but what is certain is that truly market-led companies recognize that they need to always be in touch with what is happening in the marketplace. Customer needs are continually changing, often in ways that are very subtle. To innovate new forms of value for customers, accurate and timely customer insights are very important. These insights can inform everything from product innovation, product design and features, advertising campaign themes and so on (see Exhibit 4.1). For example, the famous Johnnie Walker 'Keep Walking' campaign was created after research insights which showed that modern men (their key target market) increasingly saw life as one long journey. The successful television and viral advertisement featuring the Scottish actor Robert Carlyle, is over five minutes long, serving to illustrate this journey.

For some companies, no major strategic decisions are made without first researching the market. But this activity goes far beyond commercial organizations. For example, political parties and record companies are heavy users of marketing research and often stand accused of overdependence on it to shape everything from manifestos to new albums. Therefore organizations have a huge appetite for information to help them make the correct decisions. This information can play a key role in a whole variety of choices including whether there is a market for a new product, what our current customers think of our service levels, how our brands are performing in the market,

how effective our latest promotional campaign has been and so on. This chapter will examine the types of information that are available and how they can be used to assist better decision making. Given the information age that we live in, this is a crucial activity, as organizations frequently suffer more from a surplus rather than a deficit of information. Being able to intelligently sort through all the information that is potentially available and convert it into usable customer insights is an important marketing task.

As a result, the marketing research industry is a huge one, estimated to be worth over $39.08 billion globally in 2012 and $15.64 million in Europe, or 40 per cent of the total global spend.[2] Table 4.1 provides details of levels of marketing research expenditure throughout the world. Market research also tends to follow market development. For example, some of the highest growth rates for market research have been in countries like Nigeria, Kenya, Argentina and Indonesia, whose growing economies have attracted the interest of marketers.[3] The highest expenditure per capita is to be found in Europe. Defining the boundaries of marketing research is not easy. Casual discussions with customers at exhibitions or monitoring online forums can provide

Table 4.1 Global marketing research expenditure 2012 (selected countries)

Country	Turnover in US$ million	Spend per capita in US$
UK	5,076	80.26
France	2,568	40.49
Sweden	462	48.44
Germany	3,321	40.54
Norway	149	29.63
Denmark	161	28.81
USA	13,756	43.78
Switzerland	235	29.43
Australia	733	32.18
Finland	113	20.75
Netherlands	336	20.03
Ireland	93	20.20
Belgium	197	17.76
Canada	769	22.07
New Zealand	96	21.55
Japan	2,234	17.51
Italy	749	12.31
Singapore	106	19.55
China	1,651	1.22

Source: Esomar Global Market Research, 2013.

Exhibit 4.1 BT's soap opera-style campaign for broadband services was developed using customers' insights regarding the late adopters of telecommunications

 BT Ad Insight: This soap-style advertising campaign involved the public voiting on how the storyline developed.

valuable informal information about their requirements, competitor activities and future happenings in the industry. More formal approaches include the conduct of marketing research studies or the development of marketing information systems. This chapter focuses on these formal methods of information provision.

Marketing information systems

Given the wide variety of information sources that an organization can potentially access, decisions about which types of information to gather are crucial. In the main, these are driven by what questions need to be answered. For example, if a company wants to examine whether there have been any changes in attitude towards its brand following on from recent marketing activities, it may informally monitor conversations that are happening online or more formally carry out periodic market research using customer panels that track changes in how the brand is perceived. For every research question, there is always a menu of answers and the main categories of information available are shown in Figure 4.1, which outlines the components of a **marketing information system**.
A marketing information system is defined as:[4]

> *a system in which marketing information is formally gathered, stored, analysed and distributed to managers in accord with their informational needs on a regular planned basis.*

The system is built on an understanding of the information needs of marketing management, and supplies that information when, where and in the form that the manager requires it. Marketing information system (MkIS) design is important since the quality of a marketing information system has been shown to influence the effectiveness of decision-making.[5] The MkIS comprises four elements: internal market information, market intelligence, marketing research and environmental scanning (see Figure 4.1). The last

element – environmental scanning – was discussed in Chapter 2 and each of the other elements will be examined in detail in this chapter. The volume of market information and insight that is to be managed clearly shows how important it is to effectively design and use a MkIS system.

Marketing information systems should be designed to provide information and insights on a selective basis where it is useful in assisting decisions. Senior management should conspicuously support use of the system.[6] These recommendations are in line with Ackoff's view[7] that a prime task of an information system is to eliminate irrelevant information by tailoring what is provided to the individual manager's needs. It is also consistent with Kohli and Jaworski's view that a market orientation is essentially the organization-wide generation and dissemination of, and responsiveness to, market intelligence.[8]

Marketing research is more likely to be used if researchers appreciate not only the technical aspects of research, but also the need for clarity in report presentation and the political dimension of information provision. It is unlikely that marketing research reports will be used in decision-making if the results threaten the status quo or are likely to have adverse political repercussions. Therefore, perfectly valid and useful information may sometimes be ignored in decision-making for reasons other than difficulties with the way the research was conducted. However, accurate and timely customer insights are crucial to an organization becoming a truly market-led enterprise.

Internal market information

A very good place for an organization to begin answering a research problem is by looking at what information it currently already has available to it. This can take many forms. For example, personnel working in the organization such as salespeople or customer service people may have useful information regarding what is happening in the market. What is essential is that employees are motivated to share this information and that systems are put in place to record, store and make available these customer insights. Advances in information technology mean that the retention of this type of information has improved dramatically. Internal market information is particularly useful when companies want to get to know their current customers better. To do this the following techniques are used.

Marketing databases

Companies collect data on customers on an ongoing basis. The data are stored on marketing

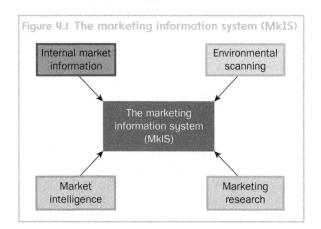

Figure 4.1 The marketing information system (MkIS)

Exhibit 4.2 Loyalty card schemes are used extensively
by organizations to build up databases of customers

Exhibit 4.2 Loyalty card schemes are used extensively
by organizations to build up databases of customers

databases, containing each customer's name, address, telephone number, past transactions and, sometimes, demographic and lifestyle data. Information on the types of purchase, frequency of purchase, purchase value and responsiveness to promotional offers may be held (see Chapter 11). For example, retailers collect these data through loyalty card schemes, which are popular with supermarkets, department stores and so on (see Exhibit 4.2). Customers collect points that can be redeemed for cash or gifts while at the same time the retailer collects valuable information about the customer each time the card is used (see Marketing in Action 4.1).

Banks have become heavy users of this type of information as they seek to manage more carefully consumers that have taken on debts such as mortgages and credit cards. Banks get information from a number of sources, including their own records, their links to other payment organizations, such as Visa and MasterCard, and specialist credit-checking agencies. Through the examination of this information, they can develop relatively accurate predictions of which customers are likely to default on a loan, or they can intervene earlier before debts become significant. For example, if consumers have switched more of their regular shopping, such as groceries, from cash to credit cards, this may indicate a cash shortage and the increased risk of a missed payment on a loan. Even consumers who opt out of loyalty card schemes can still have their purchasing patterns monitored because supermarkets, for example, can track and match debit and credit card data with till receipts.

Customer relationship management (CRM) systems

A potential problem with the growth of marketing databases is that separate ones often exist in different departments in an organization. For example, the sales department may have an account management database containing information on customers, while call-centre staff may use a different database created at a different time also containing information on customers. This fragmented approach can lead to problems, when, for example, a customer transaction is recorded on one but not the other database. Issues like this have led to the development of **customer relationship management (CRM)** systems where a single database is created from customer information to inform all staff who deal with customers. CRM is a term for the methodologies, technologies and e-commerce capabilities used by companies to manage customer relationships[9] (see Chapter 11). Good CRM systems throw up all sorts of unusual patterns in consumer behaviour, such as when Tesco found that one segment of its customers were buying beer and nappies during the same shopping trip and it was then able to target more carefully these young fathers.

The effective use of CRM allows organizations to conduct a rigorous analysis of their customers. Businesses frequently find that they are subject to the Pareto Principle or 80/20 rule, that is, that 80 per cent of their profits may come from 20 per cent of their customers. At a very simple level what this means is that some customers may be more important than others and that from a marketing point of view perhaps the company should invest more in those valuable customers. Other researchers have recommended classifying customers on the basis of their value to the organization using labels such as platinum, gold, silver and lead.[10] Silver and gold customers need to be moved up the scale while lead customers are gradually 'fired'. Customer relationship management allows firms to measure the following:

1   *Customer retention*: What proportion of customers is staying with the firm and are these the customers that it wants to retain?
2   *Customer defection*: What proportion of customers is leaving the firm? Are these the customers that firm would want to 'fire' or the ones that it would rather retain?
3   *Customer acquisition*: What proportion of new customers is arriving onto the firm's books as a result of its marketing activities?

Website analysis

Customer information can also be provided by analyzing website behaviour. Measurements of the areas of the site most frequently visited, which products are purchased and the payment method used can be made. Indeed, one of the challenges of website analysis is coping with the vast volumes of data that can be produced. Whatever the challenges of measuring the size of the audience from an advertising point of view, there are several aspects of how consumers behave while visiting a website that owners should record and monitor. First, where did they come from – for example, did they come via a search engine or from a link on another site? Second, where do they go once they are on the site? What options are selected, what visuals are viewed, and so on. How long did they spend on the website and what proportion of visitors 'bounced' away from the site within a few seconds? Did they respond to particular offers, promotions or site design changes? Most websites use Google Analytics to monitor these patterns and results are available on a daily or weekly basis (see Exhibit 4.3). And, if the company is an online retailer, what percentage of consumers proceeded to the checkout and, for those that didn't, at what stage in the buying process did they drop out?

Exhibit 4.3 Consumer behaviour on websites can be analysed using Google Analytics

Some of the key metrics for website analysis include the number of unique visitors, information on these visitors and their levels of engagement with the site. Measurement of these variables is improving all the time, although some are still open to manipulation.

Marketing in Action 4.1 Costa Coffee Club

Critical Thinking: Below is a review of a campaign conducted by Costa Coffee targeted at its Club members. Read it and critically evaluate why the promotion was so successful and the ways in which firms can use existing customer information better.

Almost all service organizations such as hairdressers, coffee shops, DIY retailers and supermarkets offer customers the opportunity to participate in a loyalty scheme or club. Some businesses use these simply as a way of rewarding regular visitors with discounts in an attempt to retain these customers. So for example, a coffee shop may have a scheme whereby every 10th coffee is free or alternatively you collect points which can be redeemed against future purchases. Increasingly even coffee shops are using sophisticated data mining to glean as much information as possible about customers in order to maximize revenues and profits. Costa Coffee used a strategy of personalized communications with its members in order to increase sales. The company has a wide variety of touch-points with its customers including in-store purchases, Facebook contact, SMS messaging and email contact. These were aggregated to develop a more accurate profile of customers ranging from

heavy, loyal users to those who were lapsing or had lapsed. Communications were tailored specifically to each of these different customer groups. For example, if heavy users visited seven times per month, double points could be offered for an eighth visit. Email was the primary means chosen as it allowed for a volume of messages at low cost and the opportunity for interaction as well as the facility to accurately measure response. Facebook was used in a similar way allowing response via SMS, Facebook or email.

The results of the campaign were significant. In-store visits increased by 47 per cent and average spend per customer rose by 50 per cent. Points redemption rates increased by 84 per cent – nine times the target set and the campaign as a whole generated £21 million in additional revenues for Costa.

Based on: Arnett (2013);[11] Direct Marketing Association (2012).[12]

Unique users (when a person visits a website) is a popular metric for measuring the number of visitors to a site. But it is problematic because 2 million unique users could mean anything from 2 million people visiting the site once, to one person visiting it 2 million times. It is impossible to know for sure. Information about website visitors is best captured by having them register to use the site where they provide details of who they are and what they are interested in. *Page views* has been a popular way of measuring website engagement but many modern websites use a technology that allows pages to update parts of themselves, such as a share-price ticker, without having to reload and redraw the rest of the page. Therefore a user spending the entire day on Yahoo! Finance, for example, counts as only one page view. Thus more emphasis is now being put on website *interactivity*. 'Duration' and 'time spent' suggest how long one or more people are interacting with a page, which in turn gives an indication of how 'engaged' they are, as does counting the number and types of comments left by visitors. We shall examine the issue of digital marketing research in more detail in Chapter 12.

Market intelligence – the 'era' of big data

Internal market information is very useful for developing deep insights about current customers but is less useful for learning about potential new customers and competitor activity. For answers to these questions, the organization needs to begin looking outward to what is happening in the marketplace. **Market intelligence** is something of a catch-all term to describe the systematic collection of data on what is happening in a market including gathering information on customers, competitors and market developments. Increasingly, the term 'big data' is used to describe the wide range of external sources of information that can be used to aid marketing decision making.[13] Everything that a modern customer does such as websites searched, social media activity, telephone use, loyalty card use, purchases made and so on leaves a trail. The collection, aggregation and analysis of all of this information is becoming increasingly sophisticated, supported by vast data storage capabilities, faster software and people equipped with the necessary analytical skills.

Big data analysis enables marketers to answer all sorts of questions about customers. Do they buy products from competitors? What other categories of products and services are they interested in? What are their hobbies and interests? For example, supermarkets might provide the credit and debit card data of their customers to an analytics firm who can then look for information that it already has on those card numbers from other companies to begin to build a profile of where customers are spending their money.[14] This can then be used to create offers designed to encourage consumers to spend more or to switch from competitors. Life insurance companies have begun to aggregate data about individuals from records like drug purchases, magazine subscriptions, credit card spending and social media activity like Facebook profiles to determine whether they have sedentary, active or risk-taking lifestyles, all which helps to determine their risk profiles. Business-to-business firms use big data to find optimal price points for the thousands of product variants that many of them offer.

A number of key characteristics have been identified to demonstrate how big data differs from other forms of data analysis that have existed up to now.[15] The first is *volume*. It is estimated that Walmart collects more than 2.5 million petabytes of data every hour from its customers' transactions. A petabyte is the equivalent of about 20 million filing cabinets worth of text. The second is *velocity*. Data provided by mobile phones, credit card transactions and consumers checking in on social media sites are now real time or almost real time. The third is *variety*. As we have seen, data are increasingly being aggregated from a wide variety of sources. However to date, big data analysis is not for everyone. For smaller organizations or those without the resources to devote to big data initiatives another source of market intelligence is secondary research.

Marketing research

If organizations cannot find the answers they are looking for through either existing internal information or market intelligence, then there is always the option of a marketing research study. **Marketing research** is defined as the systematic design, collection, analysis and reporting of data relevant to a specific marketing situation. Marketing research describes a broad range of potential activities many of which are quite different from each other and therefore it can be classified in a number of different ways. For example, distinctions are drawn between ad hoc and continuous research, custom and syndicated research and also between exploratory, descriptive and casual research.

Ad hoc and continuous research

Ad hoc research focuses on a specific marketing problem and involves the collection of data at one point in time from one sample of respondents such as a customer satisfaction study or an attitude survey.

Continuous research involves conducting the same research on the same sample repeatedly to monitor the changes that are taking place over time. This form of research plays a key role in assessing trends in the market and one of the most popular forms of continuous research is the consumer panel.

Consumer panels When large numbers of consumers are recruited to provide information on their purchases over time, together they make up a **consumer panel**. For example, a grocery panel would record the brands, pack sizes, prices and stores used for a wide range of supermarket brands. By using the same consumers over a period of time, measures of brand loyalty and switching can be achieved, together with a demographic profile of the type of person who buys particular brands. Tesco has created a Shopper Thoughts panel comprising 60,000 households some of whom are not regular Tesco customers. Part of the research process is a facility called Net Chats which is available in real time to Tesco management. Questions are posed to panel members in the morning with responses from members received by the end of the day. This complements the behavioural data available through the Tesco loyalty card programme to give the company a very complete view of the grocery shopper.

As this example shows, recent years have seen a significant growth in the use of technology in consumer panel research, with studies being conducted online or over the telephone as well as face to face. Once participants are familiar with the researchers and have indicated a willingness to participate, then these more remote research approaches can work very effectively. For example, Metro Ireland, which markets a free newspaper to Dublin commuters, set up an online panel of 2,000 18- to 44-year-old urban dwellers to which it sent six waves of questions and a series of mini-polls over 18 months. The insights derived from the panel informed Metro's decisions regarding everything from its editorial content to its marketing strategies to attract advertising.

The rapid growth of online blogs and discussion forums has given rise to a variant on the traditional customer panel. These types of discussion boards are everywhere on the Internet, discussing anything from the fat content of potato crisps to the merits of new electronic gadgets. In most instances, they have not been formally created by corporations but the frank nature of the debate that often takes place on them makes them appealing to managers (see Social Media Marketing 4.1). Some companies track these discussion groups to see what is being said about

their brands and what trends are emerging. It is also a very cost-effective form of research as much of the monitoring can be done electronically. However, because this monitoring is generally covert, it may be disturbing for participants to learn that what they have to say is being studied by companies.

Custom and syndicated research

Custom research is research that is conducted for a single organization to provide specific answers to the questions that it has. But because companies have such an appetite for market information, an industry has grown up in the provision of **syndicated or omnibus research**. This is research that is collected by firms on a regular basis and then sold to other firms. Among the most popular types of syndicated research are retail audits and television viewership panels.

Retail audits Major research firms like the Nielsen Company conduct **retail audits**. By gaining the cooperation of retail outlets (e.g. supermarkets), sales of brands can be measured by means of laser scans of barcodes on packaging, which are read at the checkout. Although brand loyalty and switching cannot be measured, retail audits can provide an accurate assessment of sales achieved by store. For example, Nielsen's BookScan service provides weekly sales data on over 300,000 titles collected from point-of-sale information from a variety of retailers.

Television viewership panels A television viewership panel measures audience size on a minute-by-minute basis. Commercial breaks can be allocated ratings points (the proportion of the target audience watching) – the currency by which television advertising is bought and judged. In the UK, the system is controlled by the Broadcasters' Audience Research Board (BARB) and run by AGB and RSMB. AGB handles the measurement process and uses 'people meters' to record whether a set is on/off, which channel is being watched and, by means of a hand console, who is watching. Because of concerns about the extent to which viewers actually watch advertising, audience measurement companies are now providing measures of the viewership of advertising breaks as well as programmes. Technological developments continue to revolutionize television audience measurement. Personal video recorders (PVRs) build up a profile of viewers' likes and dislikes, and record their favourite programmes automatically, but the box also relays every button press on its remote control back to the manufacturer, providing exact details of

Social Media Marketing 4.1 Social media and market research

Critical Thinking: Below is a review of some of the recent developments in social media research. Begin a social media conversation on a brand or topic of your choice and then monitor this conversation for a period of time. Assess what you have learned.

The rise of social media has begun to drastically change the market research landscape. Hundreds of millions of personal pages, feeds, status updates, tweets, profiles and blogs have been created and the numbers are growing all the time. To date, this potential source of market information is largely untapped but is likely to become increasingly important in the years ahead.

For example, Facebook has been described as a 'confessional' society where people are *marketing* themselves by acting out their desirable personalities. So researchers need to examine the motives behind decisions to join Facebook groups such as brand fan pages, for example. Does everyone become a Starbuck's fan for the same reason or are there different motives at play? What do the comments that they post about a brand say about it and its future prospects? Similarly, brand owners can monitor and analyse conversations on blogs or micro-blogs like Twitter. Are they broadly positive or negative? One of the most famous brand blogs became known as Dell Hell, when blogger Jeff Jarvis began writing negatively about the company and its products. What kinds of problems if any are being encountered with organizations? These types of conversations could be the genesis of anything from a new product idea to a new service solution to an advertising campaign idea. Social media sites like LinkedIn and ChubbyBrain can be used to research competitors while Google Trends and Trendpedia enable important trends to be tracked.

Conducting marketing research through social media raises many interesting possibilities. As consumers tire of being constantly surveyed and asked for their opinions, social media creates the opportunity for people to be participants in a dialogue rather than 'respondents'. Consumers are now willing to record and share information in ways never seen before, so user-generated content may be both more insightful and accurate. Comments may be more natural and spontaneous and more emotionally rich. Research techniques like netnography (online ethnography) are being developed to monitor online conversations, and social communities are being created to get a better understanding of consumer needs (see the Marketing Spotlight at the beginning of this chapter). For example, Mercedes Benz USA set up GenBenz, an online community to help it understand Generation Y who will be the Mercedes purchasers of the future. But as with offline research, issues of sampling, data collection and data analysis remain crucially important to ensure that erroneous conclusions are not drawn.

Based on: Beer (2008);[16] Cooke (2008);[17] Precourt (2010).[18]

what programmes people watch on what channels. A further challenge is presented by the growth in TV viewing on personal devices such as tablets and smartphones. Software has been developed which monitors the programming delivered from TV services like BBC iPlayer to an IP (internet protocol) address. It shows what programming is being viewed but not who is viewing it.[19]

Exploratory, descriptive and causal research

Finally, distinctions can also be drawn between exploratory, descriptive and causal research. **Exploratory research** is employed to carry out a preliminary exploration of a research area to gain some initial insights or to form some research hypotheses. It can be conducted in a variety of ways such as examining secondary data that is available, conducting a focus group interview with some key customers or depth interviews with industry experts. To develop stronger conclusions about a research problem, **descriptive research** needs to be conducted. This may involve a survey of a large sample of customers that is representative of a population as a whole and allows the researchers to be confident that their views accurately represent those of the market. Finally, **causal research** seeks to establish cause-and-effect relationships. The most popular form of causal research is experimentation where different variables are manipulated such as a packaging design or advertising theme and the effects of these changes on consumers are monitored. The processes through which these different forms of research are conducted are examined next.

Secondary research

Because the data come to the researcher 'second-hand' (i.e. other people have compiled it), it is known as **secondary research**. (When the researcher actively collects new data – for example, by interviewing respondents – this is called primary research.) Secondary research should be carried out before primary research. Without the former, an expensive primary research survey might be commissioned to provide information that is already available from secondary sources. Increasingly, a significant amount of market information is available for purchase through companies like Mintel, Euromonitor and others.

There is a very wide variety of secondary sources of data available. These include government and European Commission statistics, publishers of reports and directories on markets, countries and industries, trade associations, banks, newspapers, magazines and journals. Given the amount of potential sources of information that are available globally, for many the first port of call is an Internet search engine. The search engine business has grown dramatically in recent years and has led to expressions such as 'to google', after the popular search engine Google, entering the general lexicon. The range of sources of information available to researchers in the European Union is included in Appendix 4.1 (at the end of this chapter), which lists some of the major sources classified by research question.

Approaches to conducting marketing research

There are two main ways for a company to carry out marketing research, depending on the situation facing it. It might either carry out the work itself or employ the services of a market research agency. Where the study is small in scale, such as gathering information from libraries or interviewing a select number of industrial customers, companies may choose to conduct the work themselves. This is particularly feasible if a company has a marketing department and/or a marketing research executive on its staff. Other companies prefer to design the research themselves and then employ the services of a fieldwork agency to collect the data. Alternatively, where resources permit and the scale of the study is larger, companies may employ the services of a market research agency to conduct the research. The company will brief the agency about its market research requirements and the agency will do the rest. The typical stages involved in completing a market research study are described next; full-service agencies generally conduct all the activities described below.

The leading marketing research firms in the world are shown in Table 4.2.

Table 4.2 World's leading marketing research firms, 2012

Name	Country	Employees	Turnover (US$ million)
Nielsen Holdings NV	USA	34,000	5,429.0
The Kanter Group	UK	22,000	3,338.6
Ipsos SA	France	15,927	2,301.1
GfK SE	Germany	12,678	1,947.8
IMS Health Inc.	USA	2,580	775.0
Information Resources Inc.	USA	4,035	763.8
INTAGE Inc.	Japan	2,465	500.3
Westat, Inc.	USA	2.109	495.9
Arbitron, Inc.	USA	1,292	449.9
The NPD Group Inc.	USA	1,230	272.0

Source: Esomar, Global Market Research, 2013.

Stages in the marketing research process

Figure 4.2 provides a description of a typical marketing research process. Each of the stages illustrated will now be discussed.

Initial contact

The process usually starts with the realization that a marketing problem requires information to aid its solution. Marketing management may contact internal marketing research staff or an outside agency. Where an outside agency is being used a meeting will be arranged to discuss the nature of the problem and the client's research needs. If the client and its markets are new to the agency, some exploratory research (e.g. a quick online search for information about the client and its markets) may be conducted prior to the meeting.

Research brief

At a meeting to decide what form the research will need to take, the client explains the marketing

problem and outlines the company's research objectives. The information that should be provided for the research agency includes the following.[20]

1 *Background information*: the product's history and the competitive situation.
2 *Sources of information*: the client may have a list of industries that might be potential users of the product. This helps the researchers to define the scope of the research.
3 *The scale of the project*: is the client looking for a 'cheap and cheerful' job or a major study? This has implications for the research design and survey costs.
4 *The timetable*: when is the information required?

The client should produce a specific written **research brief**. This may be given to the research agency prior to the meeting and perhaps modified as a result of it but, without fail, should be in the hands of the agency before it produces its **research proposal**. The research brief should state the client's requirements and should be in written form so that misunderstandings are minimized.

Research proposal

A research proposal lays out what a marketing research agency promises to do for its client, and how much this will cost. Like the research brief, the proposal should be written in a way that avoids misunderstandings. A client should expect the following to be included.

1 *A statement of objectives*: to demonstrate an understanding of the client's marketing and research problems.
2 *What will be done*: an unambiguous description of the research design – including the research method, the type of sample, the sample size (if applicable) and how the fieldwork will be controlled.
3 *Timetable*: if and when a report will be produced.
4 *Costs*: how much the research will cost and what, specifically, is/is not included in those costs.

Data collection

During the main data collection phase of the study, a variety of techniques can be employed to deal with the questions under consideration. Researchers usually draw a distinction between qualitative and quantitative research. **Qualitative research**

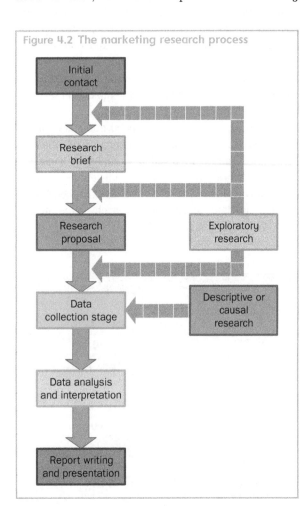

Figure 4.2 The marketing research process

Initial contact

Research brief

Research proposal — Exploratory research

Data collection stage — Descriptive or causal research

Data analysis and interpretation

Report writing and presentation

involves a semi-structured, in-depth study of small samples in order to gain deep customer insights. Some of the key qualitative techniques include focus-group interviews, depth interviews, observation studies and ethnographic research. **Quantitative research** is a structured study of small or large samples using a predetermined list of questions or criteria and the statistical analysis of findings. Typical quantitative techniques include surveys and experiments. Traditionally, qualitative research was seen as being useful during exploratory research but then needed to be supplemented by quantitative research if a descriptive study was necessary. However, this is no longer the case. The findings of many quantitative studies have proven to be erroneous while improvements in qualitative research techniques mean that they may yield more useful insights (see Table 4.3 for a breakdown of research expenditure patterns). We will now examine some of the major data collection techniques in more detail.

Focus group discussions

Focus groups involve unstructured or semi-structured discussions between a moderator or group leader, who is often a psychologist, and a group of consumers (see Exhibit 4.4). The moderator has a list of areas to cover within the topic, but allows the group considerable freedom to discuss the issues that are important to them. By arranging groups of 6–12 people to discuss their attitudes and behaviour, a good deal of knowledge may be gained about the consumer. This can be helpful when constructing

Exhibit 4.4 Focus group interviews such as this one are a very popular form of market research

questionnaires, which can be designed to focus on what is important to the respondent (as opposed to the researcher) and worded in language the respondent uses and understands. Sometimes focus groups are used to try to generate new product ideas, through the careful selection of participants who have a flair for innovation or a liking for all things new.

Focus groups take place face to face, but the rise of the Internet has led to the creation of online focus groups. The Internet offers 'communities of interests', which can take the form of chat rooms or websites dedicated to specific interests or issues (see Social Media Marketing 4.1 earlier). These are useful forums for conducting focus groups or at least for identifying suitable participants. Questions can be posed to participants who are not under

Table 4.3 Market research expenditure by type (%)*, 2012

Method	France	Germany	Holland	Ireland	Finland	Sweden	UK
Focus groups	5	4	2	15	5	7	0
Depth interview	2	3	2	5	3	7	0
Online qualitative	2	3	0	10	2	1	0
Other qualitative	2	0	6	0	1	0	9
Total qualitative	**11**	**10**	**10**	**30**	**11**	**15**	**9**
Telephone survey	10	30	15	20	24	26	9
Postal survey	2	3	6	5	10	9	5
Face-to-face	11	20	9	20	8	4	11
Online survey	22	31	36	5	32	39	27
Automated digital/electronic	27	2	0	5	8	4	0
Other quantitative	3	2	11	0	0	0	0
Total quantitative	**75**	**89**	**77**	**60**	**88**	**85**	**67**

Source: Esomar, Global Market Research, 2013.
* Figures may not add up to 100 due to rounding.

time pressure to respond. This can lead to richer insights since respondents can think deeply about the questions put to them online. Another advantage is that they can comprise people located all over the world at minimal cost. Furthermore, technological developments mean it is possible for clients to communicate secretly online with the moderator while the focus group is in session. The client can ask the moderator certain questions as a result of hearing earlier responses. Clearly, a disadvantage of online focus groups compared with the traditional form is that the body language and interaction between focus group members is missing.[21]

Depth interviews

Depth interviews involve the interviewing of individual consumers about a single topic for perhaps one or two hours. The aims are broadly similar to those of the group discussion, but depth interviews are used when the presence of other people could inhibit the expression of honest answers and viewpoints, when the topic requires individual treatment (as when discussing an individual's decision-making process) and where the individual is an expert on a particular topic. For example, depth interviews have been used to conduct research on wealthy Americans to try to understand their attitudes and opinions on money and how they spend it. This was deemed to be a method that was superior to focus groups or surveys, where it was felt that respondents would be reluctant to talk about these issues. A technique called 'snowballing' was also used, where interviewees would recommend others that they thought would be willing to participate in the research.[22]

Care has to be taken when interpreting the results of these kinds of qualitative research because the findings are usually based on small sample sizes, and the more interesting or surprising viewpoints may be disproportionately reported.

Observation

Observation research involves gathering primary data by observing people and their actions. These types of studies can be conducted in real situations such as traffic counts on public streets or in contrived situations such as hall tests where research subjects are presented with a mock shopping aisle and their behaviour is monitored. Observation studies can have a number of advantages. First, they do not rely on the respondent's willingness to provide information; second, the potential for the interviewer to bias the study is reduced; and, third, some types of information can be collected only by observation (for example, a traffic count). Observation studies are particularly popular in the retail trade where a great deal can be learned by simply watching the behaviour of shoppers in a supermarket or clothing shop. Many retail innovations including store layout and the positioning of products have arisen as a result of observation studies of consumer behaviour.

Observation studies can be conducted by either human or increasingly mechanical means, such as video recording, and may be conducted with or without the customer's knowledge. Camera phones are the latest technology to be used for observation studies, with problems arising when they are used covertly. Samsung, the world's leading manufacturer of camera phones, has even banned their use in its factories, fearing industrial espionage.[23] Some technologies allow researchers to bypass what consumers say and observe instead what they do. For example, by using eye tracking technology researchers observe which parts of an advertisement are viewed first by a subject and the design of print advertisements is greatly influenced by this kind of research. Advertisers are also extensive users of online eye tracking to monitor website behaviour and the attention paid to online display ads. Facial imaging software enables the reaction of the viewer to the advert to be measured as it can pick up smiles, frowns and so on with the result that the effectiveness of online adverts can be measured more accurately.[24] **Neuro-marketing** research, which involves observing brain responses to marketing stimuli, promises to provide an even deeper understanding of why consumers behave in the ways that they do.

Ethnographic research

One of the criticisms of research techniques like focus-group interviews is that they are somewhat contrived. Groups of people, who may or may not know each other, are brought together in boardroom-type settings and expected to provide insights into their thoughts, feelings and opinions. In such settings consumers may find it difficult or be unwilling to fully engage. As a result, many research companies are borrowing from the kinds of techniques that are employed by anthropologists and biologists, which place an emphasis on the observation of species in their natural settings. This type of research is known as **ethnographic research** and it may involve a combination of both observation and in-depth or focus-group interviewing.

In ethnographic studies, researchers decide what human behaviours they want to observe. They then go out into the field and record what consumers do, how they live their lives, how they shop, and so on (see Exhibit 4.5). For example, the UK paints brand Dulux used ethnographic research conducted in consumers' homes before launching its Perfect range of paint brushes and accessories. The research mapped the consumer journey from the anticipation when selecting colours, through to the messy decorating phase and finally to the admiration of the finished result. The research gave rise to Dulux-branded accessories such as a paint tin opener that is integrated into the brush handle (no more searching for something to open the tin), a triangular brush to make painting edges and corners easier and a soft touch grip on the metal part of the brush as this is where consumers hold it for accuracy.[25]

One of the key advantages of the ethnographic approach is that researchers often find things they didn't even realize they should have been looking for. Having recorded these activities, consumers are interviewed to try to gain insights into the motivations and attitudes that underpin their actions. When all these data have been collected, they are analysed using qualitative software packages that search for common patterns of behaviour and generate clusters of consumers. Ethnographic findings are often reported using visual as well as written means. This provides a mechanism for senior executives to get close to consumer groups they may never come into contact with in their own daily lives because of physical distance and/or social class disparities. An increasingly popular form of ethnography is online ethnographic studies or netnography (see Marketing in Action 4.2).

Exhibit 4.5 Ethnography is an increasingly popular research tool for understanding consumer behaviour

 Waitrose Ad Insight: This TV campaign featuring chef Heston Blumenthal reflects changing consumer attitudes towards home cooking and entertaining.

Surveys

Surveys remain the major market research technique (see Table 4.3) and typically involve the following key decisions.

- Who and how many people to interview: the sampling process.
- How to interview them: the survey method.
- What questions to ask: questionnaire design.

The sampling process   Figure 4.3 offers an outline of the **sampling process**. This starts with the definition of the population – that is, the group that forms the subject of study in a particular survey. The survey objective will be to provide results that are representative of this group. Sampling planners, for example, must ask questions like 'Do we interview purchasing managers in all software development firms or only those that employ more than 50 people?'

Once the population has been defined, the next step is to search for a sampling frame – that is, a list or other record of the chosen population from which a sample can be selected. Examples include the electoral register and the *Kompass* directory of companies. Researchers then choose between three major sampling methods: simple random sampling (where the sample is drawn at random and each individual has a known and equal chance of being selected); stratified random sampling (where the population is broken into groups and a random sample is drawn from each group); and quota sampling (where interviewers are instructed to ensure that the sample comprises a required number of individuals meeting pre-set conditions, such as

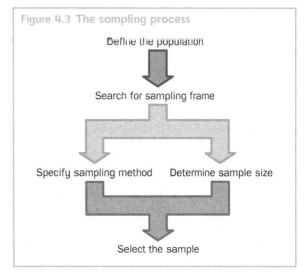

Figure 4.3 The sampling process

Define the population

↓

Search for sampling frame

Specify sampling method   Determine sample size

↓

Select the sample

Marketing in Action 4.2 Using netnography to generate new products

Critical Thinking: Below is a review of some of the netnographic research conducted in the food industry. Read it and reflect on the advantages and disadvantages of netnography as a research tool.

Symrise is a German company that is a major global supplier of flavours and fragrances for the food industry as well as cosmetic active ingredients and other raw materials. Its customers range from manufacturers in the food and beverage sector as well as the makers of nutritional supplements and also the cosmetic and pharmaceutical industries. As a B2B company, it competes with several large global rivals such as International Flavors and Fragrances, but it has sought to differentiate itself by investing in end-consumer research primarily through the means of netnography.

For example, one of its studies looked at the area of healthy nutrition and particularly the issue that many consumers perceive diet products as not tasting good. A total of 249 communities and blogs were identified and of these 16 were selected for examination in greater detail, including chefkoch.de (the largest German food community), cookinglight.com (a community for healthy living and eating) and egullet.com (a forum for gourmet food). From the thousands of posts reviewed, some key insights emerging included that more consumers wanted natural food and felt that the inclusion of artificial ingredients had got out of control; that 'light' products were a fake – when one ingredient was reduced, another was increased; that the fewer ingredients listed the better; and that many convenience foods were over-flavoured so that people have forgotten what food should taste like. These insights were used to develop a product called SymLife Sweet, an agent that enabled manufacturers to bring out the natural flavour of the food and reduce the need for added sugar. A similar analysis of the citrus drinks sector led to the development of a product called Homemade Lemonade as the netnographic research showed a strong consumer connection to homemade drinks that people had consumed as children.

Not only did the research lead to the development of new products, it also generated ideas regarding how these products should be marketed by food companies. For example, the concept of Alpine Cabin Life was used to support the marketing of SymLife Sweet as the image of natural, healthy mountain living had come through strongly in the research. This enhanced knowledge of the end consumer was a significant advantage to Symrise over its rivals. As well as providing new products for its customers, it was able to utilize its market knowledge to provide additional services such as advice and intelligence on how products should be positioned and marketed for maximum success.

Based on: Huck et al (2010).[26]

a set percentage of small, medium-sized and large companies).

Finally, the researcher must select an appropriate sample size. The larger the sample size the more likely it is that the sample will represent the population. Statistical theory allows the calculation of sampling error (i.e. the error caused by not interviewing everyone in the population) for various sample sizes. In practice, the number of people interviewed is based on a balance between sampling error and cost considerations. Fortunately, sample sizes of around 1,000 (or fewer) can provide measurements that have tolerable error levels when representing populations counted in their millions.

The survey method   Four options are available to those choosing a survey method: face-to-face interviews, telephone interviews, mail surveys or

Table 4.4 A comparison of survey methods

	Face to face	Telephone	Mail	Online
Questionnaire				
Use of open-ended questions	High	Medium	Low	Low
Ability to probe	High	Medium	Low	Low
Use of visual aids	High	Poor	High	High
Sensitive questions	Medium	Low	High	Low
Resources				
Cost	High	Medium	Low	Low
Sampling				
Widely dispersed populations	Low	Medium	High	High
Response rates	High	Medium	Low	Low
Experimental control	High	Medium	Low	Low
Interviewing				
Control of who completes questionnaire	High	High	Low	Low/high
Interviewer bias	Possible	Possible	Low	Low

online surveys. Each method has its own strengths and limitations. Table 4.4 gives an overview of these.

A major advantage of face-to-face interviews is that response rates are generally higher than for telephone interviews or mail surveys.[27] It seems that the personal element in the contact makes refusal less likely. Face-to-face interviews are more versatile than telephone and mail surveys. The use of many open-ended questions on a mail survey would lower response rates[28] and time restrictions for telephone interviews would limit their use. Probing for more detail is easier with face-to-face interviews. A certain degree of probing can be achieved with a telephone interview, but time pressure and the less personalized situation will inevitably limit its use.

Face-to-face interviews do, however, have their drawbacks. They are more expensive than telephone, mail and Internet surveys. The presence of an interviewer can cause bias (e.g. socially desirable answers) and lead to the misreporting of sensitive information. For example, O'Dell[29] found that only 17 per cent of respondents admitted borrowing money from a bank in a face-to-face interview compared with 42 per cent in a comparable mail survey.

In some ways, telephone interviews are a halfway house between face-to-face and mail surveys. They generally have a higher response rate than mail questionnaires but a lower rate than face-to-face interviews; their cost is usually three-quarters of that for face-to-face but higher than for mail surveys; and they allow a degree of flexibility when interviewing.

However, the use of visual aids is not possible and there are limits to the number of questions that can be asked before respondents either terminate the interview or give quick (invalid) answers in order to speed up the process. The use of computer-aided telephone interviewing (CATI) is growing. Centrally located interviewers read questions from a computer monitor and input answers immediately. Routing through the questionnaire is computer-controlled, thus assisting the process of interviewing.

Given a reasonable response rate, mail survey research is normally a very economical method of conducting research. However, the major problem is the potential for low response rates and the accompanying danger of an unrepresentative sample. Nevertheless, using a systematic approach to the design of a mail survey, such as the total design method (TDM),[30] has been found to have a very positive effect on response rates. The TDM recommends, as ways of improving response rates, both the careful design of questionnaires to make them easy to complete, as well as accompanying them with a personalized covering letter emphasizing the importance of the research. Studies using the TDM on commercial populations have generated high response rates.[31]

Online research is now the most popular method of conducting research, accounting for 23 per cent of all expenditure globally. The countries with the highest spend on online research as a percentage of total spend include Bulgaria (45 per cent), Canada (40 per cent), Japan (46 per cent) and Australia

(40 per cent each).[32] The Internet questionnaire is usually administered by email or signals its presence on a website by registering key words or using banner advertising on search engines to drive people to the questionnaire. The major advantage of the Internet as a marketing research vehicle is its low cost, since printing and postal costs are eliminated, making it even cheaper than mail surveys. In other ways, its characteristics are similar to mail surveys: the use of open-ended questions is limited; control over who completes the questionnaire is low; interviewer bias is low; and response rates are likely to be lower than for face-to-face and telephone interviews.

When response is by email, the identity of the respondent will automatically be sent to the survey company. This lack of anonymity may restrict the respondent's willingness to answer sensitive questions honestly. A strength of the Internet survey is its ability to cover global populations at low cost, although sampling problems can arise because of the skewed nature of Internet users. These tend to be from the younger and more affluent groups in society. For surveys requiring a cross-sectional sample this can be severely restricting.

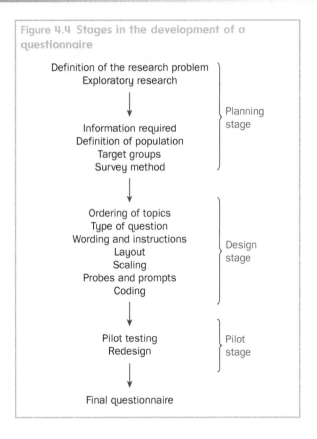

Figure 4.4 Stages in the development of a questionnaire

Questionnaire design   To obtain a true response to a question, three conditions are necessary. First, respondents must understand the question; second, they must be able to provide the information; and, third, they must be willing to provide it. Figure 4.4 shows the three stages in the development of the questionnaire: planning, design and pilot.

The planning stage involves the types of decision discussed so far in this chapter. It provides a firm foundation for designing a questionnaire, which provides relevant information for the marketing problem that is being addressed.

The design stage deals with the actual construction of the survey instrument and involves a number of important decisions. The first relates to the ordering of topics. It is sensible to start with easy-to-answer questions, in order to relax the respondent, and leave sensitive questions until last. Effective questionnaires are well structured and have a logical flow. Second, the type of question needs to be decided. Generally, three types are used: dichotomous questions (allow two possible answers, such as 'Yes'/'No'), multiple-choice questions, which allow more than two answers, and open questions, where the respondents answer by expressing their opinions.

Great care needs to be taken with both the wording and instructions used in the questionnaire and its layout. Questionnaire designers need to guard against asking ambiguous or leading questions, and

using unfamiliar words (see Table 4.5). In terms of layout, the questionnaire should not appear cluttered and, where possible, answers and codes should each form a column so that they are easy to identify.

The use of 'scales' is very common in questionnaire design. For example, respondents are given lists of statements (e.g. 'My company's marketing information system allows me to make better decisions') followed by a choice of five positions on a scale ranging from 'strongly agree' to 'strongly disagree'. 'Probes' are used to explore or clarify what a respondent has said. Following a question about awareness of brand names, the exploratory probe 'Any others?' would seek to identify further names. Sometimes respondents use vague words or phrases like 'I like going on holiday because it is nice'. A clarifying probe such as 'In what way is it nice?' would seek a more meaningful response. 'Prompts', on the other hand, aid responses to a question. For example, in an aided recall question, a list of brand names would be provided for the respondent. Coding involves the assignment of numbers to specific responses in order to facilitate analysis of the questionnaire later on.

Once the preliminary questionnaire has been designed it should be piloted with a representative

Table 4.5 Poorly worded questions

Question	Problem and solution
What type of wine do you prefer?	'Type' is ambiguous: respondents could say 'French', 'red' or 'claret', say, depending on their interpretation. Showing the respondent a list and asking 'from this list . . .' would avoid the problem
Do you think that prices are cheaper at Asda than at Aldi?	Leading question favouring Asda; a better question would be 'Do you think that prices at Asda are higher, lower or about the same as at Aldi?' Names should be reversed for half the sample
Which is more powerful and kind to your hands: Ariel or Bold?	Two questions in one: Ariel may be more powerful but Bold may be kinder to the hands. Ask the two questions separately
Do you find it paradoxical that X lasts longer and yet is cheaper than Y?	Unfamiliar word: a study has shown that less than a quarter of the population understand such words as paradoxical, chronological or facility. Test understanding before use

subsample, to test for faults. Piloting tests the questionnaire design and helps to estimate costs. Face-to-face piloting, where respondents are asked to answer questions and comment on any problems concerning a questionnaire read out by an interviewer, is preferable to impersonal piloting where the questionnaire is given to respondents for self-completion and they are asked to write down any problems found.[33] Once the pilot work proves satisfactory, the final questionnaire can be administered to the chosen sample.

Data analysis and interpretation   Basic analysis of questionnaire data may be at the descriptive level (e.g. means, frequency tables and standard deviations) or on a comparative basis (e.g. t-tests and cross-tabulations). More sophisticated analysis may search for relationships (e.g. regression analysis), group respondents (e.g. cluster analysis), or establish cause and effect (e.g. analysis of variance techniques used on experimental data).

When interpreting marketing research results, great care must be taken. One common failing is to infer cause and effect when only association has been established. For example, establishing a relationship that sales rise when advertising levels increase does not necessarily mean that raising advertising expenditure will lead to an increase in sales. Other marketing variables (e.g. sales force effect) may have increased at the same time as the increase in advertising. A second cautionary note concerns the interpretation of means and percentages. Given that a sample has been taken, any mean or percentage is an estimate subject to 'sampling error' – that is, an error in an estimate due to taking a sample rather than interviewing the entire population. A market research survey which estimates that 50 per cent of males but only 45 per cent of females smoke, does not necessarily suggest that smoking is more prevalent among males. Given the sampling error associated with each estimate, the true conclusion might be that there is no difference between males and females.

Report writing and presentation   Crouch suggests that the key elements in a research report are as follows:[34]

1   title page
2   list of contents
3   preface – outline of agreed brief, statement of objectives, scope and methods of research
4   summary of conclusions and recommendations
5   previous related research – how previous research has had a bearing on this research
6   research method
7   research findings
8   conclusions
9   appendices.

Sections 1–4 provide a concise description of the nature and outcomes of the research for busy managers. Sections 5–9 provide the level of detail necessary if any particular issue (e.g. the basis of a finding, or the analytical technique used) needs checking. The report should be written in language the reader will understand; jargon should be avoided.

Good decision making is at the heart of effective marketing. The ability to understand customer needs, to design products and services to meet those needs and to develop appropriate ways of communicating with customers all require timely and accurate market information. But marketing research is also not without its societal problems and some of these issues are raised in Marketing and Society 4.1.

Marketing and Society 4.1 Market research – fact or fiction?

Market research is one of the most visible faces of marketing. At some stage or other, nearly everyone participates in a survey, whether it is in a retail environment, a university or at home via telephone, post or, increasingly, by pressing the red button on their television remote controls. Consumers are also invited to participate in focus groups, depth interviews and ethnographic research. While all this research provides answers, it also seems to be raising some very fundamental questions.

The first concerns the widespread usage to which research is being put. It is virtually impossible now to pick up a newspaper or watch the television without seeing the results of some survey or other being presented. It may be about the most mundane of matters, such as how much time is spent cleaning the kitchen floor or who people think is the most eligible film star. The more outrageous the survey or its findings, the more likely it is to be picked up by news bulletins or discussed on radio talk shows. In other words, surveys have become the news and for 24-hour news channels they represent a relatively cheap and useful time filler. For example, many people missed the irony of Sky News charging viewers to vote by text on whether they thought they were paying too much for their mobile phone bills.

The sheer prevalence of surveys and their findings raises two other fundamental questions: who sponsored the study and how was it conducted? The former is crucial because it demonstrates that many of the surveys in the media are, in truth, public relations pieces being put out by particular companies or brands. For example, our floor cleaning survey is likely to have originated from a cleaning products company; that the majority of workers favour emailing colleagues over face-to-face meetings is likely to come from a business communications company, and so on. Sometimes, this can be relatively harmless fun but in other instances it can be very serious if the subject matter relates to food, family health and the like. The surfeit of visual, audio and print media means that there is always an outlet for these kinds of PR exercises. The consumer should take care to know who sponsored any study that receives media coverage.

After reading this chapter, you should also be critical of how studies are being conducted. What were the sampling frame and the sample size? Are the findings valid (the research measured what it intended to measure), reliable (similar findings would be found if the study was repeated) and representative (the study accurately represents the larger population)? For all the survey findings that are presented regularly, this type of detail rarely is. In its absence, it is impossible to conclude that the research was conducted scientifically. Unfortunately, time-pressed consumers rarely seek out this information and tend to take survey results at face value.

Market research suffers from other problems, too. In some instances it is used to gather competitor intelligence. Questionable practices include using student projects to gather information without the student revealing the identity of the sponsor of the research, pretending to be a potential supplier who is conducting a telephone survey to understand the market, posing as a potential customer at an exhibition, bribing a competitor's employee to pass on proprietary information, and covert surveillance such as through the use of hidden cameras. The practice of selling in the guise of marketing research, commonly known as 'sugging', also occurs from time to time. Despite the fact that it is not usually practised by bona fide marketing research agencies but, rather, unscrupulous selling companies who use marketing research as a means of gaining compliance to their requests, it is the marketing research industry that suffers from its aftermath.

Market research is an important vehicle by which organizations can learn more about their customers, and develop products and services that meet their needs. Properly conducted, it can yield invaluable insights, and can be the difference between success and failure in business. But its reputation is being sullied by the prevalence of 'bogus' surveys and other questionable practices. This raises the issue of whether research deals with the facts or is an exercise in fiction.

Reflection: Select any three studies that you have heard or seen being publicized in the media. Investigate them and evaluate the quality of the research that has been undertaken using the criteria discussed above.

Summary

This chapter has examined the nature and role of marketing information and customer insights. The following key issues were addressed.

1. The importance of marketing research and customer insights: customer insights are key if an organization is to be truly market-led. They can provide answers to all sorts of marketing questions that the organization may face.

2. The nature of marketing information systems: these are systems in which marketing information is formally gathered, stored and distributed on a regular, planned basis.

3. The three main types of market information: internal market information involves the collection and examination of data available internally to the organization; market intelligence involves the gathering of information on what is happening in the marketplace generally; while marketing research is conducted to examine specific research questions that the firm has.

4. The term 'big data' refers to the collection, aggregation and analysis of data from multiple sources in order to aid marketing decision making. The availability and suitability of new technologies has given rise to an increased use of this type of information.

5. The approaches to conducting research: marketing research can be conducted either by the organization itself or by employing the services of a professional marketing research firm. Large-scale, complex research work is best conducted by a professional firm.

6. The stages in the market research process: these include initial contact, the research brief, the research proposal, exploratory research, the main data collection phase, data analysis and report writing/presentation.

7. Qualitative research techniques: a range of semi-structured research techniques including focus groups, depth interviews, observation studies, ethnographic research and so on.

8. The four main survey methods, namely face-to-face, telephone, mail and Internet: each has its unique advantages and disadvantages, and the decision as to which to use should be guided by the nature of the study, the respondents and the cost.

Study questions

1. What are the differences between qualitative and quantitative research? Explain the roles played by each.
2. Outline the main stages in the marketing research process, identifying particularly the kinds of difficulties that might be faced at each stage.
3. Market research is being trivialized by the number of surveys that are being reported in the media. Discuss.
4. Many firms are now investing heavily in analysing their own customers through CRM and website analysis. What are the advantages and disadvantages of this trend for both firms and consumers?
5. Discuss the recent rise of ethnography and netnography as methods to study consumer behaviour. What are the ethical implications of these approaches?
6. Visit www.surveymonkey.com and learn about how to create and administer a survey.

Suggested reading

Carson, D., A. Gilmore and K. Gronhaug (2001) *Qualitative Marketing Research*, London: Sage Publications.

Graves, P. (2010) *Consumerology*, London: Nicholas Brealey.

McAfee, A. and E. Brynjolfsson (2012), Big Data: The Management Revolution, *Harvard Business Review*, **90** (10), 60–8.

McDonald, E., H. Wilson and U. Konus (2012) Better Customer Insights – In Real Time, *Harvard Business Review*, **90** (9) 102–108.

Poynter, R. (2010) *The Handbook of Online and Social Media Research: Tools and Techniques for Market Researchers*, London: John Wiley & Sons.

Ulwick, A. and L. Bettencourt (2008) Giving Customers a Fair Hearing, *Sloan Management Review*, **49** (3), 62–8.

When you have read this chapter

log on to the Online Learning Centre for
Foundations of Marketing at
www.mheducation.co.uk/textbooks/fahy5
where you'll find links and extra online study tools for marketing.

References

1. **Jawecki, G., J. Gebauer** and **S. Mathis-Alig** (2013) How Netnography Can Be Used to Unlock the Full Potential of Crowdsourcing Contests: The Case of the Mondelez Chocolate Lovers Contest, Esomar World Research: Warc.com.

2. **Esomar** (2013) *Global Market Research.*

3. **Esomar** (2013) *Global Market Research.*

4. **Jobber, D.** and **C. Rainbow** (1977) A Study of the Development and Implementation of Marketing Information Systems in British Industry, *Journal of the Marketing Research Society,* **19** (3), 104–11.

5. **Van Bruggen, A., A. Smidts** and **B. Wierenga** (1996) The Impact of the Quality of a Marketing Decision Support System: An Experimental Study, *International Journal of Research in Marketing,* **13**, 331–43.

6. **Piercy, N.** and **M. Evans** (1983) *Managing Marketing Information,* Beckenham: Croom Helm.

7. **Ackoff, R.L.** (1967) Management Misinformation Systems, *Management Science,* **14** (4), 147–56.

8. **Kohli, A.** and **B. Jaworski** (1990) Market Orientation: The Construct, Research Propositions and Marketing Implications, *Journal of Marketing,* **54**, 1–18.

9. **Foss, B.** and **M. Stone** (2001) *Successful Customer Relationship Marketing,* London: Kogan Page.

10. **Zeithaml, V., R. Rust** and **K. Lemon** (2001) The Customer Pyramid: Creating and Serving Profitable Customers, *California Management Review,* **43** (4), 118–42.

11. **Arnett, G.** (2013) Are Loyalty Cards Really Worth It?, *Guardian.co.uk,* 31 October.

12. **Direct Marketing Association** (2012) Costa Coffee Club Loyalty Programme, Warc.com.

13. **Davenport, T.** (2006) Competing on Analytics, *Harvard Business Review,* **84** (1), 98–107.

14. **Ferguson, D.** (2013) How Supermarkets Get Your Data – and What They Do with It, *The Guardian.co.uk,* 8 June.

15. **McAfee, A.** and **E. Brynjolfsson** (2012), Big Data: The Management Revolution, *Harvard Business Review,* **90** (10), 60–8.

16. **Beer, D.** (2008) Researching a Confessional Society, *International Journal of Market Research,* **50** (5), 619–29.

17. **Cooke, M.** (2008) The New World of Web 2.0 Research, *International Journal of Market Research,* **50** (5), 569–72.

18. **Precourt, G.** (2010) Mercedes Benz USA: The Move from Traditional Research to Consumer Communities, Warc.com.

19. **Asquith, R.** (2014) Why Multi-screen Television Moves the Audience Measurement Goalposts, *Guardian.co.uk,* 15 May.

20. **Crouch, S.** and **M. Housden** (1999) *Marketing Research for Managers,* Oxford: Butterworth Heinemann, 253.

21. **Gray, R.** (1999) Tracking the Online Audience, *Marketing,* 18 February, 41–3.

22. **Birchall, J.** (2005) Rich, But Not Fortune's Fools, *Financial Times,* 13 December, 13.

23. **Harper, J.** (2003) Camera Phones Cross Moral, Legal Lines, *Washington Times,* Business, 15 July, 6.

24. **Anonymous** (2011) The All-Telling Eye, *Economist,* 22 October, 90–91.

25. **Design Business Association** (2012) Dulux Perfect Accessories, Warc.com.

26. **Huck, S., J. Jonas, A. Grunhagen** and **C. Lichter** (2010), Listening to Social Media from a B2B2C Perspective: How to Strengthen the Competitive Role as 'Preferred Supplier' with Netnography, Esomar: Warc.com.

27. **Yu, J.** and **H. Cooper** (1983) A Quantitative Review of Research Design Effects on Response Rates to Questionnaires, *Journal of Marketing Research,* 20 February, 156–64.

28. **Falthzik, A.** and **S. Carroll** (1971) Rate of Return for Close v Open-ended Questions in a Mail Survey of Industrial Organisations, *Psychological Reports,* **29**, 1121–2.

29. **O'Dell, W.F.** (1962) Personal Interviews or Mail Panels?, *Journal of Marketing,* **26**, 34–9.

30. **Dillman, D.** (1978) *Mail and Telephone Surveys: The Total Design Method,* New York: John Wiley & Sons.

31. See **Fahy, J.** (1998) Improving Response Rates in Cross-cultural Mail Surveys, *Industrial Marketing Management,* **27** (November), 459–67; **Walker, B., W. Kirchmann** and **J. Conant** (1987) A Method to Improve Response Rates in Industrial Mail Surveys, *Industrial Marketing Management,* **16** (November), 305–14.

32. **Esomar** (2013) *Global Market Research.*

33. **Reynolds, N.** and **A. Diamantopoulos** (1998) The Effect of Pretest Method on Error Detection Rates: Experimental Evidence, *European Journal of Marketing,* **32** (5/6), 480–98.

34. **Crouch, S.** (1992) *Marketing Research for Managers,* Oxford: Butterworth Heinemann, 253.

Appendix 4.1: Sources of European marketing information

Is there a survey of the industry?

Euromonitor GMID Database has in-depth analysis and current market information in the key areas of country data, consumer lifestyles, market sizes, forecasts, brand and country information, business information sources and marketing profiles.

Reuters Business Insight Reports are full-text reports available online in the sectors of healthcare, financial services, consumer goods, energy, e-commerce and technology.

Key Note Reports cover size of market, economic trends, prospects and company performance.

Mintel Premier Reports cover market trends, prospects and company performance.

Snapshots on CD-Rom The 'Snapshots' CD series is a complete library of market research reports, providing coverage of consumer, business-to-business and industrial markets. Containing 2,000 market research reports, this series provides incisive data and analysis on over 8,000 market segments for the UK, Europe and the USA.

British Library Market Research is a guide to British Library Holdings. It lists titles of reports arranged by industry. Some items are available on inter-library loan; others may be seen at the British Library in London.

International Directory of Published Market Research, published by Marketsearch.

How large is the market?

European Marketing Data and Statistics Now available on the Euromonitor GMID database.

International Marketing Data and Statistics Now available on the Euromonitor GMID database.

CEO Bulletin

A–Z of UK Marketing Data

European Marketing Pocket Book

The Asia Pacific Marketing Pocket Book

The Americas Marketing Pocket Book

Where is the market?

Regional Marketing Pocket Book

Regional Trends gives the main economic and social statistics for UK regions.

Geodemographic Pocket Book

Who are the competitors?

British companies can be identified using any of the following:

Kompass (most European countries have their own edition)

Key British Enterprises

Quarterly Review – KPMG

Sell's Products and Services Directory (Gen Ref E 380.02542 SEL)

For more detailed company information consult the following:

Companies Annual Report Collection Carol: Company Annual Reports online at www.carol.co.uk

Fame DVD (CD-Rom service)

Business Ratio Reports

Retail Rankings

Overseas companies sources include:

Asia's 7,500 Largest Companies

D&B Europa

Dun's Asia Pacific Key Business Enterprises

Europe's 15,000 Largest Companies

Major Companies of the Arab World

Million Dollar Directory (US)

Principal International Businesses

What are the trends?

Possible sources to consider include the following:

The Book of European Forecasts Now available on the Euromonitor GMID database.

Marketing in Europe

European Trends

Consumer Europe Now available on the Euromonitor GMID database

Consumer Goods Europe

Family Expenditure Survey

Social Trends

Lifestyle Pocket Book

Drink Trends

Media Pocket Book

Retail Business

Mintel Market Intelligence

OECD (Organisation for Economic Co-operation and Development)

EU statistical and information sources

'Eurostat' is a series of publications that provide a detailed picture of the EU; they can be obtained by visiting European Documentation Centres (often in university libraries) in all EU countries; themes include general statistics, economy and finance, and population/social conditions.

Eurostat Yearbook

European Access is a bulletin on issues, policies, activities and events concerning EU member states.

Marketing and Research Today is a journal that examines social, political, economic and business issues relating to Western, Central and Eastern Europe.

European Report is a twice-weekly news publication from Brussels on industrial, economic and political issues.

Abstracts and indexes

Business Periodicals Index

ANBAR Marketing and Distribution Abstracts

ABI Inform

Research Index

Times Index

Elsevier Science Direct

Emerald

Wiley Interscience and Boldideas

Guides to sources

A great variety of published information sources exists; the following source guides may help you in your search:

Marketing Information

Guide to European Marketing Information

Compendium of Marketing Information Sources

Croner's A–Z of Business Information Sources

McCarthy Cards: a card service on which are reproduced extracts from the press covering companies and industries; it also produces a useful guide to its sources: *UK and Europe Market Information: Basic Sources*

Statistics

Guide to Official Statistics
Sources of the Unofficial UK Statistics

Sources: the authors thank the University of Bradford School of Management Library for help in compiling this list.

4

H&M and social media: an effective market research tool

Introduction

Sweden's Hennes & Mauritz AB, more commonly known as H&M, is a retail clothing powerhouse, famous for its reasonably priced 'fast fashion'. With six different brands sold in 3,300 stores spread out over 54 countries, the company is second only in size to its direct competitor Zara.

H&M has been ranked as one of the world's top 25 brands. It achieved this level of recognition not by luck, but rather by effective marketing and branding efforts, using and implementing the latest technology available, and carrying out good market research. In addition to its online website, the company communicates and interacts with customers through its huge social media presence. People can follow the latest fashion (and non-fashion) developments at H&M on Facebook, Twitter, Instagram, YouTube, Google+ and Pinterest, as well as on their mobile phones through apps for iPhone and Android. H&M also has a presence on China's social networks by way of Youku and Sina Weibo and via Russia's VKontakte.

As part of its marketing and branding efforts, H&M developed a social media strategy, a key component of which

states that through the effective use of social media 'millions of H&M fans and followers share ideas and opinions and get quick answers to their queries'. This allows the company to get closer to its customers, allowing for better communication and feedback, and (it is hoped) more useful marketing data. H&M collects massive amounts of raw (and technically, anonymous) information through the use of such data analysis tools as Google Analytics and Core Metrics. What allows H&M to do this is something known as 'cookies'. These are text files that are created every time you visit a particular website, and they can contain useful and valuable information about your interests and shopping habits.

The benefit of social media is that H&M can get out its message and promote its brand, while at the same time it can gather, store and interpret huge amounts of data (often referred to as 'big data'). Looking at the numbers and statistics one can't help but be amazed at the results H&M has achieved. The company has more than 14 million fans on its Facebook page alone, where it regularly posts updates promoting new products and lets customers know about upcoming promotions. It also has contests where entrants can win prizes. In addition, H&M

live streams runway fashion shows, giving fans 'an exclusive front row seat'. By keeping its Facebook page fun and dynamic, H&M enjoys a high level of interaction with customers. What seems to get people's attention the most, however, are the photo gallery updates. These normally attain 30,000 'likes' and are commented on by hundreds of people. Facebook entries result in the generation of an enormous amount of information. Studies have shown that Facebook conversations can give an indication as to the future demand and trends for a variety of products and services. An analysis of this data could very well assist H&M in identifying where fashion styles are heading and help it make more accurate forecasts regarding material needs (allowing for more efficient sourcing decisions). Furthermore, by using advanced statistical analysis on its Facebook page data, it was determined that a high level of interaction and use by people on Facebook was positively correlated with quarterly sales at H&M.

The company is extremely popular on Pinterest as well, with users interacting with the H&M brand 145,000 times in one month alone back in 2013. But an analysis of these interactions shows that there is a major problem. Many of the photos, videos and other objects that users 'pinned' to their pinboards sent people to dead H&M links when they were clicked on. In just one example, a popular pair of H&M shoes was shared almost 2,700 times among users in only in 30 days. But the link for the shoes led to a webpage that informed you that 'this item is no longer available'. Unfortunately, 'Pinterest is driving a ton of people to [H&M's] website, but they can't buy anything when they get there,' says Apu Gupta, CEO of a Pinterest data analytics firm called Curalate. Pinterest has an array of powerful analytical tools. Companies can track and monitor Pin activity, allowing them to identify and analyse trends over a given period of time. It is also possible to find out which Pins are the most popular, which ones get shared the most, who exactly interacts with them and what people associate them with. What is puzzling is that Pinterest appears to be providing a massive amount of research data regarding what is popular and what is in demand, and that H&M is not utilizing it to its full potential. This marketing data could provide insight into what customers want, what other products they might want or need, and potential markets and customers that are presently not being satisfied. This could very well be resulting in a huge amount of lost sales, in addition to a diminishing of H&M's brand among some users.

The company has also received criticism over the way it uses its Twitter feed. While seen as being efficient when it comes to posting new product and promotion information, there are complaints that the site is lacking when it comes to responding to comments or queries that users post. Research shows that H&M generally answers between five and 10 comments a day (with most of the company's responses directing users to a dedicated customer service link). This in comparison to the hundreds of customers that companies like ASOS and Nike respond to every single day. Twitter, like almost all social media outlets, has powerful analytical tools for collecting and analysing data as well. The relative lack of interaction and engagement on the part of H&M could be interpreted as a missed opportunity to 'talk' to its customers in order to gain useful insights and qualitative marketing data. One recent Twitter bright spot, however, was a Q&A session hosted by H&M 'brand ambassador' David Beckham. The legendary football player answered about 30 questions from fans, with the event being generally well received.

H&M's use of Google+, Google's social networking site that is meant to (eventually) compete with Facebook, appears to be another social media and marketing research success story. H&M has been able to gather over 2.5 million fans, making it one of the most followed brands on the service. It accomplished this through its colourful and well designed 'G+ page', which receives daily updates. The goal, according to Miriam Tappert, global social media manager at H&M, is not to duplicate the experience one would have shopping at an H&M store or online at the company's website. Rather, H&M simply wanted to 'be where our customers are, have a dialogue and share the latest fashion'. By partnering with Google it is hoped that H&M will gain access to Google's technology as well as its massive amount of market data. One powerful component of Google+ is its 'Ripples' feature. This allows companies to create interactive graphics showing how users of their G+ sites are sharing information found on those sites. This in effect allows companies to see how information 'ripples' across a network, an important marketing research tool that lets H&M see who is using its information and who possible new customers might be. It also tells them, practically in real-time, just how effective a particular marketing campaign is. This could then allow H&M to analyse the information it is receiving and make any needed adjustments to its marketing strategy. Based on their market analysis, the company could perhaps extend a successful product line or introduce a whole new range of products to attract new customers who previously were not interested in H&M (market research shows that once a consumer identifies with a fast fashion brand, they are more receptive to new product offerings from that same brand). Conversely, H&M could more quickly end unpopular promotional campaigns or product lines. As a result of effectively using all that Google has to offer, it has been reported that H&M has achieved an impressive 22 per cent increase in click-through rates.

But while H&M reportedly makes an effort to provide unique content for Google+, some critics say that a lot of what is on offer appears to be duplicated across its Facebook page, meaning that there really isn't a reason why a person would follow both. Some also note that while H&M has a large number of fans on G+, the actual interaction between people and the Google site is actually relatively low.

H&M has found other ways to use technology to connect with its customers and collect market data, entering into a partnership with the online game MyTown. This arrangement allows the company to collect information as to where a player of the game is located. If the person is playing the game on a mobile device in close proximity to an H&M store, they are awarded virtual clothing and bonus points. If they use their mobile device to scan certain products in the store, they have a chance to win prizes. A preliminary analysis of the market data received showed that of 700,000 customers who visited the game online, 300,000 eventually went to an H&M store where they scanned an item.

Another example of the power of data and its analysis come from the example of Citibank, the US financial services giant. Banks are in the enviable position of having huge amounts of information regarding the economic well-being of cities, regions and countries, and can quickly detect trends or changes in commercial activity. Citibank makes this information available to companies like H&M (and, unfortunately, Zara) for a price, in order to help them identify the best locations for new stores and centres of production.

The importance of current market research data can be further highlighted by H&M's activities with regard to social responsibility. Many studies have shown that people are becoming increasingly concerned about the environment, global warming and the future of the planet, as well as the future of the human species. Even in the USA, research shows that a majority of Americans are more concerned about the environment than they are about the economy. H&M has positioned itself well to take advantage of these studies and the data generated. The company is using social media to promote the fact that it is a responsible corporate citizen and concerned about the environment. It recently started a programme called 'Conscious', which promotes the recycling of old clothes. H&M is asking customers to bring into its stores any unwanted clothes, from any brand and in any condition, so that they can be recycled. But there is also a business side to this initiative. The company is simultaneously promoting its 'Conscious' line of clothing, which is made from environmentally sustainable material. Oddly enough, the environmental initiative was first promoted through a printed media campaign. Laura Maggs, H&M's sustainability manager, says that many people are unaware of the programme, but hopefully that will change once a planned social media campaign fully kicks in. The company is optimistic that what will be good for the planet will also be good for the H&M brand. And that a whole new market will open up as a result, providing new opportunities for revenue streams.

But H&M has found out that, while an excellent market research tool, there is also a dark side to social media. And that while good news travels slowly, bad news travels like wildfire. In spite of all of its efforts at research, data analysis and attempts at better understanding its customers, H&M has had to face several crises.

Social media and the spread of controversy

In early 2013 H&M found out just how powerful social media could be, to its detriment. Julia, a 21-year-old Swedish woman, had recently become upset over H&M's decision to sell a shirt with the face of the deceased rap star Tupac Shakur on it. She posted a negative comment on H&M's Facebook page, saying that selling a shirt with the face of a man who was convicted of sexually abusing a woman might not be the best thing for the company's image. The woman's comment received over 2,800 responses, many of them negative and some of them extremely violent, stating that she should be sexually assaulted and even murdered. One commenter gave out the woman's home address. Julia felt so threatened that she filed a complaint with the police. H&M later apologized for the way it handled the affair.

In Canada the store came under fire for selling headdresses that resembled the kind traditionally worn by the indigenous people of North America (otherwise known as Aboriginal or First Nation peoples). Many people complained that the item was culturally insensitive, and thanks to the use of social media, the story took on a life of its own. After receiving the complaints, a local company spokesperson announced that H&M would be removing the controversial item from all of its stores in Canada. H&M also had to face charges of animal cruelty. PETA (People for the Ethical Treatment of Animals) released a video showing rabbits having their hair pulled out by hand while they screamed and withered in pain. PETA purported that the practice was taking place in China and that the rabbit's hair was used to make popular angora fashion items sold in the West. H&M reassured the public that it maintains the highest ethical and moral standards when sourcing material, but shortly thereafter announced that it was halting production of all angora products. The company even faced charges of anti-Semitism after introducing a men's t-shirt that had a skull in the centre of what appears to be a Star of David (the historic symbol of the Jewish people). The controversial design was reportedly first noticed by a blogger who spread the story by Twitter, asking people to complain. H&M addressed the situation quickly, removing the questionable item from stores and offering an official apology.

Social media as a marketing tool

H&M has become adept at using social media as a powerful marketing tool, as well as an effective data mining tool. And the company appears to becoming more adept at dealing with the almost never ending controversies that seem to come with being a global brand. It is constantly promoting the fact that it is a responsible corporate citizen with a high regard for sustainability. The company has several million followers on various social media platforms, many of whom are passionate and loyal. This is both a strategic asset and a steady source of market data. In order to keep them happy it is clear that H&M needs to ensure that its brand communication is clear, reliable and consistent. And that it must continue to 'crunch the numbers' and analyse the data in order to meet customers' expectations with a continuous line of 'fast fashion' products that satisfy.

Sources

'Americans again pick environment over economic growth' by Art Swift, Gallup Poll, 20 March 2014. Accessed at: http://www.gallup.com/poll/168017/americans-again-pick-environment-economic-growth.aspx

'Fast fashion brand extensions: An empirical study of consumer preferences' by Tsan-Ming Choi, Na Liu, Shuk-Ching Liu, Mak Joseph, Yeuk-Ting To, Journal of Brand Management, 17 (7), June 2010.

'Fuzzy-set based sentiment analysis of big social data' by Raghava Rao Mukkamala, Abid Hussain and Ravi Vatrapu, working paper IT University of Copenhagen, 2014. Accessed at: http://www.itu.dk/people/rao/pubs_accepted/2014_EDOC_BigSocialData_Fuzzysets.pdf

'H&M anti-Semitic shirt draws controversy, retailer removes it from shelves' by Anny Jules, Latin Post, 28 March 2014. Accessed at: http://www.latinpost.com/articles/9674/20140328/h-m-anti-semitic-shirt-draws-controversy-retailer-removes-shelves.htm

'H&M customers wage Facebook war over Tupac shirt' by Jordan Valinsky, The Daily Dot, 8 February 2013. Accessed at: http://www.dailydot.com/news/hm-tupac-shirt-facebook-controversy/

'H&M dresses for success on Google+' Google Case Study, Google, 2012. Accessed at: http://services.google.com/fh/files/misc/google_handm_v3.pdf

'H&M fumbles on Facebook' by Jens Hansegard, The Wall Street Journal, 7 February 2013. Accessed at: http://blogs.wsj.com/corporate-intelligence/2013/02/07/hm-fumbles-on-facebook/

'H&M has the most-followed brand page on Google+' by Todd Wasserman, Mashable, 9 February 2012. Accessed at: http://mashable.com/2012/02/09/hm-google-plus-brand-pages/

'H&M launches first campaign to promote sustainability initiatives' by Sarah Vizard, Marketing Week, 10 April 2014. Accessed at: http://www.marketingweek.co.uk/sectors/retail/news/hm-launches-first-campaign-to-promote-sustainability-initiatives/4010096.article

'H&M pulls 'hipster' headdresses after complaints of cultural insensitivity' CTVNews.ca, 9 August 2013. Accessed at: http://www.ctvnews.ca/canada/h-m-pulls-hipster-headdresses-after-complaints-of-cultural-insensitivity-1.1403955#ixzz39bAfNVt0

'H&M stops making angora products after rabbit torture video' The Straits Times, 28 November 2013. Accessed at: http://www.straitstimes.com/breaking-news/world/story/hm-stops-making-angora-products-after-rabbit-torture-video-20131128?itemid=816#sthash.CIuBjobe.dpuf

'H&M suspends angora production over rabbit video' by Sarah Wolfe, Global Post, 28 November 2013. Accessed at: http://www.globalpost.com/dispatch/news/business/131128/hm-suspends-angora-production-over-rabbit-video

'H&M suspends production of items containing angora wool; footage from activists shows allegedly inhumane treatment of rabbits in China' by Jens Hansegard and Sven Grundberg, The Wall Street Journal, 28 November 2013. Accessed at: http://online.wsj.com/news/articles/SB1000142405270230474700457922574368198 4438hm.com – the H&M website

'How H&M uses Facebook, Twitter, Pinterest and Google+' by David Moth, E-consultancy LLC, 3 April 2013. Accessed at: https://econsultancy.com/blog/62450-how-h-m-uses-facebook-twitter-pinterest-and-google#i.xonzykafkeuzzy

'Know what your customers want before they do' by Thomas H. Davenport, Leandro Dalle Mule, and John Lucker, The Harvard Business Review, December 2011. Accessed at: http://iucontent.iu.edu.sa/Scholars/Information%20Technology/GruppCI.KnowWhatCustomersWant.pdf

'Murder threats push women to self-censor' The Local, 7 February 2013. Accessed at: http://www.thelocal.se/20130207/46044#.URUW4lpU6jI

'Organizational design challenges resulting from big data' by Jay R. Galbraith, Journal of Organization Design, 3 (1), 2014. pinterest.com

'Pinterest's retail problem: as more shoppers use the online scrapbook to showcase brands, retailers struggle to keep pace' by Tim Peterson, Ad Week, 4 February 2013. Accessed at: http://www.adweek.com/news/technology/pinterests-retail-problem-146988

'Social media case study: H&M' by Corely Padveen, the T2 Group, 27 June 2013. Accessed at: http://t2marketinginternational.com/social-media-case-study-hm/

'Towards a formal model of social data' by Raghava Rao Mukkamala, Abid Hussain and Ravi Vatrapu, IT University Technical Report Series TR-2013-169, November 2013. twitter.com

'What can brands learn from social media on the angora scandal?' by Olivia Standish, SalterBaxter MSLGroup. Accessed at: http://sb-tribe.com/blog/what-can-brands-learn-from-the-angora-scandal/

Questions

1. What are some of the ways in which H&M engages in market research and collects data on its customers?
2. What are some of the limitations with regard to market research and data analysis?
3. In which areas could H&M do more to collect valuable data and information on its customers?
4. Visit H&M online at hm.com. Give a critical analysis with regard to how well you believe the company's website incorporates social media. What are some steps H&M could take to make its website more useful with regard to marketing research and data collection?

This case was prepared by Tom McNamara and Irena Descubes, ESC Rennes, from various published sources as a basis for class discussion rather than to show effective or ineffective management.

Chapter 5

Market Segmentation, Targeting and Positioning

Chapter outline

Segmenting consumer markets

Consumer segmentation criteria

Segmenting organizational markets

Criteria for successful segmentation

Target marketing

Positioning

Repositioning

Learning outcomes

By the end of this chapter you will:

1   Understand what is meant by market segmentation

2   Explain the methods used to segment both consumer and organizational markets

3   Explain the criteria for effective segmentation

4   Compare and contrast the four market targeting strategies – undifferentiated, differentiated, focused and customized marketing

5   Explain the concept of positioning and the keys to successful positioning

6   Analyse the concept of repositioning and the repositioning options available to the firm

7   Critique the role of market segmentation and targeting in society.

One Direction

One of the most notable features of developing consumer markets is the emergence of younger and younger customers. Understanding and developing products and services for this quickly changing generation presents challenges and opportunities for marketers. A context in which their impact can clearly be seen is in the music industry. For example, while the pop bands of the 1970s might have appealed to teenagers, they are now designed and packaged to appeal to children, particularly, girls as young as five. Following on the success of boy bands like Boyzone and Westlife, the current dominant force in this segment of the market is One Direction.

One Direction was formed in 2010. Initially each of the five members of the group had auditioned as solo performers for the successful British reality TV series, *X Factor*. They failed to progress but were put together as a boy band and signed to Simon Cowell's Syco record label on a recording contract reputed to be worth £2 million. Concert tours and studio albums quickly followed. *Up All Night* was released in 2011, followed by *Take Me Home* in 2012 and *Midnight Memories* in 2013. The boys also found time to pack in three world tours as well as appearing at the London Olympics closing ceremony and producing live DVDs of their performances.

While their music may not be to everyone's taste, their marketing is highly effective. For example, it has been argued that as Justin Bieber had grown up, there was a gap left in the American market for 'clean-cut, wholesome, middle-class pop'. One Direction, branded as 1D, quickly became the dominant force in this market. They also fully exploited the power of social media with over 30 million Facebook fans, 19 million Twitter followers and 5 million Instagram followers in 2014. Each of the individual band members also maintains his own social media presence. This has been a particularly important part of the marketing strategy and the boys have received coaching on how to respond to messages in order to appear close and accessible as opposed to distant from fans. Interaction is high, with band members asking for suggestions about what to wear or where their next photo shoot should be. Loyal fans are given access to exclusive content. While traditionally bands have had to rely on radio play to build a following, 1D were the first group to build a global audience largely via social media.

1D have been a money-making machine since their formation. About 50 per cent of their revenues are generated from concert tours. Tickets for their shows normally sell out in minutes and it is estimated that concert sales have grossed the band close to $500 million. With their singles and albums rocketing to number one in the charts around the globe, the group is estimated to have sold in the region of 30 million albums worth a further $300 million in revenues. Other income streams include movie ticket sales, DVD sales and a wide range of merchandising products including everything from backpacks to pillows to pyjamas which alone is estimated to be worth in the region of $68 million. In short, it is estimated that 1D have earned close to $1 billion. Not bad for four years' work and a £2 million investment![1]

In our review of customer behaviour in Chapter 3, we saw that there are a variety of influences on the purchase decisions of customers. Their needs and wants vary and no matter how good a company's product or service is, not all customers will want it or will be willing to pay the same price for it. For example, some consumers may feel that saving their money in order to be able to travel to New Zealand to do a bungee jump is a good idea, while others might rather spend their money now on the latest fashions in order to look good. While both these groups of consumers may have some similarities in their preferences, they also have some key differences. Therefore, to implement the marketing concept and satisfy customer needs successfully, different product and service offerings must be made to the diverse customer groups that typically comprise a market.

The technique used by marketers to get to grips with the diverse nature of markets is called **market segmentation**. Market segmentation is defined as 'the identification of individuals or organizations with similar characteristics that have significant implications for the determination of marketing strategy'.

Thus, market segmentation involves the division of a diverse market into a number of smaller submarkets that have common features. The objective is to identify groups of customers with similar requirements so that they can be served effectively, while being of a sufficient size for the product or service to be supplied efficiently (see Exhibit 5.1). Usually, it is not possible to create a marketing mix that satisfies every individual's particular requirements exactly. Market segmentation, by grouping together customers with similar needs, provides a commercially viable method

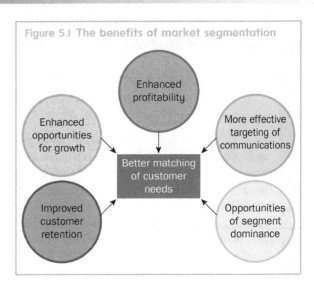

Figure 5.I The benefits of market segmentation

of serving these customers. It is therefore at the heart of strategic marketing, since it forms the basis by which marketers understand their markets and develop strategies for serving their chosen customers better than the competition. For example, a study of UK mobile phone consumers examined their attitudes to three dimensions of the purchase, namely, consumer innovativeness, the need for emotion and prestige price sensitivity. From these variables four distinct clusters or segments emerged – cognitive adopters, prestige-seeking emotional innovators, emotional adopters and prestige-seeking cognitive innovators – with implications for positioning and the use of rational or emotional appeals in marketing communications.[2]

There are a number of reasons why it is sensible for companies to segment their markets (see Figure 5.1). Most notably, it allows companies the

opportunity to enhance their profits. Many customers are willing to pay a premium for products or services that match their needs. For example, first-class air travellers regularly pay thousands of euro for long-haul flights, though the additional costs of catering for these customers is only marginally higher than that of catering for economy-class customers. In product categories like 'All-In-One' PCs, where all the key internal computer parts such as processors and graphic cards are encased with the monitor, consumers have the option of paying over €1,200 for a top of the range Apple iMac or approximately half that amount for models on offer from companies like Lenovo and Hewlett Packard. Both of these price points and product offerings will appeal to different segments of the market.

Second, through segmenting markets, companies can examine growth opportunities and expand their product lines. For example, in marketing its over-the-counter cough medicines, the Pfizer corporation offers different products for different types of cough under the Benylin brand. In its children's medicines range, it offers separate products for chesty coughs, dry coughs and night coughs, while there are five different cough brands in its adult range. Finally, in many competitive markets, companies are not able to compete across all segments effectively; by segmenting markets, companies can identify which segments they might most effectively compete in and develop strategies suited for that segment. For example, in the audio equipment business, one of the leading brands is Bose, which has built a global reputation as a manufacturer of high-quality sound systems that are only available through select stores and at premium prices. By pursuing this strategy, Bose has successfully differentiated itself from competitors like Sony, Samsung and Pioneer and, despite its premium prices, still has sales revenues of over $2 billion per annum.

Segmenting consumer markets

Consumer segmentation criteria may be divided into three main groups: behavioural, psychographic and profile variables. Since the purpose of segmentation is to identify differences in behaviour that have implications for marketing decisions, behavioural variables, such as benefits sought from the product and buying patterns, may be considered the ultimate basis for segmentation. **Psychographic segmentation** is used when researchers believe that purchasing behaviour is correlated with the personality or lifestyle of consumers. Having found these differences, the marketer needs to describe the people who exhibit them and this is where **profile segmentation** such as socio-economic group or geographic location is valuable.[3] For example, a marketer may see whether there are groups of people who value low calories in soft drinks and then attempt to profile them in terms of their age, socio-economic groupings, etc. Figure 5.2 shows the major segmentation variables used in consumer markets and Table 5.1 describes each of these variables in greater detail.

Consumer segmentation criteria

Table 5.1 shows the variety of criteria that might be considered when segmenting a consumer market. In practice there is no prescribed way of segmenting a market, and different criteria and combinations of criteria may be used. In the following paragraphs we will examine some of the more popular bases for segmentation. It is also critical for marketers to remember that consumer psychographics and behaviour patterns change over time, so that consumers do not necessarily remain in the same segments but may move between them. It is important therefore that segmentation analyses are done with the most up-to-date information.

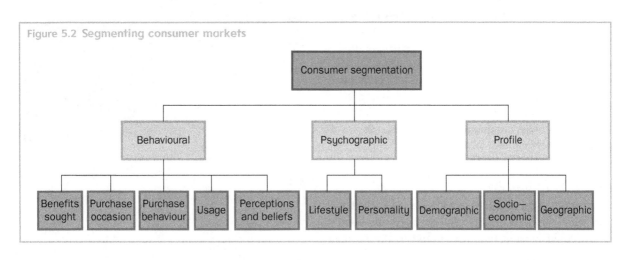

Figure 5.2 Segmenting consumer markets

Table 5.1 Consumer segmentation methods

Variable	Examples
Behavioural	
Benefits sought	Convenience, status, performance
Purchase occasion	Self-buy, gift, special occasions
Purchase behaviour	Brand loyal, brand switching, innovators
Usage	Heavy, light
Media behaviour	Primarily online, primarily offline
Psychographic	
Lifestyle	Trendsetters, conservatives, sophisticates
Personality	Conscientious, agreeable, extrovert
Profile	
Age	Under 12, 12–18, 19–25, 26–35, 36–49, 50–64, 65 and over
Gender	Female, male
Life cycle	Young single, young couples, young parents, middle-aged empty-nesters, retired
Social class	Upper middle, middle, skilled working
Terminal education age	16, 18, 21 years
Income	Income breakdown according to study objectives and income levels per country
Geographic	North vs south, urban vs rural, country
Geodemographic	Upwardly mobile young families living in larger owner-occupied houses, older people living in small houses, European regions based on language, income, age profile and location

Benefits sought

Benefit segmentation provides an understanding of why people buy in a market, and can aid the identification of opportunities. It is a fundamental method of segmentation because the objective of marketing is to provide customers with benefits that they value. For example, a basic product like toothpaste can confer a variety of benefits, ranging from decay prevention to fresh breath, and great taste to white teeth. Colgate has developed sub-brands that provide each of these benefits, such as Colgate Cavity Protection (decay prevention), Colgate Max Fresh (fresh breath), Colgate Kids (taste), Colgate Sparkling White and Ultrabrite Advanced Whitening (white teeth), and Colgate Sensitive (sensitive teeth). Luxury watch brands like Omega, Hermès and Patek Philippe convey the benefits of status and prestige to their owners as well as being considered to be a good long-term investment (see Exhibit 5.2). Focusing on benefits helps companies to spot business development opportunities.

Purchase behaviour

The degree of brand loyalty in a market is a useful basis for segmenting customers. Some buyers are totally brand loyal, buying only one brand in the product

Exhibit 5.2 This advertisement for Patek Philippe uses powerful emotional appeal to convey the benefits of ownership

Something truly precious holds its beauty forever.

group. For example, a person might invariably buy Ariel Automatic washing powder. Most customers, however, practise brand-switching behaviour. Some may have a tendency to buy Ariel Automatic but also buy two or three other brands; others might show no loyalty to any individual brand but switch brands on the basis of special offers (e.g. money-off promotions) or because they are variety seekers who look to buy a different brand each time. A recent trend in retailing is 'biographics'. This is the linking of actual purchase behaviour to individuals. The growth in loyalty schemes in supermarkets, such as the Tesco Clubcard scheme, has provided the mechanism for gathering this information. Such biographic data can be used to segment and target customers very precisely. For example, it would be easy to identify a group of customers who were ground coffee purchasers and target them through special offers. Analysis of the data allows the supermarkets to stock products in each of their stores that are more relevant to their customers' age, lifestyle and expenditure.

Usage

Another way of segmenting customers is on the basis of whether they are heavy users, light users or non-users of a selected product category. The profiling of heavy users allows this group to receive the most marketing attention (particularly promotion efforts) on the assumption that creating brand loyalty among these people will pay great dividends. Sometimes the 80:20 rule applies, where about 80 per cent of a product's sales come from 20 per cent of its customers. Skype is an example of a telecommunications company that has focused very effectively on the opportunities created by the growing need for telephone contact among people living in different parts of the world. By offering free calls over the Internet, Skype quickly built a customer base of over 600 million registered user accounts worldwide, resulting in a 13 per cent market share of international calls in just seven years.[4] However, attacking the heavy-user segment can have drawbacks if all of the competition are also following this strategy. Analysing the light and non-user categories may provide insights that permit the development of appeals that are not being mimicked by the competition. The identity of heavy, light and non-user categories, and their accompanying profiles for many consumer goods, can be accomplished by using survey information such as that provided by the Target Group Index (TGI). This is a large-scale annual survey of buying and media habits and is available in over 60 countries around the world.

Lifestyle

Lifestyle segmentation aims to categorize people in terms of their way of life, as reflected in their activities, interests and opinions. As we saw in Chapter 3, lifestyle is an important personal factor driving consumer behaviour, and advertisers have identified several different lifestyle groupings. Lifestyle is also a powerful method of segmentation as particular lifestyle groups have fairly predictable media habits (see Marketing in Action 5.1). For example, people who enjoy outdoor activities such as hiking and water sports will be likely to read magazines, watch television programmes, visit websites and join social networks dealing with these topics. Marketers can then use these media to reach their chosen segments.

An interesting example of the successful use of **lifestyle segmentation** is provided by a small US frozen foods firm, the SeaPak Shrimp Company. Although operating in a low-involvement product category that is often dominated by retailer own-brands, it identified two core but completely different lifestyle groups, namely, those that 'live-to-cook' and those that 'cook-to-live' and set about creating separate brands for each segment. The live-to-cook lifestyle has a passion for cooking, for discovering new recipes and for preparing unique meals. SeaPak surrounded these shoppers with content that enabled their passion such as access to famous chefs through online events, original seafood recipes and monthly emails. Other elements of the brand offering included higher-end non-breaded seafood products, upscale packaging and placement near the fresh seafood counter in supermarkets where these types of customers shop. For the cook-to-live group, the emphasis was on product quality and ease of preparation, with quick-bake breaded items in the frozen food section of shops. This two-segment approach yielded the firm a 15 per cent sales increase in a declining category.[5]

Age

Age is a factor that has been used in the segmentation of a host of consumer markets.[6] As we saw in Chapter 3 and the Marketing Spotlight at the beginning of this chapter, children have become a very important market believed to be worth about $1 trillion per year and now have their own television programmes, cereals, computer games and confectionery. The Gro Company's Gro Clock is an example of a successful product launch in the children's market. This market has traditionally been dominated by simple mechanical devices using static illustrations such as cartoon characters like Thomas the Tank Engine. The Gro Clock contains animated

Marketing in Action 5.1 Lululemon Athletica: Serving a Global Niche

Critical Thinking: Below is a review of the growth and development of the athletic clothing brand Lululemon. Read it and evaluate the segmentation strategy being pursued by the company. What are the strengths and weaknesses of its approach?

After 20 years in the surf, skate and snowboard business in Canada, Chip Wilson took his first yoga class and found the results exhilarating. With a passion for technical athletic fabrics he considered that the cotton clothing popular at the time was inappropriate for the stretching and sweaty activity that yoga can be. And anticipating that yoga would grow in popularity, particularly with females, he founded Lululemon in 1998 and opened his first store in Vancouver, Canada in 2000. The initial idea was that Lululemon would be not just a store but rather a community hub where people could learn about and discuss aspects of healthy living, from yoga to diet and cycling to running. While the ethos of healthy living is still central to the business, it has grown to become a large global retailer of yoga and athletic clothing with over 250 stores around the world and sales of $1.6 billion.

In building the business, Lululemon has developed a reputation for some novel marketing practices. Key among them are some of the things that it does not do – it does not use software to gather customer data, it does not use focus groups, it does not build lots of new stores and it does not offer generous discounts on its products. Instead it places a premium on staying close to its customers in the manner that it did when it was a smaller company. Senior management spend hours in stores each week observing how customers shop, listening to their complaints and then using this information to tweak products and stores. Sales staff are also trained to listen to customers, and folding tables are placed near fitting rooms so that customer comments can be heard. Stores have a large chalkboard where customers can write complaints and comments. Scarcity is a second key element of the firm's marketing strategy. A limited supply of many product lines is carried in stock so that demand for these items is high and consequently sold at full price. And a third key element of its marketing is its ambassador programme. Yoga and Pilates teachers are given free merchandise to wear while they teach in return for spreading the word about Lululemon.

The brand is also very active on social media where it can continue the conversation about healthy living on platforms like Facebook, Foursquare and Instagram. From its inception, Lululemon's target market segment has been yoga practitioners and those females interested in healthy, active lifestyles. Its products were only available up to US size 12 (European size 16), thus effectively excluding many females from its products. When it encountered some quality problems with its yoga pants in 2013, Wilson caused a storm of controversy by arguing that the products simply didn't work for some women's bodies. These comments were later retracted but the incident was generally viewed as a public relations disaster. As the company seeks to grow it has added several new lines such as a men's range and the Ivivva range for girls age 6–14.

Based on: Berg (2014);[7] Mattioli (2012);[8] Wexler (2012).[9]

imagery of the sun and the stars to communicate wake up times for very young children (see Exhibit 5.3). The product launch exceeded sales forecasts by over 300 per cent and it has quickly become a market leader in its category. Similarly, a KPMG study found that only one-fifth of fund management firms were targeting 'Generation Y' customers – that is, those born in the 1980s – even though this group will have to be more financially adept than their parents owing to changes in pension regimes.[10]

The role of children in influencing household purchasing is very significant. The expression 'pester power' is often used by advertisers to describe the process by which children subtly influence or more overtly nag their parents into buying a product. Young children are very brand aware. Studies show that over

Exhibit 5.3 The Gro Clock – a successful product launch in the children's market segment

80 per cent of children aged between 3 and 6 recognize the Coca-Cola logo.[11] The charity Childwise estimated that children in the UK spend £4.2 billion annually, demonstrating the size of the potential market.[12] It is also estimated that over two-thirds of households buying a new car are influenced in the decision by their children. Therefore Toyota in Australia has very successfully included chickens, puppies and kittens in its advertising.[13] Overt efforts by firms to target children in their marketing continues to be a significant source of controversy as shown in Marketing and Society 5.1.

As we saw in Chapter 2, age distribution changes within the European Union are having a profound effect on the attractiveness of various age segments to marketers, with people over 50 years of age likely to become increasingly important in the future. Labelled the 'grey market', people are now living longer, with life expectancies rising into the eighties in developed countries around the world. Many 'grey consumers' are healthy, active, well educated, financially independent and have a lot of leisure time, making them a very attractive market. For example, in the music business, record companies have been struggling with the fact that the core market (young people) are buying less music, preferring to download it, often for free, from file-sharing websites. Therefore, Universal Music Group brought out a CD of songs for people who grew up in the 1950s named *Dreamboats and Petticoats*. It was so successful, it was followed by a West End musical and three other albums that have sold over

2.3 million copies.[14] Other media companies such as television stations, radio stations and newspapers are increasingly realizing that the best potential for their offerings may lie with the grey market.

Social class

Social class is another important segmentation variable. As we saw in Chapter 3, social class groupings are based primarily on occupation. However, people who hold similar occupations may have very dissimilar lifestyles, values and purchasing patterns. Nevertheless, research has found that social class has proved to be useful in discriminating between owning a dishwasher, having central heating and privatization share ownership, for example, and therefore should not be discounted as a segmentation variable.[15] In addition, social classes tend to vary in their media consumption, meaning that these groups can be targeted effectively by advertisers. For example, tabloid newspapers tend to target working-class people, whereas traditional broadsheets see the middle and upper classes as their primary audience.

Geography

At a very basic level, markets can be segmented on the basis of country or regions within a country or on the basis of city size. More popular in recent years has been the combination of geographic and demographic variables into what are called **geodemographics**. In countries that produce population census data, the potential exists for classifying consumers on the combined basis of location and certain demographic (and socio-economic) information. Households are classified into groups according to a wide range of factors, depending on what is asked on census returns. In the UK, variables such as household size, online behaviour, occupation, family size and ethnic background are used to group small geographic areas (known as enumeration districts) into segments that share similar characteristics. Two of the best known geodemographic systems are ACORN (from its full title – A Classification Of Residential Neighbourhoods) produced by CACI Market Analysis and MOSAIC produced by Experian. The main ACORN groupings and their characteristics are shown in Table 5.2. CACI amalgamates a wide variety of Open Data files and commercial databases, all generally at address level. The result of classifying this data is then matched to many market research surveys and some 500 lifestyle variables to produce a detailed consumer picture of the UK. All 1.9 million postcodes are classified in this way, enabling some very precise targeting of the market. For example, for each of the groups listed

Marketing and Society 5.1 Marketing to children

Few issues in marketing generate as much heated debate and discussion as the question of marketing to children. To many it represents the ugly and sinister face of capitalism. They see companies as deliberately targeting children in their advertising and communications to encourage them to pester their parents to buy products and services that in many instances they may not be able to afford. In contrast, those in favour argue that children should be exposed to marketing communications as part of their education because we live in a consumer society and children need to understand marketing.

The opponents of marketing to children have highlighted the systematic ways in which firms target younger and younger consumers. Children are carefully researched and firms employ the skills of child psychologists to devise ways to reach inside developing minds and 'implant' brand preferences through sponsorship, advertising and product placement. Many of the products that children are encouraged to pester their parents for have negative consequences as illustrated by the dramatic growth in childhood obesity in some countries. To some commentators, the obesity problem and the fact that a firm like McDonald's is the largest owner and operator of children's playgrounds in the world is not a coincidence. Other negative consequences identified include the perpetuation of stereotypes (dolls for girls, war games for boys, etc.), the rise of materialism, the economic hardship placed on families during key gift-giving times and the sexualization of young girls (such as when Tesco offered pole dancing kits aimed at young girls on its website).

Consequently, many countries have placed restrictions on advertising to children, most notably Germany, France and the Scandinavian countries who have placed limits on both the type and amount of advertising that is allowed. However, these measures have also come in for criticism. Because of the proliferation of ways in which marketers can reach children such as through programme and video-game sponsorship, marketing in schools, using cross-national television channels and social media, marketing to children is very hard to police fairly. Others have pointed to the fact that some countries have suffered a reduction in the quality of children's programming when they have banned advertising. And anyway these critics argue that kids need to be exposed to marketing so that they can understand it and make informed decisions.

While it will continue to generate fierce debate, one thing seems certain and it is that firms under more and more competitive pressures will continue to experiment with all sorts of ways of reaching and influencing the next generation of consumers.

Suggested reading: Barber (2007).[16]

Reflection: In your view, what kinds of restrictions (if any) should be placed on advertising to children?

in Table 5.2, CACI can provide information on such things as internet usage and social media activity in the past week, brand of smartphone owned, free and paid content downloaded to mobile phone, online purchases in the past 12 months, preferred hobbies and holiday destinations and so on.

Using a similar classification system, MOSAIC Global classifies 380 million households from countries in Europe, North America and Asia Pacific. Based on the assumption that the world's cities share common patterns of residential segregation, it uses 10 distinct types of residential neighbourhood, each with a characteristic set of values, motivations and consumer preferences, to generate consumer classifications ranging from 'Comfortable Retirement' to 'Metropolitan Strugglers'. Geodemographic information has been used to select recipients of direct mail campaigns, to identify the best locations for stores and to find the best poster sites. This is possible because consumers in each group can be identified by means of their postcodes. Another area where census data are employed is in buying advertising spots on television. Agencies depend on information from viewership panels, which record their viewing habits so that advertisers can get an insight into who watches what. This means that advertisers who wish to reach a particular geodemographic group can discover the type of programme they prefer to watch and buy television spots accordingly. Advertising on

Table 5.2 The ACORN targeting classification

Categories	% in UK population	Groups	% in UK population
A: Affluent Achievers	22.5	1 Lavish Lifestyles	1.3
		2 Executive Wealth	12.4
		3 Mature Money	8.8
B: Rising Prosperity	9.1	4 City Sophisticates	3.2
		5 Career Climbers	5.9
C: Comfortable Communities	27.2	6 Countryside Communities	6.4
		7 Successful Suburbs	6.1
		8 Steady Neighbourhoods	8.3
		9 Comfortable Seniors	2.5
		10 Starting Out	4.0
D: Financially Stretched	22.5	11 Student Life	2.5
		12 Modest Means	7.4
		13 Striving Families	8.1
		14 Poorer Pensioners	4.5
E: Urban Adversity	17.7	15 Young Hardship	5.1
		16 Struggling Estates	7.9
		17 Difficult Circumstances	4.7

Source: Neighbourhood Statistics (NISRA 2011 Census) Website: www.nisra.gov.uk/ninis Contains public sector information licensed under the Open Government Licence v2.0. Sources include: Land Registry; Strategic Statistics Division; www. justice.gov.uk; DWP, 2012 Contains Crown Copyright data produced by Registers of Scotland. © Crown copyright material is reproduced with the permission of Registers of Scotland. Please see the following link for further information about this registers of Scotland Crown Copyright data: www.ros.gov.uk/public/publications/crown_copyright1.html Copyright © (2012) Care Quality Commission (CQC); Care Inspectorate for Scotland 2012; CSSIW – Care and Social Services Inspectorate Wales 2012; Regulation and Quality Improvement Authority 2012. © CACI Limited 1979 – 2014 © Crown Copyright 2013 Adapted from data from the ONS (2011 Census) and National Records of Scotland, licensed under the Open Government Licence v.1.0.

Note: Due to rounding, the percentages total 99.

social media sites like Facebook can also be targeted very specifically at customer groups based on the profile information submitted by members when they create their accounts.

A major strength of geodemographics is that it can link buyer behaviour to customer groups. Buying habits can be determined by means of large-scale syndicated surveys – for example, the TGI and MORI Financial Services – or from panel data (e.g. the grocery and toiletries markets are covered by AGB's Superpanel). By 'geocoding' respondents, those ACORN groups most likely to purchase a product or brand can be determined. This can be useful for branch location since many service providers use a country-wide branch network and need to match the market segments to which they most appeal to the type of customer in their catchment area. The merchandize mix decisions of retailers can also be affected by customer profile data. Media selections can be made more precise by linking buying habits to geodemographic data.[17]

In short, a wide range of variables can be used to segment consumer markets. Flexibility and creativity are the hallmarks of effective segmentation analysis. Often, a combination of variables will be used to identify groups of consumers that respond in the same way to marketing mix strategies.

Segmenting organizational markets

As we noted in Chapter 3, organizational markets, in contrast to consumer markets, tend to be characterized by relatively small numbers of buyers. Nevertheless, there are also many cases where it will be appropriate to segment organizational markets.

Organizational segmentation criteria

Some of the most useful bases for segmenting organizational markets are described below.

Organizational size

Market segmentation in this case may be by size of buying organization. Large organizations differ from medium-sized and small organizations in having greater order potential, more formalized buying and management processes, increased specialization of function, and special needs (e.g. quantity discounts). The result is that they may form important target market segments and require tailored marketing mix strategies. For example, the sales force may need to be organized on a key account basis where a dedicated sales team is used to service important industrial accounts. List pricing of products and services may need to take into account the inevitable demand for volume discounts from large purchasers, and the sales force will need to be well versed in the art of negotiation.

Industry

Industry sector – sometimes identified by the Standard Industrial Classification (SIC) codes – is another common segmentation variable. Different industries may have unique requirements from products. For example, software applications suppliers like Oracle and SAP can market their products to various sectors, such as banking, manufacturing, healthcare and education, each of which has unique needs in terms of software programs, servicing, price and purchasing practice. By understanding each industry's needs in depth, a more effective marketing mix can be designed. In some instances, further segmentation may be required. For example, the education sector may be further divided into primary, secondary and further education, as the product and service requirements of these sub-sectors may differ. Industry sector is a very popular method for segmenting industrial markets.

Geographic location

The use of geographic location as a basis for differentiating marketing strategies may be suggested by regional variations in purchasing practice and needs. The purchasing practices and expectations of companies in Central and Eastern Europe are likely to differ markedly from those in Western Europe. Their more bureaucratic structures may imply a fundamentally different approach to doing business that needs to be recognized by companies attempting to enter these growing industrial markets. These differences, in effect, suggest the need for regional segments since marketing needs to reflect these variations.

Choice criteria

The factor of choice criteria segments the organizational market on the basis of the key criteria used by buyers when they are evaluating supplier offerings. One group of customers may rate price as the key choice criterion, another segment may favour product performance, while a third may be service orientated. These varying preferences mean that marketing and sales strategies need to be adapted to cater for each segment's needs. Three different marketing mixes would be needed to cover the three segments, and salespeople would have to emphasize different benefits when talking to customers in each segment. Variations in key choice criteria can be powerful predictors of buyer behaviour.

Purchasing organization

Another segmentation variable is that of decentralized versus centralized purchasing, because of its influence on the purchase decision.[18] Centralized purchasing is associated with purchasing specialists who become experts in buying a range of products and are particularly popular in sectors like grocery retailing. Specialization means that they become more familiar with cost factors, and the strengths and weaknesses of suppliers than do decentralized generalists. Furthermore, the opportunity for volume buying means that their power to demand price concessions from suppliers is enhanced. They have also been found to have greater power within the decision-making unit (DMU – see Chapter 3) than decentralized buyers who often lack the specialist's expertise and status to counter the view of technical members like designers and engineers. For these reasons, purchasing organization provides a good base for distinguishing between buyer behaviour, and can have implications for marketing activities. For example, the centralized purchasing segment could be served by a national account sales force, whereas the decentralized purchasing segment might be covered by territory representatives.

Interesting opportunities often appear at the intersection of consumer and industrial markets. For example, a small German technology company called Wagner has become the biggest supplier of spray guns for painting in the USA, with an 85 per cent market share. It used its expertise, built up through working with professional painters, to make products that also appeal to DIY painters. Its vast range of 3,000 products enabled it to span both consumer and industrial markets, with prices ranging from $50 up to $2 million for large industrial systems. Though most manufacturers concentrate on industrial segments, two-thirds of Wagner's sales in the USA came from consumer spray guns.

Criteria for successful segmentation

To determine whether a company has properly segmented its market, five criteria are usually considered.

1 *Effective*: the segments identified should consist of customers whose needs are relatively homogeneous within a segment, but significantly different from those in other segments. If buyer needs in different segments are similar, then the segmentation strategy should be revised.

2 *Measurable*: it must be possible to identify customers in the proposed segment, and to understand their characteristics and behaviour patterns. For example, some personality traits, like 'extrovert' or 'conscientious', might be difficult to pin down, whereas variables like age or occupation would be more clear-cut.

3 *Accessible*: the company must be able to formulate effective marketing programmes for the segments that it identifies. In other words, it must be clear what kinds of promotional campaign might work best for the segment, how the products might best be distributed to reach the segment, and so on.

4 *Actionable*: the company must have the resources to exploit the opportunities identified through the segmentation scheme (see Marketing in Action 5.2). Certain segments – for example, in international markets – might be identified as being very attractive but the company may not have the resources or knowledge necessary to serve them.

5 *Profitable*: most importantly, segments must be large enough to be profitable to serve. This is what is meant by the clichéd expression 'Is there a market in the gap?'. Very small segments may be unprofitable to serve, though advances in production and distribution technologies mean that, increasingly, micro-segments can be profitable (see the section on customized marketing, below).

Marketing in Action 5.2 Denmark's radio

Critical Thinking: Below is an example of how a media provider can ensure that its website is perceived as fresh without using resources in constantly developing new content. Is it necessary for organizations in all types of markets to focus on reframing and refreshing content?

DR is the state-run Danish equivalent of the British BBC. DR is a full-service media provider that integrates online content with television and radio broadcasting. There are dedicated microsites for each of DR's six broadcast television channels, one of which is targeted at children and teenagers between the ages of 9 and 15. In Denmark, this age group is highly proficient in the use of the Internet and has access to the Web through smartphones, tablets and personal computers. For DR, it is important to continuously engage the target audience in order to fulfil its legal obligation as an entertainment provider. So by reframing and refreshing content, DR can make sure that the online experience that its target audience receives appears up to date without having to constantly develop completely new content.

Reframing content is straightforward: simply bundle or sub-bundle existing content and thereby reframe it to make it appear fresh. For example, DR produces a morning live show for children during every school summer holiday. This programme is then available to be streamed after the live show has finished, and the call to action is 'click here to see the live show'. Each show consists of various segments that are repeated every day, such as competitions and short sketches that follow a developing storyline. As the story develops it is possible to change the call to action to, for example, 'see Monday's episode', by simply unbundling Monday's episode from the rest of the programme.

Refreshing content consists of taking several different pieces of existing content with a common theme and bundling them together to create what consumers perceive to be fresh content. A way for DR to refresh existing content is to create 'best of' videos. After the live shows have been broadcast, DR can splice together all of the individual episodes of the story. In this way, content that is already available can be rolled into one video in a meaningful way. A new call to action can be written that emphasizes the novel aspect of the refreshed content, for example, 'click here to see all story episodes'. So by taking the original content and simply reframing or refreshing it, organizations can ensure that consumers perceive the website to be dynamic while making the marketing budget stretch further.

Target marketing

Once the market segments have been identified, the next important activity is the selection of target markets. **Target marketing** refers to the choice of specific segments to serve, and is a key element in marketing strategy. An organization needs to evaluate the segments to decide which ones to serve using the five criteria outlined above. For example, CNN targets its news programmes to what are known as 'influentials'. This is why, globally, CNN has focused so much of its distribution effort into gaining access to hotel rooms. Business people know that, wherever they are in the world, they can see international news on CNN in their hotel. Its sports programming is also targeted, with plenty of coverage of upmarket sports such as golf and tennis.

The aim of evaluating market segments is for a company to arrive at a choice of one or more segments to concentrate on. Target market selection is the choice of what and how many market segments in which to compete. There are four generic target marketing strategies from which to choose: undifferentiated marketing, differentiated marketing, focused marketing and customized marketing (see Figure 5.3). Each option will now be examined.

Undifferentiated marketing

Market analysis will occasionally reveal no pronounced differences in customer characteristics that have implications for a marketing strategy. Alternatively, the cost of developing a separate marketing mix for different segments may outweigh the potential gains of meeting customer needs more exactly. Under these circumstances a company may decide to develop a single marketing mix for the whole market. This absence of segmentation is called **undifferentiated marketing**. Unfortunately this strategy can occur by default. For example, companies that lack a marketing orientation may practise undifferentiated marketing through lack of customer knowledge and focus. Furthermore, undifferentiated marketing is more convenient for managers since they have to develop only a single product/marketing strategy. Finding out that customers have diverse needs, which can be met only by products with different characteristics, means that managers have to go to the trouble and expense of developing new products, designing new promotional campaigns, training the sales force to sell the new products, and developing new distribution channels. Moving into new segments also means that salespeople have to start prospecting for new customers. This is not such a pleasant activity as calling on existing customers who are well known and liked.

Figure 5.3 Target marketing strategies

Undifferentiated marketing

Marketing mix → Whole market

Differentiated marketing   Focused marketing

Marketing mix 1 → Segment 1

Marketing mix 2 → Segment 2 ← Marketing mix

Marketing mix 3 → Segment 3

Customized marketing

Marketing mix 1 → Customer 1

Marketing mix 2 → Customer 2

Marketing mix 3 → Customer 3

Differentiated marketing

Specific marketing mixes can be developed to appeal to all or some of the segments when market segmentation reveals several potential targets. This is called **differentiated marketing**; it is a very popular market targeting strategy that can be found in sectors as diverse as cars, hotels and fashion retailing (see Figure 5.4). For example, Arcadia's segmentation of the fashion market revealed distinct customer groups for which specific marketing mixes could be employed. In response the group has a portfolio of shops that are distinctive in terms of shop name, style of clothing, décor and ambience. In all, the company has nine separate brands including, for example, Miss Selfridge (aimed at the 18–24 age group), Dorothy Perkins (aimed at women in their twenties and thirties) and Evans (which stocks women's clothes that are size 16+). Similarly, as part of its turnaround strategy, Marks & Spencer sought to move away from one brand (St Michael) with wide market appeal to a range of sub-brands such as Autograph (an upmarket brand) and Per Una, which is aimed at fashion-conscious women up to the age of 35. A differentiated target marketing strategy exploits the differences between marketing segments by designing a specific marketing mix for each segment.

Another significant advantage is that it enables firms to achieve economies of scale and spread costs over a wide range of potential customer groups. This can be crucial in some industries like car manufacturing where complying with more stringent environmental regulations involves major costs. For example in 2013, the German manufacturer Volkswagen announced that it would be spending €84 billion over five years

Figure 5.4 Some of the key brands in the Marriott hotels portfolio, which are aimed at different segments

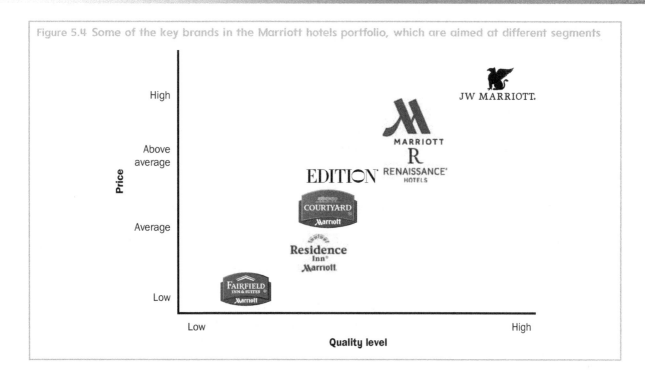

on new vehicles and technology.[19] The challenges of pursuing a differentiated marketing strategy are outlined in Marketing in Action 5.3.

Focused marketing

Just because a company has identified several segments in a market does not mean that it should serve them all. Some may be unattractive or out of step with its business strengths. Perhaps the most sensible route would be to serve just one of the market segments. When a company develops a single marketing mix aimed at one target (niche) market it is practising **focused marketing**. This strategy is particularly appropriate for companies with limited resources. Small companies may stretch their resources too far by competing in more than one segment. Focused marketing allows research and development expenditure to be concentrated on meeting the needs of one set of customers, and managerial activities can thus be devoted to understanding and catering for those needs. Large organizations may not be interested in serving the needs of this one segment, or their energies may be so dissipated across the whole market that they pay insufficient attention to their requirements.

An example of a firm pursuing a focused marketing approach is Bang & Olufsen (B&O), the Danish audio electronics firm; it targets its stylish music systems at up-market consumers who value self-development, pleasure and open-mindedness. Anders Kwitsen, the company's chief executive,

describes its positioning as 'high quality, but we are not Rolls-Royce – more BMW'. Focused targeting and cost control mean that B&O defies the conventional wisdom that a small manufacturer could not make a profit by marketing consumer electronics in Denmark.[20] In sectors like luxury goods, focused marketing is the norm (see Exhibit 5.4). For example, when Ferrari brought out its new hybrid car in 2013, it carried a price tag of £1.5 million and was primarily aimed at consumers who already owned at least five Ferraris, estimated to be a total of about 400 people worldwide.[21]

One of the challenges for focused marketers is effectively evolving their targeting strategy as the market grows. For example, the sports nutrition

Exhibit 5.4 The target market for Ferrari's hybrid car LeFerrari was existing Ferrari owners

Marketing in Action 5.3 The perils of differentiated marketing

Critical Thinking: Below is a review of some of the risks associated with differentiated marketing strategies. Read and critically evaluate both the advantages and disadvantages of this approach.

Two of the risks associated with using a differentiated marketing strategy are creating confusion in the marketplace and spreading the organization's resources too thinly. The casual clothing retailer Gap Inc. is a classic case of the former. There are different segments of the market for casual clothes ranging from those who want to shop in discount outlets to those looking for smart casual garments for work or social events. To meet the needs of these different segments, Gap Inc. acquired both the Old Navy (discount fashions) and Banana Republic chains (smart casual). But a lack of sufficient differentiation between the three brands led to cannibalization of each other's sales, with first Old Navy taking sales from Gap and then Gap taking sales from Banana Republic as it tried to position itself away from the discount retailer.

Confusion and reputational damage can also be caused by how a brand owner chooses to differentiate. From example, the leading wine brand Wolf Blass chooses to identify most of its range by the colour of the label with variants like Yellow Label and Red Label sold in supermarkets while its more exclusive wines like Gold, Grey and Platinum Label are only available in specialist wine shops. However, because all of these brands share the Wolf Blass name, some

consumers may associate the brand only with the low price (and moderate quality) wines that they see in supermarkets and not select it when choosing to buy an expensive wine.

A differentiated approach also puts great pressure on a management team to ensure that they understand and respond to the needs of different segments. Therefore when Alan Mulally took over the leadership of the Ford Motor Company he set about selling off a variety of prestigious brands that it had acquired, such as Land Rover, Jaguar, Aston Martin and Volvo, despite the fact that many of these were selling profitably. Instead, the plan was to put all the company's resources into the Ford brand under the umbrella of the OneFord strategy. For example, although the 2011 Fiesta was produced in five plants and sold in five continents, the car itself was the same. Focusing the company's energies in this way meant that Ford could generate above average profitability for its products. So while some of its peers like GM and Chrysler relied on government bailouts to stay afloat, Ford's more focused approach allowed it to survive more comfortably.

Based on: Gayatri and Madhav (2004);[22] Ritson (2010).[23]

supplements company Maximuscle traditionally focused on the narrow niche of bodybuilders but has evolved the brand through its marketing communications to target a broader base of lifestyle gym-goers and those active in sports. To do this, it was necessary to overcome consumer resistance to sports supplements which has connotations of steroids and other banned substances. Similarly low-cost airlines that have traditionally focused on budget travellers have expanded their appeal to

budget-conscious business travellers by offering some flights to primary airports like London's Gatwick and Paris Charles De Gaulle as well as offering priority boarding and access to frequent flyer, loyalty schemes.[24]

Customized marketing

The requirements of individual customers in some markets are unique, and their purchasing power sufficient to make viable the design of a discrete marketing mix for each customer. Segmentation at this disaggregated level leads to the use of **customized marketing**. Many service providers, such as advertising and marketing research agencies, architects and solicitors, vary their offerings on a customer-by-customer basis. They will discuss face to face with each customer their requirements, and tailor their services accordingly. Customized marketing is also found within organizational markets because of the high value of orders and the special needs of customers. Locomotive manufacturers will design and build products according to specifications given to them by individual rail transport providers. Similarly, in the machine tools industry, the German company Emag is a global leader in making 'multitasking' machines that cut metals used in industries like aerospace and vehicles. It practises customized marketing by manufacturing basic products at a cost-effective production site in eastern Germany but then finishing off or customizing these products in factories around the world that are located close to the customer.[25] Customized marketing is often associated with close relationships between suppliers and customers in these circumstances because the value of the order justifies a large marketing and sales effort being focused on each buyer.

Recent decades have seen a gradual growth in the potential application of customized marketing in consumer markets. The first stage in the 1980s was the development of flexible production systems initially pioneered by Japanese companies to deliver customized products such as men's suits, bicycles and golf clubs to private consumers.[26] This practice has continued with more products now being customized to the needs of particular individuals. For example, most personal computer companies allow customers to configure the products they want from a menu of options available to them. At the Mercedes Sindelfingen plant near Stuttgart, every model passing through the plant has a pre-assigned customer, many of whom configure their cars via the Internet. Furthermore, many customers take delivery of their cars at the plant rather than from a dealer as has traditionally been the case. NikeiD enables customers to design their own personal versions of Nike shoes and apparel. Initially only available online, Nike has followed up the success of this service by opening NikeiD studios in Nike Town stores around the world. Consumers create designs in the studio which can then be delivered either via the Nike Town stores or direct to their homes.

Advances in technology are continuing to facilitate developments in customized marketing in consumer markets. The consumption of media and entertainment is increasingly customized. Services like those offered by Netflix means that the consumption of television and movies is highly individualistic. Online content aggregators play a similar role. Music streaming services like Spotify and Pandora create an individual listening experience while news apps like Flipboard and Zite collect stories from around the Web and tailor them to user preferences. An interesting feature of these apps is that they use software which tracks the news items that users read, like and share and then feeds more of these types of content to them further personalizing the experience. New developments such as 3D printing create the potential for a much wider range of customized products. Already this form of manufacturing is being deployed to create body tissues using living cells.[27] Using a process known as additive manufacturing, objects are created first from blueprints that can be adjusted and customized on a computer screen, and are then 'printed' out one layer at a time until the new product is built up. Because this kind of production does not need to happen in a factory, high levels of customization and niche production will be feasible.

Customized marketing is reflective of the contemporary way of thinking about marketing as a value co-creation process based on close relationships between organizations and customers (see the discussion of the service dominant logic and relationship marketing in Chapter 7). Research has found that products customized on the basis of expressed user preferences bring about significantly higher benefits for customers in terms of willingness to pay, purchase intention and attitudes toward the product than standard products.[28]

Positioning

So far, we have examined two key aspects of the marketing management process, namely, market segmentation (where we look at the different needs and preferences that may exist in a market) and market targeting (where we decide which segment or segments of the market we are going to serve). We now arrive at one of the most important and challenging aspects of marketing: **positioning**. Positioning can be defined as:

> *the act of designing the company's offering so that it occupies a meaningful and distinct position in the target customer's mind.*

Exhibit 5.5 Diet Coke and Coke Zero: virtually identical drinks that are positioned very differently

This is the challenge that faces all organizations. All firms make products or provide services but, as we saw in Chapter 1, consumers buy benefits. Positioning is essentially that act of linking your product or service to the solutions that consumers seek and ensuring that, when they think about those needs, your brand is one of the first that comes to mind. For example, there is a segment of the car-buying market that values safety as one of its key purchasing criteria. Over the years, Swedish car manufacturer Volvo successfully positioned itself as one of the safest cars in the market through a combination of its design and its advertising messages. When asked which car they thought was the safest, Volvo was consistently mentioned by customers though technical tests showed that it was not significantly safer than other brands in the market. This is the power of effective positioning: ensuring that your brand occupies a meaningful and distinct place in the target customer's mind. Volvo typically sells over 200,000 units globally and has been consistently profitable in recent years. The clarity of Volvo's positioning contrasts markedly with that of Saab, another Swedish car brand whose image declined so badly that it had to be rescued from bankruptcy by an Asian consortium, NEVS, in 2012.

 Colgate Ad Insight: This ad targets a particular audience by showcasing one benefit.

Effective positioning created an interesting problem for Coca-Cola (see Exhibit 5.5). Though not exclusively marketed towards females, 80 per cent of Diet Coke sales are to women. Research by the company showed that men were also interested in a low-calorie drink but were reluctant to drink Diet Coke. So Coca-Cola Zero, which has been dubbed 'bloke Coke', was targeted at the male market using very male-orientated advertising. Though its ingredients are virtually indistinguishable from those of Diet Coke, its market appeal is very different.[29]

Positioning is both important and difficult. It is important because today we live in an over-communicated society.[30] Consumers are constantly exposed to thousands of marketing messages per day and as we saw in Chapter 3, as few as 5 per cent of these messages may gain the attention of the target audience. To cut through this clutter, a company needs messages that are simple, direct and that resonate with the customer's needs. Failure to gain a position in the customer's mind significantly increases the likelihood of failure in the marketplace.

Developing a positioning strategy

Deciding what position to try to occupy in the market requires consideration of three variables, namely, the customers, the competitors and the company itself. In terms of customers we must examine what attributes matter to them – there is little point in seeking a position that is unimportant from the customer's point of view. In many markets, competitors are already well entrenched, so the next challenge is to find some differential advantage that ideally cannot easily be matched. Third, as implied by the resource-based view of the firm, the company should look at building a position based on its unique attributes as this increases the likelihood that advantage can be sustained.[31]

Once the overall positioning strategy is agreed, the next step is to develop a positioning statement. A positioning statement is a memorable, image-enhancing, written summation of the product's desired stature. The statement can be evaluated using the criteria shown in Figure 5.5. Coca-Cola has become one of the world's most valuable brands through its effective exploitation of catchy positioning slogans like 'Things go better with Coke' in the 1960s and 'It's the real thing' in its 1970s advertising.

| *Clarity*: the idea must be perfectly clear, both in terms of target market and differential advantage. Complicated positioning statements

Figure 5.5 Keys to successful positioning

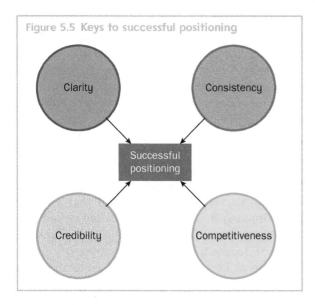

Figure 5.6 Some classic advertising slogans

'We try harder.'	Avis
'Go to work on an egg.'	Egg Marketing Board
'Guinness is good for you.'	Guinness
'Don't be vague. Ask for Haig.'	Haig Scotch Whisky
'Happiness is a cigar called Hamlet.'	Hamlet
'Heineken refreshes the parts other beers cannot reach.'	Heineken
'Beanz Meanz Heinz.'	Heinz
'It is. Are you?'	The Independent
'Just do it.'	Nike
'Think small.'	Volkswagen

Source: www.adslogans.co.uk

 Apple Ad Insight: iPad celebrates the diversity of its users and their passions.

are unlikely to be remembered. Simple messages such as 'BMW – The Ultimate Driving Machine', 'Apple – Think Different' and 'L'Oréal – Because I'm Worth it' are clear and memorable (see Figure 5.6).

2 *Consistency*: because people are bombarded with messages daily, a consistent message is required to break through this noise. Confusion will arise if, this year, we position on 'quality of service' and next year change this to 'superior product performance'. Some companies, like BMW, have used the same positioning – in BMW's case, 'The Ultimate Driving Machine' – for decades.

3 *Credibility*: the selected differential advantage must be credible in the minds of target customers. An attempt to position roll-your-own cigarette tobacco as an upmarket exclusive product failed due to lack of credibility. Similarly, Toyota's lack of credibility as an upmarket brand caused it to use 'Lexus' as the brand name for its top of the range cars.

4 *Competitiveness*: the chosen differential advantage must possess a competitive edge. It should offer something of value to the customer that the competition is failing to supply. For example, the success of the iPod was based on the differential advantage of seamless downloading of music from iTunes, Apple's dedicated music store, to a mobile player producing high quality sound.

The perceptual map is a useful tool for determining the position of a brand in the marketplace. It is a visual representation of consumer perceptions of a brand and its competitors, using attributes (dimensions) that are important to consumers. The key steps in producing a perceptual map are as follows.

1 Identify a set of competing brands.
2 Identify – using qualitative research (e.g. group discussions) – the important attributes consumers use when choosing between brands.
3 Conduct quantitative marketing research where consumers score each brand on all key attributes.
4 Plot brands on a two-dimensional map (or maps).

Figure 5.7 shows a perceptual map for seven supermarket chains. The results show that the supermarkets are grouped into two clusters: the high-price, wide product range group; and the low-price, narrow product range group. These are indicative of

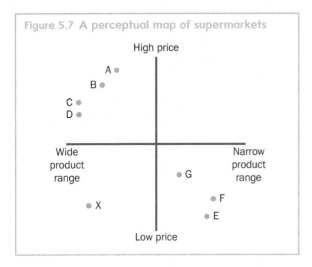

Figure 5.7 A perceptual map of supermarkets

two market segments and show that supermarkets C and D are close rivals, as measured by consumers' perceptions, and have very distinct perceptual positions in the marketplace compared with E, F and G. Perceptual maps are a visually appealing way of presenting a diverse market. They are also useful in considering strategic moves. For example, an opportunity may exist to create a differential advantage based on a combination of wide product range and low prices (as shown by the theoretical position at X).

Repositioning

Frequently, perhaps because of changing customer tastes or poor sales performance, a product or service will need to be repositioned. **Repositioning** involves changing the target markets, the differential advantage, or both (see Figure 5.8). The first option is to keep product and target market the same but to change the image of the product. For example, many companies marketing products to older customers are realizing that they need to be very careful in not portraying this group as kindly, slightly doddery souls when many remain reasonably healthy and active into old age. Therefore, the Complan brand of powdered energy drinks has changed its image from one of a caring, sickbed 'meal replacement' drink to a proactive brand with a sense of humour, by using tongue-in-cheek cartoon characters on its packaging and in its advertising, engaged in lively activities like skateboarding and crowd surfing.[32] An alternative approach is to keep the same target market but to modify the product. For example, in the intensely competitive mass car market, Ford brands like the Mondeo have had a reputation for being dull, so Ford is investing heavily in trying to make its car designs

more appealing to the consumer. A new design team was assembled and at the 2005 Frankfurt Motor Show, the new Ford Iosis was unveiled with a radical new design featuring doors that opened upwards, a sharply sloping windscreen and large wheels.

Some repositioning strategies involve retaining the product but changing the market segment it is aimed at (see Social Media Marketing 5.1). Lucozade, a carbonated drink, is a famous example of this kind of so-called 'intangible repositioning'. Manufactured by Beecham's Foods, it was initially targeted at sick children. Marketing research found that mothers were drinking it as a midday pick-me-up and the brand was consequently repositioned to aim at this new segment. Subsequently the energy-giving attributes of Lucozade have been used to appeal to a wider target market – young adults – by means of advertisements featuring leading athletes and soccer players. The history of Lucozade shows how a combination of repositioning strategies over time has been necessary for successful brand building. Several other brands have sought to repeat what Lucozade has done. For example, Rubex, the vitamin C drink, has transformed its positioning from a cold and flu drink to one that assists young people in overcoming the effects of a hard night's clubbing, while Red Bull has moved from a drink associated with clubbing to a more mainstream energy drink. Cadbury's has sought to reposition Roses and Flake into the rapidly growing premium chocolate segment, while Jose Cuervo spent $65 million on a promotional campaign entitled 'Vive Cuervo' (Live Cuervo) to broaden the appeal of tequila, which has traditionally been associated with student parties.[33]

When both product and target market are changed, a company is said to be practising 'tangible repositioning' (see Social Media Marketing 5.1). For example, a company may decide to move up- or down-market by introducing a new range

Figure 5.8 Alternative repositioning strategies

		Product	
		Same	Different
Target market	Same	Image repositioning	Product repositioning
	Different	Intangible repositioning	Tangible repositioning

Social Media Marketing 5.1 Repositioning Burberry

Critical Thinking: Below is a review of the British luxury brand Burberry which has used social media to increase the appeal of its brand. Read it and think of other brands that have tried to reposition. Critically assess the reasons for success or failure.

Burberry is an iconic English luxury brand that was founded by Thomas Burberry in 1856. It has become a well-known global label clearly identifiable by its signature check pattern that first appeared on its trench coats in 1924. It produces a diverse product range including menswear, fragrances, cosmetics and sunglasses and achieved global sales of over €2 billion in 2013. Luxury brands pride themselves on their exclusivity and aspirational quality and as a result many have been slow to adopt social media. However, Burberry has taken the opposite approach, embracing the new channels to broaden its appeal to new, younger consumers.

Its first foray into the world of digital was labelled the 'Art of Trench', utilizing its iconic trench coat, but in a contemporary way. The idea of the campaign was that existing customers could share photographs of themselves wearing their Burberry coats in unique and interesting settings. Others could then like and share the photos through social media. Publicity for the campaign was low key in keeping with the strategy of luxury brands – the emphasis was on the viral nature of the campaign. A further popular innovation was the live streaming of catwalk shows on Facebook providing fans with behind the scenes footage and rare insights into the fashion world. Traditionally, those getting to see catwalk shows might have to wait six months before they can get their hands on the clothes. Through social media, fans were being given the opportunity to order what they saw immediately – a strategy labelled 'Runway to Reality'. This was even further enhanced by the launch of Tweetwalk in 2011 where photos of clothes were tweeted to followers before they hit the catwalk. Understanding that music and fashion go hand-in-hand, it launched 'Burberry Acoustic', a collaboration with some leading bands where fans could enjoy rare live performances through Burberry's social media platforms. In a novel use of technology, visitors to its flagship store in London can enjoy the use of complimentary iPads allowing them to relax and browse through catalogues, watch videos of the clothes on models and even purchase and pay for products should they wish. In other words, the physical store had become an extension of the online store and vice versa.

Burberry's award-winning social media strategy had many benefits. It helped to imbue the brand with values such as innovation, creativity and modernism rather than being seen as a luxury brand that was rooted in the past. It enabled it to build a very large following on social channels. For example by 2014, it had 17 million fans on Facebook and 3 million Twitter followers. And it has helped to take sales for the brand globally over the €2 billion mark for the first time.

Based on: Doran (2014);[34] Grieve et al. (2013).[35]

of products to meet the needs of its new target customers. British Midland found it necessary to use both target and product repositioning in the face of growing competition in the airline business. The company was worried about its local British image and set about transforming itself into a global airline. It joined the Star Alliance led by Lufthansa and United Airlines, and commenced a long-haul service to the USA. It also spent £15 million on a corporate rebranding initiative to change its name from British Midland to bmi to create a more international appeal.

Summary

This chapter has examined the key activities of market segmentation, market targeting and positioning. The following issues were addressed.

1. The process of market segmentation: not all consumers in the market have the same needs and we can serve them better by segmenting the market into groups with homogeneous needs.

2. There are a variety of bases available for segmenting both consumer and industrial markets, and often a combination of bases is used to effectively segment markets. In consumer markets, behavioural variables such as benefits sought and purchase behaviour are particularly powerful bases for segmentation. Choice criteria are a key factor in segmenting organizational markets.

3. The five criteria for successful segmentation: effective, measurable, accessible, actionable and profitable.

4. The four generic target marketing strategies: undifferentiated marketing, differentiated marketing, focused marketing and customized marketing. Differentiated and focused marketing have their unique strengths and weaknesses, while customized marketing continues to grow in popularity.

5. What is meant by the concept of positioning, why it is important, and the need for clarity, consistency, credibility and competitiveness in a positioning statement. Consumers buy benefits, not products or services, and positioning is the key to conveying these benefits.

6. The concept of repositioning and the four repositioning strategies: image repositioning, product repositioning, intangible repositioning and tangible repositioning. Repositioning is challenging and should be undertaken with great care.

Study questions

1. Discuss the advantages of market segmentation.

2. You have been asked by a client company to segment the ice cream market. Use at least three different bases for segmentation and describe the segments that emerge.

3. Many consumer goods companies have recently been experimenting with the possibilities of a customized target marketing strategy. What are the advantages and limitations of such a strategy?

4. A friend of yours wants to launch a new breakfast cereal on the market but is unsure how to position the product. Develop a perceptual map of the breakfast cereal market identifying brands that compete in the same space and also if there are gaps where there are currently no major brands.

5. What is the difference between positioning and repositioning? Choose a brand that has been repositioned in the marketplace and describe both its old positioning and its new positioning. Is its repositioning strategy best described as image, product, intangible or tangible repositioning?

6. Visit Experian.co.uk and review the Mosaic Global geodemographic system. Select any one Mosaic group (e.g. Sophisticated Singles) and identify some products that could be targeted at this group and what kind of marketing strategy would be most appropriate for reaching the group.

Suggested reading

Canhoto, A. I, M. Clark and **P. Fennemore** (2013), Emerging Segmentation Practices in the Age of the Social Consumer, *Journal of Strategic Marketing,* **21** (5), 413–28.

Dibb, S. and **L. Simkin** (2009) Implementation Rules to Bridge the Theory/Practice Divide in Market Segmentation, *Journal of Marketing Management,* **25** (3/4), 375–96.

Franke, N., P. Keinz and **C. J. Steger** (2009) Testing the Value of Customization: When Do Customers Really Prefer Products Tailored to Their Preferences? *Journal of Marketing,* **73** (5), 103–21.

Pine, J.B. and **J.H. Gilmore** (2000) *Markets of One - Creating Customer-unique Value through Mass Customization,* Boston, MA: Harvard Business School Press.

Ries, A. and **J. Trout** (2001) *Positioning: The Battle for Your Mind,* New York: Warner.

Yankelovich, D. and **D. Meer** (2006) Rediscovering Market Segmentation, *Harvard Business Review,* **84** (2), 122–31.

When you have read this chapter

log on to the Online Learning Centre for
Foundations of Marketing at
www.mheducation.co.uk/textbooks/fahy5
where you'll find links and extra online study tools for marketing.

References

1. **Gomez, R.** (2013) One Direction's Five Lessons in Building Customer Loyalty, *MarketingProfs.com*, 8 August; **Ibrahim, M.** (2013) Lessons Marketers can Learn from the One Direction Brand Phenomenon, *Marketingmagazine.co.uk*, 21 August; **Lawrence, J.** (2013) One Direction Could be the First Boy Band Worth $1 Billion, *BusinessInsider.com*, 2 August.
2. **Aroean, L.** and **N. Michaelidou** (2014), A Taxonomy of Mobile Phone Consumers: Insights for Marketing Managers, *Journal of Strategic Marketing*, **22** (1) 73-89.
3. **Van Raaij, W.F.** and **T.M.M. Verhallen** (1994) Domain-specific Market Segmentation, *European Journal of Marketing*, **28** (10), 49-66.
4. **Hodson, S.** (2010) Skype Commands 13 Percent of International Calls, *The Inquisitor*, 3 May.
5. **Heile, C.** (2009) Brands: Taking a Narrow View, *Brandchannel. com*, 5 January.
6. **Tynan, A.C.** and **J. Drayton** (1987) Market Segmentation, *Journal of Marketing Management*, **2** (3), 301-35.
7. **Berg, M.D.** (2014) Lululemon Scrambles to Reverse its Bad PR, *Adage.com*, 14 January.
8. **Mattioli, D.** (2012) Lululemon's Secret Sauce, *Wallstreetjournal.com*. 22 March.
9. **Wexler, E.** (2012) Brands of the Year: Lululemon Takes Local to the Next Level, *Strategy Online*. September 28.
10. **Anonymous** (2007) The Boomers' Babies, *The Economist*, 11 August, 60.
11. **Jones, H.** (2002) What Are They Playing At? *Financial Times*, Creative Business, 17 December, 6.
12. **Pidd, H.** (2007) We Are Coming for your Children, *Guardian. co.uk*, 31 July.
13. **Lindstrom, M.** (2003) The Real Decision Makers, *Brandchannel. com*, 11 August.
14. **Anonymous** (2011) Peggy Sue Got Old, *The Economist*, 9 April, 67-8.
15. **O'Brien, S.** and **R. Ford** (1988) Can We at Last Say Goodbye to Social Class? *Journal of the Market Research Society*, **30** (3), 289-332.
16. **Barber, B.** (2007) *Consumed: How Markets Corrupt Children, Infantilize Adults and Swallow Citizens Whole*, London: W. H. Norton & Co.
17. **Mitchell, V.W.** and **P.J. McGoldrick** (1994) The Role of Geodemographics in Segmenting and Targeting Consumer

Markets: A Delphi Study, *European Journal of Marketing*, **28** (5), 54-72.
18. **Corey, R.** (1978) *The Organisational Context of Industrial Buying Behavior*, Cambridge, MA: Marketing Science Institute, 6-12.
19. **Anonymous** (2014), Kings of the Road, *Economist*, 11 January 49-50.
20. **Richards, H.** (1996) Discord Amid the High Notes, *The European*, 16-22 May, 23.
21. **Ritson, M.** (2013) LeFerrari Shows LeWay Forward, *Marketing Week.com*, 9 May.
22. **Gayatri, D.** and **T. Phani Madhav** (2004) Gap and Banana Republic: Changing Brand Strategies with Fashion, Case 504-087-1, *European Case Clearing House*.
23. **Ritson, M.** (2010) Why Ford's Focus is the Best in the Business, *MarketingWeek.co.uk*, 4 August.
24. **Anonymous** (2011) In the Cheap Seats, *The Economist*, 29 January, 56.
25. **Marsh, P.** (2004) Mass-Produced for Individual Tastes, *Financial Times*, 22 April, 12.
26. **Westbrook R.** and **P. Williamson** (1993) Mass Customisation: Japan's New Frontier, *European Management Journal*, **11** (1), 38-45.
27. **Anonymous** (2014) Printing a Bit of Me, *Economist Technology Quarterly*, 8 March, 15-17.
28. **Franke, N., P. Keinz** and **C. J. Steger** (2009) Testing the Value of Customization: When Do Customers Really Prefer Products Tailored to Their Preferences? *Journal of Marketing*, **73** (5), 103-21.
29. **Madden, C.** (2007) Coca-Cola Zero: The Real Thing or the Same Thing? *Irish Times*, 16 March, 12.
30. **Ries, A.** and **J. Trout** (2001) *Positioning: The Battle For Your Mind*, New York: Warner.
31. **Fahy, J.** (2001) *The Role of Resources in Global Competition*, London: Routledge.
32. **Dowdy, C.** (2005) Advertisers Smoke Out Images of Pipes and Slippers, *Financial Times*, 7 November, 30.
33. **Silver, S.** (2003) Tequila Tries to Get Out of the Slammer, *Financial Times*, 22 May, 15.
34. **Doran, S.** (2014) How Burberry Does Digital, *LuxurySociety. com*, 10 January.
35. **Grieve, J., A. Idiculla** and **K. Tobias** (2013) Entrenched in the Digital World, *BusinessToday.com*, 3 February.

Rolex: the symbol of personal achievement

Luxury brands are often associated with the core competences of creativity, exclusivity, craftsmanship, precision, high quality, innovation and premium pricing. Rolex, the leading name in luxury wristwatches, has been viewed as a symbol for prestige and performance for over a century. The crown logo of the Rolex brand symbolizes the superiority of the product and the sense of personal achievement associated with wearing a Rolex. Rolex was placed top on the list of Super brands in 2013 for a second consecutive year. This consumer survey rates leading products based on reputation, quality, reliability and distinction of offerings, based on the emotional and functional benefits they provide when compared with competitors. Rolex has maintained its position as a market leader in the luxury watch market by engaging in a very successful segmentation, target marketing and positioning strategy. However, this strategy presents a new challenge to Rolex, as it faces the difficult task of becoming the watch choice of a generation of younger consumers.

History

Rolex was founded in 1905 by German, Hans Wilsdorf and Alfred Davis. Wilsdorf and Davis was the original name of what later became the Rolex Watch Company. Hans Wilsdorf registered the trademark name 'Rolex' in Switzerland in 1908. The name Rolex was conceived as it was easy to pronounce in every language

and short enough to figure on the dial of the watch. At that time, Swiss workshops produced mostly pocket watches as it was still difficult to manufacture small enough movements that could be used in a wristwatch. In 1910, a Rolex watch was the first wristwatch in the world to receive the Swiss Certificate of Precision, granted by the Official Watch Rating Centre in Bienne. In 1914, Kew Observatory in Great Britain awarded a Rolex wristwatch a class 'A' precision certificate which until that point had been reserved exclusively for marine chronometers. This led to Rolex watches becoming synonymous with precision. Wilsdorf later relocated Rolex to Geneva in 1919. In 1926, Rolex took a major step towards developing the world's first waterproof wristwatch named the Oyster. The Oyster watch featured a sealed case providing optimal protection. The following year the Oyster was worn by Mercedes Gleitze, a young English swimmer who swam the English Channel. The watch remained in perfect working order after the 10-hour swim. This gave rise to the use of testimonials by Rolex to convey the superiority of the brand. In 1931, Rolex invented the world's first winding mechanism with a perpetual rotor. This system remains at the origin of every modern automatic watch. In the early 1950s, Rolex developed professional watches whose function went beyond that of simply telling time. The Submariner, launched in 1953, was the first watch guaranteed waterproof to a depth of 100 metres. In the same year, the expedition led by Sir Edmund Hillary, equipped with the Oyster Perpetual, became the first to reach the summit of Mount Everest.

Before his death in 1960, Hans Wilsdorf created a private trust run by a board of directors to ensure the company could never be sold. Today, Rolex is the largest single luxury watch brand, with estimated revenues of around $4.5 billion in 2013 and annual production of between 650,000 and 800,000 watches. Rolex has remained independent even as many major competitors have sought the shelter of conglomerates. Rolex currently has 28 affiliates worldwide and maintains a network of 4,000 watchmakers in over 100 countries. According to Forbes (2013), Rolex has an estimated brand value of $7.4 billion.

The watch industry

The world of luxury is not just exclusive, it is highly secretive too. Several of the large luxury brands are privately held, like Rolex, and therefore are not required to report annual or quarterly results. Many publicly listed companies (e.g. Louis Vuitton and Gucci) are part of much bigger companies which makes assessing the individual performance of these brands difficult to do with any accuracy. Many brands have responded to competition by merging into conglomerates focused on vertical integration. LVMH Moët Hennessy Louis Vuitton, the world's largest luxury goods company, includes watch brands such as Tag Heuer, Zenith and Dior Watches. Compagnie Financière Richemont, the world's third largest luxury goods maker, owns watch brands such as Cartier, Baume and Mercier, Piaget, Jaeger-LeCoultre, and Officine Panerai. Well-known brands Movado, Patek Philippe and Breitling remain essentially independent. In terms of watches, Switzerland possesses close to 100 per cent of the luxury market value which represents 48 per cent of the watch market value.

Recent trends in the luxury market

Exports of Swiss watches dropped 22 per cent in 2009 which represented the biggest drop since the Great Depression. However, the 2009 crisis proved short-lived. As early as the following year, the watch industry returned to its growth trajectory at lightning speed. Double-digit growth rates were recorded in 2010, 2011, and 2012 (+22.2 per cent, +19.4 per cent, +11.0 per cent respectively) despite the strength of the Swiss franc and the Euro crisis. In 2012, watch exports reached a record value of CHF 21.4 billion. Global interest for luxury watches grew +3.3 per cent, led by BRIC markets (+33.0 per cent). The three largest markets were China (25.6 per cent market share), the United States (19.5 per cent market share) and the United Kingdom (8.6 per cent market share). Global demand growth was fuelled by BRIC markets with the highest year-to-year increases in China (+36 per cent), Brazil (+29.4 per cent), Russia (+28.5 per cent) and India (+19.7 per cent). Early signs of demand decline were seen mostly in developed, mature, Western markets. The United States decreased by −11.6 per cent and Europe by −8.3 per cent. Rolex continues to lead the global ranking thanks to number one spots in mostly developed, mature markets (the USA, India, Europe and the Middle East). Omega's continuing leadership in large, strongly developing markets (China, Brazil, Russia, Japan, Asia Pacific, Latin America) has helped it slowly but surely gain ground on industry leader Rolex, with the gap between the two expected to close further.

Importance of emerging markets

In particular, the Swiss watch industry owes its success to its foresight in actively targeting growth in the emerging markets. By far the biggest contribution to the growth of Swiss watch exports over the past decade has come from Asia. In overall terms, the Asian countries were responsible for around 70 per cent of the rise in exports from 2000–12. In 2000, Swiss exports of small watches to China amounted to just CHF 16.8 million. Since then, the value of annual exports has multiplied by a factor of 97 and totalled CHF 1.6 billion in 2012. After many years of spectacular growth, Swiss exports of small watches to China began to fall abruptly in the middle of 2012. Reasons include anti-corruption measures and restrictions on advertising, as well as slower economic growth in China. On account of further improvements in people's living standards and the dismantling of trade barriers (under the free trade agreement), China is likely to continue growing as an export destination. Similarly, due to rising incomes and growing prosperity, other emerging markets such as Vietnam, India, Russia, Ukraine, Malaysia, South Korea and Mexico will offer substantial growth opportunities for the watch industry over the next few years. Brazil, South Africa and Turkey also offer opportunities. Whether Rolex can indeed exploit the potential that exists in these emerging markets remains to be seen due to a number of potential challenges.

Challenges for Rolex

Rolex faces a number of significant challenges in the luxury market which will be outlined below.

Over-dependence on current target market

This represents the greatest challenge for Rolex. Rolex is faced with building relevance among a younger audience. A new generation of affluent consumers is needed to generate a vital source of business in both established and emerging markets. Unfortunately, many younger consumers see Rolex as an older status symbol and not a contemporary icon of achievement. A large majority view Rolex as the watch choice of their predecessors and parents. The average Rolex customer is 45+ and Rolex now needs to build interest, relevance and aspiration among consumers in their 30s and younger, in order to drive long-term growth. Rolex is in jeopardy of being seen as an older symbol of personal wealth, instead of a crowning symbol of timeless human achievement. Similarly, Rolex has been characterized as having a more 'male' identity and the brand still sells the majority of its watches to men. The opportunity of increasing its presence in the female segment has been identified as an area for development, but the company still appears to have difficulty in attracting new female customers. The positioning strategy that has been so successful for Rolex is in danger of isolating a new generation of consumers. Rolex faces a similar challenge of exploiting its target market in new emerging markets.

Counterfeit

Like many high-priced, brand-name accessories, Rolex watches are among the most counterfeited brands of watches, illegally sold on the street and on the Internet. According to the FH – Federation of the Swiss watch industry – counterfeit causes damage of CHF 800 billion to Swiss watchmakers. These fake watches are mainly produced in China due to the ease in copying the general design (EU figures show that 54 per cent of fakes seized in 2004 originated in China) and retail anywhere from $5 upwards to $1000 for high end replicas fabricated in gold. It is estimated that over 75 per cent of all replica watches produced annually are copies of Rolex Oyster Perpetual designs. It is widely accepted that the number of counterfeits on the market is larger than the number of original pieces. This figure serves as proof of the brand's aspirational quality.

Rolex positioning

Distribution

Rolex maintains its positioning strategy by limiting production, even as demand increases. For luxury goods, scarcity in the marketplace can influence value, spur demand and contribute to long-term appreciation. Rolex also ensures that its watches are sold only in designated stores. The crystal prism that indicates a store is an 'Official Rolex Dealer' is highly prized. Rolex seeks dealers with a high-end image, relatively large stores, and attractive locations that can provide outstanding service. Maintaining this standard is not always easy. Rolex previously had a dispute with Tiffany because the retailer was imprinting

its name on the Rolex watches it sold. When Tiffany refused to stop, Rolex dropped Tiffany as an official retailer. Similarly, in the 1990s, as part of an effort to control sales of their goods in the grey market, Rolex cancelled agreements with 100 dealers. More recently Rolex fought a lengthy court battle with online retailer eBay seeking an injunction to prevent the sale of Rolex-branded watches by the online auctioneer. The Supreme Court stated in its decision that eBay must take preventative measures to ensure that no counterfeit goods are sold under the pretence of being authentic Rolex watches.

Branding

Rolex has also focused on maintaining the purity of its brand image. Many luxury-goods makers have used their original product as a springboard for brand extensions (e.g. Cartier and Mont Blanc) while others have licensed their brand to other manufacturers. Rolex has, so far, not diversified into the production of parallel products. However, Rolex did launch the Tudor brand, aimed at competing with Tag Heuer and other competitors within the accessible luxury market. For example, the price tag on a typical Rolex started at $2,000 and could go as high as $180,000 whereas a Tudor watch ranges from $850 to $4,000 (see Table C5.1 for price segmentation). There is no direct reference to the Tudor brand on the official Rolex website and as it is owned by Rolex, no financial information is made available to the public. The clear distinction between both brands has prevented any dilution of the value of the Rolex brand in the luxury market. However, the launch of Tudor in this market segment has contributed to Rolex being ineffective at reaching a younger market.

Communications

Rolex uses a number of marketing communication tools to effectively convey its positioning strategy. Print advertising in upmarket publications such as the *Financial Times* and *Vogue* remain popular. Sponsorship and testimonials remain central to Rolex marketing communications. Rolex aims to select people who have achieved something so that Rolex can reinforce the similar values of the brand. Rolex has links to the Arts (Michael Bublé), motor sports (Jackie Stewart), equestrian, exploration, skiing and yachting. Rolex has had a long association with golf since 1967, when Arnold Palmer became a testimonee. Today it sponsors major

Table C5.1 Typical price segmentation in the watch industry

Price category	Definition	Technology*	Brand examples
Over CHF3,000 (over EUR2,000)	'Exclusive luxury' segment	M	*Patek Philippe, Breguet*
Between CHF500 and CHF3,000 (between EUR350 and EUR2000)	'Accessible luxury' segment	M/Q	*Rado, Zenith, IWC*
Between CHF200 and CHF500 (between EUR150 and EUR350)	Mid-priced segment	Q/M	*Tissot, Maurice Lacroix*
Below CHF200 (below EUR150)	Low-priced segment	Q	*The Swatch, Coach*

Source: Pictet, FH
*Q = Quartz movement; M = Mechanical movement; Bold typeface indicates dominant technology.

events such as the US Open, Augusta Masters and the Ryder Cup and in a bid to attract a younger generation of consumers, Rolex has sponsored current players such as Ricky Fowler, Adam Scott and Martin Kaymer. Rolex remains a partner of the Wimbledon tennis tournament since 1978, with the Rolex clock synonymous with the scoreboard on Centre Court. Similarly, Rolex is robustly involved in philanthropy. It is the initiator of a mentoring programme, the Rolex Mentor and Protégé Arts Initiative, launched in 2002, as well as the Rolex Awards for Enterprise launched in 1978. Rolex also boasts almost 2.7 million Facebook users. These carefully selected methods of communication all reinforce the positioning of Rolex as a luxury brand.

Conclusion

In the future Rolex will face greater competition, particularly in Asia and other emerging markets, as competitors search for new ways to gain market share. The large luxury goods conglomerates enjoy certain advantages over an independent firm like Rolex. Many have restructured operations to take advantage of size and significantly reduce cost, enjoying synergies in advertising and marketing. The conglomerates may also be more willing to source from Asia, where labour costs are considerably lower than Switzerland. Crucially, these conglomerates also have successful brands targeted at a younger market. With an ageing

target market and difficulty in attracting a younger consumer base Rolex could become a prisoner of its own strategy. The strategy has been so well defined that it would be difficult for the company to change radically or become more innovative. It might be difficult to communicate any new strategy to customers without confusing them, leaving some market opportunities unattainable in the future.

Questions

1. Evaluate the alternative bases that Rolex might use to segment its market. Which base would you recommend and why?

2. Evaluate the current market targeting strategy being used by Rolex. Is it appropriate?

3. Discuss the key factors contributing to the success of Rolex's positioning strategy.

4. 'Rolex could become a prisoner of its own strategy.' Critically evaluate the advantages and disadvantages of implementing a repositioning strategy for Rolex.

This case was prepared by David Cosgrave, Limerick University from various published sources as a basis for class discussion rather than to show effective or ineffective management.

Part 2

Creating Customer Value

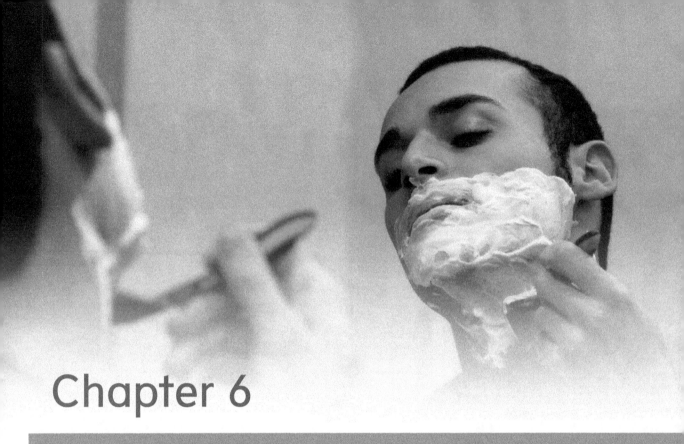

Chapter 6

Value through Products and Brands

Chapter outline

What is a product?

Product differentiation

Branding

Building brands

Managing brands

Managing product and brand portfolios

Managing brands and product lines over time:
the product life cycle

New product development

Learning outcomes

By the end of this chapter you will:

1   Understand what is meant by a product in marketing terms

2   Explain the differences between products and brands

3   Analyse the alternative ways of differentiating products

4   Evaluate the key aspects of building and managing a successful brand

5   Critique the role of brands in society

6   Analyse how to manage a diverse product or brand portfolio

7   Understand how product performance evolves over time

8   Explain the importance of innovation and the new product development process.

MARKETING SPOTLIGHT

Gillette

When it comes to the leading consumer brands, Gillette is right up there at the top of the list. It has dominated the global shaving market for over 100 years and it sets the benchmark for innovation in the sector. Despite its focus on one primary product category it has built a brand that is ranked in the Top 20 in terms of value in the world. And though faced with pressures from own-labels and other low price competitors, it continues to enjoy some of the juiciest margins in consumer marketing. How has it managed to achieve all this?

The story starts in New York in the late 1800s with an individual who had the interesting name of King Camp Gillette. King began his professional life as a travelling salesman but innovation fascinated him and, in 1895, he came up with the disposable razor. It was a stroke of genius that was to serve the company that he founded very well for years to come. By separating the razor and the blades, Gillette created a business model that has been imitated everywhere from printers to coffee to music. The hardware (in this case the razor) is sold very cheaply or given away for free but the software (the blades) are expensive. The principle is that once the 'hardware' is purchased or in use, consumers will not change and will continue to buy the expensive 'software'. It has been estimated that the profit margins on replacement blades can be anything up to 3,000 per cent, making Gillette a lot of money.

While this core model remains the key to Gillette's success today, the company has never forgotten the importance of continuous product innovation. For example, in 1990, Gillette launched the Sensor with spring-loaded blades meaning that the blades could recede into the cartridge head allowing for a closer shave and resulting in fewer cuts. This was followed in 1998 with the Mach 3, the world's first three-blade razor, which required fewer strokes resulting in less skin irritation. A new five-bladed razor, the Gillette Fusion was launched in 2006.

Along with product innovation, Gillette has invested very heavily in brand building. As far back as the early 1900s, Gillette was using famous baseball players to endorse its products. Its other major launches have relied on endorsements from celebrity sportspeople of the day such as David Beckham for the Mach 3 and Tiger Woods, Roger Federer and Thierry Henry for the Gillette Fusion. Celebrities like Jennifer Lopez are the face of the Venus range of shaving products for women. In its advertising, Gillette communicates the emotional value of its products by associating them with successful men. Its famous 'the best a man can get' global advertising campaign featured men that successfully balanced work, play and their home lives.

In recent years, Gillette has faced some new challenges. First is increased price competition from online brands such as DollarShaveClub and own-brands such as Lidl and Aldi. And second, the market has changed with a more casual unshaven look as well as the growth of full beards becoming popular again. But opportunities also abound. While facial hair might be making a comeback, body shaving by men and women is growing so Gillette Body Razor was launched in 2014.[1]

As we saw in Chapter 1, the essence of marketing is the delivery of value to some customer group. Products and brands are the embodiment of that value proposition. For example, until recently, two of the dominant brands in the mobile phone business were Nokia and BlackBerry. In the early part of this century, Nokia was the undisputed global leader in the rapidly growing mobile phone industry. It led the way in consumer markets with innovative designs, the most extensive product range and a strong brand proposition, namely, 'connecting people'. In terms of the decade from 2000 to 2009, Nokia accounted for over one third of all mobile phones sold globally, far ahead of its nearest rival, Motorola. The Canadian brand, BlackBerry was more favoured by business professionals as it contained a full QWERTY keyboard and a facility for checking and responding to emails. So powerful was its appeal that it earned itself the nickname 'Crackberry' – a reference to the addictiveness of the drug crack cocaine. Towards the end of the last decade, these two brands were also the leaders in the then emerging smartphone business, Nokia with 39 per cent and BlackBerry a further 20 per cent of the market in 2009. But their failure to match the innovativeness and market orientation of brands like Apple and Samsung has meant that their decline since then has been swift and, in terms of total global sales in 2013, Nokia was ranked ninth with BlackBerry dropping out of the top 10 altogether.

This chapter will deal with all these core marketing issues. First, we will begin by examining what we mean by the term 'product' and then explaining the difference between a product and a brand, which is one of the most important distinctions that students of marketing must grasp. Then we will take a comprehensive look at the different aspects of managing modern brands. Many firms, such as global corporations like Diageo or Colgate, can have an extensive range of brands, so we will also examine how to manage these portfolios of brands or products. As the example of brands like Nokia and BlackBerry shows, the demand for products can change very rapidly, so we will look, too, at how to manage products and brands effectively over time. An important element of this is innovation and ensuring a steady supply of new products, which is also discussed.

What is a product?

Conventionally, when thinking about products, people tend to think of tangible items such as a mobile phone, a plasma screen television or a kettle and so on. These are all products but in marketing terms, the definition of what comprises a product is much broader. A visit to a theme park like Legoland is a product, so is a sports star like Usain Bolt, so is the running of the bulls in Pamplona, the fund-raising efforts of the International Red Cross and the political activities of the Liberal Democratic party. In marketing terms, any form of value that is offered in exchange for money, votes or time is a product. In recent years, we have seen an increase in the marketing of ideas. For example, **social marketing** has emerged as a field of study due to the increase in marketing efforts behind socially beneficial causes such as the reduction in obesity and alcoholism and the promotion of wilderness protection, human rights and so on.

One of the most effective ways to think about products is in terms of their mix of tangible and intangible components (see Figure 6.1). Some products are high on tangible components and the company's marketing of these products places a great deal of emphasis on these tangible elements. Those at the intangible end of the spectrum are usually referred to as services and in Chapter 7 we will focus more specifically on the types of marketing efforts that are employed when creating value through service, experiences and relationships. But it is important to remember that almost all value offerings combine elements of both tangible and

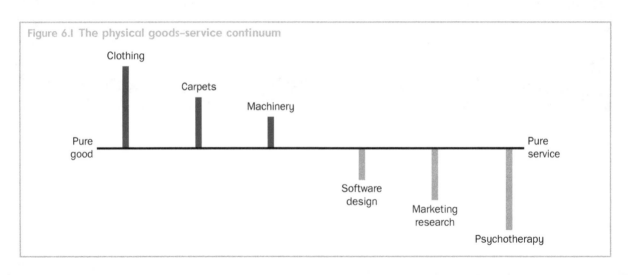

Figure 6.1 The physical goods–service continuum

Exhibit 6.1 Years of brand development by Adidas means that its three stripe logo is instantly recognizable

Exhibit 6.1 Years of brand development by Adidas means that its three stripe logo is instantly recognizable

to satisfy customer needs by providing some form of benefit or value. **Brands**, on the other hand, fulfil the very important function of distinguishing the offering of one company from those of others in a competitive environment (see Exhibit 6.1). The word 'brand' is derived from the old Norse word 'brandr', which means 'to burn' as brands were and still are the means by which livestock owners mark their animals to identify ownership.[2] As we shall see below, branding has become an ever more important aspect of marketing. This is due to the fact that the technical differences between products are becoming fewer and fewer. For example, the competing brands of many basic consumer electronics like DVD players may all be made in the same factory on the same production line. The technical features of the product are mainly the same – the only element that differs is the name. In these situations, value is derived less from the actual product and more from the brand associations. The power of brands to affect perceptions is particularly noticeable in blind product testing, where customers often fail to distinguish between competing offerings even though they may have a high level of loyalty to one brand. The power of brands over products can also be seen in the way that some products are more commonly known by the brand name than by the product name.

intangible components. Apple markets innovative handheld items like smartphones and tablets but the experience of the Apple store is an important part of its offering. A consultation with a psychotherapist is largely an intangible, mental activity but it will take place in a physical setting such as a consultation room (that probably contains a couch!).

The next important distinction that needs to be made is between products and brands. As we saw above a product can be anything that has the capacity

Product differentiation

To understand fully both the nature of the product offering and how it can be best distinguished from those of competitors, it has been customary to think in terms of the different levels of product (see Figure 6.2). At the most basic level, there is the core benefit

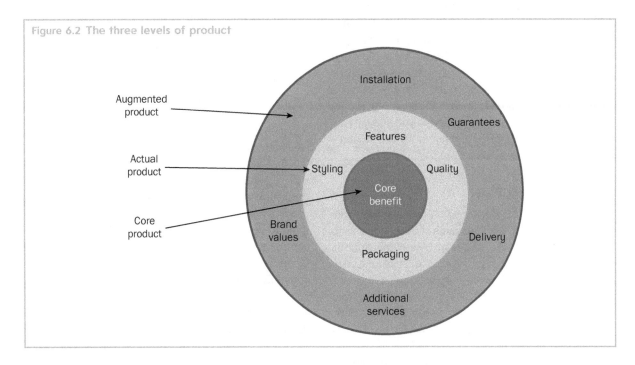

Figure 6.2 The three levels of product

Augmented product

Actual product

Core product

Installation

Guarantees

Features

Styling   Quality

Core benefit

Brand values

Delivery

Packaging

Additional services

provided by the product, such as cars that provide transportation or telephones that provide a means of communication. Products will quickly decline if the core benefit can be met most effectively in another way as we saw in the case of Nokia above. Around the basic benefit is the 'actual product' the consumer purchases, which comprises certain features, styling, and so on. For example, a Neff electric oven is an actual product, which is a blend of design, style, features and packaging assembled to meet the needs of the market. There is also a third level of product, namely the 'augmented product'. This is the additional bundle of benefits that are added to a product, and typically include elements like guarantees, additional services and additional **brand values**. For example, the Lexus GS includes extras like a keyless entry system, air-conditioned front seats, Bluetooth connectivity for mobile phones, parking-assist sensors and a rear electric sunshade. Product differentiation can take place at any of these three levels.

Core differentiation

The most radical product differentiation takes place at the core level and usually arises when there are significant technological breakthroughs. Therefore, the core benefit of keeping track of our appointments has moved from paper diaries to electronic ones stored on PCs or mobile phones with significant implications for paper diary manufacturers like Filofax. Similarly, the music industry has been transformed many times as technological changes enabled consumers to switch first from albums to CDs and then from CDs to digital downloading and streaming. The first change meant a significant rise in profits for music companies, the second, a significant fall. Core differentiation also occurs due to shifts in strategic thinking. For example, for years, airlines have been trying to outdo each other by competing on actual differentiation such as expanding menu items on flights. Low-cost carriers have made huge inroads in the business by simply focusing again on the core benefit, namely, moving people from one location to another and by removing – or charging customers for – any extras.

Actual differentiation

Actual differentiation occurs when organizations aim to compete on the basis of elements of the product such as its quality, its design, its features or its packaging. Quality is a key aspect of the product and has long been positively associated with corporate performance. It refers to both the fact that a product is free from defects and that it meets the needs of customers. Around the world, most companies look to the uniform standards of the International Organization for Standardization (ISO) for quality guidelines through its various certifications such as ISO 9001. Operational systems such as total quality management (TQM) are employed to emphasize the relentless pursuit of quality. Problems with quality regularly undermine the marketing efforts of companies. For example, Toyota is one of the most renowned brands in the world but it has suffered significant quality problems involving both the acceleration and braking of some of its car brands in 2009 and 2010. In all, a total of over 9 million Toyota vehicles have had to be recalled resulting in damage to the brand as well as potentially expensive legal judgments against it. Product safety is particularly crucial in industries such as food, transport and medicines. How firms deal with these problems is also very important.

 Tropicana Ad Insight: This ad shows how it aims to differentiate itself through the quality of its products.

With the increased difficulty of differentiating products based on their features many companies turn to elements like product design. For example, Evian is one of Europe's leading bottled water brands, but its position was being eroded by a range of local competitors in different countries. Water bottles had traditionally been designed to meet the needs of retailers allowing for easy storage on shelves, but Evian's research had indicated that consumers wanted a bottle that fitted with their lifestyles. It released a new looped bottle cap and demand in France tripled in the year of the bottle's launch.[3] Other leading firms like Dyson, Apple and Sony are renowned for their design capability. Key to effective design is a deep understanding of customer lifestyles and preferences.

Packaging involves all those decisions on the kind of container or wrapper used for the product. In the past, the primary purpose of packaging was simply to protect the product but in modern marketing it has a much more significant role in terms of attracting attention, carrying information about the product and conveying elements of the product's positioning. For example, the packaging of Apple products is highly distinctive with a focus on style and minimalism. Organizations frequently change their product packaging as part of their marketing strategy but this is a difficult and risky thing to do. For example, the fair trade tea and coffee company Cafédirect, changed its packaging in 2009 to draw a clearer link between its products and the actual farmers who grow them to reflect the product's authenticity. A major packaging change may mean that some existing customers no longer recognize or can find the product.

There are several important ethical dimensions to packaging as well. Slack packaging describes the situation where products are packaged in oversized containers giving the impression that they contain more than they actually do. Accurate labelling is also a significant issue, particularly in the case of food products. For example, in the UK, the 'country of origin' is only the last country where the product was 'significantly changed'. So oil pressed from Greek olives in France can be labelled 'French' and foreign imports that are packed in the UK can be labelled 'produce of the UK'. Consumers should be wary of loose terminology. For example, Bachelors Sugar Free Baked Beans actually contain 1.7g of sugar per 100g, Kerry LowLow Spread, which is marketed as low in fat, contains 38g of fat per 100g and Walkers Lite crisps are a hefty 22 per cent fat. Attempts by consumer groups to have labelling systems that highlight this information have been resisted by leading manufacturers and retailers, who favour a system whereby levels of sugar, fats and salt are given as a percentage of an adult's 'guideline daily amount'.[4] Similarly EU legislation aims to outlaw vague claims such as 'vitalize your body and mind' (Red Bull) or 'cleanse and refresh your body and soul' (Kombucha).[5]

Augmented differentiation

Finally, organizations may choose to differentiate their offerings on the augmented dimensions. Most differentiation efforts take place at this level (see Marketing in Action 6.1). Firms are constantly looking

---

Marketing in Action 6.1 Ziggo: finding a new basis to compete

Critical Thinking: Below is a review of Ziggo's augmented differentiation strategy. Read it and consider other examples of augmented differentiation that you can think of.

Ziggo is a major cable operator in the Netherlands providing cable television, broadband Internet and telephone services to both residential and commercial customers. Competition in this market is intense with similar or overlapping services provided by both Internet and telephone companies. Chief among Ziggo's competitors were multinational operators like Tele2 and UPC as well as the former government-owned operator, KPN. Ziggo sought to differentiate itself from this competition by pursuing an augmented differentiation strategy. While most operators compete based on 'actual' dimensions like the quality and extent of their networks, it took a different approach through investing in its brand and positioning itself as an entertainment company rather than simply an access provider.

Key to this strategy was the decision not to focus on actual product dimensions. For example, it chose not to talk about its landline telephone connections as this is a declining business with consumers switching to mobile. Similarly, though high-speed Internet is an important attribute, specifications are not of interest or are irrelevant to the average consumer. It is also difficult to gain a competitive advantage on this dimension as rival firms can also claim high Internet speeds. Instead it chose to make interactive television (iTV) the centrepiece of its marketing campaign, as this enabled Ziggo to communicate more powerful emotional themes. iTV puts the customer in control – they could choose to watch what they wanted, when they wanted. To convey this message, it created a series of commercials featuring Dutch celebrities and showing them watching their ideal night's television (because they can choose to watch what they want).

The campaign was highly successful. Sales of its 'All-In-One' bundle rose from 260,000 to 675,000 in one year, propelling it from the number three position in the market to market leader. Brand awareness rose from 69 per cent to 86 per cent over the course of the campaign. Perceptions of the Ziggo brand also improved with the campaign driving increases in attributes such as 'is a company I can trust', 'is a company that knows my needs', and 'gives me a positive feeling'. By focusing on the augmented elements of its business, Ziggo was able to steal a march on its competitors.

Based on: Anonymous (2011).[6]

for new features that they can add which will give them an advantage in the marketplace. For example, mobile phone manufacturers are constantly trying to improve dimensions like screen size and resolution, weight and portability, navigation features and reliability. However, these types of advantages are often short-lived, being quickly imitated by competitors or becoming standard parts of the offering of all major rivals. As a result, firms are putting greater efforts into intangible changes which cannot be so easily imitated. These intangible elements are captured in the brand and it is to this key decision that we now turn.

Branding

Developing a brand is difficult, expensive and takes time. We have seen that brands enable companies to differentiate their products from competitive offerings, but we must look at the benefits of brands for both organizations and consumers in more detail.

The benefits of brands to organizations

Strong brands deliver the following benefits to organizations.

Company value

The financial value of companies can be greatly enhanced by the possession of strong brands. The concept of **brand equity** is used to measure the strength of the brand in the marketplace and high brand equity generates tangible value for the firm in terms of increased sales and profits. For example, Nestlé paid £2.5 billion (€3.6 billion) for Rowntree, a UK confectionery manufacturer – a sum six times its balance sheet value. However, the acquisition gave Nestlé access to Rowntree's stable of brands,

including KitKat, Quality Street, After Eight and Polo (see Exhibit 6.2).

Consumer preference and loyalty

Strong brand names can have positive effects on consumer perceptions and preferences. This in turn leads to brand loyalty where satisfied customers continue to purchase a favoured brand. Over time some brands, such as Apple, Harley-Davidson and Virgin, become cult brands: consumers become passionate about the brand and levels of loyalty go beyond reason[7] (see Social Media Marketing 6.1). The strength of brand loyalty can be seen when companies try to change brands, such as Coca-Cola's proposed introduction of New Coke, or when the brand is threatened with extinction such as Bewley's Cafés in Dublin.[8]

Barrier to competition

The impact of the strong, positive perceptions held by consumers about top brands means it is difficult for new brands to compete. Even if the new brand performs well on blind taste tests, this may be insufficient to knock the market leader off the top spot. This may be one of the reasons that Virgin Coke and Lucozade Cola failed to dent Coca-Cola's domination of the cola market.

High profits

Strong, market-leading brands are rarely the cheapest. Brands such as Kellogg's, Coca-Cola, Mercedes, Apple and Intel are all associated with premium prices. This is because their superior brand equity means that consumers receive added value over their less powerful rivals. Strong brands also achieve distribution more readily and are in a better position to resist retailer demands for price discounts. Research into return on investment for US food brands supports the view that strong brands are more profitable. The number one brand's average return was 18 per cent, number two achieved 6 per cent, number three returned 1 per cent, while the number four position was associated with a minus 6 per cent average return on investment.[9]

Base for brand extensions

A strong brand provides a foundation for leveraging positive perceptions and goodwill from the core brand to brand extensions. Examples include Pepsi Max, Lucozade Sport, Smirnoff Ice and Google Scholar. The new brand benefits from the added value that the brand equity of the core brand bestows on the extension.

Exhibit 6.2 This very clever outdoor advertisement is for KitKat, one of Nestlé's very powerful brands

Social Media Marketing 6.1 Facebook fans and brand communities

> **Critical Thinking:** Below is a review on the growth of Facebook fan pages. Read it and evaluate the pages where you are currently a fan. Why have these pages appealed to you? Reflect on your level of attachment to the brand or organization.

Brand communities have been formally defined as a 'specialized, non-geographically bound community based on a structured set of relationships among admirers of a brand'. Some have emerged organically and in other instances leading brands have attempted to create communities of followers. Among the most famous have been cult brands like Harley-Davidson

The Harley Owners Group – initially set up to counter the damage to the company's image caused by an association with Hell's Angels – consists of 866,000 members who organize bike rides, training courses, social events and charity fund-raisers. They pore over motorcycle magazines and wear Harley-branded gear to feel like rugged individualists. Over 250,000 attended the brand's centenary, held in Milwaukee in 2003.

Facebook has become the new vehicle through which brands can communicate with their communities of fans. The largest Facebook brand fan communities in 2013 were:

1 Facebook – 91.3 million fans
2 YouTube – 74.0 million
3 Coca-Cola – 64.2 million
4 MTV – 44.8 million
5 Disney – 44.0 million
6 Red Bull – 37.6 million
7 Converse - 36.4 million
8 Starbucks – 34.4 million
9 Oreo – 33.2 million
10 Playstation – 32.2 million

Facebook pages can be used for brand communications, running competitions, handling complaints, new announcements and so on. The creation of original, entertaining and shareable content such as videos and applications is critical to the popularity of a fan page. Pages also provide a forum for fans to share stories about the brand, to show how it is a part of their lives and to connect with like-minded devotees.

Several different metrics can be used to assess the overall effectiveness of a Facebook page. Total fan numbers are important but so also are the trends in these numbers. Many pages are growing in popularity while others are falling quickly. This is influenced by levels of page engagement which can also be measured in a variety of ways including number of posts, number of comments, participation in competitions, and so on. Some leading brands, nervous about possible negative commentary, do not allow fans to post comments on their official pages. These companies see their page more as a channel of communication to customers rather than a forum that is created by both the brand owners and its community of users. As such, Facebook pages may lure brand owners into thinking that they have a brand community when in reality they do not. True brand communities have a much higher level of connection and engagement with their favoured brands.

Based on: Balwani (2009);[10] Shayon (2011).[11]

The benefits of brands to consumers

Brands also provide consumers with a variety of benefits as follows.

Communicates features and benefits

In the first instance, brands are a source of information about a product. Through their associated marketing communications, they communicate information about a product and its benefits which assist consumers in making a buying decision. The associated brand elements also make it easier for consumers to identify products.

Reduces the risk in purchasing

As we saw in Chapter 3, consumers experience a range of potential risks when they are making a purchase, including functional risks (that the product does not perform to expectations), financial risk (that it is not worth the price that is paid) as well as social risk (that the product produces social embarrassment). Brands reduce these risks because consumers can trust the brands they choose based on past experiences (see Exhibit 6.3).

Simplifies the purchase decision

As we have seen already, we live in an over-communicated society where consumers are faced with a proliferation of product choices. To rationally evaluate all these options is impossible, so brands make consumers' lives easier by providing shortcuts for product choices. Trusted and preferred brands are purchased again and again giving rise to the notion of brand loyalty.

Symbolic value

Most importantly of all, brands provide consumers with the opportunity for self-expression. Brands of clothing, music, cars, perfume and so on are powerful indicators of the consumer's personality-type. For example, recent research has demonstrated the role of brands in signalling one's desirability to potential mates.[12]

Brands are not just a consumer phenomenon. They are also increasingly important in the worlds of industrial and technology marketing. For example, although many people would not recognize a microprocessor, the chances are that they have heard of Intel, one of the world's leading technology firms which has invested heavily in branding. But it is not something that is simple, as Microsoft found in its forays into brand building. An advertising campaign featuring its founder Bill Gates and comedian

Exhibit 6.3 Purchases such as car tyres carry several risks as this advertisement for one of the leading brands Continental demonstrates

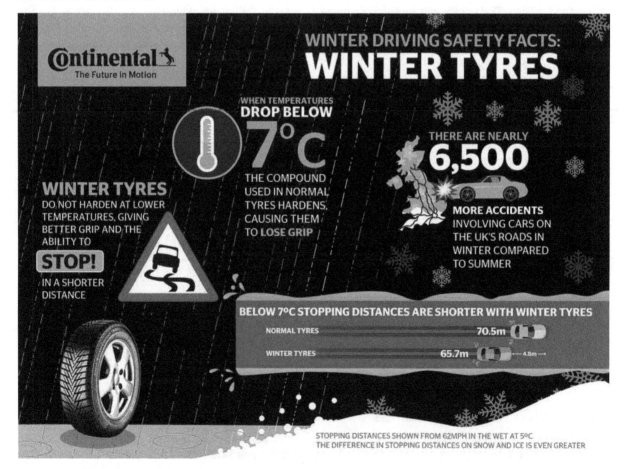

Marketing and Society 6.1 Brand values and the value of a brand

Inherent in the notion of a brand is the concept of value. When a consumer chooses a certain brand, they are doing so on the basis that a given brand delivers a certain level of value. But how accurate is this perception? For example, when a consumer buys a leading brand of running shoe, is she buying a higher level of value than if she bought a lesser-known brand or a cheaper running shoe? Consumers who are brand loyal would typically argue that a leading brand equates with better quality, but the research evidence does not always support this position. For example, a study published in the British Journal of Sports Medicine in 2007 showed that low- to medium-cost running shoes in each of three brands provided the same (if not better) cushioning of in-shoe pressure than high-cost running shoes.[13] A high-price brand, in this case, does not equate to greater levels of value as measured by product quality.

Critics of branding argue that brands do not provide value but rather an illusion of value. Vast sums are spent creating brands that are essentially not really all that different. Consumers pay more for leading brands in the belief that these are superior to other brands in terms of quality and specifications, when often this is not the case. A way out of this dilemma is to fully understand what we mean by consumer value. As shown in Chapter 3, consumers choose products for rational as well as emotional reasons. Brands are selected not only for their technical attributes but also for personal and social reasons. Should a consumer not have the option to select a brand if that brand, for example, makes them feel good about themselves or gives them the feeling that they are impressing their peers? Consumer societies are about choice and, increasingly, consumers have the information that they need to make informed choices. But, despite this, the debate concerning the real value of brands is likely to continue to rage into the future.

Suggested reading: Adamson (2006);[14] Klein (2000).[15]

Reflection: Critics of marketing contend that brand creation is unnecessary. Consider the points above and decide how you would respond.

Jerry Seinfeld confused many consumers.[16] The widespread development of brands in politics, popular culture and elsewhere means that the ethical dimensions of branding have taken on even greater importance (see Marketing and Society 6.1).

Building brands

Building brands involves making decisions about the brand name and how the brand is developed and positioned in the marketplace.

Naming brands

Three brand name strategies can be identified: family, individual and combination.

A **family brand name** is used for all products – for example, Philips, Heinz and Google. The goodwill attached to the family brand name benefits all brands, and the use of the name in advertising helps the promotion of all of the brands carrying the family name. The risk is that if one of the brands receives unfavourable publicity or is unsuccessful, the reputation of the whole range of brands can be tarnished. This is also known as 'umbrella branding'. Some companies create umbrella brands for part of their brand portfolios to give coherence to their range of products. For example, Sony has created PlayStation for its range of video game consoles.

The **individual brand name** does not identify a brand with a particular company – for example, Procter & Gamble does not use its company name on its brands Duracell, Head & Shoulders, Pampers, Pringles, and so on (see Table 6.4 later). This may be necessary when it is believed that each brand requires a separate, unrelated identity. In some instances, the use of a family brand name when moving into a new market segment may harm the image of the new product line. One famous example is the decision to use the Levi's family brand name on a new product line – Levi's Tailored Classics – despite marketing research information which showed that target customers associated the name Levi's with casual clothes, thus making it incompatible with the smart suits the company was launching. This mistake was not repeated by Toyota, which abandoned its family brand name when it launched its up-market executive car, the Lexus.

In the case of combination brand names, family and individual brand names are combined. This capitalizes on the reputation of the company while allowing the individual brands to be distinguished and identified (e.g. Kellogg's All Bran, Nokia Lumia, Microsoft Windows 8).

Much careful thought should be given to the choice of brand name since names convey images. For example, Renault chose the brand name Safrane for one of its executive saloons because research showed that this brand name conveyed an image of luxury, exotica, high technology and style. The brand name Pepsi Max was chosen for the diet cola from Pepsi targeted at men as it conveyed a masculine image in a product category that was associated with women. So, one criterion for deciding on a good brand name is that it evokes positive associations.

Another important criterion is that the brand name should be memorable and easy to pronounce. Short names such as Esso, Shell, Daz, Ariel, Swatch and Mini fall into this category. Interesting examples of name shortening are taking place online. Facebook has used the domain name for Montenegro – .me – for fb.me. There are exceptions to this general rule, as in the case of Häagen-Dazs, which was designed to sound European in the USA where it was first launched. A brand name may suggest product benefits – as in the case of Right Guard (deodorant), Alpine Glade (air and fabric freshener) and Head & Shoulders (anti-dandruff shampoo) – or express what the brand is offering in a distinctive way, such as Toys R Us. Technological products may benefit from numerical brand naming (e.g. Audi A4, Airbus A380, Yamaha YZF R125). This also overcomes the need to change brand names when marketing in different countries.

Some specialist companies have been established to act as brand-name consultants. Market research is used to test associations, memorability, pronunciation and preferences. The value of a good brand name can be seen in the prices paid for some of the top domain names in the world, such as diamond.com ($7.5 million), vodka.com ($3 million) and cameras. com ($1.5 million).[17] It is important to seek legal advice to ensure that a brand name does not infringe an existing brand name. Interesting controversies can arise relating to brand names and trademarks such as Victoria Beckham's efforts to stop Peterborough United Football Club trademarking their decades-old nickname 'Posh'. More controversially, some companies are also trying to obtain the legal rights to slogans – such as Nestlé for the KitKat slogan 'Have a Break'.

Legal protection for a brand name, brand mark or trade character is provided through the registration of **trademarks**. As brands assume greater importance so too does their legal protection. The Nike swoosh, the Starbuck's mermaid and the Apple icon are all highly valuable to their owners and these registered trademarks can be legally protected from copying by rivals. For example, Apple Computers won a court case against Apple Corporation – the owners of the Beatles Music company who had sued against its use of the apple logo. Trademarks also need to be protected online. Search advertising regulations allow firms to use trademarks as keywords and in display ads, increasing the costs of trademark protection for brand owners.[18]

Table 6.1 summarizes those issues that are important when choosing a brand name, while Table 6.2 shows how brand names can be categorized.

Developing brands

Building successful brands is an extremely challenging marketing task. In fact, of Britain's top 50 brands, only 18 per cent have been developed since 1975.[19] This also implies that when a brand becomes established, it tends to endure for a very long time. Table 6.3 lists the world's leading brands, some of which are over 100 years

Table 6.1 Brand name considerations

A good brand name should:	
1	evoke positive associations
2	be easy to pronounce and remember
3	suggest product benefits
4	be distinctive
5	use numerals when emphasizing technology
6	not infringe an existing registered brand name

Table 6.2 Brand name categories

People:	Cadbury, Mars, Heinz
Places:	Singapore Airlines, Deutsche Bank
Descriptive:	I Can't Believe it's Not Butter, The Body Shop, T-mobile
Abstract:	KitKat, Kodak, Prozac
Evocative:	Egg, Orange
Brand extensions:	Dove Deodorant, Virgin Direct, Playtex Affinity
Foreign meanings:	LEGO (from 'play well' in Danish), Thermos (meaning 'heat' in Greek)

Source: adapted from Miller, R. (1999) Science Joins Art in Brand Naming, *Marketing*, 27 May, 31–2.

old, so we can see that brand building is a long-term activity. There are many demands on people's attention; generating awareness, communicating brand values and building customer loyalty usually takes many years, which is why the rapid rise to prominence of brands like Amazon and Google is so admirable. Similarly, the Korean company, Samsung has moved from being seen as a company that produced cheap televisions and microwave ovens to a leading global premium brand in sectors like mobile phones, memory chips and flat panels. This was achieved through doubling its marketing spend to $3 billion, advertising that showed the company's prowess in technology, product placement in futuristic films like *Matrix Reloaded* and sponsorship of the Athens Olympics, which increased general awareness of the brand.[20] The value of the Samsung brand is now greater than that of the once dominant Sony. League tables like those presented in Table 6.3 are also illustrative in charting both the demise of venerable brands like Toyota, Gap, BlackBerry, Hewlett Packard and Cisco, and the rise of powerful new brands like Visa, Amazon and UPS. Management must be prepared to provide a consistently high level of brand investment to establish and maintain the position of a brand in the marketplace. Unfortunately, it can be tempting to cut back on expenditure in the short term, particularly when there is a downturn in the economy. Such cutbacks need to be resisted in order for the brand to be supported, as it is one of the key drivers of shareholder value.[21]

Figure 6.3 is an analytical framework that can be used to dissect the current position of a brand in the marketplace, and to form the basis of a new brand positioning strategy. The strength of a brand's position in the marketplace is built on six elements: brand domain, brand heritage, brand values, brand assets, brand personality and brand reflection. The first of these, brand domain, corresponds to the choice of target market (where the brand competes); the other five elements provide avenues for creating a clear differential advantage with these target consumers. These elements are expanded on briefly below.

1 *Brand domain*: the brand's target market, i.e. where it competes in the marketplace.
2 *Brand heritage*: the background to the brand and its culture. How it has achieved success (and failure) over its life (see Exhibit 6.4). For example, English

Table 6.3 The top 20 most valuable brands worldwide

Company	2013 brand value ($ billions)	Country of origin	% change from 2012
Apple	185.07	USA	1
Google	113.67	USA	5
IBM	112.54	USA	−3
McDonald's	90.26	USA	−5
Coca-Cola	78.42	USA	6
AT&T	75.51	USA	10
Microsoft	69.82	USA	−9
Marlboro	69.38	USA	−8
Visa	56.06	USA	46
China Mobile	55.39	China	18
General Electric	55.36	USA	21
Verizon	53.00	USA	8
Wells Fargo	47.79	USA	20
Amazon	45.72	USA	34
UPS	42.75	USA	15
ICBC	41.12	China	−1
Vodafone	39.71	UK	−8
Walmart	36.22	USA	5
SAP	34.37	Germany	34
Mastercard	27.82	USA	34

Source: Millward Brown.

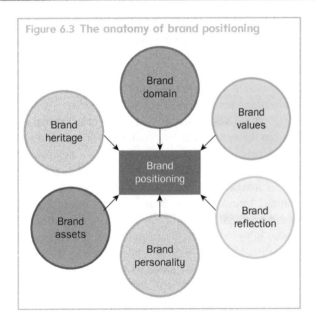

Figure 6.3 The anatomy of brand positioning

4 *Brand assets*: what makes the brand distinctive from other competing brands (symbols, features, images and relationships, etc.).

5 *Brand personality*: the character of the brand described in terms of other entities, such as people, animals or objects (See Marketing in Action 3.1). Celebrity endorsement of brands gives them personality. Sales of Kia Kaha, a small New Zealand-based company, were significantly boosted when Michael Campbell won the US Open golf tournament wearing its clothing.[22]

6 *Brand reflection*: how the brand relates to self-identity; how the customer perceives him/herself as a result of buying/using the brand.

Brand managers can form an accurate portrait of how brands are positioned in the marketplace by analysing each of the elements listed above. Brand building is expensive and great care needs to be taken with brand investment decisions. A classic case in point has been the decision by Gap to change its logo (see Marketing in Action 6.2).

wines like Chapel Down have been successful despite the country's lack of a wine heritage.

3 *Brand value*: the core values and characteristics of the brand.

Exhibit 6.4 This Audi advertisement demonstrates the brand's heritage with the slogan 'a sporty car full of history'

Audi R8. A sporty car full of history.

A la vanguardia de la técnica   Audi

Evian Ad Insight: The brand successfully uses viral advertising as part of its marketing strategy.

Marketing in Action 6.2 Gap's logo disaster

Critical Thinking: Below is a review of the failed attempt to redesign the Gap logo. Read it and discuss the extent to which a logo redesign was the correct response to Gap's problems. What initiatives should it have taken?

Gap is a leading US casual clothing brand. Its parent company, Gap Inc. was founded in San Francisco in 1969 and its range of casual clothes and accessories for men, women and children has become popular right around the world. However, due to its rapid global expansion, problems in brand management and increased competition, its sales and profits began to slide during the 2000s. One of its strategic responses was to unveil a new logo for the brand in 2010. Out went its iconic blue box logo to be replaced by the word Gap with a blue box located behind the p.

In doing so, Gap adopted an interesting approach. It quietly unveiled the new logo on its website without any fanfare and waited to see what kind of response came from customers and brand fans. Almost immediately, it was apparent that the new logo was not going to be well received and was criticized for being bland, uninspiring and more reminiscent of a technology company than a fashion retailer. Some of the most trenchant criticism argued that it fitted Gap perfectly – a brand that had lost its way and lacked vision and creativity!

Also devastating were two Twitter accounts @OldGapLogo and @Gap Logo that began a satirical dialogue with each other including tweets from @OldGapLogo that said 'Help I've Been Taken Hostage!' Within three days, Gap had reverted to its original logo on its website claiming that it was listening and responding to the views of its fans. It then commenced a crowd-sourcing project – inviting its Facebook and Twitter fans to suggest new ideas for its logo. But in another twist and all within just seven days, it announced that it was withdrawing its crowd-sourcing project as well.

The manner in which the new Gap logo was introduced and then scrapped, led many to claim that this was a deliberate and clever ploy on the part of the company to engineer publicity about the brand in the news and on social media. However, with hindsight it is clear that it was a major logo redesign disaster. Marka Hansen, president of Gap North America who oversaw the project, resigned in February 2011.

Based on: Anonymous (2010);[23] Ritson (2010);[24] Sauer (2010).[25]

Managing brands

Once brands have been established, several important management decisions need to be made. The first of these is whether or not to extend or stretch the brand. A **brand extension** is the use of an established brand name on a new brand within the same broad market. For example, the Anadin brand name has been extended to related brands: Anadin Extra, Ultra, Soluble, Paracetamol and Ibuprofen. **Brand stretching** is when an established brand name is used for brands in unrelated markets. Among the most famous examples of brand stretching is the Virgin brand which began life as Virgin Music (music publishing) and Megastores (music retailing) but grew to encompass over 200 businesses in everything from financial services to modelling to rail travel.

The question of whether or not, the same brand can be marketed in the same way across geographic boundaries is an important decision facing brand managers when an organization internationalizes. The expansion of economic unions and the growing globalization of business are forces that seem to favour the use of standardized or **global branding** strategies, which help to reduce campaign costs and generate global uniformity for brands. Major multinational corporations adopt different approaches to the global/local choice. Unilever has cut its brand portfolio from over 1600 down to just 400 big brands that are marketed across international boundaries. Similarly, the luxury goods group, LVMH, cut its range from 73 in 2000 to 58 in 2006. Other companies have spent heavily on renaming local brands such as Mars' decision to rename Marathon as Snickers, and P&G's decision to rename its popular Fairy laundry detergent as Dawn, with the aim of giving these brands global consistency.

In contrast, the German consumer group Henkel is going in the opposite direction. Like Unilever, Henkel has grown through the acquisition of local companies, but rather than focusing on global leaders it maintains a portfolio of national and international brands. Persil, its premium brand in the laundry detergent business, is not suitable for the US market where washing machines on average use more water at lower temperatures than Europe, so for this reason it paid $2.9 billion for the Dial group in 2003 to acquire the US washing powder, Purex. After the failure of Fa, its range of personal care products, in the USA, it acquired the deodorants Right Guard, Soft & Dri and Dry Idea from P&G for $275 million. In the company's view, Americans tend to prefer to suppress sweating, while continental Europeans want to conceal any odour without blocking perspiration, illustrating the kinds of differences that can exist between markets.

Finally, a popular strategy for some companies today is co-branding where two brands are combined. This may take the form of **product-based co-branding** or **communications-based co-branding**. Product-based co-branding involves the linking of two or more existing brands from different companies to form a product in which both brand names are visible to the consumer. There are two variants of this approach. **Parallel co-branding** occurs when two independent brands join forces to form a combined brand such as HP and Apple iPod to form the HP iPod. **Ingredient co-branding** is where one supplier explicitly chooses to position its brand as an ingredient of a product. Intel is one of the best-known ingredient brands through its popular slogan 'Intel inside', seen on PCs worldwide.

There are a number of advantages to product-based co-branding. First, the co-branding alliance can capture multiple sources of brand equity and therefore add value and provide a point of differentiation. Combining Häagen-Dazs ice cream and Bailey's liqueur creates a brand that adds value through distinctive flavouring that is different from competitive offerings. Second, a co-brand can position a product for a particular target market. For example, Volkswagen teamed up with Trek mountain bikes to develop the Jetta Trek, a special edition of the Volkswagen Jetta. The car was equipped with a bike rack and a Trek mounted on top, and appealed to some 15 million mountain bikers. Finally, co-branding can reduce the cost of product introduction since two well-known brands are combined, accelerating awareness, acceptance and adoption.[26]

Communications-based co-branding involves the linking of two or more existing brands from different companies or business units for the purpose of joint communications. For example, one brand can recommend another, such as Whirlpool's endorsement of Ariel washing powder.[27] Also the alliance can be used to stimulate interest or provide promotional opportunities, such as the deal between McDonald's and Disney, which gives the former exclusive global rights to display and promote material relating to new Disney movies in its outlets. Communications alliances are very popular in sponsorship deals, such as Shell's brand name appearing on Ferrari cars.

Whatever basis is used to differentiate products in a market, three important product management issues remain, namely, managing large portfolios of products and brands, managing products over time and developing new products. We now turn to each of these questions.

Managing product and brand portfolios

Some companies have a large portfolio of products or brands (see Table 6.4). They can be described in terms of a company's product line and mix. A **product line** is a group of products that are closely related in terms of their functions and the benefits they provide (e.g. Dell's range of personal computers or Samsung's line of television sets). The *depth* of the product line refers to the number of variants offered within the product line. A 'product mix' is the total set of brands or products marketed in a company. It is the sum of the product lines offered. Thus, the *width* of the product mix can be gauged by the number of product lines an organization offers. Philips, for example, offers a wide product mix comprising the brands found within its product lines of televisions, audio equipment, DVDs, camcorders, and so on. Coca-Cola, for example, is deemed to be more vulnerable to market trends than its rival Pepsi because of its greater dependence on sales of sugary drinks, whereas Pepsi has a broader portfolio of drinks and food.

The process of managing groups of brands and product lines is called **portfolio planning**. This can be a very complex and important task. Some product lines will be strong, others weak. Some will require investment to finance their growth, others will generate more cash than they need. Somehow companies must decide how to distribute their limited resources among the competing needs of products so as to achieve the best performance for the company as a whole. Specifically, management needs to decide which products to invest in, hold or withdraw support from.

The Boston Consulting Group's (BCG's) growth-share matrix is a technique borrowed from strategic management that has proved useful in helping companies to make product mix and/or product

Table 6.4 Sample brand portfolios of leading companies

Johnson & Johnson	Procter & Gamble	Nestlé	Unilever	L'Oréal	Diageo
Band-Aid	Always	Nescafé	Omo	Vichy	Guinness
Neutrogena	Bounce	Perrier	Surf	Garnier	Baileys
RoC	Duracell	Juicy Juice	Comfort	La Roche-Posay	Smirnoff
Johnson's	Pantene	KitKat	Domestos	Maybelline	J&B
bebe	Pampers	Stouffer's	Cif	Lancôme	Bundaberg
Clean & Clear	Tampax	Purina	Dove	Ralph Lauren perfumes	Captain Morgan
Aveeno	Crest	Milo	Timotei	Helena Rubinstein	Pimm's
Acuvue	Vicks	Nespresso	Toni & Guy	Giorgio Armani perfumes	Ciroc
Pepcid	Head & Shoulders	Carnation	Knorr	Cacherel	Tanqueray
Tylenol	Gillette Fusion	Lean Cuisine	Ben & Jerry's	Biotherm	Blossom Hill
Imodium	Camay	Buitoni	Lipton	The Body Shop	Archers
Visine	Hugo	Nesquik	Vaseline	Diesel	Bells
Splenda	Cover Girl	Häagen Dazs	TRESemme	Redken	Piat d'Or
Benecol	Old Spice	Chef	Hellmann's		Bertrams VO
Listerine	Pringles	Smarties	Axe		Hennessey
	Oral B	Friskies	Lux		
	Gucci	Dreyer's	Brylcreem		
	Mexx	Poland Spring	Bertolli		

line decisions (see Figure 6.4). The matrix allows portfolios of products to be depicted in a 2x2 box, the axes of which are based on market growth rate and relative market share. The size of the circles reflects the proportion of revenue generated by each product line. Market growth rate forms the vertical axis and indicates the annual growth rate of the market in which each product line operates; in Figure 6.4 this is shown as 0–15 per cent although a different range could be used depending on economic conditions.

Market growth rate is used as a proxy for market attractiveness.

Relative market share refers to the market share of each product relative to its largest competitor, and is shown on the horizontal axis. This acts as a proxy for competitive strength. The division between high and low market share is 1. Above this figure a product line has a market share greater than its main competitor. For example, if our product had a market share of 40 per cent and our main competitor's share was 30 per cent

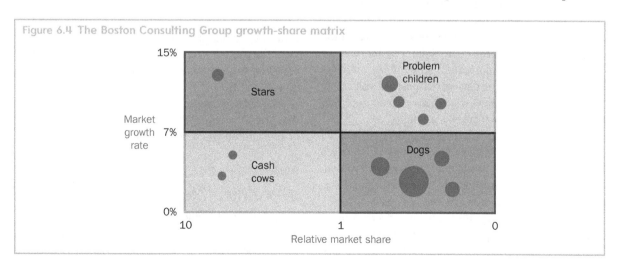

Figure 6.4 The Boston Consulting Group growth-share matrix

this would be indicated as 1.33 on the horizontal axis. Having plotted the position of each product on the matrix, a company can begin to think about setting the appropriate strategic objective for each line.

The market leaders in high-growth markets are known as *stars*. They are already successful and the prospects for further growth are good. Resources should be invested to maintain/increase the leadership position. Competitive challenges should be repelled. These are the cash cows of the future (see below) and need to be protected.

Problem children (also known as *question marks*) are cash drains because they have low profitability and require investment to enable them to keep up with market growth. They are so called because management has to consider whether it is sensible to continue the required investment. The company faces a fundamental choice: to increase investment (build) to attempt to turn the problem child into a star, or to withdraw support, either by harvesting (raising the price while lowering marketing expenditure) or divesting (dropping or selling it). In a few cases a third option may be viable: to find a small market segment (niche) where dominance can be achieved.

The high profitability and low investment associated with high market share in low-growth markets mean that *cash cows* should be defended. Consequently, the appropriate strategic objective is to hold sales and market share. The excess cash that is generated should be used to fund stars, problem children that are being built, and research and development for new products. For example, the C&C group sold its soft drinks business (a cash cow) to Britvic for €249 million, a deal aimed to fund its star division: cider.[28]

Dogs are weak products that compete in low-growth markets. They are the also-rans that have failed to achieve market dominance during the growth phase and are floundering in maturity. For those products that achieve second or third position in the marketplace (*cash dogs*) a small positive cash flow may result and, for a few others, it may be possible to reposition the product into a defendable niche. For the bulk of dogs, however, the appropriate strategic objective is to *harvest* – that is, to generate a positive cash flow for a time – or to *divest*, which allows resources and managerial time to be focused elsewhere.

The strength of BCG's growth-share matrix is its simplicity. Once all of the company's products have been plotted it is easy to see how many stars, problem children, cash cows and dogs there are in the portfolio. Cash can be allocated as necessary to the different product lines to ensure that a balanced portfolio is maintained. For example, the world's biggest maker of alcoholic drinks, Diageo, sold off its food businesses such as Burger King in order to focus on its global brands in whisky, vodka and stout. However, the tool has also attracted a litany of criticism.[29] Some of the key problems with using the technique are as follows.

1   The matrix was based on cash flow but perhaps profitability (e.g. return on investment) is a better criterion for allocating resources.
2   Since the position of a product on the matrix depends on market share, this can lead to an unhealthy preoccupation with market share gain. In addition, market definition (which determines market share) can be very difficult.
3   The matrix ignores interdependences between products. For example, a dog may need to be marketed because it complements a star or a cash cow (it may be a spare part or an accessory, for example). Alternatively, customers and distributors may value dealing with a company that supplies a full product line. For these reasons dropping products because they fall into a particular box may be naive.
4   Treating market growth rate as a proxy for market attractiveness, and market share as an indicator of competitive strength is to oversimplify matters.

There are many other factors that have to be taken into account when measuring market attractiveness (e.g. market size, the strengths and weaknesses of competitors) and competitive strengths (e.g. exploitable marketing assets, potential cost advantages) besides market growth rates and market share. This led to the introduction of more complex portfolio matrices such as the McKinsey/GE market attractiveness–competitive position matrix, which used a variety of measures of market attractiveness and competitive strength.

The main contribution of the portfolio matrices generally has been to demonstrate that *different products should have different roles* in the product portfolio (see Marketing in Action 6.3). For example, to ask for a 20 per cent return on investment (ROI) for a star may result in underinvestment in an attempt to meet the profit requirement. On the other hand, 20 per cent ROI for a cash cow or a harvested product may be too low. However, the models should be used only as an aid to managerial judgement, and other factors that are not adequately covered by the models should be considered when making product mix decisions.

Managing brands and product lines over time: the product life cycle

Both individual brands and product lines need to be managed over time. A useful tool for conceptualizing the changes that may take place during the time that a

Marketing in Action 6.3 Apple's portfolio decisions

Critical Thinking: Below is a review of some of the leading product lines in Apple's portfolio. Read it, plot along the lines mentioned on a BCG matrix and advise Apple on what it should do.

Apple Inc's success over the past two decades has been nothing short of extraordinary. For example in 2008, it was ranked as the 41st largest company in the world with a market capitalization of $126 billion. By 2013, it was the world's number one company worth $416 billion. In 2013, it was the world's most admired company for the seventh year in a row and it is also the world's most valuable brand. Its iconic founder Steve Jobs died in 2011; he is credited with much of the organization's success. But with Jobs no longer at the helm it faces the next chapter of its story with some classic product portfolio decisions to be made.

Apple began life in 1976 as a personal computer maker and computing has always been a key part of the business with brands such as Macintosh in 1984, the Powerbook in 1991 and the iMac in 1998. Desktop computers, printers, peripherals and related hardware remain a core part of its business. It competes with a variety of other well-known brands such as Dell, Lenovo and Hewlett-Packard in a market that has been relatively stagnant in recent years and was forecast to decline in the region of 6–8 per cent in 2014.

Personal computers are losing ground as more and more consumers switch to tablet devices. Apple launched its first tablet – the iPad – in 2011 and this has been rapidly followed by further iterations such as the iPad 2, the iPad Mini and the iPad Air. This is a business that grew by over 50 per cent in 2013 but growth forecasts for 2014 were showing a fall-off in demand with lower growth rates of approximately 20 per cent

predicted. Significant competition in this sector was coming from brands like Samsung, Sony, Google, Lenovo, Microsoft and Amazon.

A key element in the turnaround of Apple after its struggles during the 1990s was the launch of its range of personal music players starting with the iPod in 2001. This was again followed by a variety of other products such as the iPod Shuffle, the iPod Nano, the iTouch and a range of accessories. Through linking these products with its music distribution business iTunes, Apple dominated the MP3 business seeing off competition from brands like Sony and Creative. However, sales of MP3 players fell by 22 per cent in the UK between 2011 and 2012 and are expected to fall further in the coming years as smartphones provide the same function while allowing users to do a whole lot more.

Apple launched its first smartphone – the iPhone – in 2008 and it is one of the major players in this growing global business along with the leading brand, Samsung, and other major players such as LG, Lenovo and Huawei. However, it is losing ground to its rivals in this business as consumers prefer the Android operating system over Apple's iOS system.

Through the launches of products like the iMac, the iPod and the iPhone, Apple has built itself a reputation as a global leader in product innovation. While it has expressed an interest in new product areas such as television and smartwatches, there have been no significant new launches in recent years.

product is on the market is called the **product life cycle**. The classic product life cycle (PLC) has four stages (see Figure 6.5): introduction, growth, maturity and decline.

The PLC emphasizes the fact that nothing lasts forever. For example, the drop in demand for elaborate tea services has seen dramatic declines at the makers of porcelain and fine bone china products, like Royal Worcester and Royal Doulton. Portable data storage devices like floppy disks, zip disks and

USB sticks have all rapidly become popular and then faded out of popularity just as quickly. There is a danger that management may fall in love with certain products, as in the case of a company that is founded on the success of a particular product. Sony persisted with developing new iterations of its PlayStation video games console even though many consumers switched to playing games on smartphone apps. The PLC underlines the fact that companies have to

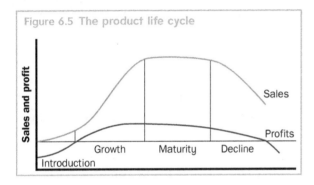

Figure 6.5 The product life cycle

accept that products need to be terminated and new products developed to replace them. Without this sequence, a company may find itself with a group of products all in the decline stage of their PLC. A nicely balanced product array would see the company marketing some products in the mature stage of the PLC, a number at the growth stage and the prospect of new product introductions in the near future.

The PLC emphasizes the need to review marketing objectives and strategies as products pass through the various stages. Changes in market and competitive conditions between the PLC stages suggest that marketing strategies should be adapted to meet them. Table 6.5 shows a set of stylized marketing responses to each stage. Note that these are broad generalizations rather than exact prescriptions, but they do serve to emphasize the need to review marketing objectives and strategies in the light of environmental change.

Introduction

When a product is first introduced on to the market its sales growth is typically low and losses are incurred as a result of heavy development and initial promotional costs. Companies will be monitoring the speed of product adoption and, if it is disappointing, may terminate the product at this stage.

The strategic marketing objective is to build sales by expanding the market for the product. The brand objective will be to create awareness so that customers will become familiar with generic product benefits. The product is likely to be fairly basic, with an emphasis on reliability and functionality rather than special features to appeal to different customer groups. Promotion will support the brand objectives by gaining awareness for the brand and product type, and stimulating trial. Advertising has been found to be more effective at the start of the life of a product than in later stages.[30] Typically, price will be high because of the heavy development costs and the low level of competition. Distribution will be patchy as some dealers will be wary of stocking the new product until it has proved successful in the marketplace.

Growth

This second stage is marked by a period of faster sales and profit growth (see Exhibit 6.5). Sales growth is fuelled by rapid market acceptance and, for many products, repeat purchasing. Profits may begin to decline towards the latter stages of growth as new rivals enter the market attracted by the twin magnets of fast sales growth and high profit potential. For example, the Internet search engine business grew rapidly and delivered very high profits for some incumbent firms like Google. But the profitability of this sector attracted a range of new entrants, such as Jeteye.com, Blinkx.com and Icerocket.com, all of which provided new and innovative search solutions but failed to dislodge Google from its dominant position. Similarly, in developed countries, the growth in pet ownership has given rise to a rapidly growing pet products and pet services sector. The end of the growth period is often associated with 'competitive shake-out', whereby weaker suppliers cease production.

The strategic marketing objective during the growth phase is to build sales and market share. The

Table 6.5 Marketing objectives and strategies over the product life cycle

	Introduction	Growth	Maturity	Decline
Strategic marketing objective	Build	Build	Hold	Harvest/manage for cash
Strategic focus	Expand market	Penetration	Protect share	Productivity
Brand objective	Product awareness/trial	Brand preference	Brand loyalty	Brand exploitation
Products	Basic	Differentiated	Differentiated	Rationalized
Promotion	Creating awareness/trial	Creating awareness/ trial repeat purchase	Maintaining awareness/ repeat purchase	Cut/eliminated
Price	High	Lower	Lowest	Rising
Distribution	Patchy	Wider	Intensive	Selective

strategic focus will be to penetrate the market by building brand preference. To accomplish this task the product will be redesigned to create differentiation, and promotion will stress the functional and/ or psychological benefits that accrue from the differentiation. Awareness and trial are still important, but promotion will begin to focus on repeat purchasers. As development costs are defrayed and competition increases, prices will fall. Rising consumer demand and increased sales-force effort will widen distribution.

Maturity

Sales will eventually peak and stabilize as saturation occurs, hastening competitive shake-out. Mobile phone adoption rates, for example, have surpassed 100 per cent in most European countries. The survivors now battle for market share by introducing product improvements, using advertising and sales promotional offers, dealer discounting and price cutting; the result is strain on profit margins, particularly for follower brands. The need for effective brand building is felt most acutely during maturity and brand leaders are in the strongest position to resist pressure on profit margins.[31] Careful strategic decisions are very important in mature markets. For example, the falling profitability of Starbucks in 2007 was attributed to decisions that sought to grow the business too rapidly (it has now over 17,000 outlets worldwide) in a mature market, which has led to market saturation and poor control over cafés.[32]

Decline

During the decline stages – when new technology or changes in consumer tastes work to reduce demand for the product – sales and profits fall. Suppliers may decide to cease production completely or reduce product depth. Promotional and product development budgets may be slashed, and marginal distributors dropped as suppliers seek to maintain (or increase) profit margins. Products like cathode ray tube (CRT) televisions have fallen out of favour as consumers have switched to flat-panel screens. For example, Dixons dropped the price of a CRT television from £1300 in 2004 to £300 in 2005, and the range still failed to sell.[33]

A key ethical consideration is the speed with which many products move through the product life cycle. For example, mobile phone models and computer software become quickly outdated. Fast fashion retailers like Zara aim to change the range of clothing in their retail outlets every two weeks. This 'planned obsolescence' is a significant boon for organizations as consumers need to repurchase updates or new models and discard old ones. Critics argue that this kind of consumption is not only expensive from the consumer's point of view but significantly wasteful from society's viewpoint. Clothes or computers that are perfectly 'fit for purpose' are being discarded simply because newer models are available.

Like BCG's growth-share matrix, the PLC theory has been the subject of a significant amount of criticism. First, not all products follow the classic S-shaped curve. The sales of some products 'rise like a rocket then fall like a stone'. This is normal for fad products such as Rubik's cubes, which in the 1980s saw phenomenal sales growth followed by a rapid sales collapse as the youth market moved on to another craze. Blockbuster movies have a similarly short life cycle. For example, *X-Men, The Last Stand* grossed $123 million in its first four days in cinemas, which was more than it earned for the remaining four months of its run.[34] Second, the duration of the PLC stages is unpredictable. The PLC outlines the four stages a product passes through without defining their duration. For example, e-books languished in the introduction stage of the product life cycle for longer than anticipated before finally taking off. Clearly this limits its use as a forecasting tool since it is not possible to predict when maturity or decline will begin. Finally, and perhaps most worryingly, it has been argued that the PLC is the *result* of marketing activities, not the cause. Clearly, sales of a product may flatten out or fall simply because it has not received enough marketing attention, or because there has been insufficient product redesign or promotional support. Using the PLC, argue its critics, may lead to inappropriate action (e.g. harvesting or dropping the product) when the correct response should be increased marketing support (e.g. product replacement, positioning reinforcement or repositioning). Like many marketing tools, the PLC should not be viewed as a panacea to marketing thinking and decision making, but as an aid to managerial judgement.

Nevertheless, the dynamic nature of brands and product lines focuses attention on the key marketing challenge of developing new products and services. It is to this issue that we turn next.

New product development

The introduction of new products to the marketplace is the lifeblood of corporate success. But new product development is inherently risky. Pharmaceutical companies research hundreds of molecular groups before coming up with a marketable drug and less than 2 per cent of films account for 80 per cent of box office returns.[35] However, failure has to be tolerated; it is endemic in the whole process of developing new products. One of the outcomes of the innovative process is the large number of interesting product ideas that emerge that never go on to be commercially successful and join lists such as the top 20 most useless gadgets (see Table 6.6).

Some new products reshape markets and competition by virtue of the fact that they are so fundamentally different from products that already exist. However, a shampoo that is different from existing products only by means of its brand name, fragrance, packaging and colour is also a new product. In fact four broad categories of new product exist.[36]

1 *Product replacements*: these account for about 45 per cent of all new product launches, and include revisions and improvements to existing products (e.g. the Ford Focus replacing the Fiesta), repositioning (existing products such as Lucozade being targeted at new market segments) and cost reductions (existing products being reformulated or redesigned so that they cost less to produce).

2 *Additions to existing lines*: these account for about 25 per cent of new product launches and take the form of new products that add to a company's existing product lines. This produces greater product depth. An example is the launch by Weetabix of a brand extension, Oatibix, to compete with other oat-based cereals.

3 *New product lines*: these total around 20 per cent of new product launches and represent a move into a new market. For example, in Europe, Mars has launched a number of ice cream brands, which made up a new product line for this company. This strategy widens a company's product mix.

4 *New-to-the-world products*: these total around 10 per cent of new product launches, and create entirely new markets. For example, the video games console, the MP3 player and the camcorder have created new markets because of the highly valued customer benefits they provided.

Of course, the degree of risk and reward involved will vary according to the new product category. New-to-the-world products normally carry the highest risk since it is often difficult to predict consumer reaction. Often, market research will be unreliable in predicting demand as people do not really understand the full benefits of the product until it is on the market and they get the chance to experience them. For example, initial market testing yielded very negative results for products like Red Bull and Nespresso coffee machines which went on to become global leaders. At the other extreme, adding a brand variation to an existing product line lacks significant risk but is also unlikely to proffer significant returns (see Table 6.7 for a list of the world's most innovative companies).

Table 6.6 Top 10 most useless gadgets

| 1. Electric nail files |
| 2. Laser-guided scissors |
| 3. Electric candles |
| 4. Soda stream |
| 5. Foot spas |
| 6. Fondue sets |
| 7. Hair crimpers |
| 8. Egg boiler |
| 9. Electric fluff remover |
| 10. Electric carving knife |

Source: *Irish Times*

Table 6.7 The world's most innovative companies 2014

Company	Business
1. Google	Information technology
2. Bloomberg Philanthropies	Charitable foundation
3. Xiaomi	Consumer electronics
4. Dropbox	Information technology
5. Netflix	Entertainment
6. Airbnb	Travel
7. Nike	Sporting goods
8. Zipdial	Telecommunications
9. Donorschoose.org	Charitable foundation
10. Yelp	Consumer reviews

Source: Fast Company

Managing the new product development process

New product development is expensive, risky and time consuming – these are three inescapable facts. A seven-step new product development process is shown in Figure 6.6. Although the reality of new product development may resemble organizational chaos, the discipline imposed by the activities carried out at each stage leads to a greater likelihood of developing a product that not only works, but also confers customer benefits. We should note, however, that new products pass through each stage at varying speeds: some may dwell at a stage for a long period while others may pass through very quickly.[37]

Idea generation

The sources of new product ideas can be internal to the company: scientists, engineers, marketers, salespeople and designers, for example. Some companies use the **brainstorming** technique to stimulate the creation of ideas, and use financial incentives to persuade people to put forward ideas they have had. 3M's Post-it adhesive-backed notepaper was a successful product that was thought of by an employee who initially saw the product as a means of preventing paper falling from his hymn book as he marked the hymns that were being sung. Because of the innovative culture within 3M, he bothered to think of commercial applications and acted as a product champion within the company to see the project through to commercialization and global success.

Sources of new product ideas can also be external to the company and the turnaround at P&G was largely attributable to its chief executive officer (CEO) A.G. Lafley setting a goal that 50 per cent of innovation in the company should come from external sources.[38] Examining competitors' products may provide clues to product improvements. Distributors can also be a source of new product ideas directly, since they deal with customers and have an interest in selling improved products. A major source of good ideas is the customers themselves. Their needs may not be satisfied with existing products and they may be genuinely interested in providing ideas that lead to product improvement. For example, the Dutch electronics group Philips employs anthropologists and cognitive psychologists to gather insights into the desires and needs of people around the world to enable it to compete more effectively with Asian rivals.[39] Internet-based social communities are a powerful source of innovation, with like-minded individuals willing to share ideas and innovations for the common good. Companies like Lego and Walkers have worked with consumers to generate new products and the open source software movement is one of the most powerful examples of consumer-led innovation.

In organizational markets, keeping in close contact with customers who are innovators and market leaders in their own marketplaces is likely to be a fruitful source of new product ideas. These 'lead customers' are likely to recognize required improvements ahead of other customers as they have advanced needs and are likely to face problems before other product users. Some innovations such as GE's Light Speed VCT, which provides a three-dimensional image of a beating heart, and Staples' Wordlock, a padlock that uses words instead of numbers, have been developed in co-operation with lead customers.

A 2006 study by IBM of global chief executives found that, overall, employees were the most significant source of innovative ideas, followed by business partners, customers and consultants – in that order.[40]

Screening

Once new product ideas have been developed they need to be screened in order to evaluate their commercial value. Some companies use formal checklists to help them judge whether the product

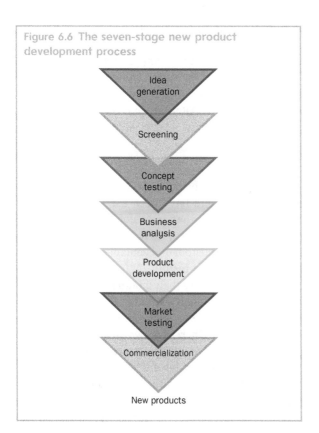

Figure 6.6 The seven-stage new product development process

Idea generation

Screening

Concept testing

Business analysis

Product development

Market testing

Commercialization

New products

idea should be rejected or accepted for further evaluation. This ensures that no important criterion is overlooked. Criteria may be used that measure the attractiveness of the market for the proposed product, the fit between the product and company objectives, and the capability of the company to produce and market the product. Other companies may use a less systematic approach, preferring more flexible open discussion among members of the new product development committee to gauge likely success.

Concept testing

Once a product idea has been deemed worthy of further investigation, it can be framed into a specific concept for testing with potential customers. The concept may be described verbally or pictorially so that the major features are understood. In many instances the basic product idea will be expanded into several product concepts, each of which can be compared by testing with target customers. **Concept testing** thus allows the views of customers to enter the new product development process at an early stage. The buying intentions of potential customers are a key factor in judging whether any of the concepts are worth pursuing further.

Business analysis

Estimates of sales, costs and profits will be made, based on the results of the concept test, as well as on considerable managerial judgement. This is known as the **business analysis** stage. In order to produce sensible figures a marketing analysis will need to be undertaken. This will identify the target market, its size and projected product acceptance over a number of years. Consideration will be given to various prices and the implications for sales revenue (and profits) discussed. By setting a tentative price this analysis will provide sales revenue estimates. Costs will also need to be estimated. If the new product is similar to existing products (e.g. a brand extension) it should be fairly easy to produce accurate cost estimates. For radical product concepts, the process is more difficult.

When the quantity needed to be sold to cover costs is calculated, *break-even analysis* may be used to establish whether the project is financially feasible. *Sensitivity analysis*, in which variations from given assumptions about price, cost and customer acceptance, for example, are checked to see how they impact on sales revenue and profits, can also prove useful at this stage. 'Optimistic', 'most likely' and 'pessimistic' scenarios can be drawn up to estimate the degree of risk attached to a project.

Product development

This stage involves the development of the actual product. It is usually necessary to integrate the skills of designers, engineers, production, finance and marketing specialists so that product development is quicker, less costly and results in a high-quality product that delights customers. Costs are controlled by a method called target costing. Target costs are worked out on the basis of target prices in the marketplace, and given as engineering/design and production targets.

A key marketing factor in many industries is the ability to cut time to market by reducing the length of the product development stage. There are two reasons why product development is being accelerated. First, markets such as those for personal computers, consumer electronics and cars change so fast that to be slow means running the risk of being out of date before the product is launched. Second, cutting time to market can lead to competitive advantage. For example, Zara's ability to reduce time to market for new styles gave it a competitive advantage in the fashion industry.

Product testing concentrates on the functional aspects of a product, as well as on consumer acceptance. Functional tests are carried out in the laboratory and in the field to check such aspects as safety, performance and shelf-life. Products also need to be tested with consumers to check their acceptability in use. Care at this stage can avoid expensive product recalls as we saw earlier in the case of Toyota. 'Paired companion tests' are used when the new product is used alongside a rival so that respondents have a benchmark against which to judge the new offerings. Alternatively, two (or more) new product variants may be tested alongside one another.

Market testing

Up to this point in the development process, although potential customers have been asked if they intend to buy the product, they have not been placed in the position of having to pay for it. **Market testing** takes measurement of customer acceptance one crucial step further than product testing, by forcing consumers to put their money where their mouth is, so to speak. The basic idea is to launch the new product in a limited way so that consumer response in the marketplace can be assessed. There are two major methods: the simulated market test and **test marketing**.

Simulated market tests take a number of forms, but the main idea behind them is to set up a realistic market situation in which a sample of consumers choose to buy goods from a range provided by the organizing company (usually a market research organization). For example, a sample of consumers may be recruited to buy their groceries from a mobile supermarket that visits them once a week. Simulated market tests are useful as a preliminary to test marketing by spotting problems, such as in packaging and product formulation, that can be rectified before test market launch. They can also be useful in eliminating new products that perform so badly compared with the competition in the marketplace that test marketing is not justified.

When the new product is launched in one, or a few, geographical areas chosen to be representative of its intended market, this is known as test marketing. Towns or television areas are chosen in which the new product is sold into distribution outlets so that performance can be gauged face to face with rival products. Test marketing is the acid test of new product development since the product is being promoted as it would be in a national launch, and consumers are being asked to choose it against competitor products as they would if the new product went national. It is a more realistic test than the simulated market test and therefore gives more accurate sales penetration and repeat purchasing estimates.

However, test marketing does have a number of potential problems. Test towns and areas may not be representative of the national market, and thus sales projections may be inaccurate. Competitors may invalidate the test market by giving distributors incentives to stock their product, thereby denying the new product shelf space. Also, test markets need to run for long enough to enable the measurement of repeat purchase rates for a product since this is a crucial indicator of success. One of the main advantages of test marketing is that the information it provides facilitates the 'go/no go' national launch decision.

Commercialization

The final stage of this rigorous process is the launch of the product in the marketplace. As an indication of the scale of the process, Hewlett Packard generates 1,800 raw ideas per year with the goal of examining 200 in detail and then commercializing two.[41] An effective commercialization strategy relies on marketing management making clear choices regarding the target market (*where* it wishes to compete), and the development of a marketing strategy that provides a differential advantage (*how* it wishes to compete). These two factors define the new product positioning strategy, as discussed in Chapter 5.

An understanding of the **diffusion of innovation** process is a useful starting point for choosing a target market (see Figure 3.5).[42] Particularly important is the notion that not all people or organizations who comprise a market will be in the same state of readiness to buy a new product when it is launched. For example, some consumers will be much quicker to adopt a new technology like a smartphone than others. Firms launching new products initially aim to target innovators and early adopters. For example, innovators are often adventurous and like to be different; they are willing to take a chance with an untried product. In consumer markets they tend to be younger, better educated, more confident and more financially affluent, and consequently can afford to take a chance on buying something new. In organizational markets, they tend to be larger and more profitable companies if the innovation is costly, and have more progressive, better-educated management.

In summary, bringing out new products and services is the key to long-term corporate success. It is a risky activity, but a systematic approach is likely to improve the chances of success.

Summary

In this chapter we have explored a number of issues involved in the marketing of products and brands. The following key issues were addressed.

1. In marketing terms, products are anything that delivers benefits and value to a consumer and all products contain some tangible and some intangible elements.

2. The important distinction between products and brands. A product is anything that is capable of satisfying customer needs. Brands are the means by which companies differentiate their offerings from those of their competitors.

3. The three different levels of product, namely, the core, the actual and the augmented product and how differentiation can take place at any of these levels.

4. The key aspects involved in building brands, including decisions regarding the brand name, and developing and positioning brands. Firms can choose from family, individual and combination brand names, and developing the brand requires key decisions regarding its customer value proposition.

5. The challenge of managing a diverse group of products and brands, and the role of portfolio planning in assisting with this process. Many firms own significant portfolios of products and ongoing decisions need to be made regarding which ones should be invested in and which should be wound down.

6. The challenge of managing products and brands over time and the role of the product life cycle concept in assisting with this process. Products at different stages of growth require different marketing strategies and, despite its weaknesses, the product life cycle offers a helpful way of thinking about these decisions.

7. The importance of new product development and the process by which products are taken from the idea stage through to commercialization. Careful management is required during all the main stages, including idea generation, screening, concept testing, business analysis, product development, market testing and commercialization.

Study questions

1. Explain the difference between a product and a brand.
2. Think of five brand names. To what extent do they meet the criteria of good brand naming as laid out in Table 6.1? Do any of the names legitimately break these guidelines?
3. Examine a product like bottled water through the lens of the core, actual and augmented product. What types of differentiation strategies are being used by brands in this sector? Can you suggest any new sources of differentiation?
4. The product life cycle is more likely to mislead marketing management than provide useful insights. Discuss.
5. Many companies comprise a complex group of business units, which in turn often have wide product lines. Discuss the techniques available to the marketer for managing this complexity.
6. Outline the main stages in the new product development process, identifying the potential sources of failure at each stage.
7. Visit www.rdtrustedbrands.com. Review the most trusted brands in different categories in your area. How do these brands go about building this trust?

Suggested reading

Batra, R., A. Ahuvia and **R. Bagozzi** (2012) Brand Love, *Journal of Marketing,* **76** (March), 1–16.

Edelman, D. (2010), Branding in the Digital Age, *Harvard Business Review,* **88** (12), 62–9.

Gladwell, M. (2000) *The Tipping Point: How Little Things Can Make a Big Difference,* London: Abacus.

Hill, S., R. Ettenson and **D. Tyson** (2005) Achieving the Ideal Brand Portfolio, *Sloan Management Review,* **46** (2), 85–91.

Holman, R., H. Kaas and **D. Keeling** (2003) The Future of Product Development, *McKinsey Quarterly,* **3**, 28–40.

Ind, N., O. Iglesias and **M. Schultz** (2013) Building Brands Together: Emergence and Outcomes of Co-creation, *California Management Review,* **55** (3), 5–26.

Moon, Y. (2005) Break Free From the Product Life Cycle, *Harvard Business Review,* **83** (5), 86–95.

When you have read this chapter

log on to the Online Learning Centre for *Foundations of Marketing* at
www.mheducation.co.uk/textbooks/fahy5
where you'll find links and extra online study tools for marketing.

References

1. **Hughes, M.** (2013) Gillette Campaign Asks, How Does Superman Shave?, *Forbes.com,* 28 May; **Neff, J.** (2012) Gillette Shaves its Prices as it's Nicked by Rivals Both New and Old, *AdAge.com,* 9 April; **Ritson, M.** (2009) Gillette's Razor Sharp Strategy, *Marketingmagazine.co.uk,* 24 June.

2. **Keller, K.** (2003) *Strategic Brand Management,* Upper Saddle River, NJ: Pearson.

3. **O'Shaughnessy, H.** (2007) Getting a Good Look, *Innovation,* June, 26–30.

4. **Pope, C.** (2007) New Labels Hit a Red Light, *Irish Times,* 15 January, 13.

5. **Hegarty, S.** (2003) You Are What You Think You Eat, *Irish Times,* Weekend Review, 19 July, 1.

6. **Anonymous** (2011) Ziggo All-In-1 (Triple Play): From Access Provider to Entertainment Company, Emap Limited: Warc.com.

7. **Roberts, K.** (2004) *The Future Beyond Brands: Lovemarks,* New York: Powerhouse Books.

8. **Healy, A.** (2004) Campaigners Appeal for Cafes to be Rescued, *Irish Times,* 25 November, 6.

9. **Reyner, M.** (1996) Is Advertising the Answer? *Admap,* September, 23–6.

10. **Balwani, S.** (2009) 5 Elements of a Successful Facebook Fan Page, Mashable.com, 30 March.

11. **Shayon, S.** (2011) BMW, Clinique and Audi Top Facebook Luxury Brands Ranking, Brandchannel.com, 6 June.

12. **Anonymous** (2011) I've Got You Labelled, *The Economist,* 2 April, 74.

13. **Clingham, R., G.P. Arnold, T.S. Drew, L.A. Cochrane** and **R.J. Abboud** (2007) Do You Get Value for Money When You Buy an Expensive Pair of Running Shoes? *British Journal of Sports Medicine,* October, 1–5.

14. **Adamson, A.** (2006) *Brand Simple: How the Best Brands Keep it Simple and Succeed,* New York: Palgrave Macmillan.

15. **Klein, N.** (2000), *No Logo,* London: HarperCollins

16. **Waters, R.** (2008) Microsoft Says 'We're human too', *Financial Times,* 9 September, 16; **Anonymous** (2008) Postmodern Wriggle, *The Economist,* 13 September, 72.

17. **Palmer, M.** (2007) What's in a Name? A Lot if it's Your Domain, *Financial Times,* 14 March, 24.

18. **O'Connor, R.** (2010) Question Marks over Trademarks, *Marketing Age,* 4 (1), 49–51.

19. **Brady, J.** and **I. Davis** (1993) Marketing's Mid-life Crisis, *McKinsey Quarterly,* 2, 17–28.

20. **Anonymous** (2005) As Good As It Gets, *The Economist,* 15 January, 60–2.

21. **Doyle, P.** (2000) *Value-based Marketing,* Chichester: John Wiley & Sons.

22. **Richards, H.** (2005) A Clothing Hit – On the Back of a Golfing Hero, *Financial Times,* 13 July, 16.

23. **Anonymous** (2010) Is This Clever Crowdsourcing or a Genuine Brand Gaff? *MarketingWeek.co.uk,* 21 October.

24. **Ritson, M.** (2010) Is this Gap's Idea of 360 Degree Branding? *MarketingWeek.co.uk,* 13 October.

25. **Sauer, A.** (2010) Gap Rebrands Itself into Oblivion, Brandchannel.com, 6 October.

26. **Brech, P.** (2002) Ford Focus Targets Women with *Elle* Tie, *Marketing,* 8 August, 7.

27. **Keller, K.** (2003) *Strategic Brand Management,* Upper Saddle River, NJ: Pearson.

28. **Brown, J.M.** (2007) Soft Drinks Sale to Britvic Enables C&C to Concentrate on High Margin Alcohol, *Financial Times,* 15 May, 22.

29. See, e.g., **Day, G.S.** and **R. Wensley** (1983) Marketing Theory with a Strategic Orientation, *Journal of Marketing,* Fall, 79–89; **Haspslagh, P.** (1982) Portfolio Planning: Uses and Limits, *Harvard Business Review,* January/February, 58–73; **Wensley, R.** (1981) Strategic Marketing: Betas, Boxes and Basics, *Journal of Marketing,* Summer, 173–83.

30. **Vakratsas, D.** and **T. Ambler** (1999) How Advertising Works: What Do We Really Know? *Journal of Marketing,* **63**, January, 26–43.

31. **Doyle, P.** (1989) Building Successful Brands: The Strategic Options, *Journal of Marketing Management,* 5 (1), 77–95.

32. **Anonymous** (2008) Starbucks v McDonald's: Coffee Wars, *The Economist,* 12 January, 54–5.

33. **Rigby, E.** and **A. Edgecliffe-Johnson** (2006) Dixons to Pull the Plug on Old Fashioned TV Sets, *Financial Times,* 19 January, 4.

34. **Anonymous** (2007) Endless Summer, *The Economist,* 28 April, 69–70.

35. **Anonymous** (2011) Fail Often, Fail Well, *The Economist,* 16 April, 66.

36. **Booz, Allen** and **Hamilton** (1982) *New Product Management for the 1980s,* New York: Booz, Allen & Hamilton.

37. **Cooper, R.G.** and **E.J. Kleinschmidt** (1986) An Investigation into the New Product Process: Steps, Deficiencies and Impact, *Journal of Product Innovation Management,* June, 71–85.

38. **O'Dea, A.** (2008) Open for Innovation, *Marketing Age,* September/October, 22–6.

39. **Tomkins, R.** (2005) Products That Aim Straight For Your Heart, *Financial Times,* 29 April, 13.

40. **Anonymous** (2007) The Love-In, *The Economist,* Special Report on Innovation, 13 October, 18.

41. **Lillington, K.** (2008) Taking Invention Out of the Lab, *Innovation,* May, 32–4.

42. **Rogers, E.M.** (1983) *Diffusion of Innovations,* New York: Free Press.

Carlsberg: changing an iconic slogan

In 2011, Carlsberg, one of the world's premium beer brands, engaged in its most significant makeover since the beer's origination in 1847. Carlsberg decided to call time on the famous 'probably the best lager in the world' tagline. Carlsberg Group's revised campaign 'That calls for a Carlsberg' was rolled out simultaneously across over 140 markets and is visible from packaging through to point-of-sale and other marketing communications. This rebranding came about as part of a global overhaul of the lager aimed at boosting the drink's appeal to younger drinkers in current and emerging markets.

History of Carlsberg

In 1835, following the death of his father, J.C. Jacobsen took over full responsibility for his father's brewery aged 24. In 1847, to cope with the increasing demand for his beer, J.C. Jacobsen established Carlsberg. The first brew was carried out on 10 November 1847 and sold under the name Carlsberg Lager Beer. The lager beer was an undisputed success, and from the first test brews until 1861, production increased from 300 barrels to more than 20,000 barrels. Carlsberg first began exporting in 1868, when a single test sample was sent to a grocer in Edinburgh, Scotland. Jacobsen became internationally recognised as a brewing pioneer by introducing science into brewing. In 1873, Jacobsen was awarded a prestigious progress medal for brewing. He repeated this success at the 1878 World Trade Exhibition in Paris, where he took the Grand Prix. In 1875, J.C. Jacobsen established the Carlsberg Laboratory, to study the malting, brewing and fermenting processes, and one year later the Carlsberg Foundation, which remains central to the group's organisational structure. Today the foundation serves as an important part of Carlsberg's governance structure. The foundation must hold at least 51 per cent of the votes and more than 25 per cent of the share capital.

The Carlsberg Laboratory has been at the forefront of breakthroughs in brewing. In 1883, the species of yeast used to make lager (Saccharomyces carlsbergensis) was discovered at the Carlsberg laboratory. This achievement revolutionized brewing. Jacobsen offered samples of the new pure yeast to breweries all over the world rather than maintaining the discovery as a source of competitive advantage. This point has been illustrated in some of Carlsberg's most recent advertising campaigns. Other notable achievements from the laboratory included the discovery of a method of analysing nitrogen and protein in food and feedstuff, the establishment of the concept of pH and research into the dynamic nature of proteins. One of the laboratory's most recent achievements is the development of a new type of barley. The new Null-LOX barley is being tipped as a source of competitive advantage for Carlsberg, since it will be able to keep beer fresh for a longer time while also providing better foam for the beer. As part of the global relaunch of the Carlsberg brand, Null-LOX is currently being rolled out across its markets.

Currently, the Carlsberg Group is one of the leading brewery groups in the world employing more than 43,000 people, with a large portfolio that includes more than 500 brands. These brands vary significantly in volume, price, target audience and geographic penetration. The brand portfolio includes the well-known international premium brands Carlsberg, Tuborg, Baltika and Kronenbourg 1664, and strong local brands such as Ringnes (Norway), Feldschlösschen (Switzerland), Lav (Serbia) and Wusu (Western China). The strength of the Group's brand portfolio is highlighted by the fact that Baltika, Carlsberg and Tuborg are among the six biggest brands in Europe, with Baltika ranked as

Table C6.1 Carlsberg Group: main market information

Our market			Market data			Consumption characteristic		Our position		Our operations
Western Europe	Population (millions)	Est. GDP/capita PPP (USD)	Est. real GDP/growth (%)	Inflation avg. consumer prices(%)	Per capita beer consumption(litres)	On-trade share of market approx(%)	Market position (no.)	Market share(%)	Breweries
Demark	5.6	37,794	0.1	0.8	78	27	1	51	1
Sweden	9.6	40,870	0.9	0.2	51	20	1	33	1
Norway	5.1	55,398	1.6	1.8	46	20	1	54	2
Finland	5.5	35,863	-0.6	2.4	84	15	1	53	1
France	63.7	35,680	0.2	1.0	29	22	1	29	1
Switzerland	8.1	45,999	1.7	-0.2	57	43	1	43	1
UK	63.8	37,229	1.4	2.7	70	51	4	15	1
Poland	38.5	21,118	1.3	1.4	96	11	3	19	3
Germany	81.8	39,468	0.5	1.6	103	19	2	16	2
Italy	61.0	29,598	-1.8	1.6	27	38	4	7	2
Portugal	10.6	22,930	-1.8	0.7	46	55	1	48	1
The Baltics	6.3	21,420	1.5-4.0	0.7-3.5	72-90	5-7	1	30-41	4
South East Europe	30.2	17,551	-4.2-2.0	-0.8-8.5	38-81	18-53	2-3	15-26	5
Eastern Europe									
Russia	141.4	18,083	1.5	6.7	59	9	1	39	10
Ukraine	45.5	7,422	0.4	0.0	55	11	2	27	3
Belarus	9.3	16,106	2.1	17.5	51	4	1	29	1
Kazakhstan	17.2	14,133	5.0	6.3	30	31	2	32	1
Azerbaijan	9.3	10,789	3.5	3.7	6	20	1	73	1
Asia									
China	1,360.8	9,828	7.6	2.7	40	46	1	-55	39
Vietnam	89.7	4,001	5.3	8.8	40	55	2	34	6
Laos	6.8	3,066	8.3	7.4	39	44	1	98	2
Cambodia	15.4	2,573	7.0	2.9	30	37	1	66	1
Nepal	27.9	1,506	3.6	9.9	2	81	1	71	1
India	1,243.3	3,991	3.8	10.9	2	16	3	8	6
Malaysia	30.0	17,526	4.7	2.0	6	77	2	45	1
Singapore	5.4	62,428	3.5	2.3	22	75	2	18	-
Hong Kong	7.2	52,687	3.0	3.5	24	29	2	25	-

number one. Kronenbourg also features within the top 10. The Carlsberg Group's brands are sold in more than 150 markets. The Carlsberg Group competes in three regions: Northern and Western Europe, Eastern Europe and Asia. In Northern and Western Europe, the Carlsberg Group is the second largest brewer with market leader positions in a large number of countries and significant positions in others. The Carlsberg Group holds a strong number one position in Eastern Europe. The Carlsberg Group states its ambition is to be the fastest growing global beer company.

Challenges in the global beer market

The global beer industry has consolidated dramatically over the past 10 years. In 2000 the top 10 brewing companies accounted for 37 per cent of the global market. By 2010 this had risen to 63 per cent. Acquisitions within the industry have given rise to the emergence of four global brewing giants: ABInBev, SABMiller, Heineken and Carlsberg. These four companies account for an estimated 48 per cent of all beer consumed worldwide. One of the paradoxes of the consolidation of the global beer industry has been the proliferation of brands and brand extensions, and the fact that there are still no real global beer brands. The growth of emerging markets often driven by local brands has limited the development of truly international brands. Perhaps the biggest consequence of the economic downturn has been the acceleration of the decline in on-premise consumption in favour of off-premise. Generally, on-premise consumption in the southern European markets and in the UK accounts for half or more of total beer consumption, whereas in the northern and eastern European countries off-premise consumption is much more prevalent, accounting for approximately 80 per cent or more of total beer consumption. In Asia, the consumption patterns are more fragmented.

Reasons for change

So why has Carlsberg launched this new campaign? Carlsberg's famous tagline, 'Probably the best beer in the world' was created in 1973 by Saatchi and Saatchi with the voiceover for the original by Orson Welles. This tagline remains popular and easily recognizable to consumers. However, while global brand recognition was high under this tagline, sales of Carlsberg were worrying. The *Wall Street Journal* reported that the Carlsberg brand represented only 10 per cent of the company's total revenues, with the majority of revenue coming from the sales of local brews in individual markets. Carlsberg has made no secret of its desire to establish the brand as a global icon, with unity of image and marketing message seen as key to achieving this much sought after status. There is also the possibility of significant cost savings in a 'glocal' approach. Another valid reason for the new slogan is that the phrase 'probably the best lager in the world' does not translate well. The playful humour associated with the tagline is lost on consumers with

the 'probably' message becoming a source of confusion in relation to the quality of the beer in some markets. Given that Carlsberg seeks fresh growth in Eastern Europe and Asia, a new unified tagline seems appropriate. However, this new campaign represented a significant risk for the company considering that the UK market delivered 40 per cent of the Carlsberg brand's profits. In order to prevent a negative reaction Carlsberg have said that the phrase will continue to appear on the UK packaging. However, the 'If Carlsberg did' aspect of the campaign which portrays idealized versions of everyday life has been cancelled.

'That calls for a Carlsberg'

The global relaunch of the Carlsberg brand was announced on 5 April 2011, after a two-year process. Carlsberg aimed to add a greater sense of essence to the brand to appeal to a new generation of drinkers. The new positioning of the Carlsberg brand celebrates Carlsberg's heritage and values, while connecting with today's active, adventurous generation of beer drinkers. The proposition encourages consumers 'to step up and do the right thing', rewarding themselves with a Carlsberg for their deeds, and carries the tagline 'That calls for a Carlsberg'. Khalil Younes (senior vice president of Global, Sales, Marketing and Innovation) states that this campaign will take Carlsberg to the next level. The campaign has seen a number of changes to Carlsberg including;

- *Technological innovations.* As part of the campaign Carlsberg was keen to emphasize its rich heritage in scientific discovery, so the Null-LOX barley was developed and is being rolled out across Carlsberg's markets
- *Modernized identity.* Carlsberg brand's visual identity has been modernized to increase its appeal to today's young adult consumers. The visual identity for Carlsberg's brand positioning has been developed around four design principles: bold, authentic, modern and approachable. The Danish Royal crown has been made more simple and distinctive and allows Carlsberg to continue to tell the story of its authenticity and premium quality. The dominant green used since 1904 has been made more vibrant, while the antique gold has been replaced by a more sophisticated alloy of gold and silver. In addition, the brand's logo now carries three elements together for the first time: the Brewer's Star, the Hop Leaf and the inclusion of 'Copenhagen 1847', the city where and date when Carlsberg was first brewed. Carlsberg believes the inclusion of all three elements reiterates the brand's quality, natural and authentic credentials.
- *Embossed packaging.* The new packaging, carrying the modernized visual identity, is now being utilized across over 140 markets. Carlsberg has established an embossed bottle with a new neck-shape label as the key bottle

design across all bottle sizes. The majority of beer bottles are characterized by the brand name printed across the face of an elliptical or rectangular paper label; Carlsberg has opted to replace the conventional paper label with glass embossing of the brand name on the bottle itself. This feature aims to differentiate the brand from other beers both on the shelf and in the hands of consumers. Carlsberg has also introduced a simpler and more distinctive version of the Carlsberg Crown icon. Overall, the new bottle is meant to appear more modern and refined to appeal to a younger target market. However, competitor brands such as Heineken also feature the trademark green colour so Carlsberg cannot depend on visual identity alone to stand out.

■ *Integrated marketing communications.* A total of 350 different creative materials, including 90-second cinema spots and point of sale panels, are being utilized by Carlsberg marketers worldwide. The introduction of updated pack graphics and an embossed bottle has led to 55 production lines across the globe being specially adapted. The brewer has also created its own soundtrack that's being used in different styles and tempos across all media channels. Brands can pay upwards of £250,000 to use single songs in just one market, so the initiative will deliver significant cost savings. The campaign coincided with the announcement of Carlsberg Group's international design competition to transform the New Carlsberg Brewhouse into a Brand and Experience Centre to attract 500,000 visitors each year. As part of the repositioning Carlsberg Group announced the sponsorship of UEFA EURO 2012. The campaign strategy was devised by creative agency Fold7.

Campaign results to date

Jorgen Bulh Rassmussen, CEO, claimed Carlsberg Group aimed to double the profits of the Carlsberg brand by 2015 at the minimum. The repositioning of the Carlsberg brand, initiated in 2011, continued to be strongly supported in 2012. This major investment in a global branding strategy demonstrates Carlsberg's ambition to achieve iconic status for its flagship brand. An important event was the EURO 2012 sponsorship, which was an important driver of the 8 per cent volume growth of the Carlsberg brand in its premium markets. The brand grew across all three regions in 2012. However, in 2013 this was offset by a decline of 2 per cent. Despite challenging conditions in the

global beer market Carlsberg continues to invest strongly in the new campaign. In 2013, several brand initiatives were undertaken including the renewal of its footballing partnership with UEFA for EURO 2016 and signing three-year partnerships with the English Premier League and the Chinese Football Association Super League. Carlsberg Group has launched a major social media initiative implementing a platform allowing it to create and share content to social networks including Facebook, Google+ and Twitter for all 500 of its brands. In February 2013 Carlsberg hired Santo Advertising to replace Fold7 as its creative agency.

Conclusion

Many critics quickly labelled the decision by Carlsberg to change its famous tagline as 'probably not the best rebranding in the world'. The repositioning represents an idea that consumers can connect to on a personal level. The new slogan 'That calls for a Carlsberg' aims to create a new voice that resonates with a younger market who like to dream big and reward themselves. Difficult conditions in the global beer market mean that it is unlikely that Carlsberg will achieve Jorgen Bulh Rassmussen's objective of doubling its profits by 2015. In its continued journey towards repositioning the brand Carlsberg will have to be wary of alienating brand loyalists, particularly in northern European, and ensure that the idea behind this new campaign meets with the brand's core identity. In attempting to appeal to all its consumers globally with a single positioning strategy, Carlsberg risks connecting with none.

Questions

1. Identify Carlsberg's stage in its product life cycle before the launch of the 'That calls for a Carlsberg' campaign.
2. Carlsberg Group has a portfolio of over 500 brands varying significantly in volume, price, target audience and geographic penetration. Outline the benefits of using the Boston Consulting Group growth-share matrix to manage this portfolio to the Carlsberg Group. In what quadrant of the matrix would you place the Carlsberg brand?
3. Discuss using Figure 6.3 the effect of Carlsberg's new tagline on the positioning of the Carlsberg brand.
4. Critically evaluate the advantages and risks associated with utilizing a single global branding strategy for Carlsberg. Explain what is meant by a 'glocal' approach.

This case was prepared by David Cosgrave, Limerick University from various published sources as a basis for class discussion rather than to show effective or ineffective management.

Chapter 7

Value through Services, Relationships and Experiences

Chapter outline

The unique characteristics of services

Managing services enterprises

Relationship marketing

Experiential marketing

Marketing in non-profit organizations

Learning outcomes

By the end of this chapter you will:

1   Understand the special characteristics of services
2   Analyse the key issues in managing services enterprises
3   Explain the nature of service quality
4   Understand the nature of relationship marketing
5   Analyse the role of customer relationship management (CRM) systems in relationship marketing
6   Critique the role of marketing relationships in society
7   Explain the role of experiential marketing
8   Analyse the nature and characteristics of not-for-profit marketing.

The Van Gogh Museum

The spectrum of marketing activity is very wide. It is not confined to bars of soap, smartphones or industrial equipment but is to be found in all aspects of modern society from political parties to religions to charities. When the tried and trusted practices of marketing are applied in these different contexts, significant results can be achieved. A classic case in point is the Van Gogh Museum in Amsterdam, Holland.

The museum was established in 1973 and is dedicated solely to the works of the famous Dutch artist, Vincent Van Gogh. Born in 1853, Van Gogh was a leading post-impressionist painter who produced many famous works such as *Sunflowers, Starry Night* and *Bedroom in Arles*. But in recent years, the Van Gogh Museum faced some significant business challenges. Museums globally depend heavily on tourism and the economic recession in Europe since 2008 combined with events like the Icelandic ash cloud affected tourist numbers. In addition, financial pressures on governments in Europe mean that museums are expected to find their own sources of revenue with the result that they need to think more carefully about how they do their marketing.

Like many museums around the world, the Van Gogh Museum regularly does audience research to find out what visitors think of the experience. Generally the results are very positive with the museum scoring very highly on attributes like design and presentation, information about the objects, its permanent collection and its temporary exhibitions. So it decided to probe a little deeper to try to uncover how consumers felt emotionally about their visits. What this research uncovered was that aspects like 'it touches me' and 'it inspires me' were perceived to be of high importance by visitors and had a significant impact on audience retention. So while the museum performed well on 'functional' attributes such as design and layout, it knew that it could improve its 'emotional' appeal by enhancing the visitor experience. But it also knew that the emotional appeal of art will vary enormously from person to person so the first step was to try to understand the different customer segments that it had.

Through qualitative and quantitative research, the museum discovered six benefit segments which it labelled as trendy hedonist, wilful discoverer, classic connoisseur, intellectual specialist, docile admirer and easy-going connector. It decided to focus its marketing efforts on the latter two groups. This meant that the museum would be spacious, have clear signage and be lively, and that staff would be friendly and cordial, strengthening the visitor's sense of connection. Its brand's positioning was also altered to reflect attributes such as unpretentiousness, openness and friendliness.

This new marketing strategy proved effective in building the museum's brand and generating repeat visits by customers. The museum caters for over 1.5 million visitors per year putting it in the top 25 museums in the world.[1]

In the previous chapter, we saw that almost all goods that are offered in a marketplace contain elements that are both tangible and intangible (see Figure 6.1 earlier). Those that are high on tangible elements, we tend to think of as products and those that are high on intangible elements, we think of as services. A wide variety of activities such as going on holidays, visiting the dentist, receiving an education and getting legal advice are all generally thought of as service activities because of their high levels of intangibility. Online education, global legal services and IT consultancy means that many business and consumer services are extensively internationally traded. In 2010, the World Bank estimated that the services sector accounted for almost 71 per cent of global gross domestic product (GDP). It also found that international trade in services has been outpacing goods since the 1980s and grew by 11 per cent in 2011. Therefore, while most goods can be thought of as a combination of products and services, the high importance of services means that it is a key area of study.

The growth of services has also been accompanied by increased attention in the marketing literature. Early work on services in the 1980s highlighted the unique nature of services enterprises and these characteristics are explored below. This was followed by more detailed work on services marketing and the emergence of the relationship marketing concept which are also explored in this chapter. More recently, the concept of the service-dominant (S-D) logic was proposed to try to shift the focus of research from the production of goods to the trading of services.[2] The foundational premises of the service-dominant logic are summarized in Table 7.1. Four key propositions have emerged from this initial list. The first is that the fundamental unit of exchange is not goods but service, and that goods are merely an embodiment of service. The second is that value is co-created between the producer and user placing the concept of value-in-use to the forefront of thinking about innovation and marketing. Third, is the idea that exchange is not taking place between just two parties (a producer and consumer, for example) but rather a variety of actors in a network can be involved in value creation. Finally, value is always uniquely determined by each beneficiary. The main contribution of the S-D logic has been to propose a more holistic and integrative way of thinking about marketing activity that captures the highly networked way in which enterprises currently operate.

Table 7.1 The service-dominant (S-D) logic

Key premise	Explanation
1	Service is the fundamental basis of exchange
2	The service basis of exchange is not always apparent as it is masked by goods, money, institutions, etc.
3	Goods are a distribution mechanism for service provision
4	Resources such as knowledge and skills are the primary source of competitive advantage
5	All economies are service economies
6	The customer is always a co-creator of value
7	The enterprise cannot deliver value but only offer value propositions
8	A service-centred view is inherently customer-oriented and relational
9	All social and economic actors are resource integrators
10	Value is always uniquely determined by the beneficiary

Source: Vargo and Lusch (2008)

The unique characteristics of services

There are four key distinguishing characteristics of services, namely, intangibility, inseparability, variability and perishability (see Figure 7.1).

Intangibility

Services can be thought of as a deed, performance or effort, not an object, device or thing, and are therefore intangible.[3] This **intangibility** may mean that a customer may find difficulty in evaluating a service before purchase. For example, it is virtually impossible to judge how enjoyable a holiday will be before taking it because the holiday cannot be shown to a customer before consumption. The contrasts with physical products where, at a minimum, the customer has an opportunity to pick up a new product like a smartphone and examine how it looks and feels. Therefore products are characterized by *search* properties (they can be examined in advance) while services exhibit *experience* properties (they can be assessed only after they have been experienced) with a result that service choices are often riskier.

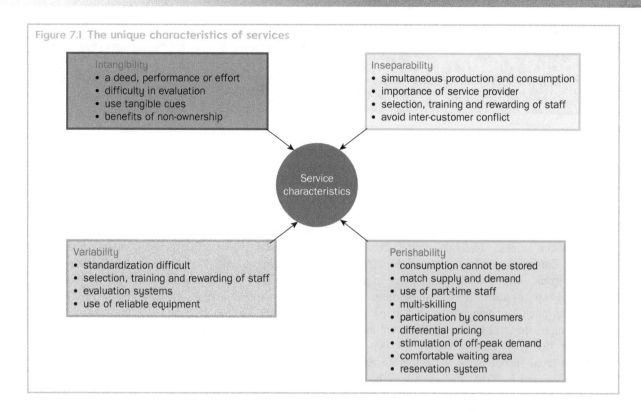

Figure 7.1 The unique characteristics of services

Intangibility
- a deed, performance or effort
- difficulty in evaluation
- use tangible cues
- benefits of non-ownership

Inseparability
- simultaneous production and consumption
- importance of service provider
- selection, training and rewarding of staff
- avoid inter-customer conflict

Service characteristics

Variability
- standardization difficult
- selection, training and rewarding of staff
- evaluation systems
- use of reliable equipment

Perishability
- consumption cannot be stored
- match supply and demand
- use of part-time staff
- multi-skilling
- participation by consumers
- differential pricing
- stimulation of off-peak demand
- comfortable waiting area
- reservation system

Some services such as a medical operation or a car service possess *credence* properties, that is, it is not possible to evaluate them even after they have been consumed which means that these types of choices are particularly difficult for consumers.[4]

The challenge for the service provider is to use tangible cues to service quality (see Exhibit 7.1). For example, a holiday firm may show pictures of the holiday destination, display testimonials from satisfied holidaymakers and provide details in a brochure of the kind of entertainment available. The staff of US-based computer services company the Geek Squad are clearly distinguishable through their short-sleeved white shirts, black ties and badges, and their colourful 'Geek Mobiles' in which they drive to house calls.[5] Service companies, like hotels, invest heavily in tangibles such as the decor of rooms and staff uniforms.

The task is to provide an indication of likely service quality. McDonald's does this by controlling the physical settings of its restaurants and by using the golden arches as a branding cue. By having a consistent offering, the company has effectively dealt with the difficulties that consumers have in evaluating the quality of a service. Standard menus and ordering procedures have also ensured uniform and easy access for customers, while allowing quality control.[6]

Intangibility also means that the customer cannot own a service. Payment is for use or performance. For example, a car may be hired or a medical operation performed. Service organizations sometimes stress the benefits of non-ownership such as lower capital costs and the spreading of payment charges.

Exhibit 7.1 This outdoor advert for NatWest uses images of its staff dressed in their uniforms to help tangiblize the brand

Inseparability

Unlike physical goods, services have **inseparability** – that is, they have simultaneous production and consumption. For example, a haircut,

Social Media Marketing 7.1 Tomorrowland music festival

> **Critical Thinking:** Below is a review of the marketing of the Tomorrowland music festival in Belgium. Read it and reflect on which of the unique characteristics of services are important in this context and how this impacts upon the marketing used by the festival.

Tomorrowland is one of the many successful boutique music festivals that characterize the European summer. Started in 2005, the electronic music festival takes place in a small town, aptly named Boom, in Belgium. It has since quickly grown into global stardom. For example, the 2012 version of the event included over 400 DJs and attracted 185,000 music fans from 75 countries. To celebrate its tenth anniversary in 2014, the event was held over two weekends and sold out its 400,000 tickets even before the line-up was announced.

Some key aspects of how the festival is marketed have been critical to its success. First, it clearly targeted a market segment of young, trendy party lovers from Belgium and around the world who have a shared passion for electronic dance music. This is a segment that differs from the more typical rock audience that characterizes summer festival goers. Second, the event is positioned as a magical journey which takes its audience into a world where anything is possible and reminds them that they are young and free. Finally, the tangible elements of the festival are designed to reflect this magical journey. For example, the theme of the 2013 festival was 'the arising of life' so the main stage was designed as a massive volcano, 140 metres wide and 35 metres high. Entry wristbands were changed from plastic to nicely designed bracelets while the pathways leading from the festival featured fire-spitting dragons and the recorded sounds of singing birds.

As is the case with services generally, the customer journey begins long before the event itself and also provides opportunities for enhancing the experience. For example in 2012, the festival partnered with Brussels Airlines to offer travel packages to the festival under the brand *Global Journey*. Aircraft were customized with the Tomorrowland livery and equipped with grass floors and DJ booths. When guests arrived they were welcomed at a Tomorrowland desk and transferred to their hotels or the festival campsite, DreamVille. Promotion tends to be heavily oriented to social media. The 2013 after movie has been viewed over 64 million times on YouTube and its official Facebook page has over 4 million fans. The festival generated a total of over 3.5 million mentions across social media in 2013 or almost 700,000 per day.

a medical operation, psychoanalysis, a holiday and a pop concert are produced and consumed at the same time (see Social Media Marketing 7.1). This contrasts with a physical good that is produced, stored and distributed through intermediaries before being bought and consumed. It also highlights the importance of the service provider, who is an integral part of the satisfaction gained by the consumer. How service providers conduct themselves may have a crucial bearing on repeat business over and above the technical efficiency of the service task. For example, how courteous and friendly the service provider is may play a large part in the customer's perception of the service experience. The service must be provided not only at the right time and in the right place but also in the right way.[7]

Often, in the customer's eyes, the photocopier service engineer or the insurance representative *is* the company. Consequently, the selection, training and rewarding of staff who are the front-line service people is of fundamental importance in the achievement of high standards of service quality. This notion of the inseparability of production and consumption means that both internal marketing and relationship marketing are important in services, as we shall see later. In such circumstances, managing buyer–seller interaction is central to effective marketing and can be fulfilled only in a relationship with the customer.[8]

Furthermore, the consumption of the service may take place in the presence of other consumers. This is apparent with restaurant meals, air, rail or coach travel, and many forms of entertainment, for example. Consequently, enjoyment of the service is dependent not only on the service provided, but also on other consumers. Therefore service providers need to identify possible sources of nuisance (e.g. noise, smoke, queue jumping) and make adequate provision to avoid inter-customer conflict. For example, a restaurant layout should provide reasonable space between tables so that the potential for conflict is minimized.

Marketing managers should not underestimate the role played by customers in aiding other customers in their decision making. A study into service interactions in IKEA stores found that almost all customer–employee exchanges related to customer concerns about 'place' (e.g. 'Can you direct me to the pick-up point?') and 'function' (e.g. 'How does this chair work?'). However, interactions between customers took the form of opinions on the quality of materials used in products, advice on bed sizes and how to move around the in-store restaurant. Many customers appeared to display a degree of product knowledge or expertise bordering on that of contact personnel.[9]

Variability

Service quality may be subject to considerable **variability**, which makes standardization difficult. Two restaurants within the same chain may have variable service owing to the capabilities of their respective managers and staff. Two marketing courses at the same university may vary considerably in terms of quality, depending on the lecturer. Quality variations among physical products may be subject to tighter controls through centralized production, automation and quality checking before dispatch. Services, however, are often conducted at multiple locations, by people who may vary in their attitudes (and tiredness), and are subject to simultaneous production and consumption. The last characteristic means that a service fault (e.g. rudeness) cannot be quality checked and corrected between production and consumption, unlike a physical product such as misaligned car windscreen wipers.

The potential for variability in service quality emphasizes the need for rigorous selection, training and rewarding of staff in service organizations. Training should emphasize the standards expected of personnel when dealing with customers. *Evaluation systems* should be developed that allow customers to report on their experiences with staff; for example, many service organizations invite feedback from customers through comment cards, online surveys and social media. Some service organizations, notably the British Airports Authority, tie reward systems to customer satisfaction surveys, which are based, in part, on the service quality provided by their staff.

Service standardization is a related method of tackling the variability problem. For example, a university department could agree to use the same software platform when developing course delivery. The use of reliable equipment rather than people can also help in standardization – for instance, the supply of drinks via vending machines or cash through bank machines. However, great care needs to be taken regarding equipment reliability and efficiency. For example, the perceived security of Internet banking facilities impacts upon consumers' willingness to use this medium for financial transactions.

Perishability

The fourth characteristic of services is their **perishability** in the sense that consumption cannot be stored for the future (see Exhibit 7.2). A hotel room or an airline seat that is not occupied today represents lost income that cannot be gained tomorrow. If a physical good is not sold, it can be stored for sale later. Therefore

Exhibit 7.2 A cleverly designed social media advertisement for the Truck festival in Oxfordshire is designed to overcome the perishability problem of events like this. If tickets are not sold by the end of the event, the opportunity to do so passes.

it is important to match supply and demand for services. For example, if a hotel has high weekday occupancy but is virtually empty at weekends, a key marketing task is to provide incentives for weekend use. This might involve offering weekend discounts, or linking hotel use with leisure activities such as golf, fishing or hiking.

Service providers also have the problem of catering for peak demand when supply may be insufficient. A physical goods provider may build up inventory in slack periods for sale during peak demand. Service providers do not have this option. Consequently, alternative methods need to be considered. For example, supply flexibility can be varied through the use of part-time staff doing peak periods. Multi-skilling means that employees may be trained in many tasks. Supermarket staff can be trained to fill shelves, and work at the checkout at peak periods. Participation by consumers may be encouraged in production (e.g. self-service breakfasts in hotels). Demand may be smoothed through differential pricing to encourage customers to visit during off-peak periods (for example, lower-priced cinema and theatre seats for afternoon performances). If delay is unavoidable then another option is to make it more acceptable, for example, by providing effective queuing systems or a comfortable waiting area with seating and free refreshments. Finally, a reservation system as commonly used in restaurants, hair salons and theatres can be used to control peak demand and assist time substitution.

In summary, intangibility, inseparability, variability and perishability combine to distinguish services from products. As we noted at the outset, products and services are not completely distinct and in most instances it is a matter of degree. For example, a marketing research study would provide a report (physical good) that represents the outcome of a number of service activities (discussions with client, designing the research strategy, interviewing respondents and analysing the results). As many firms are finding it increasingly difficult to differentiate themselves on the basis of the products, opportunities for adding value are provided by the service components (see the discussion on augmented differentiation in the previous chapter). For example, staff at a Niketown store may do much more than just assist customers with finding a running shoe that fits correctly. These stores also provide additional services such as gait analysis and advice on training and running techniques – as well as selling Nike products of course!

Managing services enterprises

Because of the unique characteristics described above, managing services enterprises involves some

special challenges. Four key issues are physical evidence, people, process and branding and we shall now examine each of these in detail.

Physical evidence

As we saw above, customers look for clues to the likely quality of a service by inspecting the tangible evidence or the **servicescape**. For example, prospective customers may look through a restaurant window to check the appearance of the waiters, the decor and furnishings. The ambience of a retail store is highly dependent on decor, and colour can play an important role in establishing mood because colour has meaning. For example, the reception area of the Petshotel chain in the USA is typically furnished with floral soft furnishings, armchairs, a wide-screen television and stainless steel bowls filled with doggie biscuits. This and its slogan, 'All the comforts of home', is designed to put pet owners at ease that their dogs will be well looked after while they are away.[10]

The layout of a service operation can be a compromise between the operation's need for efficiency and marketing's desire for effectively serving the customer. For example, the temptation to squeeze in an extra table in a restaurant or seating in an aircraft may be at the expense of customer comfort. Changes in the physical evidence are often part of a marketer's effort to reposition a brand. For example, the desire by McDonald's to improve the image of its brand has seen it invest in lime-green 'egg' chairs in many of its European restaurants, as well as putting in iPods so that customers can sit and listen to music. This moves the brand much closer to a company like Starbucks rather than its traditional competitors such as Burger King.

People

Because of the simultaneity of production and consumption in services, the firm's personnel occupy a key position in influencing customer perceptions of product quality.[11] The term **service encounter** is used to describe an interaction between a service provider and a customer. These encounters may be short and quick such as when a customer picks up a newspaper at a newsstand or long and protracted involving multiple encounters such as receiving a university education. Jan Carlzon, head of the airline SAS, called these interactions 'moments of truth'. He explained that SAS faced 65,000 moments of truth per day (that is the number of interactions between company personnel and people outside the company) and that the outcome of these interactions determined the success of the company. Research on customer loyalty in service industries has shown that only 14 per cent of customers who stopped patronizing service businesses did so because they were dissatisfied with the quality of what they had bought. More than two-thirds stopped buying because they found service staff indifferent or unhelpful.[12]

In order for service employees to be in the frame of mind to treat customers well, they need to feel that their company is treating them well. This has given rise to the idea of the *service profit chain* whereby having a happy workforce leads to having happy customers and ultimately superior profitability – a maxim that has been adopted by many leading companies such as the Virgin Group. The evidence to support the existence of a service profit chain is mixed, with some findings showing a correlation between happy staff and happy customers while others have found that having a happy workforce is more important than having happy customers in terms of profitability.[13] An important marketing task, then, is **internal marketing**, that is, selecting, training and motivating staff members to provide customer satisfaction. Without this type of support, employees tend to be variable in their performance, leading to variable service quality.

The selection of suitable people is the starting point of the process as the nature of the job requires appropriate personality characteristics. Once selected, training is required to familiarize recruits to the job requirements and the culture of the organization. Socialization then allows recruits to experience the culture and tasks of the organization. Service quality may also be affected by the degree to which staff are empowered or given the authority to satisfy customers and deal with their problems. For example, each member of staff of Marriott Hotels is allowed to spend up to £1,000 on their own initiative to solve customer problems.[14] Maintaining a motivated workforce in the face of irate customers, faulty support systems and the boredom that accompanies some service jobs is a demanding task. Some service companies give employee-of-the-month awards in recognition of outstanding service. Reward and remuneration is also important. For example, the US retailer Costco competes against Walmart in the discount warehouse sector. But its pay and conditions are far superior to its main rival and it has a staff turnover rate of 17 per cent annually compared with 70 per cent for the sector.[15]

Process

The service process refers to the procedures, mechanisms and flow of activities by which a service is acquired. The service process usually contains two elements, namely, that which is visible to the customer and where the service encounter takes place and that which is invisible to the customer but is still critical to service delivery. For example, waiting staff in a restaurant are a key part of the service encounter and they need to be well selected and well trained. How they treat customers is a key element of the service experience. But what happens in the kitchen, even though it is invisible to the customer is also critical to the service experience. Both parts of the service process need to be carefully managed.

Service process decisions usually involve some trade-off between levels of service quality (effectiveness) and service productivity (efficiency). Productivity is a measure of the relationship between an input and an output. For instance, if more people can be served (output) using the same number of staff (input), productivity per employee has risen. For example, a doctor who reduces consultation time per patient, or a university that increases tutorial group size, raises productivity at the risk of lowering service quality. Clearly, a balance must be struck between productivity and service quality. There are ways of improving productivity without compromising quality. As we saw earlier, customers can be involved in the service delivery process, such as in self-service restaurants and petrol stations, and supply and demand for services can be balanced through either capacity expansion or demand management techniques.

The service process will also be significantly influenced by the service provider's attitude towards investments in technology. Owing to some of the challenges involved in delivering services through people that we discussed above, firms have begun to look at technological solutions. For example, banks have been using automatic cash dispensers, telephone banking and Internet banking to improve the number of transactions per period (productivity) while reducing waiting times and increasing the availability of banking facilities (service quality). For many customers this means that the service encounter is no longer with a banking representative but rather a piece of technology. This may be advantageous in terms of service consistency but it also removes the opportunity to build a personal relationship with the customer, as we shall see later. The potential offered by technology has caused some service providers to focus more on productivity rather than on service quality. Significant investments have been made in outsourcing customer service to call centres from which levels of service quality is often variable leading to customer frustration and dissatisfaction.

Service branding

Because of the intangible nature of services, branding is of crucial importance. As we saw earlier in the chapter, service decisions are difficult to make because services may be high on experience and credence properties. The reputation of the service provider becomes ever more important as a result and trust is an important factor in the customer buying decision. One way for service providers to differentiate themselves is through the strength of their brand equity. The brand name of a service influences the perception of that service. Research on service organizations has identified four characteristics of successful brand names, as follows.[16]

1   *Distinctiveness*: it immediately identifies the service provider and differentiates it from the competition.
2   *Relevance*: it communicates the nature of the service and the service benefit.
3   *Memorability*: it is easily understood and remembered.
4   *Flexibility*: it not only expresses the service organization's current business but also is broad enough to cover foreseeable new ventures.

Wagamama, the successful Japanese noodle chain, literally translates as 'wilful naughty child', but the distinctiveness of its name and service has proven to be attractive in foreign markets. Credit cards provide examples of effective brand names: Visa suggests internationality and MasterCard emphasizes top quality. Obviously the success of the brand name is heavily dependent on the service organization's ability to deliver on the promise it implies. Sometimes service brand names are changed, such as the decision by Aviva, the UK's biggest insurer group, to drop its Norwich Union brand, which had existed for over 200 years, and by Eagle Star to change its name to that of its parent, Zurich (see Marketing in Action 7.1).

 Premier Inn Ad Insight: The 'Good Night Guarantee' campaign featuring Lenny Henry conveys the hotel chain's brand proposition.

Dimensions of the service brand may also be difficult to communicate. For example, it may be difficult to represent courtesy, hard work and customer care in an advertisement. Once again the answer is to use tangible cues that will help customers understand and judge the service. A hotel, for example, can show the buildings, swimming pool, friendly staff and happy customers; an investment company can provide tangible evidence of past performance; testimonials from satisfied customers can also be used to communicate services benefits. Netto, the Danish-based supermarket chain, used testimonials from six customers in its UK advertising to explain the advantages of shopping

there. External communications that depict service quality can also influence internal staff if they include employees and show how they take exceptional care of their customers.

Word of mouth is critical to success for services because of their experiential nature. For example, reading reviews written by people who have visited a resort or hotel is more convincing than reading holiday brochures. It is estimated that word of mouth can be the primary factor behind anything from 25 to 50 per cent of all consumer decisions.[17] The growth in digital and social media has significantly amplified the word of mouth effect leading to the emergence of the term electronic word of mouth or eWOM. The strength of the word of mouth effect is a function of what is said, who says it and where it is said. Content that relates directly to consumer decisions and that comes from trusted sources is likely to have a more powerful effect. However, the existence of a strong brand has been shown to moderate the strength of online customer reviews implying that service brand building remains an important activity.[18]

Managing service quality

One of the core means of providing value to customers is to focus on the issue of service quality and how it can be improved. All kinds of organizations are making increasing use of customer satisfaction research to guide their marketing activity. This type of research may range from customer comment cards, to mystery shoppers to online customer satisfaction studies. Research has shown that companies that are rated higher on service quality perform better in terms of market share growth and profitability.[19] Yet for many companies high standards of service quality remain elusive. There are four causes of poor perceived quality (see Figure 7.2). These are the barriers that separate the perception of service quality from what customers expect.[20]

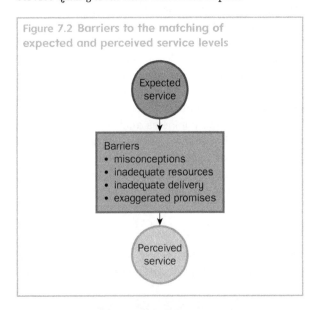

Figure 7.2 Barriers to the matching of expected and perceived service levels

Marketing in Action 7.1 Aviva: changing the brand proposition

Critical Thinking: Below is a review of a repositioning exercise conducted by the financial services group, Aviva. Read it and critically evaluate the role of the brand in the service enterprise.

As we saw earlier, the intangibility of services is a particular challenge with the result that the management of tangible cues is very important. One such cue is the brand name and service: customers around the world choose providers with which they have developed some level of trust. So any decision to change a service brand name must be considered very carefully. But at the same time service organizations in sectors like banking, consultancy and insurance expand globally through the acquisition of independent providers in different countries. Significant advantages such as uniformity and cost savings can be gained from using just one global name rather than many individual domestic ones but the process needs to carefully managed.

A case in point is the insurance provider Aviva. The company's origins go all the way back to founding of the Hand in Hand Fire & Life Insurance Society in London in 1696. The Aviva name first came into use in 2002 by which stage the insurer had grown significantly after a period of acquisitions spread throughout 21 countries around the world. Some of these companies were leaders in their own markets such as Norwich Union in the UK, Hibernian Insurance in Ireland and Commercial Union in Poland and these retained their names due to the high levels of brand recognition that they had built up. But as part of a strategy of building stronger relationships with its customers, the decision was taken in 2007 to brand all members of the group as Aviva.

The name change process required a major investment in resources by the company. A team of 700 people were directly involved and a central planning office was formed in London to oversee the project. Programme managers were put in place in each of the three countries who managed and coordinated the work of multiple teams including IT, human resources, marketing, operations and facilities. In the case of the UK, the decision was taken to make a 'big bang' change from Norwich Union to Aviva, while in Ireland and Poland the process involved moving to Hibernian Aviva and Commercial Aviva first before the full change. The name changes also created the opportunity for the company to refine its positioning as a more empathetic, customer-friendly organization in an industry that is generally perceived as being conservative and self-serving. This was captured in the slogan 'one Aviva, twice the value'. A key part of the change-over process involved appealing to the company's 54,000 employees as well as to the network of brokers (intermediaries) who sold the company's products. The effectiveness of its strategy can be gauged by its rise into the Top 20 insurance brands in the world with an estimated brand value of $5 billion.

Based on: Anonymous (2010).[21]

Barriers to the matching of expected and perceived service levels

1 **Misconceptions barrier.** This arises from management's misunderstanding of what the customer expects. Lack of marketing research may lead managers to misconceive the important service attributes that customers use when evaluating a service, and the way in which customers use attributes in evaluation.

2 **Inadequate resources barrier.** Managers may understand customer expectations but be unwilling to provide the resources necessary to meet them. This may arise because of a cost reduction or productivity focus, or simply because of the inconvenience it may cause.

3 **Inadequate delivery barrier.** Managers may understand customer expectations and supply adequate resources but fail to select, train and reward staff adequately, resulting in poor or

inconsistent service. This may manifest itself in poor communication skills, inappropriate dress and unwillingness to solve customer problems.

4   **Exaggerated promises barrier.** Even when customer understanding, resources and staff management are in place, a gap between customer expectations and perceptions can still arise through exaggerated promises. Advertising and selling messages that build expectations to a pitch that cannot be fulfilled may leave customers disappointed even when receiving a good service. Therefore, it is important not to overpromise in marketing communications.

Meeting customer expectations

A key to providing service quality is the understanding and meeting of customer expectations. To do so requires a clear picture of the criteria used to form these expectations, recognizing that consumers of services value not only the outcome of the service encounter but also the experience of taking part in it. For example, an evaluation of a haircut depends not only on the quality of the cut but also the experience of having a haircut. Clearly, a hairdresser needs not only technical skills but also the ability to communicate in an interesting and polite manner. Consequently, five core dimensions of service quality have been identified.[22]

1   *Reliability*: is the service consistent and dependable?
2   *Assurance*: that customers can trust the service company and its staff.
3   *Responsiveness*: how quickly do service staff respond to customer problems, requests and questions?
4   *Empathy*: that service staff act in a friendly and polite manner and care for their customers.
5   *Tangibles*: how well managed is the tangible evidence of the service (e.g. staff appearance, decor, layout)?

Improving service quality delivery requires an understanding of both customer expectations and the barriers that cause a difference between expected and perceived service levels. One approach has emphasized the closing of four gaps which are the main cause of service quality problems.[23]

Gap 1

This is the gap between what customers expect from a service provider and what the senior management team in the service organization thinks that customers expect. The gap is caused by senior managers being too far removed from customers – a problem that arises particularly in large organizations. Effective research of customers' expectations can be used to close this gap.

Gap 2

This is the gap between senior management perceptions and the service level criteria that they set for the organization. All organizations have some service level criteria such as the speed with which phones should be answered or the number of breakdowns that should be fixed within a day and so on. This gap can be closed by ensuring that customer service goals are an important part of the organization's targets for the planning period.

Gap 3

This is the gap between the service level targets set by the organization and the actual level of service that is delivered by front-line staff. This gap can arise due to there being inadequate resources committed to service delivery or poor selection, training and motivation of staff. Good internal marketing practices can assist in closing this gap.

Gap 4

Finally, this is the gap between what firms tell their customers to expect in their external communications and what they actually deliver. Therefore, service promises need to be managed very carefully. Overpromising causes customer expectations to rise and failure to deliver on these promises leads to dissatisfaction.

In summary, delivering service quality requires constant attention to the four potential gaps in the service delivery system. This is why consistently high levels of service are so difficult and why only very few firms, such as service leaders like Singapore Airlines and Marriott Hotels, manage to achieve them.

 Singapore Airlines Ad Insight: The 'Across the World' campaign illustrates the company's reputation for outstanding service quality.

Service recovery

Because services involve people, mistakes will inevitably occur even in the best managed service systems. Service recovery strategies should be designed to solve the problem and restore the customer's trust in the firm, as well as improve the service system so that the problem does not recur in the future.[24] They are crucial because an inability to recover service failures and mistakes loses customers directly as well as through their tendency to tell other actual and potential customers about their negative experiences. This is particularly the case where consumers have paid a great deal for a service, such as first-class airline passengers.

The first ingredient in a service recovery strategy is to set up a tracking system to identify system failures. Customers should be encouraged to report service problems since it is those customers that do not complain that are least likely to purchase again. Second, staff should be trained and empowered to respond to service complaints. This is important because research has shown that the successful resolution of a complaint can cause customers to feel more positive about the firm than before the service failure. For example, when P&O had to cancel a round-the-world cruise because of problems with its ship, the *Aurora*, it reportedly offered passengers their money back plus a discount on their next booking. Many passengers said they planned to travel on a P&O cruise in the future.[25]

Finally, a service recovery strategy should encourage learning so that service recovery problems are identified and corrected. Service staff should be motivated to report problems and solutions so that recurrent failures are identified and fixed. In this way, an effective service recovery system can lead to improved customer service, satisfaction and higher customer retention levels.

Relationship marketing

The intangible nature of services means that customers may also value having a close relationship with a service provider. For example, if a customer finds an organization that she can trust, she may want to go back to this provider again and again as this saves her having to conduct a new information search each time a purchase is made. The relationship may also benefit the service provider as it is generally believed that it is cheaper for the organization to retain its existing customers than it is to gain new ones. These elements have underpinned the concept of **relationship marketing**.

The idea of relationship marketing can be applied to many industries. It is particularly important in services since there is often direct contact between service provider and consumer – for example, doctor

and patient, hotel staff and guests (see Exhibit 7.3). The quality of the relationship that develops will often determine its length. Not all service encounters have the potential for a long-term relationship, however. For example, a passenger at an international airport who needs road transportation will probably never meet the taxi driver again, and the choice of taxi supplier will be dependent on the passenger's position in the queue rather than free choice. In this case the exchange – cash for journey – is a pure transaction: the driver knows that it is unlikely that there will ever be a repeat purchase.[26] Organizations therefore need to decide when the practice of relationship marketing is most applicable. The following conditions suggest the use of relationship marketing activities:[27]

- There is an ongoing or periodic desire for the service by the customer, e.g. insurance or theatre service versus funeral service.
- The customer controls the selection of a service provider, e.g. selecting a hotel versus entering the first taxi in an airport waiting line.
- The customer has alternatives from which to choose, e.g. selecting a restaurant versus buying water from the only utility company service in a community.

The existence of strong customer relationships brings benefits for both organizations and customers. There are six benefits to service organizations in developing and maintaining strong customer relationships.[28] The first is *increased purchases*. Customers tend to spend more because, as the relationship develops, trust grows between the partners. Second is *lower costs*. The start-up

costs associated with attracting new customers are likely to be far higher than the cost of retaining existing customers. Third, loyal customers generate a significant *lifetime value*. If a customer spends €80 in a supermarket per week, resulting in €8 profit, and uses the supermarket 45 times a year over 30 years, the lifetime value of that customer is almost €11,000. Fourth, the intangible aspects of a relationship are not easily copied by the competition, generating a *sustainable competitive advantage*. Fifth, satisfied customers generate additional business due to the importance of *word-of-mouth* promotion in services industries. Finally, satisfied, loyal customers raise *employees' job satisfaction* and decrease staff turnover.

The net result of these six benefits of developing customer relationships is high profits. A study has shown across a variety of service industries that profits climb steeply when a firm lowers its customer defection rate.[29] Firms can improve profits from 25 to 85 per cent (depending on industry) by reducing customer defections by just 5 per cent. The reasons are that loyal customers generate more revenue for more years and the costs of maintaining existing customers are lower than the costs of acquiring new ones.

Entering into a long-term relationship can also reap benefits for the customer. First, since the intangible nature of services makes them difficult to evaluate beforehand, purchase relationships can help to reduce the risk and stress involved in making choices. Second, strong relationships allow the service provider to deliver a higher-quality service, which can be customized to particular needs. Maintaining a relationship reduces the customer's switching costs and, finally, customers can reap social and status benefits from the relationship, such as when restaurant managers get to know them personally.

Relationship marketing strategies vary in the degree to which they bond the parties together. One framework that illustrates this idea distinguishes between three levels of retention strategy based on the types of bond used to cement the relationship.[30]

1 *Level 1*: at this level the bond is primarily through financial incentives – for example, higher discounts on prices for larger-volume purchases, or frequent flyer or loyalty points resulting in lower future prices. The problem is that the potential for a sustainable competitive advantage is low because price incentives are easy for competitors to copy even if they take the guise of frequent flyer or loyalty points.

2 *Level 2*: this higher level of bonding relies on more than just price incentives and consequently raises the potential for a sustainable competitive advantage. Level 2 retention strategies build long-term relationships through social as well as financial bonds, capitalizing on the fact that many service encounters are also social encounters. Customers become clients, the relationship becomes personalized and the service customized. Characteristics of this type of relationship include frequent communication with customers, providing personal treatment like sending cards, and enhancing the core service with educational or entertainment activities such as seminars or visits to sporting events. Some hotels keep records of their guests' personal preferences such as their favourite newspaper and alcoholic drink.

3 *Level 3*: this top level of bonding is formed by financial, social and structural bonds. Structural bonds tie service providers to their customers through providing solutions to customers' problems that are designed into the service delivery system. For example, logistics companies often supply their clients with equipment that ties them into their systems.

Customer loyalty and retention

Relationship marketing strategies focus attention on the important issue of customer loyalty. At the most basic level, it has been suggested that a potential ladder of loyalty exists and that customers progress up or down this ladder (see Figure 7.3). The firm's marketing activity may revolve around trying to move customers up this ladder until they become advocates or partners of the organization. Advocates are an important group because they not only purchase an organization's products but they actively recommend it to their friends and colleagues. At the top of the ladder are partners who trust and support the organization and actively work with it.

The ladder of loyalty also helps organizations to reflect on the different types of loyalty that may exist. For example, some customers may continue to engage in high levels of repeat business with an organization but this may happen for reasons of inertia rather than true loyalty. This has occurred in sectors like retail banking where consumers have demonstrated a reluctance to switch. Similarly, many of the loyalty schemes run by organizations aim to attract and retain customers on a purely financial basis. Again, this is not true loyalty with customers tending to engage in repeat business only for as long

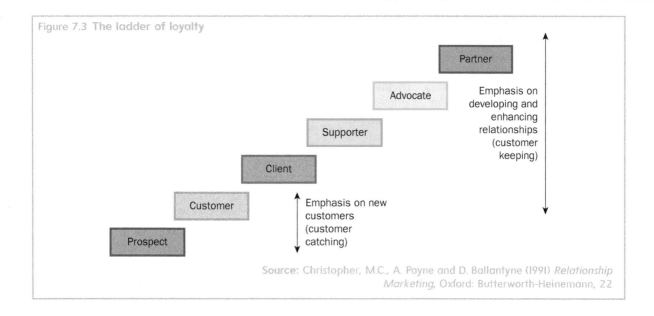

Figure 7.3 The ladder of loyalty

Partner

Advocate

Supporter

Client

Customer

Prospect

Emphasis on developing and enhancing relationships (customer keeping)

Emphasis on new customers (customer catching)

Source: Christopher, M.C., A. Payne and D. Ballantyne (1991) *Relationship Marketing*, Oxford: Butterworth-Heinemann, 22

as the financial incentives remain. A much greater understanding of customers' needs and a willingness to meet those needs on an ongoing basis is required for true loyalty to occur.

Finally, the link between customer loyalty and profitability is a very important one in marketing. Associations between a small increase in customer retention and a large increase in profitability have been identified.[31] This has been explained by the propensity of loyal customers to spend more with the organization and the decreased cost of serving such customers. However, other research has highlighted that this relationship may be more complex. For example, in some instances it has been found that long-standing customers are only marginally profitable while some short-term customers have been highly profitable.[32] This reaffirms that it is the nature of loyalty rather than the length of time customers have been with a firm that is most important.

Experiential marketing

Allied to the provision of service quality and relationships, the creation of customer experiences is another avenue for organizations to deliver value for customers, as we saw in the marketing spotlight at the beginning of the chapter. It aims to capitalize on consumer trends in the Western world, where experiences are perceived by many as being more important than the ownership of goods. Through **experiential marketing**, organizations either partner with existing events or create entirely new ones.

For example, one of the most popular forms of experiential marketing has been the increased association of brands with events like rock concerts and music festivals. This allows marketers to use relevant ways of communicating with audiences for such events, such as through social media and word-of-mouth marketing. The Guinness brand has been associated with the Witnness music festival in Ireland, where even the altered spelling of the word 'witness' highlighted the Guinness association. Pre-publicity for the event also featured a play on the idea of a witness. Consumers and the media joined in a search for clues and were invited to participate in the discovery of Witnness. This generated huge publicity about the event and the various acts that would be performing there. Because the target audience was considered to be marketing literate and cynical with regard to corporate marketing efforts, this approach was more subtle and gave consumers a feeling of ownership and involvement with the event.

Experiential marketing has also become very popular within the retail trade as stores and locations seek to find new ways of appealing to potential customers. The focus has moved from being a venue where products are sold to one where consumers can have a shopping experience or where they can shop as part of other activities. Many major shopping malls now have cinemas attached, others have leisure facilities such as gymnasiums and swimming pools, and some have theatres and galleries. Luxury store Prada, New York, has a cultural performance space, Louis Vuitton's Paris flagship store has an art gallery and a bookstore, while Gucci's Ginza store in Tokyo also has an art gallery as well as an event space. Nespresso has opened a number of Nespresso Boutiques to create the 'ultimate coffee experience'.

The ideal experiential marketing effort is an ownable, sensory brand experience that makes customers feel like the product or service is theirs. These motivated customers then become product advocates, who influence family, friends and co-workers to try the product. For example, Delta Airlines has developed its SKY360 lounge in New York to create a customer experience. Visitors to the lounge are met by actual flight attendants and ticket agents. They sample food items available on Delta and are asked to try new entertainment systems that are built into the backs of seats. The lounge has WiFi connections and computer terminals for anyone who wants to book a flight with Delta.[33]

Marketing in non-profit organizations

Non-profit organizations attempt to achieve some other objective than profit. This does not mean that they are uninterested in income as they have to generate cash to survive. However, their primary goal is non-economic – for example, to provide cultural enrichment (an orchestra), to protect birds and animals (Royal Society for the Protection of Birds, Royal Society for the Prevention of Cruelty to Animals), to alleviate hunger (Oxfam), to provide education (schools and universities), to foster community activities (community associations), and to supply healthcare (hospitals) and public services (local authorities). Their worth and standing is not dependent on the profits they generate. They are discussed in this chapter as most non-profit organizations operate in the services sector. Indeed, non-profit organizations account for over half of all service provision in most European countries.

Marketing is of growing importance to many non-profit organizations because they need to generate funds in an increasingly competitive arena. Even organizations that rely on government-sponsored grants need to show how their work is of benefit to society; they must meet the needs of their customers. Many non-profit organizations rely on membership fees and donations, which means that communication to individuals and organizations is required, and they must be persuaded to join or make a donation. This requires marketing skills, which are increasingly being applied. As we saw in Chapter 1, political parties, universities, hospitals and aid agencies are now frequent users of marketing.

Characteristics of non-profit marketing

There are a number of characteristics of non-profit marketing that distinguish it from that conducted in profit-orientated organizations.[34]

Education vs meeting current needs

Some non-profit organizations see their role not only as meeting the current needs of their customers but also educating them in terms of new ideas and issues, cultural developments and social awareness. **Social marketing** is the term that is used to describe efforts, mainly by public sector organizations, to encourage positive social change such as healthy eating, reduced cigarette and alcohol consumption, safe sex, safe driving, human rights and racial equality (see Exhibit 7.4). Commercial marketing techniques such as consumer research, segmentation and marketing mix development are frequently used to achieve these types of goals.

Multiple publics

Most non-profit organizations serve several groups, or publics. The two broad groups are *donors*, who may be individuals, trusts, companies or government bodies, and *clients*, who include audiences, patients and beneficiaries.[35] The need to satisfy both donors and clients is a complicated marketing task. For example, a community association may be partly funded by the local authority and partly by the users (clients) of the association's buildings and facilities. To succeed, both groups have to be satisfied. The BBC has to satisfy not only its viewers and listeners, but also

Exhibit 7.4 Advertisements such as this one focus on important social issues such as cancer prevention

YOU KNOW THE FIVE SIGNS OF BREAST CANCER, RIGHT? (YES, FIVE)

Breast cancer kills 1,000 women a month and it doesn't always start with a lump.

Knowing the five most common warning signs – and catching them early – could just save your life.

Text GUIDE to 70500 for your FREE Touch Look Check guide today

the government, which decides the size of the licence fee that funds its activities. Non-profit organizations need to adopt marketing as a coherent philosophy for managing multiple public relationships.[36]

Measurement of success and conflicting objectives

For profit-orientated organizations success is ultimately measured in terms of profitability. For non-profit organizations, measuring success is not so easy. In universities, for example, is success measured in terms of research output, number of students taught, the range of qualifications or the quality of teaching? The answer is that it is a combination of these factors, which can lead to conflict – more students and a larger range of courses may reduce the time available for research. Decision making is therefore complex in non-profit-orientated organizations.

Public scrutiny

While all organizations are subject to public scrutiny, public-sector non-profit organizations are never far from the public's attention. The reason is that they are publicly funded from taxes. This gives them extra newsworthiness and they have to be particularly careful not to become involved in controversy. For example, some charitable organizations in Ireland suffered a collapse in funding in 2013 when it emerged that donations were being diverted to top up the salaries of senior executives.

Marketing procedures for non-profit organizations

Despite these differences, the marketing procedures relevant to profit-orientated organizations can also be applied to non-profit organizations. Target marketing, differentiation and tactical marketing decisions need to be made. We will now discuss these issues with reference to the special characteristics of non-profit organizations.

Target marketing and differentiation

As we have already discussed, non-profit organizations can usefully segment their target publics into donors and clients (customers). Within each group, sub-segments of individuals and organizations need to be identified. These will be the targets for persuasive communications and the development of services. The needs of each group must be understood. For example, donors may judge which charity to give to on the basis of awareness and reputation, the

confidence that funds will not be wasted on excessive administration, and the perceived worthiness of the cause (see Marketing in Action 7.2). The charity needs, therefore, not only to promote itself but also to gain publicity for its cause. Its level of donor funding will depend upon both these factors. The brand name of the charity is also important. 'Oxfam' suggests the type of work the organization is mainly concerned with – relief of famine – and so is instantly recognizable. 'Action in Distress' is also suggestive of its type of work.

Market segmentation and targeting are key ingredients in the marketing of political parties. Potential voters are segmented according to their propensity to vote (obtainable from electoral registers) and their likelihood of voting for a particular party (obtainable from door-to-door canvassing returns). Resources can then be channelled to the segments most likely to switch votes in the forthcoming election, via direct mail and doorstep visits. Focus groups provide a feedback mechanism for testing the attractiveness of alternative policy options and gauging voters' opinions on key policy areas such as health, education and taxation. By keeping in touch with public opinion, political parties have the information to differentiate themselves from their competitors on issues that are important to voters. While such marketing research is unlikely to affect the underlying beliefs and principles upon which a political party is based, it is a necessary basis for the policy adaptations required to keep in touch with a changing electorate.[37]

Developing a marketing mix

The pricing of services provided by non-profit organizations may not follow the guidelines applicable to profit-orientated pricing. For example, the price of a nursery school place organized by a community association may be held low to encourage poor families to take advantage of the opportunity. Some non-profit organizations exist to provide free access to services – for example, the National Health Service in the UK. In other situations, the price of a service provided by a non-profit organization may come from a membership or licence fee. For example, the Royal Society for the Protection of Birds (RSPB) charges an annual membership fee; in return members receive a quarterly magazine and free entry to RSPB bird watching sites. The BBC receives income from a licence fee, which all television owners have to pay. The level of this fee is set by government, making relations with political figures an important marketing consideration.

Marketing in Action 7.2 Comic Relief

Critical Thinking: Below is a review of the marketing approach used by the UK charity, Comic Relief. Review it and evaluate the reasons for its success.

One charity that has been highly innovative in its marketing over the years is Comic Relief. The UK-based charity was set up in 1985 with the goal of bringing about positive and lasting change in the lives of poor and disadvantaged people. From its inception, it has used the power of marketing to build its brand and generate funds to enable it to carry out its work. Comic Relief was launched live on the BBC1 television programme the *Late, Late Breakfast Show* broadcasting from a refugee camp in Sudan on Christmas Day! As well as creating a high level of awareness, the contrasting lives of the camp dwellers and the viewers sent out a powerful message on a day that is traditionally associated with sharing and giving.

Another very innovative idea was the launch of Red Nose Day (RND) in 1988. As the name suggests, RND is a day that involves wearing plastic/foam red noses that are available through distributors such as Sainsbury's and Oxfam in return for a donation. RND is the main fundraising vehicle for Comic Relief. The first RND was a national day of comedy. In partnership with the BBC, normal television programming was suspended and comedians and celebrities gave their time for free to host a live telethon to raise funds interspersed with comedy sketches and entertainment. The event raised £15 million for the charity. The idea captured the public imagination and has almost become a semi-holiday with schools for example hosting red-themed days where pupils can wear something red instead of or with their uniforms. Red Nose Day 2013 raised over £100 million.

As the charity has grown it has expanded into using a wide variety of other fundraising mechanisms. A series of charity singles have been recorded by leading artists of the day many of which reached number one in the singles charts. In 2000, the author J K Rowling wrote two Harry Potter books exclusively for Comic Relief raising over £17 million. In recent years the trend has been for well-known celebrities to take on physical challenges to raise funds. In 2009, nine musicians and TV presenters climbed Mount Kilimanjaro in Africa while the comedian, John Bishop, raised £4 million by cycling, rowing and running from Paris to London in five days.

Social media has also become a centrepiece of the organization's communication strategy. The link with high-profile celebrities (who already have their own large followings on social media) has enabled Comic Relief to reach large audiences and gain a 96 per cent brand awareness level in the UK. Fundraising events also generate highly shareable content. But it also means that the organization is not immune from criticism. One of its fundamental premises is the 'golden pound principle'. That is, every pound donated is spent on charitable causes while operating costs such as staff salaries are covered by corporate sponsors or the interest earned on monies not yet distributed. This was a source of controversy in 2013 when it emerged that some of its stock market investments included owning shares in companies manufacturing arms, tobacco and alcohol. This decision to invest in businesses that many of their donors would not invest in themselves, proved very controversial and was reversed in 2014.

Like most services, distribution systems for many non-profit organizations are short, with production and consumption simultaneous. This is the case for hospital operations, consultations with medical practitioners, education, nursery provision, cultural entertainment and many more services provided by non-profit organizations. Such organizations have to think carefully about how to deliver their services with the convenience that customers require. For example, Oxfam has 750 shops around the UK that sell second-hand clothing, books, music and household items that have been donated to it. It has also formed alliances with online retailers such as abebooks.co.uk to list and sell secondhand books, from which Oxfam receives a commission.

Many non-profit organizations are adept at using promotion to further their needs (see Social Media Marketing 7.2 and Exhibit 7.5). The print media are popular with organizations seeking donations for worthy causes such as famine in Africa. Direct mail is also used to raise funds. Mailing lists of past donors are useful here, and some organizations use lifestyle geodemographic analyses to identify the type of person who is more likely to respond to a direct mailing. Non-profit organizations also need to be aware of publicity opportunities that may arise because of their activities. Many editors are sympathetic to such publicity attempts because of their general interest to the public. Sponsorship is also a vital income source for many non-profit organizations.

Public relations have an important role to play in generating positive word-of-mouth communications and establishing the identity of the non-profit

Exhibit 7.5 The Rainforest Alliance 'Follow the Frog' viral video has been viewed over 4.5 million times on YouTube and in tone and content is an example of a really effective promotion for a charitable organization

organization (e.g. a charity). Attractive fundraising settings (e.g. sponsored lunches) can be organized to ensure that the exchange proves to be satisfactory to donors. A key objective of communications efforts should be to produce a positive assessment of the fundraising transaction and to reduce the perceived risk of the donation so that donors develop trust and confidence in the organization and become committed to the cause.[38]

Summary

In this chapter, we examined the particular issues that arise when marketing services businesses. The following key issues were addressed.

1. There are four unique characteristics of services, namely intangibility, inseparability, variability and perishability. As a result marketers must find ways to 'tangibilize' services, must pay attention to service quality, must find ways to ensure service consistency, and must find ways to balance supply and demand for services.

2. The four key elements of managing services enterprises, namely, physical evidence, people, process and service branding.

3. Internal marketing to frontline employees is critical to the success of a service organization and great attention needs to be paid to their selection, training and motivation. Employee empowerment is a key element of service quality and service recovery.

4. Service quality is an important source of value creation. Essentially, it involves measuring how service perceptions match up against the expectations that customers have of the service provider and taking the types of remedial action necessary to close any service delivery gaps.

5. Relationship marketing is another important source of value creation. Organizations can engage in marketing activities that raise levels of attitudinal loyalty.

6. Value can also be created through the provision of customer experiences which can be used to improve the consumer's relationship with the organization.

7. Non-profit organizations attempt to achieve some objectives other than profit. Their two key publics are donors and clients; the needs of these two groups often conflict. In managing this complexity, non-profit organizations use conventional services marketing techniques.

Study questions

1. Discuss the implications of the unique characteristics of services for the marketing activities of services enterprises.
2. What are the barriers that can separate expected from perceived service? What must service providers do to eliminate these barriers?
3. Discuss the role of service staff in the creation of a quality service. Can you give examples from your own experiences of good and bad service encounters?
4. Discuss the benefits to organizations and customers of developing and maintaining strong customer relationships.
5. Select any three music, sport or cultural events that you have attended in the past year. What industry partners were involved in the events and what role did they play in each one?
6. How does marketing in non-profit organizations differ from that in profit-orientated companies? Choose a non-profit organization and discuss the extent to which marketing principles can be applied.
7. Visit www.yelp.com and www.tripadvisor.com. Discuss the impact of the existence of these websites on organizations that provide good and poor levels of service.

Suggested reading

Ahmed, P.K. and **R. Mohammed** (2003) Internal Marketing: Issues and Challenges, *European Journal of Marketing*, **37** (9), 1177–87.

Berry, L.L., V. Shankar, J. Turner Parish, S. Cadwallader and **T. Dotzel** (2006) Creating New Markets Through Service Innovation, *Sloan Management Review*, **47** (2), 56–63.

Dixon, M., K. Freeman and **N. Toman** (2010) Stop Trying to Delight Your Customers, *Harvard Business Review*, **88** (7/8), 116–22.

Gronroos, C. and **P. Vioma** (2013) Critical Service Logic: Making Sense of Value Creation and Co-Creation, *Journal of the Academy of Marketing Science*, **41**, 133–50.

McDermott, L., M. Steed and **G. Hastings** (2005) What is and What is Not Social Marketing: The Challenge of Reviewing the Evidence, *Journal of Marketing Management*, **21** (5/6), 545–53.

Moeller, S. (2010) Characteristics of Services – A New Approach Uncovers Their Value, *Journal of Services Marketing*, **24** (5), 359–68.

Vargo, S. L. and **R. F. Lusch** (2008) Service-dominant Logic: Continuing the Evolution, *Journal of the Academy of Marketing Science*, **36**, 1–10.

When you have read this chapter

log on to the Online Learning Centre for
Foundations of Marketing at
www.mheducation.co.uk/textbooks/fahy5
where you'll find links and extra online study tools for marketing.

References

1. **Van de Wiel, L.** and **S. Brox** (2013), Emotion and Inspiration at the Van Gogh Museum: How Emotion-Based Visitor Research can Create Engaging Brand Experiences, *Esomar Congress*, September 2013.
2. **Vargo, S. L.** and **R. F. Lusch** (2004), Evolving a New Dominant Logic for Marketing, *Journal of Marketing*, **68** (1), 1–17; **Vargo, S. L.** and **R. F. Lusch** (2008), Service-dominant Logic: Continuing the Evolution, *Journal of the Academy of Marketing Science*, **36**, 1–10.
3. **Berry, L.L.** (1980) Services Marketing is Different, *Business Horizons*, May–June, 24–9.
4. **Zeithaml, V.** (1984) How Consumer Evaluation Processes Differ Between Goods and Services, in C.H. Lovelock (ed.) *Services Marketing*, Engelwoods Cliffs, NJ., Prentice-Hall, 191–9.
5. **Foster, L.** (2004) The March of the Geek Squad, *Financial Times*, 24 November, 13.
6. **Edgett, S.** and **S. Parkinson** (1993) Marketing for Services Industries: A Review, *Service Industries Journal*, **13** (3), 19–39.
7. **Berry, L.L.** (1980) Services Marketing is Different, *Business Horizons*, May–June, 24–9.
8. **Aijo, T.S.** (1996) The Theoretical and Philosophical Underpinnings of Relationship Marketing, *European Journal*

of Marketing, **30** (2), 8–18; **Grönoos, C.** (1990) *Services Management and Marketing: Managing the Moments of Truth in Service Competition*, Lexington, MA: Lexington Books.

9. **Baron, S., K. Harris** and **B.J. Davies** (1996) Oral Participation in Retail Service Delivery: A Comparison of the Roles of Contact Personnel and Customers, *European Journal of Marketing*, **30** (9), 75–90.

10. **Birchall, J.** (2005) Top Dogs Lead the Way as Pet Market Grooms and Booms, *Financial Times*, 3 August, 28.

11. **Rafiq, M.** and **P.K. Ahmed** (1992) The Marketing Mix Reconsidered, *Proceedings of the Annual Conference of the Marketing Education Group*, Salford, 439–51.

12. **Schlesinger, L.A.** and **J.L. Heskett** (1991) The Service-driven Service Company, *Harvard Business Review*, September–October, 71–81.

13. **Anonymous** (2007) Doing Well By Being Rather Nice, *The Economist*, 1 December, 74; **Mitchell, A.** (2007) In the Pursuit of Happiness, *Financial Times*, 14 June, 14.

14. **Bowen, D.E.** and **L.L. Lawler** (1992) Empowerment: Why, What, How and When, *Sloan Management Review*, Spring, 31–9.

15. **Birchall, J.** (2005) Pile High, Sell Cheap and Pay Well, *Financial Times*, 11 July, 12.

16. **Berry, L.L., E.E. Lefkowith** and **T. Clark** (1980) In Services: What's in a Name? *Harvard Business Review*, September–October, 28–30.

17. **Bughin, J., J. Doogan** and **O. J. Vetvik** (2010) A New Way to Measure Word of Mouth Marketing, *McKinsey Quarterly*, April.

18. **Nga, N.H., S. Carson** and **W. Moore** (2013) The Effect of Positive and Negative Online Customer Reviews: Do Brand Strength and Category Maturity Matter? *Journal of Marketing*, **77** (6), 37–53.

19. **Buzzell, R.D.** and **B.T. Gale** (1987) *The PIMS Principles: Linking Strategy to Performance*, New York: Free Press, 103–34.

20. **Parasuraman, A., V.A. Zeithaml** and **L.L. Berry** (1985) A Conceptual Model of Service Quality and its Implications for Future Research, *Journal of Marketing*, Fall, 41–50.

21. **Anonymous** (2010) Aviva: Creating a Global Brand in a 300 Year Old Market, *The Marketing Society*, Warc.com.

22. **Parasuraman, A., V.A. Zeithaml** and **L.L. Berry** (1985) A Conceptual Model of Service Quality and its Implications for Future Research, *Journal of Marketing*, Fall, 41–50.

23. **Berry, L.L., A. Parsuraman** and **V.A. Zeithaml** (1988) The Service-Quality Puzzle, *Business Horizons*, **31** (5), 35–44.

24. **Reichheld, F.F.** and **W.E. Sasser Jr** (1990) Zero Defections: Quality Comes To Services, *Harvard Business Review*, September–October, 105–11.

25. **Reinartz, W.J.** and **V. Kumar** (2002) The Mismanagement of Customer Loyalty, *Harvard Business Review*, **80** (7), 86–94.

26. **Egan, C.** (1997) Relationship Management, in Jobber, D. (ed.) *The CIM Handbook of Selling and Sales Strategy*, Oxford: Butterworth-Heinemann, 55–88.

27. **Berry, L.L.** (1995) Relationship Marketing, in Payne, A., M. Christopher, M. Clark and H. Peck (eds) *Relationship Marketing for Competitive Advantage*, Oxford: Butterworth-Heinemann, 65–74.

28. **Zeithaml, V.A.** and **M.J. Bitner** (2002) *Services Marketing*, New York: McGraw-Hill, 174–8.

29. **Reichheld, F.F.** and **W.E. Sasser Jr** (1990) Zero Defections: Quality Comes To Services, *Harvard Business Review*, Sept-Oct, 105–11.

30. **Berry, L.L.** and **A. Parasuraman** (1991) *Managing Services*, New York: Free Press, 136–42.

31. **Kasper, H., P. van Helsdingen** and **W. de Vries Jr** (1999) *Services Marketing Management*, Chichester: Wiley, 528.

32. **Witzel, M.** (2005) Keep your Relationship with Clients Afloat, *Financial Times*, 31 January, 13.

33. **Borden, J.** (2008) Experiential Marketing Takes the Industry by Storm in 2008, *Marketing Week*, 15 January, 23–6.

34. **Bennett, P.D.** (1988) *Marketing*, New York: McGraw-Hill, 690–2.

35. **Shapiro, B.** (1992) Marketing for Non-Profit Organisations, *Harvard Business Review*, September–October, 123–32.

36. **Balabanis, G., R.E. Stables** and **H.C. Philips** (1997) Market Orientation in the Top 200 British Charity Organisations and its Impact on their Performance, *European Journal of Marketing*, **31** (8), 583–603.

37. **Butler, P.** and **N. Collins** (1994) Political Marketing: Structure and Process, *European Journal of Marketing*, **28** (1), 19–34.

38. **Hibbert, S.** (1995) The Market Positioning of British Medical Charities, *European Journal of Marketing*, **29** (10), 6–26.

IKEA: a unique service experience

Introduction

IKEA is a Scandinavian company famous for its minimalist and modern furniture and accessories. The company is also famous for making customers walk miles through its giant stores, pick out and find the furniture they want themselves, drag it to the check-out counter, load it into their cars, and then assemble it at home with directions that don't have any words. Not the ideal service experience by any stretch of the imagination. But for some strange reason, people love their interactions with the company, making IKEA the largest furniture retailer in the world (an estimated 10 per cent of European homes have at least one item that was purchased from IKEA).

The foundation to IKEA's marketing strategy is to provide the same level of service (and hence, the same experience) in every country in which IKEA operates (similar to what McDonald's does). This involves selling almost the exact same items at the same (relative) prices in every store in every country.

While thought of as a retailer of household furnishings, IKEA sees itself as more of a service company, providing its customers a meaningful, and memorable, shopping experience. The goal is to 'create a better everyday life for the many people'. The way they do it is through well designed furniture. The company's founder, Ingvar Kamprad, believed that furniture should have three things: function, quality and a low price. It bothered him that well designed furniture always seemed to be expensive and only available to the rich. To solve this problem Kamprad came up with a concept called 'democratic design'. Its goal was to develop a broad selection of home furnishings that was both well designed and intuitive to use, of good quality and at a low enough price to be readily accessible to the vast majority of people (the 'democratic' in democratic design). To accomplish this goal, IKEA insisted that the people who design the furniture work directly on the shop floor with the people who make the furniture. Democratic design would go on to infuse itself into the corporate culture of IKEA and become an integral part of the company's brand and image, and hence its service experience. It relies on respect for social values (treating stakeholders with respect), respect for the planet (efforts at reducing waste, recycling, sustainable sourcing, etc.) and respect for the customer (providing value and quality to as many people as possible). Things that readily identify with IKEA and its brand.

A key component of how IKEA manages the way customers encounter and experience its service is the way its stores are configured. Visitors are required to take a tortuous path indicated with arrows (known technically in marketing as a 'servicescape') that forces them to pass through almost every section of the store, tempting them each step of the way with another functional, practical and reasonably priced item that would be just perfect for their home. It is interesting to note that this 'natural tour' concept was originally developed when the average IKEA store had 19,000 square metres of surface space. The current average is 40,000 square metres. But while some people complain about the 'safari' IKEA forces them to go on, there is a method to the apparent madness. The floor plan and store configuration is specifically designed to encourage people to touch, interact with and experience the items for sale, and imagine what they would feel like in their own home. This is aided by the strategic placement of what are called 'experience rooms' throughout the store. These are small mock-up apartments or rooms that let you see and feel what an item will be like before you buy it, allowing for a greater emotional experience as well. IKEA extended this concept to include kitchens with its innovative 'kitchen planner''. What this allows shoppers to do is to build a kitchen using actual measurements from their own homes and then see what it would look like on a computer. This added service provides customers with what is known as a 'hyper-real' experience, and is an extremely important marketing tool. Stores are also explicitly designed to provide the same levels of customer service and quality, with equivalent staff to customer ratios being maintained no matter where a store is located.

As a result of this detail to service and experience, many customers seem to have a love affair with IKEA. And for some strange reason, doing unpaid labour at one of its stores appears to be one of the main attractions. An example of this dedication and devotion could be found in Ireland back before the financial collapse of 2008. During the housing bubble, people who had just bought a new house would often fly to Scotland on a cheap Ryanair flight in order to shop at IKEA (Ireland's restrictive zoning laws at the time prevented IKEA from building a local furniture warehouse). Few companies can boast of such brand loyalty. Some believe that these extreme levels of devotion have to do with the way customers are intimately involved in the IKEA 'experience'. Because people have to find an item themselves, carry it home and then put it together with their own hands, the result can be an increase in the personal value that an item holds for the customer who bought it (a phenomenon known as the 'IKEA effect'). The fact that people are willing partners in IKEA's transport and production system (and, in effect, a form of free outsourced labour) is a vital component of the company's business model, as well as how the company is able to offer low prices and still make a profit. Oddly enough, it might also be the reason why people identify so strongly with its brand.

Many customers feel like they have a personal relationship with IKEA, and the company does everything possible to foster and protect this feeling through targeted experiential marketing initiatives. One of the most imaginative of these involved inviting 100 fortunate guests to a sleepover party held at a store in Essex in the UK. The idea was inspired by a Facebook group calling itself 'I wanna have a sleepover in IKEA'. The group gathered almost 100,000 followers and caught the attention of IKEA's corporate headquarters. The overnight visitors had to be at least 25 years old, and pyjamas were mandatory. The event featured gifts and games, and there was an expert on hand to give sleep and bedding tips. This was not the first over-night event for IKEA. Previously, the company hosted a 'girls' night out' at one of its stores in Australia. Fifty female fans were chosen from the company's Australia Facebook page for a night of films, food and furniture demonstrations. But the event that has to belong in the 'experiential marketing hall of fame' was when IKEA built a temporary fully furnished apartment in a Paris Metro station. Five people were invited to live on display in the apartment for almost a week in order to show just how functional and pleasant a small apartment could be when fitted out with IKEA furnishings. People who followed the promotion on Facebook were also given a chance to win a one night's stay in the apartment.

These events were impressive in that they combined several elements of effective marketing. As Lois Blenkinsop, IKEA's UK public relations and internal communications manager put it, 'Social media has opened up a unique platform for us to interact directly with our customers. Listening to what they want is what we do best, and the Big Sleepover is just one example of how we're using such instant and open feedback to better inform our marketing activity.' IKEA's use of original and pioneering experiential marketing techniques is believed to go a long way towards building and maintaining the loyalty of its customers. What was particularly innovative about IKEA's use of social media in these instances was that it brought its virtual community and local community together. This allowed the company to observe and listen to its customers first hand, giving the company valuable primary data that could be the basis for new ideas and new products.

In addition to its effective use of social media, the company is also proficient at using and adapting technological innovations to provide high service levels and a satisfying customer experience. One value adding service that IKEA provides is a mobile phone app that allows you to see, virtually, what an item would look like in your house before you buy it. Claudia Willvonseder, global marketing manager, IKEA Global Retail Services, says that in the area of marketing her company is primarily a low tech one. She argues that the company doesn't think in terms of 'online' or 'offline', but rather in terms of what is the message they want to get across. IKEA believes that its marketing and brand image can be promoted and received through any medium. That said, print is still a huge component of marketing at IKEA, with 210 million catalogues a year being distributed (making it twice as popular as the bible).

Relationship marketing is another area that IKEA takes very seriously. It starts the minute you enter a store and interact with an employee. By having an enjoyable shopping experience in which you are left to explore the store at your own pace and leisure, by having attractive and well-priced meals available, by having a play area for small children and by creating an overall pleasant environment and product presentation, IKEA believes that relationships are built. And while the company can start and maintain a conversation with customers through social media, it is in the actual stores where relationships are made and cemented. The goal is not so much to make a one-time sale, but rather to engage a customer (or possible customer) by clearly showing them IKEA's value proposition, and hopefully develop a long-term relationship with them. The fact that shoppers are co-creating the value with IKEA through their involvement and work only seems to enhance the service experience, and thus make it easier to develop these relationships. It is in the successful management of these relationship building interactions and experiences that IKEA appears to excel.

IKEA appreciates and values its customers' business, and in an effort to retain and satisfy its shoppers the company has a loyalty programme called 'IKEA Family', which is targeted at regular retail customers. The programme is not points based, but rather focuses on exclusive deals, offers and events available only to card members (again, putting a focus on trying to enhance 'the experience'). IKEA also has a loyalty plan for small businesses. For commercial customers who join up, IKEA offers personalized service and support, as well as attractive financing options. There are also free professional and entrepreneurial workshops and networking events.

In addition to its efforts to retain and reward customers, IKEA also tries to please its employees. To further motivate workers and improve service levels, the company has bonus, profit sharing and pension schemes. An estimated 136,000 of IKEA's worldwide employees are expected to benefit from the pension bonus scheme in 2014 alone.

IKEA is also concerned with maintaining its strong corporate brand and culture. This means that it takes internal marketing very seriously, making sure that employees are well trained and well motivated, and that all of the company's stakeholders have the same corporate vision and values. One way in which IKEA achieves this stakeholder alignment is through its 'IKEA Way' or IWAY initiative. Simply put, it is a list of principles that all people must respect if they want to be a part of IKEA.

IKEA's customers and fans are the envy of other companies around the world. But there is a reason for this loyalty and devotion. IKEA takes great steps to ensure that the experience they have when they enter a store is the best it can possibly be. Great efforts are made to develop and foster relationships with customers. One example is when the company changed the font that it used in its catalogue. Fans wasted no time making their dissatisfaction with the changes known on social media. IKEA's reaction? It changed the font back to the original on the very next catalogue. It is this kind of attention to detail that allows IKEA to excel at providing value through service and flawlessly managed customer experiences and relationships.

Questions

1. What are some of the ways in which IKEA provides its customers with a unique service experience?
2. What does IKEA do in order to retain and reward customers?
3. How does IKEA ensure that its customers get the same service level and experience no matter what store or country they shop in?
4. Is IKEA a provider of goods or services? Explain.

This case was prepared by Tom McNamara and Irena Descubes, ESC Rennes, from various published sources as a basis for class discussion rather than to show effective or ineffective management.

Sources

'A Six-Day Parisian Stay, Courtesy of Ikea via AdvertisingAge-Experiential Marketing', The KMAC Group, 11 January 2012. Accessed at: http://kmacgroup.ca/a-six-day-parisian-stay-courtesy-of-ikea-via-advertisingage-experiential-marketing/

'A standardised approach to the world? IKEA in China' by Ulf Johansson and Asa Thelander, *The International Journal of Quality and Service Sciences*, 1 (2), 2009.

'Boom Time's Inflation Proves Stubborn in Ireland' by Brian Laverty, *The New York Times*, 16 November 2004. Accessed at: http://www.nytimes.com/2004/11/16/business/worldbusiness/16irishinflation.html?position=&_r=0&adxnnl=1&pagewanted=print&adxn nlx=1407423949-iXQV3QJNbYkk0EjbPT9rZw

'Consumer Behavior Analysis of Braşov Residents Regarding the Choice of Furniture Products Produced by Multinational Companies' by Neacşu Nicoleta Andreea and Bârbulescu Oana, 'Ovidius' University Annals, Economic Sciences Series, XIII (2), 2013.

'Defining Gamification – A Service Marketing Perspective' by Kai Huotari and Juho Hamari, Proceedings of the 16th International Academic MindTrek Conference, 3–5 October 2012.

'Experiential Marketing – Innovative Idea IKEA Hosts Sleepover For 100 Lucky Facebook Fans via PSFK' by Alice Chan, The KMAC Group, 3 January 2012. Accessed at: http://kmacgroup.ca/experiential-marketing-innovative-idea-ikea-hosts-sleepover-for-100-lucky-facebook-fans-via-psfk/

'How Retail Brands Are Using Technology To Provide Added Value To Consumers' by Steve Olenski, *Forbes*, 25 November 2013. Accessed at: http://www.forbes.com/sites/steveolenski/2013/11/25/how-retail-brands-are-using-technology-to-provide-added-value-to-consumers/ikea.com

'Ikea: 25 facts' by Harry Wallop, *The Telegraph*, 31 October 2012. Accessed at: http://www.telegraph.co.uk/finance/newsbysector/retailandconsumer/9643122/Ikea-25-facts.html

'Ikea launches employee loyalty program', *Retailing Today*, 19 December 2013. Accessed at: http://www.retailingtoday.com/article/ikea-launches-employee-loyalty-program

'Ikea to introduce new loyalty programme for London based businesses', *Business Matters*, 14 May 2013. Accessed at: http://www.bmmagazine.co.uk/news/18116/ikea-to-introduce-new-loyalty-programme-for-london-based-businesses/

'Ikea builds loyalty with a pension bonus scheme' by Natasha Browne, *WorkPlace Savings and Benefits*, 10 March 2014. Accessed at: http://www.wsandb.co.uk/wsb/profile/2333261/ikea-builds-loyalty-with-a-pension-bonus-scheme

'Relationship Marketing', Marketing-Schools.org, 2012. Accessed at: http://www.marketing-schools.org/types-of-marketing/relationship-marketing.html

'Small details that make big differences: A radical approach to consumption experience as a firm's differentiating strategy' by Ruth N. Bolton, Anders Gustafsson, Janet McColl-Kennedy, Nancy J. Sirianni and David K. Tse, *The Journal of Service Management*, 25 (2), 2014.

'Success factors in new service development and value creation through services' by B. Edvardsson, A. Gustafsson and B. Enquist, B., in D. Spath and K.-P. Fahrich (eds), *Advances in Service Innovation*, Berlin, Springer Book, 2005.

'The service excellence and innovation model: lessons from IKEA and other service frontiers ' by Bo Edvardsson and Bo Enquist, *Total Quality Management*, 22 (5), May 2011.

Chapter 8

Value through Pricing

Chapter outline

Key considerations when setting prices

Other factors influencing price-setting decisions

Managing price changes

Customer value through pricing

Learning outcomes

By the end of this chapter you will:

1 Understand the key considerations when setting an initial price

2 Understand how consumers respond to pricing cues

3 Explain how several key factors influence price-setting decisions

4 Critique the impact of pricing on consumers and society

5 Describe the major issues involved in managing pricing decisions over time

6 Understand the strategic role of pricing.

Netflix

Movies have been an enduringly popular means of relaxation and entertainment for people around the world. However, the ways in which movies are consumed has been undergoing some significant change in recent decades. The main distribution channel for new titles was the cinema and popular new releases could expect a long run there. But the manufacture of first video recorders (VCRs) and then DVD players took movies out of the cinema and into the home. If you missed the movie during its cinema run – no problem, pick up the video or DVD and watch it later at your leisure. Video and DVD rental chains sprang up meet this demand. One of the most famous of these was Blockbuster and its iconic blue and yellow stores were a regular feature of the suburban retail landscape from the USA to Australia to Japan to Europe. The business model for video rental was attractive. During the release period, titles were not available for sale so renting was the only option. Companies like Blockbuster bought titles at low cost and split the revenues in the ratio of 60:40 with the studios.

However, as the arrival of the Internet changed the distribution model for music and books, it also opened up new possibilities for movie rental. Into this space moved a California based company called Netflix. The idea for Netflix is said to have come to the company's founder when he was charged $40 in fines for the movie that he was returning which was long after its due date. The inconvenience of having to pick up and return movies to a fixed location could be overcome by using a postal delivery system. Customers ordered online creating a list of movies to rent. Once a title was sent, they could hold onto it for as long as they wished but could only obtain new titles by returning previously held ones in a prepaid envelope. At the outset, Netflix adopted a pricing strategy similar to offline stores, charging customers a flat rental fee similar to those of Blockbuster and others. But this proved unappealing to customers who could pay the same price and get a movie straight away in a physical store. Netflix decided to move to a monthly subscription service. This proved to be a masterstroke and was particularly appealing to frequent movie watchers who could now watch as many films as they liked for a set monthly fee.

The online rental system also possessed other advantages. When initially signing up for the service, subscribers provided some details of their preferences so Netflix could then recommend movies that they may not have considered. While popular releases accounted for up to 70 per cent of the rentals at offline stores, they represented less than 30 per cent at Netflix. It had done a better job than any of its competitors in getting to know its customers' preferences and making useful recommendations to them. Its customer churn rate (the number of customers cancelling subscriptions) had fallen to just 3 per cent by 2006. And the impact of this strategy can be seen in Netflix generating revenues of over $4 billion in 2013 while its erstwhile competitor Blockbuster ceased trading the following year.

Pricing strategy was, and will continue to be, key to Netflix's success. For example, in 2011, Netflix had a DVD by mail and online streaming plan for $9.99 per month. However, that year it decided to make the following price changes. Customers could avail of either service alone for $7.99 per month or continue to have both for $15.99 – in essence a 60 per cent price increase. Customers were outraged, many cancelled their subscriptions and the company's stock price fell sharply. But in 2014, it was again looking at new price changes aimed at different market segments. For example, a new $6.99 was offered that allowed streaming to just one screen while an $11.99 monthly plan allowed four simultaneous streams and was aimed at families.[1]

Setting prices and managing prices over time is another set of important decisions that must be made by the organization. Several factors are likely to have an influence in these decisions. If input costs such as the price of energy in the form of electricity or oil are rising, then these input costs may need to be passed on to the customer in terms of increased prices. But if customers are struggling because of an economic downturn, they may be unwilling to accept these increased prices and therefore decide to consume less, thereby reducing organizational sales. And then there is also the role played by competitors. Pricing decisions need to take account of the prices being offered by competitors for alternative products or potential substitutes. Some of these firms may also be seeking to differentiate themselves based on the prices that they charge and will therefore tend to defend their price positions very aggressively.

All these dimensions need to be considered in terms of the principal relationship between price and the ultimate goal of the business, which is profit. This was starkly illustrated by the example of the Harry Potter series of books which have been the best-selling books of all time. But such was the demand for the books that each of the different sales channels such as major chains like Tesco and KwikSave, online retailers like Amazon and specialist book stores like Waterstones competed aggressively to get as big a share of the market as possible. The major competitive tool used was special price reductions on the books, with the result that some retailers made very little overall profit on the sales of this successful series. The importance of the price–profit relationship is also illustrated by the launch of the Mercedes A Class model in Germany. Initially, the company had chosen a price tag of DM29,500, based on the belief that the DM30,000 mark was psychologically important. However, after further market research that examined the value offered to customers in comparison with competitor brands such as the BMW 3 series and the VW Golf, the price was set at DM31,000. Mercedes still hit its sales target of 200,000, but the higher price increased its income by DM300 million per year.[2]

In many businesses, greater price competition is becoming a fact of life, with the use of technology helping to drive down costs, greater levels of globalization and retail competition helping to depress price levels, and developments like the Internet and the introduction of the euro giving rise to greater levels of price transparency (see Exhibit 8.1). Economic downturns focus further attention on price levels and increase demands for greater price

transparency so that consumers can understand the true cost of goods such as personal loans or telephone services. As a result, firms must think carefully when setting prices initially and when adjusting them to changing circumstances.

Key considerations when setting prices

Shapiro and Jackson[3] identified three methods used by managers to set prices (see Figure 8.1). The first of these – cost-based pricing – reflects a strong internal orientation and, as its name suggests, is based on costs. The second is competitor-orientated pricing, where the major emphasis is on the price

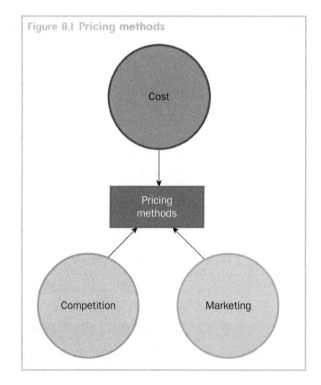

Figure 8.1 Pricing methods

levels set by competitors and how our prices compare with those. The final approach is market-led pricing, so called because it focuses on the value that customers place on a product in the marketplace and the nature of the marketing strategy used to support the product. In this section we will examine each of these approaches, and draw out their strengths and limitations.

Cost-based pricing

Cost-based pricing is a useful approach to price setting in that it can give an indication of the minimum price that needs to be charged in order to break even. Cost-based pricing can best be explained by using a simple example (see Table 8.1). Imagine that you are given the task of pricing a new product and the cost figures given in Table 8.1 apply. Direct costs such as labour and materials work out at €2 per unit. As output increases, more people and materials will be needed and so total costs increase. Fixed costs (or overheads) per year are calculated at €200,000. These costs (such as office and manufacturing facilities) do not change as output increases. They have to be paid whether 1 or 200,000 units are produced.

Once we have calculated the relevant costs, it is necessary to estimate how many units we are likely to sell. We believe that we produce a good-quality product and therefore sales should be 100,000 in the first year. Therefore total (full) cost per unit is €4 and using the company's traditional 10 per cent mark-up a price of €4.40 is set.

So that we may understand the problems associated with using **full cost pricing**, we should assume that the sales estimate of 100,000 is not reached by the end of the year. Because of poor economic conditions or as a result of setting the price too high, only 50,000 units are sold. The company believes that this level of sales is likely to be achieved next year. What happens to price? Table 8.1 gives the answer: it is raised because cost per unit goes up. This is because fixed costs (€200,000) are divided by a smaller expected sales volume (50,000). The result is a price rise in response to poor sales figures. This is clearly nonsense and yet can happen if full cost pricing is followed blindly. A major UK engineering company priced one of its main product lines in this way and suffered a downward spiral of sales as prices were raised each year, with disastrous consequences.

So, the first problem with cost-based pricing is that it leads to an increase in the price as sales fall. Second, the procedure is illogical because a sales estimate is made *before* the price is set. Third, it focuses on internal costs rather than the customer's willingness to pay. And, finally, there may be a technical problem in allocating overheads in multi-product firms. Nevertheless the cost-based approach is popular in practice. For example, Apple aims to cover costs plus receive a 40 per cent margin on all its new product launches.

The real value of this approach is that it gives an indication of the minimum price necessary to make a profit. Once direct and fixed costs have been measured, 'break-even analysis' can be used to estimate the sales volume needed to balance revenue and costs at different price levels. Therefore, the procedure of calculating full costs is useful when other pricing methods are used since full costs may act as a constraint. If they cannot be covered then it may not be worthwhile launching the product. In practice, some companies will set prices below full costs (known as direct cost pricing or **marginal cost pricing**). As we saw in the previous chapter this is a popular strategy for services companies. For example, where seats on an aircraft or rooms in hotels are unused at any time, that revenue is lost. In such situations, pricing to cover direct costs plus a contribution to overheads is sensible to reduce the impact of excess capacity, although this approach is not sustainable in the long term.

Table 8.1 Cost-based pricing

Year 1	
Direct costs (per unit)	= €2
Fixed costs	= €200,000
Expected sales	= 100,000
Cost per unit	
Direct costs	= €2
Fixed costs (200,000 ÷ 100,000)	= €2
Full costs	= €4
Mark-up (10 per cent)	= €0.40
Price (cost plus mark-up)	= €4.40
Year 2	
Expected sales	= 50,000
Cost per unit	
Direct costs	= €2
Fixed costs (200,000 ÷ 50,000)	= €4
Full costs	= €6
Mark-up (10 per cent)	= €0.60
Price (cost plus mark-up)	= €6.60

Competitor-orientated pricing

Competitor-orientated pricing may take any one of three forms:

1　where firms follow the prices charged by leading competitors
2　where producers take the going-rate price
3　where contracts are awarded through a **competitive bidding** process.

Some firms are happy simply to benchmark themselves against their major competitors, setting their prices at levels either above, the same as or below them (see Exhibit 8.2). This is very popular in the financial services area where, for example, the price of a loan (that is, the interest rate) is often very similar across a wide range of competitors. It can be a risky approach to take, particularly if the firm's cost position is not as good as that of its competitors (see 'Cost-based pricing' above).

In other circumstances, all competitors receive the same price because it is the going rate for the product. **Going-rate prices** are most typically found in the case of undifferentiated commodities such as coffee beans or cattle meat. The challenge for the

marketer in this situation is to find some creative ways of differentiating the product in order to charge a different price.

In addition, many contracts are won or lost on the basis of competitive bidding. The most usual process is the drawing up of detailed specifications for a product and putting the contract out to tender. Potential suppliers quote a price, which is known only to themselves and the buyer (known as a 'sealed bid'), or the bidding may take place in a public auction where all competitors see what prices are being bid. All other things being equal, the buyer will select the supplier that quotes the lowest price. A major focus for suppliers, therefore, is the likely bid price of competitors. Increasing price pressures, European competition legislation and the growing use of technology has resulted in more and more supply contracts being subject to competitive bidding. For example, traditionally, many hospital supply companies sold directly to doctors and nurses in hospitals, which meant that suppliers invested in developing selling skills and building relationships with these customers. Now, the norm is that supply contracts are put out to tender, with the winning bidder often securing the contract for a period of three

Exhibit 8.2 The launch price of the PlayStation 4 much more closely matched that of competitors than did its predecessor the PlayStation 3 which was priced significantly above the competition and did not reach sales targets as a result

to five years. Thus supply firms have had to develop skills in different areas such as tender preparation and pricing. Online auctions present suppliers with a whole new set of demands (see Chapter 3).

The main advantage of the competitor-orientated pricing approach is that it is simple and easy to use, except in the case of competitive bidding, where it may be difficult to guess what prices competitive bids will come in at. Increased price transparency in Europe, brought about by the introduction of the euro and the growing use of the Internet as a tool for comparing prices, will perhaps increase the level of attention being given to competitor-orientated pricing. It also suffers, however, from two significant flaws. First, it does not take account of any differential advantages the firm may have, which may justify its charging a higher price than the competition. As we have seen, the creation of a differential advantage is a fundamental marketing activity, and firms should seek to reap the rewards of this investment. Second, as noted above, competitor-orientated pricing is risky where a firm's cost position is weaker than that of its competitors.

Market-led pricing

A key marketing consideration when setting prices is estimating a product's value to the customer. In brief, the more value a product gives compared to the competition, the higher the price that can be charged (see Exhibit 8.3). Simply because one product costs less to make than another does not imply that its price should be less (see Marketing in Action 8.1). The logic of this position is borne out by Glaxo's approach when it launched Zantac, an ulcer treatment drug. It set the price for the drug at 50 per cent more than that of SmithKline Beecham's Tagamet, which was then the world's best-selling drug. Thanks to its fewer side effects, Zantac overtook Tagamet and the resulting superior revenues transformed Glaxo from a mid-sized UK company to a global powerhouse.[4]

In this section we shall explore a number of ways of estimating value to the customer. Marketers have at their disposal three useful techniques for uncovering customers' value perceptions: **trade-off analysis**, experimentation and **economic value to the customer (EVC)** analysis.

Trade-off analysis

Measurement of the trade-off between price and other product features – known as trade-off analysis or conjoint analysis – enables their effects on product preference to be established.[5] Respondents are not asked direct questions about price but instead product profiles consisting of product features and price are described, and respondents are asked to name their preferred

Exhibit 8.3 Products like those from luxury brand company Prada command premium prices due to their association with high value

profile. From their answers the effect of price and other product features can be measured using a computer model. For example, respondents are shown different combinations of features such as speed, petrol consumption, brand and price in the case of a car and asked which combinations they prefer. This exercise enables one to measure the impact on preferences of increasing or reducing the price. Companies like 3M, who are renowned for their product innovation, use trade-off analysis at the test marketing stage for new products. Different combinations of variables such as the brand, packaging, product features and price are tested to establish the price level customers are prepared to pay.[6]

Experimentation

A limitation of trade-off analysis is that respondents are not asked to back up their preferences with cash expenditure. Consequently, there can be some doubt whether what they say they prefer would be reflected in an actual purchase when they are asked to part with money. 'Experimental pricing research' attempts to overcome this drawback by placing a product on sale at different locations with varying prices. Test

Marketing in Action 8.1 Why buy a Swiss watch?

Critical Thinking: Below is a review of the premium prices that continue to be commanded by Swiss watches. Read it and critically reflect on the high prices commanded by Swiss watch brands despite the presence of many cheaper alternatives.

Switzerland is the country most associated with watches. It boasts an impressive array of global brands including Omega, TAG Heuer, Rolex, Patek Philippe, Swatch and many others. The average Swiss watch costs $685. A Chinese one costs about $2. Why does this situation persist?

Answering this question places a focus again on the benefits that consumers look for in the products and services that they consume. Yes watches tell the time but the $2 watch does just as good a job of doing that as the $685 one. It does not seem to make sense to pay the higher price but this situation clearly demonstrates that price is not all about costs and competitors. As we saw in Chapter 3, there are many powerful emotional drivers of consumer behaviour. Ironically, much of the appeal of Swiss watches is down to their very high price. Most consumers choose one of these brands simply because they

can afford to do so and their appeal is particularly strong in the Middle East and Asia where there are ever growing populations of customers who want to be able to show that they can.

Switzerland has a long and proud tradition of fine watchmaking. Knowledge and craftsmanship in component design and watchmaking has been developed and refined over the generations. The image of the craftsman working in a small firm in a tiny Alpine village endures despite the fact that the industry is dominated by one large firm – Swatch – which owns some of the aforementioned brands and supplies many of the components to other manufacturers. The continued success of Swiss watches in the face of significant low cost competition is down to their enduring heritage and the powerful emotional appeal of their brands.

Based on: Anonymous (2013);[7] Minder (2014).[8]

marketing (see Chapter 6) is often used to compare the effectiveness of varying prices. For example, the same product could be sold in two areas using an identical promotional campaign, but with different prices between areas. The areas would need to be matched (or differences allowed for) in terms of target customer profile so that the result would be comparable. The test needs to be long enough so that trial and repeat purchase at each price can be measured. This is likely to be between 6 and 12 months for products whose purchase cycle lasts more than a few weeks.

EVC analysis

Experimentation is more usual when pricing consumer products. However, industrial markets have a powerful tool at their disposal when setting the price of their products: economic value to the customer (EVC) analysis. Many organizational purchases are motivated by economic value considerations since reducing costs and increasing revenue are prime objectives for many companies. If a company can produce an offering that

has a high EVC, it can set a high price and yet still offer superior value compared to the competition. A high EVC may be because the product generates more revenue for the buyer than competition or because its operating costs (such as maintenance, operation or start-up costs) are lower over its lifetime. EVC analysis is usually particularly revealing when applied to products whose purchase price represents a small proportion of the lifetime costs to the customer.[9]

For example, assume a manufacturer is buying a robot to use on its production line. The robot costs €100,000 but this represents only one-third of the customer's total life-cycle costs. An additional €50,000 is required for start-up costs such as installation and operator training, while a further €150,000 needs to be budgeted for in post-purchase costs such as maintenance, power, etc. Assume also that a new product comes on the market that due to technological advances reduces start-up costs by €20,000 and post-purchase costs by €50,000. Total costs then have been reduced by €70,000 and the EVC that the new product offers is €170,000 (€300,000 – €130,000). Thus the EVC figure is the total amount that the customer would have to pay to make the total life-cycle costs of the new and existing robot the same. If the new robot was priced at €170,000 this would be the case – any price below that level would create an economic incentive for the buyer to purchase the new robot.

The main advantage of market-led pricing is that it keeps customer perceptions and needs at the forefront of the pricing decision. However, in practice it is sensible for a company to adopt an integrated approach to pricing, paying attention not only to customer needs but also to cost levels (cost-based pricing) and competitor prices (competitor-orientated pricing).

Other factors influencing price-setting decisions

Aside from the basic dimensions of cost, competitive prices and customer value, various aspects of the firm's marketing strategy will also affect price-setting decisions. In particular, marketing decisions such as positioning strategies, new product launch strategies, product-line strategies, competitive marketing strategies, distribution channel strategies and international marketing strategies will have an impact on price levels.

Positioning strategy

As we saw in Chapter 5, a key decision that marketing managers face is positioning strategy, which involves the choice of target market and the creation of a differential advantage. Each of these factors can have an enormous impact on price. Price can be used to convey a differential advantage and to appeal to a certain market segment. Leading European retail chains such as Aldi and Lidl target cost-conscious grocery shoppers through a policy of lowest prices on a range of frequently purchased household goods. At the other end of the spectrum, many firms will charge very high prices in order to appeal to individuals with a high net worth. Products such as yachts, luxury cars, golf club memberships, luxury holidays, and so on, are sold in this way. Massimo Dutti, the fashion brand that is part of the Inditex group, is targeted at the 25–50-year-old age group and is priced higher than sister companies like Zara but lower than the luxury fashion brands, leading to it being labelled as 'credit-crunch fashion'.

Price is a powerful positioning tool because, for many people, it is an indicator of quality. But recent research in the field of behavioural economics has demonstrated that consumers experience significant difficulties when they attempt to judge price and quality in an objective way. For example, one experimental study involved participants being subjected to electric shocks. During the course of the treatment, one part of the sample were administered a pill that costs $2.50 per dose while another subset received a pill that cost 10 cents. In the former case, all participants experienced pain relief compared with only half of the 10 cent group. In reality, both groups had simply received a vitamin C capsule but clearly the higher price had influenced the participant's perception of the product.[10] In short, this demonstrates that a higher price can lead to a perception of higher quality though that may not actually be the case.

 Rimmel Ad Insight: The London Glam' Eyes campaign reflects the company's new positioning.

Because price perceptions are so important to customers, many companies engage in what is called **psychological pricing** – that is, the careful manipulation of the reference prices that consumers carry in their heads. Consequently, the price of most grocery products ends in '.99' because the psychological difference between €2.99 and €3.00 is much greater than the actual difference.

New product launch strategy

When launching new products, price should be carefully aligned with promotional strategy. Figure 8.2 shows four marketing strategies based on combinations of price and promotion. Similar matrices could also be developed for product and distribution, but for illustrative purposes promotion will be used here. A combination of high price and high promotion expenditure is called a 'rapid skimming strategy'. The high price provides high-margin returns on investment and the heavy promotion creates high levels of product awareness and knowledge. The launches of Microsoft's Xbox and Apple's iPod and iPhone are examples of a rapid skimming strategy (see Marketing in Action 8.2). A 'slow skimming strategy' combines high price with low levels of promotional expenditure. High prices mean big profit margins, but high levels

Figure 8.2 New product launch strategies

	Promotion	
	High	Low
Price High	Rapid skimming	Slow skimming
Price Low	Rapid penetration	Slow penetration

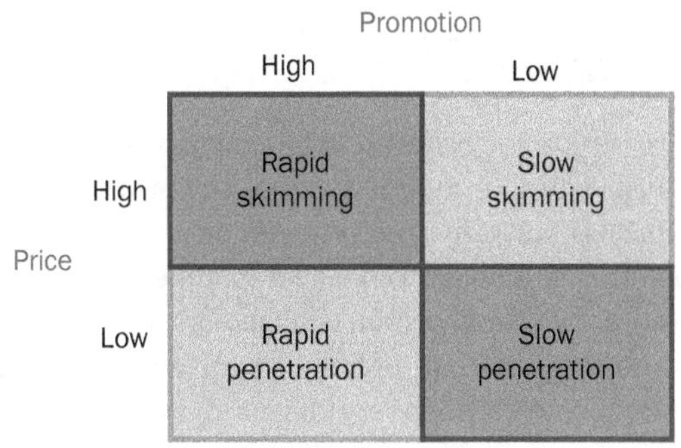

Marketing in Action 8.2 Skimming the market

> **Critical Thinking:** Below is a review of price skimming strategies in some popular product categories. Read it and critically evaluate the pros and cons of price skimming from both the firm's and the customer's point of view.

In a number of product markets, like phones, MP3 players and games consoles, rapid skimming strategies are becoming ever more prevalent. A particular case in point was the Apple iPhone. An 8-gigabyte version of the phone was launched in July 2007 with a price tag of $599. But, by just September of that year, its price had fallen by $200 and a new 16-gigabyte model was launched on the market at a price of $499. Innovators and early adopters who had purchased the phone at the full initial price were outraged and were ultimately offered a $100 gift voucher by Apple.

The iPhone is an example of a classic rapid skimming strategy. Buzz marketing was used intensively to generate demand for the product, with a promise that it would do for mobile phones what the iPod had done for MP3 players. Its ease of use, combined with its functionality and its Apple 'cool', were extolled in blogs, reviews and commentaries. This low-cost form of promotion, combined with a high initial price, meant high profits for Apple. By 2011, Apple still only commanded a mere 4 per cent of the global mobile phones market in terms of sales but took in over 50 per cent of all profits in the industry.

There are several explanations for the rise in the use of rapid skimming strategies. The first is the cost of production. Products like the iPhone represent the convergence of several technologies, such as music players, computers and telecommunications. Packing all this functionality into one product is expensive. Second is the speed of imitation by competitors. Innovative new designs are now very quickly reverse-engineered and replicated, with new low-cost versions quickly reaching the shop floor. A rapid skimming strategy is the best way to recoup the high costs of research and development before competitors erode margins. Finally, consumer behaviour also plays an important role. The desire to be the first person with a new product is a strong feature of today's consumers, as demonstrated by the queues that frequently form for new phones, games consoles and fashion items. Price does not seem to be a major factor for these early adopters, and technology companies are exploiting this.

However, managing a skimming strategy is easier said than done. Drop the price too quickly and you risk the wrath of customers, as Apple did. Drop the price too slowly, as Sony did with its PlayStation 3, and you risk losing out on sales and market penetration. On the back of the global success of its PlayStation 2, Sony launched the PlayStation 3 at a price of $600 in 2006, compared with $399 for the Microsoft Xbox and $249 for the Nintendo Wii. By the time the PlayStation 3 brand was eventually retailing at $399 one year later, Sony had seen its dominant position in the global games console market eroded and it had fallen to number three behind Microsoft and Nintendo. The timing of pricing decisions is critical for the success of new products.

Based on: Anonymous (2011);[11] Sanchanta (2007);[12] Stern (2008).[13]

of promotion are believed to be unnecessary, perhaps because word of mouth is more important and the product is already well known or because heavy promotion is thought to be incompatible with product image, as with cult products. One company that uses a skimming pricing policy effectively is German car components supplier Bosch. It has applied an extremely profitable skimming strategy, supported by patents, to its launch of fuel injection and anti-lock brake systems.[14] Companies that combine low prices with heavy promotional expenditure are practising a 'rapid penetration strategy'. In a break with its traditional policy of rapid skimming, Apple changed to a rapid penetration strategy with its launch of the iPad due to intense competition with rival tablets makers. Finally, a 'slow penetration strategy' combines low price with low promotional expenditure. Own-label brands use this strategy: promotion is not necessary to gain distribution and low promotional expenditure helps to maintain high profit margins for these brands. This price/promotion framework is useful when thinking about marketing strategies at launch.

The importance of picking the right strategy was illustrated by the failure of TiVo in the UK. TiVo makes personal video recorders (PVRs), which are high-technology recorders capable of storing up to 40 hours of television and with features such as the facility to rewind live television programmes and memorize selections so that favourite programmes are automatically recorded. But the product failed to take off and TiVo has withdrawn from the UK market. Part of the reason for the failure is that consumers did not seem to fully understand what PVRs could do and therefore could not justify spending in the region of £300 plus a monthly subscription fee for a recorder. Some analysts estimated that the product should have been priced in the region of £100 for it to take off, suggesting that a penetration rather than a skimming strategy would have been more appropriate.[15]

High price (skimming) strategies and low price (penetration) strategies may be appropriate in different situations. A skimming strategy is most suitable in situations where customers are less price sensitive, such as where the product provides high value, where customers have a high ability to pay and where they are under high pressure to buy. However, setting the price too high can lead to problems generating sales. For example, when Nissan launched its 350Z sports car, it was priced at levels similar to top sports cars like the Porsche Boxster and BMW Z4. However, poor sales levels forced it to cut its retail price by €10,000, a move that brought it closer to the next level of sports cars like the Mazda RX-8. Penetration pricing strategies are more likely to be driven by company circumstances where the company is seeking to dominate the market, where it is comfortable to establish a position in the market initially and make money later, and/or where it seeks to create a barrier to entry for competitors.

 Kindle Ad Insight: This ad clearly conveys Kindle's benefits and price proposition.

Product-line strategy

Marketing-orientated companies also need to take account of where the price of a new product fits into its existing product line. Where multiple segments appear attractive, modified versions of the product should be designed, and priced differently, not according to differences in costs, but in line with the respective values that each target market places on a product. All the major car manufacturing companies have products priced at levels that are attractive to different market segments, namely, economy cars, family saloons, executive cars, and so on. In 2009, iTunes abandoned its long-standing strategy of charging a flat fee of 99 cents per song download in favour of a three-tier structure with songs priced at 69 cents, 99 cents and $1.29 to appeal to different market segments.

Some companies prefer to extend their product lines rather than reduce the price of existing brands in the face of price competition. They launch cut-price 'fighter brands' to compete with the low-price rivals. This has the advantage of maintaining the image and profit margins of existing brands. For example, the department store John Lewis launched its value range to compete with the lower price offerings of retailers like Tesco. Intel, a global leader in the semi-conductor industry brought out the Celeron, a cheaper version of its better known Pentium chips, to meet the growing demand from low cost personal computer manufacturers.[16] By producing a range of brands at different price points, companies can cover the varying price sensitivities of customers and encourage them to trade up to the more expensive, higher-margin brands. However, this strategy must be pursued carefully as they also risk cannibalizing the sales of their existing brands (see Chapter 5).

Competitive marketing strategy

The pricing of products should also be set within the context of the firm's competitive strategy. Four strategic objectives are relevant to pricing: build, hold, harvest and reposition.

Build objective

For price-sensitive markets, a build objective for a product implies a price lower than that of the competition. If the competition raise their prices we would be slow to match them. For price-insensitive markets, the best pricing strategy becomes less clear-cut. Price in these circumstances will be dependent on the overall positioning strategy thought appropriate for the product.

Hold objective

Where the strategic objective is to hold sales and/or market share, the appropriate pricing strategy is to maintain or match the price relative to the competition. This has implications for price changes: if the competition reduces prices then our prices would match this price fall.

Harvest objective

A harvest objective implies the maintenance or raising of profit margins, even though sales and/or market share are falling. The implication for pricing strategy would be to set premium prices. For products that are being harvested, there would be much greater reluctance to match price cuts than for products that were being built or held. On the other hand, price increases would swiftly be matched.

Reposition objective

Changing market circumstances and product fortunes may necessitate the repositioning of an existing product. This may involve a price change, the direction and magnitude of which will be dependent on the new positioning strategy for the product.

The above examples show how developing clear strategic objectives helps the setting of price and clarifies the appropriate reaction to competitive price changes. Price setting, then, is much more sophisticated than simply asking 'How much can I get for this product?' The process starts by asking more fundamental questions like 'How is this product going to be positioned in the marketplace?' and 'What is the appropriate strategic objective for this product?' Answering these questions is an essential aspect of effective price management.

Channel management strategy

When products are sold through intermediaries such as distributors or retailers, the list price to the customer must reflect the margins required by them. Some products, such as cars, carry margins of typically less than 10 per cent, therefore car dealers must rely on sales of spare parts and future servicing of new cars to generate returns. Other products, such as jewellery, may carry a margin of several hundred per cent. When Müller yoghurt was first launched in the UK, a major factor in gaining distribution in a mature market was the fact that its high price allowed attractive profit margins for the supermarket chains. Conversely, the implementation of a penetration pricing strategy may be hampered if distributors refuse to stock a product because the profit per unit is less than that available on competitive products.

The implication is that pricing strategy is dependent on understanding not only the ultimate customer but also the needs of distributors and retailers who form the link between them and the manufacturer. If their needs cannot be accommodated, product launch may not be viable or a different distribution system (such as direct selling) might be required (see Chapter 9).

International marketing strategy

The firm's international marketing strategy will also have a significant impact on its pricing decisions. The first challenge that managers have to deal with is that of **price escalation**. This means that a number of factors can combine to put pressure on the firm to increase the prices it charges in other countries. These include the additional costs of shipping and transporting costs to a foreign market, margins paid to local distributors, customs duties or tariffs that may be charged on imported products, differing rates of sales taxes and changes to the price that may be driven by exchange rates and differing inflation rates. All of these factors combine to mean that the price charged in a foreign market is often very different to that charged on the home market. For example, a 16GB Apple iPhone 5s in Brazil costs the equivalent of the average monthly income in the country's major cosmopolitan areas or just over 2,000 reais, making it the most expensive place in the world where Apple has stores. This is largely due to tariffs and state and federal taxes on imports.

While international prices are often higher, they can also be lower if circumstances dictate that low prices are necessary to gain sales, as would be the case in countries where levels of disposable income are low. In such instances it is important for firms to guard against **parallel importing** – this is when products destined for an international market are re-imported back into the home market and sold through unauthorized channels at levels lower than the company wishes to charge. For example, the online music company CD Wow was fined £41 million when it was charged with selling cut-price CDs in the UK that it had imported from Hong Kong. But trading of products across borders within the European Union is legal, so companies like Chemilines have been able to build a successful business importing pharmaceuticals from EU accession states for sale in the UK, where prices can be up to 30 per cent higher.[17]

While most firms seek to standardize as many elements of the marketing mix as possible when operating internationally, pricing is one of the most difficult to standardize for the reasons outlined above. Sometimes the price differences are driven by cost variations, but sometimes they are also due to the absence of competitors or different customer value perceptions, which can lead to accusations of ripping off customers. Now that international prices are much easier to compare through, for example, the introduction of the euro, price differences across markets have become much more controversial (see Marketing and Society 8.1).

Marketing and Society 8.1 What is a fair price?

Price is one of the most hotly debated aspects of marketing. News reports regularly present stories of price variations for products across Europe, leading to claims that some consumers are being unfairly ripped off by companies charging inflated prices. For example, one study found that consumers in Ireland pay €10.99 for four Gillette Mach-3 blades compared with just €6.84 in London, that they pay €9.39 for a packet of Pampers newborn nappies compared with only €4.79 in the Netherlands, and that they pay higher prices for several other well-known brands.[18] These variations are difficult to justify, given the nature of modern consumer markets. Global pharmaceutical companies have been accused of overcharging for critical medicines, particularly in the world's poorer countries where diseases like HIV and AIDS are rampant. Telecommunications companies charge significant premiums for calls made or texts sent while roaming in other countries. And international travellers have complained for years about being ripped off by taxi companies, car hire firms, hotels and other service outlets when they visit new countries.

There are several ways in which organizations can exploit consumers by overcharging for goods and services. One of the most common is price fixing, which is illegal and banned throughout Europe. Rather than compete on price, companies collude with each other to ensure that everyone charges the same or similar prices. For example, 14 retailers in Germany, including leading chains like Metro, Edeka and Rewe, were investigated in 2010 on suspicion of working with manufacturers of products like confectionery, pet food and coffee to fix minimum price levels. It is the job of regulatory authorities like the Competition Authority of Ireland and the Office of Fair Trading (OFT) in the UK to identify and investigate possible price collusion. For example, in 2008, the OFT investigated possible collusion between British supermarkets and their suppliers. The 'big four' supermarkets – Tesco, Asda, Sainsbury's and Morrisons – along with suppliers like Britvic, Coca-Cola, Mars, Nestlé, Procter & Gamble, Reckitt Benckiser and Unilever, were asked to hand over documents. Price fixing is most likely to be found in industries where brand differentiation is difficult, such as oil, paper, glass and chemicals.

Equally controversial is the practice of deceptive pricing – in other words, where prices are not the same as they may first appear. Low-cost airlines have been significant users of deceptive pricing. For example, quoted fares may be as low as 99 cents but when all additional items, such as taxes, baggage charges, fuel surcharges, seat charges and credit card charges, are added in, fares may end up being well in excess of €70. These companies are also users of opt-outs. That is, unless consumers specifically opt out of additional items like travel insurance they will be charged for these as well. Furthermore, many of the headline low-fares offers are very limited in their availability, often restricted to just a few seats. EU regulators have targeted the industry to clean up its act on pricing. Airlines must now give a clear indication of the total price and extra charges have to be indicated at the start rather than the end of the booking.

All this means that consumers need to be very careful when judging the price of a good or service. Ultimately this debate rests on the issue of price and value. Consumers can vote with their feet. If they feel that a price is excessive, in most cases they can switch to substitute products or to other vendors. Consumers need to inform themselves and companies need to take great care in setting price levels. As this chapter shows, pricing must be an integral part of a company's marketing strategy.

Reflection: Consider the points made above and discuss the contention that firms will always charge as much as they possibly can unless forced to do otherwise.

Managing price changes

So far, our discussion has concentrated on those factors that affect pricing strategy but, in a highly competitive world, managers need to know when and how to raise or lower prices, and whether or not to react to competitors' price moves. First, we will discuss initiating price changes before analysing how to react to competitors' price changes.

Three key issues associated with initiating price changes are: the circumstances that may lead a company to raise or lower prices, the tactics that can be used, and estimating competitor reaction. Table 8.2 illustrates the major points relevant to each of these considerations.

Circumstances

Marketing research (for example, trade-off analysis or experimentation) which reveals that customers place a higher value on the product than is reflected in its price could mean that a price increase is justified. Rising costs, and hence reduced profit margins, may also stimulate price rises. Another factor that leads to price increases is excess demand. This regularly happens, for example, in the residential property market where the demand for houses can often grow at a faster pace than houses can be built by construction companies, resulting in house price inflation. A company that cannot supply the demand created by its customers may choose to raise prices in an effort to balance demand and supply. This can be an attractive option as profit margins are automatically widened. The final circumstance when companies may decide to raise prices is when embarking on a harvest objective. Prices are raised to increase margins even though sales may fall.

In the same way, price cuts may be provoked by the discovery that a price is high compared to the value that customers place on a product, by falling costs and by excess supply leading to excess capacity. A further circumstance that may lead to price falls is the adoption of a build objective. When customers are thought to be price sensitive, price cutting may be used to build sales and market share, though doing so involves the risk of provoking a price war.

Tactics

There are many ways in which price increases and cuts may be implemented. The most direct is the 'price jump', or fall, which increases or decreases the price by the full amount in one go. A price jump avoids prolonging the pain of a price increase over a long period, but may raise the visibility of the price increase to customers – see the Marketing Spotlight at the beginning of this chapter. This happened in India, where Hindustan Lever, the local subsidiary of Unilever, used its market power to raise the prices of its key brands at a time when raw materials were getting cheaper. As a result, operating margins grew from 13 per cent in 1999 to 21 per cent in 2003. Subsequently, though, sales fell sharply due to competition from P&G and Nirma, a local brand, as well as consumer disaffection.[19] Using staged price increases might make the price rise more palatable but may elicit accusations of 'always raising your prices'. This frequently happens in sectors like utilities and broadband services.

A one-stage price fall can have a high-impact dramatic effect that can be heavily promoted but also has an immediate impact on profit margins. When the demand for hotel beds fell globally after the terrorist attacks on New York in 2001, the industry reacted by slashing hotel rates to try to generate business. One of the effects was that it proved to be difficult to raise rates again when the recovery took place.[20] As a result, the hospitality industry has been less willing to make big rate cuts as a result of the global economic downturn. Staged price reductions have a less dramatic effect but may be used when a price cut is believed to be necessary although the amount needed to stimulate sales is unclear. Small cuts may be initiated as a learning process that proceeds until the desired effect on sales is achieved.

'Escalator clauses' can also be used to raise prices. The contracts for some organizational purchases are

Table 8.2 Initiating price changes

	Increases	Cuts
Circumstances	Value greater than price Rising costs Excess demand Harvest objective	Value less than price Excess supply Build objective Price war unlikely Pre-empt competitive entry
Tactics	Price jump Staged price increases Escalator clauses Price unbundling Lower discounts	Price fall Staged price reductions Fighter brands Price bundling Higher discounts
Estimating competitor reaction	Strategic objectives Self-interest Competitive situation Past experience	

drawn up before the product is made. Constructing the product – for example, a new defence system or motorway – may take a number of years. An escalator clause in the contract allows the supplier to stipulate price increases in line with a specified index (for example, increases in industry wage rates or the cost of living).

Another tactic that effectively raises prices is **price unbundling**. Many product offerings actually consist of a set of products for which an overall price is set (for example, computer hardware and software, an airline flight, etc.). Price unbundling allows each element in the offering to be priced separately in such a way that the total price is raised. A variant on this process is charging for services that were previously included in the product's price. For example, manufacturers of mainframe computers have the option of unbundling installation and training services, and charging for them separately, while low-fares airlines charge for baggage, check-in, etc. separately. Alibaba.com, the world's largest online platform for trade between businesses, moved from a uniform membership package to a new structure that involved a basic membership fee and charges for additional services such as factory audits and keyword searching – a move that significantly raised the company's profits.[21]

Yet another approach is to maintain the list price but lower discounts to customers. In periods of heavy demand for new cars, dealers lower the cash discount given to customers, for example. Similarly if demand is slack, customers can be given greater discounts as an incentive to buy. However, there are risks if this strategy is pursued for too long a period of time. For example, owing to poor sales of its car models, GM pursued a four-year price discounting strategy in the US market, with disastrous effects. The net effect of this strategy was to take the total in incentives available to the buyer to over $7,000, or over 20 per cent off the suggested retail price of the car.[22] The resulting price war with Ford and Chrysler, who followed with similar schemes, hurt profits. But, more worryingly, the effect of the campaign seemed to be that GM customers simply brought forward purchases that they were going to make anyway to avail themselves of the discounts, and customer attention switched to price rather than the value offered by the product.[23]

Quantity discounts can also be manipulated to raise the transaction price to customers. The percentage discount per quantity can be lowered, or the quantity that qualifies for a particular percentage discount can be raised.

Those companies contemplating a price cut have three choices in addition to a direct price fall.

1 A company defending a premium-priced brand that is under attack from a cut-price competitor may choose to maintain its price while introducing a fighter brand. The established brand keeps its premium-price position while the fighter brand competes with the rival for price-sensitive customers.
2 Where a number of products and services that tend to be bought together are priced separately, price bundling can be used to effectively lower the price. For example, televisions can be offered with 'free three-year repair warranties' or cars offered with 'free service for two years'.
3 Finally, discount terms can be made more attractive by increasing the percentage or lowering the qualifying levels.

Reacting to competitors' price changes

Companies need to analyse their appropriate reactions when their competitors initiate price changes. Three issues are relevant here: when to follow, what to ignore and the tactics to use if the price change is to be followed. Table 8.3 summarizes the main considerations.

When to follow

When competitive price increases are due to general rising cost levels or industry-wide excess demand, they are more likely to be followed. In these circumstances the initial pressure to raise prices is the same on all parties. Following a price rise is also more likely when customers are relatively price insensitive, which means that the follower will not gain much advantage by resisting the price increase. Where brand image is consistent with high prices, a company is more likely to follow a competitor's price rise as to do so would be consistent with the brand's positioning strategy. Finally, a price rise is more likely to be followed when a company is pursuing a harvest or hold objective because, in both cases, the emphasis is more on profit margin than sales/market share gain.

When they are stimulated by general falling costs or excess supply, price cuts are likely to be followed. Falling costs allow all companies to cut prices while maintaining margins, and excess supply means that a company is unlikely to allow a rival to make sales gains at its expense. Price cuts will also be followed in price-sensitive markets since allowing one company to cut price without retaliation would mean large sales gains for the price cutter. This has happened in the UK toiletries market where Boots has failed to follow Tesco in aggressive price cutting on products like shampoo and skin cream, suffering significant sales losses as a result. The image of the company can also affect reaction to price cuts. Some companies position themselves as low-price manufacturers or retail outlets. In such circumstances they would be less likely to allow a price reduction by a competitor to go unchallenged

Table 8.3 Reacting to competitors' price changes

	Increases	Cuts
When to follow	Rising costs Excess demand Price-insensitive customers Price rise compatible with brand image Harvest or hold objective	Falling costs Excess supply Price-sensitive customers Price fall compatible with brand image Build or hold objective
When to ignore	Stable or falling costs Excess supply Price-sensitive customers Price rise incompatible with brand image Build objective	Rising costs Excess demand Price-insensitive customers Price fall incompatible with brand image Harvest objective
Tactics Quick response Slow response	Margin improvement urgent Gains to be made by being friend	Offset competitive threat High customer loyalty

for to do so would be incompatible with their brand image. Finally, price cuts are likely to be followed when the company has a build or hold strategic objective. In such circumstances an aggressive price move by a competitor would be followed to prevent sales/market share loss. For example, Amazon has dropped the price of its Kindle e-reader from $350 in 2009 to under $150 in 2011 in response to price competition from other e-readers such as Barnes & Noble's Nook (see Exhibit 8.4). In the case of a build objective, the response may be more dramatic, with a price fall exceeding the initial competitive move. For example, Vodafone halved the monthly tariff for wireless datacards from £30 to £15, which put it on a par with 3, the industry leader, in a bid to grow its share of the mobile data services market.

When to ignore

In most cases, the circumstances associated with companies not reacting to a competitive price move are simply the opposite of the above. Price increases are likely to be ignored when costs are stable or falling, which means that there are no cost pressures forcing a general price rise. In the situation of excess supply, companies may view a price rise as making the initiator less competitive and therefore allow the rise to take place unchallenged, particularly when customers are price sensitive. Companies occupying low-price positions may regard a price rise in response to a price increase from a rival to be incompatible with their brand image. Finally, companies pursuing a build objective may allow a competitor's price rise to go unmatched in order to gain sales and market share.

Price cuts are likely to be ignored in conditions of rising costs, excess demand and when servicing price-insensitive customers. Premium-price positioners may be reluctant to follow competitors' price cuts for to do so would be incompatible with their brand image.

Exhibit 8.4 The Amazon Kindle has pursued a strategy of aggressively reducing its price in response to competition from other e-readers

For example, some luxury brands, such as Lacoste, have suffered heavily because of pursuing a strategy of discounting when faced with excess capacity while competitors chose not to follow.[24] Finally, price cuts may be resisted by companies using a harvest objective.

Tactics

If a company decides to follow a price change, it can do this quickly or slowly. A quick price reaction is likely when there is an urgent need to improve profit margins. Here, the competitor's price increase will be welcomed as an opportunity to achieve this objective.

In contrast, a slow reaction may be the best approach when a company is pursuing the image of customers' friend. The first company to announce a price increase is often seen as the high-price supplier. Some companies have mastered the art of playing low-cost supplier by never initiating price increases and following competitors' increases slowly.[25] The key to this tactic is timing the response: too quick and customers do not notice; too long and profit is foregone. The optimum period can be found only by experience but, during it, salespeople should be told to stress to customers that the company is doing everything it can to hold prices for as long as possible.

If a firm wishes to ward off a competitive threat, a quick response to a competitor's price fall is called for. In the face of undesirable sales/market share erosion, fast action is needed to nullify potential competitor gains. However, reaction will be slow when a company has a loyal customer base willing to accept higher prices for a period so long as they can rely on price parity over the longer term.

Customer value through pricing

Price leadership has become the central value proposition for firms in a wide variety of industries (see Exhibit 8.5). For example, in grocery retailing, the German hard discounters Aldi and Lidl have led the way. Similar strategies have been pursued by the likes of Primark and TK Maxx in apparel retailing, Ryanair and easyJet in air travel, Lenovo in personal computers and so on (see Social Media Marketing 8.1). Because these firms aim to continually offer the best prices in the marketplace, the various issues described in this chapter take on particular importance. Offering low prices means that profit margins may be tight unless firms can find ways to drive their cost base down or find additional product/service elements that they can charge handsomely for. The three tools that firms have at their disposal to assist in this challenge are cost management, **yield management** and **dynamic pricing**.

Cost management

Cost control is critical for firms that attempt to lead on price as their success in controlling costs has a direct impact on profit margins. For example, retailers like Walmart and airlines like Ryanair have a reputation about being fanatical in their search for ways of reducing cost. One of the first costs to be removed by some airlines was the practice of selling seats through

Exhibit 8.5 This hugely popular viral advert for DollarShaveClub.com has helped to build awareness of its value offering. Viral advertising is particularly popular with low price businesses due to its low cost

Social Media Marketing 8.1 Primark: low price clothing

Critical Thinking: Below is a review of the operations of the apparel discounter, Primark. Read it and critically evaluate the strengths and weaknesses of its approach.

Price competition has become a feature of many industries and none more so than clothing. One brand which has capitalized on this trend is Primark, a company that was formed in Ireland as Penneys – where it still trades under that name – and has grown to encompass almost 300 outlets through Europe. Its primary competitive weapon is the low price of its garments and it regularly features shirts, tops and underwear that retail for just a few euros each. Customers are not just value shoppers but also those that purchase high-price items and then buy basics and accessories in Primark. So popular is its offering that when it opened its outlet at Marble Arch in London, thousands of customers queued outside and when the doors opened some staff were injured in the stampede that resulted.

Though its garments are manufactured in many of the same factories that its competitors use, Primark looks to achieve cost savings primarily in its retail outlets. Staff levels are low and pay rates are lower than the sector generally. As a result, its outlets tend to be characterized by piles of unsorted clothes which are appealing to both bargain hunters and a turn off for other shoppers in equal measure. Its shops also tend to be in low-cost locations on the edge of major urban centres and carry a much wider range of items than competitors, achieving economies of scale. For example, it built a 100,000 square foot store in Manchester in 2001 and stores like this encourage volume shopping. Primark spends very little on advertising and instead uses social media and word of mouth to build its reputation. It has built up almost 3 million followers on Facebook through a combination of quirky posts, conversational items and focusing on fashionable items of interest to its audience.

Low-price operators like Primark have given rise to the concept of disposable fashion. But they have also been the subject of much criticism. The main focus of attention has been the poor working conditions of staff in low-cost countries where the products are made. The collapse of a clothing factory in Dhaka, Bangladesh with the loss of over 1,000 lives in 2013 highlighted the extent of the problem. Primark paid compensation and emergency aid to the victims and has adopted a supplier code of conduct. But the demand by consumers for low-price products has seen it go from strength to strength.

Based on: Shawcross (2014).[27]

travel agents and paying them a margin of up to 10 per cent which was incorporated into the price. Most airline seats are now booked directly by customers online. Services like catering and check-in are outsourced, flights go to small regional airports where landing charges are low and, in extreme instances like Ryanair, flight crews buy their own uniforms and pay for their training. The Norwegian low-cost carrier, NAS, bases its planes and hires staff in Spain, has its back office in Latvia and its IT department in Ukraine.[26] Along with this type of aggressive cost management, low price operators seek as much scale as possible in order that fixed costs can be spread over a larger number of units and thus reduced.

Yield management

Another tool in the armoury of low price competitors is yield management which is the monitoring of demand or potential demand patterns. It is very popular in services businesses like travel and hotel accommodation. Levels of demand are tracked electronically on a daily basis. Therefore, over the course of a year, this information can be stored and used to set prices for rooms or flights which vary from day to day for the next year. It is also possible to track enquiries and use this information to make decisions regarding potential demand levels.

Dynamic pricing

An interesting aspect of many low-price companies is their level of profitability. For example, despite its reputation for low prices, Ryanair is the most profitable airline in Europe. Aside from their attention to costs, a key reason for their success is their flexible approach to pricing which is known as dynamic pricing. This means that prices are adjusted continually, based on demand and potential demand. Therefore, while prices on some flights may be cheap, on others they may be high if these flights coincide with peak holiday periods or major sporting events. Also, if demand for particular flights were to rise quickly for any reason, prices are quickly adjusted upwards. Through the application of technology and the close monitoring of demand patterns, many 'low-price' operators demonstrate a very flexible approach to price!

Summary

Price is a key aspect of the organization's marketing strategy and is also the core value proposition for some businesses. In this chapter the following key issues were addressed.

1. There are three bases upon which prices are set, namely cost, competition and market value. We noted that all three should be taken into account when setting prices. Costs represent a floor above which prices must be set to build a viable business, while competition and customers will influence the overall height of prices.

2. That the pricing levels set may also be influenced by a number of other marketing strategy variables, namely, positioning strategy, new-product launch strategy, product-line strategy, competitive strategy, channel management strategy and international marketing strategy.

3. That marketers need to make decisions relating to initiating price changes or responding to the price changes made by competitors. Whether prices are rising or falling, various factors need to be taken into account and these are important decisions as they affect the overall profitability of the firm.

4. That there are key issues surrounding the ethics of price setting. Price fixing is illegal, and other unethical practices such as deceptive pricing and product dumping are frequently targeted by regulators. Greater levels of price transparency are assisting consumers to avoid being exploited by unscrupulous companies.

5. Price may be the core value proposition offered by some businesses. In these cases organizations employ a combination of cost management, yield management and dynamic pricing to generate high profitability levels.

Study questions

1. Accountants are always interested in profit margins; sales managers want low prices to help push sales; and marketing managers are interested in high prices to establish premium positions in the marketplace. To what extent do you agree with this statement in relation to the setting of prices?
2. Why is value to the customer a more logical approach to setting prices than cost of production? What role can costs play in the setting of prices?
3. To what extent do you use price to judge the potential quality of an item that you are considering purchasing? Critically reflect on the pros and cons of using price as a decision cue in this way.
4. Discuss how a company pursuing a build strategy is likely to react to both price rises and price cuts by competitors.
5. Discuss the specific issues that arise when pricing products for international markets.
6. Visit www.vodafone.co.uk, www.o2.co.uk, www.orange.co.uk and www.easymobile.co.uk and compare the prices these companies charge for their products. How difficult is it to make an accurate comparison of the cost of a mobile phone package? Why do you think this is so?

Suggested reading

Baker, W., M. Marn and **C. Zawada** (2010) Do You Have a Long-Term Pricing Strategy? *McKinsey Quarterly*, October, 1–7.

Bertini, M. and **J. Gourville** (2012) Pricing to Create Shared Value, *Harvard Business Review*, **90** (6), 96–104.

Bryce, D., J. Dyer and **N. Hatch** (2011) Competing Against Free, *Harvard Business Review*, **89** (6), 104–11.

Davis, G. and **E. Brito** (2004) Price and Quality Competition between Brands and Own Brands: A Value Systems Perspective, *European Journal of Marketing*, **38** (1/2), 30–56.

Mohammed, R. (2005) *The Art of Pricing: How to Find the Hidden Profits to Grow Your Business*, London: Crown Business.

Sahay, A. (2007) How Dynamic Pricing Leads To Higher Profits, *Sloan Management Review*, **48** (4), 53–60.

When you have read this chapter

log on to the Online Learning Centre for
Foundations of Marketing at
www.mheducation.co.uk/textbooks/fahy5
where you'll find links and extra online study tools for marketing.

References

1. **Bachman, J.** (2014) Netflix Customers Get Ready, Higher Prices are Coming, *Businessweek.com*, 24 January; **Rogowosky, M.** (2014) Netflix Price Increase: Is There a Billion Hidden in Those Couch Cushions? *Forbes.com*, 21 April.

2. **Lester, T.** (2002) How to Ensure that the Price is Exactly Right, *Financial Times*, 30 January, 15.

3. **Shapiro, B.P.** and **B.B. Jackson** (1978) Industrial Pricing to Meet Customer Needs, *Harvard Business Review*, November–December, 119–27.

4. **London, S.** (2003) The Real Value in Setting the Right Price, *Financial Times*, 11 September, 15.

5. **Kucher, E.** and **H. Simon** (1987) Durchbruch bei der Preisentscheidung: Conjoint-Measurement, eine neue Technik zur Gewinnoptimierung, *Harvard Manager*, **3**, 36–60.

6. **Lester, T.** (2002) How to Ensure that the Price is Exactly Right, *Financial Times*, 30 January, 15.

7. **Anonymous** (2013) An industry ripe for a shake-up, *Economist. com*, 16 February.

8. **Minder, R.** (2014) Swiss Watchmakers Skeptical of Digital Revolution, *newyorktimes.com*, 25 March.

9. **Forbis, J.L.** and **N.T. Mehta** (1979) Economic Value to the Customer, *McKinsey Staff Paper*, Chicago: McKinsey and Co., February, 1–10.

10. **Ariely, D.** (2008) *Predictably Irrational*, London: HarperCollins Publishers.

11. **Anonymous** (2011) Blazing Platforms, *The Economist*, 12 February, 63–4.

12. **Sanchanta, M.** (2007) A Price Cut Too Late for PlayStation 3, *Financial Times*, 6 December, 25.

13. **Stern, S.** (2008) Keep the Focus on Value or You Will Pay the Price, *Financial Times*, 27 May, 12.

14. **Simon, H.** (1992) Pricing Opportunities – and How to Exploit Them, *Sloan Management Review*, Winter, 55–65.

15. **Cane, A.** (2003) TiVo, Barely Used . . ., *Financial Times, Creative Business*, 25 February, 12.

16. **Ritson, M.** (2009) Should You Launch A Fighter Brand? *Harvard Business Review*, **87** (10), 86–94.

17. **Jack, A.** (2005) Drugs Groups Seek Cure for Irritation of Parallel Trading, *Financial Times*, 10 August, 18.

18. **Cullen, P.** (2007) Cheated at the Checkout, *Irish Times, Weekend Review*, 28 July, 1.

19. **Anonymous** (2004) Slow Moving: Can Unilever's Indian Arm Recover From Some Self-Inflicted Wounds? *The Economist*, 6 November, 67–8.

20. **Blitz, R.** (2008) Hotels Keep Door Shut to Big Rate Cuts, *Financial Times*, 27 November, 28.

21. **Hille, K.** (2010) Alibaba Marketing Push Brings Results, *Financial Times*, 11 August, 18.

22. **Simon, B.** (2005) GM's Price Cuts Drive Record Sales, *Financial Times*, 5 July, 28.

23. **Simon, B.** (2005) Detroit Giants Count Cost of Four-year Price War, *Financial Times*, 19 March, 29.

24. **Dowdy, C.** (2003) Wealth, Taste and Cachet at Bargain Prices, *Financial Times*, 9 October, 17.

25. **Ross, E.B.** (1984) Making Money with Proactive Pricing, *Harvard Business Review*, November–December, 145–55.

26. **Anonymous** (2013) Here Come the Vikings, *Economist*, 27 April, 53–54.

27. **Shawcross, J.** (2014) The Rise and Rise of Primark, *Money.aol. co.uk*, 23 March.

8

The Jelly Bean Factory (Aran Candy): post-acquisition reflections on international pricing

Aran Candy's mission statement:

> *To produce and market the best gourmet jelly beans in the world, at affordable prices, with a reliable & efficient service, and long term customer care.*

Aran Candy specializes in the manufacture and worldwide distribution of high-quality gourmet jelly beans exporting over 98 per cent of its production to 55 markets around the world.[1] The company, which achieved a turnover of €12 million in 2013, produces beans under 'The Jelly Bean Factory[R]' brand at its state-of-the-art plant in Blanchardstown, Dublin, for supply to Europe, the Middle East, the Far East, Australia, New Zealand and Canada. It has sales offices in Britain and Bahrain and its product is available in over 45,000 stores in the UK alone, including Tesco, Debenhams, Boots, and W.H. Smith.[2]

Introduction

In late May 2014 Peter Cullen ('The Old Bean') and his son Richard Cullen ('The Young Bean'), Joint CEOs of Aran Candy,

sat in the boardroom of their company. They had just advised fellow board members of the takeover terms under which Scandinavian confectionery firm Cloetta AB (STO:CLAB) was to acquire Aran Candy. A consideration of €15.5 million in cash for an initial 75 per cent stake had been agreed, with the remaining 25 per cent to be acquired in 2016 for a price based on 2015 result targets. Under the terms of the deal Richard would continue as managing director. Post-meeting they toasted the takeover and exchanged reminiscences of some of the more memorable strategic challenges they had faced over the years. In particular they vividly recalled a major challenge to their UK export sales due to a severe weakness of sterling relative to the euro. It was January 2009 and sterling had weakened by almost 30 per cent vis-à-vis the euro over the previous 12 months, effectively forcing an equivalent cost increase on Aran Candy. As a matter of urgency a review of strategic pricing options for their confectionery products in the UK market was required and this item topped the agenda at Aran Candy's first board meeting of 2009.

The sterling debacle (2008–09)

The year 2008 had begun with an exchange rate of €1 = £0.74130; by the year end it stood at €1 = £0.95250 (see Figure C8.1). Peter and Richard both knew that even with the right product, promoted correctly and distributed through appropriate channels, the effort was doomed to failure if the product was incorrectly priced. Both were aware that continued action by the Bank of England to depreciate sterling had the potential to inflict grave damage on their export business. A strategic response to the lost price competitiveness in the UK market was urgently needed. At their meeting of January 2009 the board sought a clear vision of the strategic responses available to them from which one or more could be prioritized.

Background and history

Aran Candy was founded by Peter and Richard Cullen in the late 1990s. Peter had significant prior experience of the confectionery industry. In 1973 he accepted the position of marketing manager and minority 10 per cent stakeholder of Shannon Confectionery, a company in which he was later appointed managing director. On leaving the firm in 1985, his next career move, in partnership with his brother-in-law, was to acquire Clara Candy, makers of Cleeves Toffees, from the receiver. They soon brought it back to profitability. Despite generating up to 9 per cent net profit in its best years, over-exposure to a weakening UK market in 1994 caused the company to run into cash flow difficulties,

and ultimately to losses in 1996. On 23 December 1997, as the plant closed for Christmas, Banque Nationale de Paris sent in the receivers. Cullen, then 52, was the largest creditor and lost IR£350,000 (€444,000) personally. Shortly afterwards, Dunhills Plc, a subsidiary of Haribo, a German confectionery firm, purchased the building and machinery of Clara Candy, and took on most of its 105 former employees.[3]

In 1998, Aran Candy was established on a shoestring budget and initially was run from a room in the Cullens' home in Killiney, Dublin. Given his experiences with Clara Candy Cullen had vowed never to manufacture again. All production was outsourced to former rivals in Spain, Belgium and the Netherlands, and sold on a commission basis. Cullen Senior recalls, 'We had one computer, a phone and a fax. We kept costs to nil and took out nothing for at least six months.'[4] Circumstances, however, forced an alternative sourcing strategy on them when, in 2004, their main supplier in the Netherlands decided to sell up. A production facility which became available in the north-east of England looked a likely solution; however, before the deal was signed, the owner sold to a rival bid from a property developer. All was not lost. A sell-off of the factory contents left Cullen in possession of the manufacturing equipment at a knock-down price. Now all that was needed was premises to house the machinery. After some frenetic searching, a suitable unit became available in the IDA Business and Technology Park in Blanchardstown, Dublin. A fitting-out of the premises followed, staff including some ex-Clara and Haribo employees fully trained in production, safety and hygiene standards were recruited and production began in August 2005.[5]

Figure C8.1 Euro/pound sterling (GBP) exchange rate (January 2008–December 2008)

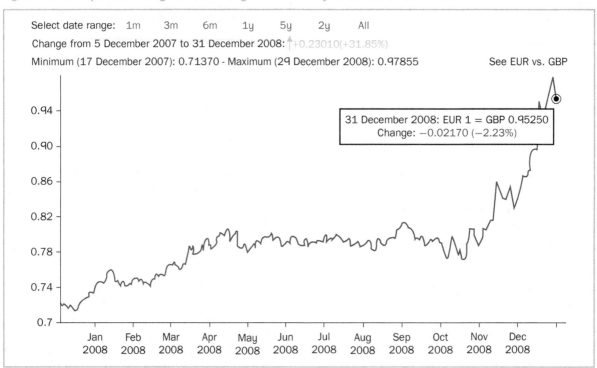

Select date range: 1m   3m   6m   1y   5y   2y   All

Change from 5 December 2007 to 31 December 2008: ↑+0.23010(+31.85%)

Minimum (17 December 2007): 0.71370 - Maximum (29 December 2008): 0.97855   See EUR vs. GBP

31 December 2008: EUR 1 = GBP 0.95250
Change: −0.02170 (−2.23%)

Production and product range

Jelly beans are believed to be a contemporary variant of Turkish Delight, which itself dates to biblical times. Jelly beans were developed in eighteenth-century France and are linked to Easter, with their egg-like shape symbolizing new birth.[6] Aran Candy is dedicated to producing gourmet jelly beans, a variety produced from a recipe containing sugar, glucose syrup, modified food starches, water, citric acid, fumoric acid, glazing agents shellac bees wax and carnaula wax, flavourings, acidity regulator sodium citrate and colours. The finished bean, which is available in 36 flavours, takes two weeks to produce. Aran Candy Gourmet Jelly Beans are softer, smaller and contain fewer calories than other varieties. The company's 150,000 sq ft factory had been extended three times in recent years and current production runs at 12 million beans a day.

At the time of the sterling debacle production was running at some 10 million beans per day sold in a variety of pack sizes and formats. Sachets were available in 25g and 50g sizes and the standard tube was 125g. Jars with an after-use had proved popular with customers, and three jar sizes were offered in the product range, a 600g, a 900g and a 1.5kg 'spaghetti' jar. In addition, the 600g jelly bean machine (for which 600g refill bags were available) had proved popular with customers. All products from The Jelly Bean Factory are GMO, gelatine, gluten and nut free and all are also Halal compliant. (See Exhibit C8.1 for a selection of The Jelly Bean Factory products.)

Exhibit C8.1 Example of a product from The Jelly Bean Factory

The UK sugar confectionery market [7]

The UK sugar confectionery market grew by 2 per cent in current value terms in 2013, to £1.68 billion. Cadbury UK Ltd, with 2013 UK sales of £335 million, was the dominant player with a 19.9 per cent share of the market. Haribo Dunhills, Nestlé, Perfetti Van Melle UK Ltd and Mars UK Ltd were the other main competitors, with 2013 market shares of 12.5 per cent, 12 per cent, 5.8 per cent and 5.2 per cent respectively (see Table C8.1).

Unit prices in the sugar confectionery sector rose by 3 per cent in 2013, partially due to the rising commodity price of sugar and also due to firms in the sector taking steps to moderate the effects of an anticipated fall in volume sales. A feature of the market during the period was the negative press sentiment about the health dangers of excessive sugar consumption. Many UK adults expected to eat sweets less often and many parents, seeking to inculcate healthy eating habits, are actively discouraging their children from purchasing them. Although many leading brands offered sugar-free options they represented a small proportion of the total sugar confectionery retail value sales.

Cadbury UK Ltd had exploited this trend by introducing the Australian Natural Confectionery Company brand of healthier sweets, a product containing no artificial colours or flavours, aimed at parents looking for more permissible treats for their family. They also had introduced a reduced sugar version of their long established Maynards Wine Gums brand.

Nestlé had launched a range of sugar confectionery products containing real fruit juice, with no artificial colourings or flavourings and positioned as a 'better for you' alternative to standard confectionery products. They also launched the Nestlé

Table C8.1 Sugar confectionery company shares 2007–13

% Retail value	2007	2010	2013
Cadbury UK Ltd	23.54*	21.66	19.90
Haribo Dunhills (Pontefract) Plc	10.41	8.98	12.48
Nestlé UK Ltd	10.86	11.98	12.07
Perfetti Van Melle UK Ltd	–	5.33	5.75
Mars UK Ltd	–	4.68	5.23
Swizzels Matlow Ltd	3.35	3.66	3.58
Ernest Jackson Ltd	3.08	2.40	2.39
Tesco Plc	2.42	2.64	2.42
Asda Group Ltd	2.23	2.44	2.20
Leaf United Kingdom Ltd	1.62	1.87	2.01
Benedicks (Mayfair) Ltd	3.00	1.82	1.74
Total retail value sales (£)	**1.50b**	**1.55b**	**1.68b**

*2007 = Cadbury Trebor Bassett Ltd
Source: Euromonitor International 2008–14

Go Free promotion, whereby consumers could earn free football, swimming and tennis lessons using vouchers from the packaging of Milkybar, Jelly Tots, Smarties, Fruit Gums or Fruit Pastilles products, taking advantage of the trend towards a healthier and more active lifestyle.

Despite an EU Commission decision, in late 2011, authorizing the use of stevia sweetener, major players were slow to integrate it into recipes fearing the resultant change in flavour could compromise customer loyalty and jeopardize sales.

The smoking ban in enclosed public places, introduced across the whole of the UK in 2007, continued to have a positive impact on the sugar confectionery sector, with many adults reverting to consumption of mints and sweets in lieu of cigarettes.

Options

Addressing the January 2009 board meeting Richard Cullen began by outlining a range of strategic pricing options available to counteract the loss of competitiveness due to the adverse movement in exchange rates. What the meeting had to do was to consider the pros and cons of each option and judiciously select among them. One option was to withdraw temporarily from the UK market and give priority to exports to relatively strong currency countries. When the sterling exchange rate returned to a more favourable level the UK market could be re-entered. A second option was to trim profit margins and use marginal cost pricing until matters improved. Richard was aware that if sterling valuation continued to be undermined by the Bank of England's quantitative easing process, then this option could prove costly. A third option was to improve productivity and engage in vigorous cost reductions, although Richard was conscious of the challenges of doing this in what was already a lean production facility. Switching sourcing and production overseas to take advantage of more attractive currency exchange rates and factor prices was another option, especially if it was anticipated that sterling would remain weak. Aran Candy could also engage in non-price competition by improving quality and introducing new products. Introducing product with only natural colours and no artificial flavours might not only take advantage of the trend towards natural ingredients but also serve to enhance margins. Another option, relying on the theory of just noticable difference (JND),* would require a reduction in the net weight of product supplied while holding price constant.

---

* JND refers to the smallest detectable change in a stimulus. In pricing JND refers to the magnitude of a price change before it is noticed by a consumer. In some cases a reduction in product weight may be less noticeable to the consumer than an equivalent increase in price.

In line with this strategy Aran Candy might refresh packaging or introduce pack innovations, perhaps a 100g tube or larger jar sizes. A final option would be to seek a price increase in the UK although Richard was conscious that such a strategy might be resisted by powerful channel partners. Having witnessed the significant adverse effects of the sterling depreciation, Richard knew that Aran Candy jobs depended on making a timely and appropriate strategic response.

References

1. **Newenham, P.** (2014) Eur 15.5m for share of Aran Candy, *The Irish Times*, Finance, 29 May, 3.
2. **The Irish Examiner** (2014), Spilling the beans on company's sweet success, 10 February.
3. **Costello, R.** (2006) How I Made It: Success at Second Bite Tastes Sweet, *Sunday Times*, 4 June, business.timesonline.co.uk/tol/business/article671302.ece?print=yes&randum=12 (accessed 16 May 2011).
4. **Costello, R.** (2006) How I Made It: Success at Second Bite Tastes Sweet, *Sunday Times*, 4 June, business.timesonline.co.uk/tol/business/article671302.ece?print=yes&randum=12 (accessed 16 May 2011).
5. **Daly, G.** (2008) The Jelly Bean Giants, *Sunday Business Post*, 27 April.
6. Adapted from **eHow Careers & Work Editor**, How to Make Jelly Beans, www.ehow.com/how_2084964_make-jelly-beans.html (accessed 16 May 2011).
7. This section relies heavily on data from *Euromonitor International* (2008) and (2014).

Questions

1. Discuss ways in which changes in the macro-environment have impacted on the sugar confectionery market.
2. Discuss the risks faced by an exporting company with a strong domestic currency.
3. List the different pricing strategies Aran Candy may employ in the UK given the severe weakness of sterling relative to the euro.
4. Are there any non-pricing strategies open to Aran Candy to respond to the depreciation in sterling?
5. Which strategy would you recommend for Aran Candy to deal with the weakness of sterling relative to the euro? Justify your choice.

This case was prepared by Dr Michael Gannon, Marketing Group, DCU Business School, Ireland, from various published sources as a basis for class discussion rather than to show effective or ineffective management.

Part 3

Delivering and Managing Customer Value

Chapter 9

Distribution: Delivering Customer Value

Chapter outline

Types of distribution channel

Channel integration

Retailing

Key retail marketing decisions

Physical distribution

Learning outcomes

By the end of this chapter you will:

1 Understand the different types of distribution channel for consumer goods, industrial products and services

2 Analyse the three components of channel strategy – channel selection, intensity and integration

3 Analyse the five key channel management issues – member selection, motivation, training, evaluation and conflict management

4 Explain the different kinds of retail store formats

5 Critique the impact of retail formats on society

6 Analyse the key retailing management decisions

7 Explain the key issues in managing the physical distribution system.

John Lewis

In a retail landscape characterized by global franchises and the huge store sizes of companies like Carrefour and Walmart, John Lewis stands apart. Though its first store was opened in 1864, the chain remains limited to just 43 outlets operating throughout the UK. It is positioned as an up-market department store retailing menswear, women's wear, children's wear, electrical goods and a home and garden range. Compared with its leading competitor, Marks & Spencer, John Lewis had adopted a very low-key approach to marketing. The company had no marketing director on the board, a limited marketing budget and its main marketing activities were associated with new store openings.

But all that began to change after the global financial crisis of 2008. The British economy was in recession, unemployment was rising and consumer confidence was hit hard. John Lewis' performance suffered with sales and profits falling faster than competitors'. In a situation like this, the company has a range of options. For example, cutting its prices was one option and this would have also fitted well with its slogan of 'never (being) knowingly undersold'. But instead it chose a bolder approach. It hired a new marketing director in 2009 and invested in a major new marketing campaign.

The first step in the campaign involved conducting research to understand its existing customer base better. John Lewis shoppers tended to be 25–55 years old, ABC1 and spanning life stages from pre-families to empty nesters. They were house-proud, fashionable and demanding. They tended to be more value conscious than price conscious and saw John Lewis as an outlet that they visited infrequently when they needed something. Most significantly the research revealed that while the John Lewis brand was trusted, it was not loved. This critical insight was the driver behind a decision to invest heavily in an emotional advertising campaign centered on the key Christmas shopping period.

Its Christmas 2009 campaign was entitled 'remember the feeling' and was based on the universal idea that when you get a present that you love you feel like a child again. In this way, John Lewis was positioned as a more thoughtful place to shop. Emotional elements like music and storytelling also became a big part of this and future campaigns. Television was the main medium used due to its strength in communicating emotional values and reaching large audiences. The campaigns evoked a huge response on social media with many people commenting on how the ads made them cry and they have been viewed over 10 million times on YouTube. The campaigns changed attitudes towards the brand which was seen as more modern and offering great service. Sales rose strongly between 2009 and 2012 leading to market share reaching record levels of over 26 per cent by 2012. This was during a period when almost 150 UK retailers ceased trading. John Lewis' courageous decision to invest in marketing during a period of decline appeared to pay off handsomely.[1]

John Lewis Ad Insight: A successful use of emotional appeal in Christmas advertising.

As we have seen throughout the book, several activities need to be conducted in order for organizations to market themselves effectively, including generating customer insights, developing differential products and services, pricing them correctly and communicating with customers. Important decisions also need to be made regarding how products and services are made available to customers. For example, in consumer markets significant shifts in buying habits are taking place such as online purchasing and the increased proportion of expenditure on foods being absorbed by supermarkets. In general, products need to be available in adequate quantities, in convenient locations and at times when customers want to buy them. In this chapter we will examine the functions and types of distribution channel, the key decisions that determine channel strategy, how to manage channels, the nature of retailing and issues relating to the physical flow of goods through distribution channels (physical distribution management).

Producers need to consider the requirements of **channel intermediaries** – those organizations that facilitate the distribution of products to customers – as well as the needs of their ultimate customers. For example, success for Müller yoghurt in the UK was dependent on convincing a powerful retail group (Tesco) to stock the brand. The high margins that the brand supported were a key influence in Tesco's decision. Without retailer support, Müller may have found it uneconomic to supply consumers with its brand. Clearly, establishing a supply chain that is efficient and meets customers' needs is vital to marketing success. This supply chain is termed a **channel of distribution**, and is the means by which products are moved from the producer to the ultimate customer. Gaining access to distribution outlets is not necessarily easy. For example, in the consumer food products sector, many brands vie with each other for prime positions on supermarket shelves (see Exhibit 9.1).

An important aspect of marketing strategy is choosing the most effective channel of distribution. The development of supermarkets effectively shortened the distribution channel between producer and consumer by eliminating the wholesaler. Prior to their introduction, the typical distribution channel for products like food, drink, tobacco and toiletries was producer to wholesaler to retailer. The wholesaler would buy in bulk from the producer and sell smaller quantities to the retailer (typically a small grocery shop). By building up buying power, supermarkets could shorten this chain by buying direct from producers. This meant lower costs to the supermarket chain and lower prices to the consumer.

Exhibit 9.1 Eye-level is the best position to have in a shopping aisle and brands will compete aggressively to gain and hold these positions. Eye tracking technology is increasingly used by researchers to understand what captures the attention of customers

The competitive effect of this was to drastically reduce the numbers of small grocers and wholesalers in this market. By being more efficient and better at meeting customers' needs, supermarkets had created a competitive advantage for themselves which they have been able to retain for many years.

We will now explore the different types of channel that manufacturers use to supply their products to customers, and the types of function provided by these channel intermediaries.

Types of distribution channel

Whether they be consumer goods, business-to-business goods or services, all products require a channel of distribution. Industrial channels tend to be shorter than consumer channels because of the small number of ultimate customers, the greater geographic concentration of industrial customers and the greater complexity of the products that require

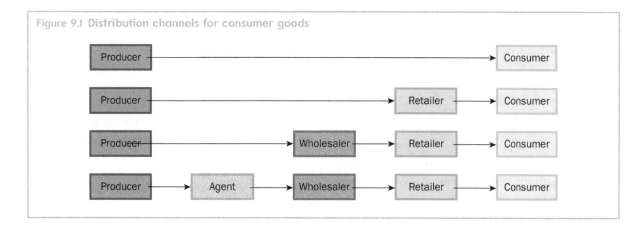

Figure 9.1 Distribution channels for consumer goods

close producer/customer liaison. Service channels also tend to be short because of the inseparability of the production and consumption of many services.

Consumer channels

Figure 9.1 shows four alternative consumer channels. We will now look briefly at each one in turn.

Producer direct to consumer

This option may be attractive to producers because it cuts out distributors' profit margins. Direct selling between producer and consumer has long been a feature of the marketing of many products, ranging from the sale of fruit in local markets to the sale of Avon Cosmetics and Tupperware plastic containers. It is a form of distribution that is starting to grow rapidly again (see Exhibit 9.2). Concerns over food quality in supermarkets and a growing market for organic foods have seen a rapid rise in farmers' markets in Europe. And of course, in the past 20 years or so, the Internet has been the great new direct distribution medium for products ranging from books and music to DVDs to air travel, and so on. This has had huge implications for traditional retailers like bookshops, music shops and travel agents, many of whom have suffered falling sales or have ceased trading.

Producer to retailer to consumer

For a variety of reasons, a producer may choose to distribute products via a retailer to consumers. Retailers provide the basic service of enabling consumers to view a wide assortment of products under one roof, while manufacturers continue to gain economies of scale from the bulk production of a limited number of items. For many people, retailing is the public face of marketing, and large in-city and out-of-town shopping centres have become popular venues for consumers to spend their leisure time. For example, the Mall of

the Emirates in Dubai features an indoor ski resort providing a host of winter activities, a Magic Planet family entertainment centre, a shark-filled aquarium and cinemas. As we shall see later in the chapter, retailers have become increasingly sophisticated in their operations and dominate many distribution channels. For example, supermarket chains exercise considerable power over manufacturers because of their enormous buying capabilities, and have been expanding into other areas of retailing like financial services, music distribution, and so on.

Producer to wholesaler to retailer to consumer

The use of wholesalers makes economic sense for small retailers (e.g. small grocery or furniture shops) with limited order quantities. Wholesalers can buy in bulk from producers, and sell smaller quantities to numerous retailers (this is known as 'breaking bulk'). The danger is that large retailers in the same market have the power to buy directly from producers and thus cut out the wholesaler. In certain cases, the buying power of large retailers has meant that they can sell products to their customers more cheaply than a small retailer can buy from the wholesaler. Longer channels like this tend to occur where retail oligopolies do not dominate the distribution system. In some Asian countries, like Japan, distribution channels can involve up to two and three tiers of wholesalers who supply the myriad small shops and outlets that serve Japanese customers.[2] Many of these wholesalers provide additional services to their customers (the retailers) such as collecting and analysing customer data which can be used to get better deals from producers.[3]

Producer to agent to wholesaler to retailer to consumer

This is a long channel, sometimes used by companies entering foreign markets, who may delegate the task of selling the product to an agent (who does not take title to the goods). The agent contacts local wholesalers (or retailers) and receives a commission on sales. Companies entering new export markets often organize their distribution systems in this way.

Business-to-business channels

Common business-to-business distribution channels are illustrated in Figure 9.2. A maximum of one channel intermediary is used under normal circumstances.

Producer to business customer

Supplying business customers direct is common practice for expensive business-to-business products such as gas turbines, diesel locomotives and aero-engines. There needs to be close liaison between supplier and customer to co-create products and solve technical problems, and the size of the order makes direct selling and distribution economic.

Producer to agent to business customer

Instead of selling to business customers using their own sales force, a business-to-business goods company could employ the services of an agent who may sell a range of goods from several suppliers (on a commission basis). This spreads selling costs and may be attractive to those companies that lack the reserves to set up their own sales operations. The disadvantage is that there is little control over the agent, who is unlikely to devote the same amount of time selling these products as a dedicated sales team.

Producer to distributor to business customer

For less expensive, more frequently bought business-to-business products, distributors are used; these may have both internal and field sales staff.[4] Internal staff deal with customer-generated enquiries and order placing, order follow-up (often using the telephone) and check inventory levels. Outside sales staff are more proactive; their practical responsibilities are to find new customers, get products specified, distribute catalogues and gather market information. The advantage to customers of using distributors is that they can buy small quantities locally.

Producer to agent to distributor to business customer

Where business customers prefer to call upon distributors, the agent's job will require selling into these intermediaries. The reason why a producer may employ an agent rather than a dedicated sales force is usually cost-based (as previously discussed).

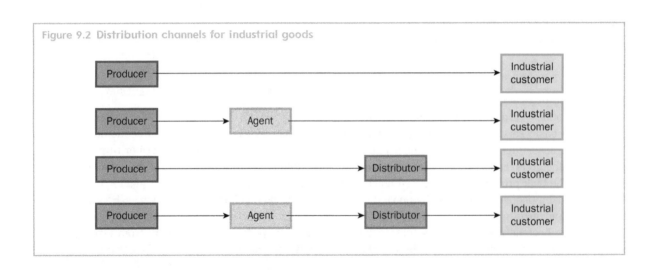

Figure 9.2 Distribution channels for industrial goods

Services channels

Distribution channels for services are usually short, either direct or via an agent (see Figure 9.3). Since stocks are not held, the role of the wholesaler, retailer or industrial distributor does not apply.

Service provider to consumer or business customer

The close personal relationships between service providers and customers often means that service supply is direct. Examples include healthcare, office cleaning, accountancy, marketing research and law.

Service provider to agent to consumer or business customer

A channel intermediary for a service company usually takes the form of an agent. Agents are used when the service provider is geographically distant from customers, and where it is not economical for the provider to establish their own local sales team. Examples include insurance, travel, secretarial and theatrical agents.

Channel strategy and management

The design of the distribution channel is an important strategic decision that needs to be integrated with other marketing decisions. For example, products that are being positioned as upmarket, premium items are usually only available in a select number of stores. **Channel strategy** decisions involve the selection of the most effective distribution channel, the most appropriate level of distribution intensity and the degree of channel integration. Once the key channel strategy decisions have been made, effective implementation is required. Channel management decisions involve the selection, motivation, training and evaluation of channel members, and managing conflict between producers and channel members.

Channel selection

Ask yourself why Procter & Gamble sells its brands through supermarkets rather than selling direct. Why does Mitsui sell its locomotives direct to train operating companies rather than use a distributor? The answers are to be found by examining the following factors that influence channel selection. These influences can be grouped under the headings of market, producer, product and competitive factors.

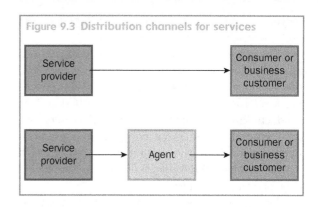

Figure 9.3 Distribution channels for services

Market factors

Buyer behaviour is an important market factor; buyer expectations may dictate that a product be sold in a certain way. Buyers may prefer to buy locally or online. Failure to match these expectations can have catastrophic consequences, as illustrated by the experience of entertainment retailers, who continue to struggle as more and more consumers switch to digital downloading. Similarly innovative technologies are changing the way consumers obtain their news. Platforms like Flipboard scan the Internet and aggregate content in a magazine style format based on each individual user's interests. These types of developments have implications for both magazine and newspaper publishers and the retail outlets through which these print editions are sold.

The geographical concentration and location of customers also affects channel selection. The more local and clustered the customer base, the more likely it is that direct distribution will be feasible. Direct distribution is also more prevalent when buyers are few in number and buy large quantities such as in many industrial markets. A large number of small customers may mean that using channel intermediaries is the only economical way of reaching them (e.g. department stores). Buyers' needs regarding product information, installation and technical assistance also have to be considered. For example, products that require facilities for local servicing, such as cars, often use intermediaries to carry out the task.

Producer factors

When a producer lacks adequate resources to perform the functions of the channel, this places a constraint on the channel decision. Producers may lack the financial and managerial resources to take on channel operations. Lack of financial resources may mean that a sales force cannot be recruited and sales agents and/or distributors are used instead. Producers may feel that they do not possess the customer-based skills to distribute their products, and prefer to rely on intermediaries instead.

The desired degree of control of channel operations also influences the selection of channel members. The use of independent channel intermediaries reduces producer control. For example, by distributing their products through supermarkets, manufacturers lose total control of the price charged to consumers. Furthermore, there is no guarantee that new products will be stocked. Direct distribution gives producers control over such issues.

Finally, an important decision for producers is whether they want to push their product through the channel or rather market to the end consumer, who then 'pulls' the product through the channel. The former requires investing heavily in trade support to ensure that products are carried and given desired shelf space. The latter means that marketing is targeted at the end user, who through their demand for the product, ensures that it is carried by middlemen. This has raised important ethical issues in the medical profession because of the increased consumer advertising of products by pharmaceutical companies. By building well-known brands like Viagra, Prozac and Vioxx, pharmaceutical companies have been accused of driving consumers to demand products that are not always necessary, in effect pulling them through the channel despite possible objections by medical practitioners. For example, the US drug firms Merck and Schering-Plough have been embroiled in controversy since a study concluded that their joint cholesterol drug, Vytorin, is no more effective than generic versions costing a third of its price. The drug had been aggressively marketed by these two companies.[5]

Product factors

Large and/or complex products are often supplied direct to the customer. The need for close personal contact between producer and customer, and the high prices charged, mean that direct distribution and selling is both necessary and feasible. Perishable products, such as fruit, meat and bread, require relatively short channels to supply the customer with fresh stock. Bulky or difficult to handle products may require direct distribution because distributors may refuse to carry them if storage or display problems arise.[6] A significant proportion of products which can digitized such as books, music, video, software and education are distributed through online channels (see Social Media Marketing 9.1).

Competitive factors

An innovative approach to distribution may be required if competitors control traditional channels of distribution –

for example, through franchise or exclusive dealing arrangements. Two available alternatives are to recruit a sales force to sell direct or to set up a producer-owned distribution network (see the information about administered vertical marketing systems, a topic discussed later in this chapter under the heading 'Conventional marketing channels'). Producers should not accept that the channels of distribution used by competitors are the only ways to reach target customers. Direct marketing provides opportunities to supply products in new ways, as many online companies have shown. For example, traditional channels of distribution for personal computers through high-street retailers were circumvented by direct marketers such as Dell, which used direct-response advertising to reach buyers. The emergence of the more computer-aware and experienced buyer, and the higher reliability of these products as the market reached maturity, meant that a local source of supply (and advice) was less important. However, by pursuing this strategy, Dell was not as effective in reaching corporate customers as some of its major competitors, which continued to use computer resellers. In a break with tradition, Dell announced in 2007 that it was broadening its business model to include computer resellers for the business market as well as Walmart to reach the consumer market in the USA.

The process by which producers or service providers bypass intermediaries and deal directly with final consumers is known as **disintermediation**. In certain sectors and driven largely by online retailing it has been occurring very frequently. For example, travel agents traditionally operated as an intermediary between consumers and airlines and holiday companies charging commissions of up to 10 per cent for their services. Now however, most consumers book their flights and holidays directly online either from airlines or from online travel websites such as Expedia, Travelocity and Lastminute.com. Major holiday companies such as Dream Holidays and Holidays4UK ceased trading and established distributors like Thomas Cook were forced to undertake dramatic restructuring programmes.

Distribution intensity

The choice of distribution intensity is the second channel strategy decision. The three broad options are intensive, selective and exclusive distribution. We will look at each of these now.

Intensive distribution

By using all available outlets, **intensive distribution** aims to provide saturation coverage of the market.

Social Media Marketing 9.1 Shutterstock: images of everything!

Critical Thinking: Below is a review of Shutterstock – one of the many new types of distributors emerging due to the growth of online business. Read it and critically reflect on the advantages and disadvantages of its business model.

The growth of social media has given rise to an army of online publishers generating blogs, ezines, forums and websites. These productions are enhanced by the inclusion of images but simply grabbing pictures off the Internet exposes users to copyright violation issues. As a result the market for images has grown and Shutterstock has become one of the market leaders in this nascent business.

The company was founded by Jon Oringer in 2003 and his first investment was an $800 Canon Rebel camera. With it he took 30,000 images, uploaded them onto his website and his business was in operation. Customers could either buy the rights to use a single image or pay a subscription to use up to 25 images per day. This option was then expanded to allow unlimited downloads. The company's primary customers are businesses operating in creative industries that Oringer reached through search advertising and direct sales. Shutterstock's business model meant that, unlike many start-ups, it got paid first making it instantly profitable

and it has generated revenue growth in excess of 30 per cent per year since its formation. The company went public in 2012 with revenues in excess of $230 million.

On the supply side, the opportunity was opened to any photographer anywhere to submit photos and they were paid from 25 cents to $120 if these were downloaded. But its decision to provide feedback to photographers on what was and was not selling was innovative and helped it to generate a supply for photos that customers were looking for. By 2014, 55,000 photographers around the world were uploading 30,000 images per day giving the company a total database of over 30 million images. Since 2006, the company has included video images in its library and in 2014 it decided to expand its business with the launch of Shutterstock Music, giving musicians everywhere the opportunity to make money from the music that they create.

Based on: Anonymous (2014)[7]; Bertoni (2013).[8]

With many mass-market products, such as snacks, foods, toiletries, beer and newspapers, sales are a direct function of the number of outlets penetrated (see Exhibit 9.3). This is because consumers have a range of acceptable brands from which they choose and, very often, the decision to purchase is made on impulse. If a brand is not available in an outlet, an alternative is bought. The convenience aspect of purchase is paramount. New outlets may be sought that hitherto had not stocked the products, such as the sale of alcoholic drinks and grocery items at petrol stations.

Selective distribution

Selective distribution also enables market coverage to be achieved. In this case, a producer uses a limited

number of outlets in a geographical area to sell its products. The advantages to the producer are: the opportunity to select only the best outlets to focus its efforts on building close working relationships, to train distributor staff on fewer outlets than with intensive distribution, and, if selling and distribution are direct, to reduce costs. Upmarket, aspirational brands like Hugo Boss and Raymond Weil are often sold in carefully selected outlets. Retail outlets and industrial distributors like this arrangement since it reduces competition. Selective distribution is more likely to be used when buyers are willing to shop around when choosing products. This means that it is not necessary for a company to have its products available in all outlets. Products such as audio and video equipment, cameras, clothing and cosmetics may be sold in this way.

Problems can arise when a retailer demands distribution rights but is refused by producers. This happened in the case of Superdrug, a UK discount store chain that requested the right to sell expensive perfume but was denied by manufacturers, which claimed that its stores did not have the right ambience for the sale of luxury products. Superdrug maintained that its application was refused solely because it wanted to sell perfumes for less than their recommended prices. A Monopolies and Mergers Commission investigation supported current practice. European rules allow perfume companies to confine distribution to retailers who measure up in terms of decor and staff training. Manufacturers are not permitted to refuse distribution rights on the grounds that the retailer will sell for less than the list price.[9]

Exclusive distribution

Exclusive distribution is an extreme form of selective distribution in which only one wholesaler, retailer or business-to-business distributor is used in a particular geographic area. Cars are often sold on this basis, with only one dealer operating in each town or city. This reduces a purchaser's power to negotiate prices for the same model between dealers, since to buy in a neighbouring town may be inconvenient when servicing or repairs are required. It also allows very close co-operation between producer and retailer over servicing, pricing and promotion. The right to exclusive distribution may be demanded by distributors as a condition for stocking a manufacturer's product line. Similarly, producers may wish for exclusive dealing where the distributor agrees not to stock competing lines.

Exclusive distribution arrangements can restrict competition in a way that may be detrimental to consumer interests. The European Court of Justice rejected an appeal by Unilever over the issue of exclusive outlets in Germany. By supplying freezer cabinets, Unilever maintained exclusivity by refusing to allow competing ice creams into its cabinets.[10] However, the European Court rejected an appeal by the French Leclerc supermarket group over the issue of the selective distribution system used by Yves Saint Laurent perfumes. The judges found that the use of selective distribution for luxury cosmetic products increased competition and that it was in the consumers' and manufacturer's interests to preserve the image of such luxury products.

Channel integration

Channel integration can range from conventional marketing channels – comprising an independent producer and channel intermediaries – through a franchise operation to channel ownership by a producer. Producers need to consider the strengths and weaknesses of each system when selecting a channel strategy.

Conventional marketing channels

The producer has little or no control over channel intermediaries because of their independence. Arrangements such as exclusive dealing may provide a degree of control, but separation of ownership means that each party will look after its own interests. Conventional marketing channels are characterized by hard bargaining and, occasionally, conflict. For example, a retailer may believe that cutting the price of a brand is necessary to move stock, even though the producer objects because of brand image considerations.

A manufacturer that, through its size and strong brands, dominates a market may exercise considerable power over intermediaries even though they are independent. This power may result in an **administered vertical marketing system** where the manufacturer can command considerable co-operation from wholesalers and retailers. For example, the big Hollywood studios have tried to carefully manage the distribution of movies through a sequence of cinema, video/DVD sale, video/DVD rental to pay-per-view television and finally free television to maximize their returns. Pfizer created some controversy when it sought to change its drug distribution arrangements in the UK, which would see all its products distributed through one company, UniChem. Other wholesalers sought to have the action deemed anticompetitive, while retailers were also concerned about the possible emergence of a single, powerful wholesaler.[11]

In recent years retailers have exerted significant control in an administered vertical marketing system. For example, when the retail entrepreneur Philip Green bought the Arcadia group in 2002, he wrote to all suppliers setting out new terms and conditions, imposing a retrospective 1.25 per cent discount and lengthening the number of days taken to pay suppliers from 28 to 30. He then consolidated the number of suppliers completely, delisting some and increasing the work given to others.[12] Grocery retailers have been particularly strong in their channels with firms like Tesco, Carrefour and Walmart achieving positions of significant dominance. A key way in which these retailers hurt other channel members is through the development of their own retailer brands or private labels. Outlets like Aldi, Lidl and Marks & Spencer sell primarily their own branded products rather than manufacturer brands. Tesco has a range of own brands from its high-end *Finest* range to its *Organics* and *Value* ranges. In relatively undifferentiated product categories like milk, pasta, ready meals, refuse bags and aluminum foil, private label penetration levels have been very high posing particular problems for manufacturers. However, manufacturers have done a much better job of holding their dominant positions in sectors like beer, toothpaste and cosmetics.

Franchising

A legal contract in which a producer and channel intermediaries agree each member's rights and obligations is called a **franchise**. Usually, the intermediary receives marketing, managerial, technical and financial services in return for a fee. Franchise organizations such as McDonald's, Domino's Pizza, Hertz and the Body Shop combine the strengths of a large sophisticated marketing-oriented organization with the energy and motivation of a locally owned outlet, and hence have been highly successful in building global businesses. Although a franchise operation gives a degree of producer control there are still areas of potential conflict. For example, the producer may be dissatisfied with the standards of service provided by the outlet, or the franchisee may believe that the franchising organization provides inadequate promotional support. Goal conflict can also arise.[13] A franchise agreement provides a **contractual vertical marketing system** through the formal co-ordination and integration of marketing and distribution activities.

Three economic explanations have been proposed to explain why a producer might choose franchising as a means of distribution.[14] Franchising may be a means of overcoming resource constraints whereby the cost of distribution is shared with the franchisee. It may also be an efficient system for overcoming producer/distributor management problems, because producers may value the notion of the owner-manager who has a vested interest in the success of the business. Finally, franchising may be a way for a producer to access the local knowledge of the franchisee. Franchising may therefore be attractive when a producer is expanding into new international markets. The biggest franchises operating in Europe are listed in Table 9.1.

Franchising can occur at four levels of the distribution chain.

1 *Manufacturer and retailer*: the car industry is dominated by this arrangement. The manufacturer gains retail outlets for its cars and repair facilities without the capital outlay required with ownership.

2 *Manufacturer and wholesaler*: this is commonly used in the soft drinks industry. Manufacturers

Table 9.1 Europe's top franchises (by unit numbers), 2013

Rank	Franchise	Business	Country of origin
1	7 Eleven	Convenience stores	USA
2	Subway	Food: sandwich bars	USA
3	McDonald's	Restaurants	USA
4	Kumon Institute of Education	Children's education	Japan
5	KFC	Restaurants	USA
6	Spar	Convenience stores	Netherlands
7	Europcar	Car rental and leasing	France
8	Pizza Hut	Restaurants	USA
9	Burger King	Restaurants	USA
10	Mexx	Clothing and footwear	Netherlands

Source: www.franchiseeurope.com

such as Schweppes, Coca-Cola and Pepsi grant wholesalers the right to make up and bottle their concentrate in line with their instructions, and to distribute the products within a defined geographic area.

3 *Wholesaler and retailer*: this is not as common as other franchising arrangements, but is found with car products and hardware stores. It allows wholesalers to secure distribution of their product to consumers.

4 *Retailer and retailer*: an often used method that frequently has its roots in a successful retailing operation seeking to expand geographically by means of a franchise operation, often with great success. Examples include Subway, Best Western, Pizza Hut and KFC (see Exhibit 9.4).

Channel ownership

Channel ownership brings with it total control over distributor activities. This establishes a **corporate vertical marketing system**. By purchasing retail outlets, producers control their purchasing, production and marketing activities. In particular, control over purchasing means a captive outlet for the manufacturer's products. For example, the purchase of Pizza Hut and KFC by Pepsi has tied these outlets to the company's soft drinks brands.

Exhibit 9.4 This clever outdoor advertising campaign by the McDonald's franchise demonstrates how widespread its outlets are

so much flavor
the bun
called for backup

100% pure beef

i'm lovin' it

The benefits of control have to be balanced against the high price of acquisition and the danger that the move into retailing will spread managerial activities too widely. Nevertheless, corporate vertical marketing systems have operated successfully for many years in the oil industry where companies such as Shell, Texaco and Statoil own not only considerable numbers of petrol stations but also the means of production.

Channel management

Channels need to be managed on an ongoing basis once the key channel strategy decisions have been made. This involves the selection, motivation, training and evaluation of channel members, and the resolution of any channel conflict that arises.

Selection

The selection of channel members involves two main activities: first, the identification of potential channel members and, second, development of selection criteria. A variety of potential sources can be used to identify candidates, including trade sources such as trade associations and participation at exhibitions, talking to existing customers and/or to the field sales force, and taking enquiries from interested resellers.[15] Common selection criteria include market, product and customer knowledge, market coverage, quality and size of sales force (if applicable), reputation among customers, financial standing, the extent to which competitive and complementary products are carried, managerial competence and hunger for success, and the degree of enthusiasm for handling the producer's lines. In practice, selection may be complex because large, well-established distributors may carry many competing lines and lack enthusiasm for more. Smaller distributors, on the other hand, may be less financially secure and have a smaller sales force, but be more enthusiastic and hungry for success.

Motivation

Once they have been chosen, channel members need to be motivated to agree to act as a distributor, and allocate adequate commitment and resources to the producer's lines. The key to effective motivation is to understand the needs and problems of distributors, since needs and motivators are linked. For example, a distributor who values financial incentives may respond more readily to high commission than one who is more concerned with having an exclusive territory. Possible motivators include financial rewards, territorial exclusivity, providing resource support (e.g. sales training, field sales assistance,

provision of marketing research information, advertising and promotion support, financial assistance and management training) and developing strong work relationships (e.g. joint planning, assurance of long-term commitment, appreciation of effort and success, frequent interchange of views and arranging distributor conferences). In short, the management of independent distributors is best conducted in the context of informal partnerships.[16]

Training

Channel members' training requirements obviously depend on their internal competences. Large supermarket chains, for example, may regard an invitation by a manufacturer to provide marketing training as an insult. However, many smaller distributors have been found to be weak on sales management, marketing, financial management, stock control and personnel management, and may welcome producer initiatives on training.[17] From the producer's perspective, training can provide the necessary technical knowledge about a supplier company and its products, and help to build a spirit of partnership and commitment.

Evaluation

Channel member evaluation has an important impact on distributor retention, training and motivation decisions. Evaluation provides the information necessary to decide which channel members to retain and which to drop. Shortfalls in distributor skills and competences may be identified through evaluation, and appropriate training programmes organized by producers. Where a lack of motivation is recognized as a problem, producers can implement plans designed to deal with the root causes of demotivation (e.g. financial incentives and/or fostering a partnership approach to business).[18] It needs to be understood, however, that the scope and frequency of evaluation may be limited where power lies with the channel member. If producers have relatively little power because they are more dependent on channel members for distribution, then in-depth evaluation and remedial action will be restricted. Where manufacturer power is high through having strong brands, and many distributors from which to choose, evaluation may be more frequent and wider in scope. Evaluation criteria include sales volume and value, profitability, level of stocks, quality and position of display, new accounts opened, selling and marketing capabilities, quality of service provided to customers, market information feedback, ability and willingness to keep commitments, attitudes and personal capability.

Managing conflict

Finally, given that producers and channel members are independent, conflict will inevitably occur from time to time (see Marketing in Action 9.1). First, such discord may arise because of differences in goals – for example, an increase in the proportion of profits allocated to retailers means a reduction in the amount going to manufacturers. For instance, when Irish tour operator Budget Travel cut the commissions it paid to travel agents for selling its holidays from 10 to 5 per cent, its subsequent research found that many agents were omitting Budget from the list of choices being presented to customers. Its response was to reach out directly to the end consumer through a €1 million multimedia campaign urging consumers to consider Budget as one of their potential travel choices.[19] However, this campaign was unsuccessful and the firm subsequently ceased trading.

Second, in seeking to expand their businesses many resellers add additional product lines. For example, UK retailer WH Smith originally specialized in books, magazines and newspapers but has grown by adding new product lines such as computer

---

Marketing in Action 9.1 Conflict in the channel!

Critical Thinking: Below are some examples of distribution channel conflict. Read the text and consider the drivers and potential solutions for this kind of conflict.

Channel conflict is commonplace in a variety of industries and frequently arises due to the conflicting goals of the channel members. A case in point is the book industry which has undergone significant disruption in recent years. In the world of printed books, publishers usually set the retail price of the book. This protected their margins but allowed retailers little flexibility in how much they charged for their titles. Legal challenges in many parts of the world succeeded in having this fixed price law removed allowing discounting and special deals by retailers. As e-books grow in popularity, the price points for books have become a source of controversy again. For example, the powerful online retailer Amazon has been pushing for the opportunity to discount freely and offer other features like a lending library for customers of 'Prime', its quick delivery service. But many publishers are resisting, fearing that Amazon will drive down the price of e-books eroding their margins in the same way that Apple's iTunes store eroded profitability in the music industry. For example, publishers in France are protected by the Lang Law which insists on fixed book prices and have used it as part of their defence in disputes with Amazon. Regulators in France passed what became dubbed as the 'Anti-Amazon' law in 2014, preventing the online retailer from offering free shipping on books which was seen as a means of circumventing the fixed pricing laws.

Trouble also frequently erupts between the partners in a franchise operation. For example in the soft drinks industry, leading firms like Coca-Cola and Pepsi Cola manufacture cola concentrate, which is then sold to independent licensed bottling companies, which hold exclusive contracts for particular geographic territories. They in turn manufacture the finished products, which are packaged in bottles and cans, and distributed directly to retail outlets such as shops, supermarkets and vending machines. But pressure from large retailers looking for direct supplies from the drinks manufacturers has put pressure on this arrangement. Consequently, when Walmart asked that Coca-Cola distribute its Powerade brand to Walmart warehouses rather than to individual stores, bottlers in the USA reacted angrily. Sixty independent bottlers filed a lawsuit against Coca-Cola and Coca-Cola Enterprises, fearing that the move would be the first in a shift away from the direct delivery model and would ultimately threaten their future. Coca-Cola had initially accepted Walmart's proposal as it feared that not doing so would mean that the giant retailer would begin selling an own-label version of the drink. After some disruption to the supply chain, the bottlers settled with Coca-Cola, and agreed to develop and test new distribution and customer service systems.

Based on: Anonymous (2014);[20] Ward (2007).[21]

disks, DVDs and software supplies. This can cause resentment among its primary suppliers, who perceive the reseller as devoting too much effort to selling secondary lines. This problem can also work in reverse. Small newsagents in Ireland asked the Competition Authority to review the system whereby wholesalers insisted that they carry a full range of magazine titles, with the result that many were left unsold, increasing the costs to the retailer.[22]

Third, in trying to grow their business, producers can use multiple distribution channels, such as selling directly to key accounts or other distributors, which may irritate existing dealers. For example, Alanis Morissette's record company, Maverick Records, created a significant amount of channel conflict in North America when it gave exclusive rights for the sale of her *Jagged Little Pill* album to Starbucks, which was allowed to sell the album for six weeks in its then 4,800 stores before it became available elsewhere. HMV reacted by removing all the artist's music from the shelves of its Canadian stores.[23] For digitized products such as music and software, online distribution is significantly cheaper making it very difficult for physical stores to compete with this channel which is often a source of conflict.

Finally, an obvious source of conflict is when parties in the supply chain do not perform to expectations. For example, DSG International, the owner of the PC World and Currys retail chains, claimed that its poor financial performance in 2007 was partly attributable to a lack of promotional support by Microsoft for its new Vista operating system, which left it with thousands of unsold computers that had to be heavily discounted. This type of conflict is also very common in the telecommunications business where mobile and fixed-line operators buy bundles of time on networks for resale to their customers. Any increase or reduction in these wholesale prices can have a significant impact on their profitability.

There are several ways of managing conflict. Developing a partnership approach calls for frequent interaction between producer and resellers to develop a spirit of mutual understanding and co-operation. First, sales targets can be mutually agreed, and training and promotional support provided. Second, staff may need some training in conflict handling to ensure that situations are handled calmly and that possibilities for win/win outcomes are identified. Third, where the conflict arises from multiple distribution channels, producers can try to partition markets. For example, Hallmark sells its premium greetings cards under its Hallmark brand name to upmarket department stores, and its standard cards under the Ambassador name to discount retailers.[24] Fourth, where poor performance is

the problem, the most effective solution is to improve performance so that the source of conflict disappears. Finally, in some cases, the conflict might be eliminated through the purchase of the other party or through coercion, where one party gains compliance through the use of force such as where a large retailer threatens to delist a manufacturer. The merger between Procter & Gamble and Gillette was seen by many as a move to put these two manufacturers on an equal footing with giant retailers like Walmart.

Retailing

Most retailing is conducted in stores such as supermarkets and department stores, but non-store retailing, such as online, mail order and automatic vending, also accounts for a large proportion of sales. Many large retailers exert enormous power in the distribution chain because of the vast quantities of goods they buy from manufacturers (see Marketing and Society 9.1). This power is reflected in their ability to extract 'guarantee of margins' from manufacturers. This is a clause inserted in a contract that ensures a certain profit margin for the retailer, irrespective of the retail price being charged to the customer. One manufacturer is played against another, and own-label brands are used to extract more profit.[25]

Major store and non-store types

Supermarkets

Supermarkets are large self-service stores, which traditionally sell food, drinks and toiletries, but the broadening of their ranges by some supermarket chains means that such items as non-prescription pharmaceuticals, cosmetics and clothing are also being sold. As Tesco seeks further growth beyond groceries, it has moved into a variety of new businesses including savings and insurance products, mobile and broadband telecoms as well as legal services. Carrefour, Europe's biggest retailer is renowned for its huge hypermarkets. In 2010, its average store size was 10,000 square metres stocking a vast array of food and non-food items. The main attractions of supermarkets are their convenient locations, wide product ranges and competitive prices. Supermarket operators are skilled marketers who use a variety of techniques such as psychological research, sensory experiences and loyalty schemes to capture a significant share of the market.

Department stores

Department stores are titled thus because related product lines are sold in separate departments, such as men's and women's clothing, jewellery, cosmetics, toys

Marketing and Society 9.1 Supermarket power

Love them or hate them but you cannot ignore them. Supermarkets are part of the way we live and they have gained enormous power over time. For example, the top four supermarkets in Britain – Tesco, Sainsbury's, Asda and Morrisons – account for over 76 per cent of all grocery purchases. Tesco is the biggest with 658 large supermarkets and over 1,800 convenience stores, and even in a period of declining performance, it was able to report profits of almost £1.5 billion in 2013. It takes £1 of every £8 spent by consumers in the UK. In other countries, levels of supermarket concentration are even higher. For example in Australia, the two biggest chains Coles and Woolworths control 70 per cent of the market and 23 cents in every dollar spent by consumers there goes to businesses owned by either of these two companies.

Many critics contend that this level of power is unacceptable. For example, suppliers argue that it puts them in a very difficult position because they are dependent on the supermarkets for their sales. If the supermarket demands lower supply prices, participation in special promotions or is slow to pay, there is usually very little that suppliers can do about it. As a result, many small suppliers cease trading which in turn means that their suppliers also suffer. From society's point of view, this is a worrying development. Branches of large supermarkets may argue that they bring employment to a local community. But over time other local businesses may be unable to compete with these supermarkets and local suppliers may cease trading, resulting in a loss of employment and economic activity in these communities. For example, in the 12 months to June 2005, 2,000 convenience stores closed down in the UK when supermarkets moved in.

Supermarkets also counter that they deliver value to customers by providing a wide range of products at low prices. But again this has led to unsustainable practices such as shipping food products from large scale suppliers in different parts of the world ahead of using local suppliers that leave a smaller carbon footprint. Lobby groups continue to campaign against the growth of supermarkets, and competition authorities around the world regularly conduct investigations of their activities. And in 2011, riots broke out in Bristol, UK, over the opening of a new Tesco store. It would appear that the controversy surrounding supermarkets is likely to run on for some time to come.

Reflection: Consider the arguments for and against supermarkets. Put forward your own point of view.

and home furnishings. In recent years such stores have been under increasing pressure from discount houses, speciality stores and the move to out-of-town shopping. Nevertheless, many continue to perform well in this competitive arena through a strategy of becoming one-stop shops for a variety of leading manufacturer brands, which are allocated significant store space.

Speciality shops

As their name suggests, these outlets specialize in a narrow product line. Many town centres, for example, have shops selling confectionery, cigarettes and newspapers in the same outlet. Many speciality outlets, such as Tie Rack and Sock Shop, sell only one product line. Specialization allows a deep product line to be sold in restricted shop space. Some speciality shops, such as butchers and greengrocers, focus on quality and personal service. Speciality shops can, however,

be vulnerable when tastes change or competition increases. For example, speciality sports retailers such as JJB Sports have collapsed as the blending of sportswear and fashion, driven by cultural icons such as David Beckham, has opened up the market to a host of other retailers such as fashion shops and supermarkets.

Discount houses

Discount houses sell products at low prices by accepting low margins, selling high volumes and bulk buying. For example, 'pound shops' sell a wide range of items such as fashion accessories, toys, stationery and tools for €1, and operate on low margins of 2–3 per cent. Good location and rapid product turnover are the keys to success. Low prices, sometimes promoted as sale prices, are offered throughout the year. Many discounters operate from out-of-town retail warehouses with the capacity to stock a wide range of merchandise. The UK pound shop, Poundland is Europe's biggest discount house. The company was founded in 1990 and by 2012 had 400 outlets throughout the UK, many in high-street locations.[26]

A growing form of discount retailing is factory outlet stores. These are usually out-of-town shopping locations comprising a wide range of manufacturer-owned retail shops that carry out-of-season stock or unsold products from department stores that are heavily discounted. Some of these outlet malls are repositioning themselves as premium outlets (rather than factory outlets) and feature prestigious brand names such as Versace, Gucci, Dolce & Gabbana, Ralph Lauren, Yves Saint Laurent and so on.

Category killers

These retail outlets have a narrow product focus, but an unusually large width and depth to that product range. Category killers emerged in the USA in the early 1980s as a challenge to discount houses. They are distinct from speciality shops in that they are bigger, and carry a wider and deeper range of products within their chosen product category; they are distinct from discount houses in their focus on only one product category. Examples of category killers are Toys R Us (toys), Nevada Bob's Discount Golf Warehouses (golf equipment), Woodies (DIY), Halfords (bicycles and auto accessories) and IKEA (furniture) (see Exhibit 9.5).

Convenience stores

Convenience stores, true to their name, offer customers the convenience of a close location and long opening hours every day of the week. Because they are small they may pay higher prices for their merchandise than supermarkets, and therefore have to charge higher prices to their customers. Some of these stores, such as Spar, join buying groups to gain some purchasing power and lower prices. The main customer need they fulfil is that of top-up buying – for example, when a customer is short of a carton of milk or loaf of bread. Societal changes, such as rising divorce rates, decreasing family sizes, long commuting times and time-poor consumers, have all combined to help revitalize the convenience store sector. Consumers are once again favouring quick, convenient purchases, as offered by convenience stores, over a big weekly shop at a supermarket. Consequently, major retailers like Tesco and Sainsbury's have been aggressively buying into this sector.

Catalogue stores

This type of retail outlet promotes its products through catalogues, which are either mailed to customers or available in-store or online for customers to view on-site (see Chapter 11). Purchase is in city-centre outlets where customers fill in order forms, pay for the goods and then collect them from a designated place in the store. In the UK, Argos is a successful catalogue retailer selling a wide range of discounted products such as electrical goods, jewellery, gardening tools, furniture, toys, car accessories, sports goods, luggage and cutlery.

Mail order

This non-store form of retailing may also employ catalogues as a promotional vehicle, but the purchase transaction is conducted via the mail (see Chapter 11). Alternatively, outward communication may be by direct mail, television, magazine or newspaper advertising. Increasingly, orders are being placed by telephone or over the Internet, a process that is facilitated by the use of credit cards as a means of payment. Goods are then sent by mail. Otto-Versand, the German mail-order company, owns Grattan, a UK mail-order retailer, and has leading positions in Austria, Belgium, Italy, the Netherlands and Spain. Its French rival, La Redoute, has expanded into Belgium, Italy and Portugal. Mail order offers the prospect of pan-European catalogues, central warehousing and processing of cross-border orders.

Automatic vending

Offering such products as drinks, confectionery, soup and newspapers in convenient locations, 24 hours a day, vending machines are particularly popular in some

Exhibit 9.5 This clever advert is by the Swedish firm IKEA, a hugely successful category killer in the furniture industry

Free

for babies born 9 months from today.

To celebrate Valentine's Day, IKEA is offering parents-to-be a free cot if your baby is born on 14 November 2013. Limit of one cot per baby. Proof of birth must be provided. Voucher must be presented to redeem offer. Delivery not included.

SNIGLAR cot
Normally $99
74x137xH84cm.
Beech.

Happy Valentine's Day
(see you in 9 months)

IKEA

countries, such as Japan. No sales staff are required, although restocking, servicing and repair costs can be high. Cash dispensers at banks have improved customer service by permitting round-the-clock financial services. However, machine breakdowns and out-of-stock situations can annoy customers.

Online retailing

Online retailing is one of the fastest-growing forms of distribution, and is proving particularly popular for products like electrical goods, groceries, clothing/footwear and music/video. It can take any of three major forms. First, in pure online retailing scenarios, the product is ordered, paid for and received online in a completely electronic transaction. Any product that can be digitized can be retailed in this way. Second, products can be ordered online and then distributed either through the postal system or through the use of local distribution companies in the case of groceries or wine, for example. Finally, most leading retailers have an online presence. For example, the top retailers that have a significant presence both online and offline include Tesco, Marks & Spencer, Argos, Next, Carrefour and Aldi. These retailers work hard to link both channels. For example, Argos customers can select products from the Argos catalogue, order online and pick them up from a local outlet.

Increasingly, retailers are opting for a dual online and offline channel. As well as established retailers selling via their websites, businesses that started life online are also increasing their physical presence. For example, Kiddicare, which is owned by Morrisons in the UK, purchased 10 superstore locations while Zolando, the German fashion website, has also been opening physical stores. Despite the growth of online banking, banks with the most branches in their networks are the most successful in building their revenues and profitability. Physical stores play an important brand awareness and brand building role for online retailers.

Online retailers possess several advantages which help to explain their rapid rise. First is the issue of location which is a central part of the competitive advantage of many offline retailers who made early investments and captured the best locations. However, in an online environment, location becomes less important. Second is flexibility. Online stores are open 24 hours per day, every day of the year, offering customer convenience. Product range is a significant advantage of online retailers. Physical bookstores, video game shops and so on are limited by the number of titles that they can carry making supply choices very important. Online retailers have relatively unlimited carrying capacity as their products are stored in huge warehouses, with other online affiliates or in digital

formats such as e-books with the result that they can potentially offer almost any niche product a consumer may be looking for. Fourth, the cost of doing business is relatively lower for an online retailer. Small players can establish a web presence relatively cheaply while offline retailers have to invest in store locations, shop fittings, sales personnel and so on. Finally, online businesses have access to a global market and one of the key marketing challenges is finding ways of driving customers from all over the world to your webstore.

Key retail marketing decisions

A retail outlet needs to be thought of as a brand involving the same set of decisions we discussed when we looked at branding in Chapter 6. Retailers need to anticipate and adapt to changing environmental circumstances, such as the growing role of information technology and changing customer tastes. However, there are a number of specific issues that relate to retailing, and are worthy of separate discussion.

Retail positioning

Retail positioning – as with all marketing decisions – involves the choice of target market and differential advantage. Targeting allows retailers to tailor their marketing mix (which includes product assortment, service levels, store location, prices and promotion) to the needs of their chosen customer segment. Differentiation provides a reason to shop at one store rather than another. A useful framework for creating a differential advantage has been proposed by Davies, who suggests that innovation in retailing can come only from novelty in the process offered to the shopper, or from novelty in the product or product assortment offered to the shopper.[27] The catalogue shop Argos in the UK has offered innovation in the process of shopping, whereas Next achieved success through product innovation (stylish clothes at affordable prices). Hard discounters like Aldi and Lidl stock primarily own-label products, which are sold at competitive prices (product innovation). This is the dominant retail form in Germany, where discounters have a 40 per cent market share, and is growing rapidly in other European countries. Toys R Us is an example of both product and process innovation through providing the widest range of toys at one location (product innovation) and thereby offering convenient, one-stop shopping (process innovation).

Store location

Conventional wisdom has it that the three factors critical to the success of a retailer are location, location and location. Convenience is an important issue for many shoppers, and so store location can have a major bearing on sales performance. Retailers have to decide on regional coverage, the towns and cities to target within regions, and the precise location to select within a given town or city. The choice of town or city will depend on such factors as correspondence with the retailer's chosen target market, the level of disposable income in the catchment area, the availability of suitable sites and the level of competition. The choice of a particular site may depend on the level of existing traffic (pedestrian and/or vehicular) passing the site, parking provision, access to the outlet for delivery vehicles, the presence of competition, planning restrictions and whether there is an opportunity to form new retailing centres with other outlets. For example, Starbucks has sought to locate its coffee shops on the side of the street most favoured by commuters going to work, based on the notion that consumers would not cross a busy street for a coffee. Also, two or more non-competing retailers (e.g. Sainsbury's and Boots) may agree to locate outlets together in an out-of-town centre to generate more pulling power than each could achieve individually. Having made that decision, the partners will look for suitable sites near their chosen town or city.

Product assortment

Retailers have to make a decision on the breadth and depth of their product assortment. A supermarket, for example, may decide to widen its product assortment from food, drink and toiletries to include clothes and toys: this is called 'scrambled merchandising'. For example, currently in the UK, supermarkets sell 24 per cent of all CDs, 8 per cent of books and 40 per cent of all newly released DVDs, which has implications for specialist CD/DVD and book retailers.[28] Scrambled merchandising becomes a basis through which retailers can differentiate themselves. Therefore, we see companies like McDonald's offering DVD rentals, Gap selling CD mixes, Starbucks selling music and Tesco selling Starbucks coffee!

Within each product line, a retailer can choose to stock a deep or shallow product range. Some retailers, like Tie Rack, Sock Shop and Toys R Us, stock one deep product line. Department stores, however, offer a much broader range of products, including toys, cosmetics, jewellery, clothes, electrical goods and household accessories. Some retailers begin with one product line and gradually broaden their product assortment to maximize revenue per customer. For example, petrol stations broadened their product range to include motor accessories and, more recently, confectionery, drinks, flowers and newspapers. Services like hot food and car washes offer much greater profit margins than the sale of petrol. A

by-product of this may be to reduce customers' price sensitivity since selection of petrol station may be based on the availability of other products there rather than the fact that it offers the lowest price.

Own-label branding gives rise to another product decision. Major retailers may decide to sell a range of own-label products to complement national brands. Often the purchasing power of these large retail chains means that prices can be lower and yet profit margins higher than for competing national brands. This makes the activity an attractive proposition for many retailers. For example, the electrical retailer DGSi which owns retail brands like Currys and PC World has developed a range of own-brands with the launch of Essential, Logik, Advent and Sandstrom. As the name suggests Essentials offers entry level household items such as kettles and fridges while Sandstrom is a premium range of TVs and other electrical goods.[29]

Price

Price is a key factor in store choice for some market segments. Consequently, some retailers major on price as their differential advantage. This requires vigilant cost control and massive buying power. A recent trend is towards the 'everyday low prices' favoured by retailers, rather than the higher prices supplemented by promotions that are supported by manufacturers. Retailers such as B&Q, the do-it-yourself discounter, maintain that customers prefer predictable low prices rather than occasional money-off deals, three-for-the-price-of-two offers and free gifts. Supermarket chains are also pressurizing suppliers to provide consistently low prices rather than temporary promotions. This action is consistent with the desire to position themselves on a low price platform. For example, in France, Carrefour has introduced a system whereby the bonuses of store managers are linked to whether prices are lower than those of comparable retailers. The importance of price competitiveness is reflected in the alliance of European food retailers called Associated Marketing Services. Retailers such as Morrisons (UK), Ahold (the Netherlands), ICA (a federation of Swedish food retailers), Migros (Finland), Delhaize Group (Belgium) and others have joined forces to foster co-operation in the areas of purchasing and marketing of brands. Their range of activities includes own branding, joint buying, the development of joint brands and services, and the exchange of information and skills. A key aim is to reduce cost price, since this accounts for 75 per cent of the sales price to customers.[30]

Store atmosphere

Atmosphere is created by a combination of the design, colour and layout of a store. Both exterior and interior design affect atmosphere. External factors include architectural design, signs, window displays and use of colour, which create an identity for a retailer and attract customers. The Body Shop, for example, projects its environmentally caring image through the green exterior of its shops, and through window displays that focus on environmental issues. Interior design also has a major impact on atmosphere. Store lighting, fixtures and fittings, and layout are important considerations. Colour, sound and smell can affect mood. Department stores often place perfume counters near the entrance, supermarkets may use the smell of baking bread to attract customers and upmarket shirt companies like Thomas Pink even pump the smell of freshly laundered linen around their stores. In addition, supermarkets often use music to create a relaxed atmosphere, whereas some boutiques use pop music to draw in their target customers.

Multi-sensory marketing describes an approach being adopted by retailers to appeal to as many senses as possible (see Marketing in Action 9.2).

As we saw in Chapter 7, the rise of experiential marketing has placed a significant focus on store atmospherics as retailers strive to create a shopping experience for consumers. Shoppers are considered to have three attention zones.[31] The first zone operates at a distance of 30 feet from the shopper, and requires the retailer to use a combination of sound, colour, scent and motion to attract potential buyers. At 10 feet what is important is placement on a shelf and an ability to stand out from competitors, placing a premium on how well manufacturers influence the distribution process. And, at 3 feet, the consumer is already holding a potential choice or reaching out for it, so it is the look and feel of the product or its packaging that is important.

Marketing in Action 9.2 The Hollister experience

Critical Thinking: Below is a review of Hollister's marketing strategy. Read it and critically evaluate the extent to which it uses multi-sensory marketing.

Hollister, the clothing company owned by Abercrombie & Fitch (A&F) is a prime example of the trend in retailing towards using multi-sensory marketing to enhance the customer experience. The company was founded in 2000 with the aim of appealing to young consumers. To do this, it decided to embrace the surfing lifestyle, as the sport was becoming increasingly popular and seen as cool. To do this, it even went as far as creating a back story that the company was the brainchild of J.M. Hollister, founded in 1922 and inspired by the laid back, California culture. It was positioned as an aspirational lifestyle destination – in other words, though it may not appeal to the true surfing community, it would appeal to the larger masses who aspired to that lifestyle.

Much of the chain's success is credited to its in-store experience. The exterior of the shops is meant to look like beach shacks with shuttered windows and a boardwalk to the entrance. As a result, Hollister shops stand out from other outlets in a shopping mall. The interior is dimly

lit with spotlights above the merchandise and divided into two sections, 'Dudes' and 'Bettys'. In 2007, the company outfitted its stores with flat-screen TVs that play a live feed to the surf conditions at Huntington Beach pier. Stores are scented with the company's signature SoCal fragrance and it plays music (surfing tunes of course!) at between 80–85 decibels – just under the legal requirement which would force it to provide auditory safety equipment for staff. In the middle of the shops is a lounge area complete with chairs, surf and other general interest magazines and potted palm trees.

The company's international growth has been rapid. By 2013, it had almost 600 outlets mainly in the USA and Canada but also in the UK, France, Spain, Germany, Italy and a number of other European countries. It was also the largest selling brand in the A&F group, generating sales of over $760 million.

Based on: Anonymous (2013);[32] Hunter (2008);[33] Marcus (2010).[34]

Physical distribution

Earlier in this chapter we examined channel strategy and management decisions, which concern the choice of the correct outlets to provide product availability to customers in a cost-effective manner. Physical distribution decisions focus on the efficient movement of goods from producer to intermediaries and the consumer. Clearly, channel and physical distribution decisions are interrelated, although channel decisions tend to be made earlier. Physical distribution is defined as a set of activities concerned with the physical flows of materials, components and finished goods from producer to channel intermediaries and consumers. It is a business that has become increasingly complex as customers such as Walmart, Tesco and others extend their global reach. This has given rise to mergers between logistics companies such as that involving Exel and Tibbet & Britten, as companies seek to provide integrated solutions for their clients ranging from warehouse management to home delivery.[35]

Distribution aims to provide intermediaries and customers with the right products, in the right quantities, in the right locations, at the right time. Distribution problems caused by, for example, a move to a new warehouse frequently impact on corporate performance. Physical distribution activities have been the subject of managerial attention for some time because of the potential for cost savings and improving customer service levels. Cost savings can be achieved by reducing inventory levels, using cheaper forms of transport and shipping in bulk rather than small quantities. For example, Benetton's blueprint for reviving its fortunes has been predicated on getting clothes from the factory to the shop rail faster to enable it to compete with fast fashion retailers like Zara and H&M.[36] Customer service levels can be improved by fast and reliable delivery, including just-in-time (JIT) delivery, holding high inventory levels so that customers have a wide choice and the chances of stock-outs are reduced, fast order processing, and ensuring that products arrive in the right quantities and quality. Physical distribution management concerns the balance between cost reduction and meeting customer service requirements. Trade-offs are often necessary. For example, low inventory and slow, cheaper transportation methods reduce costs but lower customer service levels and satisfaction.

As well as the trade-offs between physical distribution costs and customer service levels, there is the potential for conflict between elements of the physical distribution system itself. For example, low-cost containers may lower packaging costs but raise the cost of goods damaged in transit. This fact, and the need to coordinate order processing, inventory and transportation decisions, means that physical distribution needs to be managed as a system, with a manager overseeing the whole process..

The key elements of the physical distribution system are customer service, order processing, inventory control, warehousing, transportation and materials handling.

Customer service

It is essential to set customer service standards. For example, a customer service standard might be that 90 per cent of orders are delivered within 48 hours of receipt and 100 per cent are delivered within 72 hours. Higher customer service standards normally mean higher costs as inventory levels need to be higher. In some cases, customers value consistency in delivery time rather than speed. For example, a customer service standard of guaranteed delivery within five working days may be valued more than 60 per cent within two and 100 per cent within seven days. Customer service standards should be given considerable attention for they may be the differentiating factor between suppliers: they may be used as a key customer choice criterion. Methods of improving customer service standards include improving product availability, improving order cycle time, raising information levels and improving flexibility. An example of raising information levels is the kind of service now being provided online by courier companies like Federal Express and UPS, which offer their customers a facility whereby they can log on and get immediate updates on delivery status. However, in modern global supply chains, the outsourcing of activities means a lack of control, which can impact on customer service. For example, a small disruption in its material supplies from Southeast Asia affected Zara's service levels and sales in 2005.

 DHL Ad Insight: The 'Speed of Yellow' campaign illustrates the value the logistics company creates for its customers.

Order processing

This relates to the question of how orders are handled. Reducing time between a customer placing an order and receiving the goods may be achieved through careful analysis of the components that make up order processing time. A computer link between the salesperson and the order department may be effective. Electronic data interchange can also speed order processing time by checking the customer's credit rating, and whether the goods are in stock, issuing an order to the warehouse, invoicing the customer and updating the inventory records.

Inventory control

Inventory control deals with the question of how much inventory should be held. A balance has to be found between the need to have products in stock to meet customer demand and the costs incurred in holding large inventories. Having in stock every conceivable item a customer might order would normally be prohibitively expensive for companies marketing many items. Decisions also need to be taken about when to order new stocks. These order points are normally before stock levels reach zero because of the lead time between ordering and receiving inventory. The JIT inventory system is designed to reduce lead times so that the order point (the stock level at which re-ordering takes place), and overall inventory levels for production items, are low. The more variable the lead time between ordering and receiving stocks, and the greater the fluctuation in customer demand, the higher the order point. This is because of the uncertainty caused by the variability leading to the need for **safety (buffer) stocks** in case lead times are unpredictably long or customer demand unusually high. How much to order depends on the cost of holding stock and order-processing costs. Orders can be small and frequent, or large and infrequent. Small, frequent orders raise order-processing costs but reduce inventory carrying costs; large, infrequent orders raise inventory costs but lower order-processing expenditure.

Warehousing

This part of the distribution chain involves all the activities required in the storing of goods between the time they are produced and the time they are transported to the customer. These activities include breaking bulk, making up product assortments for delivery to customers, storage and loading. Storage warehouses hold goods for moderate or long time periods, whereas distribution centres operate as central locations for the fast movement of goods. Retailing organizations use regional distribution centres where suppliers deliver products in bulk. These shipments are broken down into loads that are then quickly transported to retail outlets. Distribution centres are usually highly automated, with computer-controlled machinery facilitating the movement of goods. A computer reads orders and controls the fork-lift trucks that gather goods and move them to loading bays. Further technological advances are likely to have a

significant impact on warehousing and the movement of goods through the supply chain. Warehousing strategy involves the determination of the location and the number of warehouses or distribution centres to be used. The trend is towards a smaller number of ever larger warehouses. For example, the UK retailer Boots closed its 17 regional distribution centres in favour of a £70 million automated warehouse in Nottingham. At the extreme, some retailers are seeking single distribution centres for the whole of Europe), with locations such as Moissy-Cramayel in France measuring the size of 350 football pitches.[37]

Transportation

This refers to the means by which products will be transported; the five major modes are rail, road, air, water and pipeline. Railways are efficient at transporting large, bulky freight on land over long distances and are often used to transport coal, chemicals, oil, aggregates and nuclear flasks. Rail is more environmentally friendly than road, but the major problem with it is lack of flexibility. Motorized transport by road has the advantage of flexibility because of direct access to companies and warehouses. This means that lorries can transport goods from supplier to receiver without unloading en route. However, the growth of road transport in Europe, and particularly the UK, has received considerable criticism because of increased traffic congestion, damage done to roads by heavy juggernauts and the impact on the environment. The key advantages of air freight are its speed and long distance capabilities. Its speed means that it is often used to transport perishable goods and emergency deliveries. Its major disadvantages are high cost, and the need to transport goods by road to and from air terminals. Water transportation is slow but inexpensive. Inland transportation is usually associated with bulky, low-value, non-perishable goods such as coal, ore, grain, steel and petroleum. Ocean-going ships carry a wider range of products. When the cost benefits of international sea transportation outweigh the speed advantage of air freight, water shipments may be chosen. But some industries, such as fashion retailing, have seen production move from low-cost countries like China to Eastern Europe and Turkey because it takes 22 days by water to reach the UK from China compared with five days from Turkey. So, although the cost of production is lower in China, the fast turnaround of fashion items makes sea transportation unappealing. Finally, pipelines are a dependable and low-maintenance form of transportation for liquids and gases such as crude petroleum, water and natural gas.

Materials handling

Materials handling involves the activities related to the movement of products in the producer's plant, warehouses and transportation depots. Modern storage facilities tend to be of just one storey, allowing a high level of automation. In some cases robots are used to conduct materials-handling tasks. Lowering the human element in locating inventory and assembling orders has reduced error and increased the speed of these operations. For example, the pharmaceuticals distributor Cahill May Roberts has replaced a paper-based system with Vocollect voice technology whereby material handlers speak to computers to confirm the products that they have collected rather than making paper records. It distributes in the region of 180,000 product units per day to pharmacies in Ireland and accurate records are critical because of the nature of the products being dealt with.[38] Two key developments in materials handling are unit handling and containerization. Unit handling achieves efficiency by combining multiple packages on pallets that can be moved by fork-lift trucks. Containerization involves the combination of large quantities of goods (e.g. car components) in a single large container. Once sealed, such containers can easily be transferred from one form of transport to another.

Summary

In this chapter we have examined the key issue of delivering products and services to customers. In particular, the following issues were addressed.

1. There are important differences in the structure of consumer, industrial and service channels. Consumer channels tend to be longer and involve more channel partners, while many industrial and service channels are direct to the customer.

2. Channel strategy involves three key decisions, namely, channel selection, distribution intensity and channel integration. These decisions must be made in line with the firm's overall marketing strategy. For example, positioning decisions may drive the number and type of channel members selected to distribute a product and the extent to which they are controlled.

3. The key channel management issues are the selection and motivation of middlemen, providing them with training, evaluating their performance and resolving any channel conflict issues that may arise. Effective support for channel members is often necessary to achieve marketing objectives.

4. There is a diverse range of retail types, including supermarkets, department stores, speciality shops, discount houses, category killers, convenience stores, catalogue stores, mail order, vending machines and online retailing.

5. The key retail marketing decisions include retail positioning, store location, product assortment, price and store atmosphere. Many retailers are strong brands in their own right and need to be managed as such. Technology has enabled some Internet retailers to achieve major competitive advantages in their markets.

6. Physical distribution concerns decisions relating to customer service, order processing, inventory control, warehousing, transportation and materials handling, which impact on the efficiency and effectiveness of the supply chain. Cost and customer service are two conflicting pressures that impact upon the structure and management of the physical distribution system.

Study questions

1. A friend of yours who has been pursuing pottery as a hobby has just formed a business selling a range of gift items. Advise the founder on her options for distributing the company's products.

2. Evaluate the three distribution intensity options that are available to an organization. In what kinds of circumstances might each be used?

3. Describe situations that can lead to conflict between channel members. What can be done to avoid and resolve conflict?

4. Discuss the impact of the growth of online retailing on other retail formats.

5. Discuss the reasons why more and more distribution channels are being characterized by a small number of large central distribution centres rather than by a large number of relatively small outlets.

6. Visit www.starbucks.com and www.costa.co.uk. Compare and contrast these two coffee chains in terms of the major retail marketing decisions such as retail positioning, product assortment, store location and store atmospherics.

Suggested reading

Anderson, C. (2006) *The Long Tail: The New Economics of Culture and Commerce*, London: Random House Books.

Corstjens, J. and **M. Corstjens** (1995) *Store Wars: The Battle for Mindspace and Shelfspace*, New York: John Wiley & Sons.

Ferdows, K., M.A. Lewis and **J. Machuca** (2004) Rapidfire Fulfillment, *Harvard Business Review*, **82** (11), 104–11.

Jerath, K. and **J. Zhang** (2010) Store within a Store, *Journal of Marketing Research*, **47** (4), 748–63.

Myers, J.B., A.D. Pickersgill and **E.S. Van Metre** (2004) Steering Customers to the Right Channels, *McKinsey Quarterly*, **4**, 36–48.

Rigby, D. (2011) The Future of Shopping, *Harvard Business Review*, **89** (12) 64–75.

When you have read this chapter

log on to the Online Learning Centre for
Foundations of Marketing at
www.mheducation.co.uk/textbooks/fahy5
where you'll find links and extra online study tools for marketing.

References

1. **Anonymous** (2013) John Lewis: Harnessing the Power of Emotion, Emap Inc. Warc.com; **Bold, B.** (2013) John Lewis' Epic Journey: The Evolution of its Christmas Campaigns from 2007-2013, *Marketingmagazine.co.uk*, 7 November; **Burrell, I.** (2013) First View: John Lewis Christmas Commercial: The Bear and the Hare, *Independent.co.uk*, 8 November.

2. **Fahy, J.** and **F. Taguchi** (1995) Reassessing the Japanese Distribution System, *Sloan Management Review*, Winter.

3. **Anonymous** (2011) The Co-op Strikes Back, *The Economist*, 29 January, 58.

4. **Narus, J.A.** and **J.C. Anderson** (1986) Industrial Distributor Selling: The Roles of Outside and Inside Sales, *Industrial Marketing Management*, **15**, 55 62.

5. **Anonymous** (2008) Shock to the System, *The Economist*, 2 February, 67-8.

6. **Rosenbloom, B.** (1987) *Marketing Channels: A Management View*, Hinsdale, IL: Dryden, 160.

7. **Anonymous** (2014) Moving Pictures, *Economist.com*, 14 March.

8. **Bertoni, S.** (2013) Silicon Valley's First Billionaire Aims to Dominate Images on Web, *Forbes.com*, 10 September.

9. **Laurance, B.** (1993) MMC in Bad Odour Over Superdrug Ruling, *Guardian*, 12 November, 18.

10. **Anonymous** (1993) EC Rejects Unilever Appeal on Cabinets, *Marketing*, 25 February, 6.

11. **Jack, A.** (2007) Wholesalers to Seek Injunction on Pfizer's Drug Distribution Plan, *Financial Times*, 1 March, 4.

12. **Voyle, S.** (2003) Supply Chain Feels Fresh Pressure, *Financial Times*, 28 April, 23.

13. **Helmore, E.** (1997) Restaurant Kings, or just Silly Burgers? *Observer*, 8 June, 5.

14. **Hopkinson, G.C.** and **S. Hogarth Scott** (1999) Franchise Relationship Quality: Microeconomic Explanations, *European Journal of Marketing*, **33** (9/10), 827-43.

15. **Rosenbloom, B.** (1987) *Marketing Channels: A Management View*, Hinsdale, IL: Dryden, 160.

16. **Shipley, D.D., D. Cook** and **E. Barnett** (1989) Recruitment, Motivation, Training and Evaluation of Overseas Distributors, *European Journal of Marketing*, **23** (2), 79-93.

17. See **Shipley, D.D.** and **S. Prinja** (1988) The Services and Supplier Choice Influences of Industrial Distributors, *Service Industries Journal*, **8** (2), 176-87; **Webster, F.E.** (1976) The Role of the Industrial Distributor in Marketing Strategy, *Journal of Marketing*, **40**, 10-16.

18. See **Pegram, R.** (1965) *Selecting and Evaluating Distributors*, New York: National Industrial Conference Board, 109-25; **Shipley, D.D., D. Cook** and **E. Barnett** (1989) Recruitment, Motivation, Training and Evaluation of Overseas Distributors, *European Journal of Marketing*, 23 (2), 79-93.

19. **Coyle, D.** (2004) Budget Travel Accuses Agents of Blacklisting, *Irish Times*, 16 November, 16; **Coyle, D.** (2005) Challenges Circle Overhead for Tour Operator, *Irish Times Business*, 7 January, 22.

20. **Anonymous** (2014) Burying the Hachette, *Economist*, 31 May, 58.

21. **Ward, A.** (2007) Coca-Cola's Bottlers Settle Dispute Over Distribution, *Financial Times*, 13 February, 2.

22. **Slattery, L.** (2007) Concern at Merger Plan for Distributor Eason, *Irish Times*, 29 January, 18.

23. **Sexton, P.** (2005) A Music Sales Storm is Brewing in a Coffee Shop, *Financial Times*, 21 June, 14.

24. **Hardy, K.G.** and **A.J. Magrath** (1988) Ten Ways for Manufacturers to Improve Distribution Management, *Business Horizons*, November-December, 68.

25. **Krishnan, T.V.** and **H. Soni** (1997) Guaranteed Profit Margins: A Demonstration of Retailer Power, *International Journal of Research in Marketing*, **14**, 35-56.

26. **Bloom, J.** (2012) How Did Pound Shops Change the UK?, BBC. com, 11 December.

27. **Davies, G**. (1992) Innovation in Retailing, *Creativity and Innovation Management*, I (4), 230.

28. **Rigby, E**. (2006) Supermarkets Prepare to Beef Up Non-Food Ranges, *Financial Times*, 21 February, 5.

29. **Baker, R**. (2010) DSGi Ready to Do Battle With Consumer Brands, *MarketingWeek.co.uk*, 3 August.

30. **Elg, U**. and **U. Johansson** (1996) Networking When National Boundaries Dissolve: The Swedish Food Sector, *European Journal of Marketing*, **30** (2), 62–74.

31. **Roberts, K**. (2006) *The Lovemarks Effect: Winning in the Consumer Revolution*, New York: Powerhouse Books.

32. **Anonymous** (2013) Abercrombie & Fitch Report Record Sales and Strong Earnings Growth, *Online.wsg.com*, 22 February.

33. **Hunter, J**. (2008) How Hollister Co. Stole Surf: Eight Years After Abercrombie & Fitch Invaded the Surf Market, What Can Be Done to Defend Against Them?, *Business.Transworld.net*, 7 August.

34. **Marcus, M**. (2010) Abercrombie Tries to Ride Hollister to New Highs, *Forbes.com*, 17 February.

35. **Felsted, A**. and **S. Goff** (2004) Going Global is Crucial to Deliver Goods, *Financial Times*, 17 June, 27.

36. **Anonymous** (2003) Benetton Starts 'Dring' Drive, *Financial Times*, 10 December, 33.

37. **Pickard, J**. (2005) Growing Trend sees Warehouses Swell, *Financial Times*, 17 August, 25.

38. **Lillington, K**. (2008) Giving Voice to New Technology, *Irish Times Health Supplement*, 29 January, 4.

Cinnabon: on a roll across all channels

THE COMPANY

Founded in Seattle in 1985 and now based in Atlanta, Cinnabon, Inc. is the market leader among cinnamon roll bakeries. In 2004, US food parent company AFC Enterprises Inc. sold the Cinnabon unit of its business to Focus Brands Inc. for over $30 million. Focus Brands Inc. is an affiliate of the buyout firm, Roark Capital Group, based in Atlanta and is the umbrella company that also owns Carvel ice cream, Schlotzsky's Sandwich Shop, Auntie Anne's Pretzel Company and Moe's Southwest Grill.

Cinnabon produces fresh, aromatic, oven-hot cinnamon rolls, as well as a variety of other baked goods and speciality beverages. Cinnabon currently operates more than 1,200 franchised locations across 56 countries worldwide, primarily in high traffic venues such as shopping malls, airports, train stations, travel plazas, entertainment centres and military establishments.

Cinnabon is also a multichannel licensor, partnering with other companies to provide brand licensed products at food-service and retail venues (e.g. Burger King, Taco Bell). Other channels include entertainment (e.g. casinos and theme parks), shopping (e.g. in malls), grocery (where the company's cinnamon is included in other products) and travel (e.g. airports and travel plazas). Sales are expected to top $1 billion at year end 2013-14 achieved across over 60,000 distribution points through the multiple channels. The brand positions itself worldwide as offering a 'special indulgence' using cinnamon as a key ingredient to provide customers with a sensory taste experience. There are 70 Cinnabon branded products including new additions such as Pinnacle Cinnabon Vodka and Airwick Cinnabon air fresheners and candles.

In 2014-15 the company will be opening 230 new outlets; 125 in the USA and a further 105 international ones giving a total of 632 domestic and 567 international retail outlets. This builds on the already impressive growth of 2013-14 which saw an additional 210 outlets open, with 100 of these in international markets.

Leadership and culture

Since 2011 the company has been led by Kat Cole, appointed president at age 32. Highly entrepreneurial in character, Cole instils an action-oriented culture of 'can-do' in her corporate team of 43 across the Cinnabon corporate operation. She encourages staff to experiment, to challenge the status quo and to have no fear of failure. She states that the franchise operation, given the relatively small size of each outlet, is 'small and nimble' and that the company can respond quickly to opportunity and be creative in that response. Constantly opportunity focused, Cole underlines that new ideas come from many sources, including the company's resident advisory forum, their head chef and food innovation team, the marketing team and not least the customers and Cole herself. New products can take a year to come to market while augmentation and smaller changes can be rolled out in a few months. Cole recently launched Cinnabon vodka which may seem initially like a poor fit for a bakery company but flavoured vodka is a rapidly growing market in the USA and the distinctive cinnamon flavour used by the company in its products is already established through the famous baked goods range. Cole remains an accessible presence in the company for customers as well as staff. As a 'digital native' she has a strong presence on social media and manages her own LinkedIn and Twitter dialogue. In terms of the company's social media presence she actively contributes to it displaying an authenticity and visibility that is unusual for executives at her level.[1] The company is very focused on building a presence through both social media (Facebook, LinkedIn, YouTube, Foursquare) and traditional channels (TV, press) as well as having industry credibility and profile enhanced through effective PR in the industry press (e.g. *Restaurant News, Franchise Help, Food Network*).

The company's mission, vision and strategy are communicated thus:

- Mission: Make Our Guest Say WoW!
- Vision: To Become One of the World's Greatest Food Brands
- Strategy: Build World Class Food Brand through Strong Global Franchise System and High Quality Multi Channel Growth

The growth strategy is multi-faceted and includes the following actions:

1. Build the Brand: Achieve Relevance & Differentiation
2. Multi Channel Work, Products, Remodels
3. Operate Awesome Bakeries: WoW our Guests!
4. Operational Excellence & Accountability
5. Build Franchise Partner Profitability
6. Expand our Points of Distribution
7. Grocery, Club, Retail, Franchise
8. Positively impact our employees and our communities.

The market

The global baked goods industry is expected to exceed $310 billion in 2015, according to research from Global Industry

[1] For example, Cole participated in the US version of the television series *Undercover Boss* shortly after starting at the company.

Analysis. The market for baked and pastry goods is being driven by changing lifestyles, which leaves consumers little time to prepare meals leading to an increase in snacking. Busy consumers are increasingly quick to buy convenient baked snack foods such as wraps and sandwiches. In 2013, the US bakery sector's market size accounted for revenues exceeding $75 billion (Euromonitor International, 2014). The UK bakery sector is worth £3.6 billion and is one of the largest markets in the food industry. Total UK volume at present is just under 4 billion units; the equivalent of almost 11 million loaves and packs is sold every single day. Within the Bakery-Café segment of this sector is the 'snack' sub-segment which is where Cinnabon's products would be officially classified. The snack market has been enjoying high single digit growth in recent years while Bakery-Café has been thriving.

The Bakery-Café industry is heating up as consumers warm to the idea of moderately priced, high quality menu offerings. Bakery cafés specialize in serving flour-based baked goods and complementary food items such as sandwiches, salads and soups for immediate consumption. The industry has surged ahead since the recession and outperformed the overall food service sector, driven largely by changing consumer preferences. Consumers are increasingly demanding healthy, gourmet and custom-made cuisine at an affordable price. Based on these trends, industry revenue is expected to grow at an impressive rate of 6.5 per cent per year on average over the five years to 2013. As operators add more stores in 2013 and consumer awareness of this relatively new segment increases within the food sector, industry revenue is expected to jump 7.2 per cent in 2013 to $7.1 billion.

According to IBISWorld Industry Analyst Andy Brennan, 'The industry has undergone heavy consolidation over the past five years as major chains such as Panera Bread, Einstein Bros. Bagels and Tim Hortons have expanded rapidly.' The franchise model most of the major players operate under has accommodated the rapid growth in establishments as operators require less capital and take on lower risk while growing market share. A number of small, independent bakery cafés which have traditionally serviced local markets have been pushed out of the industry, unable to compete with the geographic reach and marketing spend of the major chains. The Bakery-Café sector is expected to continue on a growth trajectory over the next five years as many of the same trends that have influenced the industry continue. As the largest industry operators continue to expand their market presence, smaller operators are expected to be forced out of the market to an even greater extent. Small local bakery cafés are therefore expected to struggle the most in this industry and IBISWorld expects that they will continue to have to fend off larger operations to maintain their markets.

The customer

A Cinnabon's customer is motivated to impulse purchase a Cinnabon product as a 'treat or indulgence'. Signature products are targeted by time of day with tasty treats tailored for morning, mid-day and late afternoon snacking. Cole talks about the role of the company in offering customers 'permission to indulge' and highlights the importance of 'guest first' in the training provided to franchise outlet staff.

The fact that the Cinnabon product range is largely bought on impulse means that the retail environment must be conducive to that quick sale. In practice this means having the Cinnabon product range well displayed – 'customers eat with their eyes first', says Cole – and also support merchandizing must be well positioned based on traffic flow patterns in the respective outlets. However, the Cinnabon proposition also extends beyond the tangible product and service differentiation is important to Cinnabon and to Cole. In that customer-oriented service environment the sales process is more fully enabled and enhanced by the pervasive aroma of cinnamon. Indeed, the #1 driver for purchase has been found to be aroma so the ovens are constantly baking through the day and filling the air of the outlets with the smell of cinnamon.

The Cinnabon proposition

Over 60 per cent of Cinnabon's sales come from its core product – the cinnamon Classic roll (see Exhibit C9.1). Beverages account for 15–20 per cent of revenues in the UK while in the EU this is closer to 35 per cent given higher levels of coffee consumption.[2] Beyond the core product, the product portfolio also includes baked goods such as the Minibon, Cinnabon Bites, Caramel Pecanbon, CinnaPacks and Cinnabon Stix – all made with the company's signature Makara cinnamon.

Distribution and delivery

Cinnabon operates a multichannel distribution system. The product is typically sold in high customer traffic contexts. Cole classifies these as:

- Entertainment (casinos, theme parks): characterized by an infrequent customer visit pattern, high permission to

indulge and offering the highest financial return to the company.
- Travel (airports): characterized by relatively infrequent customer visit patterns, medium permission to indulge and offering the second highest level of unit sales.
- Shopping (malls): characterized by high levels of customer visit patterns, and relatively lower obvious permission to indulge.

In addition, there are 1,200 flagship retail outlets / bakeries and 200 domestic express / mini-bakeries. These focus on licensed and manufactured products. The company has established partnerships with Pillsbury, Kellogg's, Burger King and Taco Bell.

The average customer sale in-bakery is valued at $6 (food and beverage). In the franchise operation of 1,200 outlets, 200 million unit sales are delivered annually, the 50,000 grocery outlets deliver 400 million unit sales and within food service, 10,000 outlets deliver 400 million unit sales annually. Income streams are variable across platforms however as in grocery and food-service Cinnabon only receives a royalty from their licence agreement with that distributor.

As to the challenges of managing a multichannel global brand, there are many. One is around preserving the brand's positioning as the company extends into many channels. Cole explains, 'In a market like Houston Texas, for example, you can get Cinnabon branded products at Taco Bell or Burger King or you can visit an entire Cinnabon bakery franchise location which made the system famous with our aroma and broadest variety of beverages and baked goods or you could visit a "Pilot Flying J" truck stop or a Schlotzsky's restaurant that both have tiny Cinnabon bakeries inside of them. No matter where you are going, or your appetite, in that one single city there are many different ways to engage with the brand at varying price points and environments. As more products go to market a challenge is continuing to protect the exact aromas, flavours and attributes that made the brand famous and that consumers are likely seeking in these alternative products.' She continues, 'As Cinnabon launches more products that are sold by other restaurant chains now we are distancing the end product from its origin, and so that puts more hands, and more brands, into the process increasing the likelihood for divergence from the core brand values or poor execution of the proposition. Resources and systems are in place to measure the end user experience. We research the consumer's brand impression after experiencing products across channels and feedback loops mean we have continuous improvement of the process and therefore we can refine and improve consumer experiences as a result.'

In the digital age Cole proposes that multichannel coordination is as important within traditional media initiatives as it is within social media communication. All restaurants and retailers who partner with Cinnabon communicate for mutual advantage through social media. Cole explains, 'We tweet each other's posts forward, "like" and connect each other's communities so that we are bringing communities who love the brand together to create mutual benefit across other products

Exhibit C9.1 The Cinnabon classic roll

[2] Excludes sales for new Vodka product

and all channels. You would think that there would be risk of cannibalization, or concern from one company or brand that may open up visibility to other retailers or brands that we could hurt the sales of that product. But we have found the opposite is actually true, as the brand becomes more relevant and the entire market pie increases!'

Growth ambitions

Cole sees great potential for the franchise operation delivering through the rapidly expanding 'travel centres' on the US highway network ('truck stop cafes' on the UK's motorway system). Such travel centres or plazas are developing rapidly in the US and of new franchise outlets opened last year by Cinnabon over a third of these were in highway travel centres – in 2014-15 this figure will rise to almost half. Adapting how the Cinnabon product is packaged and delivered through these more mobile/transitional contexts is a current focus for the company. The company is also innovating around 'portable packaging' which, given changing consumption patterns, would allow some Cinnabon products to be consumed 'on the go'. Under Cole's opportunity-driven leadership Cinnabon continues to strive for innovative distribution and delivery solutions that will differentiate the company from emerging international competition well into the future.

Suggested reading

Berry, L.L., Shankar, V., Turner Parish, J., Cadwallader, S. and Dotzel, T. (2006) Creating New Markets through Service Innovation, *Sloan Management Review*, 47 (2), 56–63.

Bitner, M.J. (1992) Servicescapes: The Impact of Physical Surroundings on Customers and Employees, *Journal of Marketing*, 56, April, 57–71.

Levitt, T. (1983) After the Sale is Over, *Harvard Business Review*, September–October, 87–93.

Read, S., Sarasvathy, S., Dew, N., Wiltbank, R. and Ohlsson, A.V. (2011) *Effectual Entrepreneurship*, Routledge, Chapter 11, 96–105.

Questions

1. Thinking about the distribution channels for Cinnabon how would you categorize their model by channel (i.e. consumer, industrial, service) and by strategy (i.e. selection, distribution intensity and integration)?
2. Where does customer value accrue through Cinnabon's distribution system and what is the role of the service staff member in creating such value at the point of delivery?
3. As Cinnabon expands its product range and embraces new partnership arrangements what do you see as the challenges for managing the essence of the Cinnabon brand?
4. In the digital age how is Cinnabon integrating social media into its delivery model to customers?

This case was prepared by Mark Durkin and Lynsey Hollywood, Ulster Business School, University of Ulster, Northern Ireland from various published sources as a basis for class discussion rather than to show effective or ineffective management.

Chapter 10

Integrated Marketing Communications I: Mass Communications Techniques

Chapter outline

Integrated marketing communications

Stages in developing an integrated communications campaign

Advertising

Sales promotion

Public relations and publicity

Sponsorship

Other promotional techniques

Learning outcomes

By the end of this chapter you will:

1 Explain the concept of integrated marketing communications (IMC)

2 Understand the stages involved in developing and conducting an integrated marketing communications campaign

3 Analyse the nature and role of advertising in the IMC mix

4 Critique the role of advertising in society

5 Analyse the roles played by sales promotion, public relations and sponsorship in the IMC mix

6 Explain the roles played by exhibitions, product placement, ambient advertising and guerrilla marketing in the IMC mix.

Coca-Cola: share a Coke

Advertising is perhaps the most public face of marketing. Television advertising in particular has the power to shock, to annoy and to make people laugh or cry. Ads are analysed, talked about, shared on social media and complained about to the relevant authorities. Advertising is a key part of popular culture both influencing the way we live and reflecting it. Songs that are used as the soundtracks to ad campaigns frequently return to the top of the music charts and television shows like *Mad Men* document life in the industry, or at least how it used to be.

Coca-Cola is a company that has been long renowned for its advertising work. Founded in 1886, it has dominated the global soft drinks industry for over a century. Its brand is still one of the most highly valued in the world, estimated to be worth over $78 billion in 2013. Advertising has always been a key part of the Coca-Cola success story. In particular, it has been admired for being able to capture the spirit of each new generation maintaining its appeal and relevance despite the many changes that have taken place in society over that time

An example of this ability to capture the essence of an age is its campaign, Share a Coke. The idea was originally trialled in Australia in 2011 and was an immediate success. It increased traffic to the Coca-Cola Facebook page by 870 per cent and generated a 39 per cent growth in likes. As a result of the campaign, sales grew by 7 per cent, a significant level of increase in a mature product category. The core of the campaign is the inclusion of a first name on the label of each bottle. Customers are then invited to share a Coke with a person who has that name. It is a strategy that taps into some core elements of human nature particularly among Coke's core audience of teens and young adults. Being socially connected is very important for this group and Coke's goal was to make its brand the centrepiece of the formation and development of these relationships. It also taps into one of the most personal things about all of us – our first names, indirectly connecting us with a brand that we may have forgotten about.

The business case for the Share a Coke campaign was a strong one. When the campaign was first run in Australia, the company's brand health measures there were very good but its sales were falling. In other words, consumers reported that they liked the Coke brand but this was not translating into purchases. Largely due to the economic downturn, consumers were switching to private label brands or consuming branded products like Coke less often. The two-fold objectives of the campaign were to get people talking about Coca-Cola and consuming the brand more often. The simple idea of putting first names on the packaging created a high level of social buzz and the opportunity for sharing images of the Coke brand on social media platforms. Once again Coca-Cola was at the centre of popular culture. The campaign has been rolled out worldwide with similar levels of success, demonstrating the global power of a good idea.[1]

As well as deciding what form of value an organization is proposing to offer its customers, it is also important to make a series of decisions regarding how this value is going to be communicated in the marketplace. As we saw in Chapters 3 and 5 particularly, these are very important decisions owing to the sheer volume of marketing messages that are currently aimed at consumers and the likelihood that many of these messages will not even be attended to, not to mention affect recipients in the ways that might be intended. This makes the study of marketing communications one of the most fascinating aspects of marketing as we seek to answer questions regarding what kinds of messages we should create and how we should communicate them. There are two major classes of tools available to the marketer. Mass communications techniques such as television advertising or sponsorship can be used, and these kinds of techniques will be the focus of this chapter. In addition, many organizations use direct communications techniques such as mobile marketing and social networking, and these direct and online techniques are examined in Chapter 11.

The overall range of techniques available to the marketer is usually known as the 'promotional mix' and comprises seven main elements.

1   *Advertising*: any paid form of non-personal communication of ideas or products in the prime media (television, press, posters, cinema and radio).
2   *Sales promotion*: incentives to consumers or the trade that are designed to stimulate purchase (competitions, special offers).
3   *Publicity*: communications for a product or business by placing information about it in the media without paying for the time or space directly (media interviews, blogs).
4   *Sponsorship*: the association of the company or its products with an individual, event or organization.
5   *Direct marketing*: the distribution of products, information and promotional benefits to target consumers through interactive communication in a way that allows response to be measured.
6   *Digital marketing*: the distribution of products, information and promotional benefits to consumers and businesses through digital technologies. Digital marketing is growing rapidly and is examined in detail in Chapter 12.
7   *Personal selling*: oral communication with prospective purchasers with the intention of making a sale.

In addition to these key promotional tools, the marketer can also use a wide range of other techniques, such as exhibitions, events, product placement in movies, songs or video games and more recent techniques like ambient marketing, guerrilla marketing and buzz marketing. Given the potentially wide menu of communications choices that the organization has, it is important that these decisions are consistent with all other elements of marketing such as branding, pricing and distribution in order to ensure a consistent positioning in the marketplace. If several different communications tools are being used, it is also important that they are consistent with and complement each other. This is what is meant by the concept of integrated marketing communications (IMC).

Integrated marketing communications

Each of the seven major promotional tools has its own strengths and limitations; these are summarized in Table 10.1. Marketers will carefully weigh these factors against promotional objectives to decide the amount of resources they should channel into each tool.

Usually, the following five considerations will have a major impact on the choice of the promotional mix.

1   *Resource availability and the cost of promotional tools*: to conduct a national advertising campaign may require several million euro. If resources are not available, cheaper tools such as direct marketing or publicity may have to be used.
2   *Market size and concentration*: if a market is small and concentrated then personal selling may be feasible, but for mass markets that are geographically dispersed, selling to the ultimate customer would not be cost-effective. In such circumstances advertising or direct marketing may be the correct choice.
3   *Customer information needs*: if a complex technical argument is required, personal selling may be preferred. If all that is required is the appropriate brand image, advertising may be more sensible.
4   *Product characteristics*: industrial goods companies tend to spend more on personal selling than advertising, whereas consumer goods companies tend to do the reverse.
5   *Push versus pull strategies*: a **distribution push** strategy involves an attempt to sell into channel intermediaries (e.g. retailers) and is dependent on personal selling and trade promotions. A **consumer pull** strategy bypasses intermediaries to communicate to consumers directly. The resultant consumer demand persuades intermediaries

Table IO.I Key characteristics of seven key promotional mix tools

Advertising
■ Good for awareness building because it can reach a wide audience quickly
■ Repetition means that a brand positioning concept can be effectively communicated; television is particularly strong
■ Can be used to aid the sales effort: legitimize a company and its products
■ Impersonal: lacks flexibility and questions cannot be answered
■ Limited capability to close the sale
Personal selling
■ Interactive: questions can be answered and objections overcome
■ Adaptable: presentations can be changed depending on customer needs
■ Complex arguments can be developed
■ Relationships can be built because of its personal nature
■ Provides the opportunity to close the sale
■ Sales calls are costly
Direct marketing
■ Individual targeting of consumers most likely to respond to an appeal
■ Communication can be personalized
■ Short-term effectiveness can easily be measured
■ A continuous relationship through periodic contact can be built
■ Activities are less visible to competitors
■ Response rates are often low
■ Poorly targeted direct marketing activities cause consumer annoyance
Digital communications
■ Global reach at relatively low cost
■ Relatively easy to measure effectiveness
■ A dialogue between companies, and their customers and suppliers can be established
■ Catalogues and prices can be changed quickly and cheaply
■ Convenient form of searching for and buying products
Sales promotion
■ Incentives provide a quick boost to sales
■ Effects may be only short term
■ Excessive use of some incentives (e.g. money off) may damage brand image
Publicity
■ Highly credible as message comes from a third party
■ Higher readership than advertisements in trade and technical publications
■ Lose control: a press release may or may not be used and its content distorted
Sponsorship
■ Very useful for brand building and generating publicity
■ Provides an opportunity to entertain business partners
■ Can be used to demonstrate the company's goodwill to its local community or society in general
■ Popular due to the fragmentation of traditional media

to stock the product. Advertising and consumer promotions are more likely to be used.

As the range of promotional techniques expands, there is an increasing need to coordinate the messages and their execution. This problem is often exacerbated by the fact that, for example, advertising is controlled by the advertising department, whereas personal selling strategies are controlled by the sales department, leading to a lack of coordination. This has led to the adoption of **integrated marketing communications** by an increasing number of companies. Integrated marketing communications is the system by which companies coordinate their marketing communications tools to deliver a clear, consistent, credible and competitive message about the organization and its products. For example, Meteor Ireland's Reindeer campaign for Christmas 2008 was rolled out across television, cinema, outdoor, press, radio, online, social networking, PR, in-store and on-street. While digital marketing is a significant area of growth, most companies aim to create campaigns that have both online and offline dimensions. The application of this concept of integrated marketing

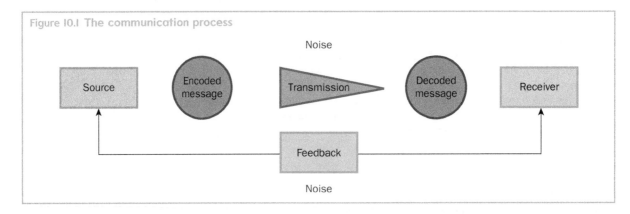

Figure I0.I The communication process

communications can lead to improved consistency and clearer positioning of companies and their brands in the minds of consumers.

The traditional model of the communication process is shown in Figure 10.1. The source (or communicator) encodes a message by translating the idea to be communicated into a symbol consisting of words or pictures, such as an advertisement. The message is transmitted through media, such as television or the Internet, which are selected for their ability to reach the desired target audience in the desired way. 'Noise' – distractions and distortions during the communication process – may prevent transmission to some of the target audience. The vast amount of promotional messages a consumer receives daily makes it a challenge for marketers to cut through this noise. When a receiver sees or hears the message it is decoded. This is the process by which the receiver interprets the symbols transmitted by the source. Communicators need to understand their targets before encoding messages so that they are credible, otherwise the response may be disbelief and rejection. In a **personal selling** situation, feedback from buyer to salesperson may be immediate as when objections are raised or a sale is concluded. For other types of promotion, such as advertising and sales promotion, feedback may rely on marketing research to estimate reactions to commercials, and increases in sales due to incentives.

Stages in developing an integrated communications campaign

For many small and medium-sized firms, marketing communications planning involves little more than assessing how much the firm can afford to spend, allocating it across some media and, in due course, looking at whether sales levels have increased or not. It is clear that to avoid wasting valuable organizational resources, marketing communications should be planned and evaluated carefully. The various stages involved in doing this are outlined in Figure 10.2.

The process begins by looking at the firm's overall marketing strategy, its positioning strategy and its intended **target audience**. What is the firm trying to achieve in the marketplace and what role can marketing communications play? If, for example, the firm is trying to reposition a brand or change consumer attitudes, then advertising is likely to play an important role in this, but it must be integrated with the other marketing mix elements. Objectives need to be set for the IMC campaign and they should be quantifiable. For example, the objective is to increase sales by a given amount or to increase awareness among the youth market by a given percentage. Only after these stages are complete should the company begin thinking about what it is going to say (the message decisions) and where it is going to say it (the media decisions). These are complex decisions, which are discussed in detail in this and the next chapter. A budget for the

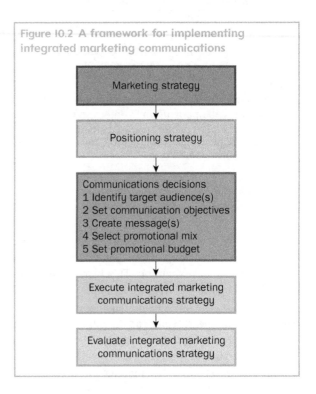

Figure I0.2 A framework for implementing integrated marketing communications

Marketing strategy

Positioning strategy

Communications decisions
1 Identify target audience(s)
2 Set communication objectives
3 Create message(s)
4 Select promotional mix
5 Set promotional budget

Execute integrated marketing communications strategy

Evaluate integrated marketing communications strategy

campaign needs to be agreed, usually at board level in the company. Then after the campaign has been run, it is imperative that it is fully evaluated to assess its effectiveness. We will now examine some of the key mass communications techniques in more detail.

Advertising

Advertising is very big business. In 2014, global advertising expenditure was estimated to be worth $524 billion, with almost two-thirds of all this expenditure taking place in Europe and North America.[2] There has long been considerable debate about how advertising works. The consensus is that there can be no single all-embracing theory that explains how all advertising works because it has varied tasks. For example, advertising that attempts to make an instant sale by incorporating a return coupon that can be used to order a product is very different from corporate image advertising that is designed to reinforce attitudes. One view of advertising sees it as being powerful enough to encourage consumers to buy by moving them through the stages of awareness, interest, desire and action (known by the acronym AIDA). This is known as the **strong theory of advertising** and it implies that advertising is targeted at a largely passive consumer and is capable of moving them through a series of stages in a fairly linear fashion. An alternative approach – the awareness, trial, reinforcement (ATR) model – sees a key role of advertising as being to defend brands, by reinforcing beliefs so that existing customers may be retained. This is referred to as the **weak theory of advertising**. It implies that most purchase choices are based on habit and that the purpose of advertising is largely defensive. Advertising is likely to have different roles depending on the nature of the product and the degree of involvement of the customer.

More recent perspectives from consumer culture theory (see Chapter 3) interpret consumer advertising more in terms of the transfer of meaning. In other words, advertising acts as a source of meanings through which we express ourselves and communicate with others. For example, marketing communications may have social meaning and consumers differentiate themselves from others by consuming particular products (see Exhibit 10.1). Research has found that the brands of clothes worn by people have an impact on cooperation from others, job recommendations and even collecting money when soliciting for a charity.[3] However one chooses to explain it, one should not underestimate the power of advertising. For example, Covergirl's

Lashblast mascara advertising campaign featuring Drew Barrymore generated sales that were 70 per cent higher than expected.

Developing advertising strategy

Each of the steps identified in Figure 10.2 is appropriate irrespective of whether the firm is conducting an advertising campaign, a **direct marketing** or **sales promotion** campaign; all that changes is the detail involved. Here we examine some specific advertising issues.

Defining advertising objectives

Although, ultimately, advertising is a means of stimulating sales and increasing profits, a clear understanding of its communication objectives is of more operational value. Advertising can have a number of communications objectives. First, it can be used to *create awareness* of a brand or a solution to a company's problem. Awareness creation is critical when a new product is being launched or when the firm is entering a new market. For example, *The Economist* magazine, which primarily targets wealthy executives, ran a cinema campaign entitled 'The Economist – Let Your Mind Wander' to create awareness among younger readers. Second, advertising can be used to *stimulate trial*, such as car advertising encouraging motorists to take a test drive. Third, and as we saw in Chapter 5, advertising is used to help *position products* in the minds of consumers, such as L'Oréal's repeated use of the slogan 'Because I'm worth it' or Ronseal's 'It does exactly what it says on the tin'. Other objectives of advertising include the *correction of misconceptions* about a product or service, *reminding* customers of sales or special offers, and *providing support* for the company's sales force.

Setting the advertising budget

The amount that is spent on advertising governs the achievement of communication objectives. There are four methods of setting advertising budgets. A simple method is the *percentage of sales* method, whereby the amount allocated to advertising is based on current or expected revenue. However, this method is weak because it encourages a decline in advertising expenditure when sales decline, a move that may encourage a further downward spiral of sales. Furthermore, it ignores market opportunities, which may suggest the need to spend more (not less) on advertising. For example, in response to declining sales in 2011, Nokia reduced its advertising and promotional expenditure for 2012 by 25 per cent. This corresponded to an almost identical drop in demand for its products with sales in 2012 slumping by 27.5 per cent.[4] Major consumer brands typically spend in the region of 10–15 per cent of sales on marketing.

Alternatively, companies may set their advertising budgets based upon matching competitors' expenditures, or using a similar percentage of sales figure as their major competitor. This is known as the *competitive parity* method. Again this method is weak because it assumes that the competition has arrived at the optimum level of expenditure, and ignores market opportunities and communication objectives. Sometimes firms make a decision on the basis of what they think they can afford (the *affordability* method). While affordability needs to be taken into account when considering any corporate expenditure, its use as the sole criterion for budget setting neglects the communication objectives that are relevant for a company's products, and the market opportunities that may exist, to grow sales and profits.

The most effective method of setting advertising budgets is the *objective and task* method. This has the virtue of being logical since the advertising budget depends upon communication objectives and the costs of the tasks required to achieve them. It forces management to think about objectives, media exposure levels and the resulting costs. In practice, the advertising budgeting decision is a highly political process.[5] Finance may argue for monetary caution, whereas marketing personnel, who view advertising as a method of long-term brand building, are more likely to support higher advertising spend. During times of economic slowdown, advertising budgets are among the first to be cut, although this can be the time when advertising expenditure is most effective. However, research has shown that maintaining or increasing promotional expenditures during a recession can have a positive impact on sales, market share and profitability[6] (see for example the Marketing Spotlight at the beginning of Chapter 9).

Message decisions

The **advertising message** translates an organization's basic value proposition into an **advertising platform**; that is the words, symbols and illustrations that are attractive and meaningful to the target audience. In the 1980s, IBM realized that many customers bought its computers because of the reassurance they felt when dealing with a well-known supplier. The company used this knowledge to develop an advertising campaign based on the advertising platform of reassurance/low risk. This platform was translated into the advertising message 'No one ever got fired for buying IBM'. As we shall see below, the choice of media available to the advertiser is vast, therefore one of the challenges of message formulation is to keep the message succinct and adaptable across various media. For example, a recent campaign for eBay just focused on the word 'It'. Imagery of the word 'It' appeared on posters, print and television, and migrated online as a viral campaign. The 'It' was finally revealed as part of eBay's slogan, 'Whatever it is, you can get it on eBay'.[7]

Most of those who look at a press advertisement read the headline but not the body copy. Because of this, some advertisers suggest that the company or brand name should appear in the headline otherwise the reader may not know the source of the advertisement. For example, the headlines 'Good food costs less at Sainsbury's' and 'United Colors of Benetton' score highly because in one phrase or sentence they link a customer benefit or attribute with the name of the company. Even if no more copy is read, the advertiser has got one message across by means of a strong headline.

Messages broadcast via television also need to be built on a strong advertising platform. Because television commercials are usually of a duration of 30 seconds or less, most communicate only one major selling appeal which is the single most motivating and differentiating thing that can be said about the brand. A variety of creative treatments can be used, from *lifestyle*, to *humour*, to *shock* advertising. Cosmetics brands like Estée Lauder have traditionally favoured the lifestyle approach (showing the brand as being part of an attractive lifestyle) to advertising though many have now moved to using top models and celebrities in their advertising (*testimonials*) (see Exhibit 10.2). *Sexual imagery* remains a popular attention-getting tactic in advertising, though recent research casts doubt on its effectiveness.[8] *Comparative advertising* is another popular approach frequently used by companies like low-cost airlines, supermarkets and banks to demonstrate relative price advantages (see Marketing in Action 10.1). It can be a risky approach as it often leads to legal battles over claims made, such as the legal action between Asda and Tesco over the former's claim that it was 'officially' the lowest price supermarket.[9]

Television advertising is often used to build a brand personality. The brand personality is the message the advertisement seeks to convey. Lannon suggests that people use brand personalities in different ways, such as acting as a form of self-expression, reassurance, a communicator of the brand's function and an indicator of trustworthiness.[10] The value of the brand personality to consumers will differ by product category and this will depend on the purpose served by the brand imagery. In 'self-expressive' product categories, such as perfumes, cigarettes, alcoholic drinks and clothing, brands act as 'badges' for making public an aspect of personality ('I choose this brand [e.g. Michael Kors] to say this about myself ').

Television advertising has long been the staple method of promoting consumer brands, although it now faces many challenges. Technologies like digital recorders enable viewers to avoid watching the commercial breaks and the multiplicity of channels available means that it is harder for advertisers to reach large audiences. The growing trend towards multitasking may well mean that consumers are also online at the same time as they are watching television further reducing attention. Advertisers have responded to these trends in a number of ways. First there is the creation of live adverts. For example, Honda and Channel 4 combined to produce the first live television advertisement in 2008. A live sky-diving jump was broadcast in which 19 stuntmen spelt out the car maker's brand name in an advert that had the slogan 'Difficult is worth doing'. The pre- and post-publicity surrounding the initiative also benefited Honda. Second, there is the growth of **consumer-generated advertising**, where brands hold competitions inviting consumers to submit adverts or to participate in the creation of adverts. The risk of adopting this approach is that some user-generated content may be negative but many organizations feel it is worth giving up some control in order to enhance the relationships that consumers have with brands. The clothing brand Diesel's 'Be Stupid' campaign was designed to inspire consumers to upload videos of their own stupidity online. Successful user-generated advertising tends to quickly migrate online as part of a **viral campaign**. Finally, some television advertising invites consumers to go to websites to avail themselves of special offers to take account of consumer trends towards multi-tasking.

Media decisions

Because of the proliferation of media now available to an advertiser, such as hundreds of television channels or radio stations, the media selection decision has become a very important one. Choice of media class (e.g. television versus press) and media vehicle (e.g. a particular newspaper or magazine) are two key decisions. Both of these will be examined next.

Volkswagen Ad Insight: 'The Force' campaign uses humour as an effective creative treatment.

Marketing in Action 10.1 Samsung: the next big thing is already here

Critical Thinking: Below is a review of a comparative promotional campaign run by Samsung. Critically evaluate the pros and cons of this type of advertising.

In 2011, the Samsung brand had a problem. While it had developed a great product, the Samsung Galaxy II mobile phone, it was not perceived as an innovator but rather just another smartphone brand competing against the category leader, the Apple iPhone. So it made a courageous decision – to tackle the iPhone head on and position Samsung as a brand that could be considered just as innovative as its better known rival. In the past, this kind of head-on positioning has been successful, for example, Avis and Hertz in the car rental business and also disastrous – Kronenberg's failure versus Heineken in the drinks industry. So taking on arguably the strongest brand on the planet required very careful planning and execution by Samsung.

One of the features of the smartphone business was the choice by many consumers to wait in line outside stores when new products were being released. Samsung decided to focus on this element of consumer behaviour and use it to demonstrate that waiting in line was futile when the latest technology was already here. It was a direct challenge to the iPhone 4S which was launched nine months after the Galaxy II. The aim of the advert was to be funny but not mean-spirited towards Apple so that it would appeal to all smartphone users. It showed consumers waiting in line for a launch only to be distracted by others using their Galaxy IIs. Television was the primary medium used for the campaign but it was also aired in cinemas and quickly migrated online to become a viral success. Other media used to support the campaign included public relations, digital display adverts, Samsung's Facebook page and guerrilla marketing techniques such as street teams, events and ambient advertising.

The campaign was a huge success. Samsung's Facebook audience jumped by 433 per cent in the first month of the campaign alone. It has helped to propel the brand to a position of dominance in the industry with a global market share of 32 per cent in 2013. Subsequent iterations of the campaign continued to enhance the Samsung brand while questioning Apple's ownership of the 'cool' factor. For example, one of the stars of the campaign is seen waiting in line but he tells us that he is only holding a spot for some others – who turn out to be his parents. The success of Samsung's approach has been put down to the use of humour in the campaign, the fact that it focuses on real differences between the products and that it does not mention Apple specifically though it is clear to everyone who the focus of the campaign is.

Based on: Anonymous (2013);[11] Ellet (2012);[12] Kovach (2013).[13]

Table 10.2 lists the major media class and vehicle options (the media mix). The media planner faces the choice of using television, press, cinema, outdoor, radio, the Internet and so on, or a combination of media classes. Creative factors have a major bearing on the choice of media class. For example, if the *objective* is to position the brand as having a high-status, aspirational personality, television or product placement would be better than outdoor advertising. However, if the communication objective is to remind the target audience of a brand's existence, an outdoor or an ambient campaign may suffice.

Each medium possesses its own set of creative qualities and limitations. Television can be used to demonstrate the product in action, or to use colour and sound to build an atmosphere around the product, thus enhancing its image. Although television was traditionally one of the most powerful advertising mediums, concerns about fragmentation of the television audience have led many leading advertisers to move away from it. Furthermore, recent research has again questioned whether viewers actually watch advertisements when they are on, finding that consumers may spend as little

Table 10.2 Media choices

Media class	Media vehicle
Television	Channel 4 News; Eurosport
Radio	Classic FM; Star FM
Newspapers	The Guardian; El Mundo
Magazines – Consumer	Hello; Glamour
– Business	Marketing Week; Construction News
Outdoor	Billboards; bus shelters; London Underground
Internet	Google Adwords; YouTube videos; Facebook advertising
Cinema	Particular movies
Exhibitions	Motor Show; Ideal Home
Product placement	TV programmes, songs, video games
Ambient	Street pavements; buildings

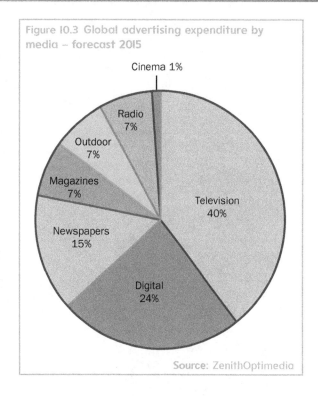

Figure 10.3 Global advertising expenditure by media – forecast 2015

Cinema 1%
Radio 7%
Outdoor 7%
Magazines 7%
Newspapers 15%
Television 40%
Digital 24%

Source: ZenithOptimedia

as 23 per cent of the time the advertisements are on watching them, with the remainder spent talking, reading, surfing between channels or doing tasks such as cleaning, ironing or office work.[14] Unilever has responded by reducing the amount of advertising it places on television, switching instead to outdoor and Internet advertising. Despite these developments, television is still the largest advertising medium (see Figure 10.3) and some research shows it plays a significant role in brand building.[15]

Press advertising is useful for providing factual information and offers an opportunity for consumers to re-examine the advertisement at a later stage. Advertisers are increasingly using colour print ads to ensure that their brands stand out. Leaders in this field include the likes of Orange and easyJet, as well as retail chains like Marks & Spencer. Colour advertising in newspapers has risen by 53 per cent as against an 8 per cent growth in mono advertising.[16] Magazines can be used to target particular markets and one growing sector is customer magazines, whereby leading brands such as BMW and Mercedes produce colour magazines of pictures and editorial about their products. Posters are a very good support medium, as their message has to be short and succinct because consumers such as motorists will normally only have time to glance at the content. Lavazza, the Italian coffee brand, is an extensive user of poster sites in airports and metropolitan areas where its

glamorous, fashion magazine-style adverts are used to build awareness and image of the brand. Outdoor advertising continues to be favoured as the growth of cities, metros and long commuting times make the medium appealing, though it is increasingly subject to regulation a subway poster for Apotek, a Swedish pharmacy brand, was equipped with ultra-sonic sensors to determine when a train was coming. When it did, the model's hair flapped in the wind to the tagline – 'make your hair come alive'. Technology is increasingly being used to catch the attention of busy consumers. Radio is limited to the use of sound and is therefore more likely to be useful in communicating factual information rather than building image, while cinema benefits from colour, movement and sound, as well as the presence of a captive audience. Cinema is a particularly good medium for brands trying to reach young audiences, as is Internet advertising.

A number of other factors also affect the **media class decision**. An important consideration is the size of the *advertising budget*. Some media are naturally more expensive than others. For example, €500,000 may be sufficient for a national poster campaign but woefully inadequate for television. The relative cost per opportunity to see (OTS) is also relevant. The target audience may be reached much more cheaply using one medium rather than another. However, the calculation of OTS differs according to media class, making comparisons difficult. For example, in the UK, an OTS for the press is defined as 'read or looked at any issue of the publication for at least two minutes', whereas for

Exhibit 10.3 Immersive advertising inside Oxford Circus tube station

posters it is 'traffic past site'. A further consideration is *competitive activity*. A company may decide to compete in the same medium as a competitor or seek to dominate an alternative medium. For example, if a major competitor is using television, a firm may choose posters, where it could dominate, thus achieving a greater impact. Finally, for many consumer goods producers, the views of the *retail trade* (for example, supermarket buyers) may influence the choice of media class. Advertising expenditure is often used by salespeople to convince the retail trade to increase the shelf space allocated to existing brands, and to stock new brands. For example, if it is known that supermarkets favour television advertising in a certain product market, the selling impact on the trade of €3 million spent on television may be viewed as greater than the equivalent spend of 50:50 between television and the press.

The choice of a particular newspaper, magazine, television spot, poster site, etc., is called the **media vehicle decision**. Although creative considerations still play a part, cost per thousand calculations is the dominant influence. This requires readership and viewership figures. In the UK, readership figures are produced by the National Readership Survey, based on 36,000 interviews per year. Television viewership is measured by the Broadcasters' Audience Research

Board (BARB), which produces weekly reports based on a panel of 5,100 households equipped with metered television sets (people meters). Traffic past poster sites is measured by Outdoor Site Classification and Audience Research (OSCAR), which classifies 130,000 sites according to visibility, competition (one or more posters per site), angle of vision, height above ground, illumination and weekly traffic past site. Cinema audiences are monitored by Cinema and Video Industry Audience Research (CAVIAR) and radio audiences are measured by Radio Joint Audience Research (RAJAR). Adwords are sold in online auctions where the price of the word is determined by its popularity.

Media buying is a specialist area and a great deal of money can be saved on rate card prices by powerful media buyers. Media buying is generally done by specialist media-buying agencies who may be owned by a full-service advertising agency or part of a communications group. Specialist media-buying agencies have significant buying power as well as established relationships with media vehicles.

Executing the campaign

When an advertisement has been produced and the media selected, it is sent to the chosen media vehicle for publication or transmission. A key organizational issue is to ensure that the right advertisements reach the right media at the right time. Each media vehicle has its own deadlines after which publication or transmission may not be possible.

Evaluating advertising effectiveness

Measurement can take place before, during and after campaign execution. *Pre-testing* takes place before the campaign is run and is part of the creative process. In television advertising, rough advertisements are created and tested with target consumers. This is usually done with a focus group, which is shown perhaps three alternative commercials and the group members are asked to discuss their likes, dislikes and understanding of each one. The results provide important input from the target consumers themselves rather than relying solely on **advertising agency** views. Such research is not without its critics, however. They suggest that the impact of a commercial that is repeated many times cannot be captured in a two-hour group discussion. They point to the highly successful Heineken campaign – 'Refreshes the parts other beers cannot reach' – which was rejected by target consumers in the pre-test.[17] Despite this kind of criticism, advertising research is a booming business because of the uncertainty surrounding the effectiveness of new advertising campaigns.

Post-testing can be used to assess a campaign's effectiveness once it has run. Sometimes formal post-testing is ignored through laziness, fear or lack of funds. However, checking how well an advertising campaign has performed can provide the information necessary to plan future campaigns. The top three measures used in post-test television advertising research are image/attitude change, actual sales and usage, although other financial measures such as cash flow, shareholder value and return on investment are increasingly being used. Image/attitude change is believed to be a sensitive measure, which is a good predictor of behavioural change. Those favouring the actual sales measure argue that, despite difficulties in establishing cause and effect, sales change is the ultimate objective of advertising and therefore the only meaningful measure. Testing recall of advertisements is also popular. Despite the evidence suggesting that recall may not be a valid measure of advertising effectiveness, those favouring recall believe that because the advertising is seen and remembered, it is effective.

 Virgin Atlantic Ad Insight: This ad focuses on the value of service provided for customers.

Organizing for campaign development

There are four options open to an advertiser when organizing for campaign development. First, small companies may develop the advertising in *cooperation with people from the media*. For example, advertising copy may be written by someone from the company, but the artwork and final layout of the advertisement may be done by the newspaper or magazine. Second, the advertising function may be conducted *in-house* by creating an advertising department staffed with copy-writers, media buyers and production personnel. This form of organization locates total control of the advertising function within the company, but since media buying is on behalf of only one company, buying power is low. Cost-conscious companies such as Ryanair do most of their advertising work in-house. Third, because of the specialist skills that are required for developing an advertising campaign, many advertisers opt to work with an *advertising agency*. Larger agencies offer a full service, comprising creative work, media planning and buying, planning and strategy development, market research and production. Because agencies work for many clients, they have a wide range of experience and can provide an objective outsider's view of what is required and how problems can be solved. Four large global conglomerates – Omnicom, WPP Group, Interpublic and Publicis – dominate the industry. These corporations have grown in response to major multinational companies like Samsung and Nestlé, who want their global advertising handled by one firm.[18] A fourth alternative is to use in-house staff (or their full-service agency) for some advertising functions, but to use *specialist agencies* for others. The attraction of the specialist stems in part from the large volume of business that each controls. This means that they have enormous buying power when negotiating media prices, for example. Alternatively, an advertiser could employ the services of a 'creative hot-shop' to supplement its own or its full service agency's skills.

The traditional system of agency payment was by commission from the media owners. Under the commission system, media owners traditionally offered a 15 per cent discount on the rate card (list) price to agencies. For example, a €1 million television advertising campaign would result in a charge to the agency of €1 million minus 15 per cent (€850,000). The agency invoiced the client at the full rate-card price (€1 million). The agency commission therefore totalled €150,000.

Large advertisers have the power to demand some of this 15 per cent in the form of a rebate. For example, companies like Unilever and P&G have

Marketing and Society 10.1 Informing or misleading?

Advertising is everywhere; it is the means by which organizations communicate with potential customers. But many opponents argue that advertising is at best wasteful and at worst downright misleading, offensive and dangerous. On the other hand, advocates argue that, in modern societies, consumers are savvy enough to be able to assess advertising for what it is.

Misleading advertising can take the form of exaggerated claims and concealed facts. For example, Coca-Cola ran into trouble with the Australian Competition and Consumer Commission for running a 'Myth-busting' campaign about Coca-Cola that used the words 'Myth – Makes you fat. Myth – Rots your teeth. Myth – Packed with caffeine'. The commission forced the soft drinks maker to publish corrective advertisements in seven national and state newspapers charging that its claims were misleading. Similarly, broadband operators have been criticized for advertising promised download speeds that, in reality, were not delivered.

Advertising can also deceive by omitting important facts from its message. Such concealed facts may give a misleading impression to the audience. The advertising of food products like breakfast cereals is particularly susceptible to misleading advertising, such as omitting details of sugar and salt levels, or making bogus scientific claims of health benefits. Some companies, like Kellogg's, use celebrity presenters of science programmes to endorse their products, which can give the impression that claims are scientifically grounded. Many industrialized countries have their own codes of practice that protect the consumer from deceptive advertising. For example, in the UK the Advertising Standards Authority (ASA) administers the British Code of Advertising Practice, which insists that advertising should be 'legal, decent, honest and truthful'. Shock advertising, such as that pursued in the past by companies like Paddy Power, Benetton and FCUK, is often the subject of many complaints to the ASA.

Critics argue that advertising images have a profound effect on society. They claim that advertising promotes materialism and takes advantage of human frailties. Advertising is accused of stressing the importance of material possessions, such as the ownership of a car or the latest in consumer electronics. Critics argue that this promotes the wrong values in society. A related criticism is that advertising takes advantage of human frailties such as the need to belong or the desire for status. For example, a UK government White Paper has proposed a ban on junk food advertising at certain times, in the same way as cigarette and alcohol advertising is restricted.

Advertising has always been controversial and it looks as though it will continue to be so for some time to come.

Reflection: Think about your views on advertising. Do you consider it to be mainly informative and entertaining or mainly annoying and misleading?

reduced the amount of commission they allow their agencies. Given that P&G spent $9 billion in 2012 or 11 per cent of its global revenues it could probably demand very low commission levels, but these companies choose not to exercise all of their muscle as low commission rates ultimately may lead to poor-quality advertising. The second method of paying agencies is by fee. For smaller clients, commission alone may not be sufficient to cover agency costs. Also, some larger clients are advocating fees rather than commission, on the basis that this removes a possible source of agency bias towards media that

pay commission rather than a medium like direct mail or online for which no commission is payable.

Payment by results is the third method of remuneration. This involves measuring the effectiveness of the advertising campaign using marketing research, and basing payment on how well communication objectives have been met. For example, payment might be based on how awareness levels have increased, brand image improved or intentions-to-buy have risen. Another area where payment by results has been used is media buying. For example, if the normal cost per thousand to reach men in the age range 30–40 is €4.50, and the agency achieves a 10 per cent saving, this might be split 8 per cent to the client and 2 per cent to the agency.[19] Procter & Gamble uses the payment-by-results method to pay its advertising agencies. Remuneration is tied to global brand sales, so aligning their income more closely with the success (or otherwise) of their advertising.[20]

Sales promotion

As we have already seen, sales promotions are incentives to consumers or the trade that are designed to stimulate purchase. Examples include money off and free gifts (consumer promotions), and discounts and sales-force competitions (trade promotions). A vast amount of money is spent on sales promotion and many companies engage in joint promotions. Some of the key reasons for the popularity of sales promotion include the following.

- *Increased impulse purchasing*: the rise in impulse purchasing favours promotions that take place at the point of purchase.
- *The rising cost of advertising and advertising clutter*: these factors erode advertising's cost-effectiveness.
- *Shortening time horizons*: the attraction of the fast sales boost of a sales promotion is raised by greater rivalry and shortening product life cycles.
- *Competitor activities*: in some markets, sales promotions are used so often that all competitors are forced to follow suit.
- *Measurability*: measuring the sales impact of sales promotions is easier than for advertising since its effect is more direct and, usually, short term.

If sales require a 'short, sharp shock', sales promotion is often used to achieve this. In this sense it may be regarded as a short-term tactical device. The long-term sales effect of the promotion could be positive, neutral or negative. If the promotion has attracted new buyers who find that they like the brand, repeat purchases from them may give rise to a positive long-term effect.[21] Alternatively, if the promotion (e.g. money off) has devalued the brand in the eyes of consumers, the effect may be negative.[22] Where the promotion has caused consumers to buy the brand only because of its incentive value with no effect on underlying preferences, the long-term effect may be neutral.[23] An international study of leading grocery brands has shown that the most likely long-term effect of a price promotion for an existing brand is neutral. Such promotions tend to attract existing buyers of the brand during the promotional period rather than new buyers.[24]

Sales promotion strategy

As with advertising, a systematic approach should be taken to the management of sales promotions involving the specification of objectives for the promotion, decisions on which techniques are most suitable and an evaluation of the effectiveness of the promotion.

Sales promotions can have a number of objectives. The most usual goal is to *boost sales* over the short term. Short-term sales increases may be required for a number of reasons, including the need to reduce inventories or meet budgets prior to the end of the financial year, moving stocks of an old model prior to a replacement, or to increase stock-holding by consumers and distributors in advance of the launch of a competitor's product. A highly successful method of sales promotion involves *encouraging trial*. Home sampling and home couponing are particularly effective methods of inducing trial. Certain promotions, by their nature, *encourage repeat purchasing* of a brand over a period of time. Any promotion that requires the collection of packet tops or labels (e.g. free mail-ins and promotions such as bingo games) attempts to increase the frequency of repeat purchasing during the promotional period. Some promotions are designed to encourage customers to *purchase larger pack sizes*. Finally, trade promotions are usually designed to *gain distribution and shelf space*. Discounts, free gifts and joint promotions are methods used to encourage distributors to stock brands.

Selecting the type of sales promotion to use

There is a very wide variety of promotional techniques that a marketer can consider using (see Figure 10.4). Major consumer sales promotion types are money off, bonus packs, premiums, free samples, coupons and prize promotions. A sizeable proportion of sales promotions are directed at the trade, including price discounts, free goods, competitions and allowances.

Consumer promotion techniques

Money-off promotions provide direct value to the customer and therefore an unambiguous incentive to purchase. They have a proven track record of stimulating short-term sales increases. However, price reductions can easily be matched by competitors and if used frequently can devalue brand image. **Bonus packs** give added value by giving consumers extra quantity at no additional cost and are often used in the drinks, confectionery and detergent markets. The

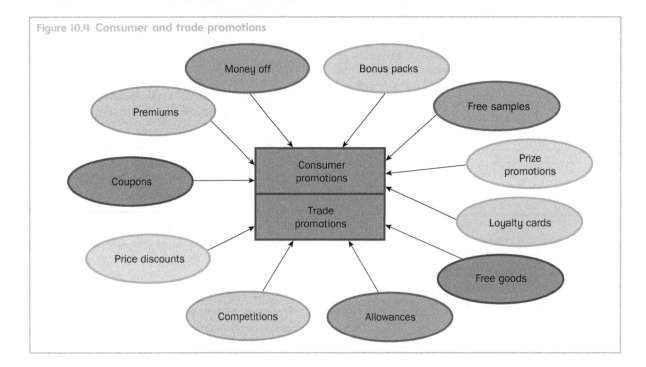

Figure 10.4 Consumer and trade promotions

promotion might be along the lines of 'Buy 10 and get 2 extra free'. Because the price is not lowered, this form of promotion runs less risk of devaluing the brand image. When two or more items are banded together the promotion is called a multi-buy. These are frequently used to protect market share by encouraging consumers to stock up on a particular brand when two or more items of the same brand are banded together, such as a shampoo and conditioner. Multi-buys can also generate range trial when, for example, a jar of coffee is banded with samples of other coffee varieties such as lattes and mochas. **Premiums** are any merchandise offered free or at low cost as an incentive to purchase a brand; they can come in three forms: free in-pack or on-pack gifts, free in-the-mail offers and self-liquidating offers, where consumers are asked to pay a sum of money to cover the costs of the merchandise. The main role of premiums is in encouraging bulk purchasing and maintaining share. Breakfast cereal manufacturers have been extensive users of in-pack and self-liquidating premiums. For example, Kellogg's 'Big Breakfast' promotion for its mini portion packs and cereal bars includes gifts, a scratchcard competition, trade incentives and extensive point-of-purchase support. A behavioural argument for the inclusion of a free gift is that it is a powerful tool in reducing buyer risk and therefore likely to lead to desired purchases or product choices.[25]

Free samples of a brand may be delivered to the home or given out in a store and are used to encourage trial. For new brands or brand extensions this is an effective, if sometimes expensive, way of generating trial. Coupons can be delivered to the home, appear in magazines or newspapers, or appear on packs, and are used to encourage trial or repeat purchase. Increasingly online coupons are being used. Daily deal websites like Groupon and LivingSocial have become very popular online destinations for bargain hunters. Coupons are a popular form of sales promotion, although they are usually less effective in raising initial sales than money-off promotions because there is no immediate saving and the appeal is almost exclusively to existing consumers.[26]

There are three main types of prize promotion: competitions, draws and games (see Social Media Marketing 10.1). These are often used to attract attention or stimulate interest in a brand. Competitions require participants to exercise a certain degree of skill and judgement and entry is usually dependent on purchase at least. For example, in an attempt to revitalize its ailing PG Tips tea brand, Unilever put 'mind game' puzzles on the backs of packs and directed entrants to a PG Tips website for solutions. Draws make no demand on skill and judgement, the result simply depends on chance.

Trade promotion techniques

The trade may be offered (or may demand) discounts in return for purchase, which may be part of a joint promotion whereby the retailer agrees to devote extra shelf space, buy larger quantities, engage in a joint competition and/or allow in-store demonstrations. An alternative to a price discount

Social Media Marketing 10.1 De Bijenkorf's crazy queues!

> **Critical Thinking:** Below is a review of an online competition run by de Bijenkorf. Read it and critically evaluate the strengths and weaknesses of this promotion.

De Bijenkorf is an upmarket department store chain in the Netherlands that was founded in 1870. Its main store is located in Amsterdam and it has nine other outlets spread throughout the country. In keeping with the strategy of similar businesses such as Harrods in London and Galleries Lafayette in Paris, it has become known for its events, its magazine and its spectacular window displays. It stocks the top international brands as well as its own brands of fashion, cosmetics, accessories, homewares and travel services. Its primary target market is females between 20 and 45 with above-average incomes.

Since 1984, de Bijenkorf has been organizing a three-day sales promotion known as 'Three Crazy Days' when a limited supply of top luxury brands are heavily discounted. A booklet outlining the items on sale is available on the first day and typically runs to 200 pages in length. Long queues of bargain hunters are a regular feature of this promotion and the atmosphere inside the stores during the sale is generally described as frenzied.

De Bijenkorf exploited the buzz surrounding its annual sale to build its Facebook fan base. It created an online game with a winning prize of a gift card worth €333 plus the advantage of being first in the door when the sale began. The game began 10 days before the actual sale and anyone ordering a sales booklet was granted immediate access to the Crazy Queue – an online version of the real thing. The game was also promoted through a variety of other channels such as Facebook, TV, radio and public relations. However, in this case queue-jumping was encouraged and one could move up the queue by challenging the person in front of you to a roll of the dice. If the challenger rolled a higher number, the players swapped places. The game proved highly addictive with participants playing throughout the night and swapping tips, advice and moral support on Facebook. In total, 15,000 people participated in the queue and over 360,000 battles were fought. The competition generated an eight-fold increase in de Bjenkorf's Facebook likes.

Based on: Anonymous (2011).[27]

is to offer more merchandise at the same price (free goods); for example, the 'baker's dozen' technique involves offering 13 items (or cases) for the price of 12. Manufacturers may use competitions, such as providing prizes for a distributor's sales force, in return for achieving sales targets for their products. Finally, a manufacturer may offer an allowance (a sum of money) in return for retailers providing promotional facilities in store (display allowance). For example, allowances would be needed to persuade a supermarket to display cards on its shelves indicating that a brand was being sold at a special low price.

The pharmaceutical industry is one of the biggest users of trade promotion. For example, in 2004, pharmaceutical companies in the USA spent $14.7 billion on marketing to healthcare professionals as against $3.6 billion on direct-to-consumer advertising activities. Trade promotions involve gifts, samples and industry-sponsored training courses. It is a highly competitive business with roughly 102,000 pharmaceutical 'detailers' or salespeople all trying to meet with the top prescribers among America's 870,000 physicians.[28]

The final stage in a sales promotion campaign involves testing the promotion. As with advertising, both pre-testing and post-testing approaches are available. The major pre-testing techniques include **group discussions** (testing ideas on groups of potential targets), **hall tests** (bringing a sample of customers to a room where alternative promotions are tested) and **experimentation** (where, for example, two groups of stores are selected and alternative promotions run in each). After the sales promotion has been implemented the effects must be monitored carefully. Care should be taken to check sales both during and after the promotion so that post-promotional sales dips can be taken into account (a lagged effect). In certain situations a sales fall can precede a promotion (a lead effect). If consumers believe a promotion to be imminent they may hold back purchases until it takes place. Alternatively, if a retail sales promotion of consumer durables (e.g. gas fires, refrigerators, televisions) is accompanied by higher commission rates for salespeople, they may delay sales until the promotional period.[29] If a lead effect is possible, sales prior to the promotion should also be monitored.

Public relations and publicity

All organizations have a variety of stakeholders (such as employees, shareholders, the local community, the media, government and pressure groups) whose needs they must take into account (see Figure 10.5). **Public relations** is concerned with all of these groups, and public relations activities include **publicity**, corporate advertising, seminars, publications, lobbying and charitable donations. PR can accomplish many objectives:[30] it can foster prestige and reputation, which can help companies to sell products, attract and keep good employees, and promote favourable community and government relations; it can promote products by creating the desire to buy a product through unobtrusive material that people read or see in the press, or on radio and television; awareness and interest in products and companies can be generated; it can be used to deal with issues or opportunities, or to overcome misconceptions about a company that may have been generated by bad publicity; and it can have a key role to play in fostering goodwill among customers, employees, suppliers, distributors and the government. For example, Belfast Zoo in Northern Ireland used a rare Barbary lion, Lily, as the centrepiece of their publicity campaign to increase visitor numbers to the zoo. Barbary lions are extinct in the wild and when Lily was rejected by her mother at birth, the cub was hand-reared at the home of the zoo keeper. Belfast Zoo set up an email account for Lily to which children could send messages and press releases and visuals tracked the cub's growth. The campaign caught the public imagination, generating £1.4 million in press coverage and raising visitor levels by almost one third.

Three major reasons for the growth in public relations are a recognition by marketing teams of the power and value of public relations, increased advertising costs leading to an exploration of more cost-effective communication routes, and improved understanding of the role of public relations. The dramatic growth of social media has further revolutionized the public relations business.

Publicity is a major element of public relations. It is defined as the communication of information about a product or organization by the placing of news about it in the media without paying for the time or space directly. The three key tasks of a publicity department are responding to requests for information from the media, supplying the media with information on important events in the organization and stimulating the media to carry the information and viewpoint of the organization.[31] Information dissemination may be through news releases, news conferences, interviews, feature articles, photo-calls and public speaking (at conferences and seminars, for example). No matter which of these means is used to carry the information, publicity has three important characteristics.

I   *The message has high credibility*: the message has greater credibility than advertising because it appears to the reader to have been written independently (by a media person) rather than by an advertiser. Because of this enhanced credibility it can be argued that it is more persuasive than a similar message used in an advertisement.

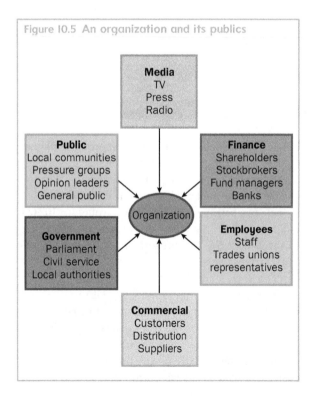

Figure 10.5 An organization and its publics

Table 10.3 Potentially newsworthy topics

Being or doing something first	
Marketing issues	**Financial issues**

New products
Research
  breakthroughs: future
  new products
Large orders/contracts
Sponsorships
Price changes
Service changes
New logos
Export success
	Financial statements
	Acquisitions
	Sales/profit
	  achievements

	Personal issues

Production issues	Training awards
	Winners of company
	  contests
	Promotions/new
	  appointments
	Success stories
	Visits by famous people
	Reports of interviews

Productivity achievements Employment changes Capital investments	
	General issues

	Conferences/seminars/
	  exhibitions
	Anniversaries of
	  significant events

2   *No direct media costs*: since space or time in the media does not have to be bought there is no direct media cost. However, this is not to say that it is cost free. Someone has to write the news release, take part in the interview or organize the news conference. This may be organized internally by a press officer or publicity department, or externally by a public relations agency.

3   *No control over publication*: unlike advertising, there is no guarantee that the news item will be published. This decision is taken out of the control of the organization and into the hands of an editor. A key factor in this decision is whether the item is judged to be newsworthy. Newsworthy items include where a company does something first, such as a new product or research breakthrough, new employees or company expansions, sponsor-ships, etc. A list of potentially newsworthy topics is provided in Table 10.3. Equally there is no guar-antee that the content of the news release will be published in the way that the news supplier had intended or that the publicity will occur when the company wants it to.

Sponsorship

Sponsorship has been defined by Sleight as:[32]

a business relationship between a provider of funds, resources or services and an individual, event or organization which offers in return some rights and association that may be used for commercial advantage.

Potential sponsors have a wide range of entities and activities from which to choose, including sports, arts, community activities, teams, tournaments, individual personalities or events, competitions, fairs and shows. Sports sponsorship is by far the most popular sponsorship medium as it offers high visibility through extensive television coverage, the ability to attract a broad cross-section of the community and to service specific niches, and the capacity to break down cultural barriers (see Exhibit 10.4). For example, the Olympics, the biggest global sporting event, attracted over $4.87 billion in broadcast fees and sponsorship for the combined 2010 Winter Games in Vancouver and the 2012 Summer Games in London. The London Organising Committee raised a further £700 million in sponsorship.[33] Such is the scramble for sponsorship opportunities that even a soccer team's pre-season tour can be sponsored; this was the case with a tour of China by Spanish club Real Madrid, which was sponsored by local cigarette company Hong Ta Shan.

Sponsorship can be very expensive. For example, being one of only six worldwide partners for the 2010 soccer World Cup in South Africa was estimated to cost $125 million. Similarly, becoming a tier one Olympic partner requires a similar scale of investment as well as a minimum eight-year commitment. Brand activation or spending associated with the sponsorship is usually at a ratio of 1:1 with the amount committed to the sponsored property.[34] Therefore organizations need to have a carefully thought—out and well-planned sponsorship strategy. The five principal objectives of sponsorship are to gain publicity, create entertainment opportunities, foster favourable brand and company associations, improve community relations, and create promotional opportunities.

Exhibit 10.4 Nike has been an extensive user of sports sponsorship in building its brand globally

Gaining publicity

Sponsorship provides ample opportunity to create publicity in the news media. Worldwide events such as major golf, football and tennis tournaments supply the platform for global media coverage. Such **event sponsorship** can provide exposure to millions of people. For example, DHL, the German-owned package delivery company, signed a deal to sponsor major league baseball in the USA. This was part of a strategy by DHL to raise its awareness level in the US market where it has a small share and which is also home to its two major global rivals, UPS and FedEx.[35] The publicity opportunities of sponsorship can provide major awareness shifts. For example, Canon's sponsorship of football in the UK raised awareness of the brand name from 40 per cent to 85 per cent among males. Similarly Texaco's prompted recall improved from 18 per cent to 60 per cent because of its motor racing sponsorship.[36]

Creating entertainment opportunities

A major objective of much sponsorship is to create entertainment opportunities for customers and the trade. Sponsorship of music, the arts and sports events can be particularly effective. For example, Barclays Capital sponsored a fashion show at London's Natural History Museum for 450 of its clients that were attending a global borrowers and investors forum. Often, key personalities are invited to join the sponsor's guests to add further attractiveness to the event. Similarly, sponsors of the Global Challenge yacht race, such as Norwich Union, BP and BT, used the event to entertain their best clients on board sponsored boats in desirable locations like Boston and Cape Town.[37]

Fostering favourable brand and company associations

A third objective of sponsorship is to create favourable associations for the brand and company. For example, sponsorship of athletes by Lucozade Sport brand reinforces its market position and its energy associations. Red Bull has built a global brand on the back of sponsorship of everything from Formula 1 motor racing to extreme sports such as cliff diving. Both the sponsor and the sponsored activity become involved in a relationship with a transfer of values from activity to sponsor. The audience, finding the sponsor's name, logo and other symbols threaded through the event, learns to associate sponsor and activity with one another. For example, the German lifestyle clothing company

Puma has entered a boat (shaped like a shoe) in the prestigious Volvo Ocean race. Footage showing the dangers and thrills faced by yachtsmen and women reflect well on the Puma brand but come at a high price as the cost of participation can reach $30 million.[38]

Improving community relations

Sponsorship of schools – for example, by providing low-cost personal computers as Tesco has done – and supporting community programmes can foster a socially responsible, caring reputation for a company. Many multinational companies get involved in community initiatives in local markets. For example, UBS has had sponsorships with the Tate art gallery, the London Symphony Orchestra and some inner-city schools like the Bridge Academy in London.

Creating promotional opportunities

Sponsorship events provide an ideal opportunity to promote company brands. Sweatshirts, bags, pens, and so on, carrying the company logo and name of the event can be sold to a captive audience. One of the attractions of O2's sponsorship of the former Millennium Dome (now known as the O2) was to showcase the latest in mobile phone technology and WiFi services as part of improving the overall visitor experience at the Dome.[39] For example, O2 customers can avoid having to get a paper ticket and instead receive a barcode on their phones that allows them access to an event. By doing so, O2 is hoping to both win new customers and persuade existing customers to buy new services. Similarly, Orange UK provided Glastonbury festival-goers with a 'Text Me Home' tent finder facility as well as a wind-powered mobile phone charger that could be attached to tents overnight.[40]

New developments in sponsorship

Sponsorship has experienced major growth in the past 20 years. Some of the factors driving the rise in sponsorship expenditure include the escalating costs of media advertising, restrictive government policies on tobacco and alcohol advertising, the fragmentation of traditional mass media, the proven record of sponsorship and greater media coverage of sponsored events.[41] Accompanying the growth of event sponsorship has been the phenomenon of **ambush marketing**. Originally, the term referred to the activities of companies that tried to associate themselves with an event without paying any fee to the event owner. Nike has been a particularly successful ambush marketer at various Olympic Games and indeed emerged as the name Asian viewers most closely associated with the Athens Games even though it was not one of the event's official sponsors.[42] The activity is legal as long as no attempt is made to use an event symbol, logo or mascot. For example, Pepsi ran an advertising campaign in 2010 featuring some of the world's most famous soccer players such as Lionel Messi playing local boys on the Serengeti plains. This was a challenge for Coca-Cola, one of the South African World Cup's major sponsors. Regulations are catching up with the ambush marketers, such as provisions in the London Olympics Bill that outlawed the words 'gold', 'summer' and '2012' in advertisements by non-sponsors of the 2012 Olympics.

The selection of an event or individual to sponsor requires that consideration is given to a number of key questions. These include the firm's communication objectives, its target market, the promotional opportunities presented, the costs involved and the risks associated with the sponsorship. The latter point is examined in Marketing in Action 10.2. As with all communications initiatives, the sponsorship should be carefully evaluated against the initial objectives to assess whether it was successful or not. For example, Budweiser beer sales in the UK were up by 18.6 per cent in the second quarter of 2010 compared with the same period in 2009 due largely to its sponsorship of the World Cup in South Africa. Its 'man-of-the-match' vote following each of the 64 games generated 1.5 million fan votes and 2.7 million fans participated in the Budweiser 'paint your face' promotion on Facebook.[43] Similarly, BT estimated that media coverage of its sponsorship of the Global Challenge yacht race covered costs by a multiple of three and the official website attracted more than 30 million hits per race. However, recent research has shown that only 35 per cent of respondents 'always or nearly always' measure their sponsorship and event marketing returns.[44]

Other promotional techniques

Because of the fragmentation of traditional audiences such as press and television, a variety of other promotional techniques are becoming more commonplace. Four popular mass communications tools are exhibitions and product placement as well as ambient advertising and guerrilla marketing, which are examined below.

Exhibitions

Exhibitions are unique in that, of all the promotional tools available, they are the only one that brings buyers, sellers and competitors together in a commercial setting. In Europe, the Cologne trade exhibitions bring together 28,000 exhibitors from 100 countries with 1.8 million buyers from 150 countries. Exhibitions are a particularly important part of the industrial promotional mix and can be a key source of information on buyers' needs and preferences.

Exhibitions are growing in their number and variety. Aside from the major industry exhibitions such as motor shows and property shows, more specialized lifestyle exhibitions are emerging in niche markets. For example, the Cosmo show, featuring cosmetics and targeting young women, attracts over 55,000 visitors. The 1999 event was the launch pad for Olay Colour (formerly Oil of Ulay) to reveal its new identity and for the launch of Cussons' new moisturizer, Aqua Source.

Exhibitions can have a variety of objectives, including identifying prospects and determining their needs, building relationships, providing product demonstrations, making sales, gathering competitive intelligence and fostering the image of the company. They require careful planning and management to ensure that they run smoothly. And a post-show evaluation needs to take place to determine their effectiveness. Fortunately, there are a variety of variables that can easily be quantified, which can be used to measure success. These include number of visitors to the stand, number of leads generated, number of orders received and their value, and so on. Following up the trade show through contact with prospects and customers is also important.

Product placement

Product placement is the deliberate placing of products and/or their logos in movies, television, songs and video games, usually in return for money. While it has been big business in some countries, like the USA, for some time, restrictions preventing product placement have only recently been relaxed in Europe. For example, Steven Spielberg's sci-fi film *Minority Report* featured more than 15 major brands, including Gap, Nokia, Pepsi, Guinness, Lexus and Amex, with their logos appearing on video billboards throughout the film. These product placements earned Dreamworks and 20th Century Fox $25 million, which went some way towards reducing the $102 million production costs of the film.[45] Corporate tie-ins with movies are also big business. For example, when the Superman 'Man of

Marketing in Action 10.2 Lance Armstrong: what am I on?

Critical Thinking: Below is a review of some examples of where sponsorships have resulted in negative publicity for the companies involved. Read it and critically evaluate whether you think it is the sponsor or the sponsee that is most negatively affected by this kind of controversy.

Sponsorship, in its modern form, is effectively a partnership between two entities. To be effective it should meet the criteria for successful relationships outlined in Chapter 7 of this book. So commercial organizations entering into these kinds of arrangements need to be very aware of the downside risks attached to associating themselves with particular individuals or events. High-profile sports people or celebrities represent the most risky partner because controversies that these people become involved in may negatively affect the brands that are associated with them. The list of instances where this has occurred is a long one. Multiple Olympic gold medal winning swimmer Michael Phelps was dropped by a range of sponsors including Kellogg's, AT&T and Rosetta Stone after footage emerged in 2009 of him smoking marijuana. Similarly, the British fashion model Kate Moss lost deals with brands like H&M, Chanel and Burberry after she also became embroiled in a drug scandal in 2005. The former American football player and movie star, O. J. Simpson was dropped by Hertz when he became a suspect in the murder of his wife and her friend.

One of the biggest falls from grace in recent times was that of the professional cyclist Lance Armstrong. What had first appeared to be a very inspiring story (which appealed to a variety of brands) subsequently turned out to be a fraud. Armstrong had been diagnosed with cancer in 1996 and after a significant period of treatment and rehabilitation he returned to his sport in 1998. Between 1999 and 2005 he won the sport's most

difficult race, the Tour de France, an unprecedented seven times in a row, a feat that had never been achieved before. One of his major partners during these successful years was Nike and in one of its adverts Armstrong directly addresses those who were suspicious of his achievements by asking 'What am I on?' His answer was that he was on his bike pushing himself and just doing it as his partner's slogan advocates. However, it subsequently transpired that he was on much more. In 2012, he was found guilty of systematic performance-enhancing drug use. He was stripped of his titles and banned from the sport for life. Though he had always maintained his innocence, he eventually appeared on American television to admit that he had lied and used banned substances.

At the height of his powers in 2005, Armstrong was earning $17.5 million per year in endorsement deals with brands including Trek Bicycles, Giro helmets, Radioshack, Anheuser-Busch, Oakley sunglasses and others. All of these brands wanted to be part of the successful Armstrong story but began to terminate deals when it became apparent that the evidence against him was overwhelming. Even Nike, a brand that has stuck with other controversial stars such as Tiger Woods and Kobe Bryant, quickly terminated their deal with him and by the end of 2012 all his corporate partners had left. As a statement by Oakley put it, 'When he joined our family he was a symbol of possibility …. We are deeply saddened by the outcome'.

Based on: Madden (2012);[46] Tredinnick (2012).[47]

Steel' movie was released in 2013, it generated an income of $160 million from 100 corporate partners. So for example, Gillette produced a video on how Superman shaves, Walmart offered patrons an exclusive screening and Hershey's Twizzler was a

Facebook promotion that let users create and star in a Superman-themed video.[48]

Similarly in the music business, when the hip-hop artist Busta Rhymes had a smash hit with 'Pass the Courvoisier', US sales of the cognac rose by 14 per cent in volume and 11 per cent in value. Allied Domecq, the brand's owner, claims it did not pay for the plug, but McDonald's is more upfront, offering hip-hop artists $5 each time they mention Big Mac in a song.[49] The value of product placement deals in the USA grew from $174 million in 1974 and was estimated to be worth $7.6 billion in 2009.[50]

Product placement has grown significantly in recent years for the following reasons: media fragmentation means it is increasingly hard to reach mass markets; the brand can benefit from the positive associations it gains from being in a film or television show; many consumers do not realize that the brand has been product-placed; repetition of the movie or television show means that the brand is seen again and again; careful choice of movie or television show means that certain segments can be targeted; and promotional and merchandising opportunities can be generated on the show's website. For example, the clothes and accessories worn by actresses in popular television shows like *Sex and the City* and *Desperate Housewives* have been in great demand from viewers and some have quickly sold out. Show producers are increasingly looking at the merchandising opportunities that their shows can present. Technological developments in the online gaming sector allow for different products to be placed in games at different times of the day or in different geographic locations, expanding the marketing possibilities available to companies. Product placement is significantly more restricted in Europe than it is in the USA, though the Audiovisual Media Services Directive adopted by the EU in 2007 permits greater levels of placement on EU television programmes but not news, current affairs, sport or children's programming.

While product placement is becoming very popular, it is important to remember that there are risks involved. If the movie or television show fails to take off it can tarnish the image of the brand and reduce its potential exposure. Audiences can become annoyed by blatant product placement, damaging the image, and brand owners may not have complete control over how their brand is portrayed. Also the popularity of product placement is fast giving rise to claims that it constitutes deceptive advertising. Lobby groups in the USA claim that one of the difficulties with product placement is that it can't be controlled by the consumer in the way the traditional advertising breaks can through zapping, and want it restricted.

Product placement is subject to the same kinds of analysis as all the other promotional techniques described in this chapter. For example, in the James Bond movie *Die Another Day*, the Ford Motor Company had three of its car brands 'starring' in the film: an Aston Martin Vanquish, a Thunderbird and a Jaguar XKR. Movie-goers were interviewed both before and after seeing the film to see if their opinions of the brands had changed. In addition, the product placement was part of an integrated campaign including public relations and advertising, which ensured that even people who had not seen the film were aware of Ford's association with it. During the film's peak viewing periods in the USA and UK, Ford's research found that the number of times its name appeared in the media increased by 34 per cent and that Ford corporate messages appeared in 29 per cent of the Bond-related coverage.[51]

Ambient advertising and guerrilla marketing

Two increasingly popular mass communications techniques are **ambient advertising** and **guerrilla marketing**. Ambient advertising generally refers to advertising carried on outdoor media that does not fall into the established outdoor categories such as billboards and bus signs. Therefore advertising that appears on shopping bags, on petrol pump nozzles, on balloons or on banners towed by airplanes, on street pavements, on overhead lockers on an aircraft and so on are classed as ambient (see Exhibit 10.5). Ambient media is only limited by advertiser imagination.

Closely related to ambient advertising is guerrilla marketing. In essence, the latter is the delivery of advertising messages through unexpected means and in ways that almost 'ambush' the consumer to gain attention. One of the most effective guerrilla marketing campaigns was that used by Carlsberg in the UK which also employed its well-known positioning slogan 'Carlsberg don't do . . . but if they did it would probably be the best . . . in the world'. The company dropped £50,000 worth of £5 and £10 notes all over London on which were stickers containing the slogan – 'Carlsberg don't do litter but if they did, it would probably be the best litter in the world'. For a small advertising investment, the brand received enormous publicity.

Ambient and guerrilla tactics tend to be used by advertisers with limited budgets or to complement a bigger budget campaign. The main strength of these techniques lies in their ability to capture audience attention though they also come in for criticism in that they add to the proliferation of advertising messages in society.

Exhibit 10.5 This very clever piece of guerrilla advertising demonstrates the possibilities of the communications tool

Summary

This chapter has provided an overview of the promotional mix and examined some important mass communications techniques. The following key issues were addressed.

1. The promotional mix is broad, comprising seven elements, namely, advertising, sales promotion, publicity, sponsorship, direct marketing, digital marketing and personal selling. Decisions regarding which combination to use will be driven by the nature of the product, resource availability, the nature of the market and the kind of strategies being pursued by the company.

2. Because of the breadth of promotional techniques available, it is necessary to adopt an integrated approach to marketing communications. This means that companies carefully blend the promotional mix elements to deliver a clear, consistent, credible and competitive message in the marketplace.

3. It is important to take a systematic approach to communications planning. The various steps involved include consideration of the company's marketing and positioning strategy, identifying the target audience, setting communications objectives, creating the message, selecting the promotional mix, setting the promotional budget, executing the strategy and evaluating the strategy.

4. Advertising is a highly visible component of marketing, but it is only one element of the promotional mix. Advertising strategy involves an analysis of the target audience, setting objectives, budgeting decisions, message and media decisions, and evaluating advertising effectiveness. Significant ethical issues surround the use of advertising, which is also undergoing many changes due to developments in technology.

5. Sales promotions are a powerful technique for giving a short-term boost to sales or for encouraging trial. Some of the most popular consumer promotion techniques include premiums, coupons, loyalty cards and money-offs, while discounts and allowances are popular trade promotion techniques.

6. Publicity plays a very important role in the promotional mix. It is the mechanism through which organizations communicate with their various publics. It has more credibility than advertising and incurs no direct media costs, but firms cannot control the content or timing of publication.

7. Sponsorship is a popular form of promotion. The most common types of sponsorship include sports, the arts, community activities and celebrities. Its principal objectives are to generate publicity for the sponsor, create entertainment opportunities and foster favourable brand and company associations.

8. Other important mass communications techniques include exhibitions, product placement, ambient marketing and guerrilla marketing, all of which play different roles in the promotional mix.

Study questions

1. What is meant by integrated marketing communications? Explain the advantages of taking an integrated approach to marketing communications.
2. Select three recent advertising campaigns with which you are familiar. Discuss the target audience, objectives and message executions adopted in each case.
3. It is frequently argued that much promotional expenditure is wasteful. Discuss the ways in which the effectiveness of the various promotional techniques described in this chapter can be measured.
4. Discuss the role of sponsorship in the promotional mix.
5. There is no such thing as bad publicity. Discuss.
6. Discuss the reasons why ambient and guerrilla marketing have become such popular promotional techniques for some product categories. What are the ethical issues surrounding the growth of these mass communications techniques?
7. Visit www.youtube.com. Examine some adverts for a brand or organization of your choice. Discuss the message that the adverts are attempting to convey, as well as the creative treatment used.

Suggested reading

Hackley, C. (2010) *Advertising and Promotion: An Integrated Marketing Communications Approach*, London: Sage.

Kitchen, P., I. Kim and D. Schultz (2008) Integrated Marketing Communications: Practice Leads Theory, *Journal of Advertising Research* 48 (4), 531–46.

Nichols, W. (2013) Advertising Analytics 2.0, *Harvard Business Review*, 91 (3), 60–8.

Raghubir, P., J. Inman and H. Grande (2004) The Three Faces of Consumer Promotions, *California Management Review*, 46 (4), 23–43.

Reinartz, W. and P. Saffert (2013) Creativity in Advertising: When it Works and When it Doesn't, *Harvard Business Review*, 91 (6), 106–12.

Robinson, D. (2006) Public Relations Comes of Age, *Business Horizons*, 49 (3), 247–56.

Ryan, A. and J. Fahy (2012) Evolving Priorities in Sponsorship: From Media Management to Network Management, *Journal of Marketing Management*, 28 (9/10), 1132–58.

Tellis, G. and K. Tellis (2009) Research on Advertising in a Recession: A Critical Review and Synthesis, *Journal of Advertising Research*, 39 (3), 304–27.

When you have read this chapter

log on to the Online Learning Centre for
Foundations of Marketing at
www.mheducation.co.uk/textbooks/fahy5
where you'll find links and extra online study tools for marketing.

References

1. **Anonymous** (2013) Coca-Cola South Pacific: Share a Coke, Emap Ltd; Warc.com; **Grimes, T.** (2013) What the Share a Coke Campaign Can Teach Other Brands, *Guardian.com*, 24 July; **O'Reilly, L.** (2013) Coke Uses Ads to Thank Consumers for 'Share a Coke' Success, *MarketingWeek.co.uk*, 11 September; **Silverstein, B.** (2013) Coca-Cola Gets Personal in Europe with 'Share a Coke' Campaign, Brandchannel.com, 15 May.

2. **Brinded, L.** (2014) World Cup 2014 to Propel Global Advertising Spend to $524bn, *Ibtimes.co.uk*, 16 June.

3. **Anonymous** (2011), I've Got You Labelled, *The Economist*, 2 April, 74.

4. **Bruell, A.** (2013) Nokia Rethinks Global Marketing as a Challenger Brand, *AdAge.com*, 3 July.

5. **Piercy, N.** (1987) The Marketing Budgeting Process: Marketing Management Implications, *Journal of Marketing*, **51** (4), 45-59.

6. **Tellis, G.** and **K. Tellis** (2009) Research on Advertising in a Recession: A Critical Review and Synthesis, *Journal of Advertising Research*, **39** (3), 304-27.

7. **Silverman, G.** (2006) Is 'it' the Future of Advertising? *Financial Times*, 24 January, 11.

8. **Anonymous** (2004) Sex Doesn't Sell, *The Economist*, 30 October, 46-7.

9. **Rigby, E**. (2005) Tesco's Victory over Asda Advert Ends Year-Long Row, *Financial Times*, 18 August, 5.

10. **Lannon, J.** (1991) Developing Brand Strategies across Borders, *Marketing and Research Today*, August, 160-7.

11. **Anonymous** (2013) Samsung Mobile USA: The Next Big Thing is Already Here, Effie Worldwide Inc: Warc.com.

12. **Ellet, J.** (2012) 3 Reasons Samsung's Latest Advertising Poking Apple is So Smart, *Forbes.com*, 20 September.

13. **Kovach, S.** (2012) Samsung is Still Crushing Apple in Smartphone Market Share, *BusinessInsider.com*, 14 November.

14. **Ritson, M.** (2003) It's the Ad Break: . . . and the Viewers are Talking, Reading and Snogging, *Financial Times Creative Business*, 4 February, 8-9; **Silverman, G.** (2005) Advertisers are Starting to Find Television a Turn-off, *Financial Times*, 26 July, 20.

15. **Terazono, E.** (2005) TV Fights for its 30 Seconds of Fame, *Financial Times*, 20 September, 13.

16. **Grimshaw, C.** (2003) Standing Out in the Crowd, *Financial Times*, Creative Business, 6 May, 7.

17. **Bell, E.** (1992) Lies, Damned Lies and Research, *Observer*, 28 June, 46.

18. **Anonymous** (2005) Consumer Republic, *The Economist*, 19 March, 63, 66.

19. **Smith, P.R.** (1993) *Marketing Communications: An Integrated Approach*, London: Kogan Page, 116.

20. See **Tomkins, R.** (1999) Getting a Bigger Bang for the Advertising Buck, *Financial Times*, 24 September, 17; and **Waters, R.** (1999) P&G Ties Advertising Agency Fees to Sales, *Marketing Week*, 16 September, 1.

21. **Roth**schild, M.L. and W.C. Gaidis (1981) Behavioral Learning Theory: Its Relevance to Marketing and Promotions, *Journal of Marketing*, **45** (Spring), 70-8.

22. **Tuck, R.T.J.** and **W.G.B. Harvey** (1972) Do Promotions Undermine the Brand? *Admap*, January, 30-3.

23. **Brown, R.G.** (1974) Sales Response to Promotions and Advertising, *Journal of Advertising Research*, **14** (4), 33-9.

24. **Ehrenberg, A.S.C., K. Hammond** and **G.J. Goodhardt** (1994) The After-effects of Price-related Consumer Promotions, *Journal of Advertising Research*, **34** (4), 1-10.

25. **Ariely, D.** (2008) *Predictably Irrational*, London: HarperCollins Publishers, 54.

26. **Davidson, J.H.** (1998) *Offensive Marketing*, Harmondsworth: Penguin, 249-71.

27. **Anonymous** (2011) De Bijenkorf: The Crazy Queue, European Association of Communication Agencies; Warc.com.

28. **Anonymous** (2005) An Overdose of Bad News, *The Economist*, 19 March, 69-71.

29. **Doyle, P.** and **J. Saunders** (1985) The Lead Effect of Marketing Decisions, *Journal of Marketing Research*, **22** (1), 54-65.

30. **Lesly, P.** (1991) *The Handbook of Public Relations and Communications*, Maidenhead: McGraw-Hill, 13-19.

31. **Lesly, P.** (1991) *The Handbook of Public Relations and Communications*, Maidenhead: McGraw-Hill, 13-19.

32. **Sleight, S.** (1989) *Sponsorship: What it is and How to Use it*, Maidenhead, McGraw-Hill, 4.

33. **Anonymous** (2012) Victors and Spoils, *The Economist*, 21 July, 20-21.

34. **Papadimitriou, D** and **A. Apostolopoulou** (2009), Olympic Sponsorship Activation and the Creation of Competitive Advantage, *Journal of Promotion Management*, **15** (1/2), 90-117.

35. **Ward, A.** (2005) DHL Goes For Home Run in Rival's Back Yard, *Financial Times*, 6 April, 31.

36. **Mintel** (1991) *Sponsorship: Special Report*, London: Mintel International Group.

37. **Friedman, V.** (2003) Banks Step on to the Catwalk, *Financial Times*, 3 July, 12.

38. **Mallet, V.** (2008) Retail Brands See Oceans of Opportunity at the Helm, *Financial Times*, 19 December, 12.

39. **Carter, M.** (2007) Sponsorship Branding Takes on New Name, *Financial Times*, 13 March, 12.

40. **O'Daly, K.** (2008) Main Event, *Marketing Age*, November/December, 46-9.

41. **Miles, L.** (1995) Sporting Chancers, *Marketing Director International*, **6** (2), 50-2.

42. **Bowman, J.** (2004) Swoosh Rules Over Official Olympic Brands, *Media Asia*, 10 September, 22.

43. **Farrell, G.** (2010) Sponsors Score with World Cup as Football Promotions Lift Sales, *Financial Times*, 16 August, 15.

44. **Meenaghan, T.** (2011) Mind the Gap in Sponsorship Measurement, *Admap*, February (available online).

45. **Anonymous** (2002) The Top Ten Product Placements in Features, *Campaign*, 17 December, 36.

46. **Madden, L.** (2012) Sponsors Who Have Dropped Lance Armstrong (And the List Goes On), *Forbes.com*, 19 October.

47. **Tredinnick, A.** (2012) Lance Armstrong Has Lost His Last Sponsor, *BusinessInsider.com*, 22 October.

48. **Morrison, M.** (2013) Superman Reboot 'Man of Steel' Snares $160M in Promotions, *Adage.com*, 3 June.

49. **Tomkins, R.** (2003) The Hidden Message: Life's a Pitch, and Then You Die, *Financial Times*, 24 October, 14; **Armstrong, S.** (2005) How to Put Some Bling into Your Brand, *Irish Times*, *Weekend*, 30 July, 7.

50. **Silverman, G.** (2005) After the Break: The 'Wild West' Quest to Bring the Consumers to the Advertising, *Financial Times*, 18 May, 17.

51. **Dowdy, C.** (2003) Thunderbirds Are Go, *Financial Times*, Creative Business, 24 June, 10.

Captain Morgan: integrating traditional and social media to build a successful brand

Introduction

Previously known as Morgan's Spiced, Captain Morgan Original Spiced Gold is a spirits brand produced by the world's leading premium drinks business Diageo. Diageo is the proud owner of some of the biggest drinks brands in the world, such as Smirnoff, Johnnie Walker, Guinness, Baileys, J&B, Jose Cuervo, Bushmills, Tanqueray and Captain Morgan.

Inspired by the 17th century Welsh buccaneer, Captain Henry Morgan (1635–88) who eventually became Governor of Jamaica, Captain Morgan Spiced Gold was first launched in the USA in 1983.[1] The Captain Morgan brand is the third biggest spirit in the USA and the fastest growing spirit brand within the top 20 globally.[2] With a presence that extends to six continents, Captain Morgan is committed to 'conquering new territories' and strengthening its position in the spirits market on a global scale.[3]

In 2013, Diageo launched a new-look bottle for Captain Morgan Original Spiced Gold in Britain, to tie it in line with its brand name and identity in other worldwide markets. This came two years after Morgan's Spiced was rebranded Captain Morgan's Spiced in Britain. The aim of the new-look brand was to put more focus on the brand's personality Sir Henry Morgan

and was backed by a £9 million marketing campaign. Central to its new brand identity was the character Captain Morgan who is used to give the brand a unique identifiable personality.[4] He is promoted as someone with a fun-loving personality, who symbolizes legendary times and fun. Diageo see him as someone who appeals to the target market for the brand – 18–24-year-olds. The addition of the Captain Morgan figurehead to the title and the label of the brand is seen to be vitally important in distinguishing the brand in the ever competitive spirits marketplace.[1]

Graham Villiers-Tuthill, Captain Morgan brand manager, emphasized, 'Captain Morgan is an iconic brand which is all about fun and partying. The Captain Morgan character has celebrity status in the US and other markets and we are introducing this rebellious, yet playful personality through our digital and on-trade activity. Captain Morgan will appeal to our consumers not only for being a well-known premium-quality brand, but also as a legendary partier.'[4] The move appears to have been a good one for Captain Morgan as in 2012 the brand saw record sales growth and became only the sixth premium spirit brand ever to sell 10 million cases in one year.[5]

Exhibit CIO.I Captain Morgan's new branding

The growth of personal and participation media

When relaunching Captain Morgan in the British market, Diageo were conscious of the fact that the global marketplace was evolving and this affected the way consumers lived and interacted with brands. As the world went online, a whole new media stream opened up to feed a dynamic marketplace. Diageo realized they had to integrate the role of social media into their 360 strategy to build a broader range of engaging activities and two-way dialogue with consumers. In addition, they began to place more emphasis on experiential marketing and social diffusion activities. Diageo wanted to forge ahead of its competition with marketing innovations in viral, digital and experience based platforms and up-weighted their spend in the digital space.[6]

Diageo has invested heavily in social media alcohol marketing. In 2010, this accounted for 21 per cent of Diageo's marketing budget. It appears to be paying off with more younger people now invested more in spirits than beer. The company extended its multi-million dollar partnership with Facebook in 2011 after reporting that Diageo brands had collectively enjoyed a 20 per cent increase in sales as a direct result of Facebook activity. Diageo's social media marketing involves the use of a multi-platform social media presence as well as smartphone apps and blogs, often alongside traditional offline marketing. These social media platforms encourage users to interact with sites via the 'like' and 'comment' and 'share' functions, posting photos of themselves and their friends on nights out.[7]

When relaunching Captain Morgan in Britain, Diageo wanted to appeal to its target market by involving them in memorable, shared experiences by using social media and online endeavours to promote the Captain Morgan brand. Diageo have become masters of leveraging new technology and new media. Diageo realized that their target audience lives online, so creating a Captain Morgan GB Facebook page was seen as a natural progression for the brand. Facebook was given a specific role within the Captain's communications strategy and the Captain Morgan Great Britain Facebook page was established (www.

facebook.com/CaptainMorganGB). The Captain would run the Facebook page and his playful tone would be maintained throughout all communications.[8]

'Live Like the Captain' campaign

In September 2013, Diageo announced that it was launching an advertising campaign for the British market worth £1.8 million as part of a significant global investment in the brand. The new marketing drive included a year-long TV advertising campaign, social media activity and point-of-sale materials for all channels including the on-trade. The campaign's strapline was 'Live Like the Captain' and showed Captain Morgan's journeys and adventures. According to Sam Newby, marketing manager for Captain Morgan at Diageo, 'It's an exciting time for Captain Morgan Original Spiced Gold as we begin to tell our epic tale and bring the legend to life with an impactful new lively and creative advertising campaign. The distinctive bottle will still contain the same legendary liquid 'Spiced Gold', but reinforce the brand's identity with a fresh new look designed to capture the imagination of consumers.'[9]

The TV advertisement

The new Captain Morgan TV advertisement aired on British television on 10 September 2013, during the England vs. Ukraine football match on ITV. It ran for a year-long media plan, encouraging consumers to 'Live Like the Captain'. The TV advertisement showcased the epic journeys, legendary adventures and charisma of Sir Henry Morgan to a contemporary audience in an attempt to bring to life the legendary figure behind the brand.[3] The TV advert showed Captain Morgan in a series of shots riding a horse, discovering treasure in a dark cave, before stripping off his shirt and being admired by women, all while being cheered on by crowds and his crew. It ends with a voiceover stating: 'Make no mistake about the man on the bottle of Captain Morgan. The man was a legend. A hero history remembers. A liver of life. A man who led with his heart and showed his crew a life more legendary. Captain Morgan. Live Like the Captain,' ending with the onscreen text 'Captain Morgan ... LIVE LIKE THE CAPTAIN ... DRINK RESPONSIBLY CAPTAIN'S ORDERS'... for the facts drinkaware.co.uk'.[10]

The controversy

Despite the popularity of the 'Live Like the Captain' TV advertising campaign, in February 2014 the TV advertisement was pulled after the UK's media regulator (the Advertising Standards Agency - ASA) upheld a complaint that the ad linked alcohol with 'aggressive behaviour'.[10] The ASA noted scenes showing the Captain driving a carriage at speed, searching a cave for treasure and emerging from the sea having apparently dived from his ship. 'We considered that those actions and the settings shown in the ad would be associated with buccaneers and seafarers renowned for drinking rum and for their disregard for authority and the well-being of others.'[11] They concluded that the depiction of the character and his actions, especially when placed alongside the slogan 'LIVE LIKE THE CAPTAIN' in an advertisement for rum, linked alcohol with daring and aggressiveness. Therefore, the ASA ordered that the advertisement could not be shown again and Diageo was warned not to employ a similar tactic for its other brands.[10]

Diageo defended the TV spot, which it credited for helping to return sales across Britain to growth after several quarters, in its latest results, claiming it was far removed from the 'real-life' of today. Diageo claimed that 'all of the scenes were set in a stylized historic way so as to educate consumers that Captain Morgan was based on a genuine historical buccaneer character and illustrated the brand's heritage in a positive and responsible light'. It pointed to the minimal appearance of the drink in the ad and said there was 'nothing to suggest' the rum enhanced the Captain's skills as a buccaneer.[12]

The website

In addition to the TV advertising campaign, Diageo encouraged their target audience to visit their complementary online site – www.livelikethecaptain.com. This site challenged young men globally to prove their skills as an ultimate charmer, first winning the heart of a 17th century countess and then partying with none other than the legend himself, Captain Morgan. Fans were transported back to Port Royal Jamaica in the year 1669, the Captain's hometown. A highly personalized and authentic experience, Facebook connect technology allowed them to become an integral part of his interactive adventure. The top performing charmers were entered into a prize draw and invited to exclusive Captain Morgan parties with the chance to meet the countess herself. A responsive design platform accessible across multiple devices, enabled the campaign to be delivered to over 140 markets in 27 languages, reaching a target audience of over 12 million people.[13]

Captain Morgan's use of social media

Captain Morgan's success is due to its ability to integrate social and traditional media and this was an approach that it used when launching the 'Live Like the Captain' campaign. Since the rebranding of Captain Morgan Spiced in Britain in 2011, Diageo has used social media, particularly Facebook, Twitter and YouTube, extensively. The Captain Morgan Facebook page is the main hub of all its social media activity. The page frequently features pictures of a real Captain Morgan, videos and regular competitions all of which are centred on Captain Morgan himself. For example, in 2011 Diageo launched the Captain's Island, a multimedia campaign which ran via Captain Morgan's Facebook page. The competition gave fans the opportunity to win an adventure to a private island where a series of competitions would give a lucky team $15,000. Using Facebook as its hub and utilising an interactive app, fans had

to collect keys to enter the campaign. These keys were available on promotional packs, online challenges and at experiential events. Each key had a unique code which when entered on the Captain Morgan Facebook page, would enter the applicant into the competition.[14]

These digital initiatives were also extended into 2012 to promote the UEFA Euro 2012. The £3 million Euro 2012 campaign featured an unofficial football anthem video and a digital app called 'Captain's Orders', which gave users the chance to win a party kit bag.[14] In 2012, Diageo ran a promotional campaign which offered anyone who bought any promotional bottle of Captain Morgan the opportunity to claim a free Captain Morgan glass tankard. In an effort to link offline and social media, consumers had to visit and like the Captain Morgan Facebook app, enter the code from the bottle's promotional collar and claim the free glass tankard. This was a great way for the brand to build Facebook likes and to get the target audience to engage with the brand via social media.[15]

With over 5.2 million likes for the Captain Morgan British Facebook page (www.facebook.com/CaptainMorganGB), Diageo are using Facebook to market rum to a digital generation. They use the Captain's distinctive personality and authentic voice to interact with fans on their level while showcasing the Captain's legendary shareable humour.[16] The brand has also recently experimented with real-time creative as well. Captain Morgan has used custom meme-style cards on Facebook to tell topical brand-themed stories daily. For example, when Prince Harry's Vegas adventures made it into the news, the Captain was sure to tell the Queen that Harry wasn't drinking with him. When news leaked that Kim and Kanye were having a baby, the Captain just happened to overhear Kanye singing 'Baby, Baby, Baby' and as Gangnam Style went global, the Captain reminded fans that Pirate Style would never go out of style.[17]

Buzz marketing

To complement the use of online and offline media, Captain Morgan has also used buzz marketing to raise the profile of the brand. The Captain Morgan character appears at public events, almost guaranteeing some media coverage. PR stunts then get fed back into social media to help further promote the brand. In a recent move, Diageo used interactive washroom technology to tie in with the 2014 World Cup. It created a game with technology specialist Captive Media where men could score a goal through radical peeing at a urinal! The Captain's Cannon washroom game is linked to media above the urinal. Consumers can compete for the accolade of 'top goal scorer' by playing hands free whilst at the urinal, using the control of their 'flow' to free the ball from the Captain's ship into the digital goal. Once the 'ammunition' has run out, each player can sign onto the national leader board using their mobile phone and tweet their score.[18] According to Samantha Newby, marketing manager for Captain Morgan Western Europe at Diageo, 'Captain Morgan is always looking for ingenious and fun ways to connect with and recruit our "crew". It is increasingly difficult for brands to stand out in bars and the Captive Media washroom technology offers an innovative way to interact with our adult audience in a fun and engaging way. The brand is then at the front of mind when consumers return to the bar, plus the game gives the guys social currency to challenge their mates to beat their score.' This campaign generated great buzz and extensive media coverage for the brand and helped complement the brand's TV and social media efforts.[19]

Conclusion

Diageo has achieved huge exposure for the Captain and the revamped Captain Morgan brand in Britain through the use of offline, online and social media for the 'Live Like the Captain' campaign. By mid-2014, the Captain Morgan Facebook page had 5.2 million likes and there was substantial press coverage of the campaign.[20] Building on this success, Diageo hopes to continue to use traditional and social media to successfully embody the brand and assist in further developing the characteristics of Captain Morgan in the British market.

References

1. http://www.businessandleadership.com/marketing/item/11577-captain-morgan-lands-in-ire
2. http://sltn.co.uk/2011/05/12/captain-aims-to-capture-success/
3. http://www.foodbev.com/news/new-18m-captain-morgan-rum-campaign#.U7B9YZRdW8A
4. http://offlicencenews.co.uk/news/fullstory.php/aid/13701/New_look_for_Captain_Morgan.html
5. http://www.morningadvertiser.co.uk/Business-Support/New-drinks-trends-for-pubs2
6. http://www.designcognition.com/2010/06/18/
7. http://alcoholireland.ie/world_news/alcohol-giants-pour-into-social-medias-digital-drinking-spaces/
8. http://www.wilsonhartnell.ie/
9. http://barmagazine.co.uk/new-design-for-captain-morgan-spiced-rum/
10. http://www.thedrinksbusiness.com/2014/02/aggressive-captain-morgan-ad-banned/
11. http://www.foodmanufacture.co.uk/Regulation/Diageo-s-Captain-Morgan-TV-advert-made-to-walk-plank
12. http://www.marketingweek.co.uk/sectors/regulation/trade-bodies/news/captain-morgan-ad-banned-for-encouraging-daring-behaviour/4009601.article
13. www.vimeo.com/81188376/
14. http://www.branditmagazine.co.uk/captain-morgans/
15. http://www.hotukdeals.com/deals/free-glass-tankard-with-captain-morgan-spiced-rum-1607407
16. http://www.tribalworldwide.co.uk/work/captain-morgan-social
17. http://www.edelmandigital.com/2013/04/30/creative-newsroom-brand-storytelling-at-the-speed-of-social
18. http://www.energypr.co.uk/blog/campaign-watch/top-pr-campaigns
19. http://barmagazine.co.uk/score-at-the-urinal-with-captain-morgans-rum-captive-media-pee/
20. https://www.facebook.com/CaptainMorganGB

Questions

1. Evaluate the importance of the Captain Morgan character to the brand's identity. Do you think the character appeals to the 18–24-year-old target market? Why?
2. Why were online and social media relied upon so heavily to promote the Captain Morgan brand in the British market? How have Diageo managed to integrate their online and offline media?
3. View the banned 'Live Like a Captain' TV ad online at https://www.youtube.com/watch?v=LEV7OImmexU or http://www.tellyads.com/show_movie.php?filename=TAI7087 . Do you think that the ASA were justified in banning this ad? Why or why not?
4. View the Captain Morgan Great Britain Facebook page (www.facebook.com/CaptainMorganGB). Comment on the various initiatives being used on this page to engage with its target market.

This case was written by Marie O' Dwyer, Lecturer in Marketing, Waterford Institute of Technology, Ireland as a basis for class discussion rather than to illustrate either effective or ineffective management.

Chapter 11

Integrated Marketing Communications 2: Direct Communications Techniques

Chapter outline

Database marketing

Customer relationship management

Direct marketing

Buzz marketing

Personal selling

Sales management

Learning outcomes

By the end of this chapter you will:

1 Understand the importance of database management as a foundation for direct marketing activities

2 Understand the role of direct marketing in the IMC mix

3 Analyse the main direct marketing techniques

4 Critique the role of direct marketing in society

5 Analyse the role of buzz marketing in the IMC mix

6 Explain the main stages in the personal selling process

7 Understand the key activities involved in sales management.

Skoda: the worst car in the country!

A key feature of modern marketing has been the moves by organizations to communicate directly with their customers on an individual basis. Technology has been a key enabler in allowing this happen. Databases of customers can be effectively stored and retrieved as needed and communications and digital media allow for a two-way conversation to take place in real time. Many businesses have a preference for sending messages directly to a recipient rather than using mass media where it is more difficult to know if the message has been received and acted upon. But to do this, organizations need to build a database of customers or potential customers in the first place. As individuals become more concerned and discerning about who they give their personal information to, this can be quite a challenging task, leading to some very innovative approaches by leading brands.

A case in point is the Czech car brand Skoda which is part of the Volkswagen group. Its Spanish subsidiary faced a big challenge due to declining demand in its local market. Spain had been hit particularly hard by the global economic recession with youth unemployment skyrocketing to 50 per cent. For example in 2007, 1.6 million vehicles were sold in Spain but by 2012 this number had more than halved to 700,000. Though Skoda was positioned as a high-quality product at an affordable price, it struggled to hold onto its small share of the market in this intensely competitive environment.

To meet this challenge, Skoda had to adopt a creative promotional strategy given its declining marketing budget. With an eye to creating an immediate impact on sales, it came up with an innovative direct marketing campaign targeting precisely those customers whose car was in need of change. Entitled 'Skoda: Change My Car' it was a competition to find the worst car in Spain. Participants registered their car on the competition website along with videos, photos and fact sheet detailing why their car should win. The winner would be chosen by public vote and the competition was publicized on social media with a leading contender posted each day. The winner got to watch their old car being destroyed as well as the keys to a brand new Skoda Yeti Fresh. The competition caught the public imagination to such an extent that the winner's car was scrapped live on a prime time television programme.

There were several positive outcomes from this campaign. First, it generated a list of almost 10,000 new prospects, almost all of which were in Skoda's target market, that it continued to communicate with via direct mail and online dialogue after the competition was finished. It proved to be an ingenious way of building up a database of potential customers. The promotion generated an 89 per cent month-on-month sales increase during the first month of the competition at a time when the general market was declining. And finally, the publicity surrounding the competition more than covered the cost of the promotion itself.[1]

Skoda Ad Insight: This innovative promotion campaign involved the public in a competition.

For many decades, mass communications techniques were favoured by marketers, and the promotional mix was heavily weighted towards tools like advertising and sales promotion. But in recent times, direct communications techniques have become very popular. There are a number of reasons for this. As we saw in the previous chapter, both the audience and the media have begun to fragment significantly, making it very difficult for companies to reach a mass market through the classic 30-second television advertisement, for example. In its place, the emergence of some new technologically based solutions, such as customer relationship management (CRM), digital marketing and social media marketing, promise a much more direct and interactive relationship with the customer. Also, one of the perennial challenges for marketers has been to justify promotional budgets, and demonstrate the impact of expenditure on awareness and sales. Direct communication techniques such as direct response advertising allow for the more effective measurement of the impact of marketing investments.

This chapter will examine direct marketing communications techniques and in Chapter 12 we will examine the rapidly developing world of digital and social media marketing in more detail. Direct marketing communications techniques rely on the availability of a database of customers, which is the foundation upon which campaigns can be built. We shall first examine database marketing and its evolution into customer relationship management. We then go on to look at the field of direct marketing itself, which has grown out of the old mail-order business. Then we will examine the growth of word-of-mouth marketing which exploits a combination of online and offline techniques. Finally, as one of the core objectives of marketing activity is to facilitate a sale, we examine the key activities of personal selling and sales management.

Database marketing

A marketing database is an 'electronic filing cabinet' containing a list of names, addresses, telephone numbers, and lifestyle and transactional data on customers and potential customers. Information such as types of purchase, frequency of purchase, purchase value and responsiveness to promotional offers may be held.

Database marketing is defined as:[2]

an interactive approach to marketing that uses individually addressable marketing media and channels (such as mail, telephone and the sales force) to:

- *provide information to a target audience*
- *stimulate demand, and*
- *stay close to customers by recording and storing an electronic database of customers, prospects and all communication and transactional data.*

Database marketing has some key characteristics. The first of these is that it allows direct communication with customers through a variety of media including **direct mail**, **telemarketing** and **direct response advertising**. Second, it usually requires the customer to respond in a way that allows the company to take action (such as contact by telephone, sending out literature or arranging sales visits). Third, it must be possible to trace the response back to the original communication. The potential of database marketing is enormous. For example, one supermarket analysed its sales and found that it was making a loss on a certain brand of cheese. Before cutting the line altogether, it correlated information about the people who were buying the product and found that they bought other high-ticket items and spent more on average on luxury goods. The supermarket concluded that it would make sense to continue selling the cheese in order to please these high-value customers.[3]

Computer technology provides the capability of storing and analysing large quantities of data from diverse sources, and presenting information in a convenient, accessible and useful format. The creation of a database relies on the collection of information on customers, which can be sourced from:

- company records
- responses to sales promotions
- warranty and guarantee cards
- offering samples that require the consumer to give name, address, telephone number, etc.; for example, some bands give away music for free in exchange for a valid email address
- enquiries
- exchanging data with other companies
- sales-force records
- application forms (e.g. to join a credit or loyalty scheme)
- complaints
- responses to previous direct marketing activities
- organized events (e.g. wine tastings)
- website registrations.

However, a key challenge for companies now is how to handle information overload due to the size and complexity of the data available. Winter Corporation's survey of databases found that over 90 per cent of those that it studied contained over 1 terabyte

(1000 gigabytes) of data compared with just 25 per cent in 2001. The large US retailer, Kmart had 12.6 terabytes of data covering stocks, sales, customers and suppliers, but this was not enough to save it from bankruptcy.[4] A recent study in the International Data Corporation estimated that less than 1 per cent of the world's data is actually analysed.[5]

Collecting information is easiest for companies that have direct contact with customers, such as those in financial services or retailing. However, even for those where the sales contact is indirect, building a database is often possible. For example, Seagram, the drinks company, built up a European database through telephone and written enquiries from customers, sales promotional returns, tastings in store, visits to company premises, exhibitions and promotions that encouraged consumers to name like-minded friends and colleagues.[6]

Figure 11.1 shows the sort of information that is recorded on a database. Customer and prospect information typically includes names, addresses, telephone numbers, names of key decision-makers within DMUs and general behavioural information. Transactional information refers to past transactions that contacts have had with the company. Transactional data must be sufficiently detailed to allow frequency, recency, amount and category (FRAC) information to be extracted for each customer. Frequency refers to how often a customer buys. Recency measures when the customer last bought; if customers are waiting longer before they re-buy (i.e. recency is decreasing) the reasons for this (e.g. less attractive offers or service problems) need to be explored. Amount measures how much a

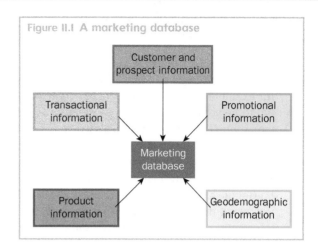

Figure 11.1 A marketing database

customer has bought and is usually recorded in value terms. Finally, category defines the type of product being bought.

Promotional information covers what promotion campaigns have been run, who has responded to them, and what the overall results were in terms of contacts, sales and profits. Product information would include which products have been promoted, who responded, when and from where. Finally, geodemographics includes information about the geographic location of customers and prospects, and the social, lifestyle and business category to which they belong. Cross-tabulating these details with transactional information can reveal the customer profile most likely to buy a particular product. Because of the amount of information held about consumers, data privacy is becoming a major issue, as discussed in Marketing and Society 11.1.

Marketing and Society 11.1 Corporations vs citizens

The advances in data tracking and storage technology mean that the amount of information that corporations and the state hold about us has never been greater. As we increase our usage of technology we leave more and more information trails behind us. Every mobile phone call that we make and the texts and emails that we send is recorded. Some governments are now requiring that operators store all this information for periods of up to three years for security purposes. As we surf the Web, click-stream analysis keeps track of where we go and what we view. Software being pioneered intercepts web page requests to build up a profile of user interests, which can then be used to target advertising. Facebook keeps track of our interests, pictures and conversations. And every time we use a store loyalty card, we enable stores to build up a picture of the kind of customer we are. The key questions that arise are how well do organizations know us, what are they doing with this information and how safe is it.

In answer to the first question, they increasingly know us very well. Database information allows organizations to build up profiles of customers. When organizations share information as, for example, members of the Nectar Card scheme can do, then consumer profiles have the potential to be very accurate because details about grocery shopping (Sainsbury's), travel and accommodation (Expedia) and credit card transactions (American Express) can all be cross-tabulated and compared. Entry into a loyalty card scheme usually requires the submission of very valuable information like employment status, number of children, number of cars you have, and so on. When all these data are mined, very accurate profiles emerge. The 2008 takeover of DoubleClick by Google also raised significant privacy issues. DoubleClick is one of the biggest users of 'cookies', small digital files that sit on computers and track the websites visited by users. When this information is combined with Google's search records, it can present a very accurate picture of a surfer's interests.

To maximize company profits, this kind of information can be used in different ways. For example, bonus points can be offered to consumers who switch purchases to high-profit items. Second, targeting is improved. For example, Gmail messages are scanned for keywords so if you use the word holiday, you may find that you get advertisements for travel companies. Third, products that offer low margins can be discontinued, which sometimes means that cost-conscious shoppers find their preferred brands are deleted and they may have to shop elsewhere, which is in effect a form of discriminatory pricing. Fourth, price changes can be tested to see how consumers react. For example, the price of a range of products might be increased for a short period and, if consumers do not react adversely, then these higher price levels might remain. Over time, a greater proportion of the store can be dedicated to higher-price items. In intensely competitive markets this is not always possible, but in sectors like grocery retailing the market is becoming dominated by a small number of very large players. Finally, in some industries like insurance, social media profiles can be used to identify and weed out high-risk customers based on their lifestyle habits.

Once consumer profiles get very accurate, the security of this information is paramount. For example, in the USA, Facebook records and loyalty card data have been presented in legal cases such as divorces to show that one side has the facility to pay more alimony. Security breaches such as this are becoming increasingly common. In 2011, Sony contacted its 70 million PlayStation Network users to confirm that hackers had carried out a massive data theft which included names, addresses, dates of birth, passwords, security questions and answers and in some cases credit card details. In 2013, 150 usernames and passwords were stolen from the technology firm Adobe who did not become aware of the theft until about two weeks after it occurred and took another two weeks to inform customers. Facebook too has been criticized for frequently changing its privacy settings or making it complicated to protect one's privacy. For example, the *New York Times* observed that users would need to navigate 50 settings with more than 150 options in order to maintain their privacy on Facebook.[7]

All this adds up to a situation where consumers need to be very aware of what information they give organizations and what permissions they give these organizations with respect to that information. Consumer rights are protected through data protection legislation. Consumers have a right to know what information organizations hold about them and who this information can be passed on to. They also have the right to opt out of marketing databases. But, in an information society, it has effectively become impossible to live a truly private life!

Suggested reading: Turow (2008).[8]

Reflection: Is it reasonable that corporations should be able to build up very accurate profiles of individuals? What are the pros and cons?

The main applications of database marketing are as follows.

1 *Direct mail*: a database can be used to select customers for mailings.
2 *Telemarketing*: a database can store telephone numbers so that customers and prospects can be contacted.
3 *Distributor management systems*: a database can be the foundation on which information is provided to distributors and their performance monitored.
4 *Loyalty marketing*: loyal customers can be selected from the database for special treatment as a reward for their loyalty (see Chapter 7).
5 *Target marketing*: groups of individuals or businesses can be targeted as a result of analysing the database.

Databases can also be used to try to build or strengthen relationships with customers. For example, Highland Distillers switched all of its promotional budget for its Macallan whisky brand from advertising to direct marketing. It built a database of 100,000 of its most frequent drinkers (those who consume at least five bottles a year), mailing them every few months with interesting facts about the brand, whisky memorabilia and offers.[9] It is these kinds of efforts to improve customer relationships that have caused the evolution of database marketing into what is now known as customer relationship management.

Customer relationship management

Customer relationship management (CRM) is a term for the methodologies, technologies and ecommerce capabilities used by firms to manage customer relationships.[10] In particular, CRM software packages aid the interaction between the customer and the company, enabling the company to coordinate all of its communications efforts so that the customer is presented with a unified message and image. CRM companies offer a range of information technology-based services, such as call centres, data analysis and website management. The basic principle behind CRM is that company staff have a single-customer point of view for each client. Customers are now using multiple channels more frequently. They may buy one product from a salesperson but another from the company website. Interactions between the customer and the company may take place in a variety of ways – through the sales force, call centres, email, distributors, websites, and so on (see Figure 11.2). For example, Heineken Ireland distributes its products through 8,000 pubs/restaurants and over 1,300 shops

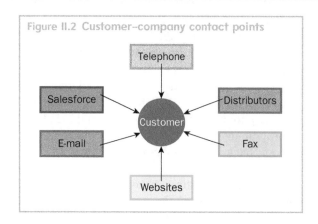

Figure 11.2 Customer–company contact points

and off-licences in Ireland. Presenting a single, up-to-date view on all these customers to all organizational staff, including a field sales force, is what a good CRM system should do.

Therefore, it is crucial that, no matter how a customer contacts a company, front-line staff have instant access to the same, up-to-date data about the customer, such as his/her details and past purchases. This usually means the consolidation of many databases held by individual departments in a company into one centralized database that can be accessed by all relevant staff. However, CRM is much more than the technology. As we saw in Chapter 7, to be effective, CRM must be integrated into the overall marketing strategy of the company. Staff must be trained on how to use the system, and accurate usage must be continually encouraged and monitored.

The key ways in which CRM systems can be used include the following.

1 *Targeting* customer and prospect groups with clearly defined propositions.
2 *Enquiry management* – this starts as soon as an individual expresses an interest and continues through qualification, lead handling and outcome reporting.
3 *Welcoming* – this covers new customers and those upgrading their relationship; it covers simple 'thank you' messages to sophisticated contact strategies.
4 *Getting to know* – customers need to be persuaded to give information about themselves; this information needs to be stored, updated and used; useful information includes attitude and satisfaction information and relationship 'health checks'.
5 *Customer development* – decisions need to be made regarding which customers to develop through higher levels of relationship management activity, and which to maintain or drop.

6 *Managing problems* – this involves early problem identification, complaint handling and 'root cause' analysis to spot general issues that have the potential to cause problems for many customers.
7 *Win-back* – activities include understanding reasons for loss, deciding which customers to try to win back, and developing win-back programmes that offer customers the chance to come back and a good reason to do so.

To date, CRM initiatives have had a very mixed success rate. Some of the factors that have been associated with success are:[11]

- having a customer orientation and organizing the CRM system around customers
- taking a single view of the customer across departments, and designing an integrated system so that all customer-facing staff can draw information from a common database
- having the ability to manage cultural change issues that arise as a result of system development and implementation
- involving users in the CRM design process
- designing the system in such a way that it can readily be changed to meet future requirements
- having a board-level champion of the CRM project, and commitment within each of the affected departments to the benefits of taking a single view of the customer
- creating 'quick wins' to provide positive feedback on the project programmes.

Direct marketing

Direct marketing is the term that is used to describe the distribution of products, information and promotional benefits to target consumers through interactive communication in a way that allows response to be measured. The origins of direct marketing lie in direct mail and mail-order catalogues and, as a result, direct marketing is sometimes seen as synonymous with 'junk mail'. However, today's direct marketers use a wide range of media, such as telemarketing, direct response advertising and email to interact with people. Also, unlike many other forms of communication, direct marketing usually requires an immediate response, which means that the effectiveness of most direct marketing campaigns can be assessed quantitatively.

A direct marketing campaign is not necessarily a short-term response-driven activity. More and more companies are using direct marketing to

develop ongoing relationships with customers (see Marketing in Action 11.1). Some estimates consider that the cost of attracting a new customer is five times that of retaining existing customers. Direct marketing activity can be one tool in the armoury of marketers in their attempt to keep current customers satisfied and spending money. Once a customer has been acquired, there is the opportunity to sell that customer other products marketed by the company. Direct Line, a UK insurance company, became market leader in motor insurance by by-passing the insurance broker to reach the consumer directly through direct-response television advertisements using a freephone number and financial appeals to encourage car drivers to contact them. Once they have sold customers motor insurance, trained telesales people offer substantial discounts on other insurance products including buildings and contents insurance. In this way, Direct Line has built a major business through using a combination of direct marketing methods.

Direct marketing covers a wide array of methods, including:

- direct mail
- telemarketing (both in-bound and out-bound)
- direct response advertising (coupon response or 'phone now')
- catalogue marketing
- inserts (leaflets in magazines)
- door-to-door leafleting.

The proportion of the promotional budget being devoted to direct marketing has been increasing steadily in recent decades. For example, in the US market alone spending on direct marketing was estimated to be worth $47 billion in 2014 with a

Marketing in Action 11.1 O2's priority customers

> **Critical Thinking:** Below is a review of Telefonica O2's Priority Moments customer loyalty programme. Read it and critically evaluate its strengths and weaknesses.

Though virtually everyone uses a mobile phone, telecommunications is an intensely competitive business. For example, mobile operators compete in an undifferentiated business whereby they rent space on an existing network and resell it to end users. As a result, the sector is characterized by high levels of competition, frequent price promotions and switching between operators is relatively easy as end users can keep their existing phone numbers leading to low levels of customer loyalty.

To try to counteract this, Telefonica O2 UK focused on a campaign designed to appeal to its existing customers who were invited to register on its website for *Priority Moments* (see Exhibit 11.1). Once their hobbies and interests were recorded, they received offers tailored specifically to their passions. The key aim of this campaign was to make the offers more special and suited to the needs of their customers rather than just be one of the many daily deals that were available from other businesses. Four levels of offer were created, namely, Extraordinary Moments (unique experiences and contests

such as a free lunch at the Upper Crust restaurant chain), Extraordinary Offers (savings on everyday items such as four free Millie's Cookies), Thank Yous (targeted rewards aimed at a value segment such as Café Nero Iced Coffee on a hot day) and Headline Moments (rewards designed to create excitement at key moments such as a Christmas dinner masterclass with Jean-Christophe Novelli).

Consumers were invited to download the *Priority Moments* app where the range of offers could be viewed and redeemed. By partnering with over 30 high street brands, O2 was able to bring a range of location-based offers to its customers. So for example, if a restaurant chain was opening a new outlet, it could invite 100 priority moments customers in that area to trial new dishes and raise awareness of the outlet. The campaign was also extended to include a wide variety of small businesses, giving these businesses an opportunity to engage in low cost mobile marketing with O2's customers.

Based on: Anonymous (2013);[12] O'Reilly (2011).[13]

further $53 billion spent on telemarketing. These two promotional techniques combined accounted for over a quarter of all US advertising spending.[14] The significant growth in direct marketing activity has been explained by five factors.

1 The growing *fragmentation of media and markets*. The growth of specialist magazines and television channels means that traditional mass advertising is less effective. Similarly, mass markets are disappearing as more and more companies seek to customize their offerings to target groups (see Chapter 5).
2 *Developments in technology*, such as databases, and software that generates personalized letters, have eased the task for direct marketers. Recent developments like variable data printing (VDP)

have enabled different elements within direct mail documents, including text, pricing, offers, images and graphics, to be uniquely personalized.
3 *Increased supply of mailing lists*. List brokers act as an intermediary in the supply of lists from list owners (often either companies that have built lists through transactions with their customers, or organizations that have compiled lists specifically for the purpose of renting them). List brokers thus aid the process of finding a suitable list for targeting purposes.
4 *Sophisticated analytical techniques* such as geodemographic analysis (see Chapter 5) can be used to pinpoint targets for mailing purposes.
5 The *high costs* of other techniques, such as **personal selling**, have led an increasing number of companies to take advantage of direct

marketing techniques, such as direct response advertising and telemarketing, to make sales forces more cost-effective.

Direct marketing activity, including direct mail, telemarketing and telephone banking, is regulated by a European Commission Directive that came into force at the end of 1994. Its main provisions are that:

- suppliers cannot insist on prepayments
- customers must be told the identity of the supplier, the price and quality of the product and any transport charges, the payment and delivery methods, and the period over which the solicitation remains valid
- orders must be met within 30 days unless otherwise indicated
- a cooling-off period of 30 days is mandatory and cold calling by telephone, fax or electronic mail is restricted unless the receiver has given prior consent.

Managing a direct marketing campaign

Direct marketing, as with all promotional campaigns, should be fully integrated to provide a coherent marketing strategy. Direct marketers need to understand how the product is being positioned in the marketplace as it is crucial that messages sent out as part of a direct marketing campaign do not conflict with those communicated by other channels such as advertising or the sales force.

The stages involved in conducting a direct mail campaign are similar to those for mass communications techniques described in the previous chapter (see Figure 11.3). The first step is the identification of the target audience, and one of the advantages of direct mail is that audience targeting can be very precise. For example, Tesco's loyalty card programme enabled it to build up very accurate profiles of its customers. By monitoring purchasing patterns and products selected, Tesco was able to develop a fine grained analysis of its shoppers. Like many other supermarkets it produced a quarterly magazine that was mailed out to customers featuring news items, articles, special offers and coupons. Because of its customer knowledge, it was able to produce 150,000 variants of the magazine so content and offers were targeted precisely to match readers' interests. One outcome of this was that its coupon redemption rate was over 20 per cent compared with an industry average of 0.5 per cent.[15]

The objectives of direct marketing campaigns can be the same as those of other forms of promotion: to improve sales and profits, to acquire

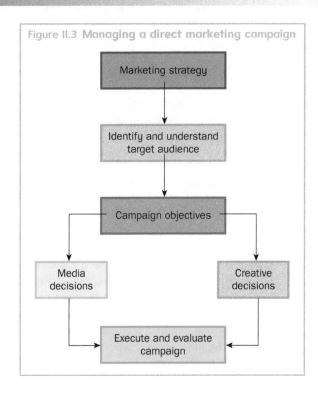

Figure II.3 Managing a direct marketing campaign

or retain customers or to create awareness (see Exhibit 11.2). However, one of the benefits of direct marketing is that it usually has clearly defined short-term objectives against which performance can be measured, which makes the evaluation of effectiveness relatively easy. For example, the Dutch bank ABM-AMRO ran a direct mail campaign aimed at the parents of young children aged 6–12 years old. It sent them a specially designed Queen's Day cash box with features to help children learn about money and an offer to put €20 in the box if they opened a Youth Account with the bank. The campaign resulted in a 200 per cent year-on-year increase in the number of accounts opened.[16]

The next major decision involves the media to be used for conducting the direct marketing campaign. Each of the major alternatives available to the marketer is discussed below. Once the media have been selected, the creative decisions must be made. The creative brief usually contains details of the communications objectives, the product benefits, the target market analysis, the offer being made, the communication of the message and the action plan (i.e. how the campaign will be run). As direct marketing is more orientated to immediate action than advertising, recipients will need to see a clear benefit before responding.

Finally, the campaign needs to be executed and evaluated. Execution can be in-house or through the use of a specialist agency. As we noted earlier,

direct marketing does lend itself to quantitative measurement. Some of the most frequently used measures are response rate (the proportion of contacts responding), total sales, sales rate (percentage of contacts purchasing), enquiry rate, cost per contact or enquiry or sale, and repeat purchase rate.

Direct mail

Material sent through the postal service to the recipient's home or business address, with the purpose of promoting a product and/or maintaining an ongoing relationship, is known as direct mail. For example, Heinz employed direct mail to target its customers and prospects. By creating a database based on responses to promotions, lifestyle questionnaires and rented lists, Heinz built a file of 4.6 million households. Each one received a quarterly 'At Home' mail pack, which has been further segmented to reflect loyalty and frequency of purchase. Product and nutritional information was combined with coupons to achieve product trial.[17] A major advantage of direct mail is its cost. For example, in business-to-business marketing, it might cost €50 to visit potential customers, €5 to telephone them but less than €1 to send out a mailing.[18]

A key factor in the effectiveness of a direct mail campaign is the quality of the mailing list. For example, in one year in the UK, 100 million items were sent back marked 'return to sender'. So the effectiveness of direct mail relies heavily on the quality of the list being used. Poor lists raise costs and can contribute to the growing negative perception of 'junk mail'. As a result, it is often preferable to rent lists from list houses rather than purchase them.

Direct mail facilitates specific targeting to named individuals. For example, by hiring lists of subscribers to gardening catalogues, a manufacturer of gardening equipment could target a specific group of people who would be more likely to be interested in a promotional offer than the public in general. Personalization is possible and the results directly measurable. Since the objective of direct mail is immediate – usually a sale or an enquiry – success can be measured easily. Some organizations, such as *Reader's Digest*, spend money researching alternative creative approaches before embarking on a large-scale mailing. Factors such as type of promotional offer, headlines, visuals and copy can be varied in a systematic manner and, by using code numbers on reply coupons, response can be tied to the associated creative approach.

Email or electronic mail shares much in common with its paper-based equivalent, direct mail. It is easy to use, costs little to produce and is virtually free to send. However, it also suffers from the same problem – junk mail or spam! Huge volumes of spam clog up email inboxes which has reduced the effectiveness of **email marketing**. It has also given rise to the concept of **permission marketing** which means that consumers opt to receive email communications from organizations. Where email is permission-based and personalized, it is much more likely to be effective. It can be used to communicate information, to build relationships through the content provided in e-zines (electronic magazines) and to generate revenues and referrals. Email communications should include some form of call-to-action (e.g. avail of a limited offer) so that their effectiveness can be measured.

Telemarketing

Telemarketing refers to the use of telecommunications in marketing and sales activities. It can be a most cost-efficient, flexible and accountable medium.[19] The telephone permits two-way dialogue that is instantaneous, personal and flexible.

Technological advances have significantly assisted the growth of telemarketing. For example, integrated telephony systems allow for callers to be easily identified. The caller's telephone number is relayed into the computer database and his/her details and account information appear on the screen even before the call is picked up. Technology has also greatly improved the effectiveness and efficiency of outbound telemarketing. For example, predictive dialling enables multiple outbound calls to be made from a call centre. Calls are only delivered to agents when the customer answers, cutting out wasted calls to answering machines, engaged signals, fax machines and unanswered calls. In addition, scripts can be created and stored on the computer so that operators have ready and convenient access to them on-screen.

Telemarketing can be used in a number of roles, and this versatility has also assisted in its growth. It can be used for direct selling when the sales potential of a customer does not justify a face-to-face call or, alternatively, an incoming telephone call may be the means of placing an order in response to a direct mail or television advertising campaign (see Marketing in Action 10.2). Second, it can be used to support the field sales force, for example, in situations where salespeople may find contacting their customers difficult given the nature of their job. Third, telemarketing can be used to generate leads through establishing contact with prospective customers and arranging a sales visit. Finally, an additional role of telemarketing is to maintain and update the firm's marketing database.

Telemarketing has a number of advantages.

I It has *lower costs* per contact than a face-to-face salesperson visit. But such has been the success of telemarketing that calls to businesses are growing significantly, with many companies moving call centre operations to low-cost countries.

2 It is *less time consuming* than personal visits.

3 The increasing *sophistication of telecommunications technology* has encouraged companies to employ telemarketing techniques. For example, digital networks allow the seamless transfer of calls between organizations.

4 Despite the reduced costs, compared to a personal visit, the telephone retains the advantage of *two-way communication*.

However, telephone selling is often considered intrusive, leading to consumers objecting to receiving unsolicited telephone calls. For example, legislation introduced in the UK in 2004 bans marketing companies from cold calling businesses, with fines of up to £5,000 for violations of the law, although this applies only to call centres located in Britain.

The widespread use of mobile and smartphones has given rise to a dramatic increase in **mobile marketing** which is the use of short messaging services (SMS), multimedia messaging services (MMS) and mobile display advertising (MDA) in marketing. Global spending on mobile advertising was estimated to be worth over $16 billion in 2013. One of the most rapidly growing forms of mobile marketing is smartphone applications (apps). For

example, the deodorant brand Lynx, which is targeted mainly at young males, developed two mobile phone apps designed to help young guys be more successful with girls as part of their 'Get in There' campaign. The apps were downloaded over 350,000 times. One study found that mobile display advertising was particularly effective when used for high involvement products.[20]

Mobile marketing has several advantages. First, it is very cost effective. The cost per message is between 15p and 25p, compared with 50p to 75p per direct mail shot, including print production and postage. Second, it can be targeted and personalized. For example, operators like Vodafone, Virgin Mobile and Blyk offer free texts and voice calls to customers if they sign up to receive some advertising. In signing up, customers have to fill out questionnaires on their hobbies and interests. Third, it is interactive: the receiver can respond to the text message, setting up the opportunity for two-way dialogue and relationship development. Fourth, it is a time-flexible medium. Text messages can be sent at any time, giving greater flexibility when trying to reach the recipient. Fifth, it can allow marketers to engage in what is known as **proximity marketing**. Messages can be sent to mobile users at nightclubs, shopping centres, festivals and universities, where recipients can immediately avail themselves of special offers. For example, the US consumer electronics retailer, Best Buy, sends special offers and deals to customer smartphones using a technology that pinpoints when they are entering a Best Buy store. Finally, like other direct marketing techniques, it is immediate and measurable, and can assist in database development.

Direct response advertising

Although direct response advertising appears in prime media, such as television, newspapers and magazines, it differs from standard advertising in that it is designed to elicit a direct response such as an order, enquiry or a request for a visit. Often, a freephone telephone number is included in the advertisement or, for the print media, a coupon response mechanism may be used. This combines the ability of broadcast media to reach large sections of the population with direct marketing techniques that allow a swift response on behalf of both prospect and company. For example, direct response advertising is used very regularly by not-for-profit organizations such as the National Society for the Prevention of Cruelty to Children (NSPCC) in order to increase the number of volunteers and donors. Macmillan Cancer Support ran a direct response campaign to drive more callers to avail of its financial and emotional support services. It's 'Good Day, Bad Day' campaign significantly increased calls to its helplines.

Direct response television has experienced fast growth. It is an industry worth £3 billion globally and comes in many formats. The most basic is the standard advertisement with telephone number; 60-, 90- or 120-second advertisements are sometimes used to provide the necessary information to persuade viewers to use the freephone number for ordering. Other variants are the 25-minute product demonstration (these are generally referred to as 'infomercials') and live home shopping programmes broadcast by companies such as QVC. Home shopping has a very loyal customer base. For example, Shoppingtelly.com, a website that offers home shoppers news and information on home shopping products, receives between 20,000 and 35,000 hits per day and some of the leading home shopping presenters, such as Paul Lavers and Julia Roberts, have their own very popular websites.[21] A popular misconception regarding direct response television (DRTV) is that it is suitable only for products such as music compilations and cut-price jewellery. In Europe, a wide range of products, such as leisure and fitness products, motoring and household goods, books and beauty care products, are marketed in this way through pan-European channels such as Eurosport, Super Channel and NBC.

As with many other forms of direct marketing, the effectiveness of campaigns is highly measurable, which is attractive to advertisers, who are also able to avail themselves of the multiplicity of digital channels in order to target adverts more carefully.

Catalogue marketing

The sale of products through catalogues distributed to agents and customers, usually by mail or at stores if the catalogue marketer is a store owner, is known as **catalogue marketing**. This method is popular in Europe with such organizations as Germany's Otto-Versand, the Next Directory in the UK, La Redoute in France and IKEA in Sweden. Many of these companies operate in a number of countries; La Redoute, for instance, has operations in France, Belgium, Norway, Spain and Portugal. Catalogue marketing is popular in some countries where, for example, legislation restricts retail opening hours. A common form of catalogue marketing is mail order, where catalogues are distributed and, traditionally, orders received by mail. Some enterprising companies, notably Next, saw catalogue marketing as an opportunity to reach a new target market: busy, affluent, middle-class people who valued the convenience of choosing products at home.

Used effectively, catalogue marketing to consumers offers a convenient way of selecting products that allows discussion between family members in a relaxed atmosphere away from crowded shops and the high street. Often, credit facilities are available, too. Catalogue marketing was originally popular with consumers living in remote rural locations, obviating the need to travel long distances to town-based shopping centres. For catalogue marketers, the expense of high-street locations is removed and there is an opportunity to display a wider range of products than could feasibly be achieved in a shop. Distribution can be centralized, lowering costs. Nevertheless, catalogues are expensive to produce (hence the need for some retailers to charge for them) and they require regular updating, particularly when selling fashion items. They do not allow goods to be tried (e.g. a vacuum cleaner) or tried on (e.g. clothing) before purchase. Although products can be seen in a catalogue, variations in colour printing can mean that the curtains or suite that are delivered do not have exactly the same colour tones as those appearing on the printed page.

Catalogue marketing is big business. IKEA distributes 46 versions of its catalogue in 36 countries and in 28 languages, accounting for 50 per cent of its total promotional budget. Increasingly, catalogues are being made available online, which reduces the costs of production and distribution, and means that they can easily be updated; 45 per cent of Next Directory's business is now conducted online.

Buzz marketing

As we have seen throughout this book, consumers can be a significant influence in the products and services purchased by other consumers. This type of word-of-mouth marketing, which is also known as **buzz marketing**, is defined as the passing of information about products and services by verbal or electronic means in an informal, person-to-person manner and has enjoyed a renaissance due to advances in technology such as email, websites and mobile phones. For example, in the USA, Nintendo recruited suburban mothers to spread the word among their friends that the Wii was a gaming console that the whole family could enjoy together.

The first step in a buzz marketing campaign involves identifying and targeting 'alphas' – that is, the trendsetters that adopt new ideas and technologies early on – and the 'bees', who are the early adopters. Brand awareness then passes from these customers to others, who seek to emulate the trendsetters. In many instances, the alphas are celebrities who either directly or indirectly push certain brands (see Social Media Marketing 11.1). For example, the Australian footwear and accessories brand UGG became popular in the US and European markets when photographs of actresses like Sienna Miller and Cameron Diaz appeared in the media wearing these products. Celebrities may be paid to endorse products or simply popularize products through their own choices.

Critical to the success of buzz marketing is that every social group, whether it is online or offline, has trendsetters. The record company, Universal, successfully promoted its boy bands Busted and McFly by targeting these trendsetters. It recruited a 'school chairman' who was given the task of spreading the word about a particular band in their

school. This involved giving out flyers, putting up posters on school noticeboards and then sending back evidence that this had been done. In return, the 'chairman' – who was typically a 12- to 15-year-old schoolgirl – was rewarded with free merchandise and a chance to meet members of the band.

Developments in technology have allowed the 'buzz' to spread very quickly. Viral marketing is popular because of the speed with which advertising gets passed on via social media and email. Companies attempt to harness this viral effect by building messages that are suitably engaging and promote an aspect of their company with content that customers want to read and send on. This requires some creativity and a good understanding of the customer base. For example, as part of its 'Campaign for Real Beauty', Dove created a short film entitled *Evolution*, which was viewed over 10 million times on YouTube.[22]

Social Media Marketing II.I Snickers tweets

Critical Thinking: Below is a review of a promotional campaign by Snickers using Twitter. Read it and critically reflect on the advantages and disadvantages of this type of viral marketing. Is it ethical that brands be promoted on social media in this way?

A key part of the approach to integrated communications is to try to leverage an idea across a range of media. So for example, when advertisers are spending large amounts of money developing a television campaign, they are also thinking about the extent to which the ad will be viewed and shared online through platforms like YouTube and Vimeo. In other instances, advertisers might run competitions on social media for consumers to come up with advertising ideas and content which are then translated into campaigns that run on traditional media. By exploiting this 'viral effect' advertisers aim to maximize the returns on their investment.

An example of a brand that has successfully used this blended approach is Snickers, the confectionery product owned by Mars. The insight that guided the campaign was that people are not really themselves when they are hungry. But before they ran a series of television

adverts based on this theme, they wanted to initially seed the idea in the minds of consumers. To do so, they partnered with a number of leading celebrities such as the footballer Rio Ferdinand and the model Katie Price who had very large followings on Twitter. These celebrities posted tweets that were entirely out of character which were then followed by showing them back on track with a tweet 'you are not you when you're hungry' and a photo of them eating Snickers. The out-of-character tweets were extensively retweeted, often by other celebrities with large followings, amplifying the viral effect of the campaign immediately. The innovative campaign was a huge success. It was estimated that it was seen by over 26 million people across all the major online and offline publications.

Based on: Barnett (2012);[23] Lewis (2014);[24] Sweney (2012).[25]

Exhibit 11.3 Dove's Real Beauty campaigns have very successfully leveraged the power of word-of-mouth marketing

Exhibit 11.3 Dove's Real Beauty campaigns have very successfully leveraged the power of word-of-mouth marketing

 Dove Ad Insight: Real beauty sketches was the biggest viral advertisng campaign of 2013.

Exhibit 11.4 Brands like Paddy Power are big creators of provocative viral content. This booth placed outside the Manchester United soccer ground was designed to poke fun at the difficulties the team was experiencing under their then manager, David Moyes

Viral marketing can be very cheap to produce and highly effective because it is transferred from peer-to-peer and is therefore less likely to be rejected by a recipient than other electronic communications (see Exhibits 11.3 and 11.4).

Once the target audience has been identified, the next key decisions, like those for all forms of promotion, are the message and the medium. The message may take many forms, such as a funny video clip or email attachment, a blog or story, an event such as a one-off concert, and so on. For example, Diageo launched Smirnoff Raw Tea in the USA with a video clip featuring a spoof hip hop song. The clip, entitled 'Smirnoff Tea Partay', has been one of the most popular on YouTube, with over 3.5 million views. The medium used for carrying the message is frequently online but could also be through offline means such as posters or flyers. But, as with all aspects of buzz marketing, the only limitation is the imagination. For example, many individuals have used parts of their bodies or their private cars to carry commercial messages.

Finally, given its novelty, evaluating the effectiveness of buzz marketing is difficult. Numbers are available regarding how many times a video clip is viewed but marketers will not be able to determine by whom.

Personal selling

The final major element of the promotional mix is personal selling. This involves face-to-face contact with a customer and, unlike advertising, promotion and other forms of non-personal communication, personal selling permits a direct interaction between buyer and seller. This two-way communication means that the seller can identify the specific needs and problems of the buyer and tailor the sales presentation in the light of this knowledge. The particular concerns of the buyer can also be dealt with on a one-to-one basis.

Such flexibility comes at a price, however. The cost of a car, travel expenses and sales office overheads can mean that the total annual bill for a field salesperson is often twice the level of a salary. In industrial marketing, over 70 per cent of the marketing budget is usually spent on the sales force. This is because of the technical nature of the products being sold, and the need to maintain close personal relationships between the selling and buying organizations.

The make-up of the personal selling function is changing, however. Organizations are reducing the size of their sales forces in the face of greater buyer concentration, moves towards centralized buying, and recognition of the high costs of maintaining a field sales team. The concentration of buying power into fewer hands has also fuelled the move towards relationship management, often through key account selling. This involves the use of a small number of dedicated sales teams, which service the accounts of major buyers as opposed to having a large number of salespeople. Instead of sending salespeople out on the road, many companies now collect a large proportion of their sales through direct marketing techniques such as the telephone or the Internet.

The three main types of salespeople are order-takers, order-creators and order-getters. Order-takers respond to already committed customers such as a sales assistant in a convenience store or a delivery salesperson. Order-creators have traditionally been found in industries like healthcare, where the sales task is not to close the sale but to persuade the medical representative to prescribe or specify the seller's products. Order-getters are those in selling jobs where the major objective is to persuade the customer to make a direct purchase. They include consumer salespeople such as those selling double glazing or insurance, through to organizational salespeople, who often work in teams where products may be highly technical and negotiations complex.

Personal selling skills

While the primary responsibility of a salesperson is to increase sales, there are a number of additional enabling activities carried out by many salespeople, including **prospecting**, maintaining customer records, providing service, handling complaints, relationship management and self-management. Prospecting involves searching for and calling on potential customers. Prospects can be identified from several sources including talking to existing customers, and searching trade directories and the business press. Customer record-keeping is an important activity for all repeat-call salespeople because customer information is one of the keys to improving service and generating loyalty. Salespeople should be encouraged and rewarded for sending customer and market information back to head office. Providing service to customers – including, for example, advice on ways of improving productivity and handling customer complaints – can also be a key sales force activity. This is particularly true in cases where the selling situation is not a one-off activity. In general, there has been a rise in the number of salespeople involved in relationship management roles with large organizational customers. Trust is an important part of relationship development and is achieved through a high frequency of contact, ensuring

promises are kept, and reacting quickly and effectively to problems (see Marketing in Action 11.2). Finally, given the flexibility of the salesperson's job, many are required to practise self-management, including decisions on call frequencies and journey routing, for example. Many people's perception of a salesperson is of a slick, fast-talking confidence trickster devoted to forcing unwanted products on gullible customers. In reality, success in selling comes from implementing the marketing concept when face to face with customers, not denying it at the very point when the seller and buyer come into contact. The sales interview offers an unparalleled opportunity to identify individual customer needs and match behaviour to the specific customer that is encountered.[26] In order to develop personal selling skills it is useful to distinguish seven phases of the selling process (see Figure 11.4). We will now discuss each of these in turn.

Preparation

The preparation carried out prior to a sales visit can reap dividends by enhancing confidence and performance when the salesperson is face to face with the customer. Some situations cannot be prepared

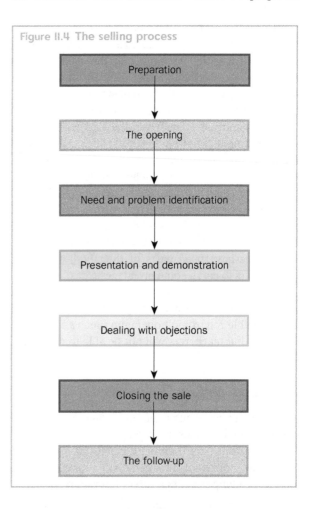

Figure II.4 The selling process

Preparation

↓

The opening

↓

Need and problem identification

↓

Presentation and demonstration

↓

Dealing with objections

↓

Closing the sale

↓

The follow-up

Marketing in Action II.2 Cisco's brave new world

Critical Thinking: Below is a review of some of Cisco's marketing efforts in the Middle East. Read it and critically reflect on the nature of modern personal selling.

Cisco Systems, the networking giant, sees a major part of its future growth coming from massive construction projects in the Middle East. One example is the creation of King Abdullah Economic City (KAEC) in Saudi Arabia. By 2020, the Saudis expect 2 million people to be living in a future metropolis supported by some of the most advanced technology that money can buy. All told, King Abdullah plans to build four brand new cities and upgrade the country's infrastructure at a cost of $6 billion over the coming years.

To tap into this vast potential, Cisco hired a well-connected local person to head the business in the country. He, in turn, hired salespeople and engineers, and got Cisco involved in major government projects. For the KAEC project, senior Cisco executives played host to the King for a demonstration of Cisco technology that allowed a person elsewhere to appear on stage as a holographic image. They realize, though, that Cisco is not just selling technology (a product feature). The real benefit is that it can help countries such as Saudi Arabia modernize their economies and become leaders in the Internet age. The company argues that,

by investing in the Internet infrastructure that Cisco sells, these governments can better educate their people, improve healthcare and boost national productivity.

To achieve this, Cisco provides consulting services to help government officials work out how best to use the Internet, and pays for training centres to produce the technicians to implement such plans. Cisco is helping the leaders of countries like Saudi Arabia imagine the future, to bring about 'country transformations' and brainstorm big ideas. One example was the call to Cisco to help with a new broadband network for Sudair city, but a Cisco executive saw the potential of the city as a hub for vast computer data centres, based on its cheap electricity rates. The electricity bill is often the biggest expense in running such centres, which are increasingly important for Internet companies like Google and Amazon. The idea was well received and helped Cisco secure a $280 million contract to create the underlying fibre-optic network for Sudair city.

Based on: Burrows (2008).[27]

for: the unexpected question or unusual objection, for example. But many customers face similar situations, and certain questions and objections will be raised repeatedly. Preparation can help the salesperson respond to these recurring situations. Salespeople will benefit from gaining knowledge of their own and competitors' products, by understanding buyer behaviour, by having clear sales call objectives and by having planned their sales presentation. This is because the success of the sales interview is customer-dependent. The aim is to convince the customer; what the salesperson does is simply a means to that end.

The opening

It is important for salespeople to consider how to create a favourable initial impression with customers as this

can often affect later perceptions. Good first impressions can be gained by adopting a businesslike approach, being friendly but not overly familiar, being attentive to detail, observing common courtesies like waiting to be asked to sit down and by showing the customer appreciation for having taken the time to see you.

Need and problem identification

Consumers will buy a product because they have a 'problem' that gives rise to a 'need'. Therefore the first task is to identify the needs and problems of each customer. Only by doing this can a salesperson connect with each customer's situation. Effective need and problem identification requires the development of questioning and listening skills. The hallmark of inexperienced salespeople is that they do all the talking; successful salespeople know how to get the *customer* to do most of the talking.

Presentation and demonstration

It is the presentation and demonstration that offers the opportunity for the salesperson to convince customers that they can supply the solution to their problem. It should focus on **customer benefits** rather than **product features**. The salesperson should continue to ask questions during the presentation to ensure that the customer has understood what he or she has said, and to check that what the salesperson has talked about really is of importance to the customer. This can be achieved by asking questions like 'Is that the kind of thing you are looking for?'

Dealing with objections

Salespeople rarely close a sale without first having to overcome customer objections. Although objections can cause problems, they should not be regarded negatively since they highlight issues that are important to the buyer. The secret of dealing with objections is to handle both the substantive and emotional aspects. The substantive part is to do with the objection itself. If the customer objects to the product's price the salesperson needs to use convincing arguments to show that the price is not too high. But it is a fact of human personality that the argument that is supported by the greater weight of evidence does not always win since people resent being proven wrong. Therefore, salespeople need to recognize the emotional aspects of objection handling. Under no circumstances should the buyer be caused to lose face or be antagonized during this process. Two ways of minimizing this risk are to listen to the objection without interruption and to employ the 'agree and counter' technique, where the salesperson agrees with the buyer but then puts forward an alternative point of view.

Closing the sale

The inexperienced salesperson will sometimes imagine that an effective presentation followed by the convincing handling of any objections should guarantee that the buyer will ask for the product without the seller needing to work to close the sale. This does occasionally happen but, more often, it is necessary for the salesperson to take the initiative. This is because many buyers still have doubts in their minds that may cause them to wish to delay the decision to purchase. Closing techniques include simply asking for the order, summarizing the key

points and asking for the order, or offering a special deal to close the sale (the concession close).

The follow-up

Once an order has been placed there may be a temptation for the salesperson to move on to other customers, neglecting the follow-up visit. However, this can be a great mistake since most companies rely on repeat business. If problems arise, customers have every right to believe that the salesperson was interested only in the order, and not their complete satisfaction. By checking that there are no problems with delivery, installation, product use and training (where applicable), the follow-up can show that the salesperson really does care about the customer.

Sales management

Because of the unique nature of the selling job, sales management is a challenging activity. For example, many salespeople spend a great deal of their time in the field, separated from their managers, while others may suffer repeated rejections in trying to close sales, causing them to lose confidence. Therefore, the two main aspects of the sales manager's job are designing the sales force and managing the sales force.

Designing the sales force

The critical design decisions are determining sales force size and organizing the sales force. The most practical method for deciding the number of salespeople required is called the 'workload approach'. It is based on the calculation of the total annual calls required per year divided by the average calls per year that can be expected from one salesperson.[28]

There are three alternative approaches to organizing the sales force. A *geographic* structure is where the sales area is broken down into territories based on workload and potential, and a salesperson is assigned to each one to sell all of the product range. This provides a simple, unambiguous definition of each salesperson's sales territory, and the proximity to customers encourages the development of personal relationships. A *product* structure might be effective where a company has a diverse product range selling to different customers (or at least different people within a given organization). A *customer-based* structure is where sales forces are organized on the basis of market segments, account sizes or new versus existing account lines. This structure enables salespeople to acquire in-depth knowledge of particular customer groups.

A growing form of customer-based sales force organization is **key account management**, which reflects the increasing concentration of buying power into fewer but larger customers. These are serviced by a key account sales force comprising senior salespeople who develop close personal relationships with customers, can handle sophisticated sales arguments and are skilled in the art of negotiation. A number of advantages are claimed for a key account structure, including that it enables close working relationships with customers, improved communication and coordination, better follow-up on sales and service, more in-depth penetration of the DMU, higher sales and the provision of an opportunity for advancement for career salespeople.

Managing the sales force

The following elements are involved in sales force management: setting specific salesperson objectives; recruitment and selection; training; **sales force motivation** and compensation; and **sales force evaluation**. These activities have been shown to improve salesperson performance, indicating the key role that sales managers play as facilitators, helping salespeople to perform better. Sales objectives are usually set in sales terms (sales quotas) but, increasingly, profit targets are being used, reflecting the need to guard against sales being bought cheaply by excessive discounting. The importance of recruiting high calibre salespeople cannot be overestimated. A study of sales force practice asked sales managers the following question: 'If you were to put your most successful salesperson into the territory of one of your average salespeople and made no other changes, what increase in sales would you expect after, say, two years?'[29] The most commonly stated increase was 16–20 per cent, and one-fifth of all sales managers said they would expect an increase of over 30 per cent. Based on extensive research, Mayer and Greenberg reduced the number of qualities believed to be important for effective selling to empathy and ego drive.[30] These are the kinds of qualities that need to be looked for in new salespeople.

It is believed by many sales managers that their salespeople can best train themselves by just doing the job. This approach ignores the benefits of a training programme, which can provide a frame of reference in which learning takes place. Training should include not only product knowledge, but also skills development. Success at selling comes when the skills are performed automatically, without consciously thinking about them, just as a tennis player or footballer succeeds.

A deep understanding of salespeople as individuals, their personalities and value systems, is the basis for effective motivation. Managers can motivate their sales staff by getting to know what each salesperson values and what they are striving for, increasing the responsibility given to salespeople in mundane jobs, providing targets that are attainable and challenging, and recognizing that rewards can be both financial and non-financial (e.g. praise). In terms of financial rewards, sales staff can be paid either a fixed salary, commission only, or on a salary-plus commission basis. Salaries provide security while commissions are an incentive to sell more as they are directly tied to sales levels. Great care must be taken in designing commission and bonus structures. For example, a Chrysler car dealership in the USA found that monthly sales for April were significantly down because salespeople who knew that they would not hit their targets for that month were encouraging customers to delay sales until May in hope of getting the May bonus.[31]

Sales force evaluation gathers the information required to check whether targets are being achieved and provides raw information that will help guide training and motivation. By identifying the strengths and weaknesses of individual salespeople, training can be focused on the areas in need of development, and incentives can be aimed at weak spots such as poor prospecting performance. Often, performance will be measured on the basis of quantitative criteria such as sales revenues, profits generated or number of calls. However, it is also important to use qualitative criteria such as sales skills acquired, customer relationships, product knowledge and self-management.

Summary

This chapter has provided an overview of direct communications techniques and digital marketing. In particular, the following issues were addressed.

I. The marketing database is the foundation upon which direct marketing campaigns are built. Databases can contain customer and prospect information, transactional information, product information, promotional information and geodemographic information. Technological developments have greatly assisted with database development.

2. Customer relationship management is an outgrowth of database marketing and describes the use of technologies to build and foster relationships with customers. CRM aims to provide an up-to-date single point of view for each customer.

3. Direct marketing is where consumers are precisely targeted through a variety of different techniques including direct mail, telemarketing, mobile marketing, direct response advertising and catalogue marketing. Direct marketing provides many advantages to companies, such as the ability to target customers directly, to run cost-effective campaigns and to allow the effectiveness of campaigns to be easily measurable.

4. Buzz marketing is an emerging marketing tool that capitalizes on the importance of word-of-mouth promotion. Greater global electronic connectivity has fostered the rise of buzz marketing.

5. Personal selling plays an important role in the promotional mix and salespeople are required to develop a range of selling skills including preparing for the sale, opening the sale, identifying customer needs and problems, presenting and demonstrating, dealing with objections, closing the sale and following up. Sales management involves designing and managing a sales team.

Study questions

I. Discuss the differences between database marketing and customer relationship management.

2. Companies now have a variety of direct marketing media that they can consider when planning a direct marketing campaign. Compare and contrast any two direct marketing media. In your answer, give examples of the kinds of markets in which the media you have chosen might be useful.

3. Data collection and retention is carried out extensively by both online and offline firms. Discuss the ethical implications of this practice.

4. What is meant by buzz marketing? Discuss the elements of an effective buzz marketing campaign.

5. Salespeople are born, not made. Discuss.

Suggested reading

Choudhury, M. and **P. Harrigan** (2014) CRM to Social CRM: The Integration of New Technologies into Customer Relationship Management, *Journal of Strategic Marketing*, **22** (2), 149–76.

Hillebrand, B., J. Nijholt and **E. Nijssen** (2011) Exploring CRM Effectiveness: An Institutional Theory Perspective, *Journal of the Academy of Marketing Science*, **39**, 592–608.

Kaikati, A.M. and **J.G. Kaikati** (2004) Stealth Marketing: How to Reach Customers Surreptitiously, *California Management Review*, **46** (4), 6–23.

Kumar, V., J.A. Petersen and **R.P. Leone** (2007) How Valuable is Word of Mouth? *Harvard Business Review*, **85** (10), 139–56.

Leibowitz, J. (2010) Rediscovering the Art of Selling, *McKinsey Quarterly*, October, 1–3.

Ramaswamy, V. and **F. Gouillart** (2010) Building the Co-creative Enterprise, *Harvard Business Review*, **88** (10), 100–9.

Shankar, V. and **S. Balasubramanian** (2009) Mobile Marketing: A Synthesis and Prognosis, *Journal of Interactive Marketing*, **23** (2), 118–29.

When you have read this chapter

log on to the Online Learning Centre for *Foundations of Marketing* at
www.mheducation.co.uk/textbooks/fahy5
where you'll find links and extra online study tools for marketing.

References

1. **Anonymous** (2013) Skoda: Change My Car, Direct Marketing Association: Warc.com.
2. **Stone, M., D. Davies** and **A. Bond** (1995) *Direct Hit: Direct Marketing with a Winning Edge*, London: Pitman.
3. **Harvey, F.** (2003) They Know What You Like, *Financial Times*, Creative Business, 6 May, 4.
4. **London, S.** (2004) Choked by a Data Surfeit, *Financial Times*, 29 January, 17.
5. **Burn-Murdoch, J.** (2012) Less than 1% of the World's Data is Analysed, Over 80% is Unprotected, *Guardian.com*, 19 December.
6. **Nancarrow, C., L.T. Wright** and **J. Page** (1997) Seagram Europe and Africa: The Development of a Consumer Database Marketing Capability, *Proceedings of the Academy of Marketing*, July, Manchester, 1119–30.
7. **Rothery, G.** (2010) About Face, *Marketing Age*, 4 (2), 22-5.
8. **Turow, J.** (2008) *Niche Envy: Marketing Discrimination in the Digital Age*, Boston MA: MIT.
9. **Murphy, C.** (2002) Catching up with its Glitzier Cousin, *Financial Times*, 24 July, 13.
10. **Foss, B.** and **M. Stone** (2001) *Successful Customer Relationship Marketing*, London: Kogan Page.
11. See **Ryals, L., S. Knox** and **S. Maklan** (2002) *Customer Relationship Management: Building the Business Case*, London: FT Prentice-Hall; **H. Wilson, E. Daniel** and **M. McDonald** (2002) Factors for Success in Customer Relationship Management Systems, *Journal of Marketing Management*, 18 (1/2), 193–200.
12. **Anonymous** (2013) Priority Moments: O2 Telefonica, European Association of Communications Agencies, Warc.com.
13. **O'Reilly, L.** (2011) O2's Priority Moments Has Cracked It, *MarketingWeek.co.uk*, 15 July.
14. **Advertising Age** (2014) Marketing Fact Pack, 14.
15. **Mukund, A.** (2003) Tesco: The Customer Relationship Management Champion, ICMR Center for Management Research 503-108-1.
16. **Anonymous** (2013), ABN AMRO: Queen's Day Cash Box, Direct Marketing Association, Warc.com.
17. **Clegg, A.** (2000) Hit or Miss, *Marketing Week*, 13 January, 45-9.
18. **Benady, D.** (2001) If Undelivered, *Marketing Week*, 20 December, 31-3.
19. **McHatton, N.R.** (1988) *Total Telemarketing*, New York: Wiley, 269.
20. **Bart, Y., A. Stephen** and **M. Sarvary** (2014) Which Products are Best Suited to Mobile Advertising? A Field Study of Mobile Display Advertising Effects on Consumer Attitudes and Intentions, *Journal of Marketing Research*, 51 (3).
21. **McCann, G.** (2003) Just Like Members of the Family, *Financial Times*, 15 January, 13.
22. **Smith, G.** and **A. O'Dea** (2007) Word of Mouse, *Marketing Age*, Autumn, 20-6.
23. **Barnett, E.** (2012) Twitter Users Angered by Rio Ferdinand's Snickers 'Adverts', *Telegraph.co.uk*, 25 January.
24. **Lewis, A.** (2014) Snickers: Hungry Tweets, Warc.com.
25. **Sweney, M.** (2012) Snickers Twitter Campaign Cleared by Ad Watchdog, *Guardian.co.uk*, 7 March.
26. **Weitz, B.A.** (1981) Effectiveness in Sales Interactions: A Contingency Framework, *Journal of Marketing*, 45, 85-103.
27. **Burrows, P.** (2008) Cisco's Brave New World, *Business Week*, 24 November, 57-68.
28. **Talley, W.J.** (1961) How to Design Sales Territories, *Journal of Marketing*, 25 (3), 16-28.
29. **PA Consultants** (1979) *Sales Force Practice Today: A Basis for Improving Performance*, Cookham: Institute of Marketing.
30. **Mayer, M.** and **G. Greenberg** (1964) What Makes a Good Salesman, *Harvard Business Review*, 42 (July/August), 119-25.
31. **Griffith, V.** (2001) Targets that Distort a Company's Aim, *Financial Times*, 21 November, 18.

Case 11
Happy Arthur's Day?

Introduction

'To Arthur' is a phrase that echoes around the world on Arthur's Day, as people raise a pint to Arthur Guinness. Arthur's Day signals the start of a day-long annual arts and music event that celebrates the creation of the 'black stuff'. Effectively a sponsorship event centred around the Guinness brand, Arthur's Day began in 2009 to mark the 250th anniversary of Guinness, a drink that is synonymous with Ireland.[1]

On Arthur's Day 2009, Guinness drinkers were asked for the first time to raise a glass to the memory of Arthur Guinness at 17:59 (5.59 pm), a reference to 1759, the year the Guinness Brewery was established.[1] The event has continued since 2009 and is now in its fourth year. Over the past four years, Arthur's Day events have been held in Dublin, Kuala Lumpur, Lagos and New York. Acts such as Tom Jones and Estelle have performed at events.[3]

The aim of Arthur's Day was to encourage people to recognize the iconic status of the brand, to make a positive statement about Guinness and to engage with both existing and new drinkers with the brand. The event was also being used to provide a positive experience for customers and to assist channel members achieve their business goals through increased revenue.

In 2009, as this was the first time the event would take place, Diageo spent millions advertising Arthur's Day across

multiple media online and offline. In particular, it invested heavily in a TV advertising campaign to raise awareness of the event. The company created the original Arthur's Day advert 'To Martha' in 2009 to raise awareness of the event and this was initially released on Facebook before debuting on Irish TV. This TV ad campaign was followed with a 'Paint the Town Black' advert campaign for Arthur's Day in 2012.[2] Each year since the event's inception, Diageo has not only invested heavily in advertising, but has also used social media (Facebook and Twitter in particular) to engage with the public and raise awareness of Arthur's Day. It continues to use advertising, sales

promotion, public relations and digital marketing and social media in an integrated manner every year to promote the event.

In 2013, an astonishing 10,000 people took part in Arthur's Day festivities in Kuala Lumpur alone. It is now even being called, 'Ireland's second national day' by some.[4] However, the future of Arthur's Day is in doubt as increasing concerns about this 'national drinking holiday' began to emerge just before Arthur's Day 2013.[5]

The backlash

Arthur's Day 2013 was shrouded in controversy, even before it began. It came under fire from health officials, parents groups, politicians and celebrities who saw the event as a cynical marketing campaign, a form of cultural misappropriation, and worse, an event which perpetuated and promoted drinking in a country which ill-needed it.[4] Much of the controversy originated in Ireland, but led to increased discussion about the appropriateness of the event worldwide. All sides agree Ireland has a deeply ingrained alcohol problem. Government statistics show that Irish households last year spent 7.7 per cent of their money, or €6.3 billion, on alcoholic drinks. That's double what they spent on clothing and more than €2,100 per adult, with women increasingly drinking hard liquor as much as men.[6]

Some critics saw Arthur's Day as a marketing exercise - the creation of a 'pseudo-national holiday' to increase sales of Guinness, without any regard to the harm caused.[7] The Irish Times has described Arthur's Day as 'a master class in how to fabricate a national holiday'. It refers to the 'faux-patriotism that comes with the celebration of a "national" drink' and the 'hagiographic treatment of Arthur Guinness as some kind of saint'. The paper warned 'If St. Patrick's Day, Christmas and Halloween are festivals that offer an excuse for a drink, Diageo has flipped the concept on its head and made the drink an excuse for a festival'.[8] Critics argue that people may like to think that they are honouring a well-loved Dubliner on Arthur's Day, but in fact they have been manipulated into helping to create further millions for Diageo's already wealthy shareholders. Diageo doesn't need the public's help to boost its bottom line. Last year its operating profits jumped to £3.2 billion sterling, primarily due to its soaring sales in emerging markets. This year, profits are expected to jump by another 9 per cent to over £3.5 billion.[3]

Effects on the nation's health

One area of concern surrounding Arthur's Day was its effects on the overstretched Irish health service, particularly on the emergency services. This concern may have emanated from a reported 30 per cent increase in ambulance call-outs in Dublin city centre alone following the 2012 event.[9] According to Alcohol Action Ireland, the national charity for alcohol-related issues, the Irish problematic relationship with alcohol costs the state an estimated €3.7 billion to deal with alcohol-related harm. The Royal College of Physicians in Ireland have also spoken out against the festival stating that Ireland already has a problem with excessive drinking.[7]

The timing of Arthur's Day has also been seen as a cause for concern. The event is not on an annual fixed date, although it is usually in late September and falls on a Thursday, a day that many people get paid and a traditional 'student night' in Dublin and many towns in Ireland. The fact that it falls during many university and college Fresher's Week is also contentious.[10]

Marketing of the arts

Along with the health debate is another debate centred on marketing and the arts. In recent years, there have been a number of musicians and artists who have spoken out against Arthur's Day. Film director Lenny Abrahamson and writer Marion Keyes have weighed in on the debate, along with folk singer Christy Moore. Moore penned a song in 2013 (which was released on Arthur's Day itself) which hit out at the event and those who promote it. In the tune, Moore describes the event as an 'alcoholiday'.

Moore isn't a lone voice in the wilderness, with Mike Scott from the Waterboys also speaking out about his dislike for the day.[9]

Boycott Arthur's Day

The controversy surrounding Arthur's Day led to the creation of a social media campaign entitled 'Boycott Arthur's Day' (BAD), which claimed national and international attention. This social media campaign was initiated because for some of those involved in the Irish music, literary and creative world, it became apparent that there was a sense that Diageo were selling Arthur's Day as a celebration of creativity. There was a feeling that there was a huge degree of cultural misappropriation involved. Many Irish and international artists have since given their support to the BAD campaign, which called on Irish citizens to 'say NO to Diageo's boozefest'.[12]

Its positive contribution

Despite the criticisms of Arthur's Day, there is still some support for the event. The proponents of Arthur's Day present it as a celebration of the pub and the music of Irish and international acts. It is seen to have positive effects in that it promotes Irish music and the arts and gives something back to society. This view was reflected in advertisements for Arthur's Day 2013 - 'Showcasing Ireland's Talent and Creativity'. The event was held in 500 music venues across Dublin and Ireland and provided people with the opportunity to hear and see some of their favourite bands on Arthur's Day, with the lure of big names such as Emeli Sandé, Bobby Womack, Manic Street Preachers and The Script. In fact, the Script frontman Danny O' Donoghue, who has been involved in Arthur's Day since the beginning, defended it as a success for live music stating 'it's a music, arts, food and culinary festival'.[13] In addition, Arthur's Day has evolved into a cultural event focused mainly on the hard-pressed pub sector, where tourism is an important factor. Guinness says the annual festivities provide a needed tonic for a 7,500-strong Irish pub network, struggling to maintain profits in the face of a five-year debt crisis that has ravaged employment and incomes.[14]

In 2009, Diageo established the Arthur Guinness Fund – an internal fund set up by the company which aims to enable and empower individuals with skills and opportunities to deliver a measured benefit to their communities. Over the past four years, Diageo has already committed €7.4 million for the fund, paid for in part by revenues derived from the global Arthur's Day celebrations.[15]

In Ireland alone, Guinness has also pledged a further €3 million over the next three to four years to the Arthur Guinness Projects. The Arthur Guinness Projects celebrate young Irish talent and creativity across the areas of the arts, music and food. To date 30 Irish social entrepreneurs have received funding as well as professional business mentoring for their projects. In the process, Guinness has turned the spotlight on the huge number of innovators in Ireland and on the enormous creative potential of the country.[15]

Although the criticism of Arthur's Day has been extensive, it may be naive to assume that Arthur's Day alone is the cause of Irish people's drinking problems. It is more complex than that – it is a deep-seated cultural issue. This is reflected in a statement made by Taoiseach Enda Kenny when asked about Arthur's Day: 'It doesn't take any particular day to have an impact on the situation in Ireland's accident and emergency departments.'[16]

Diageo's reaction

Despite the many criticisms of Arthur's Day, Diageo has defended the event, saying Guinness was showcasing emerging Irish music talent by offering them a stage at over 500 music events. The company said it had implemented a responsible drinking awareness campaign around Arthur's Day and gave clear advice to pubs creating their own events. In particular, it encouraged all 500 participating pubs to give out free water and food at the larger ticketed events.[11] In addition, Diageo reacted to this unprecedented controversy about Arthur's Day 2013 by speaking out to reassure those concerned that they would contribute towards the costs of extra policing for Arthur's Day.[17]

On 24 September, two days before Arthur's Day 2013, a live studio debate which included the Guinness executive Peter O'Brien was held on the Irish news and current affairs TV programme *Prime Time*, to discuss the pros and cons of Arthur's Day. O'Brien, who is Diageo's European corporate relations manager, emphasized that Arthur's Day is all about the pub. He stated: 'All we are doing is bringing people to the pub, it is an industry in crisis. Where else in the world can you get a major international act to play in your local pub? That's what it's

about, supporting your local pub.' He went on to say that no one was required to drink anything on the day – 'They can just go and enjoy the music.' Peter O'Brien also appeared on a number of national radio stations to speak in support of Arthur's Day and his views were widely quoted in the press.[18]

Despite all the furore prior to the day about its effects on emergency services, it was reported that there was a 50 per cent decrease in the need for emergency services when compared to Arthur's Day 2012.[4] A spokesperson for Diageo stated that the debate surrounding Arthur's Day 2013 was difficult for the company to hear, but that the event and Diageo have helped contribute to a wider debate on alcohol misuse, and therefore was beneficial.

As long as Arthur's Day continues, controversy and debate are likely to follow. The event has been praised and bashed in equal measure. The future of Arthur's Day still remains in doubt in the aftermath of the major public backlash of the 2013 festival. Diageo refuses to confirm if the festival will return next year, simply stating that no decision has yet been made, but perhaps they should keep an open mind on changing Arthur's Day next year, to focus less on pubs and pints and more on the arts.[4]

References

1. en.wikipedia.org/wiki/Arthur's_Day
2. Nudd, T. (2012) Ad of the Day: Guinness Saatchi and Saatchi Wants You to Paint the Town Black for Arthur's Day, www.adweek.com
3. Fitzgerald, R. (2012) Boycott Guinness on Arthur's Day – Or Should That Be 'Diageo Day'?, www.thehuffingtonpost.com, 26 September.
4. Duncan, P. (2013) A Black and White Issue, but Arthur's Day Continues to Produce a Stout Performance, *The Irish Times*, 27 September.
5. Pogatchnik, S. (2013) Guinness – Inspired Arthur's Day Causes Concern in Ireland, *The Star*, 26 September.
6. Toledo, P. (2013) Raising a Controversial Glass, *Buenos Aires Herald*, 30 September.
7. Alcohol Action Ireland (2013), Minister Joins in Criticism of Arthur's Day.
8. Griffin, D. (2012) Arthur's Day: Fabrication and Libation, *The Irish Times*, 27 September.
9. Barry, A. and Hosford, P. (2013) Why Are People Saying 'Down With Arthur's Day'?, www.thejournal.ie, 22 September.
10. Clifford, M. (2011) We're Buying Into Cheap Marketing Ploys, *The Irish Times*, 24 September.
11. Hallahan, C. (2013) Moore's Anti-Arthur's Day Song Gathers Momentum, www.breakingnews.ie, 23 September.
12. deBurca Butler, J. (2013) Arthur's Day – Cynical Marketing or a Boost for the Arts?, *Irish Examiner*, 26 September.
13. deBruca, D. (2013) Danny O' Donoghue: 'Stick to the Script Christy', *The Irish Mirror*, 26 September.
14. Pogatchnik, S. (2013) Arthur's Day Guinness Beer Celebration in Ireland Should Be Called 'Vomit Day' Critics Say, www.huffingtonpost.com, 26 September.
15. Donovan, C. (2013) Arthur Guinness Projects: The Fund is Just the Beginning, Hot Press, 11 July.

16. Hosford, P. (2013) Ireland's Drinking Problem Goes Beyond Arthur's Day – An Taoiseach, www.thejournal.ie, 24 September.

17. Power, A. (2013) Diageo Contribution to Policing Costs for Arthur's Day Welcome, But Doesn't Go Far Enough, www.fiannafail.ie, 26 September.

18. Finn, C. (2013) Diageo Defends Arthur's Day Saying It's a Music Festival and Celebration of the Pub, www.thejournal.ie, 23 September.

Questions

1. Comment on the objectives that Diageo is trying to achieve through the use of Arthur's Day.

2. Arthur's Day has been a hugely successful marketing event for Diageo. Highlight how Arthur's Day is a perfect example of an integrated marketing communications campaign.

3. In your opinion, was the negative backlash against Arthur's Day justified? Was Diageo's response to the negative publicity against the event sufficient?

4. Negative publicity aside, do you think that Arthur's Day has a future? Is it an event that has run its course anyway and that people have grown tired of it?

This case was prepared by Marie O' Dwyer, Waterford Institute of Technology from various published sources as a basis for class discussion rather than to show effective or ineffective management.

Chapter 12

Digital Marketing

Chapter outline

Digital natives and digital immigrants

Introduction to digital marketing

Objectives of digital marketing

Web design

Search engine optimization

Market research

Netnography

Netiquette

Social media

Campaign measurement

Future potential in digital marketing

Learning outcomes

By the end of this chapter you will:

1 Understand the development and changing trends within the digital marketing environment

2 Explain how digital marketing tools are used within market research

3 Understand basic rules and principles of the web design process

4 Evaluate the importance of social media and digital presence within integrated marketing communications (IMC)

5 Demonstrate how to measure digital marketing efforts

6 Discuss a variety of tools available within digital and social media marketing.

MARKETING SPOTLIGHT

ASOS

ASOS (As Seen on Screen) was first launched in June 2000 as an online shop for celebrity inspired fashion products and has since grown into a 'global online fashion and beauty retailer (...) shipping to 234 countries and territories'.[1] If this still doesn't prove how big digital business can be it attracts 29.5 million unique visitors a month (excluding mobile visitors) and has 8.6 million active customers.[2] That's only slightly less than the population of Saudi Arabia or Malaysia. Where does ASOS's power come from? ASOS launched with a focus on the digital presence of its brand, investing heavily in the website, social media channels and in providing a great service; that mission has continued as the company has grown. After launching in the UK in 2000, ASOS expanded internationally launching local language sites aggressively throughout 2010 and 2011, culminating in the launch of its Chinese language site in 2013, bringing its total to nine (Chinese; Russian; Australian; Italian; Spanish; American; German; and French). The utilization of new channels of social media and following customer trends online has produced excellent results. Throughout its history it has been the recipient of many awards, including 'Best Online Retailer'.[1]

ASOS's case shows how much a brand can achieve online only, and how important a digital presence is now. One of the most interesting campaigns from ASOS is its 2012 Summer Sale which achieved a return on investment of 2000 per cent and increased its Facebook follower base by 33 per cent (over 211,000 new likes).[3] Every professional marketer dreams of such numbers.

Sale time is crucial for all fashion retailers, trying to ensure that customers pick their brand over those of competitors. With strong competition from brands like Primark, New Look, H&M, Topshop, Zara and others, ASOS used the element of anticipation to increase interest in its sale in advance. It tried to recreate the same excitement for sales as experienced with bricks and mortar stores: 'people camping outside a store waiting for the doors to open'.[3] To get a place in the queue for earlier access to sale pages, you had to be an ASOS Facebook follower. You could also push your way towards the front of the queue by participating in various activities/games developed by ASOS. The main aim of the games was to spread the buzz about the sale, getting more followers on the page and effectively raising awareness of the sale and the campaign.

The results were more than impressive, one of them bringing the most revenue for ASOS in a single day at that time.[3]

ASOS Ad Insight: Consumers are engaged with campaigns through Facebook.

Digital natives and digital immigrants

In the digitalized era it's particularly difficult to bring anyone's attention to a printed book or to something longer than 140 characters. But it's a traditional way to transfer knowledge. This actually shows the main difference between digital natives and immigrants. Digital natives were born in an era in which digital technology has always existed.[4] To become successful marketers we need to meet the needs of both digital natives and immigrants, so in this chapter we will highlight some concepts of digital marketing and good practices which will address the needs of both groups.

First of all, who is a **digital native**? In 2001 Marc Prensky used this term to describe new a generation of students, who have 'spent their entire lives surrounded by and using (...) all the toys of digital age'.[5] On the other hand, there are **digital immigrants**, those who used to hand write their letters, and wait for newspapers to be printed to check for the news. It seems to be pretty obvious, but it will affect how marketers communicate with those two groups of consumers. Understanding the difference now will help us to develop and run successful marketing campaigns (both traditional and digital). A good example of how quickly consumers' mindsets change is to check the Beloit College Mindset List.

According to Beloit College, young consumers (students) are accustomed to instant access, and therefore lack the patience of scholarship. They need to discover knowledge in books and journals and other sources which are offline. At the same time, older consumers although they can use digitally provided information, often prefer tangible materials like books, leaflets, etc.

Introduction to digital marketing

The growth of digital technologies in the last decades has been remarkable (see Table 12.1). The number of people around the world with some form of access to the Internet is growing rapidly and, in the developed world in particular, consumers have high-speed access through multiple devices. The amount of time spent 'online' is also growing exponentially.

The digital environment allows many options for communications between a business and its customers. It can accommodate B2C, B2B, C2B and C2C communications (see Figure 12.1). This shift from one-way communication between organizations and customers was a major trigger for the development of digital marketing as we know it now.

Although the majority of consumers currently interact with brands online, the commercialization of the Internet didn't start until the late 1990s. After all Amazon.com wasn't launched until 1995! Since then we have observed a lot of changes and the rapid growth of the digital world. This growth is often linked to the term Web 2.0, but what does it actually mean? And what was Web 1.0?

Web 2.0 encompasses a range of changes that were introduced to the World Wide Web in the late 1990s. Before looking at the effective use of digital tools in our marketing campaigns, it's worth clarifying some main characteristics of Web 2.0. A Web 2.0 site includes the following:

- customers have their profile pages including selected data like age, sex, location, etc. and they are the most important entities in the system
- the ability to create networks between customers, through links, likes, friends, etc.
- the ability to post rich content in the form of photos, videos, blogs, comments, etc.

Table 12.1 World Internet usage

World regions	Internet users	Penetration (%)	% Growth 2000–12	% of Total users
Africa	167,335,676	15.6	3,606.7	7.0
Asia	1,076,681,059	27.5	841.9	44.8
Europe	518,512,109	63.2	393.4	21.5
Middle East	90,000,455	40.2	2,639.9	3.7
North America	273,785,413	78.6	153.3	11.4
Latin America/ Caribbean	254,915,745	42.9	1,310.8	10.6
Oceania/ Australia	24,287,919	67.6	218.7	1.0
World total	2,405,518,376	34.3	566.4	100.0

Source: InternetWorldStats (2012) *World Internet Usage Statistics – The Internet Big Picture* [online] available from: http://www.internetworldstats.com/stats.htm [June 2014].

Figure 12.1 Online communication options

	Supplier of content	
	Business	Customer
Business	B2B Covisint.com	C2B Priceline Consumer feedback Communities
Customer	B2C Amazon Company websites iTunes Kelkoo	C2C Facebook YouTube Twitter Skype Blogs

Receiver of content (vertical label on left side)

■ other more complex technical features including a 'public API to allow third-party enhancements', 'mash-ups', the embedding of various rich content types (e.g. Flash videos), and communication with other users through internal e-mail or IM systems.[6]

Digital media revolutionized B2B and B2C communications, but Web 2.0 gave a voice to customers. From businesses' perspective, they have gained new ways to communicate with each other as well as with customers, streamlining certain processes like ordering, purchasing, etc. It also gave companies an opportunity to establish relationships with new partners and suppliers. One of the novel applications of digital media has been the growth of C2B activity. An example is a freelancer-hiring website where people can advertise their skills and companies may 'purchase' them for their projects. Another, popular example is when customers write reviews of their experiences with companies. They don't need to carry any monetary value for the customer, but may enhance their status on the particular service, or bring other benefits (think about eBay, Amazon, etc.). Finally, digital media has revolutionized how people communicate and connect with each other giving rise to massive growth in C2C activity. People trade with each other on eBay and some generate a living through full-time trading. Others make a living playing poker online. Consumers are no longer just the recipients of what businesses have to offer.

Ebay Ad Insight: This campaign puts across the company's core value in an online world.

Even though marketers are not required to understand the technicalities of the Internet, it is worth gaining some basic knowledge in this area. This may prove priceless when working on online campaigns with Web designers and developers; it will support an understanding of what is required and how the final campaign should be implemented. This chapter will look at digital marketing from both angles: business oriented and technical.

Objectives of digital marketing

Before we move to the 'how to', it's important to clarify what we want to achieve with the digital presence. Without setting clear objectives, companies may invest a lot of money in a Web, mobile or social media presence without seeing any profit from it.

Similarly to traditional offline campaigns, any planning starts with situation analysis (audit) and the definition of objectives (see Chapter 1). This works exactly the same for any online campaigns, whether they are independent or integrated with an offline campaign. Successful marketers must clearly understand the benefits of an online presence. There are five objectives of e-marketing as defined by Chaffey and Smith:[7]

1 *Sell* – Grow sales through wider distribution. A new online channel allows marketers to reach customers that couldn't be previously reached offline. There is no limit with the store space online, a wider variety of products may be displayed and offered to customers, therefore increasing sales.

2 *Serve* – Add value through extra benefits for customers online. Give them better customer service, or a discount for buying products online. Customers online may also be offered gift wrapping of products, free delivery, etc. as part of their online experience.

3 *Speak* – Get closer to customers through creating a dialogue with them. Listen to their suggestions or ask for their opinion on a variety of aspects like products, design of the website, etc. Engaging in a dialogue with customers makes them feel important and has a positive influence on their brand loyalty.

4 *Save* – Save cost through limiting print, store and rent costs. There are many options here: emailing customers will reduce print and postage costs; there's no need to open, equip and staff another brick and mortar store, etc. These savings may then be redirected into enhancing customers' experience or adding extra services.

5 *Sizzle* – Extend the brand online through enhancing the online experience using interactivity with

customers. Ensure confidentiality and safety of customers to gain their trust and loyalty.

This 5S model is the basics of all digital activity marketers may undertake. Being online for the sake of it is not a good business practice. Marketers should decide which objectives to focus on, as this will direct all the activity online. This decision needs to support the strategy of the company. They also need to make sure that digital activity is never treated as a separate entity. Any activity online needs to complement offline marketing actions. (See Chapters 10 and 11 about IMC.)

Lack of clear objectives often leads to poor design, development and management of the online presence. Errors such as broken links, false information, etc. cause customers to turn away from the company and search for the product or service elsewhere. Sloppy e-marketing impacts negatively on brand reputation and customer trust (see Figure 12.2).

Web design

In this section we will focus on the basic principles of online presence design. We will also focus on web design, bearing in mind that the principles discussed may also be applied to the design of mobile sites and apps. The design of an online presence needs to be directed by two key elements: business objectives derived from current situation analysis; and target audience requirements (customers, suppliers, staff and other stakeholders).

Building the website based solely on the creative skills of designers or marketers is ineffective. Online design is an iterative process and is rarely done right the first time. To achieve user-centred design and effective ways to communicate with the audience, online research of their needs, as well as reviews and testing, should be factored into management of the website. (For details of how to utilize an online presence in market research see later in this chapter and in Chapter 4.)

The target audience of the designed website influences the structural and interactive elements. There are clear differences in web design approaches for different age groups, as illustrated in Figure 12.3.

Needs and behaviours of adults differ from those of teenagers or young children (this also shows the difference between digital natives and digital immigrants). Therefore factors such as interactivity, topics and content style need to be designed specifically for the target audience of the website.

Research of the target audience is also crucial for other reasons. There are many stereotypes regarding people's ability to use technology but often they are not necessarily true. Many teenagers are not super tech savvy; similarly, not all adults are clueless about the Internet. Surprisingly, young people

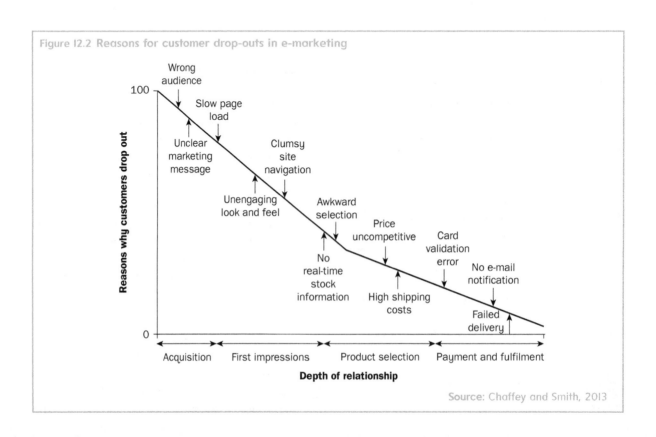

Figure 12.2 Reasons for customer drop-outs in e-marketing

Source: Chaffey and Smith, 2013

Figure 12.3 Age group differences

	Hunting for things to click	Tabbed browsing	Scrolling	Search	Patience	Animation and sound effects
Kids (3–12)	😊	☹️	☹️	☹️	😐	😊
Teens (13–17)	😐	😐	😊	☹️	☹️	😐
College students (18–24)	☹️	😊	😊	😊	☹️	☹️
Adults (25–64)	☹️	😐	😊	😊	😊	☹️

key:

😊 Enjoyable, interesting and appealing, or users can easily adjust to it.

😐 Users might appreciate it to some extent, but overuse can be problematic.

☹️ Users dislike it, don't do it, or find it difficult to operate.

Source: Loranger and Nielsen, 2013.

tend to perform worse in finding information and completing tasks online. Evolution of education and accessibility of information has resulted in a lowering of teens' reading skills and less sophisticated research strategies. The pace of life that they are used to also dramatically lowers their levels of patience.[8]

Another important factor to be considered for the online design process is the intended access device. Sites designed for mobile devices, such as mobile phones or tablets, will differ from the websites intended for desktop computers. This need comes mainly from the time required to load a page on such devices and the size of the screen. The initial solution used by web designers focused on duplicating the content and creating a separate website for each single device. This however is a less common practice now, and is replaced by responsive web design (RWD). RWD is 'a combination of fluid grids and images with media queries to change layout based on the size of a device viewport. It uses feature detection to determine available screen capabilities and adapt accordingly'.[9] With the introduction of responsive web design marketers can focus on the development of a single web place, rather than ensuring consistency of information presented on sites created for various devices.

Once the end user and the objectives of an online presence have been identified, the actual design begins. The first rule of effective design is to focus not only on how it looks but also on how it works. After all we want our customers to be able to find what they are looking for and complete the task online, whether it's buying online or contacting the company. In many cases, less is more, with the best example being www. gov.uk which received the Design of the Year 2013 award (see Exhibit 12.1).[10]

The GOV.UK design is perfect for the target audience – a wide range of citizens with a variety of queries and technical abilities – and for the purpose of the website – providing information about a

Exhibit 12.1 The UK government's website

variety of government-related services. There's no need for flashy images or video clips. Simple, clear design will not delay page loading time, and white background provides high contrast for ease of access (particularly for vision impaired users).

Basic elements of effective web design

Presentation

As with any other communication tool: make it professional and clear. Steve Krug[11] demonstrated that users online act instinctively and they don't want to spend time learning how to use a new website. With this in mind, marketers shouldn't be afraid to follow the standards (fonts, consistency in colour scheme, presentation of links, position of logo, use of breadcrumbs, etc.). Users are goal-oriented and have little patience with websites which they can't use. With the amount of information online, if they can't find it in one place, they will move to another. Standardization of certain aspects of design gives them a feeling of mastery and empowerment leading to successful completion of the task.[12, 13]

Page width and length need to be considered as important factors of design. Some pages will be printed by users, therefore designers need to consider the amount of content on a such page. Printers work with a maximum width of 750 pixels, and any content above this will be chopped. As for the length, users shouldn't have to scroll down the page to find vital information.

Pictures, graphics and video clips should complement the website rather than be the main element. It's not good for SEO (see later in this chapter) to overload the website with visual elements. In a case of online communications, a picture doesn't necessarily 'paint a thousand words'. (See Marketing in Action 12.1 for a simple introduction to encoding graphic elements of a website in HTML.)

Usability

Usability focuses on assessing how easily the user can complete their task online. Tasks may differ from finding information (address of the store, particular product, etc.) to completing the purchase or contacting the author of the page. In simple terms, usability deals with user friendliness online or user experience. Usability of a website's user interfaces was defined by ISO 9241-151 as:

> The effectiveness, efficiency and satisfaction with which specified users achieve specified goals in particular environments:

- *effectiveness: the accuracy and completeness with which specified users can achieve specified goals in particular environments;*
- *efficiency: the resources expended in relation to the accuracy and completeness of goals achieved;*
- *satisfaction: the comfort and acceptability of the work system to its users and other people affected by its use.*[14]

Usability was considered by computer engineers much earlier than by marketers. However, what they described informs successful marketing endeavours. Two usability experts Jakob Nielsen and Bruce Tognazzini focus on ensuring that a well-designed website should focus on the user (the customer). Each element of the website should be relevant, up-to-date, accessible and clear for the user. Both of them are also strong advocates of simplicity and consistency of design.[15, 16]

Consistency for marketers refers not only to the website itself but reaches further. Websites should serve as part of an offline campaign and agree with branding in general. This way the online presence of the company is part of IMC. Also, ensuring consistency between online and offline channels gives the customer the sense of familiarity and recognition while online and enhances their satisfaction (see Exhibit 12.2).

Navigation

According to Gerry McGovern[17] 'good navigation is ugly and functional'. Navigation on the website is not there to be pretty, but to allow the visitor to find their way around. Think about a dictionary:

Exhibit 12.2 A brand which utilizes consistency on a large scale is IKEA, a Swedish furniture giant. Its highly recognized logo and colour scheme is the same in all countries that it operates in. Apart from keeping the same design for marketing materials, both offline and online, the design and layout of the stores is kept consistent.

an A–Z order is not pretty or inventive, but it works perfectly. The same applies to websites, so the navigation (menus, breadcrumbs, links, footer) needs to be familiar and easy to use. Good navigation will help customers to find what they need, navigate back if they make a mistake and reduce the times when disappointed customers leave the website because they got lost.

Testing

Before launching a website online, it needs to be tested for errors and performance. Due to the multiplicity of web browsers and devices used, companies need to ensure that every visitor to their website will see it exactly as intended. Rushing through this process is not advisable as premature launch may lead to lost transactions, errors on the page and ultimately unsatisfied customers.

Reviews and maintenance

As mentioned before, the design process doesn't finish once the website is online. At this stage customers become testers, so their opinions need to be heard, and marketers need to react to them and their suggestions. Errors and non-working parts need to be fixed immediately; suggestions for improvement should be considered and addressed if appropriate. Constant dialogue with customers will lead to customer satisfaction and loyalty.

Therefore, according to Vila and Kuster[18] a well-designed website will increase customers' confidence, attitude and satisfaction, lowering perceived risk and ultimately leading to increased purchase intention (see Figure 12.4).

Content strategy and copywriting

We need to remember that writing for the Web differs significantly from the writing we are used to. The reason for this is simple: people don't read on the Web: '79% of people scan the new page and only 16% read it word by word.'[19]

Pulizzi and Barrett[20] recommend that companies need to change their mindset to implement a successful content strategy. They recommend using BEST principles for creating the content for online media:

- **B**ehavioural – is there a purpose in the content? What action do you want to trigger in customers?
- **E**ssential – don't publish content that will become just space filler. If your customers visit a page that is about nothing, they will leave and never come back.

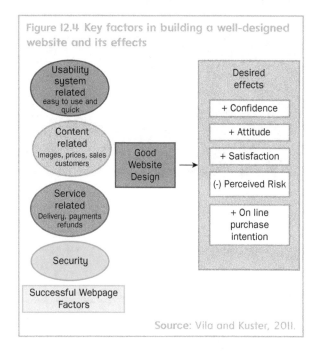

Figure 12.4 Key factors in building a well-designed website and its effects

Source: Vila and Kuster, 2011.

- **S**trategic – your content delivered online needs to support your overall business objectives and be an integral part of your marketing activity.
- **T**argeted – don't use the same content across a variety of platforms. Each platform attracts different people for a reason, so make sure your content is always relevant for them. (Adapted from Chaffey and Smith.)[7]

Writing for the Web is difficult, and writing for mobile devices is even more challenging. Therefore, marketers need to understand how to write to engage with users. General consumers don't like business jargon, and convoluted words. Focusing on the benefits of the product or service in simple words (but avoiding being patronising) will work much better. Users rarely read the full content of the website; they prefer to scan it.[21, 22] Eyetracking studies determined that users scan the page in an F-pattern; they scan/read through upper sections of the content, and then they go through the left side of the content in a vertical movement. See Exhibit 12.3 for an example of a heatmap – the most read parts of the websites are in red, followed by yellow, and least-viewed areas are blue. Grey areas didn't attract any users.

The last crucial aspect of good content writing is making sure that it's grammatically correct and spell checked. Grammar and spelling mistakes negatively affect the credibility and reputation of the business. Knowledge of basic HTML coding (see Marketing in Action 12.1) can speed up the process of removing such errors from the website.

Exhibit 12.3 Eyetracking research results

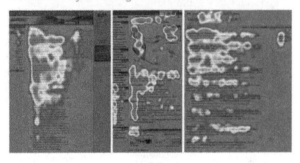

Source: Nielsen Norman Group, 2006.

Marketers with access to CMS can access web articles and make small changes without involving web developers.

Search engine optimization

Many companies make the mistake of investing a lot of money in new systems, software, animations and other wow-for-now elements. They believe that a brand new content management system (CMS) or more flash/video content will miraculously solve problems with their old website, like lack of visitors

Marketing in Action 12.1 HTML code

Critical Thinking: Below is some basic HTML code used on a website. Read it and think about how the knowledge of HTML may help marketers in the development of their company's website and how you would implement this knowledge if you were designing a site.

Marketers often find computer programming boring and not useful. We don't need to become a computer engineer to be good with digital marketing, but having some basic knowledge can help us and streamline small changes and achieve improvements in our online presence.

Below we see how a very simple website has been coded using HTML. This is what the computer or search engine 'sees' when checking the website.

```
<!DOCTYPE html>

<html>

<head>

<!-- your webpage info goes here -->

  <title>My First Website</title>

        <meta name="author" content="your name" />
        <meta name="description" content="" />
        <meta name="keywords" content="your keywords">

<!-- you should always add your stylesheet (css) in the head tag so that it starts loading
before the page html is being displayed -->

        <link rel="stylesheet" href="style.css" type="text/css" />

</head>
```

```
<body>
<!-- webpage content goes here in the body -->
        <div id="page">
                <div id="logo">
                        <h1><a href="/" id="logoLink">My First Website</a></h1>
                </div>
                <div id="nav">
                        <ul>
                                <li><a href="#/home.html">Home</a></li>
                                <li><a href="#/about.html">About</a></li>
                                <li><a href="#/contact.html">Contact</a></li>
                        </ul>
                </div>
                <div id="content">
                        <h2>Home</h2>
                        <p>
                                This is my first webpage! I was able to code all the HTML
and CSS in order to make it. Watch out world of web design here I come!
                        </p>
                        <p>
                                I can use my skills here to create websites for my business,
my friends and family, my CV, blog or articles. As well as any games or more experiment
stuff (which is what the web is really all about).
                        </p>
                </div>
```

```
                    <div id="footer">

                        <p>

                            Webpage made by <a href="/" target="_blank">[your
name]</a>

                        </p>

                    </div>

                </div>

        </body>

        </html>
```

HTML code for a simple website (Codecademy, 2014). If you want to have a quick practice go to http://www.codecademy.com/courses/my-first-webpage/0/1 and try to create your own website.

All this code is needed to produce a website looking like this:

The finished website (Codecademy, 2014).

This is how a search engine 'spider' will see any image on the website:

<img border="0" src="/images/holiday.jpg" alt="Dubrovnik" width="304" height="228">

While the user see this:

Therefore use images carefully. We will come back to this in the 'Search engine optimization' section.

or a high bounce rate (measurements for digital marketing are discussed later in this chapter). What they forget about is the crucial element of successful marketing – up-to-date and appropriate content (as discussed earlier in the chapter). SEO is actually the best way of showing the importance of content.

Search engine optimization (SEO) involves achieving the highest position or ranking in the organic listing on the search engine's results page.[7] The position of any page is determined by the algorithm of the search engine, which matches keywords entered by the user with keywords on the websites.

If companies don't want to spend time on enhancing their search engine results page position, they can pay to appear at the top of the results page (see Exhibit 12.4). Paid links can be easily distinguished on the page as they appear in the right column or on top of the list with the small 'Ad' icon. This may affect how the customer perceives such a link. Some may distrust paid links, and therefore they ignore them and move to organic (not paid for) links further down the page. Paid advertising on search engines might be considered a short-term solution (or as part of a high impact campaign, such as sale or raising brand recognition), but in the long term focusing on improving an organic score may be more valuable for the brand. Search engine advertising works for a limited number of keywords, while optimizing our web content can increase the range of keywords that will display our page high in the results.

Search engines use 'spiders' that visit all existing websites and collect various data about them. They view your website's code, rather than the pretty interface that you can see (see the HTML code section above). When they go through a website, they are looking for keywords and try to classify your website among all the others. To make sure that the spider visits a page and stores the up-to-date details about

it, content needs to be updated regularly. (See the section about content earlier.)

There are a lot of 'tips and tricks' sources available, giving marketers advice on how to improve SEO. Much of this is a guessing game, as search engine algorithms are well guarded secrets. Although we don't have the actual algorithm, there are still several areas that are known for being important for successful SEO.

Some main areas to have in mind when designing SEO for any online channel (Web, mobile, social media) are as follows:

1. *Content is the king* – it's the content of the page that influences a position on the search results page. We need to make sure it's relevant and up-to-date. Spiders like text, not flash, images or animations. (See the section on HTML code in Marketing in Action 12.1.)
2. *Keywords* – if the company makes teddy bears, this is what they should be writing about online. Teddy bear and all synonyms should appear in the title, description and throughout all elements of the website, page, etc. Those shouldn't be abused though; spiders are too clever for such tricks nowadays. Utilising metadata (the bit in HTML code in section head) is good practice as this is the first place where spiders will look.
3. *Links* – links to and from the website are important as they help the spider to place it within the network of websites. This is where the web designer/developer will need to worry more than marketers.
4. *Images and other visual content* – if marketers are working with CMS, they probably ignored the 'image description' box many times. It should be avoided. As we said before, spiders can't see through an image or a video, the 'image description' is all they care about and if this is left blank, the image will not be able to improve the position in the search engine results. (See the HTML section above for images coding.)

Market research

Digital technologies offer new ways to gather data about consumers. In this section we will discuss the main ways in which the Internet is used as a market research tool. We will not be redefining the basic terms of marketing research as they are covered in Chapter 4.

The Internet can support the collection of both primary and secondary data. The amount of data stored on servers and that uploaded online daily is a great source of information about the market and consumers (see Table 12.2).

Exhibit 12.4 Google results page

Table 12.2 Examples of data sources online

Secondary data	
Data about companies and organizations: ■ Directories ■ Companies webpages (including social media) ■ MR companies and databases ■ Government data ■ Research results ■ Official statistics and reports ■ Website and services analytics ■ Etc. Data about consumers: ■ Blogs ■ Social media pages ■ Databases ■ Browser data (site activity) ■ Search history ■ Purchase history ■ Etc.	
Primary data	
Qualitative	Quantitative
■ Skype, Google Hangouts, What's up, QQ, Snap chat – variety of communicators ■ Chats, discussion forums, group discussion tools, etc. ■ Email conversations ■ Mystery shoppers	
■ Video clips ■ Activity capturing software, user experience recording ■ Netnography – online observations	■ Online surveys (Survey Monkey, etc.) ■ Log files ■ Database records

Online data collection usually helps to save money and time. Reach using the Internet allows a wider geographical coverage, with reduced travel cost and rental of research space among other benefits. While the benefits of researching online are similar to those known for offline research, we need to consider the disadvantages of such an approach. Online research requires a more careful design to take account of the following issues:

■ quality
■ reliability
■ validity
■ ethics (see Marketing and Society 12.1)
■ representativeness of sample.

While research involving companies and organizations is less likely to face these issues, research on customers tends to be harder. The perceived anonymity of users online has a big impact on their behaviour and honesty in online research.

User experience research is deeply rooted in usability studies and user interface research. Although rather technical it allows marketers a better choice of

research method for their studies. Usability studies are a great source of information for marketers as they deliver knowledge about the behaviour of people while online and how they interact with the page or other web services.

The marketing research process online is similar to one conducted offline. One of the crucial stages is selection of the most appropriate method, which will ensure collection of the most suitable data for the problem and to ensure we reach the intended sample. By asking questions like 'what do people do?' and 'what do people say?', marketers may determine what will become the source of their data (see Figures 12.5 and 12.6).

Netnography

Netnography is a research methodology developed as a result of the growing penetration of the Internet around the world (see Table 12.1). It is based on ethnographic research techniques and is used mainly for researching behaviours of online communities and individuals. Netnography is a research approach which allows marketers to observe communities

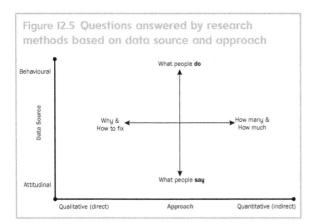

Figure 12.5 Questions answered by research methods based on data source and approach

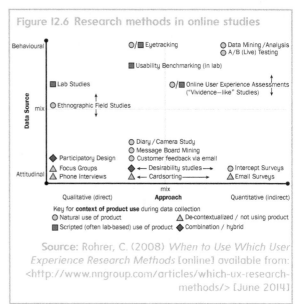

Figure 12.6 Research methods in online studies

Source: Rohrer, C. (2008) *When to Use Which User Experience Research Methods* [online] available from: <http://www.nngroup.com/articles/which-ux-research-methods/> [June 2014]

and individuals online without affecting data by the research process (see the 'Observation' and 'Ethnographical research' sections of Chapter 4). This process allows marketers to collect rich qualitative and quantitative data through mining of blogs, social media platforms, forums, chat rooms, etc.

Netnography is used to reach niche communities and individuals. It allows marketers to collect data about a group's behaviours, culture and even language specific to its members. There is however a question of the reliability of collected data. Perceived anonymity online gives users the opportunity to hide or modify their usual behaviours and opinions.

Netnography is also a subject of criticism as many companies used data obtained online without following the rules of ethical research (see Marketing and Society 12.1). Researchers online should still disclose their presence and the purpose of data collection.

Even with existing issues about accepting netnography as a new research approach, the value of this method can't be underestimated. When used well it delivers data allowing marketers to understand their customers better, and therefore meet their expectations more accurately.

Netiquette

What is netiquette, and why is it important? Netiquette is simply a network etiquette, so a set of rules on how to behave when online.

Etiquette is:

- a conventional requirement as to social behaviour; properties of conduct as established in any class or community or for any occasion
- a prescribed or accepted code of usage in matter of ceremony, as at a court or in official or other formal observances
- the code of ethical behaviour regarding professional practice or action among the members of a profession in their dealings with each other.[23]

Netiquette regulates how any user online should behave. Initially netiquette rules were relevant to each individual online, but it's also worth considering behaviours of professionals and companies online.

The set of basic netiquette rules below (adapted from Virginia Shea)[24] applies to both individual users as well as companies that operate online. With them in mind certain blunders and mistakes may be avoided, which then translates into better reputation, enhanced brand image and loyalty of customers.

- *Rule 1.* Remember the human – even though when online the only interaction you have is with the computer/mobile/tablet screen, we shouldn't forget that the final receiver of our message is a person. When communicating online we need to think about whether we would say the same words to the person's face. If not, maybe we shouldn't say it online either.
  The online world gives the opportunity to communicate with a variety of people but the interposition of the machine shouldn't make us forget basic manners.
- *Rule 2.* Adhere to the same standards of behaviour online as in real life – in real life we obey the law, or as market researchers we behave ethically towards our participants. Why not do the same online? We definitely should (see Marketing and Society 12.1).
- *Rule 3.* Know where you are in cyberspace – we need to behave differently in professional emails (with employers, lecturers, etc.) and in personal

Marketing and Society 12.1 Why do so many companies forget the rules?

With the success of the Internet and social media, many companies included this new tool as part of their marketing strategy. They also discovered that they can buy product or service reviews from people, to increase their positive rating online. Sockpuppeting (when people create fictional identities online and promote content) is a term which is not new. Many big companies like Microsoft and Amazon were involved in or accused of this practice. Why is it considered unethical? The Federal Trade Commission (FTC) provided clear guidelines when pitching online. The consumer has the right to see when the content online is a genuine opinion of a happy/unhappy customer, and when they read or watch a promotional messages. Think about it as similar to product placement on TV. So if a blogger or social media user receives a freebie from any company in exchange for a review they need to clearly disclose such information.

A recent example of unethical behaviour online comes from Facebook. The company was involved in research on users' emotions by changing their News Feed to reinforce positive or negative emotions such as love and hate. Nearly 700,000 people were affected by this research in 2012. Through manipulating messages on Facebook, researchers found that what people saw on social media could reinforce their emotions offline. However, without 'informed consent' from participants many researchers argue that such behaviour is unethical and shouldn't take place. (To read more go to James Grimmelmann's blog post 'As Flies to Wanton Boys', see the suggested reading section.)

There are also examples of unethical behaviour when conducting direct market research. Some companies forget about one of the main principles of research while online, which is anonymity. Researchers need to remember that personal details of participants in online studies should not be used for any follow-ups without obtaining the explicit permission to do so from the participants. Design of online surveys and studies needs to be done carefully, to ensure that companies receive participants' consent for quoting their responses for purposes outside of research (e.g. positive quotes from customers for marketing materials) and if any follow-up contact is anticipated, the participants should be notified about such a possibility before they undertake the research.

Anonymity online created many opportunities for individuals and companies to cross the line of ethical behaviour. However, as researchers and professionals, marketers need to have in mind that bending and breaking the rules could negatively impact brand and reputation, so the same ethical rules should apply to both online and offline activity.

Reflection: Critically evaluate why ethical behaviour online is important and how it reflects on brand image. How can you use the ethical practices of a company of your choice to gain customers' trust?

emails (to our friends, family, etc.). If we join an online community like a discussion forum or online game the good practice is to observe first, before posting ourselves. There's also no excuse for poor spelling or grammar online!

- *Rule 4*. Respect other people's time and bandwidth – this rule applies to many aspects of an online presence. If you send an email keep it short and to the point. The speed of reading online is approximately 25 per cent slower than when reading printed text.[25] Also copying emails to 'everybody' is poor practice. If it's not relevant

to somebody, they shouldn't receive the message. When on a discussion forum read existing posts first as the answers are sometimes already posted, so don't ask the same questions again. For social media platforms we shouldn't think we are centre of cyberspace. Don't overshare or post every 5 minutes without a clear need. This applies to all other areas as well.

- *Rule 5*. Anonymity – we think that we are completely anonymous online. It's a mistake. All our actions may be tracked back to us and particularly in a professional setting this is worth remembering. An extension of this rule is the fact of permanence online. Even if we delete some content, there's always a way of accessing this information. It may not be an easy task to accomplish, but it's possible. As professionals we also don't want our competitors to use our mistakes to their advantage.

- *Rule 6*. Privacy – protect yours and respect the privacy of others. Make sure your passwords are kept secure, and any confidential data is stored on a secured server or disc. Privacy goes both ways as well: don't invade the private online space of others.

These basic rules are mostly common sense when we think about the offline world, but are often forgotten online. Getting into the habit of well-mannered behaviour online is crucial, particularly if we want to keep our good reputation and image.

Social media

The Chartered Institute of Public Relations (CIPR) defines social media as:

> *Social media is the term commonly given to Internet and mobile-based channels and tools that allow users to interact with each other and share opinions and content. As the name implies, social media involves the building of communities or networks and encouraging participation and engagement.*[26]

A simplified definition of social media comes from Chaffey and Smith: it is 'online content created by people'.[7]

Social media differs from traditional media (TV, newspapers, magazines, film) as it's relatively inexpensive and changes people from readers into contributors and publishers. Development of Web 2.0 technologies and social media changed the way organizations, communities and individuals share and discover content online. Communication moved from monologue (one-to-one) to dialogue (many-to-many). The main principles of social media are:

- *Reach* – social media enables a global audience reach, without significant resource investment.
- *Accessibility* – social media is available free to anyone with access to a computer, laptop, mobile phone, tablet or any other device connected to the Internet.
- *Usability* – social media doesn't require any specialist skills or training for its users. The use of social media is intuitive, but it also gives

the opportunity for highly skilled individuals to showcase their skills.

- *Immediacy* – social media offers a 'real-time' dialogue between users. There's no time delay as with traditional media (design, print time).
- *Permanence* – social media is more flexible to changes than traditional media as it offers options to edit or remove published content. However, even with this flexibility all published content should be prepared carefully as anything published will be seen by many users before the change can be made.

The variety of social media tools available allows companies to engage with those channels which are closely related to their strategic objectives. Social media platforms have been classified by Smart Insights[27] into 10 categories (see Figure 12.7):

1. Social networks – main platforms for interaction.
2. Social bookmarking – platforms which allow users to save interesting stories and articles from the Internet. These platforms rate the most popular links to promote them to other users.
3. Social publishing – platforms which allow users to publish articles, or comment and discuss content published by others.
4. Social niche publishing – niche communities can share their interest-specific content via social media.

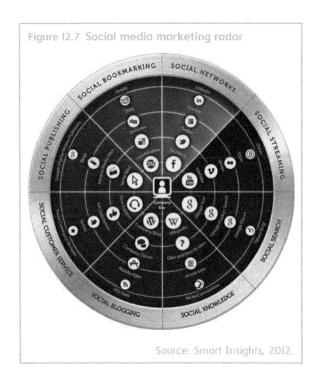

Figure 12.7 Social media marketing radar

Source: Smart Insights, 2012.

5 Social customer service – mainly review platforms and customer-support forums.

6 Social blogging – platforms to allow publishing of longer text, rich media, etc.

7 Social knowledge – reference platforms like Wikis or Yahoo! Answers.

8 Social search – search engines enabling users to rate search results or customize their search results page.

9 Social streaming – platforms for publishing of rich media such as pictures, video or podcasts.

10 Social commerce – mainly relevant to the retail industry for product ratings and reviews and sharing deals. (Adapted from Chaffey and Smith.)[7]

Selecting the right social media channel is crucial for success. This choice shouldn't be dictated by the organization's preference but by the target market. Even with the amount of social media channels available we will only focus on three here – Facebook, Twitter and blogs – as they are commonly used by many companies and differ significantly (see Figure 12.8).

Facebook

Facebook is one of the biggest social media portals and is used by many companies already. Like any other social media channel it increases brand exposure. Through engagement with customers (conversations) it can increase web traffic to company websites, help build relationships with the audience and positively affect customer loyalty. Facebook offers a variety of ways for companies to utilize this platform, such as fan pages, groups, applications, targeted advertising. Facebook also offers a measurement tool, Facebook Insights, which provides some analytics for fan pages.

A brand which successfully uses Facebook is ASOS. Its fan page is part of its integrated marketing activity (the integration with Twitter, website and other online platforms – see the Marketing spotlight at the start of this chapter). The company offers customer service advice and competitions and shows product ranges. Through its conversations with customers it builds relationships and directs traffic to the company's website.

Twitter

The focus of Twitter is slightly different to Facebook's. Although it's still used for generating conversations and building relationships, Twitter serves as a tool to connect, not only with customers, but also with experts in the industry and partners, and helps to build our position within the industry. Due to the tweet size limitation, direct product or

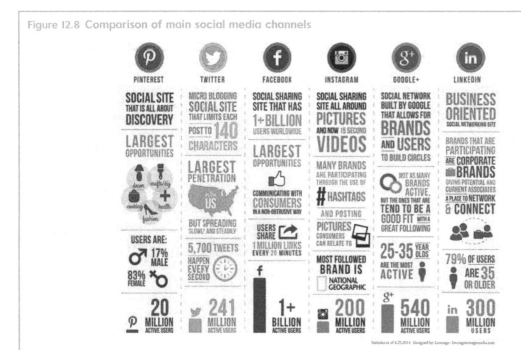

Figure 12.8 Comparison of main social media channels

service promotion is not often used on Twitter. Reputation management, customer service and participating in customer conversations are the main uses of this platform. B&Q has a successful Twitter presence with DIY tips and customer advice. Its social media presence is linked to its website and other promotional materials.

Another popular application of Twitter is the use of #hashtags during events or TV shows (see Exhibit 12.6). Immediacy of this platform allows for real-time comments and opinions and some shows engage their cast members to participate in the dialogue with viewers.

Blogs

Blogs are one of the oldest forms of social media and we can trace back their roots to the 1990s. They started as online diaries of individuals, but with time more and more businesses utilized them as another way to connect to their customers. There are several blogging platforms available with a variety of templates, topics and support available. Lack of limitations for published blog content (in comparison to other social media tools) encourages creativity and innovation. Building up a blog audience is difficult and time consuming. Many professionals are authors of blogs. Through this activity they establish their reputation as experts in their industries and increase exposure of their name (brand). They can attract new job opportunities or partnerships this way.

Also companies may use blogs as part of their marketing activity. Disney Parks blog (http://disneyparks.disney.go.com/blog/) has stories from holidaymakers, sharing updates, competitions and stories from the resorts. Through the blog people can find out more about resorts and read about any upcoming events.

As with the platforms discussed above, other social media tools can be successfully utilized by individuals and businesses as part of their marketing activity. To select the most appropriate platform, marketers need to consider the audience, type of content, strengths and weaknesses of each platform and resources that they can dedicate for this task. Not all platforms are equally suitable for all industries; therefore a careful selection is required to avoid wasting time and money. Marketers also need to have in mind the constant development of new technologies, and pay attention to any innovative ideas that may become popular in the future. (See 'Future potential of digital marketing' later in this chapter.) The challenge for

organizations and individuals is to ensure that their social media presence becomes integrated as part of their marketing activity. It's not good practice to copy the same content over to all platforms, as each platform operates differently, and to achieve best results all messages need to be platform-specific. It's also better for the organization to focus its efforts and resources on one most suitable platform to achieve higher audience engagement on a single platform.

Campaign measurement

Digital marketing is no different from traditional marketing and companies need to measure the profitability of their activities. The digital footprint left by every person online is a source of important data. The amount of data that can be captured by online systems is almost infinite, but it's important to identify metrics that are a source of vital data for overall campaign performance.

Measurement of a company's online presence is an area, next to web design, where marketers need to work closely with IT experts. The task for marketers is to identify relevant metrics, and then analyse data, while IT experts need to implement and retrieve data from the analytics system. Companies can get data about how many website visits they have had, how many fans or followers they have on social media channels and how many times an app was downloaded. These basic measures are available to us by default and there's no need to set anything special. But for more complex data like bounce rates, visit duration, new/returning visitors, conversion rates, etc. (see Table 12.3) additional software may be required.

There are many solutions available both free and licensed, like Google Analytics, Web Trends, Adobe Site Catalyst, Coremetrics and many more. A careful evaluation is required before the decision to purchase new software is made. Analytics tools are not cheap, as many of them need to be customized (the licensed or hosted ones), and therefore the cost is higher. Additionally, the decision to purchase analytics software should be driven by the linked profitability of the business and specific business decisions informed by newly obtained data.

Analytics software may analyse a company's online presence overall (website, app, social media) and produce reports on valuable metrics (see also Chapter 1).

If a company can't afford to purchase expensive software, it can always go for open source analytics solutions. They may have more limited functionality

Table 12.3 Some main metrics and dimensions used online

Metrics and dimensions	Definition
Bounce rate	The percentage of visitors to a website who leave the site after viewing only one page.
Conversion rate (Goal Conversion Rate All)	The percentage of sessions which resulted in a conversion to at least one of your goals.
Average session duration	The average duration of user sessions represented in total seconds.
Ad clicks	The total number of times users have clicked on an ad to reach your property.
Cost per click	Cost to advertiser per click. Applies for paid advertising.
Click through rate	Click through rate for the ad. This is equal to the number of clicks divided by the number of impressions for the ad (e.g. how many times users clicked on one of the ads where that ad appeared).
Cost per conversion	The cost per conversion (including ecommerce and goal conversions) for the site.
ROI	Return on investment is overall transaction profit divided by derived advertising cost.
Page views per session	The average number of pages viewed during a session on your site. Repeated views of a single page are counted.
Average search depth	The average number of pages people viewed after performing a search on your site.
Time on page	How long a user spent on a particular page in seconds. Calculated by subtracting the initial view time for a particular page from the initial view time for a subsequent page. Thus, this metric does not apply to exit pages for your site.
Dimension	'A descriptive attribute or characteristic of an object that can be given different values. For example, a geographic location could have dimensions called Latitude, Longitude or City Name. Values for the City Name dimension could be San Francisco, London or Singapore.'
Metrics	'Individual elements of a dimension which can be measured as a sum or a ratio. For example, the dimension City can be associated with a metrics like Population, which would have a sum value of all the residents of the specific city.'[29]

Source: Most definitions provided by Google Analytics.[30]

compared with expensive products, but can deliver enough information to provide some metrics on digital marketing.

For measuring social media activity, certain platforms provide built-in analytics tools (e.g. Facebook Insights – see Figure 12.9 below). Social media metrics can be divided into three main categories:[4]

1 Activity (input) metrics – these metrics show how much input the company has into the social media activity (e.g. number of posts, frequency, type of posts).
2 Interaction (response) metrics – these metrics show how our target audience engages with our social media content such as number of fans/ likes/ followers, comments, shares, virality, tags, mentions, etc.
3 Performance (outcome) metrics – these metrics focus on outcomes of our activity, such as financial, satisfaction etc.

For a quick list of how many things you can measure on social media, visit David Berkowitz's 100 Ways to Measure Social Media.[28]

Future potential in digital marketing

Many professionals are asking the same question: where will digital marketing go next? Unfortunately, this is probably one of those questions with no clear answer. Technology races forward and the next 'big thing' may be just around the corner. In 1997 Peterson et al. made a very valid point: 'No one can predict with certainty what the ultimate impact of the Internet will be on consumer marketing. There is virtually no information on how, or to what extent, consumers will use the Internet in the context of marketing or what new marketing paradigms will prove viable.'[31] In this section we will look at some technologies that are available, but not yet used on a large scale. These new technologies increasingly rely on mobile devices; their success therefore depends on many factors, one of them being variations around the world in smartphone adoption and geographical coverage of 3G and 4G networks. Below we will discuss some tools that vary on adoption and popularity levels but have great potential for marketers. Some of them have already

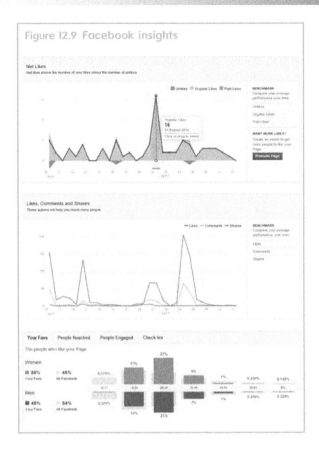

Figure 12.9 Facebook insights

been used successfully by companies, some are very popular in certain parts of the world, while others are still being evaluated by practitioners and consumers.

Augmented reality (AR) is a tool which overlays reality with highly interactive content. With the use of AR, opportunities for marketers are almost endless. Why then is everybody not yet using it? First of all, there's a variety of apps able to read and interpret AR content, so any investment in AR content needs to have a particular app in mind and therefore there is an increased risk of failure in cases where customers don't use the chosen app. Secondly, as with many other new technologies, it requires a significant investment with little guarantee of profit. Both of these lead to Catch 22 situations: why would consumers download the AR reading app, if there's not much to be scanned? And why include AR in a campaign if consumers don't look around for this type of content? Therefore adoption of AR on a large scale is still uncertain.

Note: If you want to see what AR can do, try Blippar, Aurasma, Wikitude World Browser, Google Ingress, Layar, and many more. Be careful, some of them you need to pay for.

Augmented reality developed from location-based services which are better known. Examples include Facebook check-in, TripAdvisor and Foursquare (in the UK this tool is still rarely used by marketers in comparison to the US market).

Foursquare 'helps you find the perfect places to go with friends'.[32] With over 50 million people worldwide it works as a type of customer-generated promotion. When customers check in at a shop or restaurant and rate the product or service, they act as brand advocates. The brand receives 'free' exposure, and the customer can get a discount, make their opinion known online, and earn a position on the Foursquare site. However, as mentioned before, Facebook offers similar functionality and is more popular; why then should the customer download a new app, and start building their presence from scratch?

Another interesting concept in mobile technologies is quick response (QR) codes. (See 'Ad Insight' QR codes in this book.) These work in a similar way to well-known bar codes. Once scanned the code triggers some behaviour on a mobile device, such as launching a website, app, etc.[33] The beauty of QR codes lies in their simplicity. They use a mobile phone camera and a free-to-download app. It doesn't matter which app the customer has, QR codes work with all of them (unlike AR content). It also doesn't require big investment to add QRs to a company's campaigns. Even with all these advantages, not many marketers utilize QR codes at present. Some perceive QR as an 'ugly' thing, but these little squares are more than just useful. They offer interactivity without complexity or the cost of other mobile technologies.

Near field communication (NFC) was meant to replace QR codes. NFC 'allows devices to interact via radio frequencies when they are brought into close proximity to one another'.[33] The most popular use of NFC at the moment is contactless payment cards (see Exhibit 12.7). Is NFC really better than QR codes? Opinions vary. NFC requires special parts in your phone, and at present not many manufacturers include it in their devices as standard (not even Apple). Even if you have it in your phone, you still need to invest in special chips in your promotional materials.

Exhibit 12.5 Contactless payment

To summarize this section, marketers constantly need to make sure that they follow new developments in technology. Any new tool may revolutionize digital marketing in the same way as MySpace was replaced with Facebook. We need to keep our eyes open but also make sure we don't adopt any of the tools without assessing their usefulness for the brand and the potential return.

Marketing in Action 12.2 The dark side of online communities

Critical Thinking: Below are examples of how online communities can have a negative impact on society. Marketers need to avoid any negative associations with a brand. Critically evaluate how the brands can get involved in the responsible use of digital technologies and how can they encourage consumers to do the same.

Are you able to give up your online life for a full 24 hours? Are you sure? No Facebook, Snapchat, Twitter, YouTube, online games, Skype… If you are able to spend a day without your digital identity – congratulations. More and more people are addicted to the Internet and digital communication. Researchers in Maryland conducted a study on US students who displayed symptoms similar to drug and alcohol addictions when asked to give up all media for one day.[34] The scale of the problem is growing and although only online gaming disorder has been officially recognized by the American Psychiatric Association, there is a lot of discussion on the potentially harmful impact of the Internet and social media on users.[35]

'Online community' is a term which describes a group of people interacting primarily online. The term is wider than social media communities, as it also covers interest groups or gaming communities, etc. All of them function in a similar way. They gather people of similar interests or characteristics and provide them with facilities to communicate. Involvement in such communities may be beneficial for us but can also show how detrimental abuse of the Internet can be. One of the first shocking examples was a Korean man who died after playing online games for 50 hours with few breaks.[36]

Online games also led to the rise of Gold Farmers. The highly competitive world of online games (mainly MMORPG – massively multiplayer online role-playing games) created the need for a constant online presence. As the game doesn't pause when the player is offline, Gold Farmers offer to sell experience points, game items, etc. But Gold Farmers are not official representatives of game developers. They are players (mainly from China) who spend an extensive amount of time playing games and then selling their achievements to others. There are many clips on YouTube which talk about the issue of Gold Farmers.

Another problem in online communities is cyberbullying. This is 'a form of bullying which takes place online or through mobile phone. Problems include stolen identity, threats, blackmail, gossip, abusive comments, nasty pictures'.[37] As people feel more anonymous online, many are freer in their actions than they would be offline and some of them use it to bully others. Cyberbullying is still a relatively new issue and therefore is not currently regulated by law in several countries. In the context of marketing we can observe a form of cyberbullying in hate tags where people vent out their dissatisfaction with the brand, product or service. British Airways, McDonald's, Ryanair, Tesco and Luton Airport have all faced negative reactions from customers on social media. Comments from dissatisfied customers can be really strong as usually they are published during or immediately after the customer experiences the upsetting situation. These comments tend to use strong language, and need to be treated by companies carefully.

Summary

In this chapter we have examined the important issues of digital marketing. The following key issues were addressed:

1. Digital marketing is a dynamic area of marketing which is constantly changing and giving marketers new ways to communicate with consumers. Digital marketing revolutionized communication from monologue to dialogue, where customers are empowered to express their opinions.

2. Digital marketing is a complex area of marketing covering websites, mobile apps, social media and any other online presence. To achieve effectiveness marketers should have a basic understanding of some of the technical aspects of computer systems and Internet technologies.

3. Digital marketing should always be a part of the IMC of the organization and not be treated as a separate entity. An online presence can enhance any traditional campaign and marketing activity of the company.

4. Content online is more important and effective than an overload of visual and interactive elements. Therefore copywriting and content management should be at the centre of digital marketing.

5. Digital marketing can enhance the market research process, providing valuable data about customers and their behaviour.

6. Social media is an exciting opportunity for marketers and is a useful tool for communications. The variety of platforms available requires careful consideration to achieve the highest return on investment. Social media is only relatively free, as although software is free, management time is costly.

7. Newest developments in the subject go for more interactivity and mobility of technology. Marketers need to observe new developments as they may become popular in a short period of time.

8. There are some ethical concerns around digital marketing and online communities. Companies need to ensure that the ethical procedures online are equally strict as for those offline, as this has implications for brand image and reputation.

Study questions

1. Discuss changes in the digital environment that you have noticed in the past 5–10 years. What is your opinion about current trends in the field?
2. Select two of your favourite brands and visit their websites. Evaluate the content of the websites according to web design principles.
3. Search for 'student holidays' (or anything else) in a web browser (Google, Bing, Yahoo). Go to the third results page and select one of the links. Evaluate the content of this website and recommend changes to improve the search engine position.
4. Think about the social media platforms you are using. Discuss how companies may utilize these platforms (in a new way) to promote their products and services.
5. For the company of your choice, analyse and discuss its current social media presence. Did it select the best possible platform to meet its objectives? Can you suggest a better solution?
6. Think about a local SME with no social media presence at the moment. Analyse whether setting up this channel of communication could enhance its business. Discuss with justification what would be the best solution for the SME.
7. Discuss how companies may integrate their online and offline campaigns. What are the benefits of such an approach?

Suggested reading

If you wish to learn some basic HTML go to http://www.w3schools.com/html/html_examples.asp

For tips on writing for the web visit Gerry McGovern's page http://www.gerrymcgovern.com/homepage

Rowles, D. (2014) *Mobile Marketing*, Kogan Page: London.

Beloit College (n.d.) *The Beloit College Mindset List for the Class of 2014* [online] available from: http://www.beloit.edu/mindset/previouslists/2014/ [June 2014]

Chaffey, D. and **Smith, P.R.** (2013) *E-marketing Excellence: Planning and Optimizing your Digital Marketing*, 4th ed., Routledge: Oxon.

Charlesworth, A. (2014) *Digital Marketing. A Practical Approach*, Routledge: Oxon.

Grimmelmann, J. (2014) *As Flies to Wanton Boys* [online] available from: http://laboratorium.net/archive/2014/06/28/as_flies_to_wanton_boys [July 2014]

Tuten, T. and **Solomon, M.** (2014) *Social Media Marketing*, Pearson: Harlow.

When you have read this chapter

log on to the Online Learning Centre for *Foundations of Marketing* at
www.mheducation.co.uk/textbooks/fahy5
where you'll find links and extra online study tools for marketing.

References

1. **ASOS** (2014) *About us* [online] available from: http://www. asos.com/infopages/pgeaboutus.aspx?r=2 [June 2014].

2. **Mintel** (2014) *ASOS sales rise 25% in Q3* [online] available from http://store.mintel.com/uk-retail-briefing-june-2014 [August 2014].

3. **The Marketing Society** (2013) *2012: ASOS Social Media – Case Study* [online] available from: https://www.marketingsociety. com/the-library/2012-asos-social-media-case-study-highly-commended [June 2014].

4. **Tuten, T.** and **M. Solomon**. (2014) *Social Media Marketing*, Pearson: Harlow.

5. **Prensky, M.** (2001) Digital Natives, Digital Immigrants, *On the Horizon*, **9** (5), 1–6.

6. **Cormode, G.** and **B. Krishnamurthy** (2008) Key differences between Web 1.0 and Web 2.0, *First Monday*, **13** (6).

7. **Chaffey, D.** and **P.R. Smith** (2013) *E-marketing Excellence. Planning and Optimizing your Digital Marketing*, 4th ed., Routledge: Oxon.

8. **Loranger, H.** and **J. Nielsen** (2013) *Teenage Usability: Designing Teen-targeted Websites* [online] available from: http://www.nngroup.com/articles/usability-of-websites-for-teenagers/ [accessed June 2014].

9. **Wroblewski, L.** (2011) *Multi-Device Design: An Evolution* [online] available from: http://www.lukew.com/ff/entry.asp?1436 [accessed August 2014].

10. *Financial Times* (2013) UK Government Website Wins Design Award [online] available from: http://www.ft.com/cms/s/2/529f6ab4-a5ce-11e2-b7dc-00144feabdc0.html#slide0> [accessed July 2014].

11. **Krug, S.** (2006) *Don't Make Me Think! A Common Sense Approach to Web Usability*, New Riders: Berkeley, CA.

12. **Nielsen, J.** (2004) *The Need for Web Design Standards* [online] available from: http://www.nngroup.com/articles/the-need-for-web-design-standards/ [June 2014].

13. **Nielsen, J.** (2004) *Mastery, Mystery and Misery: the Ideologies of Web Design* [online] available from: http://www.nngroup. com/articles/ideologies-of-web-design/ [July 2014].

14. **ISO** (2008) *Ergonomics of Human-System Interaction. Guidance on World Wide Web User Interfaces* [online] available from: https://www.iso.org/obp/ui/#iso:std:iso:9241:-151:ed-1:v1:en [accessed June 2014].

15. **Nielsen, J.** (1995) *10 Usability Heuristics for User Interface Design* [online] available from: http://www.nngroup.com/articles/ten-usability-heuristics/ [accessed July 2014].

16. **Tognazzini, B.** (2014) *First Principles of Interaction Design* (Revised and Expanded) [online] available from: http://asktog.com/atc/principles-of-interaction-design/.

17. **McGovern, G.** (2009) *How to Create Clear Web Navigation Menus* [online] available from: http://giraffeforum.com/wordpress/2009/11/15/how-to-create-clear-web-navigation-menus/ [accessed July 2014].

18. **Vila, N.** and **I. Kuster** (2011) Consumer Feelings and Behaviours Towards Well Designed Websites, *Information and Management*, **48** (4–5), 166–77.

19. **Nielsen, J.** (1997) *How Users Read on the Web* [online] available from: http://www.nngroup.com/articles/how-users-read-on-the-web/ [accessed June 2014].

20. **Pulizzi, J.** and **Barrett, T.** (2010) *Get Content. Get Customers*, McGraw-Hill, Columbus, OH.

21. **Estes, J.** (2013) *User-Centric vs. Maker-Centric Language: 3 Essential Guidelines* [online] available from: http://www.nngroup.com/articles/user-centric-language/ [accessed July 2014].

22. **Nielsen, J.** (2013) *Website Reading: It (Sometimes) Does Happen* [online] available from: http://www.nngroup.com/articles/website-reading/ [accessed July 2014].

23. **Dictionary.com** *Etiquette* [online] available from: http://dictionary.reference.com/browse/etiquette?s=t [accessed August 2014].

24. **Shea, V.** (1996) *Netiquette*, Albion Books: San Rafael.

25. **Nielsen, J.** (1996) In defence of print [online] available from: http://www.nngroup.com/articles/in-defense-of-print/ [accessed August 2014].

26. **CIPR** (2013) *Social Media Best Practice Guide* [online] available from: http://newsroom.cipr.co.uk/download/ciprsocialmediaguidelinesfinal-2013.pdf [accessed July 2014].

27. **Smart Insights** (2012) *The Social Media Marketing Radar* [online] available from: http://www.smartinsights.com/social-media-marketing/social-media-strategy/social-media-marketing-radar/ [accessed July 2014].

28. **Berkowitz, D.** (2009) *The Who, What, Where, When, Why, and How of the 100 Ways to Measure Social Media* [online] available from: http://www.marketersstudio.com/2009/11/the-who-what-where-when-why-and-how-of-the-100-ways-to-measure-social-media.html#more [accessed July 2014].

29. **Google Support** (2014) *Dimensions and Metrics* [online] available from: https://support.google.com/analytics/answer/1033861?hl=en-GB [accessed July 2014.

30. **Google Analytics** (2014) *Dimensions and Metrics Reference* [online] available from: https://developers.google.com/analytics/devguides/reporting/core/dimsmets [accessed July 2014].

31. **Peterson, R.A., S. Balasubramanian** and **B.J. Bronnenberg** (1997) Exploring the Implications of the Internet for Consumer Marketing, *Journal of the Academy of Marketing Sciences*, **24** (4), 329–46.

32. **Foursquare** (2014) *About* [online] available from: https://foursquare.com/about [accessed July 2014].

33. **Rowles, D**. (2014) *Mobile Marketing*, Kogan Page: London.

34. **Siew, W**. (2010) *US Students Suffering from Internet Addiction: Study* [online] available from: http://uk.reuters.com/article/2010/04/23/us-internet-addicts-life-idUSTRE63M4QN20100423 [accessed June 2014].

35. **Chamberlin, J**. (2011) Facebook: friend or foe?, *Monitor Staff*, **42** (9), 66.

36. **BBC** (2005) *South Korean Dies After Games Session* [online] available from: http://news.bbc.co.uk/2/hi/technology/4137782.stm [accessed June 2014].

37. **BullyingUK** (2014) *What is Cyber Bullying*? [online] available from: http://www.bullying.co.uk/cyberbullying/what-is-cyberbullying/ [accessed June 2014].

Net-A-Porter: digital by design

Introduction

Launched in 2000 by former fashion editor Natalie Massenet in London, Net-A-Porter.com is now the leading global e-tailer in luxury fashion for women. Since 2010 it has been owned by the Swiss luxury conglomerate the Richemont group. Net-A-Porter.com is a luxury fashion destination where editorial and e-tail merge in an interactive, shoppable magazine. This case seeks to establish the digital marketing strategies used by the company which have allowed it to obtain this prominent status.

Establishing an ecommerce site

Purchasing clothing and accessories without trying or touching products is not a new issue for fashion retailers. Mail order retailing, established in the Victorian era, offered an alternative channel for retailers to reach their customers for over 100 years and online retailing is the 21st century version. While it was not difficult for Massenet to obtain start-up funding for the venture, raising £1.2 million from contacts with private investors in the latter part of the 1990s, it was challenging to gauge support

from luxury brands who were not particularly interested in making their products available on the Internet in its early days. Most believed that exceptional customer service and the ability to feel, smell and experience luxury goods in a traditional retail environment was unrivalled and necessary when maintaining loyalty and charging customers a premium for branded and designer products. Working hard to convince brands of the relevance and opportunities the Internet held, Massenet was keen to develop an online platform that would service the needs of time poor, affluent women. Well educated, prosperous women with busy, successful working lives who wanted luxury fashion quickly but lacked immediate access to products they had seen in magazines through advertising and editorial.

In the early days a number of key brands such as Marc Jacobs, Michael Kors and Chloé endorsed Massenet's vision and agreed to be distributed through the website. Through the boom years of the 2000s sales increased rapidly and were attributed to an understanding of this new type of customer; speedy availability of the most desired products and great customer service in a premium and pioneering online environment. As the Internet and digital marketing have advanced over the past 15 years so has Net-A-Porter's ability to adapt to the opportunities and challenges of the digital age.

Initially Net-A-Porter's main form of communication to potential customers was via email newsletters; they became the arbiter of good taste and the go-to website for selective, luxury fashion in affluent markets. The brands themselves, stylists and editors set the pace; the information was sent out to potential and existing database of self-selected customers. Massenet's experience working for *Tatler*, a high-end glossy fashion and society magazine, allowed the appropriate tone and approach. The content was rich in visuals and had an editorial, informative feel without being flashy, sensational or patronizing.

The customer

The magazine for superwomen

Jada Pinkett Smith interviewed on Net-A-porter.com
August 2014

Today's target female customer is global, mobile, fashion forward and willing to spend money on luxury clothing, accessories and beauty products. Her household income is around £170,000 per annum and she will travel abroad approximately 11 times per year. Net-A-Porter.com has over 3 million daily page views with nearly 400,000 daily unique visitors. The average time a visitor spends on the site is 4.39 minutes with a bounce rate of approximately 30 per cent, both impressive figures for a fashion e-tailer. The top five visitors by country are from Japan, the USA, the UK, Germany and France (www.alexa.com). To cater to the growing global consumer and 24/7 access the company opened new offices in New York, Hong Kong and Shanghai in 2012 and regional websites in France, Germany and China. Data compiled from page visits and online sales gives the company a clear indication of customers' location, average spend and the most popular brands and their products. This information is crucial to developing their seasonal buying strategy, customer retention and promotional planning.

A shoppable magazine

The landing page for the website is not instantly recognisable as a retail store front, nestling moving wish-list imagery on a live feed with editorial articles, photo shoots and subtle advertising. Although the page changes daily the content focuses on the weekly online magazine – *The EDIT*. The use of this title suggests key fashion pieces picked out by Net-A-Porter, saving viewers time trawling through pages and pages of products to make their selection. One advantage of online retailing is the vast selection of products that can be offered without the expensive associations of in-store operations such as storage and security. Net-A-Porter stocks over 500 designers (brands) and approximately 12,000 products or SKUs (stock-keeping units) at any one time with product categories split by clothing, bags, footwear, lingerie and beauty products.

The product pages are the 'shop front' and when selling expensive luxury products this requires important consideration; they are highly visual with flawless photography and copy content offering an online stylist with editorial content and personal contact. The pages are clear and precise but speak with authority; by limiting the photographs to three this does not overwhelm the customer or make the page too busy. The copy is written in a Net-A-Porter voice with 'Editors notes and details' and a 'How to wear it' area followed by 'You may also like', and while these are sales tactics it is clear that they pertain to understanding the customer and what might appeal to their tastes.

Much of the communication is presented in a traditional magazine type format which gives an informative, soft selling approach but at every point there is the opportunity to click and 'shop the story', 'shop the video' or 'shop [the celebrity / model / interviewee's] shoot'. One click leads directly to the shop front and product listing pages. For customers in London and New York a same day delivery service is offered.

Competitors

Many of Net-A-Porter's competitors have long established bricks and mortar stores and more recently developed strong online presence for retailing and communication. Department stores like Selfridges and Harvey Nichols are aggressively marketing themselves as omni-channel retailers creating a seamless experience for customers at every point of service. As Net-A-Porter does not have a physical presence on the high street it is vital that it maintains a consistent route to its customers through online contact and excellent customer service.

Engaging the customer

It is essential for Net-A-Porter to write original copy with key words to increase SEO Web searches on organic listings. As it stocks many well-known brands the website must stand out from competitors stocking the same or similar product. From an SEO perspective, Net-A-Porter prioritizes key words such as designer names over product categories because its customer is highly brand aware and often looking for the 'must have' piece of the season, exclusive or limited editions.

SEO through a key word search is a crucial strategy to attract potential shoppers browsing the Internet but engagement through daily emails is essential for the company to foster a longer term relationship with its target customers. Updates on new fashion products, editorial stories and sales are sent to those that have signed up for emails but are not necessarily existing customers. Converting readers to customers is the key. Emails are titled with subjects such as 'meet the new multitaskers' recommending clothes that transfer from day wear to evening wear when life is busy. 'Fall-proof your closet now' instilling a little bit of fear but offering a solution so the customer feels in control, assertive and proactive in her image and wardrobe management.

Daily emails are often linked together in a theme; during a particular hot weather spell, titles such as 'we have a style dilemma' or 'workwear dilemmas solved' engage the potential customer as a fashion authority and solve their 'problem' at the same time. Successful emails have a 'call to action' (CTA) using key words that resonate with the reader with the intention of converting them into purchasers. For an online retailer, educating customers and gaining their trust is critical to conversion. Even when the customer cannot see email images viewed through their smartphone, phrases such as 'The Edit Magazine: Read and Shop' and 'Shop the Edit now' are clear messages.

Social media

Previously, information about fashion styles and trends flowed one way – from the website to the customer. This information was controlled by the fashion brands, their publicists (PR) and journalists. Information coming from the consumer was mostly statistical, where the product was purchased and how much it cost. However, with the advent of social media and user-generated content this information was more readily available. Fashion information became democratic and the buyers, stylists and brands could now get real-time feedback on their selections and were not just reliant on products selling or not. The advent of social networking sites such as Facebook and Twitter opened up a two-way interaction with the target customer. In 2009 Net-A-Porter joined Twitter and Facebook and now has 627,000 followers and 1.2 million likes respectively. Other social media websites including Pinterest, Tumblr, Google+ and YouTube are also used by Net-A-porter but the choice of social network must be appropriate to the brand and target customer.

Net-A-Porter's frequent online activity through tweets and posts creates an online buzz, generates loyalty and engagement. Viewers interact with the retailers through social media campaigns. Facebook 'likes' and comments by customers and Twitter retweets and favourites by professionals and industry experts are ways of measuring marketing communication successes. Net-A-Porter can gain insights into existing and potential customer attitudes, behaviour and motivations to purchase luxury goods as well as real-time fashion trends. Social media alone is a relatively inexpensive form of promotion but it is difficult to see its return in financial terms and it may be limited to sales figures of products highlighted through social media sites.

Net-A-Porter Live feed

> BE INSPIRED, 31693 shoppers online, NET-A-PORTER LIVE, What the world's most stylish women are buying now

www.Net-A-Porter.com August 2014

Social media engagement opens the opportunity for multiple online conversations, allowing companies greater access to the consumers' opinions but also gives a voice to the consumer to influence the retailer and fellow shoppers. In 2011 Net-A-Porter launched a live feed on the landing page which shows the viewer what other site visitors around the world are putting on their virtual wish list or in their shopping bag. This sparks curiosity,

competitiveness and creates a buzz around what people are buying. It appeals to the social aspect of online retailing, while also creating shopper profiles from around the world.

New developments in technology

> Technology is at the heart of what we do. If you come to our offices, we look like Google. We have hackathons. It's what we talk about. But we're also obsessed with fashion, service logistics, operations, automation and content.

Natalie Massenet interviewed for *Forbes* in 2014

Interactive and mobile technology has also evolved considerably over the past five years. As technological first movers Net-A-Porter's first iPhone app was developed in July 2009 followed by iPad magazine a year later. This was the company's first reference to mobile commerce. It established itself as not just a trusted retailer of luxury goods but showed that it understood the technological developments of mobile Internet devices. The company believed that smartphones and tablets would become essential to accessing fashion information and shopping and socializing on the move was just as important. A further enhancement of Net-A-Porter's digital presence was the launch of the YouTube TV channel in 2012, reporting news, fashion shows and events around the world.

A return to traditional media?

In 2014 Net-A-Porter launched a bi-monthly print magazine, *Porter*, to rival traditional glossy magazines such as *Vogue* and *Elle*. Although a traditional magazine format, it allows the customer to buy items featured in the magazine in one place: net-a-porter.com as opposed to trawling websites and stores to find a stockist. Despite being a luxurious high end publication, the magazine could be considered today's version of the mail order catalogue, updated bi-monthly and a feeder to the commercial site. The magazine also gives the company the opportunity to generate lucrative advertising revenue from the brands that it stocks and those with potential to be stocked on the transactional website. The launch of the *Porter* magazine has now established the company as a modern media brand, with online sales, YouTube TV channel and shopping apps.

Sources

http://www.drapersonline.com/digital/timeline-Net-A-Porter-under-mark-sebba/5062901.article#.U-JNfvldWSo

http://www.vogue.co.uk/person/natalie-massenet

http://www.forbes.com/sites/carolinehoward/2014/05/28/the-power-women-who-are-reinventing-the-way-you-shop-online/

http://www.alexa.com/siteinfo/Net-A-Porter.com

http://www.independent.co.uk/news/media/press/the-mag-trade-netaporters-new-glossy-magazine-set-to-be-a-serious-rival-to-vogue-9113140.html

Questions

1. Summarize how Net-A-Porter has established and maintained its position as the leading luxury fashion online retailer in the UK.

2. How much of Net-A-Porter's success can be attributed to the role Massenet played in the beginning and why is her vision important for an online retailer?

3. Evaluate the email marketing campaigns by either signing up for the emails or discuss the ones above.

4. Suggest a series of key words that might be appropriate and relevant to attract the target customer for SEO and email content. Explain why there may be a difference.

5. What are the advantages and disadvantages for a luxury ecommerce site such as Net-A-Porter when using social media?

This case was prepared by Fiona Armstrong-Gibbs, Liverpool John Moores University from various published sources as a basis for class discussion rather than to show effective or ineffective management.

Glossary

ad hoc research a research project that focuses on a specific problem, collecting data at one point in time with one sample of respondents

administered vertical marketing system a channel situation where a manufacturer that dominates a market through its size and strong brands may exercise considerable power over intermediaries even though they are independent

advertising any paid form of non-personal communication of ideas or products in the prime media (i.e., television, the press, posters, cinema and radio, the Internet and direct marketing)

advertising agency an organization that specializes in providing services such as media selection, creative work, production and campaign planning to clients

advertising message the use of words, symbols and illustrations to communicate to a target audience using prime media

advertising platform the aspect of the seller's product that is most persuasive and relevant to the target consumer

ambient advertising any out-of-home display advertising that does not fall into normal outdoor categories

ambush marketing any activity where a company tries to associate itself or its products with an event without paying any fee to the event owner

attitude the degree to which a customer or prospect likes or dislikes a brand

awareness set the set of brands that the consumer is aware may provide a solution to a problem

beliefs descriptive thoughts that a person holds about something

benefit segmentation the grouping of people based on the different benefits they seek from a product

bonus pack pack giving the customer extra quantity at no additional cost

brainstorming the technique whereby a group of people generate ideas without initial evaluation; only when the list of ideas is complete is each one then evaluated

brand a distinctive product offering created by the use of a name, symbol, design, packaging, or some combination of these, intended to differentiate it from its competitors

brand equity a measure of the strength of the brand in the marketplace

brand extension the use of an established brand name on a new brand within the same broad market

brand stretching the use of an established brand name for brands in unrelated markets

brand values the core values and characteristics of a brand

business analysis a review of the projected sales, costs and profits for a new product to establish whether these factors satisfy company objectives

business mission the organization's purpose, usually setting out its competitive domain, which distinguishes the business from others of its type

buying centre a group that is involved in the buying decision; also known as a decision-making unit (DMU) in industrial buying situations

buzz marketing the passing of information about products or services by verbal or electronic means in an informal person-to-person manner

catalogue marketing the sale of products through catalogues distributed to agents and customers, usually by mail or at stores

causal research the study of cause and effect relationships

cause-related marketing the commercial activity by which businesses and charities or causes form a partnership with each other to market an image, product or service for mutual benefit

chain of marketing productivity the processes through which marketing activities contribute to the performance of the firm

channel integration the way in which the players in the channel are linked

channel intermediaries organizations that facilitate the distribution of products to customers

channel of distribution the means by which products are moved from the producer to the ultimate consumer

channel strategy the selection of the most effective distribution channel, the most appropriate level of distribution intensity and the degree of channel integration

choice criteria the various attributes (and benefits) people use when evaluating products and services

classical conditioning the process of using an established relationship between a stimulus and a response to cause the learning of the same response to a different stimulus

cognitive dissonance post-purchase concerns of a consumer arising from uncertainty as to whether a decision to purchase was the correct one

cognitive learning the learning of knowledge, and development of beliefs and attitudes without direct reinforcement

communications-based co-branding the linking of two or more existing brands from different companies or business units for the purposes of joint communication

competitive bidding drawing up detailed specifications for a product and putting the contract out to tender

competitor analysis an examination of the nature of actual and potential competitors, their objectives and strategies

competitor targets the organizations against which a company chooses to compete directly

concept testing testing new product ideas with potential customers

consumer culture theory (CCT) views consumption less as a rational or conscious activity and more as a sociocultural or experiential activity that is laden with emotion

consumer panel consumers who provide information on their purchases over time

consumer pull the targeting of consumers with communications (e.g. promotions) designed to create demand that will *pull* the product into the distribution chain

consumer-generated advertising advertising messages created for brands by consumers

continuous research conducting the same research on the same sample repeatedly to monitor the changes that are taking place over time.

contractual vertical marketing system a franchise arrangement (e.g. a franchise) tying producers and resellers together

control the stage in the marketing planning process or cycle when the performance against plan is monitored so that corrective action can be taken, if necessary

core strategy the means of achieving marketing objectives, including target markets, competitor targets and competitive advantage

corporate vertical marketing system a channel situation where an organization gains control of distribution through ownership

culture the traditions, taboos, values and basic attitudes of the whole society in which an individual lives

custom research research conducted for a single organization to provide specific answers to the questions that it has

customer analysis a survey of who the customers are, what choice criteria they use, how they rate competitive offerings and on what variables they can be segmented

customer benefits those things that a customer values in a product; customer benefits derive from product features (see separate entry)

customer relationship management (CRM) the methodologies, technologies and e-commerce capabilities used by companies to manage customer relationships

customer satisfaction the fulfilment of customers' requirements or needs

customer value perceived benefits minus perceived sacrifice

customer value proposition a clear statement of the differential benefits offered by a product or service

customized marketing a market coverage strategy where a company decides to target individual customers and to develop separate marketing mixes for each

database marketing an interactive approach to marketing, which uses individually addressable marketing media and channels to provide information to a target audience, stimulate demand and stay close to customers

decision-making process the stages that organizations and people pass through when purchasing a physical product or service

depth interviews the interviewing of consumers individually for perhaps one or two hours with the aim of understanding their attitudes, values, behaviour and/or beliefs

descriptive research the systematic examination of a marketing question in order to draw conclusions

differentiated marketing a market coverage strategy where a company decides to target several market segments and to develop separate marketing mixes for each

differentiation strategy the selection of one or more customer choice criteria, and positioning the offering accordingly to achieve superior customer value

diffusion of innovation the process by which new products or services are adopted in the marketplace

digital immigrant a person who was born before the wide spread of digital technologies and has adopted them to some extent in their life, but digital tools are still 'foreign' to them

digital marketing the achievement of marketing objectives through the use of digital technologies

digital native a person who is very comfortable with using digital technologies, as he/she was born during or after the general introduction of these technologies. Such a person's exposure to technology started at a very early age or at birth

direct mail material sent through the postal service to the recipient's house or business address, promoting a product and/or maintaining an ongoing relationship

direct marketing (1) acquiring and retaining customers without the use of an intermediary; (2) the distribution of products, information and promotional benefits to target consumers through interactive communication in a way that allows response to be measured

direct response advertising the use of the prime advertising media, such as television, newspapers and magazines, to elicit an order, enquiry or a request for a visit

disintermediation the elimination of marketing channel intermediaries by product or service providers

distribution analysis an examination of movements in power bases, channel attractiveness, physical distribution and distribution behaviour

distribution push the targeting of channel intermediaries with communications (e.g., promotions) to *push* the product into the distribution chain

dynamic pricing the frequent adjustment of prices in response to patterns of demand

economic value to the customer (EVC) the amount a customer would have to pay to make the total life cycle costs of a new and a reference product the same

effectiveness doing the right thing, making the correct strategic choice

efficiency a way of managing business processes to a high standard, usually concerned with cost reduction; also called 'doing things right'

email marketing the achievement of marketing objectives through the use of email communications

environmental scanning the process of monitoring and analysing the marketing environment of a company

ethics the moral principles and values that govern the actions and decisions of an individual or group

ethnographic research an approach to research that emphasizes the observation/interviewing of consumers in their natural setting

event sponsorship sponsorship of a sporting or other event

evoked set the set of brands that the consumer seriously evaluates before making a purchase

exaggerated promises barrier a barrier to the matching of expected and perceived service levels caused by the unwarranted building up of expectations by exaggerated promises

exclusive distribution an extreme form of selective distribution where only one wholesaler, retailer or industrial distributor is used in a geographical area to sell the products of a particular supplier

exhibition an event that brings buyers and sellers together in a commercial setting

experiential marketing the term used to describe marketing activities that involve the creation of experiences for consumers

experimentation the application of stimuli (e.g. two price levels) to different matched groups under controlled conditions for the purpose of measuring their effect on a variable (e.g., sales)

exploratory research the preliminary exploration of a research area prior to the main data collection stage

family brand name a brand name used for all products in a range

focus group a group, normally of six to eight consumers, brought together for a discussion focusing on an aspect of a company's marketing

focused marketing a market coverage strategy where a company decides to target one market segment with a single marketing mix

franchise a legal contract in which a producer and channel intermediaries agree each other's rights and obligations; the intermediary usually receives marketing, managerial, technical and financial services in return for a fee

full cost pricing pricing so as to include all costs, and based on certain sales volume assumptions

geodemographics the process of grouping households into geographic clusters based on such information as type of accommodation, occupation, number and age of children, and ethnic background

global branding adopting a standardized approach to marketing in all the countries that the brand is available

going-rate prices prices at the rate generally applicable in the market, focusing on competitors' offerings rather than on company costs

group discussion a group, usually of six to eight consumers, brought together for a discussion focusing on an aspect of a company's marketing strategy

guerrilla marketing capturing the attention of consumers by the creation of highly unusual and unexpected forms of promotional activity

hall tests bringing a sample of target consumers to a room that has been hired so that alternative marketing ideas (e.g., promotions) can be tested

horizontal electronic marketplaces online procurement sites that cross several industries and are typically used to source low-cost supplies such as MRO items

inadequate delivery barrier a barrier to the matching of expected and perceived service levels caused by the failure of the service provider to select, train and reward staff adequately, resulting in poor or inconsistent delivery of service

inadequate resources barrier a barrier to the matching of expected and perceived service levels caused by the unwillingness of service providers to provide the necessary resources

individual brand name a brand name that does not identify a brand with a particular company

industry a group of companies that market products that are close substitutes for each other

information framing the way in which information is presented to people

information processing the process by which a stimulus is received, interpreted, stored in memory and later retrieved.

information processing approach sees consumption as largely a rational process – the outcome of a consumer recognizing a need and then engaging in a series of activities to attempt to fulfil that need

information search the identification of alternative ways of problem solving

ingredient co-branding the explicit positioning of a supplier's brand as an ingredient of a product

inseparability a characteristic of services, namely, that their production cannot be separated from their consumption

intangibility a characteristic of services, namely, that they cannot be touched, seen, tasted or smelled

integrated marketing communications the concept that companies co-ordinate their marketing communications tools to deliver a clear, consistent, credible and competitive message about the organization and its products

intensive distribution the aim of intensive distribution is to provide saturation coverage of the market

interactive television (iTV) advertising invites viewers to 'press the red button' on the remote control handset to see more information about an advertised product

internal marketing selecting, training and motivating employees to provide customer satisfaction

just-in-time (JIT) the JIT concept aims to minimize stocks by organizing a supply system that provides materials and components as they are required

key account management an approach to selling that focuses resources on major customers and uses a team selling approach

lifestyle the pattern of living as expressed in a person's activities, interests and opinions

lifestyle segmentation the grouping of people according to their pattern of living as expressed in their activities, interests and opinions

lifetime value of a customer recognition by the company of the potential sales, profits and endorsements that come from a repeat customer who stays with the company for several years

macroenvironment a number of broader forces that affect not only the company but the other actors in the environment, e.g. social, political, technological and economic

marginal cost pricing the calculation of only those costs that are likely to rise as output increases

market intelligence the systematic collection and analysis of publicly available information about consumers, competitors and marketplace developments

market segmentation the process of identifying individuals or organizations with similar characteristics that have significant implications for the determination of marketing strategy

market testing the limited launch of a new product to test sales potential

market-driven or outside-in firms seek to anticipate as well as identify consumer needs and build the resource profiles necessary to meet current and anticipated future demand

marketing the delivery of value to customers at a profit

marketing audit a systematic examination of a business's marketing environment, objectives, strategies and activities, with a view to identifying key strategic issues, problem areas and opportunities

marketing concept the achievement of corporate goals through meeting and exceeding customer needs better than the competition

marketing environment the actors and forces that affect a company's capability to operate effectively in providing products and services to its customers

marketing information system a system in which marketing information is formally gathered, stored, analysed and distributed to managers in accordance with their informational needs on a regular, planned basis

marketing mix a framework for the tactical management of the customer relationship, including product, place, price, promotion (the 4Ps); in the case of services, three other elements to be taken into account are process, people and physical evidence

marketing objectives there are two types of marketing objective – strategic thrust, which dictates which products should be sold in which markets, and strategic objectives, which are product-level objectives, such as build, hold, harvest and divest

marketing orientation companies with a marketing orientation focus on customer needs as the primary drivers of organizational performance

marketing planning the process by which businesses analyse the environment and their capabilities, decide upon courses of marketing action and implement those decisions

marketing research is the systematic design, collection, analysis and reporting of data relevant to a specific marketing situation.

marketing structures the marketing frameworks (organization, training and internal communications) on which marketing activities are based

marketing systems sets of connected parts (information, planning and control) that support the marketing function

mass customization the opposite to mass production, which means that all products produced are customized to the predetermined needs of a specific customer

media class decision the choice of prime media (i.e., the press, cinema, television, posters, radio) or some combination of these

media vehicle decision the choice of the particular newspaper, magazine, television spot, poster site, etc.

microenvironment the actors in the firm's immediate environment that affect its capability to operate effectively in its chosen markets – namely, suppliers, distributors, customers and competitors

misconceptions barrier a failure by marketers to understand what customers really value about their service

mobile marketing the creation and delivery of marketing messages through mobile devices

modified re-buy where a regular requirement for the type of product exists and the buying alternatives are known but sufficient (e.g. a delivery problem has occurred) to require some alteration to the normal supply procedure

money-off promotions sales promotions that discount the normal price

neuro-marketing the application of brain research techniques to the study of marketing issues

new task refers to the first-time purchase of a product or input by an organization

operant conditioning the use of rewards to generate reinforcement of response

packaging all the activities involved in designing and producing the kind of container or wrapper for the product

parallel co-branding the joining of two or more independent brands to produce a combined brand

parallel importing when importers buy products from distributors in one country and sell them in another to distributors who are not part of the manufacturer's normal distribution; caused by significant price differences for the same product between different countries

perception the process by which people select, organize and interpret sensory stimulation into a meaningful picture of the world

perishability a characteristic of services, namely that the capacity of a service business, such as a hotel room, cannot be stored – if it is not occupied, there is lost income that cannot be recovered

permission marketing marketers ask permission before sending advertisements or promotional material to potential customers; in this way customers 'opt in' to the promotion rather than having to 'opt out'

personal selling oral communication with prospective purchasers with the intention of making a sale

personality the inner psychological characteristics of individuals that lead to consistent responses to their environment

place the distribution channels to be used, outlet locations, methods of transportation

portfolio planning managing groups of brands and product lines

positioning the choice of target market (*where* the company wishes to compete) and differential advantage (*how* the company wishes to compete)

premiums any merchandise offered free or at low cost as an incentive to purchase

price (1) the amount of money paid for a product; (2) the agreed value placed on the exchange by a buyer and seller

price escalation the additional costs incurred in taking products to an international market, including transportation costs, distribution costs, taxes and tariffs, exchange rates and inflation rates

price unbundling pricing each element in the offering so that the price of the total product package is raised

product a good or service offered or performed by an organization or individual, which is capable of satisfying customer needs

product features the characteristics of a product that may or may not convey a customer benefit

product life cycle a four-stage cycle in the life of a product, illustrated as a curve representing the demand; the four stages being introduction, growth, maturity and decline

product line a group of brands that are closely related in terms of the functions and benefits they provide

product placement the deliberate placing of products and/or their logos in movies and television programmes, usually in return for money

product-based co-branding the linking of two or more existing brands from different companies or business units to form a product in which the brand names are visible to the consumer

production orientation a business approach that is inwardly focused either on costs or on a definition of a company in terms of its production facilities

profile segmentation the grouping of people in terms of profile variables such as age and socio-economic group so that marketers can communicate to them

promotional mix advertising, personal selling, sales promotion, public relations and direct marketing

prospecting searching for and calling upon potential customers

proximity marketing the localized wireless distribution of advertising content associated with a particular place

psychographic segmentation the grouping of people according to their lifestyle and personality characteristics

psychological pricing taking into consideration the psychological impact of the price level that is being set

public relations the management of communications and relationships to establish goodwill and mutual understanding between an organization and its public

publicity the communication of a product or business by placing information about it in the media without paying for time or space directly

qualitative research a semi-structured, in-depth study of small samples in order to gain insights.

quantitative research a structured study of small or large samples using a predetermined list of questions or criteria

reasoning a more complex form of cognitive learning where conclusions are reached by connected thought

reference group a group of people that influences an individual's attitude or behaviour

relationship marketing the process of creating, maintaining and enhancing strong relationships with customers and other stakeholders

repositioning changing the target market or differential advantage, or both

research brief written document stating the client's requirements

research proposal a document defining what the marketing research agency promises to do for its client and how much it will cost

retail audit a type of continuous research tracking the sales of products through retail outlets

retail positioning the choice of target market and differential advantage for a retail outlet

reverse marketing the process whereby the buyer attempts to persuade the supplier to provide exactly what the organization wants

rote learning the learning of two or more concepts without conditioning

safety (buffer) stocks stocks or inventory held to cover against uncertainty about resupply lead times

sales orientation a business approach that focuses on the development of products and services and the aggressive selling of these offerings as the key to its success

sales promotion incentives to customers or the trade that are designed to stimulate purchase

sales-force evaluation the measurement of salesperson performance so that strengths and weaknesses can be identified

sales-force motivation the motivation of salespeople by a process that involves needs, which set encouraging drives in motion to accomplish goals

sampling process a term used in research to denote the selection of a subset of the total population in order to interview them

search engine optimization (SEO) the practice of adjusting the website's structure and content to improve the position with which it turns up in a web search

secondary research data that has already been collected by another researcher for another purpose

selective attention the process by which people screen out those stimuli that are neither meaningful to them nor consistent with their experiences and beliefs

selective distortion the distortion of information received by people according to their existing beliefs and attitudes

selective distribution the use of a limited number of outlets in a geographical area to sell the products of a particular supplier

selective retention the process by which people retain only a selection of messages in memory

self-concept the beliefs a person holds about his or her own attributes

semiotics the study of the correspondence between signs and symbols and their roles in how we assign meanings

service encounter any interaction between a service provider and a customer

servicescape the environment in which the service is delivered and where the firm and customers interact

shareholder value the returns to a company's shareholders, which grow when the company increases its dividends or its share price rises

social marketing the use of commercial marketing concepts and tools in programmes designed to influence the individual's behaviour to improve their well-being and that of society

social media marketing the use of social media for communicating with and engaging customers online

societal marketing concept the idea that a company's marketing decisions should consider consumers' wants, the company's requirements, consumers' long-term interests and society's long-run interests

sponsorship a business relationship between a provider of funds, resources or services and an individual, event or organization that offers in return some rights and association that may be used for commercial advantage

straight re-buy refers to a purchase by an organization from a previously approved supplier of a previously purchased item

strategic business unit a business or company division serving a distinct group of customers and with a distinct set of competitors, usually strategically autonomous

strategic issues analysis an examination of the suitability of marketing objectives and segmentation bases in the light of changes in the marketplace

strategic objectives product-level objectives relating to the decision to build, hold, harvest or divest products

strategic thrust the decision concerning which products to sell in which markets

strong theory of advertising the notion that advertising can change people's attitudes sufficiently to persuade those who have not previously bought a product to buy it; desire and conviction precede purchase

SWOT analysis a structured approach to evaluating the strategic position of a business by identifying its strengths, weaknesses, opportunities and threats

syndicated research research that is collected by firms on a regular basis and then sold to other firms

target audience the group of people at which an advertisement or message is aimed

target market a segment that has been selected as a focus for the company's offering or communications

target marketing selecting a segment as the focus for a company's offering or communications

telemarketing use of telecommunications in marketing and sales activities

test marketing the launch of a new product in one or a few geographic areas chosen to be representative of the intended market

trademark the legal term for a brand name, brand mark or trade character

trade-off analysis a measure of the trade-off customers make between price and other product features, so that their effects on product preference can be established

undifferentiated marketing a market coverage strategy where a company decides to ignore market segment differences and to develop a single marketing mix for the whole market

value chain the set of the firm's activities that are conducted to design, manufacture, market, distribute and service its products

value-based marketing a perspective on marketing that emphasizes how a marketing philosophy and marketing activities contribute to the maximization of shareholder value

variability a characteristic of services, namely that being delivered by people the standard of their performance is open to variation

vertical electronic marketplaces online procurement sites that are dedicated to sourcing supplies for producers in one particular industry

vicarious learning learning from others without direct experience or reward

viral campaigns the creation of entertaining messages designed to be electronically transferred from person to person

viral marketing electronic word of mouth, where promotional messages are spread using electronic means from person to person

weak theory of advertising the notion that advertising can first arouse awareness and interest and encourage some customers to make a trial purchase as well as providing reassurance and reinforcement; desire and conviction do not precede purchase

yield management the monitoring of demand or potential demand patterns with a view to adjusting prices

Author index

Companies and brands index

Note: Page locators in **bold** refer to main entries and those in *italics* refer to illustrations

Subject index